Building an Intranet with Windows NT 4

Scott Zimmerman

with

Tim Evans

sams net

201 West 103rd Street
Indianapolis, Indiana 46290

Copyright © 1996 by Sams.net Publishing

FIRST EDITION

International Standard Book Number: 1-57521-137-8

Library of Congress Catalog Card Number: 96-68589

99 98 97 96   4 3 2 1

Interpretation of the printing code: the rightmost double-digit number is the year of the book's printing; the rightmost single-digit, the number of the book's printing. For example, a printing code of 96-1 shows that the first printing of the book occurred in 1996.

Composed in AGaramond and MCPdigital by Macmillan Computer Publishing

Printed in the United States of America

President, Sams Publishing	*Richard K. Swadley*
Publishing Manager	*Mark Taber*
Managing Editor	*Cindy Morrow*
Marketing Manager	*John Pierce*
Assistant Marketing Manager	*Kristina Perry*

Acquisitions Editor
Beverly M. Eppink

Development Editor
Fran Hatton

Software Development Specialists
Bob Correll
Cari Skaggs

Production Editor
Mary Inderstrodt

Copy Editors
Heather Stith
Angie Trzpacz
Faithe Wempen

Technical Reviewers
Ramesh Chandak
Michael Marlow

Editorial Coordinator
Bill Whitmer

Technical Edit Coordinators
Lorraine Schaffer
Lynette Quinn

Resource Coordinator
Deborah Frisby

Formatter
Frank Sinclair

Editorial Assistants
Carol Ackerman
Andi Richter
Rhonda Tinch-Mize

Cover Designer
Tim Amrhein

Book Designer
Alyssa Yesh

Copy Writer
Peter Fuller

Production Team Supervisor
Brad Chinn

Production
Bruce Clingaman, Brad Herriman, Ayanna Lacey, Paula Lowell, Susan Van Ness

Overview

Contents

Preface

The World Wide Web is an amazingly powerful tool for communicating. This power results from the ease with which information (the merchandise of the Information Age) can be obtained and shared on the Web. *Building an Intranet with Windows NT 4* shows you how to put that power to work processing information in new and creative ways within your company or organization.

To me, the word Intranet means nothing more than the usage of Web technology, such as a Web browser and server, in a local network environment. But what you can achieve with an Intranet stretches way beyond the ordinary capabilities of a typical Local Area Network.

In my opinion, every business, large and small, needs an Intranet. And when it comes to cost and ease-of-use, there is no network operating system better than Windows NT on which to build an Intranet. Windows NT 4 is not only capable of exceptional performance, but it is also very reliable and secure.

A fascinating thing about the Intranet is that one can be built so inexpensively. The fact that Web browsers (such as Internet Explorer) are both free and easy to use helps to make the decision a no-brainer. Indeed, I can't think of any parallel in business history where there has been a similar opportunity for a single employee to help guide his or her company to such a revolutionary and cost-effective new level of productivity!

This book goes way beyond the basics of using an Intranet, and into the realm of actually inventing, creating, and managing an Intranet. Until now, setting up an Intranet or Internet Web site has required deep knowledge of several Internet protocols and lots of experience. Many people still assume that you need to be a UNIX system administrator to run a Web server. Not only is this untrue, but I believe that no other book will show you how easy it really is.

Web technology evolves extremely fast. I have made every effort to verify that the information in this book is accurate at the time of printing. I have also endeavored to pack this volume with the most useful information you are likely to need. I hope you will find that the numerous cross-references to other sections in the book and to the World Wide Web itself is a valuable aid to furthering your understanding.

Good luck in your efforts. I'll be happy to hear of your questions and success stories.

Scott Zimmerman

San Diego, June, 1996

Dedication

Dedicated to all who walk softly on this Earth.

–S.Z.

Acknowledgments

As with any technical book, this book could not have been completed without the help of many others. I owe my deepest thanks to Tim Evans of DuPont Corporation for writing the first version of this book, geared more toward the UNIX platform. So many of the ideas in this book, and significant sections of the writing, are based on his deep networking experience and his excellent book "Building an Intranet," also published by Sams.net.

Next on my list is Christopher Brown, for being so knowledgeable and kind at the same time. Chris runs his own Web services company (`http://www.fbits.com`) and he introduced me to all the behind-the-scenes Web technology when we wrote our first two books for Sams.net.

I am honored by the permission from Martijn Koster to include some of his research material on Internet robots and for donating his time to help review the work on robots and security. Hershey Quintana contributed research and graphic editing.

Richard Graessler was especially helpful with the software engineering for various PERL scripts. No less thanks goes to J.J. Allaire for providing the software and documentation for Cold Fusion; Ken Nesbitt for providing the shareware version of WebEdit; and Chris Wensel for providing CGI Perform.

Special thanks to: Software.com for providing the trial version of Post.Office; and the authors of the many other fine software packages we include on the CD-ROM—too numerous to name here. I hope my gentle readers will appreciate the hard work that goes into the creation of all the software needed to make a Web site tick.

I also owe my gratitude to the members of the `webserver-nt@DELTA.PROCESS.COM` listserver, for without their advice (in fact, anyone I ever talked to about Windows NT and the Internet), my knowledge of the Web would not be what it is today.

About the Author

Scott Zimmerman has been developing software for 15 years. He has programmed in over two dozen languages, primarily C++ and Visual Basic. His full-time hobby is being the Software Engineering Manager with Azron, Incorporated. The Azron team produces an award-winning client/server system for wireless electronic medical records on Windows 95 and Windows NT. Zimmerman has also co-authored, with Christopher Brown, *Web Site Construction Kit for Windows NT* and *Web Site Construction Kit for Windows 95*, published by Sams.net. His interests include nature conservation, science, and technology. He can be reached at `http://www.hqz.com` where he helps with the technical aspects of running a Windows NT Web services company, or by e-mail at `scottz@sd.znet.com`. (In a previous career, he won the World Overall Frisbee Championships eight times and still holds the Guinness World Record for the longest throw of any object at 1257 feet.)

The Contributing Authors

Tim Evans is the author of *Building an Intranet*. He is a network administrator at the DuPont Corporation, where he led the development of a corporate-wide Web of 35 servers in locations throughout the world. Completely isolated from the Interent as a whole, the DuPont-wide Web serves corporate, scientific, and manufacturing information to customers inside the company. Evans has more than 10 years experience as a UNIX system and network administrator.

Christopher L. T. Brown (`clbrown@netcom.com`) is a Senior Chief in the U.S. Navy. For the past 15 years, he has worked in the Naval Command Control and Communications. Brown has written programs in several computer languages including BASIC, Pascal, C, and C++. In addition to proprietary operating systems, he has worked with UNIX, Macintosh, DOS, Windows, Windows NT, and Windows 95. During the past three years, Brown has dedicated most of his time to evaluation and operation of Windows NT as an Internet platform. In addition to his Navy career, he runs a World Wide Web publishing and consulting company called Final Bit Solutions, which maintains an active Internet Web server as part of its services. Brown's interests include cryptography, surfing, skiing, and wildlife.

Billy Barron (`billy@metronet.com`; `http://www.utdallas.edu/~billy`) is currently a New Technology Specialist for the University of Texas at Dallas and has an MS in Computer Science from the University of North Texas. He has written and edited so many books that he can't remember them all anymore. Some examples are *Internet Unleashed 1996*, *Web Site Adminstrator's Survival Guide*, and *Tricks of the Internet Gurus*.

Lay Wah Ooi (`ooi@pobox.com`) is a Computer Systems Engineer at Titan Spectrum Technologies. She graduated with a Computer Science degree from the University of North Texas. Lay Wah has contributed to Sams.net Publishing's *Internet Unleashed*, and was also a technical editor for *Java Unleashed.*

Tell Us What You Think!

As a reader, you are the most important critic and commentator of our books. We value your opinion and want to know what we're doing right, what we could do better, what areas you'd like to see us publish in, and any other words of wisdom you're willing to pass our way. You can help us make strong books that meet your needs and give you the computer guidance you require.

Do you have access to CompuServe or the World Wide Web? Then check out our CompuServe forum by typing GO SAMS at any prompt. If you prefer the World Wide Web, check out our site at http://www.mcp.com.

> **Note:** If you have a technical question about this book, call the technical support line at (800) 571-5840, ext. 3668.

As the team leader of the group that created this book, I welcome your comments. You can fax, e-mail, or write me directly to let me know what you did or didn't like about this book—as well as what we can do to make our books stronger. Here's the information:

Mark Taber   newtech_mgr@sams.mcp.com
Fax: 317/581-4669
Mail: Comments Department
                  Sams Publishing
                  201 W. 103rd Street
                  Indianapolis, IN 46290

Introduction

This book is your complete guide to building a very economical Intranet—quickly, professionally, and securely. It is intended for savvy and aspiring employees who want to lead their companies to new levels of achievement and accelerate their own careers in the process. Hey, if you've gotten this far, you are obviously somewhat of a visionary. And in that case, wouldn't an introduction any less bold then be a bit of a let down?

Who This Book Is For

Suppose you are savvy and aspiring but you are considering this book because you want to learn more about networking and Web technology. In particular, you want to study client/server networking on a very cool operating system named Windows NT. (And in case you haven't already noticed, Microsoft is posting new Internet products and technologies on their Web site so fast that NT is getting more and more cool every week.)

Although it would be helpful if you already have a basic understanding of Windows NT, that isn't essential beforehand, because this book covers all the necessary information for building your own Web server. In addition to being an extremely powerful operating system, Windows NT is also quite intuitive. Most tasks can be easily accomplished with point-and-click mouse commands.

> **Note:** What is meant by *client* and *server?* The server is the computer that serves as a repository of information or provides a service when the client computer makes a request for the information or service. Sometimes the terms are arbitrary because both computers can provide information for, and make requests of, each other. Of course, the requests are usually initiated by humans. When you request to view a document on a server, the computers might actually carry out dozens of low-level client/server commands using protocols such as TCP/IP and HTTP.

Do I Need to Know Programming or Protocols?

HTML (Hypertext Markup Language) and HTTP (Hypertext Transfer Protocol) are the languages of the Web, in a sense. Despite its name, HTML isn't actually considered a programming language. After you read Chapter 5, "What You Need to Know About HTML," you will see just how easy it is. I'll continue to explore HTML with you throughout the book, and by the time you finish, you will be very familiar with it. But do not fear; you do not need to know a programming language before you start.

In addition to plenty of HTML code, I'll discuss several programs written in C++, Perl, and Visual Basic. All the programs are ready to run, so the reader does not need to know programming in order to use them. However, I also include the source code so that those familiar with these languages can study the programs for further information or to make enhancements. Again, knowledge of programming would be helpful, but it is not essential.

This book does not cover the Internet protocols in any significant way. I expect people who have a background in this area will be able to use this book as a guide to building their own Intranet. For those without a background in internetworking, you still should have no trouble getting your Intranet up and running with the software and examples that are provided. The subject of Web technology is a very large topic—too large to completely cover in one book. You might find that additional research into Internet protocols and security will be helpful in the long run. You will find some useful references in Appendix C and in the Bibliography.

Why Windows NT?

There are many reasons to use Windows NT as your Intranet Web server operating system. NT offers superior reliability and security coupled with the familiar Windows user interface. NT runs on powerful and inexpensive hardware. When buying a computer to run NT, you have many excellent options depending on the bang-for-the-buck you want and can afford because the engineers at Microsoft were progressive enough to design NT to run on several hardware platforms. Today, this includes everything from Intel 486 to IBM PowerPC to MIPS to DEC Alpha. And because of multithreading, NT will continue to deliver exceptional performance under heavy user loads.

With TCP/IP and remote access software built into the operating system, NT is one of the easiest operating systems to use for an Intranet/Internet. Right out of the box, you can be surfing your Web, and the World Wide Web, in no time. When you consider the other benefits of NT, such as scalability, security, performance, and manageability, you've got an ideal platform to create an Intranet/Internet server that anyone can connect with. And there are hundreds of commercial, freeware, and shareware client and server programs for NT, in most every category, available on the Internet to help you get the most out of your project. Several are included on the CD-ROM with this book.

What Makes Windows NT Scalable?

Microsoft advertises Windows NT as *scalable,* but what does that mean? I look at it this way: NT can run on several platforms, from low-end to high-end. It can also run on SMP (Symmetric Multiprocessing) machines with up to 16 CPUs. Finally, because it is portable, you never know when they will announce a version that runs on another new platform, such as they did with version 3.51 for the PowerPC. So if you find that your server is being overstressed by an increasing user base, you have three options without dropping your existing software:

◆ Move the operating system to a faster computer in the same platform family. (Any operating system can do this.)

◆ Move it to a machine containing multiple processors. (Few operating systems can do this.)

◆ Move it to another platform altogether. (Almost no other operating system can do this!)

About the Intranet

At home and at work, you and I and millions of others have found the World Wide Web irresistible, most often for recreational and personal reasons. Even the most commonly used buzzword describing how people use the Web—surfing the 'net—implies a recreational nature about the activity. It's gotten so that some corporate officials worry about just what it is their employees are doing when they're supposed to be working. Are they really searching for work-related resources, or just surfing? And, more importantly, what does or can this phenomenon mean to my business?

Once the novelty of the Web has worn off a bit, you wonder about its potential value as a business or educational tool. Can this slick, seductive technology be put to work inside your company, organization, or institution, to some useful, real-work end? Can you capture the enthusiasm with which your employees surf the Web and channel it into their daily duties? Can you share information about your organization with its members—employees, students, and other insiders—using this glamorous and easy-to-use mechanism? The answer to those questions is an unqualified "Yes" in all cases, and the nuts and bolts of doing so is what this book is all about.

Setting up a corporate Intranet requires you to look under the surface of the Web for new and meaningful ways it can be used. Despite its glamour and accessibility for many users, the Web is essentially a passive experience. People use their Web browsers to look at things—documents, spreadsheets, images, videos, and the like. For the most part, however, there's very little a Web surfer can actually do with what he sees. Yes, Web pages can be saved, or printed, and there's potential value in doing so. Many Web pages contain valuable information, and pointers to other information. The information obtained from reading a Web page can often be used for some work-related purpose. Still, the whole Web experience remains passive: people look at static, unchanging things. You may have wondered why this attractive and easy-to-use interface can't somehow be put to work doing something active and real in a corporate or organizational environment that somehow contributes to the realization of the organization's mission.

You're not alone in asking these questions. In a recent survey by Business Research Group, reported in the *Wall Street Journal* (November 7, 1995), nearly a quarter of 170 medium- and large-sized companies surveyed are already setting up corporate Intranets using World Wide Web technology, while another 20 percent are actively considering doing so. *LAN Times* magazine on January 22, 1996 pointed to a Zona Research study stating that 200,000 Intranets will be installed during 1996 and triple that number in 1997!

What This Book Is About

Organizations do more than sell the goods and services they produce. All organizations, even noncommercial ones, have to manage themselves, buying supplies, running a physical plant, managing employees and their benefits, and otherwise keeping organizational house. Most other Web-related books pay little attention to how Web technology can be directly used by a company or other organization in fulfilling these missions. Usually, they provide a few simple examples of some kind or other, then trail off with vague statements (or even small-print footnotes) to the effect that the reader should be able to use her imagination to come up with ways to apply the books' examples to her own organization.

This book is about how commercial and noncommercial organizations can put Web technology to work inside their organization to do their real, everyday work.

This book will show how Web technology and related TCP/IP networking technology can be used to create information resources that can be actively used in the daily operation of a business, an educational institution, or any other organization. I'll provide examples ranging from simple, everyday office tools to sophisticated databases. I'll include step-by-step instructions that show you exactly how to implement useful Web features you can use in your daily work, or in the daily work of your company. Once you have set up your Intranet, your users will be able to use their Web browsers and other applications to help them perform their regular work duties.

Using Web Technology to Create Your Intranet

WWW technology can provide a familiar, user-friendly front end to a wide range of information ranging from libraries of personnel and technical documents to data warehouses full of corporate statistics, to scientific and technical data. This data can not only be accessed with Web browsers, but can also be actively manipulated as needed. Web technology can provide front ends to commercial database applications, with both query and data-entry capabilities. Custom computer application programs can be wrapped up inside an easy-to-use Web interface, with Web-based online help a mouse click away. Users can collaborate with others on work-related projects and share scientific data and other information, again using familiar Web technology.

Because Web browsers have built-in support for many kinds of network services, you'll be able to extend your Intranet to include many other facilities. Most of these facilities are based on no-cost and low-cost software (much of which is available on the Intranet CD-ROM with this book), and they provide strong and inexpensive alternatives to commercial groupware packages (like Microsoft Exchange and Lotus Notes). These value-added services will be useful in your organization, providing facilities that can be accessed using a Web browser via simple point and click.

The Intranet CD-ROM

The accompanying CD includes many useful files and programs to help you craft and maintain your Intranet. As you read the book, you'll notice the icon you see beside this paragraph for references to files and programs on the CD. Be sure to read and follow installation instructions and all licensing/copyright restrictions.

Conventions Used in This Book

Throughout this book I have made use of a few conventions developed by the good folks at Sams.net to assist you in recognizing important pieces of information. These include special highlighting methods for information displayed by your computer and for information you need to type in yourself.

Typographical conventions used in this book.

Typeface	Meaning
Computer Type	There are a number of Internet addresses, filenames, directory paths, and World Wide Web URLs defined throughout this book that are printed in computer type to make them easier to recognize.
Bold Computer Type	Text printed in bold computer type represents information you need to type at your keyboard while working with the various programs discussed in this book.
Italic	When you encounter a word printed in italic, this indicates that you are about to examine a new concept.

Icons Used Throughout the Book

Note: Information printed in Note boxes provides you with additional points of interest relating to the topic currently being discussed.

Tip: Tips offer additional suggestions about the use of programs and services.

Warning: Warning messages are designed to make you aware of important issues that may affect set up of your Intranet or general Internet issues.

And now, let's get started.

> **Note:** The information in this book is based on beta software. Since this information was made public before the final release of the product, there may be some changes to the product by the time it is finally released. After final product has begun shipping, we encourage you to visit our website, `http://www.mcp.com/sams` for an electronic update starting 09/01/96.
>
> Additionally, if you have access to the Internet, you can always get up-to-the-minute information about Windows NT Server and Windows NT Workstation direct from Microsoft at the following locations:
>
> ```
> http://www.microsoft.com/ntserver
> http://www.microsoft.com/ntworkstation
> ```

PART

Intranet
Fundamentals

CHAPTER 1

Understanding Web Technologies

I'd like to begin each chapter with a brief overview of what's ahead. These lists might help you determine whether you would like to skim through any material that you are already familiar with.

- ◆ Overview of the World Wide Web and the Internet
- ◆ World Wide Web client software, which this book calls *browser* software
- ◆ World Wide Web server software
- ◆ How the Web fits into the worldwide TCP/IP Internet
- ◆ Related TCP/IP networking technologies and how they fit into an Intranet
- ◆ Microsoft ActiveX Technology comes to the Internet

By now it's hard to imagine how anyone can have missed learning at least something about the World Wide Web and the Internet. Mass-circulation newspapers and magazines and broadcast media feature the Internet regularly. You often see Web page addresses (known as *Uniform Resource Locators*, or URLs) in television commercials and printed advertisements. The story of the meteoric rise of Netscape Communications Corporation on the stock market jumped from the financial page to the front page. Universities, businesses, and other organizations have rushed to "get on the Web," while entrepreneurs have moved equally quickly to take advantage of this rush by setting up shop on the shoulders of the Information Superhighway, hawking everything from Internet connections to Web-page authoring to Web-related conferences.

You probably bought this book because you've been using the Web and you see the potential to use its technology on an Intranet within your organization. If you're wondering what an Intranet is, you might think of it as "the Web on a LAN" (Local Area Network). Obviously, there is much more to it than such a simplistic definition. The rest of this book is all about exploring the limitless possibilities of building and using an Intranet. Using Windows NT as the server, of course.

> **Note:** For now, I assume you know the meaning of Web URLs, such as `http://www.somecompany.com`. If not, you might want to scan ahead to Chapter 5, "What You Need to Know About HTML" for an in-depth discussion about the different flavors of URLs and how they work.

This chapter is an overall introduction to the Web, and it lays a foundation for the rest of the book. Because you've probably seen similar introductory material before, I'll put a particular spin on the whole subject in this chapter by pointing to some of the things you'll be able to do on your Intranet. As you read the chapter, think of using your Web browser within your company to view your own company information instead of outside Web pages. Your corporate Intranet, then, is the implementation of World Wide Web services within your organization.

Overview of the World Wide Web and the Internet

The explosion of interest in the Internet is being driven by an even more explosive growth of the Web. Nevertheless, and this isn't meant merely in a pedantic sense, the Internet was here first and has been for more than 20 years. The Internet can be loosely defined as those computers and networks, worldwide, that are interconnected using TCP/IP (Transmission Control Protocol/Internet Protocol).

A Brief History of TCP/IP and the Internet

In the 1970s, the United States Department of Defense (DoD) contracted with researchers at the University of California at Berkeley and a company named BBN to develop networking for DoD computers worldwide. The primary objectives of the research project were to develop computer networking that

◆ Worked on a variety of computer hardware.

◆ Operated over different communications media to link both individual computers and computer networks.

◆ Was robust enough to automatically reconfigure itself in the event of network failures.

More than after-the-fact Cold War speculation, the last of the points relates to the possibility of large parts of the DoD network disappearing in a nuclear war and the need for the network to withstand it. In fact, today's Internet does exactly that: If a large portion of the network were to disappear because of some massive hardware failure, the rest of the network would simply find a way around the service interruption and keep on working! It's pretty amazing.

Even though the DoD funded most of the development of what came to be known as TCP/IP networking, the free thinkers at Berkeley managed to get permission to redistribute the network software they developed and the specifics of its protocols written into the contract with DoD. At about the same time, Berkeley was developing its own revised version of the UNIX operating system software, which it had licensed from AT&T (where UNIX was invented) as a research project. In short, TCP/IP networking was dropped right into BSD (Berkeley Software Distribution) UNIX, which was then made available to other academic institutions, also for research purposes, for the mere cost of a computer tape.

The wide distribution of these BSD tapes to other colleges, universities, and research institutions was the beginning of the Internet. TCP/IP networking not only allows individual computers to be linked into a network, but it also allows networks of computers to be linked to other networks with the appearance that all the computers on all the linked networks are on the very same *internet*.

> **Note:** The word *internet* with a lowercase *i* refers to interconnected networks, perhaps on a university campus; whereas *Internet* with a capital *I* refers to the global interconnected network in which anyone can participate.

Universities began building local networks, linking them together, and connecting their local networks with remote networks at other locations or other institutions—laying the foundation for today's Internet explosion. The DoD built its own private Internet, called MILNET, using TCP/IP, and many other U.S. Government agencies set up networks as well, some of which eventually became part of the Internet.

TCP/IP Implementations

Because the implementation nuts and bolts of TCP/IP networking (that is, the detailed descriptions of the network protocols themselves) were publicly defined in documents known as *Requests for Comments*, software companies and individuals were free to develop and sell or give away their own TCP/IP software. For example, the first implementation of TCP/IP for the IBM PC was a university Master's thesis project, and the resulting software was given away; the authors went on to found FTP Software, Inc., makers of one of today's leading TCP/IP software packages, OnNet for IBM PCs and compatibles. Dozens of other vendors sell TCP/IP software for PCs and Microsoft has wisely built it into both Windows NT and Windows 95 as a standard feature.

> **Note:** If the term *network protocol* is unfamiliar to you, you might think of it as a language that one computer on the Internet can use to speak with any other computer on the Internet, even if they are of a completely different make and model. Note that the usual purpose of the phrase *computer language* describes a language between a human and a computer, but network protocols aren't really meant to be read by humans.

Although the Internet has strong foundations in UNIX, Windows NT and Windows 95 are not only capable of serving as powerful Internet or Intranet platforms, but most folks find them much easier to manage. One reason this book is written about Windows is that the number of desktop PCs running these platforms far surpasses those running all others combined. Consequently, any Intranet project will need to integrate Windows applications. This book will show you how to configure the PCs in your organization using TCP/IP and Web technology to participate on your Intranet.

In an effort to compete against Microsoft's dominance of the desktop operating systems market, several vendors (including IBM, Sun, and Oracle) have announced plans to develop inexpensive computing devices that will have TCP/IP networking built in. Not full-blown PCs, but also not dumb terminals, these Internet Appliances would include not only TCP/IP, but also graphical capabilities and World Wide Web browser software. These appliances could prove to be a valuable part of your Intranet, because they'd give users access to any Web services you might make available; and at substantially lower cost than full-capability PCs or workstations. Microsoft Vice President Paul Maritz has indicated his view that these devices will not ultimately prove to be successful at displacing the popular PC. Although that must be taken as a biased opinion, it does appear that the impact of Internet Appliances will depend on several factors:

◆ How low can the cost go? Assuming sufficient processing power to handle Web multimedia and a high-resolution monitor/adapter to support 3-D graphics; it will be very hard to get down to a suggested $500 price point. A hard disk is also very useful as a cache for storing frequently accessed Web pages.

◆ Will consumers want to pay that price for a machine without the capability to install custom applications or store confidential files locally?

Only time will answer these questions. We should hear much more as the concept and reality of Internet Appliances progresses in 1996.

Most people are familiar with the general idea of a computer network; several computers in an office or other common environment are connected together with wires to enable sharing of printers and files, and to otherwise allow communication among them. The idea of the Internet is much the same, only a lot bigger, but it also has an important extra element. TCP/IP networking allows not only the connection of local computers to each other, but also permits networks to be connected to other networks. These connections create *internets* (purposely not capitalized here), in which it appears to users that the computers on all the connected networks are part of a single, large *internetwork*. The same capabilities of sharing devices and communicating data between computers exists, but the sharing has been extended from just the computers on one network to all the systems on all the connected networks.

Interconnected networks need not be in the same location or building; they can be physically remote from each other with connections using special-purpose data lines, satellite radio, infrared radio links, cable TV wiring, or even ordinary telephone lines and modems. Remote computers appear to become local, allowing file transfers, electronic mail, printer and disk sharing, and many other features, including, of course, access to the World Wide Web.

Internet Services

As previously stated, before there was a Web there was already an Internet (now capitalized), a worldwide network of networks interconnected using TCP/IP networking. Some of the major features of the Internet include (although all of these were pre-Web, they are still used):

◆ Internet **Electronic Mail** for sending messages and attachments (including images and programs) between users on remote computers.

◆ **File transfers** between remote computers using the file transfer protocol (FTP).

◆ **Remote login services** (telnet) allowing users to log into remote computers and use them as if they were local.

◆ **Remotely searchable indexes** of information, free software, and other data.

◆ **USENET News**, the mother of all computer BBSs (bulletin board systems).

Besides these major Internet services, many others have developed over the lifetime of the Internet, some of which use combinations of the above services. Using an Internet search tool called *archie*, for example, you can search a database of free software and find its location on the Internet just by sending a specially worded e-mail message to a special address. Return e-mail services transfer files to you, much like fax-back services, when you request them via e-mail. Special-interest electronic mailing lists have developed for like-minded people who want to discuss subjects ranging from computers and networks themselves to spelunking and job searching.

Each of these (and many other) Internet services are useful and powerful tools, and all are still widely used. Even before the existence of the Web, the need for electronic mail capabilities was driving substantial growth in the Internet. Each *pre*-Web Internet service, however, has its own particular user interface to be learned. Many of these interfaces are less than friendly to non-technical users. Figure 1.1 shows an archie search using a GUI software package (called *WSARCHIE*) included on the CD-ROM with this book. Figures 1.2 and 1.3 show the same search using a Web browser and fill-in form interface to the archie service. The search term given in both cases is msie20.exe, which is the filename of Microsoft's Internet Explorer.

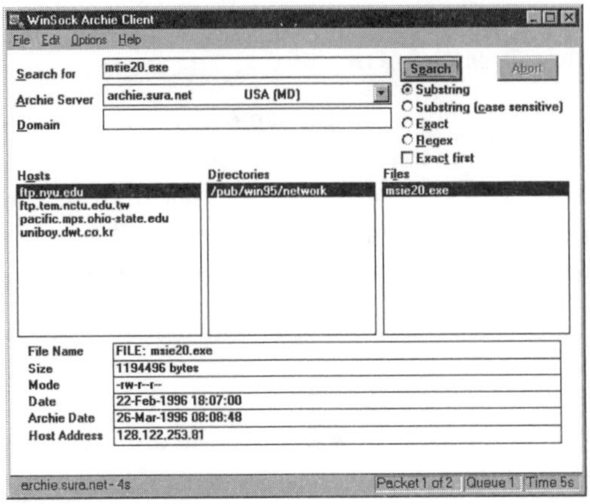

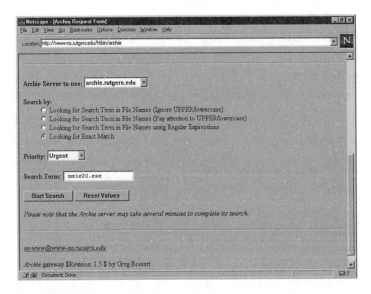

Figure 1.1. WSARCHIE interface to archie Internet search service.

Figure 1.2. Web-based archie search.

As you can see in these figures, the Web interface is significantly more accessible; the difference literally speaks for itself. Instead of a raw list of anonymous FTP servers and lengthy directory paths, you see a nicely formatted list of locations with the ability to download the located file just by clicking the link. Even though the WSARCHIE program is a very nice GUI, you still have to turn around and use FTP, a completely different service with a different user interface, to retrieve the file you want. Even assuming you can find the data you want, which Internet program do you use to access it? And where did you put the obscure set of instructions for this particular program? Actually using the *ante*-Web Internet then was not an easy proposition, particularly for casual computer users.

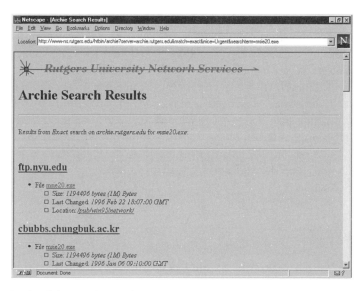

Figure 1.3. *Results of Web-based archie search.*

The Birth of the Web

In 1993, Tim Berners-Lee and other researchers at the European Particle Physics Lab (*Conseil Europeen pour la Recherche Nucleaire*, or CERN) in Geneva, Switzerland, developed a means of sharing data among their colleagues using something they called *hypertext*. CERN users could view documents on their computer screens using new *browser* software. Special codes embedded in these electronic documents allowed users to jump from one document to another on screen just by selecting a *hyperlink*. Internet capabilities were built into these browsers. Just as a user could jump from one text document on a computer to another, he could jump from a document on one computer to a document on another remote computer. Moreover, each of the major Internet services listed above was added to the browser software. A researcher could transfer a file from a remote computer to her local system, or log into a remote system just by clicking on a hyperlink, rather than using the clumsy FTP or Telnet mechanisms. CERN's breakthrough work is the basis of today's World Wide Web and its Web server and browser software (now being maintained by the World Wide Web Consortium) were the first of their kind.

> **Note:** CERN has now moved on, or rather back, to its main mission of doing research on particle physics, but its Web-related legacy has been passed on to the World Wide Web Consortium, a group of academic and commercial organizations dedicated to the advancement of the Web. W³, as it's called, remains active in the development of the Web, and Berners-Lee is still right in the thick of things at W³. You may want to visit the W³ Web site at http://www.w3.org/.

Unlike today's Web browsers, CERN's Web browser was a *plain-text* package in which cursor keys were used to move around the computer screen and the Enter key to select hyperlinks. While it could access both hypertext documents and *ante*-Web Internet services like FTP, Gopher, and Telnet, it had no graphical capabilities. Marc Andreesen, a graduate student working part-time at the University of Illinois National Center for Supercomputer Applications, picked up CERN's work and turned it into what would become today's *NCSA Mosaic*, the first graphical Web browser with point-and-click capabilities. First developed for UNIX computer systems running the X Window graphical user interface, NCSA Mosaic was quickly ported to Microsoft Windows and Macintosh PC's. Mosaic rapidly became the proverbial "killer application" for the Internet. Just as Mosaic descended from the work at CERN, all subsequent graphical Web browsers come from this common ancestor.

Web Browsers

Besides NCSA Mosaic, there are a large number of other Web browsers, including, of course, the widely used *Netscape Navigator* package, now the leading Web browser in terms of market share, and Microsoft Internet Explorer. (Incidentally, Marc Andreesen left NCSA to co-found Netscape Communications Corporation.)

While this book concentrates on Microsoft Internet Explorer and Netscape Navigator, there are a lot of Web browser software packages to choose from besides these two. Depending on the type of workstations you have on your LAN, you may need to consider browsers written for platforms other than Windows. Netscape Navigator is available on nearly every platform and Microsoft Internet Explorer is available for Windows NT, Windows 95, Windows 3.1, and the Macintosh. Here is a quick look at just a few of the other browsers available:

- ◆ NCSA Mosaic—A full-featured free browser from the University of Illinois that runs on several operating systems, though its performance on Windows is not quite as snappy as Explorer or Navigator. It can be downloaded from this URL:

  `http://www.ncsa.uiuc.edu/SDG/Software/Mosaic/`

- ◆ Cello—A free browser from Cornell University that runs under Windows and OS/2.

- ◆ WinWeb—Shareware developed by Microelectronics and Computer Technology Corporation that runs under Windows and OS/2.

- ◆ MacWeb—Shareware developed by Microelectronics and Computer Technology Corporation that runs on Macs.

- ◆ Enhanced Mosaic—The commercial version of Mosaic from SpyGlass, Inc. It's available for PCs and Macs.

- ◆ Chimera—Freeware from the University of Nevada that runs under UNIX.

- ◆ Lynx plain-text browser—Freeware from Kansas University for UNIX systems and low-end PCs (doesn't require Windows).

- ◆ W³C (formerly CERN)—This line-mode browser is the original Web browser. It's freeware from the W³ Consortium.

> **Note:** One source for more information about the various Web browsers available on the Internet is `http://www.browserwatch.com/`.

How Web Browsers Work

Graphical or not, all Web browsers work in essentially the same way. Look at what happens when you click on a hyperlink.

◆ Your browser reads a document written in HTML and displays it for you, interpreting all the markup codes in the document.

◆ When you click a hyperlink in that document, your browser uses the Hypertext Transfer Protocol (HTTP) to send a network request to a Web server to access the new document or service specified by the hyperlink.

◆ Also using the HTTP protocol, the Web server responds to the request with the document or other data you requested.

◆ Your browser software then reads and interprets that information and presents it to you in the correct format.

As you can see, a simple click on a hyperlink starts a pretty significant series of events involving not only your Web browser software but also a Web server somewhere on the Internet. Figure 1.4 shows this sequence of events.

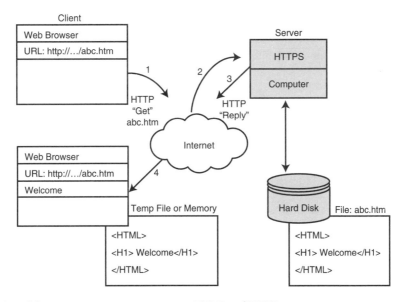

Figure 1.4. *Web browser/server communication using HTML and HTTP.*

> **Note:** For purposes of your Intranet, it's important to note that Web servers always identify the type of data they send in response to browser requests. Most of the time the data returned is text data with HTML markup, but any kind of data can be returned. This bit of information is critical to the potential capabilities of your Intranet: As long as your Web server can identify the data it's sending, your users' Web browsers can be set up to handle almost any kind of data including word processing files, spreadsheets, and the datafiles used by a wide variety of other applications. This simple-but-powerful mechanism explained in detail in Chapter 12, "MIME and Helper Applications" is what you can use to turn your Intranet into an interactive tool for getting your company's everyday work done.

Web Servers

Web browsers like Explorer or Navigator communicate over a network (including the worldwide Internet) with Web servers, using HTTP. Browsers send network messages to servers asking that specific documents or services be provided by the server. The server returns the document or service if it's available also using the HTTP protocol, and the browser receives and understands it.

There are many network protocols spoken on the Internet, each one for a specific and limited purpose. There are network protocols for electronic mail, file transfers, and other services you may have heard of, including *Gopher, Telnet,* and *WAIS.* Each of these protocols works well for its own purpose, and you can use individual programs on your computer that communicate with the protocols to locate and retrieve information on the Net. The HTTP protocol was designed to incorporate these, and other, network protocols into a single protocol. What's important to the World Wide Web user is that Web browsers speak the HTTP protocol, taking care of locating, retrieving, and, most important, interpreting the data, regardless of the actual underlying protocol or service.

Your Intranet will utilize the HTTP protocol and all the other TCP/IP protocols it subsumes to provide point-and-click access to a wide variety of your mission-critical information and services. This is an important point, and we'll come back to it in the final section of this chapter.

World Wide Web Server Software

You don't have to have a UNIX computer system to set up and run a World Wide Web server. In fact, this book will show you how easy it is to run a Web server on Windows NT. Windows NT is an order of magnitude easier to install and manage than UNIX or Netware, in my personal opinion. Windows NT is also a very powerful and secure operating system and many Web servers are available to take advantage of its features.

> **Note:** For detailed information about setting up an Internet Web site on Windows NT (Server or Workstation) or Windows 95, please consult either of these two Sams.net books which I recently co-authored with Christopher Brown: *Web Site Construction Kit for Windows NT* and *Web Site Construction Kit for Windows 95*.

This book will cover aspects of configuring Microsoft Internet Information Server (IIS). Although all of the techniques in this book will apply to any NT Web server, some of the reasons for choosing IIS is that it comes free with Windows NT Server, it is well integrated with the operating system, it includes strong security features, and it was recently rated by PC Week Magazine as the fastest NT Web server. (Of course, benchmark results are a never-ending sea change.)

Information about setting up and using a Web Server is given in Chapter 7, "Running the Intranet Web Server". Since IIS only runs on Windows NT Server, you will need to consider other software if you plan to run Windows NT 4.0 Workstation. NT Workstation 4.0 includes a peer Web server, similar to IIS. Another very good free package is the EMWAC HTTPS. It is included on the CD with *Web Site Construction Kit for Windows NT*. Two powerful commercial servers that run on NT Workstation are Purveyor WebServer and ILAR Concepts FolkWeb. You'll probably want to dedicate a high-end machine to this task, rather than trying to run a server on somebody's desktop PC while it's in use—but this really depends on how much network traffic your Intranet server will need to handle.

> **Note:** Several Windows NT Web Servers are discussed in Appendix B. For detailed information about the current features and capabilities of almost every Web server available, see http://www.webcompare.com/

Chapter 3, "The Software Tools to Build a Web" goes into more detail to help you select the hardware and software to make up your Intranet.

Commercial Web Server Software Features

With the explosive growth in numbers of Intranet and WWW server installations, most professional server software packages have been adding features at an equally fast pace. What follows is a list of some of these:

- ◆ *Encryption* of sensitive information (credit card numbers and other personal or business information for example).
- ◆ *Authentication* of users accessing the server to ensure confidentiality.
- ◆ Accurate *tracking* of who accesses the server.
- ◆ Tracking of *data retrievals*, so software and other data can actually be sold interactively over the Net.

Of course you should also be able to expect commercial-grade support from Web server software vendors. This is a potentially critical matter especially if you don't have in-house expertise in managing the software. Free software packages are invariably not free when you have to provide your own support.

Other TCP/IP Services in Your Intranet

Although we've touched on this subject once or twice earlier, it's worth specific, focused attention for your Intranet. The HTTP protocol spoken by both Web servers and browsers includes a number of other TCP/IP services:

◆ FTP (file transfer protocol)—usually used for downloading files from one computer to another.

◆ Gopher—a menu-based hierarchical information retrieval system.

◆ USENET news—provides access to the world's largest computer bulletin board system.

◆ Wide Area Information Servers (WAIS)—used for searching indexed data using keywords.

◆ Electronic mail—often used to send attached files using MIME (the subject of MIME will be covered extensively in this book).

◆ Other services such as the previously-mentioned archie service available directly or via fill-in forms using the CGI mechanism.

Because these services are built into the HTTP protocol, your Intranet can include any of them. Moreover, you can integrate any of these services without requiring your users to learn the service's native interfaces. Web browsers provide a common, point-and-click front end to all these services. You can, for example, set up an FTP server in your Intranet for distributing software updates or any other computer data. Similarly, you can use USENET news services as a means of collaboration and information sharing within your organization. In either case, your users—the people who are defined in Chapter 2, "Planning an Intranet" as your Intranet's customers—need learn only one interface, to access any of the services you're providing on your Intranet. You will see throughout this book, and especially in Chapter 11, that the Web browser is the key.

This is true regardless of whether your network is connected to the Internet. Because you need TCP/IP networking running in your corporate network in order to set up an Intranet, you can turn around and use this infrastructure to extend your Intranet. Doing so enables you to include a wide variety of other TCP/IP network services. Anonymous FTP, for example, need not be limited to the outside world; you can use it within your company just as well. Index internal data with WAIS, then make it available to your users. Use e-mail distribution lists within your company and your Web browser to read and send messages.

The upshot of this is that your Intranet need not be limited to the passive retrieval of HTML documents, or to extended use of helper applications described in this book. Because Web browsers understand virtually all TCP/IP network protocols, you're free to extend the capabilities of your Intranet to include any of the TCP/IP services that might be useful to your company's or organization's mission. Further, you can do so without incurring the organizational overhead of teaching people to use each and every different service that might be useful.

We will be discussing many of these ideas throughout the book in greater detail. And you will see that utilizing TCP/IP on your Intranet will serve you well when you are ready to open the door to the Internet. For information about using Windows NT as a router, please see Chapter 28, "Connecting the Intranet and the Internet".

Overview of Microsoft ActiveX

If you work with Windows NT or Windows 95 you've probably heard about the new Internet push from Microsoft called *ActiveX*. They announced several technologies under the umbrella of ActiveX at the Professional Developer's Conference in San Francisco in March, 1996. One day of the conference was even broadcast to dozens of theaters around the U.S. where programmers could sit and watch the "movies" as Microsoft explained their vision and demonstrated many of the new features coming soon in their software packages.

Depending on how you look at it, ActiveX is either the entire Microsoft Internet strategy rolled into one word, or it is simply a new name for the idea of fitting OLE custom controls onto the Web. Some of the trade literature has been rather confusing on this point, but mostly it is the latter. The fact that Microsoft is coming out with several other Internet plans at the same time as ActiveX, has led some to cast all of the technologies as "ActiveX". I don't know if this is what their marketing wizards are trying to accomplish, but it seems that many of the announcements do not necessarily depend on ActiveX. Here is a quick breakdown of a few of their recent initiatives:

◆ January purchase of FrontPage from Vermeer. FrontPage will supposedly be bundled with Microsoft Office as a mid-range Web content development tool.

◆ February release of the free Internet Information Server for Windows NT. We will cover the setup of this server in Chapter 7, "Running the Intranet Web Server."

◆ March beta-release of the free Internet Explorer 3.0 to serve as the platform for ActiveX on the Web. Microsoft also demonstrated a third-party technology which allows ActiveX to run in Netscape browsers for Windows.

◆ Development of Visual Basic Script to compete with JavaScript using the new scripting tags in HTML 3.0. This allows page designers a way to create custom functionality based on the ActiveX controls they embed in the HTML.

◆ Development of ISAPI, included with IIS, to offer significant performance advantages over traditional CGI on UNIX. (See Chapter 19, "Getting the Most Out of HTML with CGI" for more information.)

◆ Announcement of the Cryptography API developed by RSA to be distributed with Windows NT and Windows 95. This will allow software developers to write secure applications for the Internet.

◆ Development of ActiveVRML to bring 3D Web pages to Windows platforms. Microsoft has been doing a lot of research on realistic graphics trying to obtain PC performance comparable to high-end UNIX workstations.

◆ Release of Internet Assistant for Word, Excel, PowerPoint, and Access provides convenient document conversion from native formats to the Web and HTML.

◆ The release of Visual C++ 4.1 includes support for ActiveX and ISAPI. A related free product is the Internet Control Pack. It consists of OLE controls which give Visual C++ and Visual Basic programmers access to Winsock functionality.

◆ The purchase of dbWeb from Aspect Software Engineering, which provides relational database features in Web pages.

◆ The inclusion of a GUI Domain Name Server in Windows NT 4.0 and the expansion of the Windows networking Universal Naming Convention to include the concept of DNS.

◆ Beta-release of Sweeper, or the Windows Internet API, for developers of client applications to more easily include support for the Intranet and the Internet.

We will discuss some of these in more detail in Chapter 17, "Understanding ActiveX Technologies." Keep in mind that Netscape—and several other software vendors—already have in place competing alternatives to many of these initiatives.

Summary

I've introduced the World Wide Web in this chapter, then put a spin on it that's applicable to the use of its technology in a corporate Intranet. We've introduced the following subjects, each of which are covered in detail in other chapters:

◆ An overview of the World Wide Web and the Internet.

◆ World Wide Web client software.

◆ World Wide Web servers and their software.

◆ Related TCP/IP networking technologies and how they can be made a part of your Intranet.

◆ The new ActiveX technology from Microsoft.

Chapters 2, 3, 4, and 5 will continue introducing the tools of the Intranet and Internet. By the end of Part I, we will have laid the groundwork for building your Intranet.

CHAPTER

Planning an Intranet

◆ Learn what an Intranet is and how it is different from what you've seen on the World Wide Web

◆ Identify the customers in your company for whom your Intranet is designed

◆ Determine the kind of information you will make available on your Intranet

◆ Decide who in your organization will be the best keeper of your Intranet

◆ Consider high-level issues about the design and organization of your Intranet server(s)

◆ Identify and target your Intranet's customers and sell them on the idea of building an Intranet

This chapter is about the process by which you will plan your Intranet. Although you will no doubt find your design will change as you actually implement your Web, and the people who use it will want further changes, you should nevertheless go through this process before you begin the nuts-and-bolts work of putting it together. Planning your Intranet now will result in building it more effectively and in less overall time. To this end, we'll assume in this chapter only that you have used a World Wide Web browser (such as Netscape or Internet Explorer) and that you therefore have a general familiarity with the Web as a whole.

You'll find these subjects are closely interrelated, and that your decisions in one of these areas inevitably affect the others. As a result, the process of designing an Intranet won't turn out to be the straight-line process these bulleted items seem to suggest.

The What and Why of an Intranet

This book uses the term *Intranet* to refer to organizations' internal use of Web and Internet technology to efficiently share data and documentation. The whole purpose of the Intranet is to encourage and facilitate easy communication among employees so that they may go about their essential work more rapidly. Proper use of the Intranet can simplify many work processes and improve the goods and services produced.

In the rush to get on the Web, most organizations think in terms of making information available to people outside the organization. Many companies have installed Web servers and made them accessible on the Internet with the idea of making corporate information available to others or of selling things on the Web. Interestingly, though, the initial objective of the Web pioneers at the European Particle Physics Lab (CERN) in Geneva, was to create a means by which CERN scientists could more easily share information. Thus, the first Web was, in fact, an *Intranet*, designed to distribute information *within* an organization to the organization's own people. Without detracting from the proven business value of World Wide Web services in making information available to those outside organizations and companies, this book focuses on how purely within an organization, Web and related technology may be used to further the purpose for which the organization exists.

Your Customers

Given this premise, the definition of those who will use your Intranet is sharply different than that of those who use a company's public Web. Traditionally, when a company sets up a Web server, the intended audience is one or more of the following: the general public, current and future customers, stockholders, and even competitors. What all these have in common, of course, is that all of them are *outside* the business. Figure 2.1 shows a typical business home page offering public information, news releases, and the like about a major computer company.

Although many of Apple's employees might have an interest in this Web site, you can see that its primary focus is on presenting information to *outsiders*. General information about the company is available, as are public news releases about company earnings and activities. There's even a page about the company's people and its community service activities, and another about company environmental activities. Both contain valuable public relations information. Clearly, the potential audience of this Web site is external to that company.

By contrast, Figure 2.2 shows the home page for the University of Kansas campus-wide information center. Here the focus is on those people inside or closely associated with the organization: students, faculty, and administrators of the university. You see information about the university's campuses, calendars of events, course listings and schedules, departmental and campus organization information, and information such as the campus phone book.

Figure 2.1. *The Apple Computer home page.*

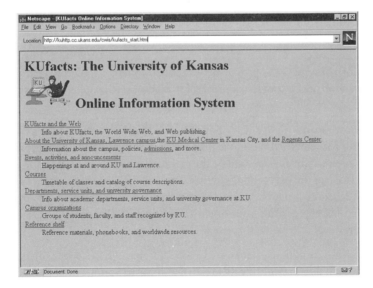

Figure 2.2. *KUFacts, the University of Kansas Online Information System.*

Although there's no doubt some of the information available on this Web server would be useful to people outside the university, its primary audience is clearly campus insiders. The campus phone book or the football schedule may be of wider interest. On the other hand, the History

Department's schedule of classes is probably of interest only to a few history students at the university who are trying to fulfill graduation requirements and/or fit a course into their schedule.

Note: You'll note the decidedly nongraphical approach taken by the university's Web site. KU is the home of Lynx, a text-only Web browser that is freely available and widely used. Nongraphical browsers are important in situations in which users have dumb terminals or other nongraphical devices that cannot display the images and other graphical features of the Web. Many times, even users of graphical browsers will put them in text-only mode for better performance, as graphics take longer to transfer over the network. Intentionally unable to support graphics, Lynx and other plain-text browsers provide the ability for users to follow hyperlinks, download files, send e-mail, read and post Usenet news articles, and access other Internet services, pretty much just as the more fortunate of us who have access to Netscape or Explorer. More information about lynx is available at `http://www.ukans.edu/about_lynx/about_lynx.html`.

Your Insiders Are Your Customers

The distinction between the intended audience of the two Web servers you've examined should now be clear. When you begin to consider the design of your Intranet, your first consideration must be a clear definition of your intended audience, your *customers*, if you will. As you've seen, KUFacts' customers are clearly different from Apple's. The university's primary business is education and research, with its primary customers being students, educators, and researchers, all of whom are members of the organization. KUFacts supports those business objectives by providing information services primarily to those customers. Apple's primary business is selling computers; its Web site customers are primarily the very same people who consume the company's products, the vast majority of whom are outside the organization.

Although your company might already have a World Wide Web server with a constituency similar to Apple's, your Intranet will take on the primary characteristics and orientation of KUFacts. Your organization's primary business might be the manufacture of ball bearings, the provision of health insurance services, or the payment of government benefits, but your Intranet's customers are not the same as the customers who buy or receive those products and services. Rather, in this case, your customers are the people inside your organization. Further, your customers are the people who make those products or provide those services.

These are critical distinctions that must be kept in view when conceiving and designing your Intranet. How you design your Intranet and what information it contains must be based on your target audience—your customers on the inside. Later in this chapter, we'll consider further focusing of the definition of this audience.

> **Note:** This book uses the term *customer* from here on to refer to the people inside your organization or company who will use the Intranet.

Your Intranet Provides Services

There are many business aspects to an Intranet. Your company provides services for one or more kinds for its employees (customers). These services may cover a wide range:

◆ Human Resources (personnel) services

◆ Material and logistical services such as office space, equipment (desks, telephones, computers, machinery, and so on), supplies, and all the physical services involved in operating an organization

◆ Information systems services

In fact, most large businesses have a formal or informal organization that reflects these services, with Material and Logistical, Human Resources, Information Systems, and other similar departments providing services to insiders. Whether your organization is a small shop, multinational corporation, government agency, or other institution, one of its business activities is the provision of these kinds of services. Looking at them is the first major step toward defining the content and layout of your Intranet.

Occasionally, this book takes a frank, customer-is-always-right point of view. Just as your business is all about selling goods or services to your outside customers, your Intranet is all about doing the same with your inside customers.

Information and Services Your Customers Need

We've just cast the people in an organization as customers of some of the organization's goods and services. In addition, we've likened the provision of those goods and services as a business activity. Let's now bring those two ideas together by thinking about the sorts of things that might go into an Intranet. Just what specific things among those goods and services might fit? Consider this question using the major breakdown of business activities listed previously.

Human Resources Services

Whether or not your company has a formal personnel department, you know there is a great deal of paperwork involved. Much of that paperwork is information your customers (remember, employees) need. There are, just to name a few:

◆ Employee manuals, codes of conduct, information about health insurance plans, pay and vacation information, procedures for buying things or getting reimbursed for expenses, and so on.

◆ Company bulletin boards papered with government notices about minimum wages and nondiscrimination policies, job announcements, work schedules, training courses, cafeteria menus, softball schedules, used-tires-for-sale notices, and a hundred other pieces of paper.

◆ Employee records of time, attendance, vital information (marital status, home address, and so on), performance reviews.

◆ Employee newsletters with company announcements and other communications.

◆ All the varied substantive and procedural documents a Human Resources department might use to hire, fire, promote, transfer, train, keep records on, and otherwise manage the employment and benefits of employees.

Here is a veritable treasure trove of information for an Intranet! Imagine how your Human Resources department might provide these kinds of information in a better, more up to date, and more easily accessible way with a World Wide Web server. You might even already have some of this information in some kind of electronic form. (Part III, "Setting Up Office Applications," discusses the conversion of existing electronic data for use on your Web server.) Employees then can use their Web browser to retrieve for themselves current copies of the documents you've previously stored in file cabinets—saving enormous amounts of time and money for both the employees who publish the information and those who need to find it and consult it.

For example, suppose an employee wants to know whether the company health insurance plan covers a particular surgical procedure. If the health plan brochure is available on your Web server, the employee can look it up herself at her own convenience and in a confidential, private way. Also, the employee nearing retirement age might want information about the pension plan, possibly even a benefit computation. Why not make it possible for him to get this information himself? Similarly, how about giving your people the opportunity to file trip reports, including requests for reimbursement of travel expenses, or apply for a job vacancy? How about the company phone book or the old-fashioned suggestion box?

Your Personnel department is a rich source of information for your Intranet.

Material and Logistics Services

Every organization, large or small, provides to its customers desks, telephones, computers, office supplies, trash removal and cleaning services, and a whole host of other related services. Fire extinguishers are serviced, parking lots and sidewalks are maintained and cleared of snow, mail is picked up and delivered, equipment and furniture is moved and repaired, and goods and services are purchased. Records are kept of all these things, some of which (Occupational Safety and Health Administration records, for example) are required by government agencies.

Here is another source of information and services your Intranet can provide. Here are some possible examples:

♦ A Web-searchable listing of excess office furniture, machinery, or computer equipment can save money in a large company, allowing people and excess equipment to be matched.

♦ Nested, clickable imagemaps (see Appendix A, "HTML and CGI Quick Reference.") of building blueprints available to building services staff can bring up increasingly detailed architectural/structural drawings of buildings and their rooms. Ditto for engineering drawings of industrial equipment and all of the underground facilities (water, heat, electricity, network connections) at a large campus.

♦ Similar, but less detailed, imagemaps can provide a graphical front end to the company telephone book allowing employees to locate each other easily. Clicking a building on a campus map can bring up the building's phone book; clicking a room in a building can bring up the names of its occupants.

♦ A wide range of fill-in forms for searching and updating inventories, filling orders, locating and ordering supplies, maintaining required records, and a hundred other tasks.

As you can see, these can range from administrative trivia (locating a used file cabinet) to essential company services. The last idea listed is especially intriguing. You've seen fill-in forms on the Web that allow you to sign electronic guest books and do searches on the Web using Web search services such as Yahoo (`http://www.yahoo.com/`) or Lycos (`http://www.lycos.com/`). Because a fill-in form is merely a means of collecting information and passing it off to a computer program for processing using the Common Gateway Interface, or CGI, you can now provide a Web interface to a plethora of services that must be requested. Bureaucracies already have hundreds of forms employees must fill out to get things or to get things done.

HTML forms can be generated in a few minutes with very few lines of simple code. (See Chapter 5, "What You Need to Know About HTML," for several examples.) When backed up with a fairly simple CGI script or database connection, HTML forms can take the information the user enters and e-mail it to data entry personnel in the Purchasing department. (See Part IV, "Advanced Intranet Publishing," for all the relevant techniques.) With a more elaborate back-end CGI script the very same simple form could be used to enter the order directly into an electronic ordering system, debit the orderer's charge code, update company inventory if the order is for capital equipment, and fire off return e-mail acknowledging the order. In fact, leaving questions of authorization aside, the information in the fill-in form could just as easily be sent via Internet e-mail or fax directly to the supplier, bypassing company purchasing altogether (though, probably, you'd want the program at least to leave a copy for them).

Information Systems Services

Your organization's Information Systems department, if you have one, is already in the business, at least in part, of providing data processing services to customers inside the company. (We use the term Information Systems Services here to mean any information your organization has stored on computers, all the way from the MIS mainframes to your desktop PCs and any services these computer systems provide.) As a result, you'll find crossover between Information Systems

Services and the two other broad categories we've drawn in this chapter. Your Personnel department, for instance, surely uses some data processing services in doing its work whether those services are on the company mainframe or on desktop PCs. In fact, all the potential customers of your Intranet, because they must have computers to access it, are already users of some of these services.

Accordingly, perhaps here is your most fertile source of resources for your Intranet. These services will then form most of the meat of your Intranet. Let's look at some ideas, all of which are covered in detail in later chapters.

- If computer use is widespread in your company, you may have a Help Desk staff that answers phone calls from users about hardware, software, and other related matters. People operating Help Desks know there are questions that come up over and over, which, not surprisingly, have the same answers. How do I set up my modem so I can dial into the office from my home PC? How do I change my password? How do I print mailing labels with my word processor? These canned answers to common questions can form the heart of an Intranet Help Desk. Using Netscape or Explorer, your Help Desk staff can use fill-in forms like the ones on Yahoo or Lycos to search for answers (and create new ones). Taken a step further, there's no reason you can't make the Intranet Help Desk available directly to users, allowing them to search for the information they need at their own convenience. As an added bonus, the Help Desk would then be available 24 hours a day, 7 days a week.

- Web-based interfaces to both commercial and homegrown database applications are available. No matter what you use a database for, it has two major functions: entering or updating information and retrieving information. Although your database application might have special screens for users to perform these functions, both of these functions can just as easily be done with Web fill-in forms and back-end CGI scripts that access the database. The advantage? Users see an interface they recognize and with which they're comfortable, because you've implemented it for many purposes in your Intranet.

- Existing word processing documents, spreadsheets, and other application datafiles can be shared using Web technology. Proper setup of your Web server and your users' Web browsers can, for example, allow a company executive to click a hyperlink and open current sales or operational data directly into his spreadsheet program for what-if analysis and then graph the results for inclusion into presentations or word processing documents.

- Scientists, engineers, and technicians can share datafiles from their computer applications on your Intranet. Chemists can fire up molecular modeling programs just by clicking a hyperlink pointing to a datafile, and engineers can bring up CAD drawings in the same way.

- You can wrap an entire custom computer application program your company uses inside a Web browser interface with built-in help for its users.

As you've read this section, you've no doubt thought about existing Information Systems resources in your company that might be made accessible on your Intranet. Just this brief listing of possibilities can lead you to think about legacy information (that is, existing documents and other data) that will be an immediate source of data you'll be able to tap to get your Intranet up and running quickly.

Who Will Do This?

We now move from thoughts about the substantive content of your Intranet to those of organizational responsibility and design. In earlier years, when MIS departments had a monopoly on data and data processing, it would have been easy to assign responsibility for Intranet setup and design: The MIS Department would do it. Today, though, the Web is based on distributed computing, and MIS probably can't control everyone's desktop PC or workstation. This presents a terrific opportunity for the consumers of Information Systems Resources, who presumably know the most about what they need to take an active role in the design and construction of your Intranet. Neither Web server setup nor the Hypertext Markup Language are rocket science. With the freely available Web server and supporting software on the CD-ROM, it's easy for almost anyone with a PC or workstation to create a Web home page and make it available.

Central Control or No Control?

This ease of setup can be both a blessing and, the MIS folks will quickly remind you, a curse. If anyone can set up a Web server and/or a home page, who will control your Intranet? This question is valid not only from an authoritarian point of view (after all, people are supposed to use their computers to do their jobs) but also from other points of view as well. Here are some issues you might have to deal with:

◆ Will you want your Intranet to have a common organization and look, or is substance all you care about?

◆ Will someone approve each and every piece of information before it goes on your Intranet, or can anyone put up anything they like?

◆ If people are free to put up anything they like, will you be concerned about inappropriate material and/or inappropriate use of your organization's Information Systems and personnel resources?

◆ Will you accept and welcome the inevitable evolution of your Intranet as you and its users figure out new things it might do?

If you've used the World Wide Web to any extent, you've recognized it as the world's largest vanity press; people can, and do, put anything they want on it. This is a sword that cuts both ways. You can find truly amazing (in all senses of the word) things on the Web, many of which may be offensive (again, in all senses of the word). How you feel about this sort of anarchy will inevitably color how you approach assigning responsibility and setting standards for your Intranet. At the same time, the fundamental nature of the Web as a distributed service provides unparalleled opportunities for individual and organizational development, and imposing a rigid, authoritarian structure on your Web might well inhibit the sort of creativity that can bring about breakthroughs in your company's work.

Organizational Models

Based on the philosophical approach you decide to take in assigning responsibility for your Intranet, there are several models you can follow. Here are three:

1. *Centralized model* with a single Web server administered by a specific organization in your company, and a formal process for developing and installing new services
2. *Decentralized model* with anyone free to set up a Web server and place resources of their choice on it
3. *Mixed model* with elements of both the centralized and decentralized models

Centralized Model

In this top-down model, all Web services are centralized. Just one computer system in your company runs a Web server. You have a specific individual or group responsible for the setup, design, and administration of the server. All Web pages (documents, forms, and so on) are designed centrally at the request of customers. Thus, if the Personnel department wanted to put employee benefit information on the Web, a formal request would be required, including content and design requests. The Web staff would, in consultation with Personnel, design and refine the employee benefits page and once the process is complete, make the page available on the Web server. Figure 2.3 shows the centralized model of Web administration with all Web-related development funneled through an approval process before any information is placed on the central Web server.

There are a number of good reasons this approach is sound. First and foremost, by focusing Web server administration, page design, and production in a single person or group, it provides the opportunity for you to develop a consistently designed Intranet. You can develop and use common Web page templates to ensure layout consistency as well as a standard set of substantive and navigational images. Users will see a coherent, well-thought-out Web server with each part consistent with your overall design, layout, and content standards.

Another strong argument in favor of the centralized model is that it simplifies the setup and administration of your Intranet. Only one computer system runs the server. All updates, both Web pages and server software, need to be applied only once. Security (see Chapter 10, "Intranet Security in Windows NT") can be focused on the single machine, which can also be physically secured. Backups are easy to do because everything that needs backing up is on the one system.

Unfortunately, there are equally strong reasons this approach is the wrong one to take. From a philosophical point of view, it runs counter to pretty much everything that's happened in data processing over the past two decades. With the rise of the personal computer and workstation, data processing has moved out of the glass-walled MIS data center and onto people's desks. Taking the centralized approach to your Intranet might satisfy the MIS diehards, but it also contradicts everything the Web stands for.

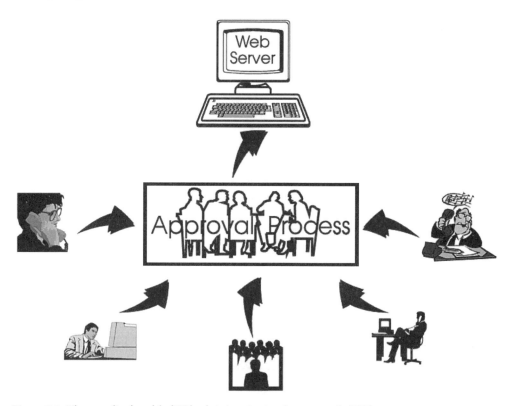

Figure 2.3. *The centralized model of Web administration involves a controlled Web server.*

More practically speaking, bureaucratized administration of your Intranet's development can choke it to death before it ever gets off the ground as endless memoranda about "standards" circulate before any real development takes place. Your primary objective in setting up an Intranet is to get information to your customers. Centralized administration can easily get bogged down in organizational and turf matters, cutting off the potential of rapid response to your customers.

Tip: It's useful to note in this connection that because your target audience is inside your company, not outside, the standards you'd apply to the former will probably be very different from those for the latter. The employee looking for help in setting up his PC probably doesn't care whether the help document he finds on your Intranet has the correctly proportioned corporate logo on it. Rather, he's interested in the substance of the document. Your company's outside Web server, aimed at a completely different audience, can—and probably will—be subject to a more rigorous set of standards.

Finally, the centralized model places all your Web eggs in a single basket. If the computer system running your Intranet server goes down, everyone is cut off. This policy requires a decision between potentially expensive downtime and expensive duplicative hardware—another hot, spare computer ready to run in the event the main system goes down. This adds not only the extra cost of the hardware and software for the system but introduces a new aspect of the administration of the system, that of making sure all changes to the primary system get mirrored to the backup.

Decentralized Model

At the other end of the spectrum lies the decentralized model. Web server software is widely available both commercially and as freeware or shareware. The software runs on desktop PCs. This software is relatively easy to set up and run. HTML, the markup language used to create Web pages with all their nice formatting and image and hyperlink capabilities, can be picked up by just about anyone in a couple of hours. Using free software or shareware, some of which is included on the accompanying CD-ROM, even a moderately experienced PC user can have a Web server up and running with some HTML documents in an afternoon. Figure 2.4 shows the decentralized model of Web administration with users free to develop their own Web documents and even set up individual Web servers.

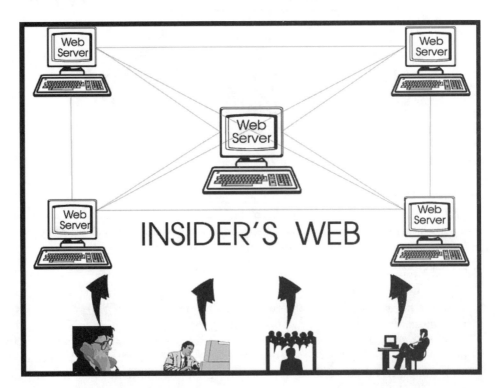

Figure 2.4. *The decentralized model of Web administration allows anyone to create useful Web services for the rest of the team.*

As with the centralized model, there are strong and weak points to this one. The most compelling argument for this model is that the user who sets up her own Web server (and who is also, you should be reminded, one of your Intranet's customers) might be the single best person to do so because she knows precisely the service she wants to provide with it. That is, if an engineer wants to share engineering drawings and technical reports with her colleagues, she and her colleagues are in the best position to decide what is to be shared and how it is best presented. In the centralized model, this customer with information to share has to negotiate the standards process before being able to get the information to her colleagues. Similarly, the Personnel Specialist who has new pension information to make available, or the Office Manager announcing the staff holiday party, is more concerned about getting the information posted than whether it's properly formatted according to some standard or whether the proper colors are used in the corporate logo.

In other words, the main advantage of the decentralized model is that it allows those who have information to share to share it quickly and with a minimum of fuss. If you're running a Web server on your PC, for instance, you can put up a new Web page on some subject in your expertise in just a few minutes. This is also the main disadvantage of the model. The fact that it is so easy to set up Web pages lends itself to what may best be termed *anarchy*, with users putting up related or unrelated (who decides which is which?) Web pages all over the company. A casual walk around the World Wide Web shows how this anarchy can and does lead from the sublime to the absurd to the obscene.

Tip: It's important also to note that the overall tone of a Web server can lead to increased or decreased support from both its customers and its sponsors. Too much anarchy often turns users off, and they just stop using the service. And, of course, there are few things that could be worse for the overall health of your Intranet than to have the president of the company stumbling across a particularly inappropriate or offensive link on some part-time employee's home page.

The nature of your organization will help you evaluate this model. Academic and research institutions might find the intellectual freedom of their researchers outweighs the high noise level of the Web created under this model. Businesses might want a tighter focus on the work at hand, finding this sort of anarchy has too much potential for abuse and/or misdirected time and effort.

Mixed Model

Somewhere between these two extremes is probably where most organizations will land when setting up Intranets. For example, you might want to establish a broad policy that your Web's primary purpose is to support a specific group of your customers and that anything consistent with that purpose is permitted. In this case, you'd rely on that part of the centralized model that dictates the overall direction and purpose of your Web but use those aspects of the decentralized model that leave most details to your customers. There will inevitably be gray areas or even outright violations of the overall policies, but you can deal with them on a case-by-case basis as *management* issues, just as you do with, say, misuse of company telephones or time-and-leave abuse.

Please don't make firm decisions on a model for administering your Intranet quite yet. You still need to focus on its primary objectives, and doing so will help you focus your decision-making on these administrative issues. In the following sections, you'll look at these questions as well as lay out some of the technical possibilities for implementing the mixed model.

Design and Layout of Your Intranet

Having considered the foregoing administrative matters, let's now turn to more interesting things: the substantive design and content of your Intranet.

What Is the Purpose of Your Intranet?

You probably bought *Building an Intranet with Windows NT 4.0* because you had some idea of what you might be able to do with an internal corporate Web server. So far in this chapter, you've established a framework that should help you bring your ideas into clearer definition. We first brought out the concept of thinking of the potential users of your Intranet as customers and provided some possibilities based on this concept. Next, we discussed some of the high-level administrative aspects of setting up and running an Intranet. By now you perhaps have a clearer focus on who your potential customers are and some definite ideas on the sorts of information you want to make available.

Statement of Purpose

Putting your ideas together into an Intranet *Statement of Purpose* is your first concrete step toward realizing your ideas. Let's look at a few example Statements of Purpose, based on the possibilities listed under the previous heading *Information and Services Your Customers Need*:

◆ Provide customers with information about their employee benefits.

◆ Give customers access to a searchable database of PC hardware and software technical support information.

◆ Provide customers a Web browser interface to the corporate inventory and ordering database.

◆ Use Web technology to enable customers to share data files from common applications.

As you can see, each of these is both specific and limited. Developing your Statement of Purpose allows you to define the task ahead of you in terms both you and your potential customers can easily grasp. There is, of course, no reason you can't write a larger Statements of Purpose incorporating several of these (or other) purposes, such as "Provide customers with Human Resources and information system services using World Wide Web technology". Such a far-reaching Statement of Purpose is certainly acceptable, provided of course that you're able to clearly define the objectives that fall under it, possibly using lower-level Statements of Purpose for each of the major subdivisions, Human Resources and Information Systems. Some people might want to start out with more limited Statements of Purpose like those listed and then expand on them later. The method you choose depends on your own ideas about what you want your Intranet to accomplish.

Besides giving you a pole star toward which to steer in developing your Intranet, your Statement of Purpose also implies some substantive choices about the work you're cutting out for yourself. For example, it's one thing to take a batch of Microsoft Word documents and put them up on a Web server as a boilerplate library (see Chapter 13, "Word Processing on the Web," and Chapter 25, "Intranet Boilerplate Library") for customers to browse and grab. Most computer-literate people can put such a library together and generate the HTML code to index it. It's quite another thing, though, to develop the CGI scripts to back up forms-based data entry and retrieval. (See Chapter 16, "Linking Databases to the Web.") The order form example mentioned earlier in this chapter is quite simple, but the program that it executes will not be. You'll need competent programmers to write the scripts in whatever programming language you choose on your system.

Implementation Goals

Once you have a Statement of Purpose, particularly if yours is a broad one like the one mentioned, you'll need to develop more concrete *implementation goals*, or specific objectives of the information and services your Intranet will provide to your customers. Following the Employee Benefits Statement of Purpose, you might, then, define a series of goals:

◆ Provide online health benefits information.

◆ Provide online job vacancy announcements, the capability of customers to read both summary and detailed information.

◆ Allow customers to enter change-of-address and/or family status information using fill-in forms.

◆ Allow customers to calculate an estimated pension benefit based on their years of service and projected earnings between now and retirement age using a fill-in form.

Your implementation goals can now be translated into clusters of specific tasks to be performed in order to implement and manage them. For example, if your job vacancy announcements are created using your word processor, they can be quickly saved in plain text form (or converted to HTML by a conversion package) then placed on your Web server. As they expire, old announcements can be removed and replaced by new ones. You'll need to designate someone to be responsible for managing the job announcements and, if necessary, train them in using HTML. Depending on the administrative model you've chosen for managing your Intranet, you might also need to train the individual in the process of actually placing the job announcements on the Web server so they become available.

Purposes and Goals Evolve

As you develop your overall purpose statement and implementation goals, bear in mind that once a Web server starts getting hits (that is, customers start using it), you and they will start thinking of new ideas you could implement using Web technology. Accordingly, you shouldn't cast your plans in stone. Rather, you'll want to leave room for evolution. Good ideas often beget other good ideas, so don't lock yourself out with a purpose statement that's too restrictive to allow new goals.

The job vacancy announcement goal example used above is a good illustration of how such a seemingly specific goal might evolve over time. You might start out with simple one-line announcements and find customers wanting more information about the positions. Adding more details to the announcements helps, but sometimes people want to be able to communicate with a real person to ask questions not covered in the announcements, so you add contact information to the announcements. Later, someone asks about using the mailto Uniform Resource Locator (see Chapter 5), and you realize you can add hyperlinks to the job announcements that allow your customers to send e-mail to the contact person just by clicking a hyperlink. Still later, customers ask why they can't just go ahead and apply for the job directly using a Web fill-in form. So it goes.

Web Design and Layout

With your Statement of Purpose and implementation goals ready, you can turn to the design and layout of your Intranet. It's useful to break this process down into two related pieces: *logical* and *physical.*

Logical Design of an Intranet

The logical design and layout is the process of arranging the information on your Intranet according to some overall plan. (Later you'll see you can reflect your logical design in your physical design.) Just as I begin the process of writing a book by organizing material with an outline, with major subjects placed into some sort of logical arrangement, your Intranet design should begin with some organizational layout. The information you're planning on placing on your Intranet often naturally breaks down into logical chunks, so you can reflect these natural divisions in its logical design. In fact, you might do well to start out with a traditional outline of the material. From the Statement of Purpose, you can generate a brief outline. Look at the following example.

ABC Company Intranet—Statement of Purpose

Provide Customers with Human Resources, Materiel and Logistics, and Information System Services Using World Wide Web Technology.

    Human Resources Information
    Employee benefits information
    Job announcements
    Other HR Information
    Material and Logistics information
    Inventory database
    Purchase orders

Building and grounds plans
Other M&L information
Information systems services
Computer hardware and software Help Desk
Boilerplate libraries
Spreadsheet data libraries
Other IS Information
Other departments
Engineering
Research
Manufacturing

Looking at this short summary outline (most of the details have been left out for space reasons of course), it's easy to see how you can organize the overall logical structure of your Intranet. Let's collapse this outline into major functional areas to make this clear.

ABC Company Home Page
Statement of Purpose:

Provide Customers with Human Resources, Materiel and Logistics, and Information System Services Using World Wide Web Technology.

Major Subdivisions of this Web:

Human Resources information
Material and Logistics information
Information systems services
Other departments

You've laid out not only the overall design of a Web, but all but written its home page as well. Using WebEdit (on the CD), you can lay this out as a home page. You don't really have to know HTML to accomplish this because the Home Page Wizard in WebEdit makes it pretty easy. After a few minutes of tinkering, I came up with the sample home page for ABC, shown in Figure 2.5. (Chapter 5 covers installing and using WebEdit.)

Tip: Your network capabilities and customers' hardware capabilities can provide important cues to help you in your Web's logical design. For example, if all your customers have high-speed (10 Mbps) LAN connections and graphical Web browsers such as Explorer or Netscape, you can take full advantage of graphics in your Intranet. If some of your customers have modem dial-up connections to your network through Windows NT Remote Access Service (RAS), you'll want to downplay graphics for performance reasons.

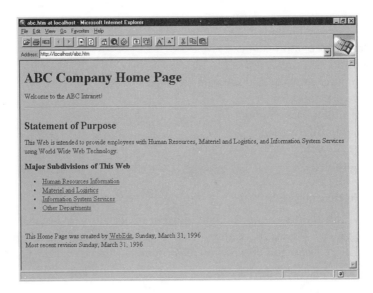

Figure 2.5. *After creating a simple Intranet home page in WebEdit, you can view it in Explorer.*

Hierarchies and Hypertext

Within this design, as you no doubt have guessed, each of the ABC Company's major subdivisions also has a home page with the information and services to be offered. This is a simple hierarchical design, and for purposes of the sort of high-level layout you're considering here, it's a good way of beginning your own Intranet design. Within your Intranet, though, you'll want to take advantage of the ability to create *hyperlinks* to other pages so your customers can get around easily and intuitively. Rigid adherence to some purely hierarchical design can limit you in Intranet design. Books are usually designed to be read sequentially, page by page, from front to back, and hierarchical design is apparent in such an arrangement. People who pick up a book expect this arrangement.

On the other hand, the World Wide Web, as you know, has introduced the concept of *hypertext*, a most assuredly non-hierarchical element. Through the use of hyperlinks, users can jump from place to place on the Web with little attention to page hierarchies or other structure. As a result, Web pages (and Web servers themselves) lend themselves to more human design. Users follow hyperlinks based on their own interests, predilections, and the needs of a given moment.

As you design your Intranet, the nice, neat hierarchical design you might lay out at the top level can handcuff you once you get down into the actual meat of your Web. You'll want to therefore be receptive to the use of nonlinear design as your Intranet develops. It's probably a good idea, for example, to include hyperlinks on pretty much every page (or every major page, at least) that allow the customer to jump back to the top-level page from anywhere without having to backtrack. Cross-references among documents are also great things to use as hyperlinks. If a document mentions another document, the user may want to see the referred-to document, and a hyperlinked cross reference allows this.

At the same time, your overall design decisions can set limits on where hyperlinks might take your customers. Many people like hypertext because it seems somehow more like how they actually think, but others are more literal in their thinking and prefer a well-organized, hierarchical structure to things. In either case, total reliance on hypertext features without any overall organization can lead to confusion and frustration and to the loss of your Intranet's customers. This is one reason that it is critical for you to involve your customers early in the process of designing your Intranet, as well as keeping them involved with a feedback loop. It's difficult, if not impossible, for you to anticipate what your customers will and will not like about their Intranet, so it's critical you get them involved in issues like design and layout. I'll go over these topics more carefully in Chapter 4, "The People Skills to Make it Work."

Physical Design of a Web

There are a number of ways to lay out the physical aspects of your Intranet. Your decisions on the administrative and logical aspects discussed in this chapter can give you important clues here as well. As suggested earlier, when discussing the centralized model of Web administration, a single computer running Web server software lends itself well to the administrative model selected. If you're using this model, you need not be concerned about the physical layout of a Web in which multiple servers in multiple locations operate; your server is inside a secure room, accessible only by its administrators. All your Web pages, and all the administration and configuration of your server, takes place in one location. This vastly simplifies server administration, maintenance, system backups, and, of course, server security.

Paradoxically, the decentralized model of Web administration, where anyone is free to set up and maintain their own Web server as part of an Intranet, is also simpler for you to administer. That is, you *don't*. Just by making the administrative decision that any user can set up a Web server and place anything on it, you've washed your hands of all these issues of physical layout, design, and server administration. Users are free to set up servers, placing documents on them according to whatever logical design they find applicable, and are responsible for doing so, as well as for maintaining their servers and documents. Any central administration can be limited to maintaining an overall home page for your Intranet with hyperlinks pointing to all the other servers. This administrative (and physical) layout can further suggest hardware and software requirements: if all your central Web server does is serve a home page with links to other servers, you don't need a powerful computer to run it.

As you can probably surmise, the mixed administrative model provides the most flexibility in both the logical and physical layout of your Intranet, while retaining your ability to manage its structure. For example, you might design an Intranet with a main server and several departmental servers. The sample Intranet used in this chapter lends itself to this setup. Each of the major subdivisions of your Intranet, corresponding to the major administrative departments of the ABC Company, can be hosted on a separate computer system running Web server software. Thus, the Personnel department would run and manage a Web server devoted to Human Resources, while Material and Logistics would run another. Having delegated the administration of those logical pieces of your Web to the departments, you can also, if you choose, delegate the physical ones. As with the decentralized model, this choice can impact your needs for hardware.

Personnel might not want the responsibility of physically maintaining a computer system, however. The decentralized model can still allow the logical layout of your Web to allow Personnel to maintain its own substantive Intranet content. The HTML language is not difficult to learn, and ABC's departments could share a single computer system running a Web server physically maintained by a dedicated individual or staff but still maintain their own documents on that server. HTML documents can be created and/or edited using almost any editing tool on desktop PCs and then uploaded to your main Web server. You can even use file-sharing mechanisms to make Web server administration completely transparent. Through appropriately secured use of the NT file system, your Web server's directories can be shared so users see them as local volumes with HTML documents directly accessible for editing. As far as the user is concerned, he's just creating or editing documents on his own PC, yet the documents are available to everyone else on your Intranet.

As with most three-choice models, your actual implementation of an Intranet is unlikely to be as clear cut as described here. It should seem clear to you that the mixed model described is what we would recommend, but there are virtually infinite variations possible. The nice, neat, logical, and/or physical division among ABC's departments probably won't fit your needs. It's more likely that Personnel will need one sort of setup, whereas Engineering might need a completely different one because the two groups have different skill sets and interests. You might find that one department wants their piece of your Intranet rigidly administered with all sorts of preset standards and procedures, whereas another department wants a completely decentralized model. Fortunately, you can accommodate both. Intranet server design and setup are anything if not flexible, and what you start out with might well change as you gain experience.

Selling Your Intranet

In this final section, you'll turn your attention to how you can get your customers to buy into your Intranet. Web technologies, or, more properly, the things that Web technology makes possible, are very seductive. The ongoing explosion of the Internet has been driven in very large part by the Web. People *really like* using Explorer or Netscape to find interesting things on the Web. As many managers are recognizing, there's a seductive, recreational aspect to the World Wide Web, as the widely used terms *playing Web* and *surfing the Web* indicate. The Web, in large respect, sells itself. This book is about using this seductive technology on an everyday basis in your company's work.

Defining Your Audience

This might seem a no-brainer. After all, your Intranet is for people within your company. Although this is generally true, a closer look reveals the fact that you need to fine tune your definition. First, unless everyone in your company has a computer (or access to one) your audience is immediately defined as the group of users who will have some sort of access to your Intranet. Even this, however, isn't a true audience definition, rather a definition of your potential audience. You still need to break this audience down based on common characteristics. The kind of work a group of individuals do can help you define their needs as customers of your Intranet. Members of a clerical pool, for example, constitute an audience for the sort of boilerplate library of documents discussed in Chapter 25. Researchers will have more interest in using your Web in their own work, perhaps as an aid in collaboration. (See Chapter 27.) Both these groups, however, fall into the larger audience of company employees with an interest in the sorts of Human Resources and/or Material and Logistics information and services described in this chapter.

Hardware Considerations

Your larger potential audience also breaks down in another way based on the capabilities of the computer hardware they'll use to access your Web. Do they all have graphical Web browser capabilities and high-speed network connections? This question raises further questions that go to both the substantive content of your Intranet and to its physical and logical nature (that is, hardware capabilities and the concomitant limits they may place on the logical design of it). Let's look at how hardware can affect your audience definition and also provide important Intranet design input.

Computer use is widespread, but not nearly universal, in organizations. Millions of people have computers on their desks at work or at home, but millions more don't. This obvious point acts to define your Intranet's audience. Further, though, even among the group of people who do have computer access, there can be a wide variation in both access and hardware capabilities. While some users have PCs with full graphical capabilities, others might be using dumb terminals with little or no graphics. In either case, a number of users may be sharing these seats.

These are important audience characteristics that speak not only to the relative ease by which your customers can access your Intranet but also to what they can see when they do access it. The user with a dumb terminal can't see graphics and can't use clickable imagemaps, so your Web design decisions must take this into account. Do you do so by not using graphics at all, dragging that part of your audience with graphical Web capabilities down to the lowest common denominator, or attempt to design a Web that everyone can use even with their hardware limits? Similarly, if large numbers of your customers share PCs or terminals—on a factory floor, for example—the timeliness and immediacy of your Intranet's information is affected, because not everyone will have easy, immediate access.

As with each of the other major subjects covered in this chapter—Intranet administration and design/layout—the characteristics of your intended audience can provide valuable help in the overall development of your Intranet.

Web Users, Web Mockups, and Focus Groups

You can help focus your audience definition and generate valuable information that can contribute to the design and content of your Intranet by involving potential customers in its development process using *focus groups*. Getting your customers involved early—and keeping them involved—

generates an investment on their part in your Intranet. This investment will pay dividends by helping you create the right Intranet, the one your customers want.

Mockups and Demos

Before you get your focus group(s) together, be sure you have something to show them. Getting a group of people together to shoot the bull about getting an Intranet going without your first having prepared some sort of presentation, is a poor way of starting out. You might have a few people who have Web experience, and some of them may already have ideas you can use, but as much as two-thirds of your focus group might never have seen the World Wide Web. If you don't have something to show them, they'll have a great deal of trouble understanding what it is you want from them.

To a person with no experience of the Web, even the crude home page shown in Figure 2.5 is a dramatic demonstration, particularly if there are hyperlinks to similar home pages for the major divisions shown on the page and an actual document or two linked into them. Even a simple demonstration can let you use that Web seductiveness we spoke of earlier to spark interest in your Intranet, getting your customers to invest early.

Encourage your demonstration participants to discuss possibilities based on what you've shown them. As mentioned repeatedly, even Web novices know the information they want from their organization. Showing them real information as well as the potential capabilities of an Intranet, will surely stimulate ideas on their part. Your focus group(s), also including your organization's information providers, should provide a lively and useful means by which you'll further define your audience and its interests. This, in turn, will help you pin down the actual kinds of information your customers will want, thereby generating audience investment and support in your Intranet.

Users and Focus Groups

You probably already have a good deal of experience with the World Wide Web and have based your own ideas about your Web on things you've seen. If you have good ideas from your own Web experiences, it's a good bet there are others in your company who have them too, or would have if you asked them to think about it. Experienced Web users who are also your potential customers are in the unique position of both knowing a lot about the capabilities and possibilities of Web technology and of knowing what they, as potential customers of your Web, want to see. Get these customers together, informally or in formal focus groups, to talk about your ideas and theirs.

Don't limit your focus groups to those with Web experience, though. The employees of a company or the members of an organization have definite ideas about the information they want. Even if they've never seen a Web browser, they can give you information that's important to your Intranet design. Similarly, don't forget to include people we might call Intranet information *resellers*. I've used the example of employee benefits and other personnel-related information in this chapter as potential Intranet content. The people in your Human Resources department who provide this information now, and who will be providing it on your Intranet, should also be part of your focus groups. They know the information they provide and probably have a good idea of how often their customers ask for it.

Summary

This chapter dealt with the overall process of designing an Intranet and covered a number of major, interrelated, topics, including

- What an Intranet is and how it is different from what you've seen on the World Wide Web
- Identification of the customers in your company for whom your Intranet is to be designed
- Determination of the kind of information you will make available on your Intranet
- Decisions on who in your company or organization (or what organizational component) is best as the keeper of your Intranet
- Consideration of high-level issues about the design and organization of your Intranet
- Targeting of your Intranet's customers and selling them on the idea of an Intranet

For more information on these topics, check out *The World Wide Web 1996 Unleashed*, by John December and Neil Randall, also published by Sams.net (ISBN 0-57521-040-1). For information on this and other Sams.net books, see the World Wide Web URL http://www.mcp.com.

The next chapter discusses Intranet infrastructure, and the hardware and software tools you'll need to get started building your Intranet.

CHAPTER

3

The Software Tools to Build a Web

◆ Computer hardware suitable for running a Web server

◆ World Wide Web server software

◆ Software tools for creating HTML pages

◆ World Wide Web browser software and helper applications that work in conjunction with Web browser software

◆ The software included on the CD-ROM

The last chapter was devoted to high-level issues involving the overall design and objectives of your Intranet. In this chapter you'll turn from abstract consideration of purpose statements and audience definition to some hardware and software specifics. Here you'll survey the software and hardware tools you need to get set up. I cover the subject of hardware (briefly) because it will affect some of your choices in software (for example, Intel versus RISC and NT Server versus NT Workstation).

Many of the software tools discussed in this chapter are available on the CD-ROM accompanying this book, although some are commercial packages. Mentions of specific commercial software packages are examples only and don't imply any endorsement of them by this author or by Sams.net.

This chapter is an overview. In subsequent chapters and appendixes, you find more detailed information about the tools discussed here. Even so, this book does not get into the internals of TCP/IP networking. I will highlight the setup of World Wide Web server software, particularly as it relates to the Intranet, but many of the technical details of Web server software are beyond our scope. Similarly, I'll refer to other Internet standard software you can integrate into your Web and leave some details to other references. Although I provide a good deal of specific setup information about several Web browser software packages, this book is not a complete reference on those packages. You'll find a variety of book-length treatments of these subjects in your favorite bookstore.

Hardware for Your Web Server

The hardware you select for your Intranet server(s) is dependent on a number of factors including your anticipated traffic levels, ease of setup, your in-house technical expertise, and other requirements. Windows NT server software is quick and easy to set up with point-and-click configuration. You can have a Web server running on a PC in just a few minutes. If you choose to use the decentralized or mixed models of Web administration described in Chapter 2, individual users can easily take advantage of this software on their own desktop PCs.

> **Tip:** Except for personal Web servers, you probably should not plan on running a Web server on a PC that is also somebody's everyday desktop machine. As a simple rule, this will help ensure the best Web server performance for your customers. However, if you are on a tight budget, reconsider that general advice in light of the expected network traffic, the processing power of the computer in question, and the frequency and complexity of the other tasks running on that machine.

> **Caution:** Before buying any hardware to run with Windows NT, it is always a good idea to make sure it is on the Windows NT Hardware Compatibility List. This document is published by Microsoft and the most current version can be browsed at their Web site: http://www.microsoft.com/ntserver/hcl/hclintro.htm.

A Respectable Intranet Server

Windows NT 4 will run on just about any 486 or greater PC with at least 16MB of RAM. At least 32 MB of RAM is recommended. (Note that support for Intel 386 machines was dropped in this latest release of NT.) There are almost as many NT configurations as there are system administrators, so I will try to stick to giving broad and budget-conscious advice in this section. Listed here is a hardware configuration that is very similar to this author's small Web site (http://www.hqz.com):

◆ Pentium-based computer in a full tower case with mouse and keyboard. You probably won't need a super high-end video card on your Intranet server, but you'll want to know whether the computer supports PCI or VLB as you consider your purchase of adapter cards. NT also runs on Alpha, MIPS, and PowerPC, and you should consider those RISC platforms if you need a high-performance Intranet server. However, most software written for Windows NT is not yet available in binary form for non-Intel machines.

◆ 250-watt power supply. This should give you enough coverage for the power draw from four disk drives, one CD-ROM drive, one tape backup, one floppy drive, VGA card, and the disk drive adapter card.

◆ 32MB RAM, at least. Windows NT runs more efficiently with 32MB than it does with 16MB because there is less need to temporarily store extra memory in pagefile.sys on the hard disk. Also, RAM access time is much faster than hard-disk access time.

◆ 15-inch or 17-inch SVGA monitor. In nearly all cases, a server needs to stay on all the time. If you aren't going to work at the computer all the time, you might want to turn the monitor off or get one of the new energy-saving monitors, which can reduce power usage by 90 percent.

◆ Network Interface Card (NIC). I have always had good luck with 3Com cards, but I can't rate them against other brands because I haven't tried any others. You need to know the type of network cabling on your LAN: Thinnet (RG-58) will need a BNC connector on the back of the card, Twisted Pair will need an RJ-45 connector, and thick coaxial cabling will require an AUI 15-pin connector. A *combo* card will support all three media types. Thinnet is good for small LANs because it doesn't entail the added expense of a hub.

◆ Internal SCSI CD-ROM drive and SCSI adapter card. NT includes terrific support for nearly all SCSI CD-ROM drives and a handful of non-SCSI CD-ROM drives. In certain cases, it installs more easily from SCSI CD-ROM drives.

◆ 512MB (minimum, 1GB recommended) hard disk drive. This is the C: drive, or the *boot* drive. You can install the operating system and all utility programs on this drive. It can be either SCSI or IDE, but once you've made an investment in a SCSI adapter card for a CD-ROM drive, you won't want to buy a separate controller card for IDE drives. Find out how many internal devices your controller card can handle. You might anticipate the future need of at least four.

◆ 1GB hard disk drive. This is the D: drive and will hold all the HTML files. This can also be SCSI or IDE. The reasons for having two physical drives are as follows: Better performance is obtained from having two platters spinning when multiple files are being loaded, and there is a gain in reliability if each drive is used less often.

◆ V.34 modem or ISDN interface. This is optional depending on whether you plan to provide Dial-Up Networking connections to the Intranet for your customers who work off-site and whether you plan to connect your Intranet to the Internet via modem. (See Chapter 28.) You can go internal or external with these devices. External modems provide status lights and save an expansion slot inside the computer for future use. V.34 is a recent modem standard ratified by the CCITT to cover data transmission speeds up to 28.8 Kilobits per second, or Kbps. You'll get the best performance out of a V.34 modem if your computer has a 16550 UART.

◆ DAT or optical backup device. Automated file backups are highly recommended.

◆ Uninterruptible Power Supply (UPS). Although optional, this is recommended for a reliable Intranet so an orderly shutdown can be conducted if power is lost on the server.

Do I Really Need to Buy a Backup Device?

If you're thinking that a tape backup is a luxury, I should point out that you are probably going to be downloading tons of software from the Internet. You'll find that new software is announced almost every day, and you'll want to take advantage of new tools to help you keep your Intranet server running efficiently.

In the event of a hard-disk failure, it is true that you can restore shrink-wrap software products from the original media, but when you consider the amount of download time it would take to recover all of your zipped packages, if they were ever lost, you'll probably agree that a backup device becomes an essential component. And if your customers are creating and storing any intellectual content on your Intranet server, the cost to re-create it could be so great that it could jeopardize the job of a system administrator who failed to back it up.

Recently, there are several exciting alternatives to tape backup: 100MB Zip drives from Iomega, 135MB EZDrives from Syquest, 1GB Jaz drives from Iomega, and 4.6GB optical drives from Pinnacle Micro are worth mentioning. These drives function at the speed of hard drives and include replaceable media in the fashion of a huge floppy drive. The Zip drives go for around $200, and three 100MB disks run about $50. The Pinnacle optical drive costs about $1,500, and the optical disks are about $200. This does add to the cost of the computer, but there is no cheaper way to add an infinite amount of quick-access storage to your system. Once you have one of these drives, all you have to do is buy more media.

Software for Your Web Server

In this section, I outline all of the tools that you will find useful in building an Intranet. Most of these packages are available on the Internet or on the CD-ROM with this book. As a Webmaster or an Intranet System Administrator, you will learn very quickly that the Internet contains a vast treasure of software to help you with your job. At the end of this chapter, I list a few helpful places you can visit online whenever you are looking for a new piece of software.

TCP/IP Networking Required

If you're already using the World Wide Web, you're already using TCP/IP, the fundamental Internet networking protocols. Only the TCP/IP networking protocols, the foundation of the world-wide Internet, support the Web over local area and wide area networks (which is the essence of an Intranet). Without TCP/IP there would be no Internet and no World Wide Web; without it on your LAN you'll have no Intranet. Designed from the very beginning to operate over different communication media, TCP/IP works on Ethernet and Token Ring LAN's; it even operates over ordinary telephone lines using modems.

Web Servers

There are dozens of excellent Web servers available for Windows NT. (Okay, so I lied a little; if you visit the URL following this sentence, you'll see that there are currently 23 Web servers available for Windows NT: `http://www.webcompare.com/server-main.html`.)

Netscape, Process, and O'Reilly have been the main players in the NT HTTP server business for more than a year. Just this year Microsoft entered the arena and promises to shake things up a bit because their Internet Information Server is free. The other vendors have lowered their prices and they do offer some features that IIS doesn't have.

Here is a quick list of a few NT Web server vendors (please see Appendix B for more information):

◆ Process Software Corporation:
  `http://www.process.com/prodinfo/purvdata.htm`

◆ EMWAC:
  `http://emwac.ed.ac.uk/html/internet_toolchest/https/contents.htm`

◆ O'Reilly & Associates:
  `http://website.ora.com/`

◆ Netscape Communications Corporation:
  `http://home.netscape.com/`

◆ ILAR Concepts:
  `http://www.ilar.com/`

◆ Internet Factory:
  `http://www.ifact.com/ifact/inet.htm`

◆ Microsoft Corporation:
  `http://www.microsoft.com/infoserv/`

◆ Questar:
  `http://www.questar.com/`

Remember, this is not intended as a complete list—just something to help you get started. I would recommend that you start with any one of these, try it for a few days, and see how far you can go with it. Chapter 7, "Running an Intranet Web Server," takes a look at IIS, but fundamentally all Web servers are similar to each other. They differentiate themselves with advanced features (such as database access), performance, security, ease of use, multiplatform support (Netscape leads in this category), and price. (IIS is the fastest according to *PC Week*, and now Microsoft claims that IIS 2.0 is 40 percent faster than version 1.0.)

HTML Editors and Tools

You can create Web pages with the Hypertext Markup Language using any text editor you want, including Windows NotePad or your favorite word processor in plain text mode. Although HTML documents are plain ASCII text with simple markup codes, you might want to use a specialized HTML editor or conversion tool. There are a wide range of these tools, and they can be broken down into several categories:

◆ Word processor *add-ons* (style sheets, templates, and macros) that allow you to use your own word processor to more easily create documents with HTML. Microsoft's Internet Assistant for Word is an example of this.

◆ Stand-alone HTML editors, some of which provide *WYSIWYG* (what you see is what you get) capabilities, rendering your HTML as you go. Kenn Nesbitt's WebEdit is an example of this. Figure 3.1 shows an example of the WebEdit Home Page Wizard.

◆ Tools to convert one sort of legacy document or another into HTML. Rtftohtml is one example. The DOS version (which will run in the NT Command Prompt window) is available for free download on the World Wide Web. A new version is promised for Windows NT soon. For more information, please see this URL:

```
http://www.sunpack.com/RTF/rtftohtml_overview.html.
```

You'll find a long listing of all sorts of HTML-related tools at this URL:
```
http://www.w3.org/pub/WWW/Tools/.
```

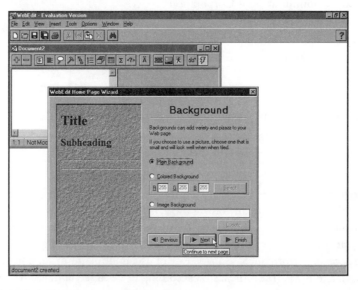

Figure 3.1. *The WebEdit HTML editor is WYSIWYG.*

World Wide Web Browsers

In case you haven't heard, Netscape Navigator is the most widely used Web browser. (About two-thirds of all WWW pages are retrieved by Netscape clients.) Netscape is a commercial package, but you can download a copy from the Netscape home page, http://home.netscape.com/. Netscape is free for people in educational and nonprofit institutions and for personal use. Commercial users must pay for the package if they use it beyond an evaluation period. For details, see the licensing information that comes with the Netscape software.

Microsoft Internet Explorer 3.0 (available in a beta version as I write this), promises to be at least good enough to keep Netscape looking over its shoulder. IE 2.0 already supports most of the new proposals in HTML 3.2, most of the Netscape proprietary extensions (except Java), and a few of Microsoft's own proprietary extensions. IE 3.0 will add Java and ActiveX support. More importantly, in terms of market share, IE 3.0 will be bundled for free with Windows NT 4, Microsoft Windows 95, and the America Online service. (Microsoft is quick to point out that business users of Navigator should send money to Netscape for the proper license fee as they expect that will give corporate bean-counters a pause to consider using IE.)

Both Netscape and Internet Explorer are highly capable Web browsers, and many users hold near-religious views on which is "best." Netscape tends to be flashier, and its Release 2 version has a number of unique features, including support for the emerging Java technology. Netscape also implements a number of proprietary extensions to the HTML language that improve document formatting, but these extensions aren't very compatible with other Web browsers. (If you use these extensions in creating Web pages for your Intranet be sure to view the pages with other browsers to ensure they're readable unless your organization standardizes on Netscape for all users.)

Selection of a Web Browser

Some of the decisions you make with respect to the design of your Intranet may have implications in Web browser selection, and vice versa. Netscape, for example, supports a significant set of semi-proprietary extensions to HTML standards, including special capabilities for image placement and font selection, along with Java and Frames support. These extensions might not be supported in other browsers, so you'll need to consider whether to use them in your Web server's HTML documents. This, in turn, affects your choice of a browser.

Specifically, if you want to take advantage of Netscape's or Explorer's HTML extensions on your Web, you'll probably want to standardize on either of these as a browser. If, at the other extreme, your Web will have large numbers of customers who don't have graphical capabilities, you might want to standardize on the *lynx* browser. This, choice, too, has implications for your Web design, because you must deal with the inability of many users to view images while still providing more-than-plain-text services to those who do have graphical browsers. The emergence of Internet appliances with built-in Web browser software could also be of relevance here.

Whether you choose to standardize on a particular browser also is a function of how you choose to administer and lay out your Intranet. The decentralized and mixed models described in the last chapter inevitably result in a wide range of Web services, some of which might use Netscape HTML extensions, for instance, while others use no special features at all. As a result, you might want to leave the choice of a Web browser to individuals.

Web Browser Helper Applications

Web browser software usually can display graphical images found on the World Wide Web. Other kinds of data, however, require the use of helper applications, also known as *external viewers*. As explained in detail in Chapter 12, "MIME and Helper Applications," Web servers and browsers use a common mechanism called MIME (Multi-Part Internet Mail Extensions) to match up types of data with helper applications. As a result, for example, although your Web browser might not be able to play an audio file you find on the Web, it can pass off that audio file to a sound-playing application on your computer.

The helper application mechanism using MIME is almost infinitely flexible. You're not limited to viewing videos. Imaginative use of this mechanism is one of the central themes of this book. I'll discuss how you can use almost any computer program as a helper application, including the standard office applications you use every day, to view and use your own organization's information. A few helper applications are provided on this book's CD-ROM.

Other Office Applications

Integration of everyday office applications into your Intranet is one of the most exciting topics you learn about in this book. I'll show you how (and how easy it is) to allow your customers to point and click using a Web browser to access live corporate information for use in their daily work. Moreover, they'll be able to do much more with that information than just look at it. Statistical data can be provided in the format your company's favorite spreadsheet package uses, for example. Managers can use their Web browsers to access this data and bring it directly into their local spreadsheet application for what-if analysis, graphing, or other manipulation of the data.

For example, you can setup Microsoft Excel as a Web helper application. All a user has to do to bring up data from the server in her local copy of Excel is click a Web page hyperlink. The browser will receive the data, identify it as an Excel spreadsheet, and hand it off to Excel for display. It's important to note a couple of things about this:

◆ The user is not just passively looking at this data. All the features of the spreadsheet package are available to use on the data; it can be manipulated, changed, recalculated, saved, printed, graphed, and so on. (Note: this is true if you use Excel itself, as opposed to the Excel Viewer application. In the latter case, the client cannot manipulate the data.)

◆ The data on the Web server, which the user downloaded into Excel, is not changed. Regardless of whether the user is running the full Excel or just an Excel viewer, the user's copy of the spreadsheet is a temporary one. If the full version of Excel is run on the client, the user can save the spreadsheet to her local machine, but it can't be saved back to the server.

Naturally, the particular applications you use will vary depending on the needs of your customers, and you might not be able to anticipate all of those needs when you are first planning your Intranet. Nonetheless, the examples provided in Part V of this book should show you how to set up your own applications.

Other Services Accessible via Web Technology

Besides the rich set of possibilities for your Intranet using helper applications, there's a wide variety of TCP/IP-based network services you can integrate into your Intranet. Although these services are commonly seen as over-the-Internet services, there's no reason you can't implement and use them locally as part of your Intranet even if your organization is not actually connected to the Internet. In fact, you should consider the ability to use these services a major dividend paid by your investment in the TCP/IP networking that underlies your Intranet. Without TCP/IP networking capabilities, you'd have no capability of using World Wide Web services, but having installed it, you now also have access to a much wider range of services that will extend and enrich your Intranet.

Web browsers know about many Internet services, including, but not limited to

◆ The File Transfer Protocol (FTP) service, used for transferring files between computers

◆ The Gopher service, a search-and-retrieval service based on hierarchical menus

◆ Usenet news, the mother of all bulletin board systems

◆ Several data indexing facilities, including WAIS (Wide Area Information Servers).

◆ Access to electronic mail (e-mail) using a Web browser.

Chapter 8, "Serving E-mail via TCP/IP," and Chapter 9, "Adding FTP and Gopher Services," discuss some of these additional, Internet-based services, where you focus on using them to provide added value to your customers in an Intranet.

Conversion Tools

The biggest source of information for your Intranet are your legacy documents: data you already have in some sort of electronic format that you might want to make available on your Intranet. A large share of these legacy documents are probably documents created by your office word processor. Although you want to set up your word processor as a Web browser helper application, a subject covered in detail in Chapter 13, "Word Processing on the Web," you also want to know how to get existing documents out of the proprietary format used by the program and into a form you can immediately use on your Intranet. Two methods are described. You can convert your documents into plain ASCII text. Second, using a two-step process, you can convert them all the way into HTML. Most of the examples here use Microsoft Word. If you are using a different word processor, you'll need to check its documentation for details on how to do these steps.

Conversion to Plain Text

The fastest and easiest thing you can do with your word processor documents is convert them to plain ASCII text. All Web browsers can read plain text files, and virtually all word processors have the capability of saving a document as a plain text file. Both Microsoft Word and WordPerfect have Save As options on the File Menu. Just select this option, and then using the scrollbar select Text Only With Line Breaks (in Word) or ASCII Text (7 bit, in WordPerfect), give the file a name, and click OK. Once you've made this conversion, your document is a plain text file you can use directly on your Web server. (Note that your original word processing format document was not changed; you created a completely new file.)

> **Note:** In WordPerfect, be sure to select ASCII Text (7 bit). Other formats are described as 8 bit, but your objective is to create plain-text files without any binary data. Seven-bit ASCII files are plain text.

Unfortunately, when you save word processing documents as plain text you lose the benefit of the special formatting features in the originals. Text enhancements such as boldface, underlining, and font selections all disappear. In addition, if you have tables or other specially formatted portions in a document, they are rearranged into something that might not resemble their original format, if not lost altogether. Graphics disappear too. So while large portions of your original documents survive the transfer intact, you can lose significant portions. Depending on the content of your original documents, the output document may well be usable on your Web, but it also may require more work.

Rich Text Format

It was the closely related problem of exchanging documents between different word processors that led Microsoft to develop the *rich text format* (RTF) for documents. RTF is an open standard for saving documents to a format that can be read by a different word processor or, as is important here, by another program on your computer. Rich text format is an enhanced, ASCII plain-text format, but which preserves your document-formatting information much like PostScript. Common document-formatting features, such as underlining, boldface, and footnotes can be preserved as a document is moved from WordPerfect to Word—for example, through the intermediary form of RTF. Both packages can save documents in Rich Text and both also read Rich Text documents, including those created by the other. Many other word processors and desktop publishing packages, such as FrameMaker and Interleaf also support saving and reading files in RTF; check your manual.

> **Note:** RTF can be used by the Exchange client included with Windows 95 to allow the creation of formatted e-mail messages. This is fine (great) on a LAN where you know if your recipient is also using Exchange, but it isn't necessarily compatible with the e-mail client that other people on the Internet might be using. If you use Exchange for article submissions to listservers and newsgroups, be sure to turn off the RTF option.

You've probably noticed both Word and WordPerfect have options in their Save As dialog to generate the other's datafile format directly, and you might wonder why RTF is needed at all. In fact, if your objective is to transfer documents between these two word processors, there is no need to use Rich Text. However, your initial objective was to get your legacy documents out of your word processor format and into HTML; RTF can help you do this.

Rich Text to HTML

Because the rich text format is publicly defined by Microsoft, anyone is free to write programs or modify existing ones to read it. This is what other word processor manufacturers have done to enable RTF compatibility in their own products. Chris Hector, at Cray Research, Inc., maintains a freely available program called rtftohtml, which converts previously saved RTF documents directly into HTML.

The current version of rtftohtml is a DOS-based program; so you must access the MS-DOS prompt to run it. (A native version for NT is promised, as well as support for most HTML 3.0 features.)

Operation of rtftohtml is amazingly simple. You supply it with the name of an RTF file, and it converts it to HTML using the same filenaming conventions as the original file. At your MS-DOS prompt, you would type the following (note the eight-character limit on the filename results in rtftohtml being called rtftohtm in DOS):

```
C:\>rtftohtm myfile.rtf
```

The program runs and unless you make a command-line error (for example, specifying a nonexistent input file), it creates the output file myfile.htm. rtftohtml supports a number of command-line options to modify its default behavior, which you can read about in the online manual for the package at this URL. You can also download this program here:

```
http://www.sunpack.com/RTF/rtftohtml_overview.html
```

While you're there, check to see if a later version is available. Note that the package not only deals with standard text formatting but also preserves tabular material, footnotes, and embedded graphics.

You'll find that rtftohtml does a superb job of basic conversion of RTF documents to HTML. Because the program is run from the command line, it will be simple for you to process several documents in a short time using a simple DOS command loop. For example:

```
C:\> for %file in (*.rtf) do rtftohtm %file
```

In this command, `%file` is called a *replaceable* parameter. The `for` loop will execute for every file in the current directory that has a file extension of `.rtf`. Each time such a file is found, the rtftohtm command will be executed on the matching filename.

Unfortunately, not every conversion is perfect, so you might find that you need to do some fiddling with the output files rtftohtml generates, particularly if you have tabular material in your documents. Maintaining table column and row alignments is a particular sticking point, as is dealing with embedded graphics, a subject covered in more detail later in the section "Image Conversion and Manipulation."

Direct Conversion to HTML

Recent Windows versions of Microsoft Word and Novell's WordPerfect allow you, with add-ons available at no cost from the vendors, to save existing documents directly in HTML. WordPerfect version 6.1 users can get Novell's WordPerfect Internet Publisher (IP) at the URL `http://hp.novell.com/elecpub/intpub.htm` or by calling WordPerfect (Internet Publisher on disk costs $9).

For Microsoft Word version 6.0 users, Internet Assistant (IA) is available at the Microsoft Web page. Internet Assistant is now also available for Word for Windows 95 but is not yet available for Macintosh Word users. As with your other documents, take care with conversions between Word version 6 and the newer one. You'll find conversion tools at Microsoft's Web site: `http://www.microsoft.com/MSOffice/MSWord/fs_wd.htm`.

Both of these packages allow you to use your familiar word processor to create HTML documents and, most importantly in the context of this chapter, to save existing documents in the HTML format. Conversions are as simple as selecting Save As from the File menu and then selecting the HTML format from the menu.

> **Tip:** Both Internet Publisher and Internet Assistant allow you to view HTML documents and see their formatting onscreen. Both also include ancillary World Wide Web browsers with which you can access Web servers and/or view HTML documents. Although both contain nonstandard HTML features, primarily to enable creating and viewing of formatting that is unique to the underlying word processor, both can render normal HTML as well.
>
> If your documents have special formatting requirements that rely on these unique features, the HTML documents these packages generate might or might not be viewable in standard Web browsers such as Netscape or Explorer. Depending on your needs, you might want to provide your users with copies of the stand-alone Microsoft Word Viewer or WordPerfect Envoy Viewer. Both of these packages can be used as stand-alone Web browsers, outside of

the word processors, allowing you to view HTML documents created by IA and IP, respectively, which contain these special formatting features. Chapter 13 shows you how to set up these packages as helper applications so your customers aren't forced into giving up their favorite Web browser just to look at a few specially formatted documents generated by IA or IP.

FrameMaker version 5 also supports direct creation of HTML-formatted documents as well as the conversion of existing frame documents in HTML. You'll also find other major desktop publishing and word processor packages are adding either direct or indirect support for HTML, though you may be required to upgrade to the current version of your particular package to get this support. See FrameMaker's home page at `http://www.frame.com/`.

Image Conversion and Manipulation

Legacy graphics files you might want to include on your Intranet generally fall into two main categories, those that are embedded in word processing documents and those that are stand-alone image files. Both are discussed here.

rtftohtml and Images

As you might imagine, rtftohtml conversions of word processing documents with embedded graphics don't quite complete the job. rtftohtml stores embedded graphics in separate files with hyperlinks added to the output HTML file pointing to the separate image files. The graphics files created by rtftohtml, however, are not immediately usable in Web pages. This is because they are stored as either Windows Metafile (WMF) or Macintosh Picture (PICT) formats (the former in Windows and on UNIX systems, the latter on Macs). The text of the hyperlinks created by rtftohtml pointing to the WMF or PICT images, however, specifies GIF image files. That is, even though rtftohtml takes your embedded images and turns them into WMF or PICT images (with filenames such as `filename.wmf`), the HTML source code it generates contains `<img src=filename.gif>` hyperlinks. As you might recall, most Web browsers support a few kinds of image formats, including GIFs, but don't support all formats, with WMF and PICT files being among the unsupported ones.

Although you can change the HTML source documents to specify `<img src=filename.wmf>`, for example, and then set up Web browser helper applications to view WMF files, this is inconvenient because anyone who might want to view your documents must also obtain and set up the correct helper applications. The solution to this problem is to run a conversion on your image files, turning them into GIF images, the most widely supported format in graphical Web browsers. There are a number of packages available to do this sort of conversion, including

◆ HiJaaK Pro (commercial; available on CompuServe: type GO INSET)

◆ ACDSEE v1.3 (image viewer; included on the CD-ROM)

◆ Paint Shop Pro v3.0 (shareware; included on the CD-ROM)

These packages take WMF or PICT files as input and convert them to the GIF (or other) format.

Other Image Conversion/Manipulation

Outside of your legacy word processor documents, you might also have stand-alone image data you'd like to use on your Intranet. Subsequent chapters in this book will extensively discuss helper applications for viewing different kinds of image files. Here, you concentrate on simple conversions of existing images into formats widely supported in Web browsers. The two most widely supported image formats for Web browsers are the *GIF* (Graphic Interchange Format) and *JPEG* (Joint Photographics Experts Group) format. Both Internet Explorer and Netscape Navigator support these formats natively.

Image Conversions from Other Applications

If you're using computer-aided drafting (CAD) packages or other application programs that create files containing images, check the package documentation for an *export* feature. Many packages allow you to save datafiles in other formats much like your word processor's Save As feature. The CorelDRAW drawing package, for example, has an Export selection on its File menu. Selecting it opens a dialog box with a range of export formats, including familiar image formats such as PC PaintBrush (PCX), TIFF, and PostScript. Once you've exported your drawing into one of these formats, you can use one of the image-conversion packages described to move the exported image files into formats directly supported by your Web browser (for example, GIF or JPEG format). As with rtftohtml, this process takes a couple of steps, but it does provide a relatively easy way to move your legacy image data into a format you can use on your Intranet.

Programming Tools for CGI

The Common Gateway Interface (CGI) is a standardized way of passing data that a user enters in Web *fill-in forms* to back-end programs (usually referred to as *CGI scripts*) you provide on your Web server. I discuss CGI, and the newer high-performance derivative, ISAPI, in Chapter 19, "Getting the Most Out of HTML with CGI." For now, let me just point out the four main parts of the CGI mechanism:

◆ Collection of user input (usually, though not always, through information typed into a Web fill-in form).

◆ Passing that information off as variables to the main program on the server lying behind the fill-in form.

- Receiving the results of the back-end program.
- Returning the results to the user in a format that is readable in the user's Web browser.

Any program you might write, using almost any programming language, can function as the back-end script as long as it can negotiate these four steps. Whether your CGI script does a simple search for a text string in a group of files or does elaborate SQL (structured query language) searches in your corporate database, these four steps apply in pretty much the same fashion. Specifically, your CGI script, running on your Web server, must be able to accept incoming data from another program (usually referred to as *standard input*) and process that incoming data in some way. Further, the results of the processing must be passed back to the CGI mechanism via *standard output,* and then formatted so a Web browser can interpret and display it. The latter step usually involves having the script create HTML (Hypertext Markup Language) data on the fly.

As noted previously, CGI scripts run on your Web server computer, and any programming language available on the server is available for you to use in creating the CGI scripts. You can write CGI scripts in the C or C++ languages, Visual Basic, or virtually any other language you want to use. The most widely used language for CGI scripts is Perl, which is available on the enclosed CD-ROM.

You'll want to learn about Perl and access important archives of no-cost Perl CGI scripts available on the Internet. To learn more about Perl, try the University of Florida's Perl Archive at `http://www.cis.ufl.edu/perl/`. Users in the UK might like to try something closer to home, such as the NEXOR Ltd Perl Page at `http://pubweb.nexor.co.uk/public/perl/perl.html`. Here are a few other Perl resources on the Net; the last one consists of a few newsgroups dedicated to Perl topics:

- `http://www.metronet.com/perlinfo/perl5.html`
- `http://www.perl.com/perl/faq/`
- `http://www.ee.pdx.edu/~rseymour/perl/`
- `comp.lang.perl`

For more information about CGI and CGI scripts, check out these URLs. First, access `http://hoohoo.ncsa.uiuc.edu/cgi/`, NCSA's Common Gateway Interface tutorial, a great place to start. Next, try Yahoo's `http://www.yahoo.com/Computers_and_Internet/Internet/World_Wide_Web/CGI__Common_Gateway_Interface/`, a high-level index of CGI resources on the Web. In both places, you'll find not only documentation on using the CGI mechanism, but also archives of CGI scripts (mostly written in Perl) people have written and made available to others for unrestricted use.

Tools of the Future: Java and VRML

Rapid development continues on the World Wide Web, with next-generation technology that might become an important part of your Intranet. Two important technologies you'll want to explore are Java and VRML.

Java

With a Java-capable Web browser, users not only can access static Web pages but also dynamically download and run Java application programs just by clicking hyperlinks. Sun's Java technology is a recipient of a November, 1995 Award for Technical Excellence in the category of Internet Tools from *PC Magazine*.

In Part III, Chapters 11 through 15 describe how you can set up common office applications as Web helper applications. This is valuable information, but Java allows the concept of helper applications to be taken an important step further. Rather than requiring each user to preconfigure a Web browser for helper applications and making sure each user has a copy of the application, Java-capable browsers actually download the application to be run (*applets*, in Java-speak) as the user clicks hyperlinks. Once downloaded, the applet runs on the user's computer. Java applets can be interactive, so the user isn't left sitting looking at a static Web page containing somebody else's idea of what they want to see. More importantly, though, Java applets can actually do something.

Java is already being put to use on corporate Intranets. National Semiconductor, for example, uses Java to enable complex searches of its database of integrated circuits by electronics systems designers building new products (see http://www.national.com). Sun's HotJava browser is not the only Java-capable Web browser. Netscape Version 2 also has Java capabilities. Microsoft has promised Java in Explorer 3.0. Spyglass, Inc., the manufacturer of Spyglass Mosaic, has signed an agreement with SunSoft for the inclusion of Java in the next release of Mosaic (though a recent announcement seems to indicate that Spyglass will be changing focus to market a Web toolkit). For Web browsers without Java capabilities, Java applets can be run using Java as a helper application.

VRML

The Virtual Reality Modeling Language is somewhat analogous to HTML, but its markup describes *three-dimensional graphics* rather than plain Web pages. VRML encodes computer-generated graphics into a compact format for transmission over a network. Using VRML browsers, users cannot only look at 3-D graphics but also use them interactively to view and move around inside *virtual worlds*. Not just for game-playing, VRML can be useful to industrial and other designers, who can examine virtual designs from a near-real perspective. Interior decorators, for example, can design a room in VRML, and then use a VRML browser to actually go inside the room and view it in three dimensions.

VRML markup itself is heavily based on Silicon Graphics' Open Inventor file format but has been adapted to include HTML hyperlink compatibility, making VRML files accessible on the World Wide Web or on the Intranet. If you plan on using VRML in your Intranet, you'll need both VRML browsers and other related tools. A good place to start is *The VRML Repository* at the San Diego Supercomputer Center, URL http://rosebud.sdsc.edu/vrml/. Here, you'll find software, including several VRML browsers/viewers, documentation, sample VRML source, and fellow VRML travelers who share your interests, as well as plenty of virtual worlds to explore for new ideas.

Microsoft Internet Explorer 2.0 (and greater) supports an add-on for ActiveVRML, which is an enhanced version of VRML that Microsoft is proposing to the Internet Engineering Task Force (IETF).

All the Server Software to Build a Great Intranet

This section provides you with a basic description of many of the programs you need to build a powerful and reliable Intranet at the lowest possible price. Many of the programs mentioned here—with the greatest exception being the Windows NT operating system itself—are included on the CD (when noted).

> **Note:** With publishing schedules being what they are, this book must go to final production sooner than the CD-ROM. Consequently, this section is by no means a complete list of the software available on the CD-ROM. And some programs might be available in a more current version.

Windows NT 4 Server and Internet Information Server 2.0

Obviously, you need the operating system and its built-in support for TCP/IP. If you run the Server version of NT 4, you will have IIS 2.0 available to you for free. However, note that the Workstation version of NT 4 is also a very capable Web server platform and it is a few hundred dollars less expensive. The Workstation version of NT cannot run IIS, but it can run several other Web servers, including the ones mentioned below.

FolkWeb HTTP Server Version 1.101

This is an excellent 32-bit Web server from Ilar Concepts, Inc. This server can be installed and serving HTML pages in less than five minutes. Although IIS comes free with Windows NT Server, FolkWeb is worthy of consideration for those readers who are running Windows NT Workstation. E-mail: support@ilar.com. Web: http://www.ilar.com/.

EMWAC HTTPS Version 0.991

This is a very well-known freeware Webserver from The European Microsoft Windows NT Academic Center for Computing Services (EMWAC). The Webserver is the main program on which a Web site is based. For a summary of other Webservers for Windows NT, including the commercial version of this program, see Appendix B. If you would like more information about EMWAC, the e-mail address is emwac-ftp@ed.ac.uk.

EMWAC WAIS Toolkit

The WAIS Toolkit enables you to create searchable indexes of the information stored on your Web site. We will describe the full operation of this amazing freeware program in Chapter 20, "Indexing Your Intranet with WAIS." E-mail `C.J.Adie@ed.ac.uk`.

Post.office Version 1.9.3b

This is an evaluation copy of commercial SMTP and POP servers that operate together as a 32-bit NT service. These servers are configured via your Web browser. This is an interesting technique that enables you to configure and administer your mail server remotely. Contact `sales@software.com` or `http://software.com`.

EMWAC Internet Mail Services Version 0.70 Beta

This is an excellent free mail server that originates at the European Microsoft Windows NT Academic Centre (EMWAC), located at Edinburgh University Computing Service. Contact `http://emwac.ed.ac.uk/` or `emwac-ims@ed.ac.uk`.

Blat Version 1.5

This is a public domain Windows command utility that e-mails a file to a user via SMTP. Blat is very useful for mailto functionality in HTML forms. (See Chapter 5 and Chapter 19.) Contact Mark Neal `mjn@aber.ac.uk` or Pedro Mendes `prm@aber.ac.uk`.

NT Perl Version 5.001

Perl (Practical Extraction and Report Language) is an interpreted language designed for scanning arbitrary text files, extracting information, and printing reports. It's also a good language for many system management tasks. Perl for NT is distributed under the GNU General Public License, which basically means that it is freeware. Despite its name, this program also runs on Windows 95. Contact Hip Communications: `http://www.perl.hip.com/`.

CGI Perform

CGI Perform is an easy-to-use Web server extension that allows you capture HTML form data into a database. The best part is that you can do this with no programming! The URL is `http://www.rtis.com`.

Cold Fusion and Allaire Forums

You have probably already heard about Cold Fusion. If you browse the Web for any length of time, you will likely land on an NT server that is using Cold Fusion as a back-end database engine. You will see in Chapter 16 that Cold Fusion is easy to use. Allaire Forums is a Web collaboration package, which is discussed in Chapter 27. Thise programs are included together on the CD-ROM. The URL is `http://www.allaire.com`.

Web Site HTML Tools

This section lists several tools that are key to building the HTML pages that comprise the heart of an Intranet. We will revisit many of these tools in subsequent chapters. Some of these are on this book's CD-ROM.

Microsoft Internet Assistant for Word Version 2.0

Internet Assistant for Word lets you browse the Web from within Word or edit your document with an HTML expert looking over your shoulder. Contact `http://www.microsoft.com`.

Microsoft Internet Assistant for Excel

Using this add-on, you can easily save your Excel spreadsheets as HTML files. Contact `http://www.microsoft.com`.

Microsoft Internet Assistant for PowerPoint

Using this add-on, you can easily save your PowerPoint slides as HTML files. Contact `http://www.microsoft.com`.

WebEdit Version 1.4

This is an excellent shareware HTML editor for Windows. Once you start putting your Intranet online (see Chapter 7), you will see that this tool can be an invaluable assistant as you create HTML pages. Contact Kenn Nesbitt, `http://www.nesbitt.com/`.

Paint Shop Pro Version 3.0

This is an excellent Windows shareware graphics program. If you want to put graphics in your HTML pages, this program can probably help. Contact `http://www.jasc.com/index.html`.

Map This! Version 1.2

This is a 32-bit Windows GUI program, written by Todd Wilson, to automate the creation of Imagemap *.map files. After you try this program, you won't believe it's free. Contact Todd Wilson via e-mail at tc@galadriel.ecaetc.ohio-state.edu or via the Web, http://galadriel.ecaetc.ohio-state.edu/tc/mt.

rtftohtm Version 3.0 for DOS

As discussed above, rtftohtm can easily convert rich text format documents into HTML documents. This comes in handy for legacy Word Processing documents that don't have a *Save As HTML* feature. For more information, contact http://www.sunpack.com/RTF/rtftohtml_overview.html.

Client Software for the Intranet and the Internet

Let's approach the topic of software from both the client side and the server side. Although a Web site needs to run server software, any Webmaster will tell you that you're also going to need good client tools to help you explore the Web and keep up with the latest developments (almost a full-time job in itself at the rate the Web is changing). The client tools discussed in this chapter (and included on the CD-ROM) will help you take advantage of all the great Internet resources that are listed throughout the book and in Appendix C, "Resources for the Windows NT Webmaster."

This section covers the highlights of the major client programs found on the CD-ROM. Also consult Appendix D for the CD-ROM directory structure and a brief description of all the software. Better yet, pop in the CD and give it a spin!

WinZip Version 6.0

Compressed files are often half their normal size and therefore travel through the Internet twice as fast. It usually takes a lot less time to compress and decompress files than it does to transmit them. WinZip provides a nice drag-and-drop graphical interface on top of the ever popular PKZIP compression technology. Some of the software included on the CD-ROM is in .zip format, and WinZip will decompress those files during installation to your hard disk. It is also very handy to keep around for all of your Internet file acquisitions. Contact Nico Mak Computing via e-mail, 70056.241@compuserve.com, or via the Web, http://www.winzip.com/winzip/.

Microsoft Internet Explorer Version 2.0

This is a very good native Web browser for Windows 95 that Microsoft has built to compete with Netscape. Future versions will be bundled with Windows 95 and Windows NT. Contact http://www.microsoft.com/ie/.

Eudora Light Version 1.5.4

Eudora is the most popular Windows e-mail client on the Internet today. Its popularity comes from its ease of use and its price; Eudora Light is free! The current version of Eudora Light is 1.5.4, and it will install as either 16-bit (on Windows 3.1) or 32-bit (on Windows 95 and Windows NT). Although Eudora is freeware, the author of this program states the following in the readme file with the software:

> If you try out Eudora and decide that you'd like to use it on a regular basis, then just send a postcard to the following address:

> Jeff Beckley
> QUALCOMM Incorporated
> 6455 Lusk Blvd.
> San Diego, CA 92121-2779
> USA

Eudora Light lacks a few of the advanced features found in the commercial version, such as automatic uuencoding of attachments and spell-checking. For more information on the 32-bit commercial version, see http://www.qualcomm.com/quest/.

News Xpress Version 1.0 Beta 4

This is an excellent shareware GUI for reading (and posting to) the Internet newsgroups. See Chapter 15, "Other Client Applications on the Intranet," for more information about using this. E-mail kenng@hk.super.net.

CuteFTP Version 1.4 Final Beta 3

This is an outstanding Windows GUI FTP client application. It supports drag-and-drop between directories, so it beats the socks off of the command prompt program included with Windows NT or Windows 95. E-mail alex@sbk.trigem.co.kr.

WSARCHIE Version 0.8

Archie is a 16-bit GUI Archie client that enables you to search Archie servers to find the contents of published FTP directories throughout the Internet. It can come in handy when you know the name of a file or program that you need, but you don't know where to go to download the file. It was written by Clifford Neuman with changes by Brendan Kehoe and George Ferguson. Contact David Woakes, david.woakes@dial.pipex.com.

Helper Applications for the Intranet Client

These free programs will help you avoid the cost of purchasing and installing the full license.

Microsoft Word Viewer

This program allows the clients to view, but not edit, Word documents retrieved by the Web browser. For further information, see `http://www.microsoft.com`.

Microsoft Excel Viewer

This program allows the clients to view, but not edit, Excel spreadsheets retrieved by the Web browser. For further information, see `http://www.microsoft.com`.

Microsoft PowerPoint Viewer

This program allows the clients to view, but not edit, PowerPoint presentations retrieved by the Web browser. For further information, see `http://www.microsoft.com`.

Installing WinZip

WinZip is shareware developed by Nico Mak Computing, Inc. It is necessary that you use some form of a Pkunzip file decompression utility in order to install many of the software programs that you find on the Internet. Most of the programs on the CD-ROM are already compressed. Also, you will usually need WinZip to help you install software that you retrieve from the Internet.

WinZip is a self-extracting archive on the CD-ROM. The file is called `WINZIP95.EXE`. The CD should have version 6.0., which runs on Windows 95 and Windows NT. It uses 32-bit code and supports long filenames. Nico Mak also makes a version 6.0 that runs on Windows 3.1. (See `http://www.winzip.com/`.)

All you need to do to install WinZip is copy the file to a `\WinZip` or `\Utilities` directory on your server and then double-click the file on the CD from within Explorer. After the file extracts itself in a DOS Prompt window, you can run the WinZip setup program. Just double-click `SETUP.EXE` in the directory in which WinZip was extracted. The setup program will install WinZip and start WinZip for you. You should see the main WinZip screen, which is shown in Figure 3.2.

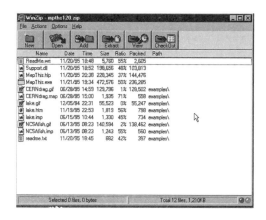

Figure 3.2. The WinZip 6.0 main window.

Other Sources for Hot Software

If you are not happy with any of software mentioned here, there is a wide variety of other products available on the Internet. In most cases, you can download immediately with your Web browser or FTP client.

Here are a few Web pages with good information to get you started searching for evaluation software and freeware available.

◆ Many Windows 95 applications will run on Windows NT 4 (WinZip is just one example), and you will want to keep abreast of software available (such as anti-virus tools) for the client machines on your LAN. A very thorough list of Windows 95 software that you can download directly from your Web browser is available at this site:

    `http://www.windows95.com/`

◆ The Consumate Winsock Apps list:

    `http://cwsapps.texas.net`

◆ The Digital Equipment Corporation FTP site:

    `http://gatekeeper.dec.com/`

◆ The World's Largest Software Archive for Windows (self-proclaimed):

    `http://www.winsite.com/`

> **Tip:** To receive biweekly news about Windows NT via e-mail, use your Web browser to fill out the form at `http://www.bhs.com/microsoft.winntnews` or send the message `subscribe winntnews` (no subject) to `winntnews-admin@microsoft.bhs.com`.
>
> To receive biweekly news about Microsoft BackOffice via e-mail, fill out the form at `http://www.bhs.com/microsoft.backofficenews/`.
>
> To receive biweekly news about Windows 95 via e-mail, subscribe to Microsoft's WinNews. To subscribe to the newsletter, send e-mail to `news@microsoft.nwnet.com` with the words `SUBSCRIBE WINNEWS` as the only text in your message.

Summary

This chapter has been a survey of the basic hardware and software infrastructure you'll need to implement an Intranet in your organization. You've learned about

- ◆ Computer hardware suitable for running a Web server
- ◆ TCP/IP networking and its essential role in any Web
- ◆ World Wide Web server software for a variety of computer systems
- ◆ Software tools for creating documents using the Hypertext Markup Language
- ◆ World Wide Web browser software for a variety of computer systems
- ◆ Common software packages, called helper applications
- ◆ How other network services that are accessible using Web technology might fit into your Web
- ◆ Tools to convert your legacy documents to HTML
- ◆ Tools for converting your existing image data
- ◆ Tools to develop CGI scripts
- ◆ Java technology to extend the helper application model
- ◆ VRML to create and view 3D virtual world steam will need.

Chapter 4 continues laying the foundation for your Intranet and talks about the people skills that your team will need.

CHAPTER

The People Skills to Make it Work

◆ Skills required for system administration
◆ Assigning administrative responsibilities in your Intranet
◆ Training, for both you and your customers
◆ Encouraging customer feedback

Here, you turn to the skill sets that you and your Intranet team will need. Most of these skills are directly related to Web matters—server administration, CGI script programming, and the like— but others are routine, computer system administration skills. As your Intranet develops into a mission-critical system for your organization, both sets of skills become crucial.

Part II, "Getting Set Up on the Server," gives you a good deal of information on Web server setup, but you'll eventually want to consult a more detailed reference. One such book is *Web Site Construction Kit for Windows NT* by Christopher Brown and me (ISBN 1-57521-047-9), published by Sams.net.

Web Server Setup and Administration

Obviously, the very first set of people skills you need are those encompassing basic Web server setup and administration. This set of skills is also probably the single most important one to the success of your Intranet. I'm referring to the areas of content design, document conversion, security control, and even CGI programming.

Your Webmaster

Your choice of a model for the administration of your Intranet (see the discussion of these models in Chapter 2, "Planning an Intranet") has important corollary choices, most importantly with respect to your need for a *Webmaster*. The Webmaster is the person with overall responsibility for setting up and maintaining your Web server(s). If you choose the centralized or mixed model, your Webmaster is the most critical part of your Web. Although many organizations add Webserver administration to the responsibilities of existing staff, a growing number of companies are creating dedicated positions. In fact, Webmastering skills are in high demand, with salaries to match. A recent survey of Webmasters in Fortune 500 companies by *Web Week* magazine showed a full two-thirds of corporate Webmasters earning more than $45,000, and nearly 40 percent with salaries over $65,000, reflecting the value companies place on their skills.

However you assign responsibilities in this area, it's vital that you recognize the value of your Webmaster(s) and ensure he has the skills he needs. This might seem to contradict earlier statements about the relative ease of basic Web server setup and the simplicity of HTML. In fact, although it's true you can set up a simple Web server on a PC using point-and-click methods and have it running in a few minutes, setup and administration of a major Web server, with fill-in forms, CGI scripts, Java applets, appropriate security, and all the other extras you and your customers will want added is considerably more involved and requires additional skills. Just as you shouldn't skimp on the hardware to run your Web server, don't expect to save money in the long run by throwing an inexperienced staffer into the job of setting up and running a major Web server. Because your Webmaster is such a vital cog in your Intranet, we'll devote a good deal of attention to the skills he or she needs.

If you're unsure where to look for your Webmaster, experienced system administrators make good choices for Webmasters because they already have many of the needed skills. You might have potential Webmasters in your MIS department. There are few experienced system administrators who don't already have these skills and knowledge, even if they've never set up a Web server—an increasingly rare situation, with the rapid growth of the Web. It can't be overemphasized that many of the most useful and important details of Web server setup are less than obvious to people who are used to installing software by double-clicking a:\setup in Microsoft Windows Explorer (or File Manager). Proper system administration of a network is part science and part art. The accumulated experience and intuition of a good system administrator can keep your Web server in top shape, tuning the performance of the server and ensuring the system is available "24-7." If your Intranet becomes mission critical, you'll want a seasoned Webmaster running it.

Look at some of the most critical skills your Webmaster will need. I'm assuming here that your Web server will be running Windows NT (and perhaps BackOffice), of course.

Web Server Setup Details

Although most Web servers come with default settings for many operational details, your Webmaster needs a good understanding of what they mean, how they might be changed, and what effects changes may have. For example, does your Web administration model allow for user accounts on the system running your Web server? If so, will you allow these users to create their own HTML documents to be served or disable the default feature of the server software that allows it? Further, if you allow users to create CGI scripts in their home directory area, it's critical that your Webmaster understand what the scripts do and educate users on the security aspects of CGI. There are a number of other details of Web server setup that need to be understood, most of which require a thorough grounding in Windows NT system administration. These include

◆ Setting the server's TCP/IP *port number* (usually 80 for Web servers).

◆ Configuring the login account under which the server will run. (It isn't a good idea to run a Web server under the system account and the administrator account that are built into NT.)

◆ Maintaining and processing the server's *logfiles.* If you don't routinely check the logfiles, how will you ever know if there are security breaches or incorrect hyperlinks in the HTML pages?

◆ Configuring and using Secure Sockets Layer on the Web server and in the browsers.

◆ Understanding the *MIME* mechanism. (See Chapter 12, "MIME and Helper Applications.")

◆ Establishing *virtual paths* on the Web server and configuring the default document to be served. A related server question is: Do you want to permit "directory browsing" when a URL with no explicit document is requested?

◆ Setting up *document indexing* on the server. (See Chapter 21.)

◆ Understanding and using *per-directory access restrictions*, including user passwords and groups and TCP/IP network address restrictions to limit access to some or all of your Web server's data.

◆ Understanding the *security* and *performance* aspects of these and other choices and how they interrelate.

You'll probably want to consult more detailed references on Web server setup and administration. A good place to start is the documentation that comes with the server software.

CGI Script Development

Creation of effective and safe CGI scripts (see Chapter 10, "Intranet Security in Windows NT") requires not only programming skills but also a fundamental understanding of NT User Administration, the Web's Hypertext Transfer Protocol (HTTP), and TCP/IP in general. Recall from Chapter 3, "The Software Tools to Build a Web," that the CGI mechanism works by taking the information entered in Web fill-in forms and passing it as *standard input* to a *back-end script* for processing. When finished, the back-end script returns the results of its run as *standard output*, usually in the form of *HTML markup*, which can be interpreted and displayed by the user's Web browser software. I'll defer the comparison of the CGI process with the ISAPI method until Chapter 19, but suffice it to say, the two are similar.

> **Note:** CGI programs are also called CGI *scripts* or *applications*. The reason they are called scripts is that they can be written in Perl or the UNIX command shell, in which case they are interpreted rather than compiled, and the Web has a strong background in UNIX. When the C language or Visual Basic is used for CGI, the terms *CGI program* or *CGI application* are preferred to CGI script. Even simpler, some people just refer to all such things as CGIs.

Simple CGI scripts might use only a couple of pieces of information, such as a simple text string for which to search and a list of files in which to search for it. More complex ones, however, might throw around a long list of input data, requiring elaborate variable handling, use of data arrays, and use of underlying operating system calls. Further, you'll want to validate data entered by users before processing it. You'll probably not be able to manage such complex scripts except in a full-feature programming language like C or Perl. Experienced system administrators already have a working knowledge of these languages, and this experience is easily portable to CGI programming. Perl is widely used for CGI scripting because of its power (including access to operating system calls), portability, and relative ease of use.

Whether you use Perl, C, or some other programming language for your CGI scripts, you need to be concerned about the security aspects of the scripts. Although you're less likely to have efforts to break the security of your Web server if your server is not on the Internet, there are still good reasons to follow good security practices. Programming languages like Perl and C include access to underlying operating system resources, including the ability to access, read, and manipulate memory and files. At the very least, you need to make sure your scripts don't inadvertently overwrite important files on your system or create memory buffer overflows when users enter incorrect information in Web fill-in forms. Curious, or in the extreme, malicious users might enter harmful system commands in Web forms; your CGI scripts need to validate the data that's entered to make sure nothing but appropriate data gets executed on the server. Even simple typographical errors are potential problems if data isn't validated. These security considerations, of course, are even more important if your Web server is accessible on the Internet.

If you are training to be a Webmaster and you want more information about Perl or C, you might want to get David Till's book, *Teach Yourself Perl in 21 Days* (ISBN 0-672-30586-0), also published by Sams.net. Sams also has a wide range of reference books on other programming languages such as *Teach Yourself C Programming in 21 Days, Premier Edition*, by Peter Aitken and Brad Jones (ISBN 0-672-30736-7).

By running your Intranet Web server on Windows NT, you'll find several choices for your CGI scripting. In addition to Perl and C, it's possible to use Visual Basic, particularly if your Web server supports WinCGI. WinCGI was developed by Bob Denny to make CGI scripting more accessible to the masses in the Web site server from O'Reilly. As another alternative, *Web Site Construction Kit for Windows NT* provides details about how you can take advantage of VB and its ease of building a database interface through ODBC (see Chapter 16 for more information about ODBC databases), in cooperation with a standard C program which performs the CGI tasks.

Java Programming Skills

Java applets are a little harder to identify because they have characteristics in common with CGI scripts, HTML documents, and Web browser helper applications. Like CGI scripts, applets are computer programs that run on the user's computer, not on the Web server. Like HTML documents, Java applets are first downloaded from a Web server by clicking a hyperlink. The client machine runs the applet and then discards it from memory when done. (It stays on the local hard disk to avoid repetitive downloading in case the same programs are needed again.) Helper applications, on the other hand, are programs that already exist on the user's computer and are run when *data* for the application is downloaded from a Web server.

Java is a completely new programming language, something like C++ in that it's object-oriented. As you might guess, it's hardware and operating-system independent. Java applets run on any computer system with a Java viewer or Java-compatible Web browser. Many of the standard features of high-level programming languages have purposely not been implemented in Java for both efficiency and security reasons. For instance, Java can't access or manipulate memory registers.

Security experts remain skeptical about the whole idea of running unknown programs in a Web browser on a corporate LAN, or even on a stand-alone PC. Remember, Java programs are automatically downloaded from sources over which a system administrator has no control. You are not being paranoid if you think this is more than a little scary, assurances about Java's built-in security features notwithstanding. Although Java applets are considered immune from external virus infection, this issue should not be taken for granted.

There is much new ground to be explored with Java for both possibilities and risks. You'll likely need to learn Java programming if you intend to use it on your Intranet, unless you know how to find ready-made code that accomplishes the task you have in mind. Moreover, you'll want to be intimately familiar with its possible security implications for your customers. For SunSoft's view on Java, along with extensive documentation, copies of the *HotJava* Web browser, and demonstration Java applets, access the Java home page (shown in Figure 4.1) at `http://java.sun.com/`. Also, Netscape has Java demos at `http://home.netscape.com/comprod/products/navigator/version2_0/java_applets/index.html`.

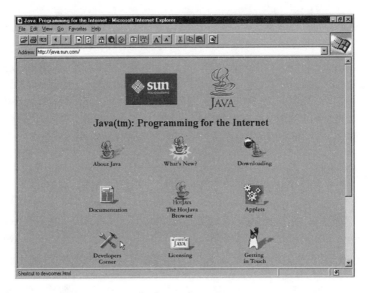

Figure 4.1. *The Sun Java Home Page is a virtual playground for Java lovers.*

Web Server Security Skills

Even if your Intranet is completely isolated from the Internet, and even if you trust all of your customers, it's still a good idea to manage your Web server(s) with routine security. If you do make your Web server(s) accessible on the Internet, doing so becomes critical. Web server software like the IIS or Purveyor packages have built-in security. To take full advantage of it you need to understand the details of server security and the NT User Manager for Domains.

As noted above, because CGI scripts run on your Web server, it's critical you make sure there are no possibilities for them to compromise the server's security through inappropriate data being passed to them by malicious users. Just like you should inspect any other software you may retrieve from the Internet or some BBS before running it, make sure any CGI scripts you may download are secure. You can only do this by inspecting and understanding the scripts' code. In practice, this means you must understand Perl because it is frequently the language of choice for CGI programming.

Your customers will likely demand to use fill-in forms on your Intranet; some of them might even want to write their own CGI scripts and/or obtain them from others. One of your security-related decisions is that of restricting CGI scripts to your server's protected filesystem or allowing users' CGI scripts to run out of their own home directories. Choosing the latter means you need to inspect the user scripts for security implications. This doesn't mean you don't trust your customers who just want to get their work done, which is the object, after all, of your Intranet. It does mean you can't necessarily expect customers to be attuned to the potential for intentional (or unintentional) misuse of CGI scripts and their security aspects. You'll want to inspect customer CGI scripts to make sure they're appropriately secure and counsel users on them.

The security of your Web server is also impacted by the administrative decisions you make with respect to managing your Web. Although it's clear in the centralized model that only authorized people can place Web documents and CGI scripts on your server, and you can take the necessary practical and management steps to enforce this policy, this is less clear in the other models.

Finally, your Web server is only as secure as the computer on which it's running. All the security precautions in the world are worth nothing if everyone in the office has the administrator password to your server, or if you haven't closed well-known security holes in the system. System and network security are meat and potatoes to experienced NT System Administrators, and security considerations alone present a strong argument for your Webmaster to have an extensive background in system administration. These considerations are especially important if your organization is connected to the Internet. The overall security of your network should be secured by a *firewall* system of some kind, and you should carefully configure the access-control features of your Web server(s) to limit access to authorized users.

By the way, the best NT System Administrators are often certified through rigorous testing by Microsoft. Individuals who can pass the test are given the badge of honor MCSE (Microsoft Certified Systems Engineer). In addition to NT configuration, MCSEs are usually skilled in at least one other technical product, such as SQL Server.

> **Note:** As the word implies, a firewall system isolates your network from the Internet, limiting access between the two networks. Usually, firewalls are set up to permit certain Internet services, such as e-mail, to enter your network but block other services that might be insecure or subject to abuse. Firewalls can also be used to selectively permit access by users in an organization to outside Internet services, such as FTP or World Wide Web servers. For more information on Internet firewalls, see *Internet Firewalls and Network Security*, by Karanjit Siyan and Chris Hare (ISBN 1-56205-437-6), published by New Riders. Many commercial firewall vendors have Web pages, including Raptor Systems (`http://www.raptor.com/`), which has just ported its Eagle product line to Windows NT, Trusted Information Systems (`http://www.tis.com/`), with its Gauntlet product line, and others. For general firewall information, including access to the home pages of a long list of firewall and security vendors, see the Firewall Product Developers Consortium Web page, maintained by the National

> Computer Security Association, at `http://www.ncsa.com/fwpdmem1.html`. The NCSA (not to be confused with the National Center for Supercomputing Applications, makers of NCSA Mosaic and the NCSA httpd server) has a home page (see Figure 4.2) with useful security information at `http://www.ncsa.com/`.

Here are a few more people skills you'll have to bring up with your Intranet team. Leaving a PC Web server running unattended in a non-secure area is an invitation to both the malicious and the curious: You might as well forget any security on that server.

Figure 4.2. *The National Computer Security Association has a great deal of information about Internet security.*

Viewer security is also a potential problem. Although you might implement access control on your Web server (which will limit user access to all or part of your Web server by specific TCP/IP addresses or by password), remember that an unattended PC that is already viewing protected documents is not secure. Let's say you plan to restrict access to certain confidential personnel information to management. You'll need to counsel management users in these security issues. For example, leaving one's desk for coffee while viewing confidential information without starting up a screen lock or taking some other security measure defeats all the Web server access controls.

General System Administration Skills

A final, catch-all set of Webmaster skills is the overall administration of your Web server system. These skills range from everyday backups of the system to performance tuning to disk-space and user account management. Although routine in some respects, the performance of these duties is a critical factor in the care and feeding of your Intranet. Even if you have hardware and software maintenance/support contracts with outside vendors, there's no substitute for the experience and intuition of a System Administrator when problems arise. Provided your System Administrator follows good backup practices, for example, restoring lost or erroneously deleted files can take just a few minutes. Webmasters and System Administrators are also important in the training of your customers in the use of your Web.

There are dozens of third-party training firms that run Microsoft certified training programs and seminars, including intensive system administration training at basic and advanced levels. A beginner needs several weeks of these courses, particularly if programming courses are required. Other alternatives include college courses in programming. (C language is a frequent course offering, even at community colleges.) You'll also find frequent one- and two-day seminars on system administration subjects such as Perl.

Management of Web Development

The decisions you make on the management of your Intranet, theoretically discussed in Chapter 2, come back into play when you consider the skill sets your people need. (Of course, this statement is easily stood on its head: The skills your people have can help you choose the administrative model and might lead you to reconsider earlier decisions.)

If you choose the decentralized model, you're deciding to leave most, if not all, of the management and development of your Web to its users, or at least to those interested enough to be setting up individual Web servers for their own data. This model also assumes the skills needed to do Web server setup, creation of HTML files, and so forth, best reside at the user level. Similarly, the need for training will be at the same level, with your customers themselves deciding who needs what in the way of training.

In the centralized model these decisions are reversed, with the delegation of responsibilities and the necessary skills focused on your Webmaster(s). Here, you and your Webmaster(s) can determine where training is required and, as noted previously, what training you can provide to your customers, to develop and manage the training process. In the more realistic mixed model, you delegate responsibilities in a more flexible fashion, based on the needs of the components of your organization.

It's also important for you to develop policies about customer contributions to your Web. Besides regular customer feedback (see the following), you should anticipate, if not solicit and welcome, resources for your Intranet that are contributed by your customers. Even if your Intranet follows the centralized model of administration, it's important you recognize that customers often have the best idea of what they want to see on it—especially if it's in their area of expertise. Empowering customer input by providing a way for them to contribute resources directly to your Intranet is a fine way of developing both customers and your Intranet and is sure to lead to further contributions.

Training

We've already mentioned general System Administration training opportunities. You'll also find a wide variety of Web-specific training offerings from commercial vendors as well as short seminars associated with major expositions and conferences. In fact, several Web-specific conferences are already occurring on a regular basis; you'll find advertisements for them in publications devoted to Web subjects and networking. Here are a few:

◆ Web Week:

```
http://pubs.iworld.com/ww-online/
```

◆ Web Developer:

```
http://pubs.iworld.com/wd-online/
```

◆ NetworkWorld:

```
http://www.nwfusion.com/
```

◆ Web Techniques:

```
http://www.web-techniques.com/
```

> **Tip:** The first and foremost technical reference that every Windows NT System Administrator should have is the Windows NT Resource Kit published by Microsoft Press. The Resource Kit for NT 3.51 totaled five volumes. If you haven't already purchased the Resource Kit, be sure you wait until the Resource Kit for NT 4 comes out, because so much of the operating system has been enhanced.

You'll find courses in Web server administration, HTML markup, CGI scripting, Perl, Java programming, VRML, network security, and so on. In these publications, you'll also, find useful articles on Web-related subjects, including technical features. Figure 4.3 shows the Web Developer magazine home page. If you want to stay up on the hottest Web technology, it is a useful place to drop by.

If you have a competent Webmaster, there is no reason not to tap her knowledge in running your own training courses on these same subjects. She'll undoubtedly be answering questions from customers on a regular basis, so you might as well formalize this relationship with training courses. Of course, Webmasters cannot only train the people who will use your Intranet, but other Webmasters as well. Don't neglect the value of the wide variety of Web-related books as training tools for users.

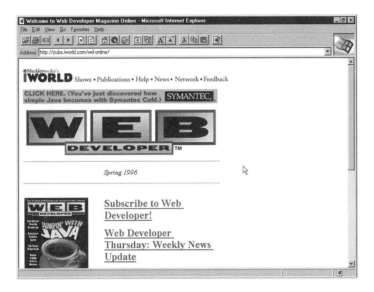

Figure 4.3. *The Web Developer magazine home page includes current news about the Web.*

Customer Feedback

In Chapter 2, I recommended use of customer *focus groups* to help define the purpose and content of your Intranet. You should continue meeting with your focus groups even after your Intranet is up and running; you might find even more valuable feedback from your customers. Also expect customer feedback outside your formal focus group arrangements.

They Inevitably Want More

Once your customers get the idea of using Web technology in their everyday work, as opposed to recreational Web *surfing*, they'll begin bombarding you with suggestions for changes and requests for new information. Listen to these suggestions and requests. As Chapter 2 suggested, your customers know best the kinds of information they want to see and how well your Web presents it. Employees often have useful ideas on how to go about doing their jobs because they are the people most intimately familiar with the jobs. Expect them to have ideas for your Intranet as well for exactly the same reason.

If you've ever designed a database application, you know the iterative design process. Even having gone through a formal process of soliciting user input on your application before you ever started its design, within minutes of the time you sit a user down in front of your prototype, he's asking questions. For example:

◆ If I can do thus-and-so query, can't I also do a that-and-so one?

◆ Wouldn't this data-entry screen be better if this box's position and that box's were reversed?

◆ This is a great report, but can't you fit it on one page? And while you're at it, how about showing the quarterly figures, too?

In other words, real users using your application—whether it's a corporate database or your Intranet— will quickly have ideas on how it can be made better. Most of their ideas will be good ones, too.

Get Them to Contribute

In your Intranet, customer ideas won't be limited to requests for new information or changes in presentation. Users will quickly recognize the *collaborative* aspects of Web technology. Chapter 27, "Collaboration on Your Intranet," discusses more about this aspect, but I should touch on it here. Chapter 2, for instance, suggested the idea of engineers and scientists sharing engineering drawings, application datafiles, and/or technical reports with colleagues by placing them on your Web. As a Web designer, you can't possibly identify this sort of specific information, but your engineer and scientist customers surely can and will.

Regardless of the administrative model you've selected for your Web, it's important you make it easy for customers to contribute resources for it. This is where the decentralized and mixed models shine: Customers using your Web can create and make their own resources available on your Web for sharing with other customers.

Simple HTML markup is easily within the grasp of just about anyone who uses a computer, as are most of the legacy data conversion tools described in Chapter 3. Point-and-click setup of a Windows Web server makes it possible for almost anyone to set up a bare-bones Web server on his desktop to share these specific resources. Just as anyone can thumb tack a notice on a cork bulletin board in the office, on your Intranet he can tack up CAD drawings of circuit boards, building blueprints, or directions to the office holiday party. You might also want to set up a free-for-all, fill-in form on your Web that allows customers to add links to their resources.

Customer contributions might turn out to be the most important aspect of your Intranet. To this end, make sure your customer training and Web-related communications emphasizes the value and continuing need for their input. It's vitally important that you create a welcoming, inclusive atmosphere. Your Intranet is, after all, for your customers. Involving them in the Intranet design process and then keeping them involved by welcoming their contributions, ensures its value, to them and to your organization. Losing this customer focus, on the other hand, will lead to your Intranet becoming stale and unused; if customers find no value, they'll go elsewhere.

Summary

This chapter has focused on the people skills you'll need in setting up, running, and using your Intranet. You've learned about

- The skills required for the setup and administration of your Intranet server(s).
- How your people skills interrelate with administrative and substantive responsibilities in your Intranet.
- Training, for both you and your customers.
- Getting and responding to customer feedback.

Chapter 5 furthers the discussion of Intranet fundamentals by diving into HTML. You will find that HTML is really pretty easy to learn, and you will see that these skills are essential to understanding the Web.

CHAPTER

5

What You Need to Know About HTML

- ◆ Basic HTML
- ◆ Installing WebEdit
- ◆ Creating lists in HTML
- ◆ Logical and physical formatting
- ◆ URLs, hyperlinks, and `mailto`
- ◆ Graphics
- ◆ HTML 2.0 forms
- ◆ Creating searchable indexes
- ◆ Server-Side Includes
- ◆ Server-push and client-pull
- ◆ Tables
- ◆ Frames
- ◆ Client-Side imagemaps
- ◆ Persistent cookies
- ◆ Style sheets
- ◆ Writing math in HTML 3.2
- ◆ Character entities

◆ HTML 3.2 resources
◆ Quick tips on HTML style

As you can see from this outline, we have a lot of ground to cover. But please do not feel intimidated by the length of this chapter; you will soon see that HTML is really quite simple. In fact, if you can use a word processor or even Windows NotePad, you can write HTML. The topics in this chapter are more or less ordered by increasing level of difficulty and (roughly) by the evolution of HTML itself. If things begin to get too advanced, just skip it and come back later. Because perhaps 90 percent of your HTML documents will consist of just the basic stuff, let's start with that.

> **Tip:** Here is a tip that might help you learn HTML by seeing how the experts write it. The next time you are browsing the Web and come across an interesting page, it's easy to find out how the page is written in HTML. Execute the View Source option of Netscape or Explorer on Web pages that can be used as examples for pages you want to create yourself. Then you can follow each line of the source window on that Web page, while referring to this chapter or Appendix A to learn about the HTML syntax.

Basic HTML

HTML files are plain ASCII text. HTML files contain two things: *content* (which is the message that you want to present) and *tags* (which are commands to the browser about how the content should appear). The content is completely up to you of course. The tags are simply an agreed-upon set of a few dozen character sequences which start with the less-than symbol (<) and end with the greater-than symbol (>). For example, one tag is <HTML>; another is <TITLE>.

> **Note:** In order to help them stand out from regular text, I will try to write all of the HTML tags in this book using uppercase. However, HTML tags are not case-sensitive, so you will often see them written in lowercase too. It is a matter of your own personal taste how you choose to write them, but one suggestion is to be consistent however you do it.

In most cases, the content must reside between a pair of similar tags. In other words, tags come in pairs to mark the beginning and ending of the text (or content) in between them. The ending tag is the same as the beginning tag, except a forward slash (/) is added like this: </TITLE>. For example:

```
<TITLE> This is my first HTML document. </TITLE>
```

When the browser loads an HTML file, the title of the document is displayed at the top of the browser application. The <TITLE> tags are used by the author of the document (sometimes called the *page designer*) to indicate the name of the file as an aid in referencing it.

HTML Comments

I oversimplified things a bit when I said that files consist only of tags and content. Some of the text in an HTML file might be considered overhead to help manage the whole process. Strictly speaking, not everything between the tags will be a part of your content. One example of what I mean by this is that you can insert comments into the HTML file. Comments are not processed or displayed by the browser; they are ignored. So why have them? Comments allow the page designer to *speak* to anyone who will edit or maintain the HTML file in the future. This brings us to a subtle but important point: HTML is like a computer language between the author and the browser program, but it also has to support person-to-person communication when viewed in its raw text format.

Comments start and end with two dash characters (--) and must be embedded between an opening tag (<!) and a closing tag (>), like this:

```
<!-- Comments can be inserted for future reference -->
```

A new addition in HTML 2.0 allows multi-line comments to be inserted in between the <COMMENT> ... </COMMENT> tags. This is rather handy when you already have a block of experimental HTML code and you want to disable it without deleting it. All you have to do is wrap it in these tags.

A Basic Template

There is a very well defined and simple outline for every HTML file. Take a look at Listing 5.1, where you see the smallest standard HTML document.

Listing 5.1. This is the basic structure of any HTML file.

```
<HTML>
<HEAD>
<TITLE> Your first HTML document </TITLE>
</HEAD>
<!-- Comments can be inserted for future reference -->
<BODY>
<H1> Hello, World! </H1>
</BODY>
</HTML>
```

Listing 5.1 is like a template just waiting for you to insert more content and tags as you see fit. First, let's talk about the new tags that are introduced here. The <HTML>...</HTML> pair marks the beginning and ending of a valid HTML document. The <HEAD>...</HEAD> pair sets off the part of the document which the browser uses internally; it isn't really displayed as part of the content in the main window of the browser. Notice that the <HEAD> section is closed before the <BODY> section begins. It is important to understand the proper nesting rules of HTML. Each pair of tags is like a sandwich, and only certain *toppings* can go in between.

The <BODY> section is the main part of any HTML file. It is where you finally get to display your message. Referring to the concept of nesting again, notice how the <BODY>...</BODY> pair starts and ends within the <HTML>...</HTML> pair. Here is one example of an invalid nesting sequence:

```
<HTML>...<BODY>...</HTML>...</BODY>
```

The <H1>...</H1> tags describe a *level one heading*. Headings are used to mark major sections in a document, sort of like chapter titles and section titles in this book. Browsers are expected to display level one headings with a larger or bolder font than any other heading level. There are six levels of headings in HTML, but <H4>, <H5>, and <H6> are seldom used. You can create heading tags in pretty much the same fashion that you would create indent levels in an outline. Because headings are included within the <BODY> section, they do display in the main window of the browser as a part of the document content. Quite often, the level one heading might simply repeat the title of the document.

From Listing 5.1 you can probably see how easy it would be to write a basic HTML document in NotePad. I'm sure you'll get the picture after you see Figure 5.1, which is the trivial document from Listing 5.1 displayed in the Internet Explorer Web browser.

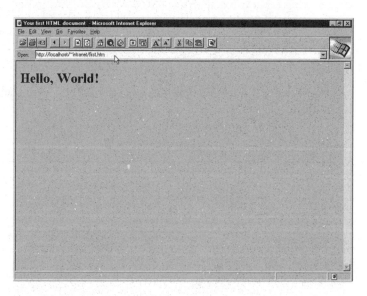

Figure 5.1. *A very simple HTML document.*

Notice in Figure 5.1 how Internet Explorer displays the title of the document in the titlebar of the browser and the level one heading, Hello World!, in the main window. So now you see how it takes nine lines of HTML code to write one simple message. Don't despair; it's usually not that bad. Once you have the basic framework in place, you can easily add more content. Let's move on to a few more basic tags.

Other Basic HTML Tags

Because most documents include text in the form of sentences within paragraphs, HTML has a pair of tags to mark the beginning and ending of a paragraph. The `<P>`...`</P>` tags serve to separate paragraph blocks with a small amount of vertical space when displayed. Starting with HTML 3.2, there are even some attributes you can use to indicate the horizontal alignment of the paragraph within the margins of the browser.

> **Note:** You might see many HTML pages that don't use the `</P>` tag. It is optional because the browser will ignore it. The `</P>` tag at the end of a paragraph has no effect on vertical spacing. Basically, the browser will supply vertical spacing whenever it encounters the `<P>` tag. The combination of these ideas leads many to think that the `<P>` tag should go at the end of a paragraph, rather than the beginning, but that is also optional. There is some HTML literature that indicates it is bad style to have paragraph text not enclosed within a pair of tags. However, if you follow an `<H1>`...`</H1>` block immediately with a `<P>` tag, the browser might cause more vertical spacing than you want.

Learning about attributes entails going one level further into the details of HTML. That's the bad news. The good news is it isn't very hard and you are rewarded with the ability to, say, center a paragraph or specify the graphic background for the whole page.

Here is an example of a paragraph with a center alignment attribute (remember, the `</P>` tag is really optional):

```
<P ALIGN="CENTER"> This paragraph will be centered horizontally. </P>
```

Note how the `ALIGN` attribute is contained within the opening tag and the value of the attribute is specified in quotes. Other possible values for the `ALIGN` attribute are: `"JUSTIFY"`, `"LEFT"`, and `"RIGHT"`.

The `<CENTER>` tag is one of the most-used Netscape extensions. All lines of text between the beginning and end of `<CENTER>` are centered between the current left and right margins. Some people consider it controversial because the `ALIGN` attribute is the standard way to achieve the same effect.

Line Breaks

Another basic tag is `<BR>`; BR stands for *break*. You can use this tag to tell the browser where you would like long lines to wrap. You might be wondering why you would need to do this. Shouldn't the browser break lines wherever you press enter in the text editor? It's actually a lot simpler (or depending on how you look at it, harder) than that. HTML treats all contiguous white space (spaces, tabs, and newlines) as one space. Really, this does us a favor because we have no idea how wide the windows of all of the client browsers are. Each browser will automatically handle issues such as word-wrap, unless we specifically ask to do it differently using `<BR>`.

Here is an example of where you would use <BR>. Suppose you wanted to print your name and e-mail address, and the date the document was last modified at the bottom of the HTML page (as is very often done). For example:

```
<P> Written by Scott Zimmerman
e-mail: scottz@sd.znet.com
modified: April 20, 1996</P>
```

Unless the browser is resized to be a very thin window, this will all appear on one long line—despite the hard carriage-returns in the HTML file. However, you can achieve a more readable effect if you add <BR> tags to the end of each line, like this:

```
<P> Written by Scott Zimmerman<BR>
e-mail: scottz@sd.znet.com<BR>
modified: April 20, 1996</P>
```

Note that there is no closing tag with <BR>, such as </BR>. By the way, Netscape also invented the <NOBR> tag, which as you might imagine, will force the browser to keep text together on the same line. The <WBR> tag allows you to tell the browser where a word break can occur, in case you have a long sequence of characters without a space. You need to use <WBR> within a block of <NOBR> text only.

Normally, <BR> just inserts a line break. Netscape has added a CLEAR attribute to <BR>, so CLEAR= "LEFT" will break the line and move vertically down until you have a clear left margin. CLEAR="RIGHT" does the same for the right margin, and CLEAR="ALL" moves down until both margins are clear of images.

Addresses

The idea of putting your address at the end of the HTML document is so common that there is even a special pair of tags just for that purpose. Instead of using <P>...</P> in the example above, you can use <ADDRESS>...</ADDRESS> instead. If you use <ADDRESS>, the text inside will also be italicized by most browsers. You could achieve the same effect with <P><I>...</I></P>, but that requires using an additional formatting tag. (I discuss the italics tag in a moment.) Other than the fact that <ADDRESS> will italicize the text, it really makes no difference whether you use it or not. (The only exception is that Internet Robots might be written in the future to read and process the text within <ADDRESS> blocks in some special fashion.)

Tip: In addition to putting the author's name and the modification date at the bottom of the HTML document, another common courtesy is to provide the user with the ability to send you e-mail just by clicking on your address. This requires the use of the mailto element, discussed below.

Horizontal Lines

The `<HR>` tag has become very popular since its introduction in HTML 2.0. Its purpose is to draw a horizontal rule (line) across the width of the page to help separate document sections. This is used for greater emphasis than the `<P>` tags.

`<HR>` comes with several fancy attributes to control the thickness and the width of the line. The width can be expressed as a percentage of the width of the browser window. For lines that are shorter than the width of the browser window, it also makes sense to apply the `ALIGN` attribute, which can take a value of `"LEFT"`, `"RIGHT"`, or `"CENTER"`.

Finally, the `SIZE` attribute takes an integer value representing browser pixel units (apparently) to control the thickness of the line. Here is an example of a typical horizontal rule:

```
<HR WIDTH=50% SIZE=5 ALIGN="CENTER">
```

Installing WebEdit

Before I get into too many details of HTML, let's take a break and install a tool that will help edit HTML files more conveniently than, say, NotePad. In this section, you'll install and use the WebEdit shareware HTML editor from the CD-ROM. This program lets you build a simple Web page with the click of a button.

> **Note:** WebEdit 2.0 is in beta testing as I write this. The CD-ROM includes the very capable version 1.4. By the time you read this, the final release of version 2.0 should be available at: `http://www.nesbitt.com/`.

WebEdit was developed by Knowledge Works, Inc. There are a lot of other HTML editors out there, but this one happens to have a very nice combination of low price and powerful, easy-to-use features.

To install WebEdit, copy the file from the CD-ROM to a temporary directory on your hard disk. Unzip the file using WinZip and run the program `SETUP.EXE` from the same directory.

The WebEdit Home Page Wizard can be used to generate the basic framework of an HTML document. Here are the steps to get your first home page on the Web in a jiffy:

1. Run WebEdit.
2. From the main menubar, choose File | Wizards | Home Page Wizard.
3. You can explore the capabilities of the Wizard, but for now let's keep it simple. Just choose the Finish button and then choose the OK button. This results in a WebEdit screen that looks like Figure 5.2. (I'm using WebEdit version 1.4 here, 2.0 is due out by the time you read this.)

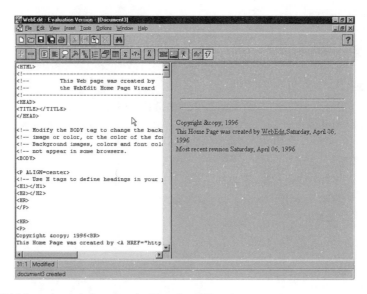

Figure 5.2. *WebEdit version 1.4 after using the Home Page Wizard.*

4. The HTML code that is automatically generated by WebEdit is shown in Listing 5.2. Now all you have to do is customize the code to suit your purposes. For now, why not simply insert your company name in between the HTML <TITLE> tag and the </TITLE> tag. For example, <TITLE> *Your Company Name Here* </TITLE>. Now do the same thing between the <H1> and </H1> tags. For example, <H1>*Your Company Name Here* </H1>.

Listing 5.2. The default.htm file created by the WebEdit Home Page Wizard.

```
<HTML>
<!------------------------------------------------->
<!--         This Web page was created by        -->
<!--         the WebEdit Home Page Wizard        -->
<!------------------------------------------------->
<HEAD>
<TITLE></TITLE>
</HEAD>

<!-- Modify the BODY tag to change the background  -->
<!-- image or color, or the color of the font.     -->
<!-- Background images, colors and font colors may -->
<!-- not appear in some browsers.                  -->
<BODY>

<P ALIGN=center>
<!-- Use H tags to define headings in your pages -->
<H1></H1>
<H2></H2>
<HR>
</P>

<HR>
```

```
<P>
Copyright &copy; 1996<BR>
This Home Page was created by
<A HREF="http://www.nesbitt.com/">
WebEdit</A>,Saturday, April 06, 1996<BR>
Most recent revision Saturday, April 06, 1996
</P>
</BODY>
</HTML>
```

5. Now you can save the file in Listing 5.2 as `default.htm` in the HTML Document Directory of the Web server. (I cover this in much greater detail in Chapter 7, "Running the Intranet Web Server.") Then, any Web browser that visits the Intranet server will retrieve this file automatically.

6. In order to give it a quick try now, you might want to open your Web browser and choose the command to open a File URL. By opening `default.htm` as a local file, you can test it in different browsers even without running a Web server.

Creating Lists in HTML

HTML has provisions for creating many types of lists. You have your choice of ordered lists, unordered lists, definition lists, directory lists, and menu lists—though I haven't seen directory lists and menu lists used very often. Ordered lists simply number the items from 1 to *n*. Unordered lists use bullets to mark each item. Definition lists are used to organize terms and their definitions, like a glossary. Menu lists are available if you want to create a menu of hyperlinks, but you can do the same thing with unordered lists. Directory lists can be used to show a listing of files, but again, unordered lists can also serve the purpose if you prefer.

The first thing you want to learn about lists is how to create a list item. Four of the five list types share one tag for specifying items in a list. That tag is `<LI>`, for list item. There is no `</LI>` closing tag because the Web browser will know that the current list item ends either at the beginning of the next list item or at the end of the entire list. (I'll get to that in a moment.)

The `<LI>` tag is so simple that we can defer an example until we get to the next section on ordered lists. One thing to bear in mind is that the `<LI>` tag does allow a few attributes, though mostly for rather specialized tasks. You can consult Appendix A, "HTML and CGI Quick Reference," for more information about `<LI>` attributes.

The next three sections discuss ordered lists, unordered lists, and definition lists. I'll follow this up with some sample code that demonstrates all the list types.

Ordered Lists

The ordered list tags simply serve as a bracket around a list of items which the browser will number. By default, ordered lists start with number 1 for the first item and continue sequentially. The ordered list tags are <OL>...</OL>. Between this pair of tags, you can place as many <LI> tags as you want.

One attribute worth mentioning for the <OL> tag is the TYPE attribute. TYPE allows you to change the default numbering scheme to use uppercase (TYPE="A") or lowercase (TYPE="a") letters instead, or you can use Roman numerals (TYPE="I"). Here is a quick example of a complete ordered list using uppercase alphabetic characters instead of numbers:

```
<OL TYPE="A"> This is an ordered list.
<LI>The browser will precede this item with A.
<LI>The browser will precede this item with B.
</OL>
```

Unordered Lists

Unordered lists are just like ordered lists, except unordered lists use the <UL>...</UL> pair of tags and the list items are preceded by bullets instead of numbers. Of course, there are various attributes, which can make it more or less interesting. The PLAIN attribute in the <UL> tag will specify that no bullets should be drawn. Or the TYPE attribute can be used to change the type of bullet that is drawn. Possible values for the TYPE attribute are "CIRCLE", "DISC", and "SQUARE".

HTML 3.2 even includes a new attribute to let you specify a graphic to be used for drawing the bullet. This would involve us in a discussion of Uniform Resource Locators (URLs), so I ask your patience until we reach that section below. In the meantime, perhaps you would like a glimpse of the syntax knowing that the description will soon follow. The SRC attribute takes the value of the URL where the graphic file resides, like this:

```
<UL SRC="http://host.domain-name.domain/bullet.gif">
```

Finally, one other HTML 3.2 attribute for unordered lists is WRAP. WRAP tells the browser whether to build a horizontal or a vertical list—for exampe, WRAP="HORIZ" or WRAP="VERT".

Definition Lists

Definition lists can be used whenever you need the style of a glossary. Definition lists are bracketed by the <DL>...</DL> pair of tags. Dictionary list items do not use the customary <LI> tag. Instead, definition list items use both the <DT> tag to introduce a *term* and the <DD> tag to begin the *definition* text accompanying that term.

The COMPACT attribute, which is new in HTML 3.2 and not universally implemented, requests the browser to use minimal vertical space between terms. There are no other attributes associated with definition lists. Please see the next section for an example of how to create a definition list.

A List of Lists

I'd like to wrap up this section on lists with one HTML file that demonstrates all the list types. Figure 5.3 shows the file as it appears in Internet Explorer. Notice that unordered lists, menu lists, and directory lists are really not very different. In fact, many browsers will put bullet items on menu lists and directory lists.

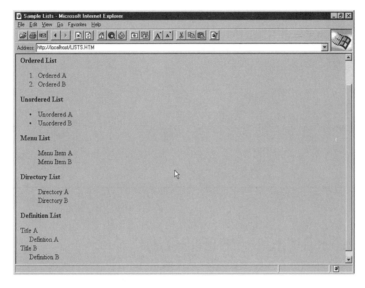

Figure 5.3. *This sample Web page demonstrates all types of basic lists.*

Listing 5.3 shows the HTML code behind Figure 5.3. The filename is LISTS.HTM, and it is on the CD-ROM in the HTML directory. You may want to use the file to cut and paste code fragments into your own HTML pages.

Listing 5.3. LISTS.HTM is simple HTML file that exercises all types of lists.

```
<HTML>
<HEAD><TITLE>Sample Lists</TITLE></HEAD>
<BODY><H1>Sample Lists</H1>

<H4>Ordered List</H4>
<OL>
<LI>Ordered A
<LI>Ordered B
</OL>

<H4>Unordered List</H4>
<UL>
<LI>Unordered A
<LI>Unordered B
</UL>
```

continues

Listing 5.3. continued

```
<H4>Menu List</H4>
<MENU>
<LI>Menu Item A
<LI>Menu Item B
</MENU>

<H4>Directory List</H4>
<DIR>
<LI>Directory A
<LI>Directory B
</DIR>

<H4>Definition List</H4>
<DL>
<DT>Title A
<DD>Defintion A
<DT>Title B
<DD>Definition B
</DL>

</BODY>
</HTML>
```

Logical and Physical Formatting

In the early days of HTML, you weren't supposed to care exactly how the browser rendered your document in terms of the fonts it had available. How could the page designer require a certain font if every browser could be running on a different platform? From Windows 3.1 to Macintosh to OS/2 to UNIX workstations, fonts are handled quite differently. Indeed, non-GUI terminals don't even have a notion of fonts—they only have one font hard-coded in ROM.

There are two types of formatting styles in HTML 2.0 (and below). Logical styles are used to indicate that your text is of a certain typical nature, such as text to appear as if it was typed on a keyboard or text that should appear like computer code. There are several of these and some of them, such as <CODE>, <SAMP>, and <KBD>, might seem redundant (which they are in most browsers).

In contrast, physical styles allow you to request a particular type of formatting regardless of the meaning of the information you want to format—for example, <B> for bold. HTML purists tend to discourage us from using the physical formatting tags because browsers (such as lynx) that don't support them will have no way to know what a useful substitute would be. I haven't had a need to use the physical styles myself, but you would think that if a browser can't support bold, it could easily be programmed to make a reasonable substitution from its available resources when it comes across the <B> tag. That would be similar to the kind of choice that the browser programmer made when he chose a rendering for, say, <KBD>.

Logical Formatting Tags

Here is a list of several logical formatting tags. (You will notice a few similarities.)

◆ `<SAMP>...</SAMP>`

These tags surround "sample" characters, which are usually displayed in a Courier font.

◆ `<CODE>...</CODE>`

These tags surround text which appears like computer code. It is usually displayed in a Courier font.

◆ `<KBD>...</KBD>`

These tags surround characters which are to be typed on a keyboard, and it usually is indicated in a Courier font.

◆ `<VAR>...</VAR>`

These tags surround text representing variable names, which are often displayed in italic.

◆ `<CITE>...</CITE>`

These tags surround text which is being quoted or cited. It is often displayed in italic.

◆ `<EM>...</EM>`

These tags surround text which is to be emphasized. It is often displayed in italic.

◆ `<STRONG>...</STRONG>`

These tags surround text which is to be strongly emphasized. It is often displayed in a bold font.

Physical Formatting Tags

Here is a list of several physical formatting tags:

◆ `<TT>...</TT>`

These tags surround text to appear in a teletype style. This usually means Courier.

◆ `<B>...</B>`

These tags surround text to appear in a teletype style. This usually means Courier.

◆ `<I>...</I>`

These tags surround text to appear in italics.

◆ `<BLINK>...</BLINK>`

These tags surround text that you want to blink. Use it with caution as many users are annoyed by it. This is a Netscape extension.

◆ `<FONT>...</FONT>`

These tags surround text that will take on a relative font size between 1 and 7. The default is 3. The `SIZE` attribute should appear within the `<FONT>` tag—for example, `<FONT SIZE=5>`. The default value of the font size can be changed for an entire document using the `<BASEFONT>` tag, which is a Netscape extension.

Other Formatting Tags

There are a couple of formatting styles that don't really fit into either of the two categories above. The difference with these tag pairs is that they are often used as containers of larger text that might contain other embedded text sections, such as paragraphs and lists.

The `<BLOCKQUOTE>` tag typically marks a larger section of quoted text than the `<CITE>` tag. In HTML 3.2, `<BLOCKQUOTE>` can be shortened to `<BQ>`. As you would expect, `<BLOCKQUOTE>` is closed with `</BLOCKQUOTE>`.

The `<PRE>` tag marks a section of text that is preformatted in terms of spaces. `<PRE>...</PRE>` can come in handy when you want to line up columns, such as in forms. An example of preformatted text in a form will be given in the section on forms. Preformatted text is usually displayed in a Courier font. We are still expected to use `<P>` to mark paragraphs within preformatted text blocks.

URLs, Hyperlinks, and `mailto`

As large as the World Wide Web is, finding things can sometimes be difficult. Fortunately, everything has an address. Every HTML page on the Web has an address. Even the graphics contained within Web pages have addresses. When you click a hyperlink in one Web page to jump to another Web page, you are simply asking your browser to retrieve a document at a new address.

URLs

Uniform Resource Locators (URLs) are used to locate documents on servers. A client computer uses a URL to request a document to be viewed. Here is the format of a fully mature URL (in practice, not all the components are required):

```
protocol://machine.domain.name:port/path/document
```

In case you haven't seen one before, here is an example:

```
http://www.hqz.com/default.htm
```

The most widely used protocol on the Web is HTTP. Accordingly, most browsers will default to using HTTP if you do not specify a protocol when you enter the name of a document to be retrieved. You have a choice of the following protocols:

- `http`—refers to a file on a World Wide Web server.
- `ftp`—refers to a file on an FTP server.
- `mailto`—used to *send* a file to a given mail address.
- `gopher`—refers to a file on a Gopher server, usually plain ASCII text.
- `news`—refers to a Usenet newsgroup article from the default NNTP server.
- `nntp`—refers to a Usenet newsgroup from a particular NNTP server.

- ◆ `file`—refers to a file on your local computer (or a network drive to which you have a shared connection).

- ◆ `telnet`—a connection to a Telnet-based service.

- ◆ `wais`—refers to a file on a WAIS server, or a search to be conducted.

It's interesting to observe that although many of these protocols were around long before the Web was invented, they have been adopted into the Web through the simple invention of URLs which support them (actually becoming a part of HTTP). The underlying Internet protocols themselves haven't changed. But their resources, previously available only via command-line programs, can now be accessed easily through a GUI browser. Because of this, the resources offered through these protocols are now more useful than ever before.

> **Note:** For more information about URLs in general, please see this URL (no pun intended):
>
> `http://www.w3.org/hypertext/WWW/Addressing/Addressing.html`

Hyperlinks

Hyperlinks in Web pages are really nothing more than a URL. The browser will underline the text of the link so the user can see that it is available as a clickable item. But the question you are probably asking in this chapter is "How do I create hyperlinks in the HTML code that I write?"

The answer is to use a pair of tags (`<A>...</A>`) for creating *anchors*. The `<A>` tag takes a very common attribute called `HREF`, which is where you specify the URL of the document to be retrieved. Between the anchor tags, you get to place any descriptive text you want the user to see. The browser will underline the descriptive text; the URL itself will not be shown in the document. (Note that most browsers will display the URL in the status bar when a user holds the mouse pointer over the anchor without clicking.) Perhaps an example will help to clear this up:

```
<A HREF="http://www.ibm.com"> Jump to the IBM home page! </A>
```

The anchor tags got their name because they started out as a way to name sections within a document that the reader might want to refer to often. This involves two steps. First, use the `NAME` attribute to mark an anchor point in the HTML file. Then you can write a hyperlink referring to the name of that anchor when you want to provide a way to make a quick jump back to it. This is very useful for creating a Table of Contents of a long HTML document.

Here is the syntax to create the anchor:

```
<A NAME="anchor"> A good place to come back to. </A>
```

And here is the syntax to create the hyperlink back to the anchor:

```
<A HREF="#anchor"> Jump back to the other place. </A>
```

Note the number sign (also called a pound sign or a sharp sign) in the HREF used to refer to the anchor. You can also refer to an anchor in another document anywhere on the Web, assuming you know the name of a valid position in that document. You can invent any name you want when you are creating an anchor—you don't have to use the word anchor, as I did.

mailto

I'd like to return to the example given earlier using the <ADDRESS> tags. Now that we know about URLs and hyperlinks, we can polish off the task of creating a standard footer in our HTML documents. When the browser sees that the user clicks on a mailto URL, a mail message dialog box is opened with the recipient's e-mail address already filled in. All the user has to do is fill in the subject and the message and click the Send button. It's a good way to elicit comments on your Web pages. It certainly makes it more likely that you will get feedback than if the user is required to write down the e-mail address and then go launch his mail client and start a new message from scratch.

Here's an HTML code fragment that could be used as a standard document footer:

```
<HR>
<ADDRESS>
This document last modified: April 20, 1996<BR>
By Scott Zimmerman<BR>
e-mail: <A HREF="mailto:scottz@sd.znet.com">scottz@sd.znet.com</A>
</ADDRESS>
```

Notice how the <A HREF...> tag is closed before the text that will appear underlined in the browser. The </A> tag is used to mark the end of clickable area in the browser.

> **Note:** Unlike HTTP and FTP URLs, it is a common syntactical mistake to include double-slash characters in a mailto URL. The correct form of a mailto URL is mailto:user@somedomain.com.

Figure 5.4 shows a sample HTML page using this code. You can see that the status bar is indicating the URL destination of the hyperlink being pointed to.

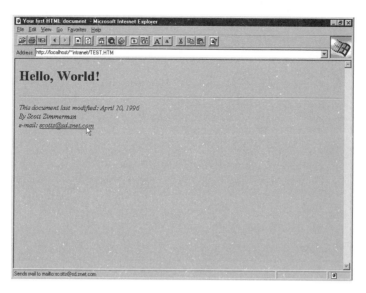

Figure 5.4. *This sample Web page demonstrates the* `mailto` *URL.*

Graphics

One of the neat things you can do with hyperlinks is include graphics in your HTML pages. Many pages on the Web use a graphic image technique to create imagemaps, which allow the user to click a region of the graphic and then have another Web page retrieved. Server-side imagemaps are beyond the scope of this book; however, I can refer you to the book *Web Site Construction Kit for Windows NT.* (It contains an entire chapter dealing with the subject of imagemaps.) I'll bring up the topic of *client-side imagemaps* later in this chapter, because they are an exciting new aspect to HTML 3.2.

You use the `<IMG>` tag to embed graphics in a Web page. There is no closing tag, such as `</IMG>`, because the attributes take care of everything. The `SRC` attribute is where you give the URL of the image document to be displayed. (Most browsers can handle a JPEG or a GIF image.) You do not need to specify a complete URL if the image is in the same directory as the HTML file. The `ALIGN` attribute allows you to specify how text will flow around the image (more about that later).

Let's dive into this with a simple example. Suppose you want to include a picture of your company guard dog on your corporate home page. Okay, maybe that's a stretch—the point isn't what's in the image, but rather, how do you write the HTML to display *any* image. Listing 5.4 is the HTML code which demonstrates a sample Web page containing a graphic image.

Listing 5.4. This HTML code demonstrates the IMG tag to embed graphics.

```
<HTML>
<HEAD>
<TITLE>Boston's Story</TITLE>
</HEAD>
<BODY>
        <H2>Welcome to Boston's Life</H2>
        Hi, my name is Boston. Here is a picture of me:
        <IMG ALIGN="top" SRC="boston.jpg">
        <H5>A Brief Autobiography</H5>
        <UL COMPACT>
                <LI>Born in Bonsall, CA March 5, 1995.
                <LI>Got my shots and went to new home in San Diego, April 30, 1995.
                <LI>Now spend time catching Frisbees and looking out the window.
        </UL>
        <HR width=80%>
        <ADDRESS>Okay, so e-mail me: boston@hqz.com</ADDRESS>
</BODY>
</HTML>
```

You might notice in Listing 5.4 that the ALIGN="TOP" attribute was used in the <IMG> tag. You can see the effect of this in Figure 5.5, which shows the sample code as it displays in Internet Explorer 2.0.

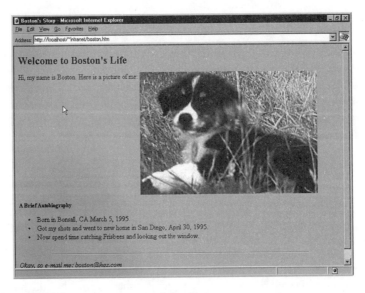

Figure 5.5. *This sample Web page demonstrates an inline image.*

More About the ALIGN Attribute

An image specified as ALIGN="LEFT" will float down and over to the left margin (into the next available space there), and subsequent text will wrap around the right side of that image. Likewise, for ALIGN="RIGHT", the image aligns with the right margin and the text wraps around the left. Here are the optional values for the ALIGN attribute:

ALIGN="TOP" aligns itself with the top of the tallest item in the line.

ALIGN="TEXTOP" aligns itself with the top of the tallest text in the line.

ALIGN="MIDDLE" aligns the baseline of the current line with the middle of the image.

ALIGN="ABSMIDDLE" aligns the middle of the current line with the middle of the image.

ALIGN="BASELINE" aligns the bottom of the image with the baseline of the current line.

ALIGN="BOTTOM" is identical to ALIGN="BASELINE".

ALIGN="ABSBOTTOM" aligns the bottom of the image with the bottom of the current line.

A Netscape Extension: `<IMG WIDTH=value HEIGHT=value>`

The WIDTH and HEIGHT attributes were added by Netscape to `<IMG>` mainly to speed up display of the document. If the author specifies these, the viewer of the document won't have to wait for the image to be loaded over the network and its size calculated. These attributes are not yet widely supported by other browsers.

The `<IMG ALT>` Attribute

It's a good idea when embedding images in HTML to use the ALT attribute to provide a description of the image. ALT gets its name because the text serves as an alternative to the image for browsers that don't have graphic capability. Here is a simple example demonstrating how a hyperlink in one document can be tied to a click an image or on the anchor text:

```
<A HREF="second.htm">
<IMG SRC="second.gif" ALT="[description of the picture]">
Jump to second.htm </A>
```

It's important to understand why there are two filenames in this code. The first filename is in the HREF attribute; this is how mouse clicks on the image are hyperlinked to documents, which could be anywhere on the Web. The second filename is the image to be displayed. In case the browser doesn't support graphics, it will instead display the text "[description of the picture]". This is also a good example of how to nest images inside of anchors.

Multimedia, MIME, and Interlaced Images

Because this is the section on graphics, I should mention that hyperlinks can point to other file types as well. You can embed audio and video into your Web pages also. This gets us into the subject of MIME, and the rest of the book will be focusing very heavily on that so I will defer it for now.

Another technique that you might have seen on the Web is the use of interlaced images. Normally, an image must be completely downloaded before it can be displayed. With interlaced images, your browser is able to display the whole image in fuzzy detail at first, but as the download progresses the image becomes more and more clear. The advantage of this is that the user can choose to cancel the download if it does not appear to be the image of interest. Transparent images are a similar technique which allows the background of the HTML page to show through the gaps in the picture. You can use Paint Shop Pro to create both transparent and interlaced images, but alas, that is also beyond the scope of this book. One source for a complete treatment of Transparent and Interlaced GIFs is *Web Site Construction Kit for Windows NT.*

HTML 2.0 Forms

The possibilities for creative form processing in HTML are endless. Perhaps as you glance at Figure 5.6, your imagination will lead you to an idea about a form that you or your office could deploy on the Intranet.

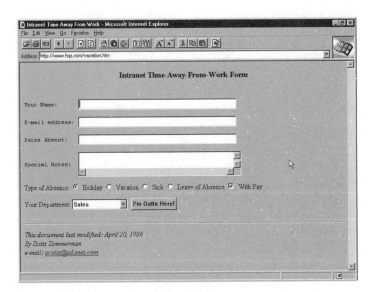

Figure 5.6. *This Intranet form is one cool way to save paper.*

The form in Figure 5.6 was created with the HTML code in Listing 5.5. The file is named `vacation.htm` on the accompanying CD-ROM.

Listing 5.5. This vacation form demonstrates all the HTML form tags.

```
<HEAD>
<TITLE>Intranet Time Away From Work</TITLE>
</HEAD>
<BODY>
<CENTER>
<H3>Intranet Time-Away-From-Work Form</H3>
</CENTER>
```

```
<FORM METHOD=POST ACTION="savedata.exe">

<PRE>
<BR>Your Name:      <INPUT NAME="name" TYPE=text SIZE=50 MAXSIZE=50>
<BR>E-mail address: <INPUT NAME="email" TYPE=text SIZE=50 MAXSIZE=50>
<BR>Dates Absent:   <INPUT NAME="item" TYPE=text SIZE=50 MAXSIZE=50>
<BR>Special Notes:  <TEXTAREA NAME="reason" ROWS=2 COLS=55 MAXLENGTH=150></TEXTAREA>
</PRE>

<P>Type of Absence:
<INPUT TYPE=radio NAME="holiday" VALUE="holiday" Checked>Holiday
<INPUT TYPE=radio NAME="vacation" VALUE="vacation">Vacation
<INPUT TYPE=radio NAME="sick" VALUE="sick">Sick
<INPUT TYPE=radio NAME="leave" VALUE="leave">Leave of Absence
<INPUT TYPE=checkbox NAME="pay" VALUE="pay" CHECKED>With Pay
</P>

<P>Your Department:
<SELECT NAME="department">
<OPTION>Accounting
<OPTION>Administration
<OPTION>Engineering
<OPTION>Marketing
<OPTION SELECTED>Sales
<OPTION>Support
</SELECT>

<INPUT TYPE=submit VALUE="I'm Outta Here!">
</P>
</FORM>

<HR>
<ADDRESS>
This document last modified: April 20, 1996<BR>
By Scott Zimmerman<BR>
e-mail: <A HREF="mailto:scottz@sd.znet.com">scottz@sd.znet.com</A>
</ADDRESS>
</BODY>
</HTML>
```

I'll have much more to say about HTML forms in Chapter 19, "Getting the Most out of HTML with CGI." For now, Table 5.1 will function as a quick introduction.

Table 5.1. HTML tags for creating forms.

`<FORM> ... </FORM>`	These tags appear within the `<BODY>` of the HTML file. Everything you code in between them will comprise the form. In addition to other HTML tags, the tags described in this section are valid within a `<FORM>` block.

continues

Table 5.1. continued

`<TEXTAREA>` ... `</TEXTAREA>`	These tags cause the browser to present a multi-line text edit box on the form. You can control the width and height in character units with the `ROWS` and `COLS` properties. As with the `<INPUT>` and `<SELECT>` tags, the `NAME` property is used to identify the data that is returned to the server for CGI processing or sent in the e-mail body if `mailto` is used.
`<INPUT>` ... `</INPUT>`	These tags define a single-line text box for strings or integers; a checkbox; a radio button; a pushbutton; and a few other varieties of controls. The `TYPE` attribute is what determines the style of `<INPUT>` control.
`<SELECT>` ... `</SELECT>`	These tags define a listbox of items from which the user can choose an item. You may use several `<OPTION>` tags within the `<SELECT>` block to present the available items.
`<OPTION>`	This tag indicates a selectable item within a `<SELECT>` block. You might also specify one of the values to be selected by default using the `SELECTED` attribute.

Creating Searchable Indexes

The `<ISINDEX>` tag is a way to let the user submit a word for the server to search for. This tag is usually placed in the `<HEAD>` section of an HTML file. When a document containing `<ISINDEX>` is first retrieved, the browser will automatically create a textbox and prompt the user to enter a keyword. When the user presses Enter, the same URL will again be requested on the server, but this time it will have supplemental text following a question mark character (which serves as a parsing delimiter). The user's keyword will be tacked onto the end of the URL (following a question mark) to enable the server to process it, search for it, and return custom results instead of the original HTML document. (See Chapter 21, "Indexing Your Intranet with WAIS," for a complete discussion of how to do this.)

Netscape has added the `PROMPT` attribute to `<ISINDEX>`. `PROMPT` has been created so the document author can specify what message is to appear before the text input field of the index. Without a custom prompt, the default is that standard message you may have come across before: `This is a searchable index. Enter search keywords:`

Further discussion of `<ISINDEX>` gets us into the topic of CGI, which is covered extensively in Chapters 19–21.

Server-Side Includes

Server-Side Includes (SSIs) are a way to have the server process your HTML file in a custom manner each time before the document is sent to a browser. This technique enables you to write more dynamic HTML. Your pages need not be delivered only as you had created them, but instead they may contain real-time information.

Here's how it works. The browser retrieves a document with a special filetype, such as `.shtml`. This special filetype serves as a clue to the server that the Web server should read and parse the file before sending it back to the client. This feature exacts a small performance penalty, so you can exclude ordinary documents by giving them filenames ending in `.htm` or `.html`. As the server reads the HTML code it searches for HTML comments with SSI commands embedded. When it finds an SSI command, the server replaces that part of the original HTML text with the output of the command before sending it to the client.

There are six basic SSI commands, though some Web servers support several additional SSI commands. Unfortunately, IIS 1.0 only supports the first of these:

- ◆ `#include`—Insert the contents of the given file into this file.
- ◆ `#echo`—Write the value of a given environment variable.
- ◆ `#fsize`—Write the size in bytes of the specified file.
- ◆ `#flastmod`—Insert the date last modified of the given file.
- ◆ `#exec`—Execute a shell command.
- ◆ `#config`—Controls the formatting of date and time strings.

Here is an example of an SSI command to insert the contents of another HTML file into the current file, replacing the SSI comment itself:

```
<!--#include file="standard.html" -->
```

The potential application of this should be obvious. Say you wish to display a corporate logo in the HTML footer of all your Intranet Web pages. You can write the HTML code that will be pasted into the `<BODY>` section and save it as a separate file, say `standard.html`. Then include that file into every document, saving you the trouble of having to modify every document when the logo or the company contact information is changed. You'll only have to edit one file and it will instantly be reflected to the next browser to retrieve any file which includes it.

Server-Push and Client-Pull

The idea behind both of these techniques is to give page designers a way to force a particular document to be updated repeatedly. Although the two techniques are quite different, the effects can be very similar. Let's start with an overview of server-push.

Server-Push

Server-push uses a variation of MIME called *multipart/x-mixed-replace* that enables each piece of data to replace the data that preceded it. This is a useful trick because the data (in this case the HTML page) isn't necessarily replaced; more likely it is just an updated version of the same page. This can be used to create an animation effect by loading a sequence of slightly different graphics.

The server will maintain the connection with the browser, and the server determines when the successive data parts are sent. If the browser is able to retrieve the subsequent images or HTML pages too quickly (which is entirely possible on an Ethernet-based Intranet), the server can insert an appropriate pause by simply delaying the transmission of each part.

Client-Pull

Client-pull is perhaps the simpler of the two techniques for dynamic self-updating documents. This technique relies on a new feature of HTML 3.2, the <META> tag. <META> should be placed within the <HEAD> section at the top of the HTML file.

Here is an example of a client-pull document that will reload every 30 seconds:

```
<HTML>
<HEAD>
<META HTTP-EQUIV="refresh" CONTENT="30">
<TITLE>Sample Client-Pull</TITLE>
</HEAD>
<BODY>
<H1>This document will automatically reload itself in 30 seconds.</H1>
</BODY>
</HTML>
```

The <META CONTENT> attribute also has the capability to retrieve a different document when the timer expires. Here is an example of how a URL can be embedded to cause the current page to load a second page:

```
<META HTTP-EQUIV="refresh" CONTENT="30; URL=http://domain.com/second.htm">
```

> **Tip:** In this section, we have barely scratched the surface of the capabilities of server-push and client-pull. For a much more thorough treatment of these subjects, please see this URL at Netscape:
>
> ```
> http://www.netscape.com/assist/net_sites/pushpull.html
> ```

Tables in HTML 3.0

Tables were the most requested feature for HTML 3.0 and 3.2. The IETF decided to stick to a powerful but simple model for creating nice looking tables. See Figure 5.7 for a very simple example of a table created in HTML 3.2, as it appears running in Microsoft Internet Explorer Version 2.0 (available on the accompanying CD-ROM).

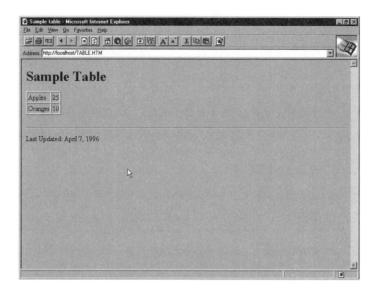

Figure 5.7. *A simple HTML 3.2 table displayed in Internet Explorer.*

The table in Figure 5.7 was created by the short HTML code shown in Listing 5.6.

Listing 5.6. This HTML 3.2 code creates a simple table.

```
<HTML>
<HEAD>
<TITLE>Sample table</TITLE>
</HEAD>
<BODY>
<H1>Sample Table</H1>

<TABLE BORDER>
<TR>
<TD>Apples</TD>
<TD>25</TD>
</TR>

<TR>
<TD>Oranges</TD>
<TD>10</TD>
</TR>

</TABLE>
<HR>
Last Updated: April 7, 1996
</BODY>
</HTML>
```

The <TABLE> tag begins the table. Here, I have added the BORDER attribute in the opening tag. Each <TR> tag defines a table row. The <TD> tags define table data elements, as you read across the table. The </TABLE> tag ends the definition of the table.

Frames in HTML 3.2

One of the most talked-about features that Netscape added to Navigator 2.0 is *frames*. As frames are yet another addition to HTML 3.2, they are not yet supported in many browsers, including Internet Explorer version 2.0. A framed Web page is much like a Web page within a Web page. Each frame can be sized separately by dragging the border between them. Indeed, each frame can even behave as a separate browser. There are many practical uses for frames.

> **Note:** Once you leave a frames page and access a page that doesn't have them (whether it's on another Web site or the same one), your frames disappear.

Frames are created by replacing the traditional <BODY>...</BODY> tags with a new pair of tags: <FRAMESET>...</FRAMESET>. The main body of the HTML file then becomes quite hollow, because the only thing you put in the <FRAMESET> block are references to other Web pages that contain the actual content to be displayed in each window. You see, you have to create a main HTML file which will govern the layout of the window panes which will load other HTML files.

Because few browsers support frames yet, it is advisable to use the <NOFRAMES>...</NOFRAMES> block as a replacement for what you would have put in the <BODY>...</BODY> block if you weren't using frames. This way, new browsers will use the <FRAMESET> tag and old browsers will still have something to chew on in the main HTML file. One technique is to simply provide an <A HREF> link in the <NOFRAMES> block to each of the framed pages.

An example should help to clear this up. Suppose you want to provide a small horizontal frame window across the bottom of your home page so that whenever someone follows a link in the top page, the bottom page will still remain. This could be a useful way to provide an omnipresent map of your site. Listing 5.7 shows the basic structure of a framed page.

Listing 5.7. This HTML 3.2 code demonstrates the <FRAMESET> tag.

```
<HTML>
<HEAD>
<TITLE>Example of Frames</TITLE>
</HEAD>

<FRAMESET ROWS="80%,20%">

<NOFRAMES>
<H1>Example of Frames</H1>
<P>This Web page is best viewed using Netscape</P>
</NOFRAMES>
```

```
<FRAME SRC="cell1.htm">
<FRAME SRC="cell2.htm">

</FRAMESET>
</HTML>
```

Notice that the `<BODY>` tag is replaced by the `<FRAMESET>` tag in a framed Web page. The `<FRAMESET>` block will either use the `<NOFRAMES>` option or it will create two horizontal windows to load other Web pages. The `<FRAMESET>` tag in this example dedicates the top 80 percent of the browser window to load the file `cell1.htm`. The bottom 20 percent loads the file `cell2.htm`.

Although many frames pages on the Web use the new capability primarily to provide navigational bars or banners, you can use them in your Intranet applications to make your ready reference pages available to your customers at all times. You can keep a list of important pages on your Intranet constantly visible—and clickable—regardless of where else in your applications your customer wanders.

> **Tip:** When you're viewing Web pages with frames, the browser's Back button on the toolbar doesn't act as you're accustomed. Hitting it takes you back to the last *non-frames* page you've visited. To get back your Back capability in a frames document, press your right mouse button. A small pop-up menu will appear with options for moving backward and forward within the frames.

Please see this URL for all the details and the syntax for creating HTML frames:

```
http://home.mcom.com/assist/net_sites/frame_syntax.html.
```

Client-Side Imagemaps

HTML 3.2 has a new graphic technique that is an alternative to server-side imagemaps. A client-side imagemap accomplishes several things. First, it enables the browser to know where a mapped image hyperlink will go so this information can be displayed to the user *before* he clicks on it. Second, this technique works for local files which are opened without using an HTTP server. Third, the server does not have to be queried for the target hyperlink of a region after a click; the browser can go straight to the new destination. Finally, the file format of server-side imagemaps is unfortunately inconsistent among different servers, but client-side imagemaps should be portable among all standard browsers.

Two new tags and one new attribute are involved in building client-side imagemaps. You must use the USEMAP attribute in the `<IMG>` tag instead of, or in addition to, the ISMAP attribute.

Here is an example of an `<IMG>` tag that is mapped by the client using client-side imagemaps:

```
<IMG SRC="mystuff.gif" USEMAP="#mystuff map">
```

In this case, the name "mystuff map" should appear elsewhere in the HTML file in a <MAP>...</MAP> block. The purpose of the <MAP> block is to define the coordinates of the regions that can be clicked in the image. The <MAP> block, which must also reside within the <BODY> or <FRAMESET> block, can contain any number of <AREA> tags. The shapes in the image can be circles, rectangles, or polygons. Listing 5.8 is the code which completes the example above.

Listing 5.8. This HTML 3.2 code demonstrates client-side imagemaps.

```
<HTML>
<HEAD>
<TITLE>Example of Client-Side Imagemaps</TITLE>
</HEAD>
<BODY>
<H1>Here is a client-side image with two hyperlinks.</H1>
<IMG SRC="mystuff.gif" USEMAP="#mystuff">
<MAP NAME="mystuff">

<AREA SHAPE=RECT COORDS="0,0,200,200" HREF="image2.htm">
<AREA SHAPE=RECT COORDS="201,201,400,400" HREF="image3.htm">

</MAP>
</BODY>
</HTML>
```

> **Note:** For the syntax of the <MAP> and <AREA> tags, the IETF proposal paper, and additional examples, please see this page at Microsoft:
>
> http://www.microsoft.com/ie/author/htmlspec/imagemap.htm

Persistent Cookies

The cookie technology invented by Netscape, and now a part of HTML 3.2, allows a browser to "remember" data about a Web page the user has visited so that the browser can return the data to the server each time it is revisited. Cookies probably got their names because computer scientists have long talked of the concept of *magic cookies,* which for lack of a better name, are like nuggets of numbers that can perform special feats when used in a proper manner inside the right program.

The need for persistent cookies in HTML is because HTTP connections only last but a fleeting moment; HTTP is a *stateless* protocol. A Web server cannot store substantial information about each client that visits because the client may not ever reappear, or it might next retrieve some other random Web page on the same server. Basically, it should be up to the client to tell the server about the status of the client.

The oft-cited reason for the invention of cookies is the shopping cart example. If you bounce around a department store Web page "picking up" several items to pay for at the "cash register," the check-out Web page is going to need to know what you have in your basket. Cookies do the trick. Cookies are sent by the server in the HTTP header. The browser simply sends the same data back whenever it visits that server. It is important for you to know that cookies are an available technique in Web page design, but as it depends somewhat on CGI programming, the syntax details are a little beyond the scope of this chapter.

> **Note:** For a thorough discussion of persistent cookies, please see the Netscape specification at
>
> ```
> http://home.netscape.com/newsref/std/cookie_spec.html
> ```

Style Sheets in HTML 3.2

HTML is intended for document *content* markup on the server-side. By design, it is not intended to provide direct control over the exact appearance of the document in the browser on the client side. One reason is portability. There is no way of controlling which browser and which font every client will have available. This state of affairs can be frustrating to graphic artists. Style sheets are intended to give page designers, or even the user of the browser, the opportunity to govern how the page is displayed in terms of fonts, colors, and other elements.

The IETF is still considering exactly how to implement style sheets in HTML 3.2. For the latest information, please visit the HTML specification:

```
http://www.ietf.cnri.reston.va.us/ids.by.wg/html.html
```

Another great place to search is

```
http://www.yahoo.com/Computers_and_Internet/Internet/World_Wide_Web/
```

Writing Math in HTML 3.2

Most of us probably haven't missed being able to write the calculus integral symbol into our HTML code. However, considering the Web got started in a physics lab, it's only natural that these features would eventually find their way into HTML. Unfortunately, these 3.0 features are just as much a moving target as style sheets. To learn more about math support in HTML 3.2, please see the section later in this chapter titled "HTML 3.2 Resources."

Character Entities

Because HTML is limited to 7-bit ASCII characters, it isn't ordinarily possible to include special symbols in documents. However, HTML has the concept of *escape codes* to provide for this. You write the ANSI number of the non-ASCII character in between &# and a semicolon. A couple of symbols are so widely used on business pages, Netscape even invented a name for them:

®—the Registered Trademark symbol; also available as ®

©—the Copyright symbol; this entity works just like ©, but now you don't have to look up the magic number anymore.

HTML 3.2 Resources

HTML 3.2 has several important new features. To name a few: frames, cookies, tables, figures (<FIG>) as a substitute for the image tag (<IMG>), support for mathematical formulae, banners, divisions, footnotes, and style sheets. You will find a quick reference to HTML in Appendix A, including tags that are specific to HTML 3.2.

> **Tip:** An excellent place on the Net to find information about the differences between HTML 2.0 and HTML 3.2 is "How to Tame the Wild Mozilla."
>
> `http://webreference.com/html3andns/`
>
> (*Mozilla* is how Netscape refers to itself in the HTTP request message.) This URL also includes late-breaking news about the Web. Definitely check it out!

Note that the specification of HTML 3.2 is still a draft. Although some parts have been stable for some time, others will undoubtedly change. The best way to track the changes to HTML is to go online to any of these sites:

◆ Netscape Communications.

`http://www.netscape.com/`

◆ Several papers and specifications on Hypertext Markup Language.

`http://www.ietf.cnri.reston.va.us/ids.by.wg/html.html`

◆ The HTML 3.2 Arena browser project (currently available for UNIX; stay tuned, a Windows version is being considered).

`http://www.w3.org/hypertext/WWW/Arena/Status.html`

◆ The HTML + specification (a little dated).

`http://www.w3.org/hypertext/WWW/MarkUp/HTMLPlus/htmlplus_1.html`

Quick Tips on HTML Style

HTML style and HTML style sheets might sound similar, but they are different subjects. Although style sheets provide some degree of control over the appearance of Web documents, the subject of style is more a topic of what to do and what not to do in Web page design (whether style sheets are used or not).

Web purists make remarks such as, "It's the content, not the presentation." That philosophy notwithstanding, Web designers obviously do have a great deal of control over many appearance factors, such as when to use a hyperlink, a bullet list, or a heading level 2. You might be tempted to think that some choices are arbitrary, but be careful. If your pages demonstrate disregard for certain accepted Web standards or are hard to read, you might not get any repeat visitors. There is a lot to be said for having good style.

Here are a few resources concerning HTML style:

◆ *Style Guide for Online Hypertext,* by the Father of the Web, Tim Berners-Lee:

`http://www.w3.org/hypertext/WWW/Provider/Style/Overview.html`

◆ *Web Style Manual,* by Patrick J. Lynch:

`http://info.med.yale.edu/caim/StyleManual_Top.HTML`

◆ *Tips for Writers and Designers,* by David Siegel:

`http://www.best.com/~dsiegel/tips/tips_home.html`

◆ *From Grass Roots to Corporate Image* by Christine A. Quinn, Director Electrical Engineering Computer & Network Services, Stanford University:

`http://www.ncsa.uiuc.edu/SDG/IT94/Proceedings/Campus.Infosys/quinn/quinn.html`

Summary

This chapter has covered a lot of ground. I concluded the tour of the basic preparations for building an Intranet, and now I'm sure you are ready to get to the real work at hand. Part II is all about building the server that will serve as the core of the Intranet.

PART

Getting Set Up on the Server

CHAPTER

6

◆

Windows NT 4 Configuration

- ◆ NT Workstation versus NT Server
- ◆ Installing TCP/IP
- ◆ HOSTS and LMHOSTS and DHCP and WINS
- ◆ Understanding UNC names
- ◆ Windows NT 4 utilities
- ◆ Understanding the Windows NT Registry

This chapter is here to give you some ideas about Windows NT configuration, but it is not intended to replace the installation documentation that comes with Windows NT. The information in this chapter covers assorted topics that might be just enough for you to go on if you have worked with other network operating systems before. If you don't consider yourself an expert in networking, this chapter alone isn't going to make you a system administrator, and I would wholeheartedly advise you to pick up a copy of *Windows NT Server Survival Guide* written by Rick Sant'Angelo and Nadeem Chagtai. I consider their book to be perhaps the best buy on the market when it comes to learning all the ins and outs of NT administration. It's also the single best book to supplement this one on an NT Webmaster's bookshelf, in my opinion.

> **Tip:** While I'm on the subject of useful sources for reference materials, I think that every Windows NT administrator should have a subscription to *Windows NT Magazine.* Each issue is packed with useful technical articles and product reviews to keep you informed about the BackOffice network.

What's the Difference Between NT Workstation and NT Server?

When buying Windows NT, you have a choice between the Server version and the Workstation version. Both are very capable, reliable, 32-bit, multithreading, preemptive-multitasking, GUI, network operating systems. In version 4, the biggest difference between the two is that the Server version now includes Internet Information Server (IIS) for free. IIS includes a high-performance Web server, an FTP server, and a Gopher server. (See Chapters 7 and 9.)

NT Workstation is more affordable than NT Server (street prices around $260 versus $675, respectively). Although the Workstation version is designed for better single-user performance, it can also reliably handle a Web server. The Server version does have several features that Workstation lacks, but most are probably not critical to building an Intranet. The following list details a few key differences:

◆ NT Server can support up to 1,000 simultaneous LAN users, whereas NT Workstation can support up to 10.

◆ Although a special Workstation license of SQL Server 6.5 is available for a single user, you must run NT Server if you expect to support several database clients. (This restriction is similar to the restriction that IIS must run on NT Server.)

◆ NT Server supports the AppleTalk LAN protocol for compatibility with Macintosh computers.

◆ The microkernel in NT Server is tweaked for faster file server performance than NT Workstation.

When dealing with Intranets, the first difference in the preceding list is not a problem. The number of Web clients that can simultaneously connect to your server is *not* the same as the number of LAN users. With either version of NT, the number of possible Intranet client connections is limited by the performance of the network, the hard disk, and other factors. The performance of the kernel system software isn't really a major problem either, unless you are planning to process hundreds of transactions per minute. Therefore, I recommend NT Workstation for those who like to save a few hundred dollars.

Installing TCP/IP

For the rest of this chapter, I'm going to assume that you have already installed Windows NT 4. One of the first things you need to do after installing NT is to get TCP/IP running as your primary network protocol. As you recall from Chapter 1, the Web requires TCP/IP. Now I must confess that I lied—sort of. Thanks to the hard-working engineers at Microsoft, Winsock 2.0, which has just been released in Windows NT 4, enables Windows network applications to run transparently on other network protocols besides TCP/IP. If you are considering not running TCP/IP on your Intranet, keep in mind that this alternate protocol feature is very new, and you should investigate it carefully before adopting it. It may take some time to determine whether all Winsock 1.1 applications will run as is on Winsock 2.0 on top of alternate protocols. Also, you would need to deploy Winsock 2.0 on all your Intranet client machines. I haven't tested this feature, and I can't see any great gain in not using TCP/IP. If you have other pre-existing protocols that you must run in addition to TCP/IP, such as NetBEUI and/or IPX/SPX, you can be confident that Windows NT Server can handle practically everything you can dish up. (Windows 95 and Windows for Workgroups 3.11 can support up to three protocols at once.)

Follow these steps to add TCP/IP to Windows NT Server 4 (similar steps apply to NT Workstation):

1. Click Start | Settings | Control Panel | Network | Protocols | Add.
2. Choose TCP/IP, as shown in Figure 6.1. Choose OK. Consider removing other protocols, such as NetBEUI and IPX/SPX, if you are sure that you do not need them on your LAN. If you can standardize on just one protocol for all the computers on your LAN, TCP/IP is a good one to choose because it is very capable.

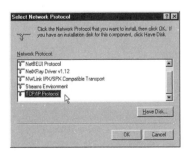

Figure 6.1. *Adding TCP/IP to the Network Protocols.*

After you have TCP/IP installed, follow these steps to configure the protocol:

1. Click Start | Settings | Control Panel | Network | Protocols | TCP/IP | Configure.
2. Click the IP Address tab as shown in Figure 6.2.

Figure 6.2. *Configuring the IP Address tab in the TCP/IP protocol.*

3. Unless another primary server exists on your network, you don't have the option of obtaining your IP address from a DHCP server (even if you decide to make this server a DHCP server for the rest of your network). You must obtain a valid static IP address for your NT server. Select the radio button that is titled Specify an IP address, and then enter your address and the mask. (The Dynamic Host Control Protocol, DHCP, is covered very lightly in the following section, and subnet masks are briefly covered in Chapter 28, "Connecting the Intranet and the Internet." Detailed treatment of these subjects is beyond the scope of this book.)

4. Click the DNS tab, and give yourself a valid host name and domain name. Depending on your network scheme, it is possible to use a NetBIOS name to refer to the server rather than a DNS host name. WINS and LMHOSTS are two ways to get that capability on a TCP/IP network (see the next section).

5. Click OK to close the Network dialog. You are prompted to restart Windows NT for the changes to take effect.

> **Note:** If the client machines on your Intranet are running Windows NT or Windows 95, you should have no trouble installing and configuring the built-in TCP/IP support that comes with those operating systems. If, however, you still have Windows for Workgroups 3.11 clients, you will need to install the free TCP/IP 32-bit stack as an add-on. You can either download the latest version from the Microsoft FTP site, or you can install it from the \Clients\Tcp32wfw directory on the Windows NT 4 Server CD-ROM. You can install it on the client machines across the LAN (assuming they are at least running NetBEUI to make an initial connection to the server).

HOSTS and LMHOSTS and DHCP and WINS

A lot of confusion exists about the difference between HOSTS and LMHOSTS. These terms refer to text files that reside in the \winnt\system32\drivers\etc subdirectory of Windows NT. I won't be covering these topics in depth here, so again, please consult *Windows NT Server Survival Guide* as a source for detailed information.

> **Tip:** I highly recommend that you create a desktop icon on your NT machine for the online books on the Microsoft Windows NT CD-ROM. Use Explorer to browse to the \support\books directory, and then drag the file server.hlp to your desktop to create a shortcut. The help files contain loads of technical information about everything from DHCP to User Manager.

In addition to the confusion concerning the difference between HOSTS and LMHOSTS, a separate confusion exists concerning the difference between WINS and DHCP. To keep the differences straight, remember that HOSTS goes with DNS, and LMHOSTS goes with WINS. Notice that I didn't mention DHCP in that sentence; the choice to run DHCP is independent of your choice to use HOSTS files or DNS.

HOSTS files can serve as a replacement for DNS if you place identical files on all the Windows clients in your LAN. HOSTS files map IP addresses to computer names, one per line. The confusion comes about because these names are TCP/IP computer names, or host names, which are quite different from the NetBIOS names you can give to Windows computers. Microsoft and IBM adopted NetBIOS in the early days of PCs to provide an efficient network protocol without forcing users to endure the headaches of TCP/IP configuration (in those days, TCP/IP required knowledge of UNIX). If you run your own DNS server on your Intranet, or if you connect to an Internet Service Provider, you won't need to suffer with the maintenance headache of the HOSTS files.

DHCP, Dynamic Host Control Protocol, stands alone in this section as a way to lease valid IP addresses from a large block to the computers on your LAN as they log into the Windows NT domain. This capability can be a plus as your LAN grows because you don't have to worry about coming up with a new address when new computers are added to the network and, more importantly, you don't have to be present to help configure the IP address when a conflict occurs (DHCP only leases available addresses).

LMHOSTS maintains NetBIOS computer name mappings to IP addresses in the same way that HOSTS maintains DNS computer name mappings. WINS plays a similar role, but in an automatic fashion, of course, so you avoid the hassle of updating and copying LMHOSTS files all over the network. The LM in the name LMHOSTS comes from LAN Manager, which was an early Microsoft network technology—the grandparent of Windows NT.

Understanding UNC Names

Once you have your LAN up and running, you're going to want to share files and printers. One of the reasons you'll want to do this is so that you can write HTML files on your own workstation before you copy them to the Web server directory on the network server (assuming, as is most likely the case, that the server is not your workstation).

In Windows NT 4, you use Explorer to share drives and files on the computer where they reside. You can still use File Manager too, if that is what you are used to from NT 3.51. Once you have shared a drive or directory, such as the WWWRoot directory where IIS is installed, you can connect to that drive from another computer on the LAN in a process called mapping a network drive. The remote drive then becomes a drive letter on your machine that you can refer to as if it were a local drive.

This process establishes a mapping, or association, between, say, drive N on your computer and drive D on the server, which is named *banana*. But if my computer is on the same LAN, I might have chosen to map the server drive D to my own drive M, not knowing that you had called it N on your computer. This difference could lead to confusion when you and I refer to files on the server because we each look at the same file and think of it with a different name.

Windows uses a very simple syntax to refer to network shared drives in a manner that avoids this potential confusion. This syntax is called UNC naming, or Universal Naming Convention. The thing that remains unique in the preceding scenario is the server name (banana) and the server's drive (D). The only problem is that the UNC syntax should not conflict with the existing syntax used for local files and directories. UNC names begin with double backslash characters to make them unique, and the colon is removed from the drive letter designation. Continuing the preceding example, drive M on my computer would have an equivalent UNC name of \\banana\d\. Drive N on your computer would have the same UNC name, which is exactly the goal of UNC names. To refer to a file in a subdirectory on drive N using UNC names, you tack on the pathname and filename as you would for a local file, for example, \\banana\d\somedir\somefile.txt.

Chapter 7 demonstrates that one reason this topic is relevant to your Intranet is that UNC names are required to make IIS virtual directories to other computers.

Windows NT 4 Utilities

Each of the tools listed in this section has its place in the toolbox that no NT Webmaster should be without. Knowing about these tools is one thing, but being familiar with them is another. Acquaint yourself with their capabilities at your earliest convenience, and you will be rewarded day in and day out.

This section introduces you to these tools' purposes and describes their basic capabilities. Most of these programs have dozens of options for all kinds of different needs and situations. It is up to you to try the programs and consult the appropriate documentation for further information.

ipconfig

If you're running on a network, ipconfig will tell you your own IP address and other facts about your Network Interface Card (NIC).

ping

You use ping to determine whether another computer running TCP/IP is reachable from your machine and how long it takes for a packet to make the round trip back to your computer.

tracert

The tracert tool is the NT console mode application equivalent to UNIX traceroute. This tool can display the entire route your IP packets take from your server to the host that you select. If you have access to the Internet, this tool can be fascinating to play with when you want to see how fast data can travel halfway around the world.

netstat

The netstat tool is handy for looking at the status of the LAN. You can see active connections to all ports and get a statistical breakdown of all connections over time.

nbtstat

To examine the status of TCP/IP connections that are using NetBIOS over TCP/IP, use the nbtstat command-line tool.

WinMSD

The handy WinMSD tool is installed in the menu system under Start | Programs | Administrative Tools | Windows NT Diagnostics. You can also run this program from the command line (winmsd.exe), but I use it so often that I created a shortcut icon on the desktop. WinMSD enables you to browse a lot of valuable system information without having to resort to separate tools.

Although WinMSD does not let you change any system parameters, it is a handy one-stop utility for information on OS version, hardware, memory, drivers, services running, drives, devices, IRQ/ port status, DMA memory, environment, and network configuration. You can print any of the information displayed or save it to a file. WinMSD also has a Tools menubar that lets you launch Event Viewer, Registry Editor, or Disk Administrator. If you ever sit down at an NT system that you are not familiar with, WinMSD is the tool to start with. (See Figure 6.3.)

Figure 6.3. Windows NT Diagnostics (`winmsd.exe`) displays the network settings.

Performance Monitor

Performance Monitor is a great GUI tool that is very easy to use after you get a little used to it. It gathers good statistics on IP/TCP/ICMP messages. This tool is your best all-around diagnostic tool for both the network (if your copy of NT is on a LAN) and the NT system itself (for example, CPU usage and disk I/O). For more information about Performance Monitor, consult the Windows NT Resource Kit.

> **Note:** To get the most out of Performance Monitor, install the SNMP service along with TCP/IP. With SNMP installed (through the Control Panel Network icon) and enabled (through the Control Panel Services icon), Performance Monitor can track IP packet statistics on your site.

Understanding the Windows NT Registry

The Registry contains important Windows NT data about user preferences and the hardware and software installed on your computer. Many of the values kept in the Registry are similar to those that you would find in the WIN.INI and SYSTEM.INI files of a machine running Windows 3.1. The Registry is a hierarchical database used to maintain configuration information for Windows NT and the users of the computer.

The Root Keys

The Registry is broken down into four subtrees. (Future versions of Windows NT might increase this number.) The root key names at the top of each subtree are prefixed with HKEY to indicate that they are handles to keys. Windows programmers speak of a *handle* as a reference to an operating system resource. A *key* is nothing more than a word by which you can look up an associated value (like a dictionary entry and its corresponding definition). The next sections cover the four root keys.

HKEY_LOCAL_MACHINE

The HKEY_LOCAL_MACHINE key contains information about the local computer system, including hardware and operating system data such as bus type, memory, device drivers, and start-up control data. This key is the subtree that you will be most concerned with.

HKEY_CLASSES_ROOT

The HKEY_CLASSES_ROOT key contains object linking and embedding (OLE) and file-class association data.

HKEY_CURRENT_USER

The HKEY_CURRENT_USER key contains the user profile for the user who is currently logged on, including environment variables, personal program groups, desktop settings, network connections, printers, and application preferences. This key always refers to a user in the subtree of HKEY_USERS.

HKEY_USERS

The HKEY_USERS key contains all actively loaded user profiles, including HKEY_CURRENT_USER and the default profile. Users who are accessing a server remotely do not have profiles under this key on the server; their profiles are loaded into the Registry on their own computers.

Editing the Registry

Many of the program configuration changes you make through the GUI in Windows NT (such as in Control Panel) will be automatically written into the Registry for you. Whenever possible, allow the friendly interface of Control Panel and other applications to write to the Registry on your behalf. Several advanced settings mentioned in this book, however, can be made only by directly editing the Registry. To make these changes, use REGEDT32.EXE (the Registry Editor) as shown in Figure 6.4.

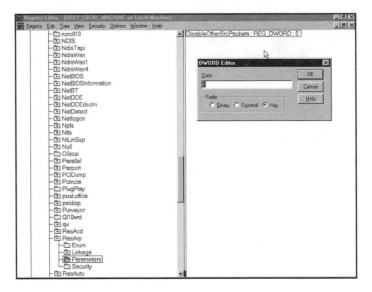

Figure 6.4. *Using the Registry Editor to change a* DWORD *value.*

> **Warning:** If you are not very careful, making changes directly to the Registry can sometimes prevent your computer from working properly. Windows NT displays a standard warning about this problem whenever you invoke the Registry Editor. The warning reads as follows:
>
> Caution: Using Registry Editor incorrectly can cause serious problems, including corruption that may make it necessary to reinstall Windows NT.

Most of the Registry values that are changed in this book are found under HKEY_LOCAL_MACHINE/ SYSTEM/CurrentControlSet.

As you navigate through the Registry with Registry Editor, you will notice that each entry in the structure is one of three things: a root key, a subtree, or a value. Value entries don't appear until you reach the end of a given subtree. Although this structure might sound complicated, the whole idea is to keep a huge amount of data organized. You'll see that the Registry serves that purpose very well, once you get used to it.

I've already discussed the four root keys. Think of subtrees as branches off of the main trunk, assuming the root keys are the main trunk. Each value entry has three parts: name, data type, and the actual value. By default, the Registry recognizes the following five types of data. The Win32 API includes functions that programmers can call to add other data types as necessary.

REG_BINARY

The REG_BINARY type is used for binary data that is uninterpreted by the Registry Editor. Such data can be interpreted either by the program that writes the entry or by a system function inside NT that will process the data at the appropriate time in the execution of the program that wrote the value. This data type can be used for values that don't fit any of the other types. Because all data in digital computers always exists in binary form, usage of the other data types is only a matter of convenience when the data can be interpreted by the Registry Editor in a human-readable form.

REG_DWORD

The REG_DWORD data type can contain 4 bytes of data. The basic unit of memory on Intel and many other computer architectures is 4 bytes, or 32 bits. This data type is useful for storing integers.

REG_EXPAND_SZ

The SZ in the REG_EXPAND_SZ stands for *string zero*, which means a NULL-terminated array of characters in C or C++. This data type indicates an expandable string of text that contains a variable that will be substituted at runtime. For example, the string %SystemRoot% appears throughout the Registry. This string will be replaced at runtime by the actual location of the Windows NT system directory.

REG_MULTI_SZ

The REG_MULTI_SZ data type is used to hold several string values, each one separated by NULL bytes.

REG_SZ

The REG_SZ data type is used to represent a simple array of characters or byte values. As you traverse the Registry, you will come across numerous examples of its use for strings of text.

Summary

Now that TCP/IP is up and running, the next chapter will bring the Intranet to life. The Web server will be the vital hub of your effort.

7

CHAPTER

◆

Running the Intranet
Web Server

◆ Configuring IIS
◆ Publishing existing documentation on your Web
◆ Web browser helper applications

With much of the theoretical material behind you, now is finally the time you can begin to establish a real Intranet. In this chapter, you'll set up the IIS Web server and take your first steps to publish existing corporate or organizational information on your Intranet. As you go through this chapter, you'll see real examples of how to jump-start an Intranet using various tools and techniques. When you finish this chapter, your Intranet will not be complete by any means, but you'll have made a good start.

Configuring IIS

Whether you downloaded IIS for free from the Microsoft Web site or obtained it from the CD-ROM with Windows NT, I'll assume at this point that you have followed the installation instructions that came with the software. Now the trick is getting it to work. Actually, depending on the state of your configuration, you may need several tricks.

By the time you read this, Microsoft will have released version 2.0 of IIS (anticipated with NT 4). Today I'm working with the beta release of version 2.0, and judging by the issues that I've faced with it and what I've heard from many other users on the Internet newsgroups, some aspects of configuration are not very intuitive. However, I think this difficulty is largely due to the fact that IIS is such a new product; the user community needs time to become aware of its features. After you get it up and running, you should be very pleased with its performance, features, and security.

Starting the Services

After installing IIS, you can run the Microsoft Internet Services Manager (shown in Figure 7.1) by choosing Start | Programs | Microsoft Internet Server | Internet Service Manager. The first thing you want to do is get the WWW Publishing Service started. Select that item in the list, and then click the triangle icon in the toolbar or choose Properties | Start Service.

If the service starts, you should be able to use your Web browser to visit the sample home page installed by IIS. (See Figure 7.2.)

But what if the service won't start? The most likely cause is that a dependency service is not already running. Unfortunately, IIS won't always tell you which service it depends on, but I learned the hard way that it is probably the Remote Procedure Call (RPC) service. In case you don't already have the RPC service running, choose Start | Settings | Control Panel | Services. Scroll down to the RPC Service, click Startup, and choose Automatic. The Automatic setting tells NT to start the service during bootup. It does not start the service immediately, and you don't need to reboot to make this setting work. Just click the Start button so your screen looks like Figure 7.3.

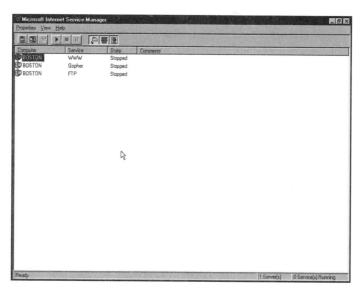

Figure 7.1. *The Microsoft Internet Services Manager with no services started.*

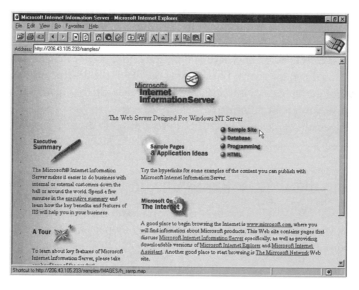

Figure 7.2. *The sample home page installed by IIS is the first place to test the WWW Publishing Service.*

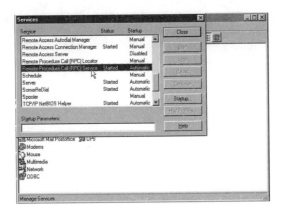

Figure 7.3. *The RPC Service should be started for IIS.*

Now you should be ready to start the WWW Publishing Service. You can either do that in the Control Panel Services dialog (while you're there), or you can do it in the IIS GUI. They both have the same effect.

> **Tip:** Currently, the best source of information for troubleshooting IIS problems is the IIS help file itself. The `admin` directory where you install IIS contains several interlinked help files. I highly recommend that you create a shortcut on your desktop for any one of the `.hlp` files in that directory. All you have to do is use Explorer (not maximized) to click the file. Still holding down the mouse button, drag the file to the desktop and let go of the mouse button. For example, because I installed IIS on my `D:` drive in a subdirectory called `IIS`, I created a desktop icon pointing to `D:\iis\admin\w3scfg.hlp`. You can always delete the shortcut icon after you've had a chance to read through the help files.

Configuring the WWW Publishing Service

After you have the WWW Publishing Service started, you can double-click the WWW item in the IIS Service Manager list to configure the Service properties. Figure 7.4 shows an example configuration of the Service tab.

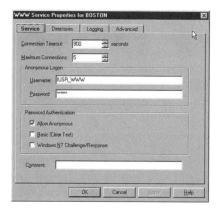

Figure 7.4. The WWW Service needs to run within the context of a User account.

The most important thing to note is that IIS created a default User account for itself when it installed. You will want to run User Manager for Domains (on NT Server) to configure the account permissions for the user that IIS creates. By default, the account name is IUSR_*computername* (where *computername* is replaced by the actual NetBEUI host name of your machine).

The purpose of this account is to let you, as the system administrator, configure the permissions of IIS when it is acting on behalf of an anonymous user. For example, if I connect with my Web browser to your WWW service, the WWW service better have Read permission to the HTML root directory so that it can send the files to my browser through HTTP. Similarly, you will want the service to have Execute permission on the directory where CGI and ISAPI applications are located.

You'll want to ensure that the user account in User Manager is maintained in a compatible manner with the Service tab in IIS. This compatibility is very important; the passwords must match, and the user account must be given the permission to log on locally. To enable the account to log on locally, follow these steps:

1. Choose Start | Programs | Administrative Tools | User Manager for Domains | Policies | User Rights. A dialog box appears.

2. Check the box labeled Show Advanced User Rights.

3. Scroll down in the drop-down list labeled Right until you see *Log on locally.* Select that item.

4. If you do not see the IUSR_*computername* account in the Grant To list box, click the Add button to add that right to that user. Your dialog should look similar to Figure 7.5 when you are done. Interestingly, the IUSR account does not need the right to log on as a service.

Figure 7.5. *The IUSR account needs the right to log on locally.*

The next step in the process is to ensure that the IUSR account has the correct permissions to access the directories containing the HTML documents. If you installed IIS on an NTFS volume (recommended), you can do this step in Explorer by right-clicking each folder that contains HTML files and then choosing Properties | Permissions.

I'll have more to say about security in Chapter 10, "Intranet Security in Windows NT," but there are a couple of other nuances that I should mention here. The IUSR account will need to have appropriate permissions within the domain if you expect it to serve documents from virtual directories on other machines in the network. To serve documents from another machine on the same LAN with the IIS machine, the virtual directory must use a UNC path. And the virtual directory must be within the same domain where IIS is running.

Configuring the WWW Service Directories

The Directories tab in the WWW Service dialog allows you to create reference names (called *aliases*) for directories on your server where you store HTML documents to be served. As you can see in Figure 7.6, there are two checkboxes in the Directories tab of this dialog. The checkboxes are self-explanatory. If you place a file named default.htm (you can choose a different default name in the dialog) in each subdirectory that is served by the WWW Service, a client browser will not need to specify the full filename in the URL.

If you check the Directory Browsing Allowed box, and you *don't* have a file named default.htm in each subdirectory under the <Home> directory, the client browser will be given a complete listing of all the files in the subdirectory that don't specify a full URL with a filename.

Figure 7.6. *The Directory configuration tab in the WWW Service dialog.*

Configuring the Logging and Advanced WWW Settings

The remaining two tabs in the WWW Service dialog deal with security: Logging and Advanced Access Control.

If you want to keep track of who is visiting your Web server, and you don't mind taking a small performance hit while the server writes that information to a file or a database, you can enable logging. As shown in Figure 7.7, the Logging dialog is very straightforward. File logging is recommended for better performance, and it should be sufficient unless you want to set up some nifty SQL queries of your own to monitor the log files. I don't imagine that logging would be a big issue on an Intranet; ideally you want all your customers to use the Web server. Logging is more for the purpose of security on an Internet Web site.

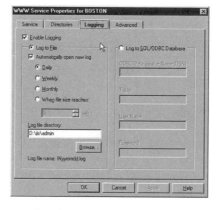

Figure 7.7. *The Logging configuration tab in the WWW Service dialog allows you to monitor who is visiting your Intranet server.*

The Advanced tab is also more of an Internet versus Intranet issue. But if you want to exclude certain machines on your LAN from having access to the Web server, you can enter those IP addresses in the dialog shown in Figure 7.8.

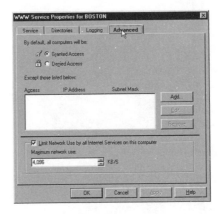

Figure 7.8. The Advanced configuration tab in the WWW Service dialog allows you to grant or deny access by IP address.

Caution: Be aware that IP filtering is not a 100-percent–reliable security measure. Through a technique known as *IP spoofing*, hackers can masquerade their packets as coming from a valid IP address and then obtain access as if they were running from a client workstation that has permission.

Publishing Existing Documentation on Your Web

Now that the IIS WWW Service is up and running, turn your attention to the documents that you will serve from your Intranet home page. The main source of information for your Intranet is the body of documents and data you already have available. This data, particularly if it's already in electronic format, will form your Intranet's foundation.

Taking Inventory

If yours is a typical organization, you probably have a lot of potential Intranet information lying around in file cabinets and on bookshelves and computer disks. Before you dive into the later sections of this book, dig up all this existing information and determine how much of it you can make available on your Intranet without too much time and effort.

Begin this process by taking inventory of the information already available in your company. Look for items such as the following:

- The company phone book
- Other informational material for employees, such as bulletin boards, job postings, and in-house newsletters or publications
- Employee benefits information
- Manuals of operational procedures
- Catalog and inventory lists
- Stored letters, memoranda, and other word processing documents from active disk drives or on backup tapes or disks
- Anything else you might find around the office, in a file cabinet, in a drawer, on a bookshelf, or even tacked on a wall or bulletin board

Casting a wide net at this point is important. Think of your Intranet as a big bank of filing cabinets, containing every piece of paper and scrap of data your company owns. You save information in filing cabinets because someone might need to look up the information in the future. The same goes for the information you'll put into your Intranet; anything that someone might need in the future is a candidate for inclusion.

After identifying the total pool of available data, the next question is which of that information can you easily make available on your Intranet? Not all of your data can be included with equal ease, so you'll need to evaluate which information is worth the time and effort necessary to make it usable on your Intranet.

The Easy Part First

Obviously, material that's already in electronic format is your prime and most accessible source of Intranet data. Within this category, old word processing documents will likely be the single best source of information, particularly if your organization uses formal electronic filing procedures of some kind. Even if you have no document-management apparatus, you'll probably find important recent documents still sitting on your hard drive or on backup tapes, just waiting to be put on your Intranet.

Your word processor's Save As feature is one of the most powerful tools for putting your word processing documents on your Intranet. All modern word processors have a Save As feature, which enables you to quickly convert the word processor's documents to plain text files, also called ASCII text files. Plain text files are directly usable in your Intranet. You can place them on your Web server as-is, with no further conversion. From there, your customers can view them with their Web browsers.

Suppose you have Microsoft Word, but you don't have Internet Assistant for Microsoft Word installed. When you choose File | Save As in the Word menu, you will see a scrollable list of file formats in which you can save documents. But if you search for plain ASCII text you won't find it—Word calls it Text Only with Line Breaks. WordPerfect has a similar option.

The default filename for converted documents in both Word and WordPerfect uses the extension .txt. You should accept this default extension because the plain text MIME data type/subtype, which uses the .txt extension, is directly supported by all Web servers and browsers. (Refer to Chapter 12, "MIME and Helper Applications," for information about MIME data types/subtypes.)

> **Note:** When you use the Save As feature, your original word processing document is not changed; you create a completely new file.

This simple Save As feature can make it possible for you to create a large library of documents for your Intranet in a very short time. Just load the document, select Save As, give your document a new name, and click OK. You may even be able to use your word processor's macro command facility to partially automate this process.

Of course, if you're part of a large operation that has a formal document-management system for its word processing documents, it's an equally simple matter for your staff to spend a morning or afternoon mass-converting documents for your Intranet. After all, you're already organized to manage your word processing data.

Either way, once you've saved your files in ASCII format, you can create an HTML document containing a list of the converted documents as hyperlinks and get your Intranet off the ground with almost no difficult work.

If you do have Internet Assistant for Microsoft Word installed (available on the CD-ROM), then you will have an additional item in the Save As Type list of the Word Save As dialog; namely HTML Document. Of course, you would think that option would be exactly what you want; however, check the result carefully because some documents might not be automatically converted the way you would expect.

Retaining Document Formatting

Unfortunately, when you save word processing documents as plain text, you lose the benefit of some of the package's special formatting features. Text enhancements like **boldface**, <u>underlining</u>, *italics*, and `font selections` all disappear. What's left are perfectly readable lines of plain text, but you'd probably like to have some of the original document's formatting back.

Besides losing formatting, you may also lose some actual content from a document when you convert it to ASCII format. Tables suffer especially in saving a document as plain text—they seldom resemble their original form when converted. Graphics usually disappear altogether. As a result, even though you've made rapid strides in creating your Intranet, you'll want to take some additional steps with at least some of your documents to preserve the documents' integrity.

The Rich Text Format (RTF) was introduced in Chapter 3, "The Software Tools to Build a Web." As you'll recall, Microsoft developed RTF as a means of enabling portability of documents among different applications, including different word processing packages. The specifications for RTF were made public and most of Microsoft's competitors in the word processor market have added support for RTF to their products. Both WordPerfect and Word support RTF as one of the document formats available through the Save As dialog box.

In just a few minutes' time, a batch of Word documents can be converted into HTML by using Word's Save As feature to create intermediate `.rtf` files. The intermediate files can then be converted to HTML using the freeware `rtftohtml` package available on the CD-ROM included with this book.

> **Note:** Chapter 3 also mentions Microsoft's Word add-on, *Internet Assistant*, which, when installed, adds HTML as an option to the Word Save As menu of file formats. Unfortunately, the author found the HTML documents created by Internet Assistant unsatisfactory, with typeface/fonts done poorly. Although Microsoft may well have upgraded Internet Assistant to resolve these problems by the time you read this, Save As RTF is a more reliable way of exporting Word documents for eventual conversion to HTML using `rtftohtm`.

If you want to populate your Intranet with useful documents as fast as you can click OK, all you need to do is save or copy the documents into the <Home> directory of the WWW Service and ensure that Directory Browsing is allowed and there is no file named `default.htm`. This procedure creates a quite unattractive, but useful, browser listing of all the documents you collect as you build your Intranet. The next step, of course, is to build a home page that contains links to and descriptions of each of the documents.

Adding Graphics

Adding graphics to your Intranet is just as easy as publishing other documents. Suppose you have various picture files lying around on your LAN in PCX or Windows BMP format (such as those created by Microsoft Paintbrush). Unfortunately, most Web browsers don't support direct viewing of `.pcx` or `.bmp` files without a helper application. Although helper application setup is quite simple in most browsers, and viewers for PCX files are widely available, you probably don't want to require all your customers to change their browser setup. A better idea is to convert the existing images into a format all Web browsers can read directly, such as `.gif` (Graphic Interchange Format) or `.jpg` (Joint Photographic Experts Group).

The Paint Shop Pro program included on the CD-ROM with this book is well-suited for the task of image conversions. You simply load the existing image, choose File | Save As, and select GIF-Compuserve in the List Files of Type drop-down list. Table 7.1 shows a list of dozens of typical image file formats that you may come across on your LAN. Paint Shop Pro (and other graphics programs available on the Internet) can handle many of these.

Table 7.1. A list of multiplatform image file formats and their customary filename extensions.

Filename Extension	File Type
AVS	AVS X image file
BMP	Microsoft Windows bitmap image file
CMYK	Raw cyan, magenta, yellow, and black bytes
EPS	Adobe Encapsulated PostScript file
EPSF	Adobe Encapsulated PostScript file
EPSI	Adobe Encapsulated PostScript Interchange format
FAX	Group 3 Facsimile
FITS	Flexible Image Transport System
GIF	CompuServe Graphics image file
GIF87	CompuServe Graphics image file (version 87a)
GRAY	Raw gray bytes
HDF	Hierarchical Data Format
HISTOGRAM	Image color histogram
HTML	Hypertext Markup Language
JBIG	Joint Bilevel Image experts Group format
JPG, or JPEG	Joint Photographic Experts Group format
MAP	Colormap intensities and indices
MATTE	Raw matte bytes
MIFF	Magick image file format
MPEG	Motion Picture Experts Group file interchange format
MTV	Ray-tracing format
NULL	NULL image
PCD	Photo CD
PCX	ZSoft IBM PC Paintbrush file
PDF	Portable Document Format
PICT	Apple Macintosh QuickDraw/PICT file
PNG	Portable Network Graphics
PNM	Portable bitmap
PS	Adobe PostScript file
PS2	Adobe Level II PostScript file

Filename Extension	File Type
RAD	Radiance image file
RGB	Raw red, green, and blue bytes
RGBA	Raw red, green, blue, and matte bytes
RLE	Utah Run-Length Encoded image file; read only
SGI	Irix RGB image file
SUN	SUN Rasterfile
TEXT	Raw text file; read-only
TGA	Truevision Targa image file
TIF, or TIFF	Tagged Image File Format
UYVY	16-bit/pixel-interleaved YUV
TILE	Tile image with a texture
VICAR	Vicar format; read-only
VID	Visual Image Directory
VIFF	Khoros Visualization Image File
X	Select image from X server screen
XC	Constant image of X server color
XBM	X11 bitmap file
XPM	X11 pixmap file
XWD	X Window system window dump image file
YUV	CCIR 601 1:1:1 file
YUV3	CCIR 601 2:1:1 files

Other Legacy Data Conversions

In addition to your word processing documents, you no doubt have other kinds of information stored in electronic format. The following sections look at how some of this legacy data can be converted for your Intranet.

Spreadsheet Data Files

Chapter 14 explains how to create a data warehouse on your Intranet with live spreadsheet data files. Because you're in a hurry to get your Intranet off the ground, though, you can get some static information from your legacy spreadsheet files up and accessible right away. As with your word processor, your spreadsheet program probably has a Save As command that enables you to save data in plain text format. Both Microsoft Excel and Lotus 1-2-3 have such features.

Both Microsoft Excel and Lotus 1-2-3 use the default filename extension .txt for converted files as well. As with the word processing files, you should accept this default because the plain text MIME data type/subtype is directly supported by all Web servers and browsers. If you're using another spreadsheet package, check its documentation for a plain text Save feature. Such files are directly usable in your Intranet, so any tabular data you have in your legacy spreadsheet files can be made available on your Intranet as quickly and easily as your word processing files.

> **Note:** Be aware that documents and databases you publish on your Intranet in the manner described in this chapter are not going to be editable files on the client side. In other words, your customers will be observing a local read-only copy. Subsequent chapters in this book show you how to extend the concept to create a powerful two-way Intranet.

Miscellaneous Legacy Data Conversions

Most relational database packages have one means or another of saving tables of data to text files you can use on your Intranet. For example, Microsoft Access has an Output To function, which can save database tables not only to plain text but also to RTF. The latter capability is interesting in that you can run the resulting RTF file through the rtftohtm program (available on the CD-ROM that comes with this book) to convert your data to HTML. Other database packages have similar features, although you may need to design a simple database report and direct its output to a plain text file to get what you want. As a result, you can export data from almost any database application for viewing in your Intranet, again with relatively minimal effort.

> **Note:** If you have legacy data in other formats, check out some of the filters and converters listed by the W³ Consortium at http://www.w3.org/pub/WWW/Tools/.

Helper Applications for Your Customers

Helper applications are computer programs to which your Web browser can pass data that it cannot display directly by itself. This sort of data typically includes audio or video, but, as you'll learn in Chapter 12, "MIME and Helper Applications," almost anything can be supported by the correct helper application.

Because you might have legacy data in video or audio format or in image formats not directly supported by Web browsers, you should provide your users with some basic helper applications. (Chapter 12 explains how to set up a means of distributing helper applications and other software/ data on your Intranet.) The following are a few you may want to obtain for your customers:

◆ Adobe Acrobat Reader

◆ Paint Shop Pro

◆ MPEGplay

◆ QuickTime

All these packages are either freeware or shareware, and the latest versions can easily be obtained on the Internet.

Adobe Acrobat Reader is a free, read-only application that can display PDF documents; you can't use it to create documents. You can retrieve the Acrobat Reader directly from Adobe's Web site at `http://www.adobe.com/Acrobat/readstep.html`, where versions are available for Windows, Macintosh, MS-DOS, and UNIX systems.

> **Note:** If you have full-capability Adobe Acrobat software, you'll want to look at Adobe's free Acrobat Plug-Ins, available at `http://www.adobe.com/`. There you'll find (among several others) WebLink, which allows Acrobat Exchange users to insert live World Wide Web hyperlinks in PDF documents. When viewing or editing these PDF files, clicking an inserted hyperlink fires up the Web browser to retrieve the link. WebLink is available only for Windows PCs and the Macintosh.

Helper Application Configuration in the Browser

Helper application setup is a subject that will be covered in a great deal of detail in later chapters. This section takes a quick look at this topic, using Netscape as an example, because you need to be able to test the documents and data that you are publishing on the Intranet.

Suppose you want a person browsing your page to be able to play a Windows Audio WAV recording of you welcoming them to your Web page. If the .wav file containing your welcome message is named `welcome.wav`, add the link with the <A> tag, just as you would add any other link on your page, as in the following line:

```
<A HREF="welcome.wav">Listen to our Welcome Message</A>
```

Of course, you can create a link to any type of file on your page, and when the person clicks the hyperlink, the file will be transported to the client application (Web browser) through HTTP. The key to all of this is that the Web browser on the receiving end of this link must be configured to handle the incoming file.

> **Tip:** Here's a very small piece of advice about HTML style. In the hyperlink preceding the previous paragraph, notice the style of the HREF text to be underlined by the browser. The way it is stated, it avoids the use of a phrase commonly seen on novice Web pages "click here". HTML author/expert Laura Lemay refers to that as "here syndrome" and points out that it makes the surrounding text less readable. In other words, readers will already know that they can click on the message, so there is no need to alter the writing style.

Most Web browsers are configured to handle *.HTML, *.HTM, *.TXT, and *.GIF files. These and other standard file types are given a MIME type. See the following sidebar for a basic discussion of MIME. For file types other than the basic ones mentioned, you just need to configure your Web browser to handle the MIME type of that associated file.

> ## What Is MIME?
>
> MIME stands for Multipurpose Internet Mail Extensions. MIME is a standard for Internet e-mail attachments and for Web multimedia documents sent through HTTP. The reason that this standard comes up in both of these applications is that both are frequently used to transfer binary files such as graphics, audio, and video.
>
> Basically, MIME encodes/decodes binary data into 7-bit ASCII using an algorithm called *base 64*. The reason it is converted to ASCII is that e-mail only supports a 7-bit word size to ensure compatibility with all computer systems on the Internet. If you would like to know all the details, see the Request For Comments. (See Appendix C.) MIME is defined by RFC 1341.

In addition to configuring your Web browser to be aware of the file type, you will also need an application capable of displaying or playing the file. For several types of multimedia files, you already have an application that can handle this job. Windows NT and Windows 95 include an application called Media Player, which can play AVI, MID, and WAV files. Just follow these steps to configure Netscape Navigator 2.0 to use Media Player:

1. Run Navigator and choose Options | General Preferences. Select the Helpers tab in the dialog box that appears. You will see a list of all the MIME types that Navigator is configured to handle.

2. Highlight the MIME type for audio/x-wav with the file extension .wav (see the right hand column). Select the Launch the Application radio button. (See Figure 7.9.)

3. Choose Browse and select MPLAY32.EXE. It should be in the Windows\System32 directory where you installed Windows NT.

4. Choose OK.

Netscape Navigator is now configured to launch Media Player any time you click a hyperlink to a file type of *.WAV. Now you can go through the same steps for *.AVI files.

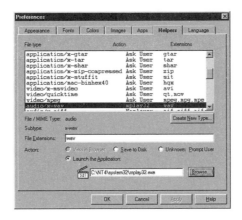

Figure 7.9. *Configuring Navigator MIME types.*

Note that in Step 2 there are other options for the Action radio button. You don't have to configure Navigator to launch an application for every MIME file type. For example, when plain text files are received by Navigator through HTTP, you can choose View in Browser or Save to Disk. Netscape Navigator is set up by default to handle many more MIME types than the ones mentioned here, including *.AU and *.AIFF files for audio.

Summary

This chapter has focused on helping you get your Intranet up and running using data you already have on hand. The main benefit of this approach, which will be extended in later chapters, is to get your Intranet online as quickly as possible. As you've seen from this chapter, you can easily start your Intranet by using just a few tools off the CD-ROM and your existing data. This chapter covered how you can

◆ Configure the WWW Publishing Service in IIS.

◆ Evaluate the information your organization is already providing for possible inclusion on your Intranet.

◆ Focus on the information that is in electronic format.

◆ Convert your legacy data so it can be immediately usable on your Intranet.

◆ Configure common Web browser helper applications for viewing your data. Part III of this book will cover this subject much more extensively.

Chapter 12, "MIME and Helper Applications," delves more deeply into important details you will need to add value to your Intranet, including some basic information about how helper applications work. This information will help you extend the helper application paradigm in new directions for your Intranet's customers.

CHAPTER

◆

Serving E-mail via TCP/IP

◆ Post.Office and SMTP
◆ Blat
◆ List servers

This chapter covers running your own e-mail server. E-mail is responsible for the greatest percentage of packet traffic on the Internet. On the Intranet, it should not be overlooked as being potentially the single greatest thing you can do to enhance employee communications.

It is customary when one is visiting a home page on the Web that comments can be e-mailed to an address of the form `webmaster@yourco.com`. If you would like to carry on this tradition, you will probably want to run your own mail server. Of course, you could also publicize your own e-mail name on your Intranet Web pages (for example, `jsmith@yourco.com`) and encourage your customers to write to you as the Webmaster.

The industry for e-mail server software on Windows NT is really heating up. Within the last year, many such packages have become available. All are very competitive in price and features. The one I chose to include with this book is Post.Office from a humbly named company called Software.Com in Santa Barbara, California.

While we're on the subject of mail, I'll also show you how to install Blat. Blat is a console program that can e-mail HTML form data. The astute reader might remember why we need console programs: They are the types of CGI application that can be launched by the Web server. CGI applications are not GUI programs.

Here's an example of what you can do with Blat. Suppose you have a suggestion box on your Intranet and you would like to encourage and track your customer feedback. In order to make it as simple as possible for your customers to express their opinions about your Intranet, you provide a convenient HTML form on your home page. When a customer fills out the form, the SUBMIT action invokes a CGI program to parse the data. Then it is passed to Blat to be e-mailed to your inbox.

Post.Office and SMTP

Post.Office is a feature-rich set of utilities. It contains RFC-compliant SMTP and POP servers that operate as 32-bit services on Windows NT. The next several sections describe pre-installation procedures for Post.Office. I strongly advise that you read through the whole chapter and through the Post.Office documentation before you begin the installation process. Post.Office is very powerful and fairly easy to use, but if you are at all like me, it might take some time for the implications of all the new terminology to sink in.

> **Note:** Post.Office uses long filenames. Although those are compatible with FAT in Windows NT 4, for security reasons, Software.Com strongly recommends that the installation drive be formatted with NTFS.

Creating an NT Login Account for the Service

Every process running under Windows NT operates with the privileges of an account (either local or part of a domain, if you're using NT Server). The Post.Office service can operate using the privileges of the built-in System account (which is the default during install) or as any local account that is preconfigured (prior to running the installation program) on the machine. This decision is primarily a security consideration. The advantage of using an account other than the built-in System account is that the default installation of Post.Office sets up permissions that will not allow other processes or accounts to access any of the Post.Office directories/files or registry information. (Additionally the Post.Office service will be unable to read, modify, and delete any system or user files.) The main disadvantage of using an account other than System is that you need to set up the local account and group, and ensure that they are not deleted, because Post.Office will not be able to run if its account is disabled.

It is recommended that you use a new account and group other than the built-in System account for sites connecting to the Internet. If you choose to use the system account, you may skip the remainder of this section and proceed to the section titled "Miscellaneous Pre-Installation Planning." When prompted for the system account, please type System (with an uppercase S).

You will need to use the User Manager (as an administrator) to create an account and group for the service to use during normal operation. The new account and group should be specifically for the Post.Office service, and should have no other members or groups. In the Windows NT User Manager, the properties of the account must have User Cannot Change Password and Password Never Expires checked, and must not have User Must Change Password at next login checked.

NT Workstation Installation Notes

You will be creating a local user and group. If the workstation is also part of an NT Domain, it is suggested that you use a local user and local group (specific to the workstation, not a member of the NT Domain). Be sure that you include only the Post.Office user in the new group and that the Post.Office user has membership in only the new Post.Office group.

NT Server Notes

On a server acting as a primary or backup domain controller, it is suggested that you use a global user/global group for the Post.Office service account. On a server that is not a PDC or BDC, use a local user/local group for the Post.Office service account.

After creating the Post.Office user and group, be sure to set the Post.Office group to be the primary group for the Post.Office user. (Under the user properties/Groups button, select the Post.Office group on the left side and click the Set Primary Groups button.) Then remove the domain users group from the list of groups for the Post.Office user. (It is added by User Manager by default.)

You must also give the account the Logon as a Service privilege. This is accomplished while still in the User Manager program. Under the Policies menu, select the User Rights option. There is a checkbox titled Show Advanced User Rights, which must be checked. Under the scrollbar titled Right:, choose Log on as a Service and add the account name (chosen above) that you created for the mail system to this privilege list. You will need to choose the Add button, Show Users, and then the Post.Office user account (it will be near the bottom of the list); then choose the Add button.

Setting Permissions for the System Directories

To ensure that the Post.Office installation program is able to give the proper permissions for operation, it is necessary that the owner of the System directories be the administrator. You can easily determine this with Explorer (or File Manager, which is still available in Windows NT 4). Select the system directory (/winnt, /winnt35, or /windows, depending on your specific installation) and select Permissions under the Security menu item. The directory owner must be administrator for the install to proceed. If this is not the case, you will need to take ownership of the directory, subdirectories, and files within—as one of the administrators. This is not a step to take lightly, so please review the Post.Office online help and additional manuals to be sure that you understand this operation.

Machine Name and Internet Protocol Number

The installation program will request the hostname (without domain name) from the TCP service. Please ensure that the hostname listed in the Control Panel | Network | Protocols | TCP/IP | Configure | DNS | hostname field is the name you are planning to use. In addition, the install program must do a reverse lookup to turn an IP number into a hostname. The file named HOSTS in \winnt\system32\drivers\etc has a list of IP numbers and hostnames. Please ensure that the proper hostname and IP numbers are listed. Sites using DNS may have only a localhost entry in this file and don't need to create a new entry if one is not present.

A sample HOSTS entry for a machine rome, in the domain software.com, with an IP address of 198.17.234.2 is

```
198.17.234.2   rome   rome.software.com
```

There are two names here for the same machine: rome and rome.software.com, separated by a space.

> **Note:** The current version of the Windows NT TCP services is case-sensitive, so use lowercase names in the HOSTS file.

Do a final check of the machine name/IP Number configuration by running a Command window and issuing these commands:

```
> ping your-host-name (example: ping rome )
Pinging host-name [IP number]
Reply from IP number ....
> ping HostName.DomainName (example: ping rome.software.com)
Pinging HostName.DomainName [IP number]
Reply from IP number ....
```

Please verify for both cases that the IP numbers returned by ping are what you think they should be and that the pings are successful. The result of a misconfigured hostname or IP number will be the inability to request forms for adding, changing, or deleting accounts—and for configuration information.

Miscellaneous Pre-Installation Planning

There are three passwords used in the installation section: the Local account password, the Postmaster password, and Mail account password. For security reasons, each of these should be different. The Local account password is used by the Service Control Program (in Windows NT) to log in the Post.Office service and give it access rights on the machine it is running. The Postmaster password is used by Post.Office to verify any administrative actions such as creating a new mail account. Your Mail account password is the password assigned to your e-mail account and allows you to retrieve your mail (as it is also your POP password), and lets you make any changes to your e-mail account (such as finger information).

Software License Number

During the installation, you will be prompted to enter a license number. If you want to proceed with the 45-day trial period, enter trial instead of a number. You will be able to rerun setup later and update your license information with a permanent, valid license number. You should purchase this from Software.Com before the trial period expires. To order, send e-mail to sales@software.com.

WWW Server Port Number

The Post.Office mail service comes with an integrated WWW Server for remote management via a Web browser. This module operates on a specific port (which is usually 80 by default for WWW Servers). If you have another WWW server (such as IIS) on the same machine already using port 80 (the default if you have not specified it), please choose another port such as 81 for Post.Office. If you do not specify another port and there is another WWW Server already using port 80, either Post.Office's WWW Server or your existing WWW Server will not start properly and will put a message in the event log explaining this. If you do choose to operate Post.Office's WWW Server on a port other than 80, you will need to specify the port number you have picked when you give the browser the URL. For example, if you choose 81, the URL will be http://yourhost:81.

Installing Post.Office

When you run the installation program from the CD-ROM with this book, you can choose to install any of the programs mentioned in Appendix D. In many cases, you can install the software directly from the CD-ROM to your hard drive; in other cases, you might want to copy the files to a temp directory on your hard drive and then execute the setup program that comes with the particular application.

The last step in the installation, after the service is operating, is to create at least one mail account for the person who will initially be acting as the postmaster (to create new accounts and change mail system parameters). Direct your WWW browser to the Post.Office WWW Server management URL and answer the questions on the form.

Post-Installation Setup

The Post.Office services should be installed and operating. You can check this from a Command window by typing

```
> finger postmaster@hostname
```

You should see

```
[hostname]
Account Name:  Mail Administrator
Email address: Postmaster@yourhost
----------
mail system administrator.
```

Configure via Your WWW Browser

Using your WWW browser, you can configure Post.Office quite easily. The URL for the server is `http://hostname:Port#` (for example, `http://oslo.software.com:81`). If you used the default port during the installation, you do not need to use the `Port#` part (for example, `http://oslo.software.com`).

You will be presented with an Authentication screen. Please use `Postmaster@yourhost` as the e-mail address and the postmaster password to get to the menus. Mail users can change their individual account information by using their personal e-mail address and mail account passwords. See Figure 8.1.

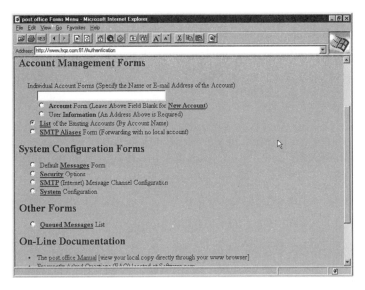

Figure 8.1. *Configuring Post.Office via HTML.*

Upon successful authentication, you will receive a list of available forms. The first step is to ask for a blank account form and create an account for yourself, and give your new account Postmaster privileges.

Creating New Mail Accounts

After installing Post.Office, add `info` and `webmaster` to the root mailbox. This will allow you to log into your mail server with a mail client such as Eudora as root and get any mail addressed to `info@yourco.com` or `webmaster@yourco.com`.

To create a new account, select the Account Form (leave the field above blank) and click the REQUEST button for the selected form. You will be presented with an empty account form. Fill this out as desired and submit when finished. Here is an annotated list of the fields:

User's Real Name: Your name (for example, Jane S. Doe).
Mail Account Password: (Used by your mail program for POP3 pickup.
Finger Information: (You can skip this for now and add later.)
Internet Addresses: `Name@host` (for example, `Jane@lhasa.software.com`).
`From Address Rewrite Style:` (You can skip for now.)
POP3-Delivery: Check Box: You will probably want POP delivery.
POP3-Username: POPName for your mail program (for example, Jane).

Setting up the Default Account

You might want to configure the Default account form to set up any commonly used parameters as defaults.

Get a List of Accounts

You can get a list of mail accounts on the system with the List of Existing Accounts form. All your accounts will be listed by account name and their first Internet address (called the *primary address* for the account).

Blat

Blat is a Public Domain Windows NT console utility that will e-mail a file to a user via SMTP. A Registry entry is generated when the program is used with the `-install` flag. This stores the address of the default SMTP server and the address of the default sender. Blat is used by CGI Perform (mentioned in Chapter 19) to mail the contents of an HTML form to whomever you choose. Post.Office comes with a similar utility called *postmail.* Postmail is also available for free at the Software.Com Web site, and it should work even if you choose to use a different mail server.

> **Note:** The binary files for Blat require the Intel 486 platform. However, source code is included (Wow!), so you can recompile the program if you need to run it on a different architecture.

Installing Blat

The files for Blat can be copied from the CD-ROM to your hard drive. Then follow these steps:

1. Copy the file `gensock.dll` to your `\WINNT\SYSTEM32` directory or to any other directory in your path. (Check if you already have this DLL; if so, copy only the DLL if the date is more recent than the existing one.)

2. Copy the file `Blat.exe` to your `\WINNT\SYSTEM32` directory or to any other directory in your path.

3. Type: `Blat -install` *yourco.com youremail@yourco.com.*

A Registry entry is generated when the program is used with the `-install` flag. This stores the address of the default SMTP server and the address of the default sender (which may be overridden with the `-f` flag).

Impersonation can be done with the -i flag, which puts the value specified in place of the sender's address in the From: line of the header. When this is done, however, the real sender's address is stamped in the Reply-To: and Sender: lines. This feature can be useful when using the program to send messages from NT users who are not registered on the SMTP host.

Blat Syntax

The Blat command line has a few variations. Here are the command types, followed by a description of each of the syntax elements.

```
Blat filename -s subject -t recipient -f address -i address

Blat -install server address senders address

Blat -h -install server address senders address
```

which sets the address of the default SMTP server.

`filename`

which is the file with the message body.

`-s subject`

which is the (optional) subject line.

`-t recipient`

which is the recipient's address.

`-c recipient`

which is the carbon copy recipient's address.

`-f sender`

which is the sender's address (must be known to the SMTP server).

`-i address`

which is a From: address, not necessarily known to the SMTP server.

`-h`

which displays this help.

`-server server address`

which overrides the default SMTP server to be used.

Note that if the -i option is used, sender is included in the Reply-to: and Sender: fields in the header of the message.

Sample `Blat` Commands

You can use `Blat` from the command line or implement your own CGI applications that call `Blat`. Here are some examples of using `Blat` from the command line:

```
Blat -install smtphost.bar.com foo@bar.com
```

sets the host and userid.

```
Blat -install smtphost.bar.com foo
```

sets the host and userid.

```
Blat -install smtphost.bar.com
```

sets the host only.

```
Blat myfile.txt -s "A file for pedro" -t foo@bar.com
```

sends a file with subject line `A file for pedro`.

```
Blat myfile.txt -s "A file for mark" -t fee@fi.com -f foo@bar.com
```

The `-f` option overrides the default sender.

```
Blat myfile.txt -s "A file for pedro" -t foo@bar.com -i "devil@fire.hell"
```

`-i` replaces `From:` line address (but leaves `Reply-To:` and `Sender:` lines).

```
Blat myfile.txt -s "animals" -t fee@fi.com -c "moo@grass.edu,horse@meadow.hill"
```

`-c` mails carbon copies to users `moo@grass.edu` and `horse@meadow.hill`.

The authors of `Blat` have very generously placed it in the public domain. This means you can use `Blat` free of charge, for any purpose you like. The source code is also available free of charge. The authors of `Blat` are Mark Neal (`mjn@aber.ac.uk`) and Pedro Mendes (`prm@aber.ac.uk`).

Electronic Mail Distribution Lists and List Servers on Your Intranet

If you've used e-mail, you probably know that you can create distribution lists of your associates' and friends' e-mail addresses, and then send messages to the lists just as if they were individual addressees. You probably also know there are thousands of special-interest Internet e-mail distribution lists, ranging from those discussing Internet Firewalls (see Chapters 10 and 28) to those discussing feminism and/or men's rights. These lists are used for communication, discussion, and collaboration among like-minded people.

Besides these distribution lists, there are automated list servers on the Internet that will do something for you if you send e-mail to them. Some list servers will automatically add your e-mail address to an e-mail distribution list (or take it off). Others will respond to specially worded e-mail messages to retrieve information for you and deliver it to you via e-mail. Special FTPMail servers will actually perform an anonymous FTP file retrieval for you while you sleep, and then deliver the file with the rest of your e-mail.

There's no reason you can't put these e-mail-based services to work in your Intranet. Web browsers are adding support for sending and reading e-mail. You can piggyback this built-in e-mail support onto both simple e-mail distribution lists and list servers, thereby providing your customers with value-added services on your Intranet.

Running a List Server

A list server (also called *listserv*) is a service program that lets its group's members broadcast e-mail messages amongst themselves. An individual user sends a single e-mail message to the server, which in turn sends it to all the other members of the listserv group.

It is somewhat beyond the scope of this chapter, however, I can briefly mention the feature set of the Software.Com list server which is a companion product to Post.Office. You can get further information from Software.Com at `http://www.software.com/` or `support@software.com`. If you try the Post.Office mail server and like it, you will probably want to contact the company and ask for the commercial release of their companion list server.

Features of Software.Com List Manager

Here is a quick look at the features of the Software.Com List Manager:

- Users can subscribe and unsubscribe via WWW or e-mail forms.
- List owners can maintain the mail list via WWW or e-mail forms.
- Subscription and unsubscription posting detection.
- Moderated and unmoderated subscriptions.
- Maximum message size limit per list.
- Maximum posts/day limit total or per subscriber.
- Header deletion/addition.
- Mail server deliver priority.
- Digesting (with time and message count triggers).
- Configurable posting policy.
- Unmoderated lists.
- Semi-moderated lists. Only list subscribers can post.
- Intro-moderated. Initial postings from a given user are moderated.

Summary

In the next chapter, you will continue building server capabilities into your Intranet when you install and configure the IIS FTP and Gopher servers. These services should not be overlooked when you are designing a complete Web site. FTP is the Internet champion of file transfers, and Gopher is an excellent means to publish textual information, especially for users who might not have graphical workstations.

CHAPTER 9

◆

Adding FTP and Gopher Services

◆ Review of MIME
◆ How an FTP server can add value to your Intranet
◆ Configuring the IIS FTP server in Windows NT 4
◆ How a Gopher server can add value to your Intranet
◆ Configuring the IIS Gopher server in Windows NT 4

In this chapter, you learn how to integrate two traditional TCP/IP network services that pre-date the World Wide Web, but that can nonetheless be important to your customers. As noted earlier, the developers of Web technology took care to build support for a number of older network services into the HTTP protocol, integrating these services into Web browsers and servers. Because you established a TCP/IP networking infrastructure for your Intranet, you easily can use these older services in it, using mostly free software.

This book began by arguing that problems of differing—and difficult-to-master—user interfaces to older networking services were prime movers in the development of the Web. Of course, the existence of the Web doesn't mean those older services no longer have value. E-mail, FTP, Gopher, Archie, WAIS, and other such services remain at the heart of the Internet.

Earlier, you saw how a Web-based front end to the Archie file-locator service vastly simplified a difficult interface, making it accessible to non-technical users. You'll learn in this chapter how you can use FTP and Gopher services in your Intranet and provide Web-based front ends to them for your customers. In doing so, you'll substantially expand the range of services available on your Intranet without requiring significant customer training.

Support for each of these services is built into both the Web network protocol and your customers' Web browsers. Integrating them into the Intranet you started building in Chapter 7, "Running the Intranet Web Server," will provide new and powerful services to your customers, making your Intranet even more valuable.

MIME and Other Intranet Services

You learned in Chapter 7 how Web servers and browsers use the MIME mechanism to identify data by MIME data types/subtypes. Also, you learned that Web servers include this identifying information in MIME data type/subtype headers when sending data back to a Web browser. You may have wondered, then, why Web browsers also have to be configured with MIME information if they already receive it from the server.

This is a good question, and the answer is fundamental to the information in this chapter. Although MIME data type/subtype information coming from a Web server may indeed be redundant to the properly set up browser, Web browsers also communicate with other kinds of Internet information services, such as FTP and Gopher. These Internet services pre-date both the World Wide Web and MIME, so they don't know anything about MIME types. Moreover, because they send back only one kind of data, not one of many kinds of data like a Web server does, they have no reason to provide any identifying information. An FTP server sends and receives data using only the FTP protocol; likewise, Gopher servers use only the Gopher protocol. These servers respond to clients by sending out data; the clients have to figure out what to do with the data. Naturally, stand-alone FTP and Gopher client software do know what type of data to expect.

Fortunately, Web browsers deal with FTP and Gopher data too, and they can use the MIME mechanism to enhance their handling of the data, even in the absence of any incoming identifying information. As mentioned before, the HyperText Transfer Protocol (HTTP), which is the Web protocol, has support for a list of older Internet services built in. This support includes both FTP and Gopher, as well as several others. Your Web browser automatically senses when it's speaking with an FTP or Gopher server and acts accordingly. As far as you're concerned, though, you're just pointing and clicking, just as you would when dealing with a Web server. If you want to retrieve a file, you just click its hyperlink. Your browser identifies the incoming data and handles it properly.

You've no doubt noticed that your Web browser often dresses up the display of FTP and Gopher server listings with identifying icons. File folder icons represent directories; other icons identify plain text and binary files. Normally, FTP servers are completely text-based, with no graphical displays. Because an FTP server, for example, has no way of telling a Web browser what sort of data is coming, Web browsers use a workaround, keying off the filename extension to a MIME data type/subtype. The set of canned icons representing different file types that you see when you connect to an FTP or Gopher server does not come from the server. Rather, these icons are a result of your browser's MIME mechanism using the filename extensions and a built-in list of MIME data types/subtypes.

Netscape, Mosaic, and Internet Explorer support a long list of standard MIME types/subtypes for communicating with non-HTTP services, such as Gopher and FTP. The browsers use a built-in set of generic icons to represent them. Table 9.1 shows a partial list of MIME types available in Netscape.

Table 9.1. MIME types/subtypes.

Content Type	Extensions	Description
text/plain	txt, text	Plain Text
text/html	html, htm	Hypertext Markup Language
application/rtf	rtf	Rich Text Format
application/x-tex	tex	TeX Document
application/x-latex	latex	LaTeX Document
application/x-dvi	dvi	TeX DVI Data
application/x-texinfo texi	texinfo	GNU TeXinfo Document
image/gif	gif	CompuServe Image
image/jpeg	jpeg, jpg, jpe	JPEG Image
image/tiff	tiff, tif	TIFF Image
image/x-cmu-raster	ras	CMU Raster Image
image/x-xbitmap	xbm	X Bitmap
image/x-xpixmap	xpm	X Pixmap
image/x-xwindowdump	xwd	X Window Dump Image

continues

Table 9.1. continued

Content Type	Extensions	Description
image/x-portable-anymap	pnm	PBM Image
image/x-portable-bitmap	pbm	PBM Image
image/x-portable-graymap	pgm	PGM Image
image/x-portable-pixmap	ppm	PPM Image
image/x-rgb	rgb	RGB Image
image/ief	ief	
application/fractals	fif	Fractal Image Format
audio/basic	au, snd	ULAW Audio Data
audio/x-aiff	aif, aiff, aifc	AIFF Audio
audio/x-wav	wav	WAV Audio
video/mpeg	mpeg, mpg, mpe	MPEG Video
video/quicktime	qt, mov	Quick Time Video
video/x-msvideo	avi	Microsoft Video
video/x-sgi-movie	movie	SGI Video
application/mac-binhex40	hqx	Macintosh BinHex
application/x-stuffit	sit	Macintosh Archive
application/x-zip-compressed	zip	Zip Compressed Data
application/x-shar	shar	UNIX Shell Archive
application/x-tar	tar	UNIX Tape Archive
application/x-gtar	gtar	GNU Tape Archive
application/x-cpio	cpio	UNIX CPIO Archive
application/octet-stream	exe, bin	Binary Executable
application/postscript	ai, eps, ps	Postscript Program
application/x-csh	csh	C Shell Program
application/x-sh	sh	Bourne Shell Program
application/x-tcl	tcl	TCL Program
application/x-troff	t, tr, roff	TROFF Document
application/x-troff-me	me	TROFF Document
application/x-troff-ms	ms	TROFF Document
application/x-troff-man	man	UNIX Manual Page
encoding/x-compress	Z	Compressed Data
encoding/x-gzip	gz	GNU Zip Compressed

You can use Netscape to view this list and the associated icons at `http://www.netscape.com/assist/helper_apps/mimedefault.html`.

> **Tip:** Web browsers' built-in lists of supported MIME types/subtypes rely solely on filename extensions when dealing with Internet services such as FTP that don't provide MIME header information. Because people are free to name files anything they want, you may encounter files on the World Wide Web that are misidentified by your browser because they've been given an extension that conflicts with your browser's built-in list. Make sure you use consistent filenaming conventions in your Intranet, following your browsers' built-in lists, to ensure that your customers don't encounter files that their browsers can't identify.

How an FTP Server Can Add Value to Your Intranet

The TCP/IP file transfer protocol (FTP) is one of the Internet's mainstays. You probably used FTP to download your first Web browser software. On UNIX, FTP is a text-based application and is not particularly user-friendly for the uninitiated. Windows NT and Windows 95 also include a command-line FTP client. But you don't have to bother with those because the CD-ROM with this book includes an excellent 32-bit GUI FTP client, named WinFTP.

> Sams.net and I obtained permission to include WinFTP just as this book was going to press. Before learning of this, this chapter had already been written including the instructions for installing and using another fine GUI FTP client named CuteFTP. Most of the information in this chapter about the FTP client program is directly applicable to WinFTP as well as CuteFTP. And of course, the information about the FTP server will work regardless of your choice of the FTP client program. CuteFTP is available for free download from the Internet.

Installing CuteFTP

To download and install CuteFTP from the CD to your hard drive, follow these steps:

1. Use your Web browser to download CuteFTP from the World Wide Web. It is available in the Winsite Archive: `http://www.winsite.com/pc/win3/winsock/cftp14b4.zip`

2. Unzip CuteFTP using the WinZip program on the CD into a directory on your hard disk and create a shortcut on your desktop for `cuteftp32.exe`. If you're upgrading from a previous release, keep your `tree.dat` file. All other files can be overwritten safely.

> **Tip:** The file `cuteftp.exe` is a 16-bit version of CuteFTP for use with Windows 3.1 or 3.11. On Windows NT and Windows 95 machines, you can safely delete this file to save disk space.

3. Copy the file `ctl3dv2.dll` into the `\WINDOWS\SYSTEM` directory (for Windows 95) or the `\WINNT\SYSTEM32` directory (for Windows NT), and then delete it from the `CuteFTP` directory.

4. Start CuteFTP and display the Options dialog (File | Options menu). Fill out the Mail Address field with your e-mail address. Click OK.

You now have one of the best FTP client applications available to assist you with file transfers.

Running CuteFTP

To use CuteFTP, you need a connection to the Internet. The first thing you will see when you run CuteFTP is the FTP Site Manager shown in Figure 9.1.

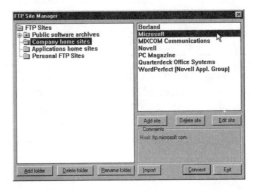

Figure 9.1. *The CuteFTP Site Manager enables you to organize the addresses of your favorite FTP sites.*

This dialog shows the predefined addresses of several anonymous FTP sites. You can easily add new sites to these folders or edit the information about existing sites. To see how this software works, try to visit the Microsoft site to download the latest version of Internet Explorer. (By the time you read this, IE version 3.0 should be available and you may want to download it in case it isn't included on the Windows NT 4 CD-ROM.)

1. Select the Company home sites folder in the left side window, and double-click the row for Microsoft in the right side window. CuteFTP shows you the login sequence in the top window, your local drive in the left window, and the remote directory structure in the right window.

2. Double-click the folder for Softlib. (See Figure 9.2.)

3. Double-click the folder for MSLFILES to display a directory with a long list of files you can download. It helps if you know the particular filename you are looking for. In this case, suppose you want to get MSIE20.EXE. (Please don't try to download this particular file because you already have it—it's on the CD-ROM with this book!) When IE version 3.0 becomes available, it will probably have a different filename, such as MSIE30.EXE. This hypothetical example illustrates how you could download a future version of Internet Explorer when one becomes available.

4. Navigate the left window pane to the local directory on your system where you would like to receive the file. For example, click the double dot icon at the top to move up one level in your directory structure. In this example, I have positioned the local directory to c:\temp in the left window pane.

5. Click the file and drag it from the right window pane to the left window pane. Then let go of the mouse button and the file transfer will begin. (See Figure 9.3.)

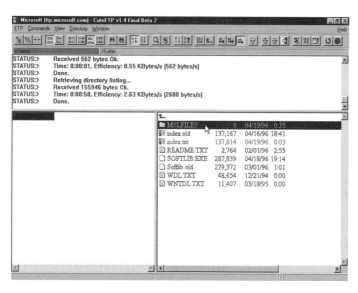

Figure 9.2. *Double-clicking the Microsoft Softlib folder takes you to that subdirectory of files on the Microsoft server.*

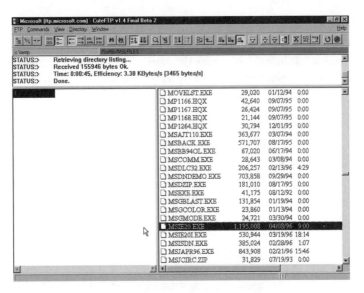

Figure 9.3. *Dragging the file from the right window to the left window will initiate the download.*

CuteFTP keeps you notified of the file transfer progress in the status bar.

> **Note:** Now that you've seen how easy it is to download a file from a remote system, you already know how to upload a file to a remote system. Basically, it is just a matter of dragging a file from your local drive (the window on the left) to the remote drive (the window pane on the right).

One other trick you might like to know about CuteFTP is how to set the default directories on the local and remote systems when a connection is established. Then you won't have to waste any time navigating the directory structures in either window pane. This trick requires you to edit the profile of the FTP site. If, for example, you wanted to edit the profile for the Microsoft site, you would perform these steps:

1. In the FTP Site Manager dialog, select Microsoft. Then choose the Edit Site button to open the dialog shown in Figure 9.4.

2. For the Initial Remote Directory, type in the server path that you would like to be placed in when the connection opens. For example, type in /softlib/mslfiles. Note that FTP originated in the UNIX world, which uses forward slashes for directory separators.

3. For the Initial Local Directory, type in the preferred path on your drive. For example, type in c:\temp. Then choose the OK button to save the edited profile.

> **Tip:** You can leave the userid and password blank for anonymous FTP sites.

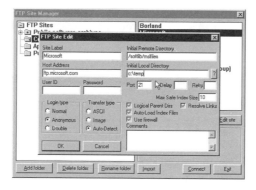

Figure 9.4. *Editing the site information for Microsoft.*

Visiting an FTP Site with Netscape Navigator

To download that same file with the FTP feature built into Netscape Navigator 2.x, perform the following steps. A similar process would apply to any Web browser that your customers might run on your Intranet.

1. Fire up Navigator, and then type this URL into the Location edit box at the top of the screen: `ftp://ftp.microsoft.com/`. Press Enter.

2. Double-click the folder for Softlib, and then double-click the folder for MSLFILES. (See Figure 9.5.)

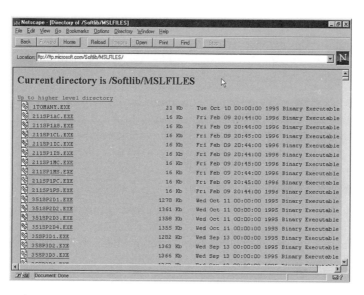

Figure 9.5. *Visiting the Microsoft FTP site with Navigator.*

> **Tip:** You can save the time of scrolling through the directories in Step 2 if you initially enter the complete URL:
>
> `ftp://ftp.microsoft.com/Softlib/MSLFILES/`

3. When you click the file you want to download, Netscape prompts you with the 32-bit Save As common dialog. All you have to do is pick the destination directory on your local drive, and the file transfer will proceed.

Whether you use your Web browser or CuteFTP, you will find that knowing how to copy Internet/ Intranet files with FTP is a very handy process to be familiar with.

How Can You Use FTP on Your Intranet?

You may have software or other data that you would like to make widely available to your customers. Setting up an FTP server on your Intranet makes this process easy. If you have Windows NT Server and IIS on your Intranet, you already have FTP server software you can use. Setting it up is fairly simple. Most of your customers will access your FTP server using their Web browsers, so they won't need to learn about FTP, or even know that they're accessing an FTP server, in order to download files.

Probably the best way to use your Intranet's FTP server is as a distribution point for Web-related software, including both browser and server software. Not only can you make it easier and faster for your customers to get the latest copy of Internet Explorer (or Netscape, if you've licensed it), but you'll also take a major load off your company's Internet connection by downloading the software from the outside once, and then having local copies of the software available on the Intranet. Your network administrators will thank you for reducing the load on their Internet link, and your customers will thank you for faster service.

You'll also do a good deed for the online community by relieving the load on the FTP server where the original software resides. Whenever a new release becomes available, you can grab a copy and make it instantly available for your customers. Major anonymous FTP servers like `FTP.ncsa.uiuc.edu`, home of NCSA Mosaic, are invariably very busy in the days immediately following a new release of Mosaic. Accesses are often denied when the system is too busy to handle all the requests for copies of the new software release.

Similarly, you can redistribute Web server software for those of your customers who may want to set up another server and make it part of your Intranet. Your FTP server is a good place to store libraries of image files for use in HTML markup for much the same reason. Be sure, however, that you read and follow licensing restrictions on the redistribution of copyrighted software, including shareware.

Configuring the IIS FTP Server in Windows NT 4

If you worked through the steps in Chapter 7 to set up the WWW Service with IIS, you should have a very easy time setting up the FTP Service in this section and the Gopher Service later in this chapter.

To configure the FTP server, follow these steps:

1. Open the Microsoft Internet Service Manager. If it isn't already running, choose Start Menu | Programs | Microsoft Internet Server | Internet Service Manager.

2. Double-click the FTP Service. If the service is not running, it will ask you if you want to start it. Choose Yes.

3. You will see the tabbed dialog to configure the FTP Service Properties that is shown in Figure 9.6. Typically, you will want to allow anonymous connections. An anonymous connection permits people to connect to your server and retrieve or upload files based on their account files and directory permissions. The IUSR_*computername* password must match exactly (case-sensitive) with the password for the same user account in User Manager for Domains.

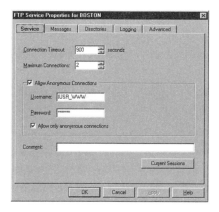

Figure 9.6. *Configuring the FTP Service properties in IIS.*

4. Click the Messages tab and configure the messages that you would like your customers to see when they visit your FTP site. Figure 9.7 shows some sample messages.

Figure 9.7. Configuring the messages that the FTP Service will display to the clients.

5. In the Directories tab, be sure to check UNIX-style directory listings for compatibility with most FTP client software. Depending on your computing background, you may think that MS-DOS style listings are better looking, but they aren't supported by many FTP clients.

6. For each directory, you can choose the Edit Properties button to enable Read and/or Write access to that directory. The root directory is called <Home> (by default it is \inetsrv\ftproot) and that is where anonymous FTP clients will be placed.

7. The Logging and Advanced tabs are identical to the WWW Service. Consult the IIS help files and Chapter 7 for further information.

Now you just need to add the files that you want to make available to your customers to the <Home> directory.

> **Note:** Internet Security Systems in Norcross, GA maintains a Frequently Asked Questions (FAQ) document about anonymous FTP setup. To grab a copy of this document, use your Web browser to go to http://iss.net. Most of the information is written with a UNIX slant, but you should still find it useful for Windows NT networks.
>
> In case you want to make your anonymous FTP server available on the Internet, the Anonymous FTP FAQ also tells you how to register it with the Archie service.

Populating Your Intranet's Anonymous FTP Server

Because setting up anonymous FTP creates a walled-off file system dedicated to your FTP server, you'll want to set up a directory structure that corresponds with the data you're distributing. Use the server's <Home> directory as the top of your file tree, with additional directories created within it based on your Intranet's needs.

Tip: Some people use the same file tree for their anonymous FTP and Web servers, putting the anonymous FTP file tree within the HTML document root file tree. This structure can make maintenance of both your Web server and your anonymous FTP server more convenient. You need to watch your directory and file permissions, though, to ensure you don't disable with one server the security you may have set up with the other. This issue is particularly relevant if you set up password-protected portions of your Web server tree, a subject covered in more detail in Chapter 10. The default installation of IIS creates separate root directories for WWW, Gopher, and FTP.

How a Gopher Server Can Add Value to Your Intranet

Before the World Wide Web burst onto the Internet stage in 1993, the sexiest Internet technology was something called Gopher. Developed at the University of Minnesota (whose athletic teams are nicknamed the Golden Gophers), Gopher was the first successful attempt to join several existing TCP/IP networking technologies into a single, easy-to-use interface.

The main Gopher interface is a plain text menu of choices. You start out at a top-level menu and work your way down a hierarchy of nested menus until you find the subject you're after. Once you find your subject, you're able to view text files on-screen and, in some cases, transfer files across the Internet to your own computer. Selecting a Gopher menu item can do one of several things:

♦ Take you to another menu of choices.

♦ Display a text document on-screen.

♦ Take you to another Gopher server in some other location.

♦ Connect you to an altogether different Internet service, such as a remote login using Telnet or FTP for file transfer.

The last two items are key to Gopher's success. By selecting a menu item, you can move transparently from one Gopher server to another one. You don't have to know anything about how to get there, the second server's Internet address, or anything else. Even more importantly, Gopher incorporates preexisting Internet services such as Telnet and FTP. As a result, you can access a remote computer for login and terminal emulation, or transfer a file using FTP, just by selecting a Gopher menu item.

If you're thinking that Gopher is beginning to sound a lot like the World Wide Web, you're right on target. You can do many of the same things with Gopher that you can do on the Web, such as jumping transparently from one computer system to another, accessing other Internet services, and even searching Gopherspace. Gopher can be seen as the Web's most immediate ancestor, with many of the same capabilities in a non-graphical interface. The Web's HTTP protocol reflects this ancestry: Gopher is one of many Internet services that is built into the World Wide Web. You can use your Web browser to access Gopher services.

> **Note:** The graphical icons shown in Gopher listings don't come from the Gopher servers. Rather, your Web browser, using the MIME mechanism and its built-in list of filename extensions/MIME type/subtype associations, generates them to dress up the display.

Why Should I Use Gopher?

If you can do everything with your Web browser that you can do with a Gopher client, you may well wonder why you would want to bother with running both on your Intranet. Gopher services have limitations not present in the Web. Most notably, you can't include graphics and hyperlinks within Gopher documents. Therefore, you can't jump directly from one document to another, though you can jump using Gopher menus. Nonetheless, there are some strong reasons for you to consider setting up Gopher services as part of your Intranet.

The primary reason is that Gopher's strongest suit is plain text files. You don't have to learn the HTML markup language, and setting up a Gopher server is substantially easier than setting up a Web server. Gopher is a favorite with many U.S. Government agencies for just these reasons. The Government generates vast quantities of plain text documents, and it's quite easy to hook them into a Gopher server. Indexing plain text files (with WAIS or other indexing tools) is easy, and Gopher can search the indices that these tools create. If a lot of the data you plan to make available on your Intranet is plain text data, Gopher is for you. You may not even need a Web server and all the time and trouble of converting documents, as described in Chapter 7. There is little reason for you to learn HTML and how to convert image data if your data is plain text and you have no images to use.

> **Tip:** The inevitable FAQ document about Gopher is at `gopher://mudhoney.micro.umn.edu/00/Gopher.FAQ`.

Configuring the IIS Gopher Server in Windows NT 4

If you implemented the steps in Chapter 7 to set up the IIS WWW Service and the steps in the previous section to configure the IIS FTP Service, you already know everything you need to know about the IIS Gopher Service. You see, Microsoft implemented the WWW, FTP, and Gopher Services in IIS so similarly that once you have learned how to configure any one of the servers, configuring another one is quite easy.

> **Note:** This chapter focuses mostly on the Microsoft IIS FTP and Gopher Services. As of this writing, IIS requires NT Server. If you are using NT 4 Workstation and you want to run an FTP or Gopher server, you still have options. The CD-ROM with this book includes the freeware EMWAC Gopher server. You might also want to consider the Serv-U FTP server for a very reasonable $20 shareware registration fee (send e-mail to: `RJB@eel-mail.mc.duke.edu` for more information).

To configure the Gopher server, follow these steps:

1. Open the Microsoft Internet Service Manager. If it isn't already running, choose Start Menu | Programs | Microsoft Internet Server | Internet Service Manager.

2. Double-click the Gopher Service. If the service is not running, it will ask you if you want to start it. Choose Yes.

3. You will see the tabbed dialog to configure the Gopher Service Properties shown in Figure 9.8. Again, the main thing you need to do here is ensure that the `IUSR_computername` account has the same password in User Manager and that you give the appropriate file and directory permissions to that user for the Gopher `<Home>` directory.

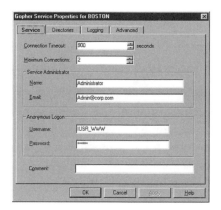

Figure 9.8. Configuring the IIS Gopher Service properties.

Creating Gopher Links

The final step in getting your Gopher server ready for your customers is to create Gopher links. Links are the items you place on Gopher menus that enable the user to jump from one place to another. A link can point to one of the following:

◆ Another Gopher menu
◆ Another Gopher server

◆ A Telnet session on a remote host

◆ A special telephone directory database known as a CSO Phone book server

◆ An FTP server

◆ A WAIS index

◆ A computer program that generates data on-the-fly when selected from a Gopher menu

> **Tip:** See the IIS help files for more information about creating Gopher links and menus. The section titled Setting Up Tag Files contains important information about the `gdsset` command-line utility. The `gdsset` utility creates hidden files that you place in the Gopher directories on your server.

Summary

This chapter has covered two of the major TCP/IP networking services that can add value to your Intranet. Your customers can access these services by using their World Wide Web browsers, and they can extend your Intranet to make it more useful to your company or organization. Although they both function as stand-alone network services, putting a Web-based front end on them can make them easy to use. In this chapter, you have done the following:

◆ Reviewed MIME from the perspective of adding services to your Intranet

◆ Learned how the FTP Service can be used in your Intranet

◆ Learned how the Gopher Service can be used on your Intranet

Don't think of these services in isolation. You can combine these services in imaginative ways to create truly unique and valuable additions to your Intranet; examples include using WAIS to index e-mail distribution list archives for subsequent search and retrieval, using Web fill-in forms, and using CGI-bin gateway scripts. These potential combinations of service, using Web browser front ends, constitute more than the simple sums of their parts; they create new, powerful applications for your Intranet.

Chapter 10 deals with Intranet security issues. Although your objective in setting up an Intranet is to make information available to your customers, you'll want to pay attention to its security, particularly if any part of your Intranet is accessible to the Internet. In addition, implementation of some Intranet security features can enhance the value of your Intranet's services.

CHAPTER 10

Intranet Security in Windows NT

- ◆ Overview of Intranet security
- ◆ Security on your Web server
- ◆ Windows NT 4 user permissions
- ◆ Secure and encrypted transactions
- ◆ Intranet CGI security
- ◆ Internet security issues
- ◆ Miscellaneous security advice

You might think that there is little reason to be concerned about security in an Intranet. After all, by definition an Intranet is internal to your organization; outsiders can't access it. Also, because one of your objectives in setting up your Intranet is to provide your customers with access to a wide variety of public documents, there might seem little need to secure access to them. These are strong arguments for the position that an Intranet should be completely open to its customers, with little or no security. You may not have considered your Intranet in any other light.

On the other hand, implementing some simple, built-in security measures in your Intranet can allow you to provide resources you may not have considered possible in such a context. For example, you can give access to certain Web pages to some people without making them available to your entire customer base by using one of several kinds of authentication. In this chapter, you learn how to use simple security measures to widen the scope of your Intranet.

Intranet security is a multifaceted issue with both opportunities and dangers, especially if your network is part of the Internet. This chapter walks through the major issues and provides detailed information on using built-in Intranet security features.

> **Warning:** Except in the sections of this chapter that are specifically devoted to Internet security issues, it's assumed your Intranet is *not* accessible from outside your organization. If you are on the Internet, the Intranet security measures discussed in this chapter may not be sufficient to secure your system. If you want to make the services and resources of your Intranet accessible from the outside, you'll need to take significant additional steps to prevent abuse and/or unauthorized access. Some of these steps are described at the end of this chapter in the section "Your Intranet and the Internet" and in Chapter 28, "Connecting the Intranet and the Internet."

Overview of Intranet Security

Many people view computer and network security in a negative light, thinking of it only in terms of restricting access to services. One major view of network security is "that which is not expressly permitted, is denied." Although this view is a good way of thinking about how to connect your organization to the Internet, you can, and possibly should, view Intranet security from a more positive angle. Properly set up, Intranet security can be an enabler, enriching your Intranet with services and resources you would not be able to otherwise provide. Such an overall security policy might be described as "that which is not expressly denied, is permitted."

This chapter takes the latter approach, presenting Intranet security in terms of its opportunities for adding value to your Intranet. For example, some of your customers may have information they'd like to make available, confidential management or financial information, for example, provided that access to it can be limited to a specified group. Without the ability to ensure that only those who have the right to see such information will have access, the custodians of such data will not be willing to put it on an Intranet. Providing security increases your organization's ability to use the important collaborative aspects of an Intranet.

The more defensive approach, preventing abuse of your Intranet, should also be considered. Organizations' needs for security in an Intranet can vary widely. Businesses in which confidentiality and discretion is the norm in handling proprietary information and corporate intellectual property have different needs than a college or university, for example. Academic institutions generally tilt toward making the free exchange of ideas a primary interest. At the same time, though, the curiosity (to use a polite word) of undergraduates imposes strong needs for security. Keeping prying sophomores out of university administration computing resources is a high priority. For example, students have been known to try to access grade records (their own or those of others) for various reasons. Adolescent pranks take on new dimensions on a computer network.

What Are the Security Features of an Intranet?

Before learning about how you can use security to enhance your Intranet, you should know what security features are available to you. These features break down into three main categories. First, you can take steps in your Web server software to set up security. Second, you can take steps with the other TCP/IP network services you've set up on your Intranet to enhance their security. Third, you can secure Windows NT Server as a network operating system irrespective of the fact that it is being used as a Web server. I address each of these categories throughout this chapter.

Another feature worthy of brief mention is that some Mosaic browsers allow you to secure the browser to limit what the customers can do with them. But this feature, referred to as *kiosk mode*, is not widely available.

Security in Your Other Intranet Applications

Although the main focus of this chapter is Web security, you can and should implement security and access controls in some of the other network services that you learned about in Chapters 8 and 9. The following are some of the steps you can take:

◆ You can limit access to your anonymous FTP server in several important ways, much like with your HTTP server, while still enabling authorized customers to upload files to it.

◆ If you choose to run a Usenet news server, you can limit access in much the same way as FTP and HTTP.

◆ You can control access to searchable Intranet indices and databases (see Chapter 21, "Indexing Your Intranet with WAIS") through password-protected Web interfaces.

◆ You can control access to Gopher services based on TCP/IP network address and set separate read and search permissions on a per-directory basis.

This chapter doesn't provide any additional information about these services. Refer to the documentation for these network packages and to the help files with the NT User Manager application to learn about how to handle access control and other security features in these other network services.

It's Your Call

It's your responsibility to determine the level of security you need on your Intranet and, of course, to implement it. Putting most of the security measures mentioned into place, as you'll learn in the following sections, is not difficult. Your primary concern will be explaining to customers how Intranet security works not so much as a limiting factor, but as an opportunity for increased use and collaboration using your Intranet. Assuring decision-makers that they can post information on your Intranet in a secure fashion can go a long way toward making your Intranet a success. At the same time, it's important to make sure both information providers and their customers understand a number of critical aspects of Intranet security, so they don't inadvertently defeat the purpose of it.

There are network security commonplaces, unrelated to Intranet security specifically, that need your attention. All the security precautions in the world can't protect your Intranet from overall poor security practices. Poor user choices on passwords always leads the list of computer and network security risks. If Bob uses his own name as his password, or his significant other's or pet's name, password-guessing is simple for anyone who knows him. Some people even write their passwords down and tape them to their keyboards or monitors—so much for the security of those passwords. You can limit access to a sensitive Web resource based on the TCP/IP network address of the boss's PC, but if the boss walks away and leaves his PC unattended without a password screen lock (a feature in many screen savers), anyone who walks into the empty office can access the protected resources.

In other words, the same good security practices that should be followed in any networked computing environment should also be made to apply in your Intranet. Not doing so negates all the possible security steps you can take and reduces the value of your Intranet. Even in the absence of malice, the failure to maintain any security on your Intranet inevitably results in an Intranet with little value to its customers.

Web Server Security

The following list summarizes the wide range of very flexible security features you can implement on your Web server:

◆ You can set your server to require a user name and password for access to Web servers, individual Web pages, and entire directories containing Web pages.

◆ You can limit access to Web servers, individual Web pages, and entire directories containing Web pages to customers on specific computer systems. In other words, access is denied unless the user is at his or her usual computer or workstation.

◆ You can organize individuals and/or computers into groups and grant access to individual Web servers, Web pages, and entire directories containing Web pages based on group membership.

◆ CGI scripts on your Web server can use any of the preceding access restrictions, though you must take care in writing them to ensure you don't make security-related mistakes.

◆ Some HTTP server software is capable of communicating with compatible Web browsers in a verifiably secure, encrypted fashion, defeating even network-level sniffers and ensuring confidential data transmission across your Intranet.

You can combine these features in a number of ways, such as requiring a password and limiting access to a group of users who must access your Web server from a specific group of computer systems. Combining two, or even all three, of these methods provides the best overall security.

User Name/Password Authentication

The first major element of Web server security is user name/password authentication. As you saw in Chapter 7, the IIS Web server provides this basic kind of security. Figure 10.1 shows what the Web browser user sees when he encounters a Web page that requires user name/password authentication for access.

Figure 10.1. *The user is prompted to enter a user name and password to gain access to a protected Web page.*

In IIS, a Web page or an entire directory tree under the Web server document root can be protected with just three easy steps:

1. Using Explorer, right-click the file or directory you want to protect. On a FAT-formatted drive, choose Properties | Permissions (the drive or directory must have sharing enabled). On an NTFS-formatted drive, choose Properties | Security | Permissions. Grant Read permission for the user or group that you want to be allowed to view the Web pages, as shown in Figure 10.2. (This step assumes that you have previously entered the users and/or groups into User Manager for Domains.)

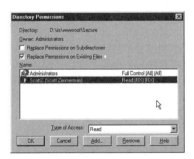

Figure 10.2. *Granting user/group permissions to a directory in Explorer.*

2. While you're in the Directory Permissions dialog in Explorer, remove the Read permission for the IUSR_*computername* account on the given file or directory. The IUSR_*computername* account is used by IIS for anonymous access.

3. Run the Microsoft Internet Service Manager and view the properties for the WWW Service. Notice three options for Password Authentication in the Service tab: Allow Anonymous, Basic (Clear Text), and Windows NT Challenge/Response. (See Figure 10.3.) For now, ensure that all three options are checked. (See following paragraph for more explanation.)

Figure 10.3. *Enabling Password Authentication in the IIS Web server.*

Now customers who want to access that directory will be faced with a dialog in their browser similar to Figure 10.1. But why did I suggest that you use all three IIS methods for password authentication? First, you probably want to keep the option for Allow Anonymous checked for the benefit of all your customers who want to access your Intranet home page. Unless, of course, you want to protect your whole Intranet!

Second, the Basic (Clear Text) option is enabled because that is all the page retrieval security that most Web browsers currently support. The Challenge/Response option is a much tighter security method provided by IIS on NT networks, but it is only compatible with Internet Explorer.

If any customers on your Intranet do have Internet Explorer, those passwords will be passed between the browser and the server in a more secure fashion if the third option is enabled. For those customers who don't have Internet Explorer, option two will provide a basic encoding (called *uuencode*) that is very simple to decipher if anyone should stick a packet sniffer on your LAN.

> **Note:** Don't confuse page retrieval security with secure transactions on the Web. The former is used to regulate whether a particular Web page is viewable by a particular customer. The latter is used to encrypt the form data that is sent back to the server by the browser after the user is done filling out a Web page that has been viewed. The Secure Sockets Layer (SSL) technology, now supported by many browsers, is an example of the latter.

Suppose your HTTP server's document root directory contains three main subdirectories named public, management, and personnel. Using NT directory permissions, you can specify that access to the management and personnel subdirectory trees requires user name/password authentication and leave public open for anyone to access without being prompted for user name and password. You can also set up more specific permissions within the protected subdirectories to further limit access to particularly sensitive documents by using user names and passwords.

Important Warnings About User Name/Password Authentication

Unless the access rules change as a user moves around on your Intranet Web pages (as with the personnel/management subdirectory in the example above), he will be prompted only once in his browser session for a user name and password. As long as he continues his browser session, he can access all of the files and directories available to him under the most recent access rule without being prompted again for his password. This situation is for convenience's sake; customers shouldn't have to repeatedly provide their user names and passwords at each step of the way when the access rule hasn't changed.

However, this situation has important ramifications if you follow it out logically. Suppose Anne, having authenticated herself to access the management subdirectory, leaves her browser session running, as most of us do. Her privileged access remains open to all the files protected by that one-time, possibly days-old, authentication. If she leaves her computer unattended when she goes to lunch or goes home for the day, without any sort of active screen or office door lock, anyone can sit down and browse the files and directories that are supposed to be limited to Anne's eyes only. This potential security breach is one that you as Webmaster can do little about and it is one that can be potentially harmful to all your work. This situation is no different from when a user leaves his workstation unattended without logging off. The most you can do is to try to educate your customers about such everyday security matters, even though they have little to do directly with the subject of your Intranet.

Authentication Based on Network Hostname or Address

Nearly all Web servers, including IIS, provide an additional authentication method that uses the TCP/IP network address of customer workstations or PCs as access criteria. As you'll learn in later chapters in the context of CGI-bin programming, every Web browser request for a document or other Intranet resource contains the numerical IP address of the requesting computer.

An important point about IP address authentication is that the Web server software blindly accepts the word of a requesting computer when it sends its IP address. There is no verification possible of this information. A curious, mischievous, or malicious person can reconfigure his computer to impersonate someone else's by changing his computer's IP address. Although this is an overall network security issue, not specifically one for your Intranet, you need to know about it because it can affect the security of your access-controlled documents. Security-minded network administrators can use special hardware and software to prevent this sort of IP spoofing, but for your Intranet's purposes, you'll probably want to combine hostname/IP address authentication with user name/password authentication.

Secure/Encrypted Transactions

You can further enhance security on your Intranet by encrypting Web transactions. When you use an encryption facility, information submitted by customers using Web fill-in forms, including user names, passwords, and other confidential information, can be transmitted securely to and from the Web server.

A wide range of proposed and/or partially implemented encryption solutions for the Web exist, but most are not ready for prime time. Of the several proposed methods, only the Secure HTTP (S-HTTP) and Secure Socket Layer (SSL) protocols have emerged in anything like full-blown form. Unfortunately, the two are usually implemented mutually exclusively, though compatibility is possible. Worse, Web browsers and servers that support one method don't support the other, so you can reliably use one or the other only if you carefully match your Web server and customers' browsers.

S-HTTP

Secure HTTP was developed by Enterprise Integration Technologies and RSA Data Security, and the public S-HTTP standards are now managed by CommerceNet, a not-for-profit consortium that is conducting the first large-scale market trial of technologies and business processes to support electronic commerce over the Internet. (For general information on CommerceNet, see `http://www.commerce.net/`.) S-HTTP is a modified version of the current HTTP protocol. It supports the following:

◆ User and Web server authentication using digital signatures, and signature keys using both the RSA and MD5 algorithms

◆ Privacy of transactions, using several different key-based encryption methods

◆ Generation of key certificates for server authentication

As with SSL, you must have a compatible Web server and browser that both support S-HTTP transactions in order to use this technology. IIS 1.0 supports only SSL.

SSL

S-HTTP seems to have been engulfed in the 1995 Netscape tidal wave. Unwilling to wait for widely accepted HTTP security standards to evolve (as it was with HTML as well), Netscape Communications Corporation developed its own Secure Sockets Layer encryption mechanism. SSL occupies a spot on the ISO seven-layer network reference below that of the HTTP protocol, which operates at the application layer. (See Table 10.1.) Rather than developing a completely new protocol to replace HTTP, SSL sits between HTTP and the underlying TCP/IP network protocols and can intervene to create secure transactions. Netscape makes the technical details of SSL publicly available. In addition, C-language source code for a reference implementation of SSL is freely available for non-commercial use. Microsoft includes SSL support in both IIS and Internet Explorer.

Table 10.1 provides a brief description of each of the seven layers of the OSI model. Note that layer 1 is contained in hardware and layers 2 through 7 are implemented in software. The list seems to be in reverse order. Network engineers generally view the flow of data as originating at the application layer and moving downward through the layers toward the hardware. Then the process is reversed when the packet arrives at the destination.

Table 10.1. An overview of the seven layers of the OSI model.

Layer	Implemented in	Description
Layer 7	Application	The program's users interact with to initiate network data transfer.
Layer 6	Presentation	Encrypts or decrypts data, packs or unpacks data, and converts data between formats.
Layer 5	Session	Determines when data transmission will start and stop.
Layer 4	Transport	Concerned with the quality of data on the circuit; includes error-checking protocols.
Layer 3	Network	Establishes the network route from the sender to the recipient.
Layer 2	Data Link	Provides for the bundling of several bits into a data frame.
Layer 1	Physical	Includes the specifications for the electrical signals and the transmission of bits.

Given Netscape's and Microsoft's collective share of the Web browser market, S-HTTP doesn't seem to have much of a chance of becoming widely available. With the exception of NCSA Mosaic, most other Web browsers have—or have promised—SSL support. Some of them are Spry's Internet in a Box and Mosaic in a Box for Windows 95 and version 2.0 and 3.0 of Microsoft's Internet Explorer for Windows 95, Windows NT, and the Macintosh. By the time you read this chapter, all these packages may have completed their SSL implementations.

> **Note:** Even though a browser may support secure transactions using SSL or S-HTTP, no transactions are actually secure except those between the browser and a compatible Web server. It's also important to note that most mechanisms for passing Web services through network firewalls (proxying, for example) don't support secure transactions unless both the proxy server and the destination server do.

The IIS online documentation includes much more detailed information about how to obtain and configure SSL.

The Common Gateway Interface (CGI) and Intranet Security

CGI is the mechanism that stands behind all the wonderful, interactive fill-in forms you'll want to put on your Intranet. Your customers demand these kinds of Intranet resources, and later chapters of *Building an Intranet with Windows NT 4* provide a number of technical tips on creating CGI scripts. You need to be aware, though, that CGI applications open potential security problems.

You can minimize much of your risk for security breaches in CGI scripting by including in your scripts explicit code for dealing with unexpected user input. The reason for this is simple: You should never trust any information a user enters in a fill-in form. Just because, for instance, a fill-in form asks for a user's name or e-mail address, there is no guarantee that the user filling in the form won't put in incorrect information. Customers make typographical errors, but probing crackers, even those inside your organization, may intentionally enter unexpected data in an attempt to break the script. To be secure, your CGI scripts have to anticipate and deal safely with unexpected input.

Other problems inherent with CGI scripts include the following:

◆ Calling outside programs, which opens up potential security holes in the external program

◆ Using server-side includes in scripts that dynamically generate HTML code. Make sure user input doesn't include literal HTML markup that could call a server-side include when your script runs.

Paul Phillips maintains a short but powerful list of CGI security resources on the Web. Check out http://www.cerf.net/~paulp/cgi-security, where you'll find a number of documents spelling out these and other risks of CGI scripting. For an extensive list of general CGI-related resources, go to Yahoo's CGI page, at http://www.yahoo.com/Computers_and_Internet/Internet/World_Wide_Web/CGI_Common_Gateway_Interface/index.html.

Your Intranet and the Internet

Is your Intranet accessible from the Internet? If so, all the security problems of the Internet are now your Intranet's problems too. Throughout this book, an implicit assumption has been made that your Intranet is private to your organization. You can, however, connect safely to the Internet and still protect your Intranet. You can even use the Internet as a means of letting remote sites in your company access your Intranet. In Chapter 28, I'll discuss how to set up NT, RAS, and your modem as a simple router between your LAN and the Internet. The following sections cover some Internet security basics.

Firewalls

It's a fact of Internet life that there are people out there who want to break into other people's networks through the Internet. Reasons vary from innocent curiosity to malicious cracking to business and international espionage. At the same time, the value of the Internet to organizations and businesses is so great that vendors are rushing to fill the need for Internet security with Internet firewalls. An Internet firewall is a device that sits between your internal network and the outside Internet. Its purpose is to limit access into and out of your network based on your organization's access policy.

A firewall can be anything from a set of filtering rules set up on the router between you and the Internet to an elaborate application gateway consisting of one or more specially configured computers that control access. Firewalls permit desired services coming from the outside, such as Internet e-mail, to pass. In addition, most firewalls now allow access to the World Wide Web from inside the protected networks. The idea is to allow some services to pass but to deny others. For example, you may be able to use the Telnet utility to log into systems out on the Internet, but users on remote systems cannot use it to log into your local system because of the firewall.

The following are a couple of good general Web resources about Internet firewalls:

◆ Marcus Ranum's Internet Firewalls Frequently Asked Questions document at `http://www.greatcircle.com/firewalls/info/FAQ.html`

◆ Kathy Fulmer's annotated list of commercial and freeware firewall packages (with many hyperlinks to firewall vendor Web pages) at `http://www.greatcircle.com/firewalls/vendors.html`

If your company is also connected to the Internet, you need to know how to make sure your Intranet isn't generally accessible to the outside world. You learned earlier in this chapter about denying access to your Web server using hostname and IP address authentication, but the fact that IP addresses can be easily spoofed makes it essential that you not rely on this mechanism as your only protection. You'll still want to rely on an Internet firewall to protect your Intranet, as well as all your other network assets. Unless your corporate network is not connected to the outside world at all, you'll probably want to ensure the security of your other Intranet services as well, including not only your Web servers, but also your FTP, Gopher, Usenet news, WAIS, and other TCP/IP network services.

Virtual Intranet

More and more companies with widely distributed offices, manufacturing sites, and other facilities are turning to use of the Internet to replace private corporate networks connecting the sites. Such a situation involves multiple connections to the Internet by the company, with the use of the

Internet itself as the backbone network for the company. Although such an approach is fraught with security risks, many organizations are using it for non-sensitive information exchange within the company. Using a properly set up firewall, companies can provide access to services inside one site's network to users at another site. Still, however, the data that flows across the Internet backbones between the corporate sites is mostly unencrypted, plain text data that Internet snoopers can easily read. Standard firewalls don't help with this situation.

A number of firewall companies have recently developed Virtual Private Network (VPN) capabilities. Essentially, VPN is an extension of standard firewall capabilities to permit authenticated, encrypted communications between sites over the Internet. Using a VPN, users at a remote site can access sensitive data at another site in a secure fashion over the Internet. All the data that flows on the public Internet backbones is encrypted before it leaves the local network, and then is decrypted when it arrives at the other end of the connection.

The most mature VPN product comes from Raptor Systems (http://www.raptor.com/) as part of the company's Eagle family of products.Other products are available from Checkpoint (http://www.checkpoint.com/) and Telecommerce (http://www.telecommerce.com/). Unfortunately, the market for Windows NT firewall products is still very young; most products are still exclusively based on UNIX.

Miscellaneous Security Advice

When people think about security on the Internet, they automatically think about firewalls, but there is a lot more to security than just firewalls. You will keep away most general pranksters by setting up your site with security in mind. The following are some miscellaneous pointers for running a secure Web site:

◆ Disable the NT Guest account in User Manager and rename the Administrator account (silly_admin, for example).

◆ Don't let server applications run as system services. Because server applications are basically listening to a port, a hacker could pass data to the well-known port. If the application is running as a system service, the application has system privileges and could, in theory, be forced to run a program that you do not want it to run. It is always best to create an account for the server application to run under so that it has only the privileges necessary to do its job.

◆ Don't put any files in the directory of an application server that you can't afford to lose.

◆ Don't provide Write permission to the CGI and ISAPI \Scripts directory to anyone but those trusted with NT administration.

◆ Use Control Panel | Networks to unbind protocols that are not essential to your LAN.

◆ Either make sure that Directory Browsing is not enabled in the IIS WWW Service tab, or make sure that you place a file named `default.htm` in your document root directory. Otherwise, users who only key in your fully qualified domain name will end up with an FTP directory listing of your document root directory, and there might be files other than your home page that you don't want them to see.

◆ Develop a security policy for users whom you allow to log into your server. What programs are they allowed to run? How often must they change their password? Are users permitted to dial out to the Internet from a private modem?

◆ Monitor your system logs carefully and often. It might be your only chance to catch strange behavior as it begins to develop. If you're lucky, you'll be able to exclude a hacker before further damage is done.

Summary

This chapter has dealt with implementing security on your Intranet. Although an Intranet is, by definition, internal to an organization, security is important not so much because it prevents things, but because it enables them. Judicious use of built-in security features of Web servers and other Intranet resources can add value to your Intranet by making new things possible. In this chapter, you have done the following:

◆ Considered the overall security aspects of your Intranet

◆ Learned how implementing security can broaden the ways in which your Intranet can be useful in your organization

◆ Learned how to use user name/password authentication to limit access to resources on your Intranet

◆ Learned about encrypted data transmission on your Intranet to protect critical information

◆ Learned important information about securing access to your Intranet in the case where your corporate network is attached to the Internet

◆ Learned how to provide and limit secure access to your Intranet from outside your immediate local network

Part III turns to the setup and use of everyday office applications as Intranet tools.

III
PART

Setting Up Office Applications

11

The Web Browser Is the Key

◆ A quick look at Netscape Navigator

◆ A quick look at Microsoft Internet Explorer

◆ A quick look at NCSA Mosaic

At first glance, many people think that a Web browser is nothing more than a container for static Web pages that are downloaded from the Internet. But look again—if either Microsoft or Netscape are even partly successful in their visions to redefine client/server computing, the browser is going to be the key. Even today, the current incarnations of Navigator and Explorer contain powerful features that go way beyond mere Web surfing, and yet they remain simple to use.

The whole foundation of this book is based on the concept (and soon your Intranet project will be too) that the browser is the key. The Web browser is the single piece of software that every desktop needs to have in order to take advantage of the Intranet. One of the reasons this is such a sweeping concept is that browsers are so cheap to deploy. Indeed, two of the most famous Web browsers, Microsoft Internet Explorer and NCSA Mosaic from the University of Illinois, are free! That's right, everyone in your organization can run a free, easy-to-use program and benefit from the increased efficiency and electronic communication made possible by the Intranet.

I assume that because you are reading this book, you will probably play a major role in establishing or leading the Intranet project in your organization. You may even be the Webmaster within your company. But whether or not you have the job title of Webmaster, you are at the very least an Intranet champion. As such, you will face the task of researching the Internet to find the right tools and technologies to usher the project through to success. Of course this book will help, but you will still need to keep up with new Web products that are being announced every day.

To keep up-to-date, you obviously need to browse the Web yourself, and you obviously need to be proficient with a Web browser. I thought it might be a good idea to glimpse at some of the features offered by the most popular browsers for Windows NT and Windows 95. This chapter might give you a few quick ideas on how you can train the masses (your customers) to use their Web browsers when your Intranet is up and rolling. If you are already familiar with using your browser, by all means skip or skim this chapter.

This chapter is by no means a complete browser tutorial or review. Rather, in the interest of brevity, I'll just cover a single interesting feature in each of the big three browsers. Obviously, they each contain many features that I don't have the space to cover here. But they all have so much in common that a discussion about any given feature in one browser can be easily applied to the other two. I hope this information will be just enough to stimulate your imagination with regard to the many other capabilities present in each browser.

Netscape Navigator

We've all heard about the Wall Street craze over Netscape. The reason for all the excitement is that Netscape currently has a very big lead in the popularity race for the best browser on the Internet. (About 80 percent of the Web pages viewed on the Internet every day are read using Netscape.) Because the Internet represents a wide open opportunity for Microsoft's competitors to attempt to reshape the software industry, the stakes are enormous.

You might think that if Mosaic and Internet Explorer are free products, few people would want to pay for Netscape Navigator. As I write this book, Netscape is giving away both the personal edition of version 2.0 and the beta version of their new 3.0 browser, but the company does expect you to pay the license fee for corporate use.

Despite the fact that Mosaic and Internet Explorer are free, there are many reasons that most Internet analysts think Navigator will probably succeed in this competitive market. The following are just a few:

◆ It contains the *de facto* and best implementation of HTML 3.2. Netscape has consistently lead the way in proposing and implementing new and useful HTML enhancements. Navigator also includes several extensions that aren't even in the proposed standard for HTML 3.2. Some Webmasters on the Internet are already advertising their home pages as being Netscape-enhanced beyond the point of backward-compatibility with other browsers.

◆ Navigator already includes support for Java. Microsoft has yet to include Java support in Internet Explorer.

◆ Navigator is truly a second-generation Web browser and has already been running on other operating systems for over a year.

◆ Netscape and Internet Explorer have a significant edge in performance over most other browsers.

◆ In addition to HTML 3.2 and Java, Navigator includes support for e-mail, newsgroups, FTP, VRML, third-party Plug-Ins, and video-conferencing. (Did I mention Java? That's the one everybody is talking about.)

> **Note:** To download a free copy for personal use of the latest release of Netscape Navigator, point your current browser to `http://www.netscape.com/`.

Reading Newsgroups in Netscape Navigator

You can read newsgroups very conveniently and send e-mail too without having to leave the comfort of Navigator. In this section, I show you how to use Netscape Navigator 2.0 to subscribe to a handy newsgroup. Suppose you would like to read daily articles about World Wide Web servers for Windows. (Hey, my sharp deductive powers must rely on what little clues I have to pick a subject that sounds like it might be of interest to you at this stage in your life.)

> **Tip:** There are so many Usenet newsgroups that it can be very overwhelming to find a good one that has information you are looking for. Fortunately, there is a Web page that will help you search for the name of a newsgroup that matches a keyword you supply. Check out this URL:
>
> `http://www.tile.net/tile/listserv/index.html`

To read the articles in the comp.infosystems.www.servers.ms-windows newsgroup with Netscape, follow these steps:

1. Run Netscape Navigator. From the main menu, choose Options | Mail | News Preferences | Servers to open the dialog shown in Figure 11.1.

2. Fill out the fields appropriate for your Internet connection and enter the address of your News server in the frame at the bottom. You can leave your name and e-mail address blank for now, unless you plan on posting articles. (Hmmm, by the way, please don't enter the same data that appears in the screen shot.) Choose OK.

3. In the URL text box labeled Go To on the main window, type in the complete path of the newsgroup you want to subscribe to. For this example, type in news:comp.infosystems.www.servers.ms-windows. Press Enter after typing in the address. Note that you need to precede the name with news:, otherwise, the browser will assume HTTP. Netscape opens its newsreader window. (See Figure 11.2.)

4. Scroll through the articles and look for headers of interest. All it takes is a single click to open an article.

Figure 11.1. Configuring Netscape Navigator to locate the NNTP server.

Note: When you are trying to quickly scan for interesting how-to articles, search for articles with Re: in the title. What often happens is that a question for help is posted by someone who is having trouble with some aspect of their computer. The good information (the answer) is usually in the reply, and the reply usually includes a copy of the original question. Of course, if you should happen to know the answer to the original question, please share your philanthropy with the rest of us and post a reply yourself.

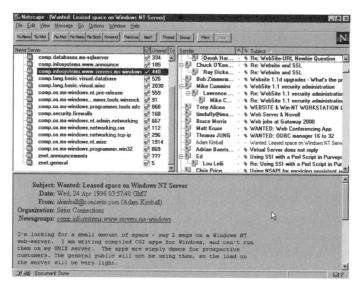

Figure 11.2. *Reading articles in a selected newsgroup is easy with Netscape Navigator.*

A Quick Look at Microsoft Internet Explorer

As I write this chapter, the current version of Microsoft Internet Explorer is 2.0. But by the time you read this chapter, version 3.0 should be available for free with Windows NT 4 and as a download from the Microsoft Web site for Windows 95 and Macintosh users.

> **Note:** To download a free copy of the latest release of Microsoft Internet Explorer, point your current browser to `http://www.microsoft.com/ie`. This URL also leads you to a wealth of information about the features and HTML tags supported by Internet Explorer.

Some of the features slated for version 3.0 of Internet Explorer are an enhanced newsreader, support for VRML (they call it *ActiveVRML*), 32-bit code optimized for multithreading on Windows NT and Windows 95, support for HTML 3.2, and support for SSL (Secure Sockets Layer). Best of all is its support for ActiveX and VBScript. ActiveX is Microsoft's name for their new vision of OLE on the Web. VBScript is a high-level language you (as a page designer) can insert in your HTML pages to process and manipulate the OLE controls embedded in the same pages. Several OLE controls (formerly called OCXs, now called ActiveX controls) are available for free from Microsoft as part of their Internet Control Pack. If that pack doesn't contain enough variety for you, dozens of other OLE control vendors have already announced support for ActiveX.

Note: To get a taste of the Microsoft ActiveX Internet Control Pack, browse to `http://www.microsoft.com/icp/`. Be aware that this page will mostly be of interest to Web page developers and client/server programmers.

Maintaining Favorite Web Pages with Microsoft Internet Explorer

The Favorites menu in Explorer allows you to easily maintain a selection list of places on the Web that you like to visit often. It saves you the trouble of having to remember and retype long URLs.

You're probably wondering why I picked such a trivial subject as this to write about Internet Explorer. First of all, some readers might not be aware of how convenient this feature is. Secondly, I wanted to expose the nature of how Microsoft chose to implement this feature. When you see that Favorites are nothing more than shortcuts in a file system folder, as are a ton of other mechanisms in the NT 4 and Windows 95 shell, you begin to realize how pervasive and powerful the concept is.

How does it work? Basically, when you are browsing the Web and come upon an interesting page that you would like to revisit, just choose Favorites | Add to Favorites from the Explorer menubar to open the dialog shown in Figure 11.3. All you have to do is click the Add button.

Figure 11.3. Saving a favorite in Internet Explorer.

The next time you want to visit that same site, you have several choices. First, you can select it from the list at the bottom of the Favorites menu. Second, you can choose Favorites | Open Favorites and select it from the list that appears in the dialog.

You can't help but notice that the dialog to reopen a Favorite page and the dialog to save a Favorite page (Figure 11.3) appear to be a common file dialog and a version of the file system Explorer program, respectively. That's the whole point; Favorites are shortcut files (with an extension of `.url`) stored in the current user's profile folder underneath the Windows system folder. See Figure 11.4 for a view of the Explorer file system where all the URL shortcut files are stored.

Knowing that these Favorite pages are stored as shortcut files opens up several new possibilities. For one thing, you can use the file system Explorer to double-click a shortcut file for a Web page that you want to browse. NT knows to launch Internet Explorer in that case, and it will take you to the Web. You also can easily drag the shortcut to your desktop if it happens to be a Web page that you like to check on daily (perhaps http://www.yahoo.com).You no doubt noticed my somewhat clumsy dance in the paragraphs above between the terms *Internet Explorer* and *file system Explorer.* If you believe that something should be done to make the software less confusing, you are not alone. In fact Microsoft has plans to make a lot of money on this very idea. Beginning in the Fall of 1996, an update to Windows 95, and probably NT 4, will integrate the file system Explorer application with the Internet Explorer Web browser. Microsoft's vision is that the Web browser should be a free part of the operating system itself.

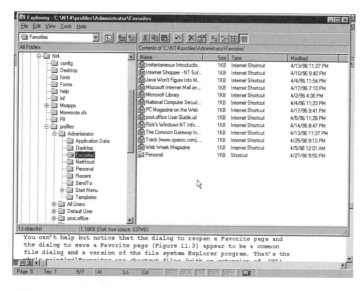

Figure 11.4. *The NT file system Explorer can retrieve URL shortcut files saved as Favorites in Internet Explorer.*

That vision achieves two purposes. First, it gives Windows users (like you and me) a very convenient way to look for files on the enormous client/server network called the World Wide Web, or even the somewhat smaller (but no less important) client/server network called the Intranet, without requiring a mental shift from the way we already browse for files on our local hard drives. Second, giving away free software helps Microsoft compete with Netscape. We win again.

NCSA Mosaic

Mosaic was invented at the University of Illinois at NCSA. NCSA stands for the National Center for Supercomputing Applications. Mosaic was the first Web browser to bring the Internet to the masses due to the way in which it made the Web easily accessible through the popular graphical environments of Windows and the Macintosh.

> **Note:** The Mosaic Web browser is available for Macintosh, UNIX, and all flavors of Windows. Mosaic can be freely downloaded for personal or internal business use from the University of Illinois Web site at the following URL:
>
> `http://www.ncsa.uiuc.edu/SDG/Software/Mosaic/`

E-Mail in Mosaic

One of the cool features about Mosaic is its capability to send e-mail to a `mailto` URL while you are browsing a Web page. Even if you don't click a `mailto` URL, you can send an e-mail message anytime you are browsing the Web and you come across something that stirs you to comment.

To configure Mosaic for e-mail and enter a simple message, follow these steps:

1. Choose Options | Preferences | Services from the Mosaic main menu to open the dialog shown in Figure 11.5. This dialog asks you for your e-mail address and the address of the SMTP server through which Mosaic will send your messages to the Internet. Enter this information, and choose OK.

2. Choose File | Send Email from the main menu. The Mail dialog shown in Figure 11.6 appears. Enter the address of the recipient, the subject, and the message. Choose the Send button and your message is on its way without you ever having to leave the browser.

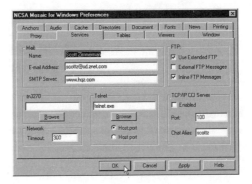

Figure 11.5. *E-mail configuration in Mosaic.*

Figure 11.6. *Sending mail in Mosaic.*

Summary

The next chapter dives into the details of how to make the Web browser and the Intranet dovetail together through the powerful and mysterious features of MIME.

CHAPTER

12

MIME and Helper Applications

◆ Web helper applications

◆ Overview of MIME (Multipurpose Internet Mail Extensions)

◆ How MIME works on the Web

◆ MIME and Web helper applications

◆ MIME and CGI

This chapter deals with some fundamentals for your Intranet. In subsequent chapters, you'll use these building blocks to help your customers access specific information in their everyday work. This chapter assumes you already have a Web server up and running, at least in a rudimentary fashion. If this is not the case, you'll probably want to get your server up, so you can see and manipulate the sample Web server and browser configuration files, which are discussed here. Refer back to Part II of this book, "Getting Set Up on the Server," and review Chapter 7, "Running the Intranet Web Server."

The configuration information that comes with the IIS 2.0 Web server software is fairly basic. It doesn't give you much in the way of troubleshooting information, nor does it go very far to explain the reasons behind certain aspects of the program. This chapter fills in this information gap. For example, a handy little section in the help file explains how to configure MIME types in the Registry, but this chapter explains why you would want to do that. This chapter also discusses the server MIME mappings in the Registry, their meaning in Web technology, and how you can use them to set up your Intranet, concepts that are central to this book.

Web Helper Applications

Web browsers like Netscape, Explorer, and Mosaic are amazing packages. They not only enable you to search the World Wide Web for interesting and useful documents, images, and other data, but they also provide a friendly interface for older Internet services such as FTP and Gopher. These browsers can display not only plain text and HTML text (and HTML hyperlinks) but also several common types of image files, even without any helper applications. But even these amazing programs have their limits. People use a mind-boggling array of different formats to store their data on computers, and new formats are being invented all the time. Your Web browser can't possibly handle all the existing kinds of data, let alone the new formats just being invented. That's where helper applications come in.

The pioneering developers of Web technology, scientists at CERN, the European Particle Physics Lab, wanted to develop some means of integrating various kinds of data into a single, user-friendly interface. Toward this end, the folks at CERN made a critical choice early in their work to allow a Web browser to call other computer programs to handle data that it can't handle itself. You probably know these other programs as *helper applications*, though some people call them *external viewers*. Whatever they're called (the term helper application is used in this book), the decision to enable Web browsers to hand off data to a different, outside program was sheer genius.

You might have already set up your browser to use helper applications for viewing Web video or listening to Web sounds. What you may not realize is that the mechanism for handing off data to helper applications is a standardized one, and you can use it for almost anything you can imagine. Helper applications aren't just for viewing video clips, as the following examples demonstrate:

◆ Your everyday word processor can function as a helper application, enabling you to distribute boilerplate documents with your Web server.

◆ You can set up your spreadsheet program as a helper application to enable your customers to download live data and then manipulate it.

◆ You can use a presentation graphics package as a helper application to open up computer-based training possibilities for your customers.

I'll come back to the specifics of setting up helper applications later in this chapter. First, though, you need to understand the mechanism by which Web browsers pass off data they can't handle internally to external programs. This subject might seem a digression from your Intranet, but understanding this subject is critical to your success.

Multipurpose Internet Mail Extensions (MIME)

The original Web developers at CERN decided on a single interface for a variety of data types. The developers implemented this decision by adopting an existing mechanism called Multipurpose Internet Mail Extensions or MIME.

As the name implies, MIME hails from the world of Internet electronic mail. E-mail is one of the oldest Internet services, pre-dating the World Wide Web by many years. E-mail is still one of the most popular Internet services and is often given as the reason organizations and people want Internet access. Despite its popularity, though, Internet e-mail has been limited by the requirement that only plain ASCII text can be used in messages. This requirement means that nontext files, such as applications, data files that include formatting (like word processor files), and other binary files, can't be e-mailed as-is. It also means that even simple non-ASCII characters, such as non-English characters used in many languages around the world, won't pass e-mail muster.

As is often the case with computers and the Internet, there are ways you can work around this limitation to get a binary data file from one place to another intact. For example, you can use the file transfer protocol (FTP) to transfer any kind of file from one computer to another over the Internet. Also, if you've used Internet e-mail to send data files very much, particularly to or from UNIX systems, you may know about the uuencode and uudecode programs. The uuencode program converts a binary file into a specially encoded ASCII text file so it can be sent by e-mail. Its companion utility, uudecode, converts the encoded file back into its original format on the recipient's end.

Neither of these workarounds is really convenient, though. Both not only require extra steps, but also a certain amount of skill and knowledge on the part of both the sender and receiver of the message—skill and knowledge that the casual e-mail user may not have. Sophisticated, user-friendly e-mail tools have developed in the past few years, and most have point-and-click features for attaching any kind of data file to a message. These tools are easy-to-use and work well for exchanging nontext data, provided both sender and recipient are using the same package.

Unfortunately, users of different proprietary-format e-mail programs, such as a cc:Mail user and a Microsoft Mail user, can't easily exchange data files through e-mail. Both cc:Mail and Microsoft Mail use a proprietary message format. Although there are gateway packages for both, they are expensive and don't always work well.

Although Lotus (manufacturer of cc:Mail) and Microsoft would have you believe that the solution to these incompatibility problems lies in your buying *their* packages for every user or buying an expensive piece of e-mail gateway software and dedicating hardware on which to run it, these solutions are inadequate in the context of the Internet. These vendors might wish they could sell their packages to every one of the millions of Internet e-mail users, but this feat is unlikely. If you need to send Internet e-mail, your fancy mail program's file attachment feature will break down sooner or later.

Enter MIME

In 1991, Nathaniel S. Borenstein of Bellcore proposed major extensions to Internet electronic mail standards. Called Multipurpose Internet Mail Extensions, or MIME, Borenstein's proposal extended the existing Simple Mail Transport Protocol (SMTP) standards to offer a "standardized way to represent and encode a wide variety of media types, including textual data in non-ASCII character sets, for transmission via Internet mail."

The MIME proposal, which was issued as Internet Requests for Comments (RFC) 1522 and 1523, amended earlier RFCs that defined the Simple Mail Transport Protocol (primarily RFC 822) to allow the attachment of virtually any kind of data file to an Internet e-mail message using a simple mechanism.

Note: The Internet has a long history of development through consensus. The TCP/IP networking protocols, developed at first with U.S. Government (Department of Defense) support, were worked out through give-and-take revolving around publicly proposed standards called *Requests For Comments*. Internet developers issued proposed standards for the nuts-and-bolts of the Internet, calling for comment from the then-small Internet community. Coordinated by the Internet Engineering Task Force (IETF), a process for building consensus for developing standards grew up, with feedback on RFCs eventually incorporated into the final standards the IETF issued. To date, more than 2,000 Internet RFCs have been issued. Many of them have made their way into final standards, guaranteeing that different vendors' TCP/IP networking applications can work together. You can find the complete set of Internet RFCs at `http://www.internic.net/ds/dspg0intdoc.html`.

RFC 822 defined the Simple Mail Transport Protocol. Anyone who wants to develop an Internet e-mail program can follow the requirements of RFC 822 to ensure the package works with all other RFC 822-compliant data file packages.

Under the terms of RFC 822, an Internet data file message has two parts:

- A header, often likened to the envelope in which you mail a letter at the post office, which contains addressing and postmark information
- A body, like the information inside the envelope, which contains the text of the message

This division of e-mail messages into a header section and a body section is critical to MIME and, as you will see later in this chapter, it is also important in World Wide Web services. Consequently, this division will be important to you in setting up your Intranet.

A header itself can be divided into separate parts, each having the same general format:

- A header name (From, To, Date, and so on) followed by a colon and a single blank space. (Multiword header names, such as Reply-To, are hyphenated.)
- The header content, such as the addressee's e-mail address, time, and sender's e-mail address.

All headers in an e-mail message are single lines. Some headers are required by RFC 822, and others are optional. The important point is that they all follow the same format, with the colon and a single blank space separating the header name and contents. You will see additional headers on your own e-mail messages, including what might be termed postmarks of all the Internet hosts that handled your message on its way to you. Even so, all follow this simple format, and the header section of all e-mail messages, regardless of how many headers there are, is separated from the body by a single blank line.

If you're interested in looking at the headers on your own e-mail messages, many mail programs (including Eudora Light) have a setup command to let you choose whether you want to see all the headers on a message. You'll see that each message contains header and body parts.

How MIME Works

As noted, the broad division of Internet data file messages into the header and body sections is always present in the format just described. Borensteins' MIME proposal, also grossly simplified here, was to extend this basic division by doing the following:

- Adding a new header type that specified whether a message was a multipart message, with some or no normal text and zero or more attachments
- Enabling the data to be encoded into a special ASCII text format, and then attached to the message body, with separating/identifying information

You can read the details of MIME in RFC 1522 and RFC 1523. In essence, the new header type allows one or more of a set of message content types to be identified and attached to messages. The content types include image, audio, video, application data, and, of course, text. In addition, a special content type allows multiple attachments of differing data types to the same message.

There are several MIME headers, including *Mime-Version*, *Content-Type*, and *Content-Length*. You can read about these headers in detail in the MIME RFCs. The important part to note is that these are just additional headers that follow the standard Internet e-mail message format.

MIME-capable mail user agents parse incoming messages for the MIME-extended headers. Based on the content type of the message and a set of user-configurable rules associating particular content types with application programs (or viewers), the MIME mail program passes attachments off to other application programs on the system that are capable of dealing with them. For example, an incoming MIME-formatted e-mail message may have an audio file attached. The recipient's MIME-compliant mail tool recognizes the sound file attachment from the extended headers in the message and fires off an audio player to play the sound. Likewise, your Web browser passes off data it cannot handle directly to helper applications on your system that can handle the data.

Mail User Agents and Mail Transfer Agents

Internet e-mail handling programs are usually divided into two categories. First, users that are creating, sending, and reading e-mail messages use Mail User Agents (MUAs). Examples of Windows GUI MUAs include Exchange (free with Windows), Eudora, and Pegasus (another very popular freeware application available on the Internet).

Usually, however, a separate program does the work of routing and delivering e-mail. These separate programs are usually referred to as Mail Transport Agents (MTAs). However, PC MUAs, like Eudora, generally have enough MTA features built in so that the mail you create gets handed off immediately to a mail server for delivery.

Similarly, MIME-compliant MUAs create MIME-formatted messages automatically. Attaching a file is simple for the user; it's usually a point-and-click operation in graphical MUAs, with the encoding handled internally by the program.

Probably the most widely used MIME-compliant MUA is the PC and Macintosh package called Eudora. It's a basic Internet e-mail package with most of the standard MUA features, but it's also MIME-compliant. A *postcardware* (meaning freeware if you send its author, Jeff Beckley, a postcard) version of Eudora Light is available on the CD-ROM that accompanies this book.

MIME and the World Wide Web

You know from using your WWW browser that you can deal with many kinds of data and Internet services. Your Web browser can display images, access Gopher and FTP services, and, when properly equipped with helper applications, play movies or audio that you find on the Web. Because you've set up a Web server of your own, you also know you can make these and other data types available on your server, and you know how to write the HTML to include them in your Web pages. You may not know, however, that the MIME mechanism just described is what makes this all possible.

To help you understand this process, this section delves more deeply into the details of MIME as it relates to Web servers, browsers, and helper applications. You'll learn how Web servers use MIME to distinguish among the types of data they're serving and how Web servers use MIME to tell Web browser clients what sort of data is being sent in every single transaction.

MIME and the Web Server

Web servers understand MIME information and provide it to Web browsers in every HTTP transaction. As described earlier in this chapter, MIME is able to identify a number of data types (called content types in the MIME discussion earlier) and subtypes. Web server software uses an extensive database of MIME content type information. With IIS, this database is in the Windows NT Registry underneath this key:

`HKEY_LOCAL_MACHINE\SYSTEM\CurrentControlSet\Services\InetInfo\Parameters\MimeMap`

Figure 12.1 displays the Registry Editor opened to this key with the MIME type for Microsoft Word documents selected in the right-hand window.

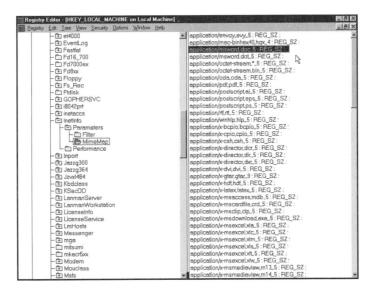

Figure 12.1. *Editing the IIS MIME map using the Windows NT Registry Editor.*

The Layout of the Server MIME Map

IIS installs over 100 MIME mappings by default. The syntax of each row in the Mime Map key is as follows:

`<mime type>,<filename extension>,,<gopher type>`

For example, the server uses the following line to tell the browser that a `.doc` file is a Microsoft Word document:

```
application/msword,doc,,5
```

Notice that the `<mime type>` field is subdivided into two parts by a forward slash. Remember from the discussion of MIME earlier in the chapter that the proposed MIME standards include a set of data types (content types) that can be attached to e-mail messages. The `<mime type>` field represents these very same data types. If you scroll down the window pane on the right side of the Registry Editor window and look at just the part of the `<mime type>` field before the slash, you can see six data types:

◆ Application

◆ Audio

◆ Image

◆ Text

◆ Video

◆ X-world

Two other common MIME types, which IIS does not install automatically, are the following:

◆ Message

◆ Multipart

These MIME types follow the conventions proposed in Nathaniel Borenstein's MIME RFCs and are the same types supported by the MIME-compliant e-mail packages listed earlier. Thus, this short list of MIME data types is incorporated into your Web server.

Of course, different kinds of data can fall into these broad categories, so the MIME data types are subdivided into MIME data subtypes. The matter to the right of the slash in the MIME map signifies subtypes of the major MIME data types. You're no doubt familiar with several kinds of images, `.gif`, `.jpeg`, and `.bmp`, for example. Thus, you'll see a number of entries for the image data type, one each for the major image subtypes, such as `image/jpeg`. Similarly, you'll see a couple of different video and audio subtypes, including `video/mpeg`.

Perhaps the largest number of subtypes are those of the application data type. As you can see from Figure 12.1, a large number of well-known application programs are listed. These range from everyday office word processors (like `application/msword`) to standard UNIX utilities (like `tar`) to special purpose packages (like PostScript). MIME provides support for all of these application programs and the mechanism to use them. If you use these applications, or any of the other applications listed in the MIME map, your Web server knows about them, and you'll be able to put them to work as a part of your Intranet by using the information in this book.

Look at the remaining data on each row of the MIME map. The MIME mechanism associates filename extensions with data types/subtypes. The right side of each row contains a filename extension to be associated with the MIME data type/subtype on the left side of the row. For example, the entry for image/gif uses the filename extension gif, and the entries for application/ postscript use several filename extensions: ai, ps, and eps.

To put this another way, the MIME map helps Web browsers tie filename extensions to specific computer programs. Your Web server knows, from the MIME map, that a .doc file is a data file for Microsoft Word, a .ps file is a PostScript document, and an .mpeg file is an MPEG (Motion Picture Experts Group) video movie. This is an important piece of information for your Intranet because now your Web server can tell your clients (that is, Explorer, Netscape, Mosaic, or another Web browser) what sort of data is coming when your customers click a hyperlink.

Clients, Servers, and MIME Types

Just as Web servers know about MIME types and include the information in every piece of data they send to Web browsers, the Web browsers understand MIME as well.

Web Servers Say What They're Sending

Web servers always precede anything they send in response to a client request (for example, when you click a hyperlink) with some preliminary header information. From the discussion about MIME headers in the e-mail context, you can probably guess that these headers contain MIME data type/subtype information. Specifically, when a Web server responds to a request from a Web browser for a document or other piece of data, the server announces to the browser in one or more headers the type of data it is sending, using the associations in the MIME map in the Registry. Thus, when you click a hyperlink pointing to a video file (volcano.mpeg, for example), the first bit of information sent back to your browser about the link is its MIME type/subtype, video/mpeg. Your browser, then, knows what sort of data is coming even before it arrives.

Web Browsers Understand MIME Types, Too

Your Web browser understands MIME and its data types/subtypes. Your browser reads the incoming MIME type header information from the Web server and decides what to do with the incoming data based on its type. For example, your Web browser knows what to do with data of the MIME type text/html (regular Web pages in HTML) or image/gif (a .gif image). It has a built-in ability to properly handle these and other common types of data. That's how you're able to read most documents you find on the Web and see most images as well.

MIME and Web Helper Applications

As noted at the beginning of this chapter, Web browsers can't possibly handle all kinds of data. You already know about common helper applications. What you might not know is that the MIME information is intimately involved with these helper applications. Web browsers use the MIME type header information they get from Web servers, using the very same set of data type/

subtype and filename extension, to pass off the data to helper applications. This process enables you to play Web movies or sound files. And this process is how, as you'll learn in later chapters, you can use MIME information to create your own associations between data and your own helper applications for your Intranet.

A MIME Conversation

The following imaginary dialog between a Web browser and Web server, written in plain English instead of in the Hypertext Transfer Protocol (HTTP) using MIME headers, illustrates what happens when a user clicks an object that the browser can't show:

User (to the browser): Click, show me this object.

Browser (to the server): Send me the data this link points to.

Server: OK, but first you should know that it is of this MIME data type/subtype. Here it comes.

Browser (to itself): Ohhhh, it's *that* kind of MIME data type/subtype. Let's see, that means I can't display it myself, so I have to send it to a helper application that understands that data type. Let me look at my list. Which one handles this MIME data type/subtype? (Note that browsers are getting more and more sophisticated at handling multiple file types internally without having to pass the data to an external helper application.)

Browser (to the selected helper application): Here, deal with this data.

Using MIME to Set Up Web Helper Applications

This section outlines the process of setting up a Web server and browsers to use helper applications. To focus on the general principles used, pretend you have a helper application called PluPerStat. You don't need to know what this program does or anything about the data it produces/uses, but assume a couple of things about it:

◆ PluPerStat has some kind of proprietary data format.

◆ PluPerStat stores its files with the filename extension `.plu`.

Edit the MIME Map on Your Web Server

Your first step in setting up PluPerStat as a helper application for your Intranet is to edit the MIME map in the Registry on your Web server to add an entry for it. Not all Web servers store the MIME map in the NT Registry. See your server documentation to make sure of the name and location of the MIME map file if you are using some Web server other than IIS.

Set Up the New Helper Application on Your Browser(s)

Before you can use PluPerStat as a helper application, you need to tell your Web browser about it and its MIME data type/subtype. Different browsers have different mechanisms for adding helper applications. The following section covers Explorer. If you're using another browser, check your documentation (if necessary). You will probably realize as soon as you read the steps for Explorer that the concepts can be easily applied to any browser.

Setting up Internet Explorer for MIME

To set up Internet Explorer 2.0 to use the imaginary PluPerStat data format, perform the following steps. Note that Explorer uses the term *file types* rather than *helper application* to accomplish the same purpose.

1. Run Explorer and choose View | Options | File Types from the main menu. You will see the dialog shown in Figure 12.2.

2. Click the New Type button to open the dialog shown in Figure 12.3.

Figure 12.2. *The Internet Explorer File Types dialog.*

3. Fill in the boxes with the appropriate information. The one thing you can't really do in this example is fill in the path to the application that will be used to open this type of file when this type of data is downloaded. But assuming you had a real application in mind, you could click the New button and fill in the path.

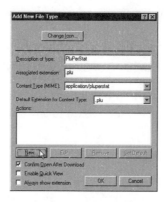

Figure 12.3. *This Internet Explorer dialog is used to add MIME types.*

4. When you've finished, click OK, and then click OK again to save the new MIME information.

Explorer is now configured to use PluPerStat as a helper application whenever it encounters the MIME type/subtype `application/x-pluperstat` or the filename extension `.plu`.

Why Include Both MIME Type and Filename Extension?

Careful readers will notice the first sentence in the preceding paragraph says "whenever it encounters the MIME type/subtype `application/x-pluperstat` *or* the filename extension `.plu`." You may wonder why it's necessary to include both the MIME type/subtype and filename extension. After all, you've learned the Web server includes this information in the MIME data type/subtype headers, so why does Explorer (or any other Web browser) have to be configured to specify both pieces of information?

Although this information is indeed redundant when communicating with a Web server, Web browsers also communicate with other kinds of Internet information servers, such as FTP and Gopher servers. These Internet services pre-date both the World Wide Web and MIME; they don't know anything about MIME types. Moreover, because they send back only one kind of data, not one of many kinds of data like a Web server, they have no reason to precede the data they send with any identifying header information at all. Because an FTP server, for example, has no way of telling a Web browser what sort of data is coming, Web browsers use a workaround, keying off the filename extension to a MIME data type/subtype. You've no doubt seen your browser display a set of canned icons, representing different file types, when you connect to an FTP or Gopher server. These icons are your browser's MIME mechanism at work, using the filename extensions it finds and a built-in list of MIME data types/subtypes.

Thus, if you're connected to an FTP server with your Mosaic browser and you click a link pointing to a file with the `.plu` extension, Mosaic can make the assumption the file is a PluPerStat data file because you've configured a helper application for this kind of data. There's no guarantee, though, that the .plu file is really a PluPerStat data file. After all, people are free to name files anything they want.

The MIME map contains a semi-official list of MIME types and filename extensions, and Web browsers are built to rely on that list. Although you added a new type, application/x-pluperstat in the example, to your browser, there's no guarantee that other Web or Internet servers won't have used the same filename extension for some other kind of data file. Still, the key point is that Web browsers have a built-in list of filename extension/MIME type associations to fall back on in the absence of any MIME header information coming from the server.

MIME and CGI

The Common Gateway Interface is a standard way of passing information from the Web fill-in forms you've seen to back-end CGI scripts or other CGI programs that deal with the data. CGI is described in detail in Chapter 19, "Getting the Most out of HTML with CGI," and Chapter 20, "Building a CGI Database System."

CGI is MIME-aware, which accounts for much of its power. CGI scripts on your Intranet can return data from your Web server in response to browser requests, in much the same way as you get data when you click a hyperlink. Although most people think of the data being returned from a Web server as being from static files on the server (such as Web pages written in HTML, images, and so on), CGI scripts and programs can generate data on the fly in response to user requests. Such requests can be, for example, based on a fill-in form. The user enters information in the form, and then clicks a Submit button. The CGI script then processes the information entered, generates a new stream of data based on the user input, and returns it to the client. Thus, a fill-in form can solicit input from a user such as search criteria in a database application, construct a query using the user data, run the query against the database, and return the results to the user's Web browser as an HTML document.

The mechanics of this CGI on-the-fly data generation use the MIME mechanism. Just as your Intranet server, sending back data in response to a mouse click on a hyperlink, precedes that data with header information containing the MIME data type/subtype of the data to be sent, your CGI scripts must return the same sort of information about the data stream they're about to send. Thus, any Perl CGI script's very first output statements might be something like the following:

```
print "Content-Type: text/html\n";
print "\n";
```

These statements give orders to generate the string of characters Content-Type: text/html followed by a newline and print a blank line. You've seen Content-Type before, just a few pages back, as well as the necessary blank line. Recall the discussion of the fundamental RFC-822 e-mail requirement: Messages must be separated into a header area and a body area with a blank line between them. What you have here is exactly the same: The CGI script generates a MIME data type/subtype header (in this case Content-Type: text/html) followed by a blank line as the very first bit of data to be returned to the Web browser.

In this example, as required in all CGI scripts that are to return data to the user's Web browser, the program informs the browser that the forthcoming data is of the MIME type text and subtype html. The rest of the data generated by the script is, in fact, text data with HTML codes. Such data can include any and all HTML markup, including URLs pointing to other Web documents, images, or even other CGI scripts. Use of variable substitution in CGI scripts, for example, can enable you to generate documents, forms, or anything else that can be flagged in HTML, all with the simple use of one MIME type/subtype header preceding the data.

This simple, yet powerful, example uses the text/html MIME type/subtype, but there is no reason your CGI scripts can't return any other valid MIME type/subtype. Provided you've set up your Web server's MIME map and your users' Web browsers have corresponding helper application setup, there's almost no limit to what you can return from your CGI scripts. For example, the preceding Perl print statements could just as well be the following:

```
print "Content-Type: application/x-pluperstat\n";
print "\n";
```

Your script would then select and return a PluPerStat data file, based on information the user enters into a fill-in form on your Intranet. This way, you can make a library of PluPerStat data available on your Web server, enable your customers to grab pieces of it using their Web browsers, and then interact with the data using the PluPerStat program itself. You've just made your Intranet something more than just a look-at-pictures-and-read-text-files server: Your customers can actually use it for their real work.

Summary

This chapter is the heart of this book. In it, you've learned the following:

- ◆ What Web helper applications are
- ◆ What MIME is and where it came from
- ◆ How the developers of the World Wide Web adopted MIME as a major part of Web technology
- ◆ How Web servers and browsers use MIME to identify and process data
- ◆ The relationship between MIME and Web browser helper applications
- ◆ The basics of helper application setup in Explorer
- ◆ How MIME and the CGI mechanism work together

The next chapter continues the discussion of MIME by showing you how to hook your office word processor into your Intranet. Later chapters talk about your own application programs and apply the information you've learned in this chapter to real programs that do real work.

CHAPTER

◆

Word Processing on the Web

◆ Understanding why the word processor is part of the Intranet

◆ Configuring the Web server for the word processor

◆ Setting up word processor documents on the Web server

◆ Setting up Microsoft Word as a browser helper application

◆ Setting up Write, WordPad, and other word processors as helper applications

◆ Getting free word processor viewers

Your word processing software is probably one of the most frequently used packages in your organization. People use it for everything from quick notes to complex, book-length documents. In this chapter, you'll learn how to set up your Intranet so that your customers can retrieve documents using their Web browser and automatically display them in their favorite word processor for revision, document assembly, or other purposes.

The chapter is organized into separate, but similar, sections devoted to Mosaic, Netscape, Word, and Windows WordPad (for Windows 95 users, or Windows Write for Windows 3.1 users). Word was chosen due to its prevalence (as a component of Microsoft Office, it can be found in nearly every workplace in America); WordPad was chosen due to the fact that it is free with Windows NT and Windows 95.

> **Note:** WordPad is a new Windows application that can handle both ASCII text and Microsoft Write documents. Versions of Windows prior to Windows 95 used Notepad and Write to accomplish these separate editing tasks, but Microsoft's consumer researchers discovered it was too confusing for novices to have separate programs for such similar tasks. Thus, WordPad can replace both Notepad and Write.

The examples in this chapter use Mosaic and Netscape—two of the most widely used Web browsers for Windows. Each section contains several screenshots, showing you step-by-step how to set up your word processor as a Web browser helper application.

If you are feeling disappointed that I didn't list your favorite application, please bear in mind that the same concepts are easily applied to just about any word processor and any Web browser you can imagine. If your organization uses multiple packages for word processing, you'll be able to get everything you need out of the separate examples to enable you to fully customize your own Intranet.

Integrating the Word Processor and the Intranet

Like most people who use computers for general office work, you probably use your word processing package more than any other application. Graphical user interfaces like Microsoft Windows integrate your word processor, along with all your other commonly used applications, into your everyday desktop allowing you to start it up with a simple mouse click.

Integrating the word processor (and other applications, as you'll learn in the next few chapters) into your Web is, in a sense, creating a whole new graphical interface for your users based on the Web browser. Some people have predicted that an overall graphical user interface based on Netscape or Explorer may eventually replace Microsoft Windows or the Macintosh desktop. Although this prediction may seem a bit farfetched, it is nonetheless both possible and simple to broaden the scope of your Web browser to tie in links to your everyday tools like your word processor, giving them a new interface with a common look and feel.

More importantly, you can use your Web server, HTML, and other tools to put together shareable libraries of word processing documents. Such libraries can be complete with searchable indices and point-and-click access through your Web browser. Locating and opening a document no longer involves finding a file and then starting up your word processor to read or edit it. Using Explorer, Netscape, or another Web browser, your customers can click a Web hyperlink for the document and have the word processor fire up with a copy of the desired document loaded.

Helper Applications

Earlier chapters talked about helper applications (also known as external viewers), which are computer programs your Web browser uses when it can't directly display the data represented by a hyperlink. For example, neither Netscape nor Explorer can play all the audio or video file formats that you might run across on the Web, but both can be set up to pass incoming audio or video data off to an audio- or video-playing helper application. When you click a hyperlink pointing to a sound or video file, your Web browser receives it from a Web server, recognizes it as a sound or video file, and hands it off to the audio or video helper application you've set up.

In this chapter, your word processor is treated as a helper application, just like a sound or video player. There's very little difference between the setup of one of these common helper applications and the setup of Word or WordPerfect, but there's a major difference in the implications of doing so. Playing video and audio on your computer may be remarkable and enjoyable, but, unless you are in the video or audio business, it accomplishes little of your substantive, everyday work. Your word processor, on the other hand, is the workhorse of many days. Integrating it into your Intranet can potentially be a major productivity enhancement that fundamentally changes the way your customers do their work.

Setting Up the Web Server for Word Processor Integration

Regardless of which word processor you use, your first steps in setting it up as a helper application involve configuring your Web server to know about your word processor's documents. With small differences, which will be explained, the instructions in this section apply to any word processor.

As you learned in Chapter 12, "MIME and Helper Applications," Web servers use the MIME mechanism to identify documents according to their MIME data type/subtype. Recall that the MIME mechanism divides data into a relatively small handful of data types, with each type further subdivided into subtypes. Word processing documents fall into the application data type. You also learned in Chapter 12 how Web servers use filename extensions to map data files on the server to a MIME data type/subtype. IIS associates filename extensions with MIME types/subtypes through the Windows NT Registry.

Editing the Registry MIME Map

As you'll recall from Chapter 12, the NT Registry holds the IIS MIME map under the following key:

```
HKEY_LOCAL_MACHINE\SYSTEM\CurrentControlSet\Services\InetInfo\Parameters\MimeMap
```

The key holds a simple list of MIME types/subtypes and associated filename extensions. (See Chapter 6, "Windows NT 4 Configuration" for some tips about how to steer a course through the Registry.) The following is a short excerpt from the default map distributed with IIS 1.0. (For a full listing, refer to the RegEdit program.)

```
application/envoy,evy,,5
application/mac-binhex40,hqx,,4
application/msword,doc,,5
application/msword,dot,,5
```

This list shows the association, for example, between the .doc filename extension and the MIME type/subtype application/msword, representing Microsoft Word. Recall that the last number on each row is the Gopher data type. Several of the IIS default MIME entries have no numbers for the Gopher type; you can add these numbers as required.

Note: The Netscape Communications server uses a different format for its MIME map and stores it in a file named mime.types. The format is more complex, but potentially easier to understand, because the two columns of each entry have labels, as shown in the following excerpt:

```
type=application/oda        exts=oda
type=application/pdf        exts=pdf
type=image/jpeg             exts=jpeg,jpg,jpe
```

As you can see, Netscape has added labels to the two columns of the mime.types file, with the left column containing not only the MIME data type/subtype (image/jpeg, for example), but also the identifying label type, followed by an equal sign (=). Similarly, the right column includes the label exts, along with the filename extensions. The Netscape mime.types file also includes an optional third column, not found in other servers' files, specifying an icon to be associated with the MIME data type/subtype. The Netscape server also provides for a secondary mime.types file, with your localizations, specified in the magnus.conf file.

If you plan to use Microsoft Word on your Intranet, and if you plan to keep the default file extension of .doc for all your Word documents, you are already set because IIS installs the Word MIME key automatically. However, to set up your Web server for other word processors, you'll need to make appropriate changes to the Registry.

As you can see in the preceding Registry excerpt, IIS also installs the .dot extension for Word document templates. If you need to use more than one file extension per application, IIS will expect them to appear on separate lines in the Registry. Normally, Word uses the filename extension .doc, although you can use anything you like. Early versions of WordPerfect had no default filename extension, but the latest releases use .wpd. If your customers are running WordPerfect, you may need to use both .wpd and one or more of your own choosing for backward compatibility.

Warning: Double-check your common filename extensions to make sure they don't duplicate any of the standard MIME entries. Otherwise, you may get unexpected results.

There is also a ready-made entry for another word processor I'll talk about later in this chapter, Windows Write (for your Windows for Workgroups customers) or Windows WordPad (for your customers running Windows 95 and Windows NT 4). The following is the IIS MIME entry for .wri files:

```
application/x-mswrite,wri,,5
```

When you're finished editing the MIME map in RegEdit, just close the application.

> **Note:** Please consult Chapter 6, "Windows NT 4 Configuration," for more information about the structure of the Windows NT Registry and how to manage it using RegEdit.

Implementing Changes in the MIME Map

Because you've changed the configuration of your Web server by editing one of its setup files, you now need to make the server aware of your changes. If your server isn't already running, it will read the changes as part of its normal start-up procedure. If IIS is already running, you can have it reread its configuration files by stopping and restarting the WWW Publishing Service. You can do this through the Internet Services Manager or through the Services icon in Control Panel.

Adding Word Processing Documents to Your Web Server

If you followed along in the preceding sections of this chapter, you've finished setting up your Web server to properly identify and serve your word processor's documents. Your next step is to populate your server with some documents.

You can transfer your documents to your Web server by using your network shared/mapped drives, FTP in binary mode, or floppy disks. Whichever method you use, it's probably a good idea to put the documents in a dedicated directory for word processing documents. If you use more than one word processor, create a separate server directory for each. After you've created these directories, you'll need to create some sort of HTML listing of them. This listing can be as simple or as complex as you like because including hyperlinks to word processing documents is exactly the same as setting up links to other kinds of documents. Using Microsoft Word as an example, a simple HTML listing might be something like the following:

```
<HTML>
<HEAD>
<TITLE>Word Documents</TITLE>
</HEAD>
<BODY>
<H1>Microsoft Word Documents</H1>
This directory contains a set of Word Documents.
Just click on one to open it up in Word.<P>
<UL>
<LI><A HREF="health.doc">Document 1</A>,
```

```
Memo about Health Insurance</LI>
<LI><A HREF="holiday.doc">Document 2</A>,
Holiday Schedule</LI>
<LI><A HREF="usedfurn.doc">Document 3</A>,
Used Office Furniture Inventory</LI>
</UL>
If you haven't already done so, you must set up your Web browser
to understand Word documents.
<A HREF="word_setup.html">Here are instructions.</A>
</BODY>
</HTML>
```

This code appears on the accompanying CD-ROM as the file Word Documents.htm. The code can be modified easily to use another word processor's documents. Figure 13.1 shows this HTML code rendered in NCSA Mosaic. As you can see, it looks like just any other Web page. Users with properly set up Web browsers can click the hyperlinks to run Word (or whatever word processor you've set up) with a copy of the selected document. Before you can use this page to load the hyperlinked Word documents, however, your Web browser must be set up to use your specific word processor as a helper application.

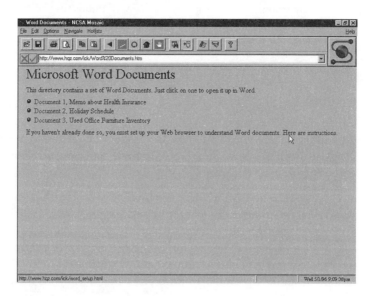

Figure 13.1. *The HTML page for Word documents as it will appear in Mosaic.*

Setting Up Microsoft Word as a Helper Application on the Client

Now that you have set up your Web server to know about Word documents and populated it with some data files from the package, your next step is to set up Word as a helper application. The concept of setting up helper applications for Web browsers is a general one, but the steps for doing it differ among browsers. The following sections go through the steps for NCSA Mosaic and Netscape. If you're using another browser, you may need to take a look at its documentation to find out how to do this procedure.

NCSA Mosaic 2.x and Word for Windows

NCSA Mosaic provides a graphical interface for setting up helper applications, although Mosaic uses the term *external viewer* rather than helper application. In Mosaic, open the Options menu, and then select Preferences. The Preferences dialog box opens. Click the Viewers tab.

As you can see in Figure 13.2, there are four fill-in boxes and several buttons that enable you to control external viewers. Figure 13.2 shows the dialog box already filled in for the Microsoft WAVE audio player.

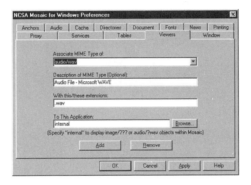

Figure 13.2. The Mosaic Viewers dialog is used to configure MIME types.

The top box, Associate MIME Type of, contains a MIME data type/subtype pair—in this case audio/wav. The second fill-in box is an optional description of the kind of data file; in this example, it's Audio File - Microsoft WAVE. The third fill-in box, With this/these extensions, contains the same information as the filename-extension information in the IIS MIME map in the Registry. The last fill-in box, To this application, is where you specify which program will function as your helper application. In Figure 13.2, the special keyword internal is used in this box to indicate that Mosaic can handle this MIME type/subtype by itself, without a helper application. Note the Browse button next to this box; you'll be using it to set up Microsoft Word as your helper application.

Now that your tour of the Viewers tab is complete, it's time to configure Microsoft Word as your helper application. Click the Add button to open up the Add Viewer dialog box shown in Figure 13.3. This box has the same four fill-in boxes as Figure 13.2, but they're blank (initially) so you can enter your own information. Knowing what you now know about Figure 13.2 and the MIME map in the Registry (from Chapter 12), you can quickly fill in these blanks:

◆ In the Associate MIME Type of box, enter `application/msword`.

◆ In the Description of MIME Type (Optional) box, enter something like `Microsoft Word Document`. Note that you're not required to enter anything in this box, although it's a good idea if you do so for future reference.

◆ In the With this/these extensions box, enter `doc wrd`. (Mosaic and Netscape, unlike IIS, can handle multiple extensions per row for the same data type.)

◆ Finally, in the To This Application box, enter the full drive and pathname to the Microsoft Word executable program. If you're not sure about this pathname, click the Browse button to locate the executable program you want. When you've found it, select it.

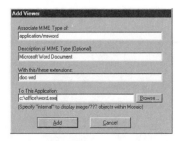

Figure 13.3. *Adding a viewer.*

Click the Add button to save your changes. You're now ready to try out your new setup. Close the Preferences dialog box by clicking OK, and then select Open Document from the Mosaic File menu. Enter the URL of a Word document on your Web server. Mosaic contacts the Web server and asks for the document. As described in detail in Chapter 12, the server sends back header information identifying the document as the MIME type/subtype `application/msword`. Mosaic reads this information, and then passes the incoming document off to Word for viewing, dynamically starting up Word with a copy of the document. At this point, you have all the features and power of Word available to you to edit, save, and print the document.

Note: It's important to note that you're working with a temporary copy of the document, not the original, which is still safe on your Web server. As a result, you're free to make any changes you want to the document without disrupting its contents for the next customer on your Intranet. The disadvantage of this system is that it lacks the potential for a collaborative documentation process. (You might have been hoping I was just about to describe such a feature.) Alas, such a feat would be a bit too magical for the Intranet to pull off all by itself. But Chapter 28, "Collaboration on Your Intranet," shows how Web collaboration is indeed possible—with a little more work and some extra software.

> **Note:** If you get errors about Word being unable to load your document, and you're sure that you've specified the correct URL on your Web server and the permissions on the file are correct, your workstation or PC may be running low on memory. Close down other open applications and/or turn off some of Word's features to conserve memory. If you are using Windows 3.1, you may also need to use a memory manager like QEMM or Microsoft Memmaker that comes with DOS. Also, make sure that the workstation isn't running any unnecessary network protocols. You obviously need TCP/IP, but you might have an opportunity to save some memory if NetBEUI and/or IPX/SPX aren't used on your LAN.

Netscape Navigator 2.x and Word for Windows

Netscape on Microsoft Windows provides a graphical interface for setting up helper applications. Open the Options menu, and then select General Preferences. The Preferences dialog box appears. Click the Helpers tab (shown in Figure 13.4).

Figure 13.4. The Netscape Helpers dialog is used to configure MIME types.

Figure 13.4 shows the scrollable File type list that contains preset helper applications; clicking one of them displays some details of the setup. In Figure 13.4, the audio/x-wav file type has been selected. The File type window should remind you of the contents of the MIME map on your Web server, with its columns specifying MIME data types/subtypes (on the left) and filename extensions (on the right).

Below the File type window, you'll see File / MIME Type, with Subtype on the next line. Below that, there's a fill-in File Extensions box. In Figure 13.4, the File / MIME Type item is filled in as audio and the subtype filled in as x-wav. The File Extensions box contains wav.

At the bottom of the dialog, there are several option buttons that enable you to choose what to do with incoming data of the MIME type/subtype application/x-wav. In Figure 13.4, Launch the

Application is selected. The bottom-most box is where you enter the name and path of the program that you want to function as your helper application. In Figure 13.4, the drive and path to the Microsoft Windows Media Player application, `mplay32.exe`, is filled in. Notice Netscape has picked up the Windows icon for `mplay32`, displaying it just to the left of the box.

To configure Microsoft Word as your helper application, click the Create New Type button in the Helpers tab to open up the Configure New Mime Type dialog box. This box has two fill-in boxes for your information about the new MIME type/subtype. In Figure 13.5, the information for Word has been filled in just like in the MIME map used by IIS.

Figure 13.5. *The Configure New Mime Type dialog is used to add Word as a Netscape helper.*

Fill in your information, and then click OK. You are returned to the Helpers tab with the MIME type information you just entered filled in. You now need to enter `doc` and `wrd` in the File Extensions box. Finally, click the Launch the Application option button and fill in the full drive and pathname to the Microsoft Word executable program. If you're not sure about this pathname, click the Browse button to locate the executable you want. When you've found it, select it. Notice that in Figure 13.6, Netscape has located and displayed the Word icon.

Figure 13.6. *The Netscape Helpers dialog after Word has been added.*

Figure 13.6 shows the Helpers tab filled in with Microsoft Word information. (Your drive and path to the Word executable program may be different than the one shown, so make sure you locate yours rather than just copying what's shown in the figure.) After you fill in all the information for your helper application, click OK to save your changes.

You're now ready to try out your new setup. Close the Preferences windows by clicking OK, and then click the Open button on Netscape's toolbar. Enter the URL of a Word document on your Web server. Netscape contacts the Web server and asks for the document. As described in Chapter 12, the server sends back header information identifying the document as the MIME type/subtype `application/msword`. Netscape reads this information, and then passes the incoming document off to Word for viewing, dynamically starting up Word with a copy of the document. At this point, you have added the power of Word into Netscape and you can edit, save, and print documents retrieved through the Intranet. Just remember, the documents are only local copies.

Setting Up Write, WordPad, and Other Word Processors as Helper Applications

The earlier procedures in this chapter described how to set up your Web server to know about Word documents and how to populate the Web server with some data files from Word; you can do the exact same procedures to use Windows Write (or WordPad) as a helper application. The steps are exactly the same except that you will use the MIME type/subtype of `application/mswrite` rather than `application/msword`, and you will change the file extension in the server MIME map from `doc` to `wri`. As discussed previously, you don't have to perform that last step following an installation of IIS. However, if you are using another Web server, you'll want to check its MIME map documentation to determine for yourself if it, too, is preconfigured for Word, WordPad, and Write. (If it's a Windows NT commercial Web server, it will probably already have Word, WordPad, Write, and dozens of other common office applications listed in its MIME map.)

The concept of setting up Write or WordPad as helper applications for Web browsers is also a general one. The exact steps differ only slightly depending on the Web browser you're using. Because I have already gone through the steps for Netscape and Mosaic, with screenshots from each browser, I'll avoid repeating myself here.

You should be able to use the general principles described in this chapter to set up other word processing packages as helper applications. As each of the previous sections has shown, the major steps in this process are as follows:

1. Add entries to the MIME map in the Registry on your Web server for your word processor's data files.

2. Place some word processor documents on your Web server.

3. Provide an HTML page on the Web server that references those documents using hyperlinks. Of course, your customers need to know the URL of that HTML page if it will lead them to the documents they seek.

4. Configure the word processor on the client computers as a helper application for your Web browser using the fill-in screens shown in this chapter.

Free Read-Only Viewers

Although I mentioned in Chapter 3, "The Software Tools to Build a Web," that some word processors can read documents created in others, and that many use RTF (Rich Text Format) as a means of converting documents from one format to another, the problem of dealing with foreign word processor documents (that is, documents created by word processing packages other than your own) is a perennial one. Each of the three major word processor manufacturers, Microsoft, WordPerfect, and Adobe's Frame Technologies, have made available free read-only viewers for their documents. These viewers include the following:

◆ Microsoft's Word Viewer for Windows, available on the CD and at the URL:

`http://www.microsoft.com/msword/fs_wd.htm`

◆ Envoy for WordPerfect on Windows, available at the following URL:

`http://wp.novell.com/busapps/win/tocen10w.htm`

◆ Frame Reader versions for UNIX, Windows, and Macintosh are available in separate directories at the following FTP site:

`ftp://ftp.frame.com/pub/techsup/product_updates`

Each of these packages reads and displays documents created by their associated word processor. You need not own the particular word processor with which these viewers are associated to use them. Although you cannot edit documents in these programs, you can save and print documents.

Although these packages work in stand-alone mode for viewing documents, you can also set them up as Web browser helper applications. In other words, you can set up your Intranet Web server to know about each of the formats, and then provide the read-only viewers to your customers instead of the full applications. That way, customers can view all the available documents regardless of whether they have the correct word processor.

Helper application setup for the viewers is exactly the same as the setup for word processors described in this chapter. Just substitute the read-only viewer as the executable program to be launched based on the MIME type/subtype of the documents.

Summary

This chapter has focused on setting up your Intranet to use common office word processors as Web helper applications. Using the information in this chapter, you can set up libraries of documents in your own word processor file format and make them available on your Web. Your customers can use their Web browsers to locate documents in the library, and then start up their word processors by clicking a Web hyperlink. Specifically, this chapter has covered the following topics within discussions of each of several major word processors and browsers:

◆ The importance of being able to retrieve documents directly into your word processor using a Web browser

- ◆ Configuration of your World Wide Web server software to understand your word processor's document files
- ◆ Configuration of your World Wide Web browser software to handle word processor documents, including viewing foreign word processor documents
- ◆ Potential uses of these capabilities

Chapter 14, "Publishing Spreadsheets on the Intranet," covers office spreadsheet packages, showing you specifically how to set up Microsoft Excel to function as a Web browser helper application. The concepts presented apply just as easily to Lotus 1-2-3 or any other spreadsheet.

CHAPTER

◆

Publishing Spreadsheets on the Intranet

- ◆ The benefits of integrating your spreadsheet and your Intranet
- ◆ Web server setup
- ◆ Adding spreadsheet data files to your Web server
- ◆ Setting up Microsoft Excel as a helper application
- ◆ Spreadsheet data file portability
- ◆ Overview of Intranet spreadsheet applications
- ◆ Indexing your spreadsheet data
- ◆ Sample Intranet spreadsheets

In Chapter 13, "Word Processing on the Web," you learned how to set up your word processor as a Web browser helper application. In this chapter, you add to that knowledge and learn how to set up your Intranet so that customers can retrieve spreadsheet data files using their Web browser and automatically open the files in their favorite spreadsheet software for revision, what-if analysis, recalculation, graphing, and more.

I focus on examples that use Excel and Explorer, Mosaic, and Netscape. If your organization uses other spreadsheet packages, you'll still be able to easily apply the ideas, if not the step-by-step instructions, in this chapter. Indeed, you can apply the ideas from this chapter and Chapter 12 to almost any computer program in the office.

Later in the chapter, I touch on the issue of portability of spreadsheet data files from one package to another. The chapter ends with a discussion of how spreadsheets can be put to great advantage on the Intranet and demonstrates some sample applications.

Why Integrate Your Spreadsheet and Your Intranet?

One of the reasons for the great success of Microsoft Windows is how well it integrates application software like spreadsheets into the desktop environment, enabling the user to start up any spreadsheet with a mouse click.

Integrating your spreadsheet in your Intranet is, in a sense, creating a new graphical interface for users based on your Web browser. Doing so allows you to tie in links to your everyday tools, like your spreadsheet, and provide a new interface with a common look and feel that's both easy and fun to use.

More importantly, you can use your Web server, HTML, your spreadsheet package, and other tools to put together shareable data warehouses of spreadsheet data files. Such libraries can be complete with searchable indices and point-and-click access through your Web browser. Locating and displaying a spreadsheet data file is no longer a process of finding a file, and then starting up your spreadsheet to read or use it. Using a Web browser, your customer can instead click a Web hyperlink and have the spreadsheet fire up with a copy of the data file loaded, all in one simple process. After the spreadsheet program has loaded the file, your customers have all the capabilities of the spreadsheet program at their disposal; they can change the data, recalculate it, graph it, print it, save it, and so on.

As with commercial groupware packages like Lotus Notes (see Chapter 28, "Collaboration on Your Intranet"), expensive data warehouse software packages are available, but you can easily replicate many of their features in your Intranet. Moreover, you can do so at a substantially lower cost and without requiring users to learn to use yet another new software package. Because they'll be using their familiar Web browser as the interface to your homegrown data warehouse and their everyday spreadsheet package to examine and manipulate the stored data, you need not purchase another package. In fact, and I realize I'm repeating myself here, one of the greatest things about the Intranet is that the Web browser is so inexpensive to deploy (Mosaic and Explorer are free).

You can store company sales or production data, for example, on your Web server in spreadsheet format, complete with formulas and macro commands. Properly set up, your Web server can provide those data files when users select hyperlinks pointing to them. Web browsers can then take the data and hand it off to your customers' spreadsheet package, which they can use to play with the numbers for forecasting or preparing presentation graphics.

Even if you use your Intranet exclusively to serve spreadsheet data files, you may well spend less money on hardware and software to do so than you would spend in buying a commercial data warehouse package. If your Web is already serving other purposes, a few minutes' work can set it up to function as an essentially free data warehouse. Although these commercial packages have features that you won't be able to replicate in your Intranet, the price of implementing those features you can replicate is certainly right, and you may find that you're able to replicate enough of these features to make it unnecessary to buy a data warehouse package.

You'll recall from earlier chapters the terms *helper application* and *external viewers* to refer to computer programs that your Web browser uses when it can't directly display a type of data that you have downloaded. In this chapter, your spreadsheet package is treated as a helper application. However, to avoid pointless repetition here in the fundamental setup and configuration of helper applications, I'll often refer you to Chapter 12, "MIME and Helper Applications," and Chapter 13, "Word Processing on the Web." The information in those chapters is all that you need to configure your Intranet to serve spreadsheets.

Web Server Setup

Regardless of which spreadsheet package you use, your first step in setting up your spreadsheet as a helper application is to configure your Web server to know about your spreadsheet's data files. With small differences, as are noted in context, the instructions in this section apply to any spreadsheet, and even to any word processor (as discussed in Chapter 13).

As you learned in Chapter 12, Web servers use the MIME mechanism to identify documents according to their MIME data type/subtype. Remember that the MIME mechanism divides data into a relatively small handful of data types, with each type further subdivided into subtypes. Spreadsheet data files fall into the application data type.

You also learned in Chapter 12 how Web servers use filename extensions to map data files on the server to a MIME data type/subtype. You associate the filename extensions with MIME types/subtypes in the Windows NT Registry on the Web server, if you are using IIS, or in a configuration text file, if you are using some other Windows NT Web servers.

> **Note:** Please refer to the section titled "Editing the Registry MIME Map" in Chapter 13 for detailed information about configuring IIS. The concepts described in that section for word processors can be applied to spreadsheets as well.

Adding Spreadsheet Data Files to Your Web Server

Assuming that you've completed the setup of your Web server to properly identify and serve your spreadsheet data files, your next step is to populate your server with some data files for your spreadsheet program. The Explorer in Windows NT 4 makes this task easy. All you have to do is share the drive or directory on the Web server, and map the drive or directory on the computer that you want to copy the files from (again using Explorer or Network Neighborhood).

To share a folder in NT, just right-click it in Explorer. That opens a context-sensitive menu. Slide the mouse down to the item called Properties at the bottom. Click the Sharing tab, and you will see a dialog very similar to one in Figure 14.1. Just click the Share As radio button to share the drive. The default share name is probably fine (in the context of this discussion), and you don't have to get into the security options (by clicking the Permissions button in this example) unless you feel the need to do so.

Figure 14.1. *Sharing a folder in the Windows NT Explorer is as easy as 1-2-3.*

Windows often enables you to do things more than one way. The context-sensitive menu from the preceding paragraph also includes an item that takes you directly to the Sharing tab. Furthermore, you can go to the Sharing tab from the Explorer menubar by choosing File | Properties | Sharing (assuming you have already selected the given file or folder in the lower left pane window).

You also can copy files through shared network drives if your Web server is in a separate domain from the data files, unless your system administrators have chosen not to configure a trust relationship between the domains for security reasons. If you have no trust relationships between domains, regardless of whether the Web server is located an inconvenient physical distance away, you can fall back to the traditional UNIX method of copying files on the network: FTP. Consult Chapter 9, "Adding FTP and Gopher Services," for information about running the IIS FTP service and then you can happily copy files to your server using an FTP client program, such as CuteFTP included on the CD-ROM with this book. Whatever method you use, you should put the files in a dedicated directory on your Web server for your particular spreadsheet package.

Next, you must create some sort of HTML listing of the data files. This listing can be as simple or as complex as you like; setting up hyperlinks to spreadsheet data files is exactly the same as setting up links to other kinds of documents. A simple HTML listing, using Microsoft Excel as an example, might be something like the following (adapted in seconds from the code in Chapter 13):

Listing 14.1. This HTML code provides links to spreadsheet files.

```
<HTML>
<HEAD>
<TITLE>Excel Spreadsheets</TITLE>
</HEAD>
<BODY>
<H1>Microsoft Excel Spreadsheets</H1>
This directory contains a set of Excel spreadsheets.
Just click on one to open it up in Excel.
<UL>
<LI><A HREF="qrtrly_sales.xls">Spreadsheet 1</A>,
Last Quarter's Sales</LI>
<LI><A HREF="qrtrly_prod.xls">Spreadsheet 2</A>,
Last Quarter's Production</LI>
<LI><A HREF="cpi_forecast.xls">Spreadsheet 3</A>,
Consumer Price Index Forecasts</LI>
</UL>
If you haven't already done so, you must set up your Web browser
to understand Excel spreadsheet data files.
<A HREF="excel_setup.html">Here are instructions.</A>
</BODY>
</HTML>
```

Setting Up Microsoft Excel as a Helper Application

Now that you have set up your Web server to know about spreadsheet data files and populated it with some actual data files from the spreadsheet program, your next step is to set up Excel as a helper application. The concept of setting up helper applications for Web browsers is a general one, but the steps for going about it differ depending on the Web browser you're using. Please see the section titled "Setting Up Microsoft Word as a Helper Application on the Client" in Chapter 13 for detailed information about how to accomplish this step in both Mosaic and Netscape. If you're using another browser, you may need to take a look at its documentation to find out how to accomplish this step.

Just keep in mind as you go that Excel uses .xls as the default extension for spreadsheet documents. You should also add .xlm to the MIME map to cover Excel macro spreadsheets that your customers have written or want to retrieve. Further, .xcl and .xlw are also widely used.

Setting Up Excel or Lotus as a Helper Application for Your Macintosh Customers

There is no requirement that every client machine on a Windows NT network be a PC. Independent of the Intranet, Windows NT 4 Server provides excellent connectivity to Macintosh computers using the AppleTalk protocol. (Obviously, to take advantage of the Intranet, a Macintosh will need to have its own TCP/IP software loaded in addition to, or instead of, AppleTalk.) If you have Macintosh users in your organization, you may need to provide them with Intranet access to spreadsheet documents. After all, once you've gone to the effort of setting up the server, you may as well get the most benefit out of it by letting everyone participate.

Macintosh users will find the process of setting up Excel or Lotus 1-2-3 as a viewer/helper application virtually identical to the process for Windows PCs. The only difference is in specifying the folder and executable names for the spreadsheet program. You can use the Browse process, just as in Windows, with the browser displaying Mac folder names in place of PC directory names.

Other Spreadsheet Packages

You should be able to use the general principles described in this chapter to set up other spreadsheet packages as helper applications. As each of the preceding sections has shown, the major steps in setting up a program as a helper application are as follows:

1. Add entries to the MIME map on your Web server for your spreadsheet's data files.
2. Set up some data files on your Web server.
3. Provide an HTML page to link to the documents.
4. Configure your spreadsheet as a helper application for your Web browser using the fill-in screens shown in Chapter 13.

Spreadsheet Data File Portability

Because your organization may use multiple spreadsheet packages, you should anticipate your customers' needs for data file portability. This section discusses two options:

◆ Supporting multiple spreadsheet formats
◆ Converting spreadsheet data to other formats

Supporting Multiple Spreadsheet Data File Formats

Your organization may use more than just a single spreadsheet program, and, if so, you're probably wondering how you make the various data files portable. Like many word processors, many spreadsheet packages can read data files in other spreadsheet programs' native formats. Excel, for example, can directly read 1-2-3 files, and 1-2-3 can read Excel files. As a result, if your company uses multiple spreadsheet packages, you can share your data among them using their capabilities to read each others' data file formats.

Warning: Be careful not to use duplicate entries in your Web server's MIME map. For example, don't do the following:

```
application/msexcel       xls xcl wks
application/lotus         wks xls xcl
application/xess3         xs3 wks
```

Web servers read the MIME map linearly, from top to bottom, until they find a match of filename extensions. With entries like those in the preceding example, your Web server's MIME type/subtype header information for .wks files will always be read as application/ msexcel. This may not be what you want if you have Lotus or Xess customers.

Each spreadsheet customer in your Web will need to configure his browser based on the spreadsheet he uses. Web browsers will override the MIME type/subtype header information they receive if you have configured them to do so.

Any new MIME type/subtype information you've added in your helper application setup in your Web browser is added to the browser's internal list. If you set up your browser to use 1-2-3 as a helper application when it encounters the filename extension .wks, it will use 1-2-3 on any file with that extension, even if one of the following things happens:

◆ The server provides no MIME type/subtype information at all, as is the case with an FTP or Gopher server.

◆ The server does provide MIME type/subtype information, but that information is for a different spreadsheet package.

In other words, your local helper application setup can both fill in missing MIME type/subtype information and override what it gets from the Web server. Suppose you've set up your Web server's MIME map to have entries like the following:

```
application/msexcel,xls,,5
application/msexcel,xlc,,5
application/lotus,wks,,5
```

Further suppose that a particular customer has only the 1-2-3 spreadsheet package on her PC. Because you know Excel can directly read 1-2-3 data files, you can extend the preceding Excel helper application setup by adding a 1-2-3 filename extension. For example, Mosaic should be set up to use Excel not only for files with the .xls, .xlm, .xlw, and .xcl extensions, but also for those with .wks. Note that you can modify the Mosaic Description of MIME Type to include a reminder of this change.

In addition to some spreadsheets being able to directly read the data files created by others, most have a Save As feature that allows you to save a native data file in some other spreadsheet package's format. Excel, for example, supports saving data files in several variations of Lotus 1-2-3's .wks format, as well as several others. Lotus has a similar feature, enabling you to save data files in Excel's .xls format.

There's also a semi-universal spreadsheet data file format many packages support, the Symbolic Link Format, that often uses a filename extension of .slk. (This format is much like the Rich Text Format used in making word processing documents portable.) You can use this format to make multiple copies of spreadsheet data files on your Web server with versions for each spreadsheet package your customers use. Alternatively, because most packages support the Symbolic Link Format, you may just want to use that format for all your data files. If you do so, be sure your Web server's MIME map and your customers' browser setup correspond.

Converting Spreadsheet Data to Other Formats

Both Excel and 1-2-3 have Save As functions that enable you to not only save spreadsheet data files in other spreadsheet formats, but also to save a spreadsheet in plain text format. Xess (for UNIX) has the same capability, along with the capability to save in PostScript format. Although recalculation and other capabilities are lost, of course, when a spreadsheet is saved in plain text or PostScript, the tabular layout and data are preserved. You can view these plain text files in your Web browser just like any other text file. You can view PostScript files with an appropriate PostScript viewer helper application.

Jordan Evans of the U.S. National Aeronautics and Space Administration has written XL2HTML, a Visual Basic for Applications (VBA) macro for Excel 5.0 that converts an Excel spreadsheet into an HTML table. Written for Excel 5.0 for Windows, the macro also works on both Macintosh Excel 5.0 and the Windows 95 version, Excel 7.0 (according to its author). A copy is on the CD-ROM that accompanies this book. You can specify a range of cells to be converted, and XL2HTML outputs HTML Table markup and retains character formatting, such as boldface, and underlining, from the original spreadsheet.

You can learn more about XL2HTML at http://www710.gsfc.nasa.gov/704/dgd/xl2html.html; instructions are included. As with spreadsheet files saved in plain text, customer interactivity (the ability to change and recalculate the spreadsheet) is lost in XL2HTML, and it would not be when using the spreadsheet program itself as a helper application. Nonetheless, you may find situations in which XL2HTML is useful for your Web.

Microsoft now has available for free download from its Web site (http://www.microsoft.com) a version of its Internet Assistant (IA) for Excel (also available on the CD-ROM that accompanies this book). Like the companion IA products for Microsoft Word and PowerPoint, this package enables you to save Office data files (in this case, Excel spreadsheets) directly to HTML format for use on your Intranet. IA supports version 5.0 of Excel in both Windows 3.1 and NT and Macintosh and version 7.0 on Windows 95.

Tip: While you're visiting the Microsoft Web site, you may also want to download a copy of a read-only Excel Viewer for Windows 95. Just as you set up Excel itself as a Web browser helper application, you can set up the Excel Viewer as one for customers who don't have their own copy of Excel. Although a version of the Excel Viewer for Windows is included on the CD-ROM with this book, you may need to obtain a more current version directly from the Microsoft Web site in the future.

Overview of Intranet Spreadsheet Applications

The rest of this chapter focuses on what you might do with spreadsheets on your Intranet. The ideas presented are meant to serve as examples; I encourage you to creatively adapt them to the specific needs of your own organization.

If you're into spreadsheets, perhaps you like to compare costs. Expensive data warehouse software packages are available from a number of vendors. These packages accumulate information from a variety of sources around an organization and provide database-like front ends, allowing searches for mostly numerical data. Data sources can include a number of different corporate databases running on different platforms. Once located, the data can be downloaded for local number crunching to users' PCs or workstations, usually in a spreadsheet package.

In this section, you'll learn about using your Intranet as a data warehouse, making full-blown, ready-to-run spreadsheet data files available to your customers. Although less capable than true data warehouse packages, your Intranet data warehouse shares many features with its larger cousins and at a much smaller price. You may find the trade-off worthwhile.

Cliché has it the spreadsheet was the first *killer app* for the PC, so it's no surprise that spreadsheet applications are used in many organizations. Individual users create and maintain their own spreadsheets, sometimes for personal use, sometimes shared. Often, the numbers used in the spreadsheets are company-wide data on sales, production, and other statistically measurable information. Collectively, your customers probably already have a great deal of useful data in spreadsheet format that could be quite valuable on your Intranet.

Of course, you probably don't want to go snooping on your Intranet customers' PCs or in their private fileserver directories for candidate spreadsheet files. But you should encourage your customers to contribute information for your Intranet. As you'll see, the collaborative aspects of making spreadsheets available on your Intranet should encourage customers to contribute. Although locating documents in this way may be a tedious, logistical problem, it's still possible, and what you find will provide the basis of your Intranet spreadsheet data.

The main principles of this activity are those already outlined, in this chapter and in others, with respect to the conversion of your legacy data for your Intranet. Where you have spreadsheet data available, you'll want to use what you learned previously to move this data quickly onto your Intranet, making it accessible via your Web server. Your customers will use their Web browsers to retrieve the data files into the spreadsheet helper applications (such as Excel, or the Excel Viewer) running on their own machines.

If you have multiple spreadsheet applications in use in your company, you may need to select a common spreadsheet data file format, such as standard Lotus format, which most other spreadsheets can read, or the exportable SYLK format. (See your spreadsheet documentation for its capabilities in this area.) Even though many, or even most, of your customers have the necessary spreadsheet software available to them, you might also want to make plain-text versions of the data files available for the benefit of customers who don't have the software. For example, a company schedule built in Excel could be saved in text format without losing the tabular formatting. Either Internet Assistant for Excel or the XL2HTML VBA script mentioned earlier in the chapter can help out with this task.

As you've learned, the basic setup of Web pages containing simple, clickable lists of available documents is quite easy. Adding a little subject matter organization is simple, too; use hyperlinks to create nested menu listings and add explanatory text to the pages. In just a few minutes, you can present a useful list of available spreadsheet data files to your customers.

For example, monthly reports can contain clickable cross-references to other documents, statistical tables, live spreadsheet data files, images, or even earlier months' reports (all with the same kinds of embedded links). Your customers can then use their Web browsers to jump from one document to another, looking for answers to questions by following promising threads. Where they come across spreadsheet data, they'll be able to look at it and even manipulate it using their own spreadsheet software as Web browser helper applications.

The more cross-references and hyperlinks you're able to add, of course, the more capabilities you'll give to your customers. To give your customers even more options for searching for specific information, you can index the contents of your spreadsheet data files. (This topic is covered later in the chapter.)

Note: Remember that helper applications, like your customers' spreadsheet application, always operate on a copy of the original spreadsheet data file. Your original remains unchanged on your Web server until you change it. Customers can freely change the data in the spreadsheet they've opened with a Web browser helper application (assuming the helper application is not a viewer only) for their own needs, all without touching the original. This situation is directly analogous to the data warehouse, where copies of corporate data are downloaded for local processing without changing the original source data. The purpose of these Intranet spreadsheets is simply to provide raw corporate data, such as sales numbers, or production numbers.

Indexing Your Spreadsheet Data

How will your customers locate spreadsheet data they want without having to go through long on-screen lists of filenames? Subject-oriented menus can help, but only up to a point. Beyond a certain number of files, such a system would become time-consuming. Chapter 21, "Indexing Your Intranet with WAIS," discusses a powerful tool for indexing data on your Intranet. This tool enables your customers to search and retrieve Intranet data from indexes of the files on the server.

If you're familiar with indexing tools on the Internet, you know that they are usually text-based. You probably wonder how binary files such as spreadsheet data files can be indexed with a text-based tool. Experimentation when reading Excel data files reveals that useful indexes can be created. Character strings in spreadsheet files (and other binary files, such as word processor documents) can be rooted out. Virtually all spreadsheet files contain some character strings, primarily as column and row labels; they would not be worth much without these labels to identify the data that the columns contain.

Spreadsheets may also contain significant amounts of text in individual cells as well as in column or row labels. Your Intranet spreadsheet files, when carefully indexed with the right indexing tools, are nearly as searchable as your plain-text data. Searching these indexes is quite fast because, unlike all-text files, the word count of text in most spreadsheet files is quite small and has a limited vocabulary.

Results of your searches show as lists of clickable Web browser hyperlinks, showing the hits on your search keywords. Just as selecting such a hyperlink pointing to a text or HTML document displays the document for viewing in your browser, so does selecting a spreadsheet data file hyperlink. The difference is the spreadsheet data file is handed off to your customer's spreadsheet helper application for viewing. And, of course, once loaded, the spreadsheet is an interactive entity your customer can use, not a static Web page that just sits there.

Tip: Mosaic gives downloaded spreadsheet data files a temporary filename (such as `mos2.wk4`). Netscape generates a completely random temporary filename for spreadsheet files you open. To save the file, give it a meaningful name and save it in a permanent place in your system.

The EMWAC WAIS package included on the CD-ROM with this book is an indexing tool that is distributed as freeware. Depending on the extent and nature of the overall library of documents on your Intranet and your customers' indexing needs, you may want also to look into commercial full-text indexing tools.

Sample Intranet Spreadsheets

Assuming you've made spreadsheet data files available on your Intranet, this section examines how your customers might use these files.

Intranet Spreadsheets Versus Data Warehouses

Because of the generic nature of data accessible from standard data warehouse applications, the numerical data customers retrieve is not in spreadsheet format, ready for them to use. Rather, it's in raw, plain text, as columns of numbers or text with the entries on each line separated by a field separator. A spreadsheet package can import such raw data, including both numerical data and text row and column headings, provided the customer tells it about the format of the incoming data.

Microsoft Excel, for example, uses its TextWizard feature to prompt the customer through the importing of the incoming data. Lotus 1-2-3 accepts only a few standard field separators and also requires row and column labels to meet a specific format. Thus, even though customers can bring rows and columns of text and data into their spreadsheet package, the resulting spreadsheet isn't of much more value than a plain tabular listing of numbers and text. Customers have to take the time to add formulas and other spreadsheet-specific features. For the imported data to be immediately useful, each customer needs to have spent time building spreadsheet templates containing the necessary housekeeping that allows imported raw data to be dealt with.

Negative-sounding comparisons between commercial data warehouse applications and spreadsheet applications on your Intranet shouldn't be taken too far. Data warehouse packages have many strong features not present in the more limited situation described in this chapter. For instance, data warehouse packages can browse a variety of sources, including multiple corporate databases, and then integrate the chosen data into a single spreadsheet for ad hoc manipulation. Canned Intranet spreadsheets can't match this capability, though it can be roughly replicated through saving and combining individual downloaded spreadsheets.

Your trade-off is between cost and features. (Cost includes more than purchase price; it also includes staff time.) If you need the advanced features an industrial-strength data warehouse package provides, you'll want to get one. Nevertheless, you don't want to ignore the ability to replicate and improve on some of these packages' features on your Intranet at very low cost. If you can get 75 percent of the features of a data warehouse package for five percent of its cost by integrating replication into your Intranet, you may still be ahead of the game, even taking into account staff costs. Only you can decide on the value of the remaining 25 percent.

Keep in mind that Web interfaces to the major data warehouse packages haven't arrived on the scene yet. Because your overall objective in using Web technology for your Intranet is to enable use of your customers' Web browsers as front ends to as much organizational data as possible, this is a critical point. Each vendor's data warehouse has its own user interface, and although these can be perfectly good, user-friendly graphical interfaces, each one is different. Customers have to learn to use the interface before it's much good to them. On the other hand, your customers already know how to use their Web browser.

The critical difference between the generic data warehouse approach and the Intranet spreadsheet approach becomes clear in this context. The spreadsheet your Intranet customers access by clicking a Web page hyperlink is already a live, ready-to-run spreadsheet in their own spreadsheet packages' formats. Formulas, spreadsheet layout, and all the other housekeeping details are already in place.

If you provide, for example, spreadsheet data files containing corporate revenue, expense, and inventory information together with appropriate formulas linking the information, customers can do quick what-if analyses by changing some of the numbers in their temporary copy of the spreadsheet or by resorting the data to get different views of it. Similarly, interactive macro commands can be built into commonly accessed spreadsheets. Thus, customers can run their spreadsheet's statistical-analysis tools (frequency distribution, regression analysis, data matrices, and so on) on a range of spreadsheet cells they interactively select.

What Can You Do with an Intranet Spreadsheet?

What can you do with an Intranet spreadsheet? The quick and easy answer to this question is, of course, anything you can do with any other spreadsheet. Although this answer is both obvious and true, it's not a sufficient answer to the question. To answer this question in the context of your Intranet, think about how your customers might use the spreadsheets you make available to them.

The World Wide Web is revolutionary, enabling technology. It provides new, easy-to-use ways for people to view and use information using their computers. Your customers use their Web browsers, not their standard operating system or windowing interface or data warehouse graphics front end, to access your Intranet spreadsheet data. Your spreadsheet data files are among all the other files available on your Intranet, all of which are accessible by a simple point and click.

By making corporate spreadsheet files available through an internal Web, you will be giving powerful new tools to your customers who use that data. Moreover, the audience of potential users of the data is also vastly increased. Customers who might never use the corporate data filed away in filing cabinets or in annual stockholders' reports, now might begin to use it, potentially benefiting themselves and your company. Putting that data in the form of Web page hyperlinks makes it accessible to everyone in your Intranet. Although doing so might lead on occasion to unqualified people acting as junior actuaries, there's much to be said for making unclassified statistical information widely available to the members of the organization.

Collaborative Aspects of Spreadsheet Sharing Through Your Intranet

As discussed in Chapter 28, spreadsheet data is yet another way in which you can enable your customers to collaborate using your Intranet. Unlike static Web pages, Intranet spreadsheets can be used by customers to do things. Even more important, a spreadsheet is an original creation, aimed at making it possible to view statistical data in some unique way, with the additional ability of refining or changing that view through what-if and other analysis. A spreadsheet is much like the results of an experiment published on your Intranet with the program the scientist wrote to perform the experiment. The data, methodology, and means of rerunning the experiment (that is, the spreadsheet itself) is made available to others who can attempt to replicate the results, possibly refine the view of them, and, of course, use them.

Customer-created spreadsheets, with results based on their unique views of common data, can be made readily accessible by their creators to the rest of your Intranet. Other customers who use these grass-roots spreadsheets are likely to offer comments and improvements to them, stimulating and feeding a collaborative process, generating new ideas, solving research or production problems, and increasing your organization's overall body of knowledge.

A Vital Business Example

Here's a story that may help you see the potential of spreadsheet/Intranet integration. Frank, a salesman for Amalgamated Enterprises can't understand why his clients have started complaining about slow delivery of the widgets he's sold them. Using his laptop, Frank plays with corporate figures in a Lotus 1-2-3 spreadsheet, discovering there's plenty of widget inventory. He probes further and hits on what he thinks might be the problem, although he isn't sure. Deciding to use the Amalgamated Enterprises Intranet to share his analysis, Frank creates a simple Web page (he's not an HTML expert, so it's pretty plain) with a link to his spreadsheet. He uploads both files to the Web server in the home office using his laptop from his motel room in Boise. The Web page points out a potentially dangerous trend in the delivery of widgets, which portends production and inventory problems. Frank has put his analysis into spreadsheet form, made the spreadsheet accessible on the Amalgamated Enterprises Intranet, and asked for comments.

If necessary, Frank can then send e-mail to key people asking them to check out his Web page at their convenience. With this simple stroke, Frank has brought everyone's attention to a problem that may threaten the business. All who want to look at Frank's data need only click his link to do so. If they want to contact Frank, who's on the road, all they need do is click a `mailto` hyperlink to send him e-mail. (Now, I'd like to keep this story as realistic as possible, so given that Frank is a salesman, let's assume that an engineer taught him how to include the `mailto` link in his HTML code.)

It's true that this same sort of collaboration could have been accomplished through any of several other means. Frank could have sent a group e-mail message with the spreadsheet(s) attached or entered it in a Lotus Notes forum. He might well have gotten a good deal of response to either, and possibly even solved his problem. Nevertheless, Frank's simple, direct Intranet presentation is quite effective. Anybody on the Amalgamated Enterprises Intranet can independently view the spreadsheet data using their own spreadsheet software and refine or change the view of the data, recalculate/reanalyze it, and otherwise seek to verify or disprove Frank's conclusions.

Other customers may generate new spreadsheet views of the original data, supporting or disproving Frank's conclusions, and make their own revised versions available on the Intranet as well, for still further collaboration and discussion by the group. Frank will be able to see the new spreadsheet versions and read his e-mail by the time he gets to Seattle the next afternoon. By the following day, the shipping bottleneck having been traced to Denver, the Amalgamated personnel locate 50 flatcars of widgets sitting forgotten on a railroad siding, and Frank's been given a fat bonus. Hooray!

Nuts and Bolts

Continuing the discussion of the widget crisis, you can see some of the possibilities for spreadsheet data on your Intranet. As already discussed, such a situation has a collaborative nature because many Intranet customers can view and verify data in a spreadsheet available through a hyperlinked Web page. Some detailed possibilities for this spreadsheet data include the following:

◆ Numerical spreadsheet data can be quickly turned into charts and graphs to further assist in visualizing the data that the spreadsheet contains.

◆ The data, including the graphs and charts, can be saved or printed locally.

◆ The spreadsheet's data can be combined with other data in new spreadsheets as a means of verifying or extending the original data.

◆ The original or modified spreadsheet data and the graphics can be exported to other applications. Excel spreadsheets and graphics can be popped right into Word documents, for example.

◆ Related corporate databases can be queried for supporting information, and new data can also be imported either into new, more elaborate spreadsheets or other documents.

◆ The generated graphics can be saved as slides for a later presentation.

◆ All the resulting documents, data files, slides, and supporting information can be fed right back onto your Intranet for customer viewing and further collaboration if desired.

Again, each of these separate activities, even for a single overall situation such as Amalgamated's widget crisis, could have been done completely outside the context of your Intranet. Certainly, the importation of spreadsheet data and graphics into word processing documents isn't anything new, nor is the creation of slides from the data using something like PowerPoint, nor is the querying of databases using the spreadsheet software. This integration is one of the primary strengths of integrated office packages such as Microsoft's or Corel's. What is new about this scenario is that it arose and was played out completely on Frank's Intranet, with one customer initiating the collaboration and others participating in the process. And the entire process used Web browsers and browser helper applications. If Frank was right in identifying shipping bottlenecks as the culprit, he helped his own sales by keeping his own clients happy, and he helped Amalgamated Enterprises by moving inventory to make room for urgent plant expansion—all using an Intranet.

Admittedly, this example is pretty contrived; not everyone can save their company from disaster wearing only a Web browser as a loin cloth. Nonetheless, it shows important possibilities for collaboration on your Intranet using lowly spreadsheet data. In a more practical sense, certainly data from multiple hyperlinked spreadsheets on your Intranet can be combined to form altogether new spreadsheets. This process is analogous to, though probably a clumsier process than, the data-warehouse browsing process described earlier, where data from various sources is combined into new spreadsheets for analysis. Spreadsheet numbers also can be turned into charts, graphs, or presentation slides or incorporated into documents, each of which can be plugged right back into your Intranet for more customer viewing and collaboration using Web browsers and helper applications.

Real-Time Intranet Data Feed with a Spreadsheet

Stockbrokers and plant engineers need access to continuously changing information. Spreadsheet packages can be connected to live stock market tickers and other live data feeds. Perhaps more widely useful than a stock market ticker, real-time spreadsheets can monitor data generated by computer controlled instruments in a manufacturing facility, refinery, or laboratory. In such a process control setting, the real-time spreadsheet monitors the instrument's data file as it grows, continuously loading incoming new data into the spreadsheet as it arrives. Whenever your Intranet customers click the link to that process-control spreadsheet, the spreadsheet package fires up as a helper application to display the latest set of data. Through the use of automatically executing macro commands, if available, your spreadsheet could automatically graph the new data as soon as it is loaded.

For example, a clickable HTML image map could be used to represent an overall process, with process control sensor icons in the image map being the hot spots. Clicking one of the sensors reads the latest spreadsheet data file containing data points that are dynamically passed to the spreadsheet graphing tool, called as a helper application.

Summary

You've learned some practical applications of spreadsheet data for your Intranet in this chapter. Use of spreadsheets as Web browser helper applications adds to your Intranet an important feature of interactivity that was heretofore lacking. This interactivity enables your customers to do their work in a completely new way. In addition, you've learned the potential value of collaboration on your Intranet using spreadsheet data as an example. The following is a review of what this chapter discussed:

◆ Why customers want to retrieve spreadsheet data files directly into their spreadsheet application using a Web browser

◆ Configuration of your World Wide Web server to understand your spreadsheet's document files

◆ Configuration of your World Wide Web browser software to handle your spreadsheet data files

◆ How to support multiple spreadsheet data formats

◆ How to survey for available existing spreadsheet data in your organization

◆ How to put your spreadsheet data together so that it's accessible to customers using a Web browser, putting what you've learned about MIME data types/subtypes and Web browser helper applications to work

◆ Indexing tools that can create searchable indexes of your Intranet spreadsheet data files

◆ How the use of interactive helper applications, such as spreadsheets, constitutes important enabling technology for your customers

◆ How a sample Intranet spreadsheet can stimulate collaboration among your customers to solve vital business problems

◆ Techniques to use your Intranet spreadsheet data for ongoing, daily work

The next chapter goes beyond the word processor and the spreadsheet to consider more Intranet office applications. Some of what's in that chapter builds on the material in this chapter and the previous two (Chapters 12 and 13).

Other Client
Applications on the
Intranet

◆ Discussion of additional helper applications
◆ Web server configuration for PowerPoint and Access
◆ Client configuration for PowerPoint and Access
◆ Reading the Usenet newsgroups with News Xpress
◆ E-mail with Exchange and Eudora

The last two chapters explained how to set up your word processor and spreadsheet packages for use on your Intranet. This chapter turns to other everyday office applications you can use in your Intranet. I cover a variety of simple and complex packages, ranging from Access and PowerPoint (key components of the ubiquitous Microsoft Office suite) to a couple of other applications that were born on the Internet: News Xpress and Eudora.

Even if you don't use Microsoft Office, there are comparable commercial, freeware, and shareware applications to those in this integrated suite of programs. Competitive office suite packages like Corel's Perfect Office and Lotus's SmartSuite have similar applications. Whether you use Microsoft Office or any other type of document-creation software, you'll undoubtedly pick up ideas on how you can use your own applications from the examples in this chapter.

One example would be the Cardfile program that used to come free with Microsoft Windows 3.1 (and earlier). You may recall that Cardfile was a very handy electronic rolodex, but it seems it is no longer included with Windows 95 and Windows NT. Perhaps your office uses a different electronic rolodex and you can set it up on the Intranet just like Access and PowerPoint.

This chapter wraps up Part III of the book by discussing a few programs you won't typically find in an office. But now that the Internet has become such a hot area, more and more corporations are being forced to learn how to send and receive e-mail and files on the Internet. And it should come as no surprise that those same applications will work just fine on the Intranet too. Eudora Light (available on the CD-ROM) is the most popular e-mail client on the Internet, partly because it is free. Microsoft Exchange is also free when you buy Windows 95 or Windows NT. This chapter discusses these programs as a very economical way to increase the efficiency of communication within your organization. To put it simply, no Intranet project should overlook the power of simple e-mail.

If you want to help your team conduct timely business research on the Internet, or if you plan to run your own NNTP server for the purpose of Intranet collaboration (see Chapter 28, "Collaboration on Your Intranet"), don't miss the opportunity to educate your customers on the potential uses of a good newsgroup reader. I'll show you how later in this chapter when I discuss News Xpress. News Xpress is a powerful and simple GUI newsgroup reader that your customers will want to be aware of. (And by the way, it is also on the CD-ROM, and it is also free, courtesy of the City University of Hong Kong.)

Note: Microsoft has recently announced a new e-mail client and newsgroup reader program for Windows 95. A beta version of the software is currently available for free download from its Web site at `http://www.microsoft.com/ie/platform/imn.htm`. Though I don't have official information, it is reasonable to suspect that the program will be made available in a commercial release by the time you read this, and it will very likely run on Windows NT 4.

Additional Office Applications on Your Intranet

Your primary objective in setting up your Intranet is to make it easy for your customers to retrieve and share information using World Wide Web technology. You can do this with the data files generated by virtually any application your customers use. As with word processing documents and spreadsheet data files, there are other ways of sharing these files, ranging from NetWare and other kinds of fileservers to passing floppy disks around the office. What's different with your Intranet is that your customers have access to shared data using their favorite Web browser, a simple front end that virtually everyone already knows how to use. Using the sample applications in this chapter on your Intranet will enable you to make important corporate information available to your customers with just a click of their mice.

For example, you could use Microsoft Access to enable access to corporate Access databases directly from your customers' World Wide Web browser. You could use Microsoft PowerPoint to distribute presentation graphics to your customers or to conduct corporate training through your Intranet. You'll come up with more ideas of your own as you go through the examples in this chapter, but first you need to go through some setup preliminaries.

If you've read through the previous three chapters, you are by now a MIME expert. I won't bore you in this chapter by repeating details of server and client MIME setup. Because you are already familiar with how to do it for the word processor and the spreadsheet, you can easily apply those same concepts and instructions to the office programs covered in this chapter. I will follow a similar, albeit much briefer, outline in this chapter, but I will refer you back to the specific sections in the previous two chapters to refresh your memory on the steps involved. Remember, very little difference exists between the setup of common helper applications that handle audio or video and the setup of PowerPoint or Access.

Web Server Setup for PowerPoint and Access

The first step in setting up PowerPoint and Access as helper applications on your Intranet is to configure your Web server to know about their data files. With small differences, as are noted in context, the instructions in this section apply not only to PowerPoint presentations and Access databases, but also to spreadsheets and word processor documents as discussed in the previous chapters.

As you learned in Chapter 12, "MIME and Helper Applications," Web servers use the MIME mechanism to identify documents according to their MIME data type/subtype. Recall that the MIME mechanism divides data into a relatively small handful of data types, with each type further subdivided into subtypes. PowerPoint and Access data files fall into the application data type. You also learned in Chapter 12 how Web servers use filename extensions to map data files on the server to a MIME data type/subtype. You associate the filename extensions with MIME types/subtypes in the Windows NT Registry on the Web server, if you are using IIS, or in a configuration text file, if you are using some other Windows NT Web servers.

Please refer to the section titled "Editing the Registry MIME Map" in Chapter 13, "Word Processing on the Web" for detailed information about configuring IIS. The concepts described in that section for word processors are exactly the same steps you need to follow to configure your server for Access and PowerPoint.

The only difference between your word processor and the applications in this chapter is that the MIME types/subtypes should look like the following in the NT Registry as viewed by RegEdit:

```
application/msaccess,mdb,,5
application/mspowerpoint,ppt,,5
```

Microsoft Access commonly uses the .mdb filename extensions for its data files, and Microsoft PowerPoint commonly uses the .ppt extension. You can use any filename extensions you want for these applications, in addition to or instead of these. If you use nonstandard ones, make sure you use them consistently, so your customers can set up their Web browsers to access the data you're providing using the right filename extensions.

> **Warning:** Double-check your filename extensions to make sure they don't duplicate any of the other MIME entries. Otherwise, your customers will see incorrect or inconsistent results.

Adding Application Data Files to Your Web Server

You've completed the setup of your Web server to properly identify and serve your application's data files. Next, you need to populate your server with the data files that you want to make available on the Intranet.

> **Note:** Please see the section titled "Adding Spreadsheet Data Files to Your Web Server" in Chapter 14, "Publishing Spreadsheets on the Intranet." That section gives advice about sharing and mapping drives on the Web server so that you can copy files conveniently from your primary workstation.

After you have the Access and PowerPoint files on the Web server, create an HTML page to describe them; this page provides your customers with clickable links to the presentations and databases. This page can be as simple or as complex as you like because including hyperlinks to presentations and databases is exactly the same as setting up links to other kinds of documents. A simple HTML listing (PowerPoint.htm), using Microsoft PowerPoint slides as an example, might be something like Listing 15.1.

Listing 15.1. PowerPoint.htm is a simple page providing links to PowerPoint documents.

```
<HTML>
<HEAD>
<TITLE>PowerPoint Slides</TITLE>
</HEAD>
<BODY>
<H1>PowerPoint Slides</H1>
This directory contains a set of Microsoft PowerPoint slides.
Just click on one to open it up in PowerPoint.
<UL>
<LI><A HREF="qrtrly_sales.ppt">Slide 1</A>, Last Quarter's Sales
</LI>
<LI><A HREF="qrtrly_prod.ppt">Slide 2</A>, Last Quarter's Production
</LI>
<LI><A HREF="cpi_fcast.ppt">Slide 3</A>, Consumer Price Index Forecasts
</LI>
</UL>
```

```
If you haven't already done so, you must set up your Web browser to
understand PowerPoint slide data files.
<A HREF="ppt_setup.html">Here are instructions.</A>
</BODY>
</HTML>
```

You've seen HTML code almost identical to this example in the preceding two chapters. This code could be just as easily adapted for your specific purposes to provide your customers with a way to get to your Access and PowerPoint data. Before you can use this page to load the hyperlinked data files, however, your Web browser must be set up to use the correct program as a helper application. The source code is available on the CD-ROM in the file PowerPoint.htm. Figure 15.1 shows this simple catalog of PowerPoint slides as it would appear running in Internet Explorer 2.0.

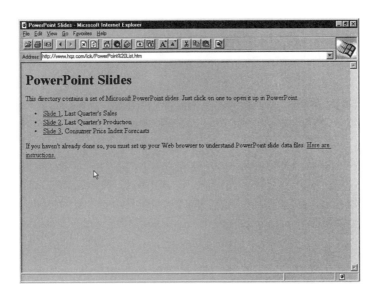

Figure 15.1. *The Intranet home page for PowerPoint slides.*

Converting PowerPoint Slides to HTML

Microsoft now has available for free download from its Web site (http://www.microsoft.com) a version of its Internet Assistant (IA) for PowerPoint. Like the companion IA products for Microsoft Word and Excel, this package enables you to save Microsoft Office data files (in this case, PowerPoint slides) directly to HTML format for use on your Intranet. Exported HTML slides include hyperlinks to all the slides in a multi-slide presentation. IA for PowerPoint currently supports Windows 95 only, but you can expect that Windows NT support will be announced as soon as Windows NT 4 is officially available.

Access and PowerPoint on the Clients

Setting up Access and PowerPoint on the clients is accomplished in exactly the same manner as setting up word processors and spreadsheets. Chapter 13 gives detailed instructions for configuring your word processor as a browser helper application. Please consult the section titled "Setting Up Microsoft Word as a Helper Application on the Client" in that chapter for the step-by-step help you need to apply to Access and PowerPoint.

Access and PowerPoint Read-Only Viewers

Microsoft has available for free download from its Web site (http://www.microsoft.com/) Access Ready-to-Run, a read-only viewer for Access database applications. (A copy is also on the CD-ROM with this book.) This package enables users who don't have a full copy of Access to read and run queries against Access databases. Access Ready-to-Run supports Windows 95 only, but it can read older Access databases.

You will also find a free PowerPoint Viewer on the CD-ROM here and at the Microsoft Web site:

http://www.microsoft.com/mspowerpoint/Internet/Viewer/default.htm

News Xpress

As an Intranet champion or as a Webmaster, you will find Usenet newsgroups a valuable resource for keeping up-to-date on the latest Web development techniques. Newsgroups are also important to help you troubleshoot problems with hardware or software. News Xpress is a freeware Usenet newsreader that allows you to easily organize the newsgroups you want to subscribe to.

Installing News Xpress

To install News Xpress from the CD to your hard drive, follow these steps:

1. Unzip News Xpress from the CD into a directory on your hard disk. You can optionally create a shortcut for nx.exe on your desktop (assuming you are running Windows 95 or NT 4).

2. If you have previously installed CuteFTP (also on the CD with this book), you can delete ctl3dv2.dll from the News Xpress subdirectory; otherwise, you will need to copy it into the \WINNT\SYSTEM directory and delete it from the News Xpress directory.

Warning: It is important that ctl3dv2.dll exist in only one directory on your system. That one location should be the \WINNT\SYSTEM directory on NT or the \Windows\System directory on Windows 95. Applications that use ctl3dv2.dll will give you a non-fatal warning message when loading and they will not look good if the DLL appears in multiple locations.

You now have one of the best Usenet newsreader client applications available to help keep you up-to-date.

Running News Xpress

Suppose you want to read articles about Microsoft SQL Server so you can learn more about how to support that key component of BackOffice. The newsgroup that you can scan to help you with this task is comp.databases.ms-sqlserver.

The following are the steps of a simple getting-started session with News Xpress 1.0:

1. Start News Xpress. From the main menu, choose Config | Setup to open the dialog shown in Figure 15.2.

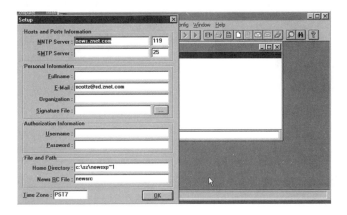

Figure 15.2. *The News Xpress Setup dialog.*

2. Enter the information that is supplied by your Internet Service Provider (ISP). The most important fields are the name of the NNTP Server and your e-mail address. The other fields can probably be left empty until you are ready to post articles or send e-mail replies. (By the way, please don't fill out your dialog with the same data shown in the screenshot.) Choose OK when you are ready to connect.

3. From the main menu, choose File | Connect. This command should connect you to the NNTP server at your ISP. This process could take a moment while News Xpress reads the names of all the newsgroups.

4. From the main menu, choose View | All Groups. It may take a while to download all the groups; after all, there are more than 16,000 out there.

5. Note that there are several good newsgroups underneath the comp.* hierarchy. Scroll down to `comp.databases.ms-sqlserver` and double-click it to subscribe and download the article headers.

6. Scroll through the articles and double-click ones that you would like to read. See Figure 15.3 for an example.

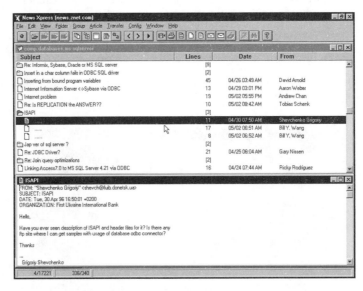

Figure 15.3. *Displaying a selected newsgroup and reading its articles is straightforward with News Xpress.*

A Quick Look at E-Mail with Microsoft Exchange

One of the first things you are going to need for your Intranet construction project is e-mail capability. You have to be able to communicate with software vendors, network consultants, contract programmers, office managers, database designers, and so on, as you go through the process of establishing a successful Intranet. For all of these reasons, you need to get your e-mail act together quickly.

The Exchange e-mail client comes with Windows NT 4 and Windows 95. Allow me to assume that you won't set up Exchange on your Web server, and that you will want to set it up on a Windows 95 machine. The following are the quick steps for configuring Exchange for Internet e-mail on a Windows 95 client machine (the steps should be almost identical for Windows NT 4 Server or Workstation):

1. Double-click the Inbox icon on the Windows 95 desktop.

2. From the Tools menu, choose Services. Check to see whether you have Internet Mail in the list. If not, choose the Add button, select Internet Mail in the next screen, and then choose OK to add the Internet Mail service to the list.

3. Select Internet Mail and choose the Properties button. Use the information supplied to you by your ISP or your network administrator to fill out this screen.

4. Other configuration options are too variable for us to cover here in a general sense. For example, ask your ISP about the SMTP server address and ask your recipients what format to use for file attachments. Choose OK to save these settings. Then choose OK again to close the Settings dialog.

5. From the main menu of Exchange, choose Compose | New Message. Fill out the Internet mail address of the recipient, type a subject, and type a message. Then choose File | Send or click the yellow envelope icon on the far left side of the button bar. If you send a message to yourself, it will take just a moment to travel round-trip to your ISP and back before it shows up in your Inbox. You can speed up the process by choosing Tools | Deliver Now Using | Internet Mail from the main menu of Exchange.

Those are the basics of Exchange. If you choose to use it as your e-mail client, you will find it to be a useful tool.

A Quick Look at E-Mail with Eudora Light

Eudora Light is on the CD with this book or you can download it from Qualcomm. Eudora is described by its author as *postcardware*, which means that he only asks you to mail him a postcard to register the product. The following are the quick steps to getting up and running with the Eudora Light e-mail client:

1. Copy the file eudor154.exe from the CD to your intended destination directory on the hard disk. Eudora doesn't have (or need) an install program, so the program files can be extracted directly into a Eudora subdirectory as opposed to the usual \temp directory. Double-click the file in Explorer to self-extract it.

2. Using Explorer, drag the Eudora.exe file to your Windows NT or Windows 95 desktop (this step is optional). Double-click the Eudora icon.

3. From the main menu of Eudora, choose Special | Settings to open the dialog you see pictured in Figure 15.4.

4. Click the Personal Information icon in the listbox on the left and fill out the information about your mail account provided to you by your ISP. This screen is really the same as the Getting Started screen except that this screen also includes your return address. It is important that you fill in the field for Return address. Usually, you will want that to be the same address as your POP account. When you are finished, choose the OK button to save these settings. Again, you may want to configure some of the other settings, depending on your situation.

5. From the Message menu, select New Message to open a dialog similar to that shown in Figure 15.5.

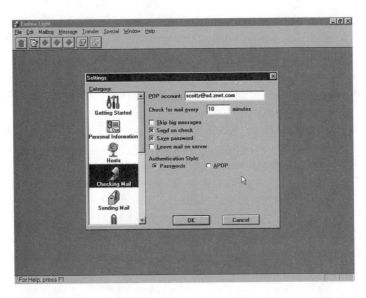

Figure 15.4. The Eudora Light Settings dialog.

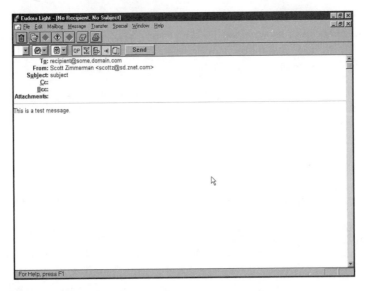

Figure 15.5. The New Message dialog in Eudora Light.

6. Fill out the fields for To and Subject, and type in a test message. When you are ready, choose the Send button.

> **Tip:** For more detailed information about the configuration and use of Eudora Light, see the file `eudora.doc`, included in the Eudora zip file on the CD. This file is the official Eudora User's Guide in Word format. You can obtain information about the latest Eudora software, including the commercial version, at this URL:
>
> `http://www.qualcomm.com/quest/QuestMain.html`

Summary

This chapter has been the last of a group of three chapters devoted to using everyday office applications as Web browser helper applications in your Intranet. You've learned about a range of useful productivity applications including the Microsoft Access database package, Microsoft PowerPoint presentation slide maker, two e-mail clients, and a Usenet newsreader.

This ends Part III of the book. By now, you have a basic understanding of the helper application mechanism, including how to use MIME data type/subtype information to integrate almost any application your customers might use on your Intranet. You should have an inkling of the virtually unlimited possibilities for your organization represented by these capabilities. Subsequent chapters build on these fundamentals to help you bring more advanced, specific capabilities into play on your Web.

IV PART

Advanced Intranet Publishing

CHAPTER

Linking Databases to the Web

- ◆ Web databases as helper applications
- ◆ Commercial Web database products
- ◆ ODBC
- ◆ Important CGI fundamentals
- ◆ Cold Fusion
- ◆ Overview of Structured Query Language (SQL)

As surely as the Intranet is changing the face of client/server application development, you can bet that organizations all over the world are striving to build Web databases. Nearly every client/server application you can imagine is based on a back-end database located on a server. And nearly everywhere you look, there is a backlog of requests for application databases that need to be built and put into service to help automate office processes.

One reason that Web technology is getting so much attention on the Intranet is that it has the potential to help alleviate the application development backlog by standardizing and simplifying the database front end. (I'm referring to our hero, the Web browser, of course.) Conveniently, the back end is simplified too. Using ODBC (Open Database Connectivity), IIS, and some simple HTML scripts, you can provide access to any legacy database system. When compared with the traditional approach of custom programming in third-generation languages, Web databases may substantially reduce implementation and maintenance costs.

As with so many other computer applications' vendors, commercial database vendors are racing to provide Web-accessible front ends to their packages. If you've struggled to build useful, user-friendly database applications using the tools your database vendor has provided or using custom programming, the idea of using a Web browser and fill-in forms as an alternative to building user interfaces from scratch is an attractive option.

In this chapter, you'll learn about a few commercial database vendors' Web products. I'll explain ODBC and the raw fundamentals of SQL programming. I'll also show you how to create user-friendly custom database applications using only IIS and HTML with no additional programming.

This chapter does not substantially cover designing and developing relational database applications. Consult your database package's documentation for that information. This chapter assumes that you are thinking of a database application you would like to access using your Web browser. Of course, you may find once you start accessing your database with your Web browser, you'll want to change the database's design. This is no different from the traditional iterative database application development process, in which you and the users try the application for awhile to see how you want to change it.

Web Databases as Helper Applications

This chapter is mostly about the subject of creating full-blown client/server database applications on the Web. But before diving too deeply into that subject, this section reviews the ideas presented in Part III, "Setting Up Office Applications." Chapters 12 through 15 showed how easy it is to set up any type of document, including a database, for Web browser access using MIME. In some cases, this simple concept may be all that you need to accomplish the task at hand.

In Chapter 15, "Other Client Applications on the Intranet," you learned how to access Microsoft Access database applications through the Web helper application mechanism. You can configure your Web server to serve complete Access databases, just as it serves any other file on the server. Your customers' Web browsers can then use their own copies of Access as a Web browser helper application to load the databases for data search and retrieval and/or export to other applications.

Note that such helper application access to a database application should be considered read-only because the Web browser downloads a temporary copy of the database to the local system. All queries made by your customer are based on the temporary copy, and any changes that he might attempt to make will not be reflected in the master copy on your Web server. Similarly, updates made to the master server won't be propagated to any client unless the client reloads the database from the Web server. Thus, you'll want to limit the capabilities of such an arrangement to running queries, generating reports, and exporting data from the application.

This limitation is more than offset by other capabilities, however. For example, if your company uses other programs, such as Microsoft Office or its individual components, you'll be able to use their capabilities to move data from one application to another. You can import information in Access databases, for example, into Word or Excel (and vice versa).

Commercial Web Databases

Whatever database package you use on your Intranet—and whatever bells and whistles it provides for developing database applications, entering queries, and generating reports—database access boils down to two broad processes:

◆ Formulating and submitting structured query language (SQL) queries or data-entry statements to the database engine.

◆ Receiving and processing the results of the query.

Whether the user hand-edits SQL queries or fills in an on-screen query or data-entry form, the objective is the same: to pass the query or new data to the database back end. Similarly, when the database spits out the results of a query or data entry, an application has to receive it and generate human-readable output (on-screen or on paper) or machine-readable output in some specific format.

Web access to these databases involves the same processes, with important differences:

◆ Your customers perform queries and data entry using fill-in Web forms (created with HTML) in which they enter query keywords or other search criteria through menu selections, click buttons, free-form text blocks, or fill-in-the-blank boxes.

◆ CGI or ISAPI applications take the information entered in the form and bundle it up into valid SQL queries or data-entry updates. They then pass it off to the database back end.

◆ The same CGI or ISAPI applications receive the results back from the database engine after processing. They format the report in HTML and pass it back to the customer's Web browser for display.

This section briefly lists a few of the commercial Web database products available for Windows NT. If you are faced with a new client/server database project, and you don't want to engineer it yourself, any of these Web tools will help. You will still have to determine the database model and the user interface (using HTML). You can find out more about these Web database products, and in some cases even download a trial version, by visiting these URLs:

◆ Cold Fusion—`http://www.allaire.com` (Cold Fusion is on the CD and is discussed more thoroughly in a special section later in this chapter.)

◆ IDC—`http://www.microsoft.com/infoserv/` (This free feature is included with IIS.)

◆ dbWeb—`http://www.microsoft.com/intdev/dbweb/` (Microsoft recently purchased Aspect Software Engineering, the company that invented this product. Version 1.1 of this product is available for free download while it is in beta development.)

◆ DataRamp—`http://dataramp.com`

◆ WebDBC—`http://www.primenet.com/`

◆ FoxWeb—`http://www.foxweb.com/` (See the following section for more information.)

◆ WebBase—`http://www.webbase.com/` (See a following section for more information.)

FoxWeb for FoxPro

FoxPro users should look at a new product from the Aegis Group called FoxWeb. This software tool interfaces Windows Web servers with FoxPro data and programs. FoxWeb overcomes the limitations of other Windows CGI approaches, which read and write temporary files to pass environment variables between processes. It works by running multiple, background Visual FoxPro instances simultaneously, each one of which can handle CGI interactions. CGI environment variables are placed into FoxPro arrays and objects for manipulation. All programming is done in FoxPro rather than in an external scripting language like Perl, so your investment in FoxPro programming can be both preserved and leveraged. You can even store reusable HTML code directly in FoxPro databases for easy retrieval, with intelligent branching capabilities.

Aegis claims substantially faster database access compared to ODBC database transactions, although ODBC database applications can also access FoxPro databases, as noted later in the section on ODBC. FoxWeb requires version 3.0 of Visual FoxPro. FoxWeb includes login/password security features.

WebBase

ExperTelligence, Inc. offers WebBase for all Microsoft Windows platforms. This package is a 32-bit HTTP server with built-in hooks for accessing databases without the use of CGI scripting.

As a Web server, WebBase can serve conventional HTML documents in response to Web browser requests. Besides this function, however, the package supports embedded SQL code in special HTML documents, which, when accessed, can contact database applications directly to run queries or data-entry commands. WebBase HTML extensions also include a macro language featuring intelligent decision-making constructs like `if-then` and `case` branching, as well as `forRow` and `forIndex` looping. A number of other useful functions are also provided, such as string-comparison/matching, math, date handling, and other logic. These features enable customized responses to Web browser requests based on user name, IP address, browser type, and the like.

WebBase enables the session state to be maintained throughout a user's session and has login/password security built in. Any ODBC database (see the next section for a discussion of ODBC) is supported (for example, Microsoft Access, Excel, SQL Server, FoxPro, dBASE III and IV, Paradox, Btrieve, as well as UNIX database servers running Sybase and Oracle).

The package can also search fielded text files as a database. Although WebBase can function as a Web server, you can also run a traditional Web server for better HTTP performance, either on the same computer or a different one, because WebBase doesn't provide all the functions of full-featured Web servers. WebBase runs on all Intel Windows platforms.

ODBC

All the previously mentioned database products support ODBC. Microsoft Open Database Connectivity (ODBC) is a standard programming interface for application developers and database systems providers. Before ODBC became a de facto standard for Windows programs to interface with database systems, programmers had to use proprietary languages for each database they wanted to connect to. Now ODBC has made the choice of the database system almost irrelevant from a coding perspective, which is as it should be. Application developers have much more important things to worry about than the syntax that is needed to port their program from one database to another when business needs suddenly change.

Through the ODBC Administrator in Control Panel, you can specify the particular database that is associated with a data source that an ODBC application program is written to use. Think of an ODBC data source as a door with a name on it. Each door will lead you to a particular database. For example, the data source named Sales Figures might be a SQL Server database, whereas the Accounts Payable data source could refer to an Access database. The physical database referred to by a data source can reside anywhere on the LAN.

Note: The ODBC system files are not installed on your system by Windows NT. Rather they are installed when you set up a separate database application, such as SQL Server Client or Visual Basic. When the ODBC icon is installed in Control Panel, the icon uses a file called `ODBCCP32.CPL`. You also can administer your ODBC data sources through a stand-alone program called `ODBCADM.EXE` (16-bit) or `ODBCAD32.EXE` (32-bit). The 16-bit and 32-bit versions maintain separate lists of ODBC data sources. The 16-bit data sources can be used only by 16-bit programs. The same goes for 32-bit data sources and 32-bit programs (unless the programmer uses an advanced technique known as thunking). On Windows NT, there is a further classification of data sources called *system data sources*. These sources can be used only by 32-bit NT services, such as IIS.

From a programming perspective, the beauty of ODBC is that the application can be written to use the same set of function calls to interface with any data source, regardless of the database vendor. The source code of the application doesn't change, regardless of whether it talks to Oracle or SQL Server. (I only mention these two as an example. ODBC drivers are available for several dozen popular database systems. Even Excel spreadsheets and plain text files can be turned into data sources.)

The operating system uses the Registry information written by ODBC Administrator to determine which low-level ODBC drivers are needed to talk to the data source (such as the interface to Oracle or SQL Server). The loading of the ODBC drivers is transparent to the ODBC application program. In a client/server environment, the ODBC API even handles many of the network issues for the application programmer.

The advantages of this scheme are so numerous that you are probably thinking there must be some kind of a catch. The only disadvantage of ODBC is that it isn't as efficient as talking directly to the native database interface (although Microsoft is planning to make ODBC the native interface of SQL Server). ODBC has had many detractors make the charge that it is too slow. Microsoft has always claimed that the critical factor in ODBC performance is the quality of the driver software that is used. In my humble opinion, this claim is valid. The availability of good ODBC drivers has improved a great deal recently.

The criticism about ODBC performance is somewhat analogous to those who said that compilers would never match the speed of pure assembly language. Of course not! But the compiler (or ODBC) gives you the opportunity to write cleaner programs, which means you finish sooner and are ready to enhance your program or optimize the section of code where it truly spends most of its execution time. Meanwhile, computer hardware gets faster every year. (As a parody of the personal career tragedy that can occur due to the ever-declining percentage of application programs being developed without any direct use of assembly language, the Microsoft Day at the Movies in April 1996 included a humorous skit showing two jobless, die-hard programmers who wanted to reinvent the Win32 common dialogs in assembly code. As I recall, they couldn't see why anyone would prefer to write one line of "slow" compiled code when pages and pages of ultra-fast assembly code could be written instead.)

Important CGI Fundamentals

The basics of CGI in this section are relevant to Web database application interfaces, and you'll want to bear them in mind as you work your way through the rest of this chapter:

◆ Each piece of data your customer enters into an HTML fill-in form (query keywords or new data entry) is available to be passed, as standard input, directly to your database engine by your CGI or ISAPI program.

◆ You can include additional data in form output using the INPUT TYPE=hidden HTML markup. You can hard-code this information into your forms or you can dynamically set it based on user behavior or other factors that the customer doesn't see, but that your CGI program might need for processing.

◆ CGI and ISAPI programs have access to a good deal of standard information in the form of environment variables. The variables include not only the customer's Web browser type, but also the TCP/IP address and hostname of the user's computer, his userid and access authentication (if the server is configured to provide it), and the MIME data type/ subtypes supported by the browser.

CGI Databases with Cold Fusion

Writing a CGI application that would interact with an off-the-shelf database would take quite a bit of programming expertise. Why take the time to write such an application or pay someone else to do it when perfectly good ones already exist? I have included on the CD-ROM a trial version of a product called Cold Fusion, which is a CGI application that allows full Web integration with any 32-bit ODBC database application. The trial version is a completely operational version; it's only limitation is that it will stop working 30 days after installation. At which time you are encouraged to buy the product if you find it useful.

You can use Cold Fusion to create a wide range of Intranet applications including company schedules, customer feedback, online order entry, event registration, searching of catalogs, directories and calendars, bulletin-board style conferencing, online technical support, and interactive training. If you have browsed the World Wide Web and come across any Windows NT servers, you probably have seen the logo saying, "Powered by Cold Fusion"; it is a popular product. Cold Fusion is sold by Allaire at http://www.allaire.com/.

You create Cold Fusion applications by combining standard HTML files with high-level database commands and a powerful CGI program that is precompiled. This method of developing Web applications is an order of magnitude faster, more robust, and more flexible than first generation, code-intensive techniques.

Cold Fusion applications can be developed very rapidly because no code (beyond simple HTML) is required. The applications are also robust because all database interactions are encapsulated in a single industrial-strength CGI script.

Cold Fusion applications are also very flexible because all formatting and presentation is done using standard HTML files that can be modified and revised at any time (as opposed to having to edit and recompile source code).

Installing Cold Fusion

The installation of the Cold Fusion demo is a snap. Just copy the file `cfafeval.exe` from the CD to a temporary directory on your hard disk. Then execute the self-extracting install program in your temporary directory. The Cold Fusion installation process will handle the rest.

> **Note:** The file `cfafeval.exe` on the CD-ROM actually includes two products: Cold Fusion 1.5 and Allaire Forums. Allaire Forums is a Web collaboration product mentioned in Chapter 27, "Collaboration on Your Intranet." These evaluation products are provided through the courtesy of J.J. Allaire.

The Cold Fusion demo application includes a complete online tutorial in HTML format that guides you through the development of several examples. You may want to spend some time with the Cold Fusion online tutorial and examples.

> **Note:** If the Cold Fusion installation of ODBC components does not complete successfully, an ODBC library was probably in use by Windows or another application during setup. In this case, restart Windows and double-click the ODBC Setup icon in the Cold Fusion Program Group to complete the installation of ODBC. To avoid this problem, you should exit all running application programs before you install new software.

The HTML Link to Cold Fusion

Suppose a fictitious ABC Corporation has a company mailing list and it's in the Microsoft Access `*.mdb` file format. Let's say that the new V.P. has decided that employees should be able to add their names to the mailing list to volunteer their free time to promote company products. With this stalwart example in mind, you will no doubt be able to think of ways you can adapt this application for your own purposes. Using Cold Fusion, you can create a form that people can fill out and have the data automatically entered into your Access MDB file. A description of the files for this project is as follows:

◆ `mlist.htm` contains the form for entering information to the database. See Figure 16.1 for the mailing list HTML page displayed in Internet Explorer 3.0. Please see Listing 16.1 for the HTML source code that provides an example of how to use Cold Fusion.

◆ `mlist.mdb` is the Access database that has a table named MLIST with columns matching the fields on the HTML form.

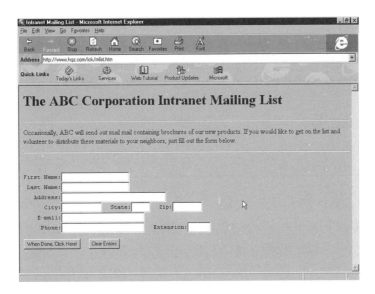

Figure 16.1. *The ABC Intranet Mailing List page for propaganda distribution.*

Listing 16.1. The `mlist.htm` file uses Cold Fusion as a CGI database application.

```
<HTML>
<HEAD>
<TITLE>Intranet Mailing List</TITLE>
</HEAD>
<BODY>

<H1>The ABC Corporation Intranet Mailing List</H1>
<HR>
<P>
Occasionally, ABC will send out snail mail containing brochures of
our new products. If you would like to get on the list and volunteer
to distribute these materials to your neighbors, just fill out the
form below.
<HR>
<FORM ACTION="/scripts/dbml.exe?Action=insert" METHOD="POST">

  <!-- Cold Fusion configuration fields -->

  <INPUT TYPE="hidden" NAME="DataSource" VALUE="Mailing List">
  <INPUT TYPE="hidden" NAME="TableName" VALUE="MLIST">
  <INPUT TYPE="hidden" NAME="NextPage" VALUE="/mlist/thanks.htm">

  <!-- Data entry fields -->

<PRE>
First Name:<INPUT NAME="FirstName" size=28>
 Last Name:<INPUT NAME="LastName" size=28>
   Address:<INPUT NAME="Address" size=45>
      City:<INPUT NAME="City" size=15>
```

continues

Listing 16.1. continued

```
State:<INPUT NAME="State" size=5>
Zip:<input NAME="PostalCode" size=10>
    E-mail:<INPUT NAME="EmailAddress" size=35>
     Phone:<INPUT NAME="Phone" size=35>
Extension:<INPUT NAME="Extension" size=7>

<INPUT Type="submit" Value=" When Done, Click Here! ">
<INPUT Type="reset" Value="Clear Entries">
</PRE>
</BODY>
</HTML>
```

Gaining CGI Database Features without Programming

To add record insert functionality to the database at your sample site, follow these steps:

1. Create a directory named `mlist` underneath your HTML document root directory. `D:\iis\wwwroot\mlist\` is an example.

2. Copy the files `mlist.htm` and `mlist.mdb` to the `mlist` directory. Since the database will be modified by the Cold Fusion CGI application, you need to ensure that the database file is located in a directory in which the `IUSR_computername` account has write permission. (The database is not required to be in the same directory as the HTML file.)

3. Modify your HTML home page to provide a link to `mlist.htm`.

4. Run the Cold Fusion Administrator (`fusionad.exe`) and create one or more ODBC data sources for MS Access, as described in the following steps. For more information on what ODBC is and how it works, see the *Cold Fusion User's Guide*.

5. Choose the Add button to display the Add Data Source dialog shown in Figure 16.2. Select the driver for the Microsoft Access driver, and then choose OK.

Figure 16.2. *Adding a data source.*

6. In the dialog box that appears, enter `Mailing List` for the Data Source Name. See Figure 16.3.

Figure 16.3. *Naming a data source.*

7. Choose the Select button to enter the path to the `mlist.mdb` file from Step 2. Choose OK to close the Select Database dialog. Choose OK again to close the ODBC Microsoft Access Setup dialog. Your Data Sources tab should appear similar to Figure 16.4.

Figure 16.4. *The result of adding the Mailing List DSN to Cold Fusion Administrator.*

8. Before closing Cold Fusion Administrator, select the Mailing List DSN in the Data Sources tab and click on the Verify button. Cold Fusion will test the DSN and the location of the physical database file.

Your site now has a link to a page that will automatically add people to your `mlist.mdb` file containing your mailing list. Now is a good time to break out your Web browser and add a few names to the list. Of course, you will need to use Microsoft Access, or a similar Access database program, to view, modify, or print out any information from the `.mdb` file. The next step is to edit and search the database from the Web.

Inserting and Updating Data with Cold Fusion

Cold Fusion's most basic functionality (inserting form data into database tables) is implemented by the addition of hidden configuration fields to HTML forms. If you are already familiar with HTML forms, this technique is extremely easy to learn. If you need a refresher course on HTML forms, please refer to Chapter 5, "What You Need to Know About HTML."

To insert or update data, you create an HTML form containing the fields in the database table that you want to insert or update. You then add three hidden fields to the form that indicate what you want Cold Fusion to do with the data entered by the user. These hidden fields are as follows:

Field Name	Purpose
DataSource	Name of the ODBC data source containing your table
TableName	Name of the table you want the form fields written to
NextPage	A URL indicating which page the user should be sent to if the submission is successful

Additional hidden fields can be specified to validate the user's entries (for example, required, numeric, date, and range-checked).

When this form is submitted to the Cold Fusion CGI program (DBML.EXE), the data entered by the user is added to the specified table and the user is routed to the specified next page.

Queries and Dynamic Pages with Cold Fusion

Cold Fusion enables you to dynamically generate HTML pages based on user queries. These queries are submitted to the Cold Fusion CGI program (DBML.EXE), which then (based on a template file specified in the query) generates the output to be sent back to the user.

The key to dynamic page generation is a small (but powerful) set of database-oriented markup tags. These tags are collectively referred to as DBML (Database Markup Language). DBML tags are very similar to HTML tags except they are database-oriented. Learning to use the DBML tags is extremely simple. Almost all of the core functionality of Cold Fusion is encapsulated in these four tags:

Tag	Purpose
DBQUERY	Submits an SQL query to the database
DBOUTPUT	Displays the result of a query, freely intermixing result set fields and HTML tags
DBTABLE and DBCOL	Displays a preformatted table containing the result set of a query

Dynamic pages are created using template files, which are composed of a mix of HTML and DBML tags that define how the user's request should be processed and what type of output should be returned.

The DBML tags are used to specify how you want Cold Fusion to interact with the database, as well as where you want to display the results of your queries. For example, you might specify that you want the SQL query SELECT * FROM Customers sent to the database and the results returned as a preformatted table.

> **Tip:** For more information about the fundamentals of Structured Query Language (SQL), see the following section titled "Overview of Structured Query Language."

The HTML tags are used both for implementing the nondatabase–driven parts of your output (for example, page header and footer) as well as for specifying how you want the results of your queries formatted. For example, you might specify that you want a field bolded or a horizontal rule drawn between each displayed record.

Depending on the nature of your data, you might decide that you would not want a link like this available to the general public. If this is the case, you'll want to place password protection on your HTML pages. Most Web servers, including IIS, enable you to password-protect your pages. (See Chapter 10, "Intranet Security in Windows NT," for more information about Intranet security.)

Overview of Structured Query Language (SQL)

Most database tasks can be accomplished with just four simple SQL statements:

◆ SELECT returns a list of matching records.

◆ DELETE deletes matching records.

◆ UPDATE modifies selected fields in matching records.

◆ INSERT adds a new row of data; values must be supplied for the required fields.

What follows are several short and sweet examples of each type of statement. In each case, it is not important to type in uppercase, but I have marked the SQL keywords in uppercase for readability. I use the terms *table1*, *field1*, and *field2* to represent placeholders for the object names that you would use in your database.

The following are some examples of the SELECT statement:

◆ SELECT * FROM *table1*

This statement will return all fields from all rows of the given table.

◆ SELECT *field1*, *field2* FROM *table1*

This statement selects all rows but only returns two fields. It is more efficient than using the * wildcard in client/server database systems because only the data in the fields you need will be copied across the network.

◆ `SELECT * FROM table1 WHERE field1 = 'abc*' AND field2 > 99`

The WHERE clause is added here to select particular rows. This example assumes that `field1` is a text field. The asterisk is used as a wildcard to match any data that begins with `'abc'`. Single quotes are needed for text constants. The AND keyword is used to also select rows in which `field2` (numeric) is greater than 99.

> **Note:** The asterisk wildcard character is specific to the Access dialect of SQL. Standard SQL uses the percent (%) character instead. Another special character that differs among SQL dialects is the date delimiter. Access SQL surrounds dates with pound signs (#), while ODBC merely requires the date to be in one of several formats (with no special delimiters).

Now that you know several varieties of SELECT, the DELETE statement is easy. The following is an example:

`DELETE FROM table1 WHERE field1 = 24`

This statement will delete all rows from the selected table that match the optional WHERE clause.

The UPDATE statement is a little trickier. It can be used to modify one or more rows of a selected table:

`UPDATE table1 SET field1 = 99 WHERE field1 = 44`

This statement will change the data in the `field1` column for all rows that currently have a `field1` value of 44. Other field=value pairs may be included as long as they are separated by commas.

The INSERT statement is also a little different from the others. Whereas the other statements operate on existing data, INSERT is used to add a new record:

`INSERT INTO table1 (field1, field2) VALUES (99, 'abc')`

Assuming that `field1` and `field2` are the only required fields, this statement creates a new row in the selected table. The order of the values must match the order of the selected column names. For example, 99 will be placed in `field1`, and `'abc'` will be placed in `field2`.

Summary

This chapter focused on Web interfaces to relational database packages. In addition, SQL and ODBC were discussed, because they form the pillars of most database projects. I talked about several vendors (but it was by no means an exhaustive list) of commercial database products for Windows NT and the Web. The chapter surveyed a fairly representative sample, some of them in detail, to at least give you a firm idea of what's possible in this rapidly growing field.

Chapter 17, "Understanding ActiveX Technologies," continues to explore the advanced Internet technologies that Microsoft is building on top of IIS. Although this chapter dealt with the creation of Web-accessible, general-purpose databases, you may find Chapter 21, "Indexing Your Intranet with WAIS," to be of similar interest as it looks at the subject of searching your Web.

17

CHAPTER

Understanding ActiveX Technologies

◆ The browser wars

◆ NT Server Internet components

◆ Three-tiered HTML authoring tools

◆ ActiveX redefines client/server computing

◆ C++ and Java development tools

◆ Powerful application programming interfaces

◆ Security

On December 7, 1995 Microsoft rushed to the Net! In a major press conference to announce their Internet vision, Chairman Bill Gates paraphrased a historical quote from the same date when he alluded that he felt as if a sleeping giant had been awakened.

He was referring both to the rapidity with which the Internet phenomenon had come upon the software industry—and to Microsoft's own lack of attention to that fact. As so many players in the software industry already consider Microsoft to be too large for its own good, the onslaught of changes being brought on by the Internet was seen by several competing companies as an opportunity to seize the initiative. One company in particular, Netscape, was (and is) doing exactly that. Until Microsoft woke up, it looked as though Netscape would dominate the Internet almost unchallenged. For example, Netscape's premier product, Navigator, is preferred by 80 percent of all Web surfers.

Users of the Internet, the Web, and Intranet technologies stand to gain a great deal from the competition between Netscape and Microsoft. The rush of both companies to bring out new and improved products is further fueling the need for trained professionals like you and me.

Because this book is about Windows NT and the Web, and because I try hard to keep abreast of all of Microsoft's product developments, I have shaped this chapter around Microsoft's recent Internet technology announcements. Its bevy of new Internet products is perhaps best summed up by the name, and strategy, of ActiveX, even though that is really only one piece of the overall Web that Microsoft is weaving.

Please understand that any perceived lack of information in this book about Netscape products should by no means be considered a vote to ignore those technologies. That would be a perilous mistake to make as Netscape will continue to influence major standards and be a preeminent force on the Web for a long time to come. I applaud Netscape for helping pave a superhighway we can all enjoy, and I celebrate the opportunity to work in an industry with innovators such as Netscape. But space and time limitations being what they are, I can only cover so much in one book.

The Browser Wars

No matter how you talk about the Internet, the conversation always winds back to the Web browser. As you have seen repeatedly throughout this book, we are living in a time when the Web browser has the potential to radically change the way we use computers. Netscape wants to own the browser market. Their Internet ally, Sun Microsystems, intends to help them reach that goal by getting everyone to use the Java language everywhere. (Java is being developed by Sun as a possible replacement for C++ and object-oriented client/server programming.) If their collective strategy works, they stand to get the largest piece of the Internet software pie. Because no one ever figured out how to cut into Microsoft's operating systems and applications pie, the thinking goes, why not just bake a new pie? In other words, client/server computing delivered through Web browsers is a way to reduce, some say even eliminate, the need for mass market desktop operating systems like Windows 95!

Microsoft realized that when it came out with Internet Explorer 1.0 at the time Windows 95 was released in August 1995. But Explorer was largely considered an insignificant free program that had no chance of competing with Navigator on features and power. Netscape had already produced many popular versions of Navigator. Navigator also ran on several operating system platforms (including Apple and UNIX), and it supported all of the Netscape HTML extensions (of course).

In early 1996, both Netscape and Microsoft released their version 2.0 Web browsers. Although Microsoft invented and supported a few interesting HTML extensions, IE 2.0 was still nowhere close to earning the popularity that the Web had bestowed upon Navigator.

Microsoft needs more than one new release of software to catch up to Netscape in browser popularity. Both Microsoft and Netscape know this fact, and software engineers at both companies are working late into the night to bring out the 3.0 versions of their respective browsers (both are expected by the time you read this).

As I put the final words into this book, both Netscape and Microsoft have released beta versions of their new 3.0 browsers. The competition continues to heat up. The June 3, 1996 issue of WebWeek magazine carries a story which points out that Microsoft has decided to integrate Macromedia's Shockwave into Explorer 3.0. In addition, with the URL parental blocking feature (useful on the corporate Intranet as well), support for HTML 3.2 style sheets, and ActiveX, Microsoft is claiming that they have the leg up. Meanwhile, Netscape has added CoolTalk (teleconferencing), LiveAudio, LiveVideo, Live3D (using VRML, or Virtual Reality Markup Language), and they have enhanced their Java and JavaScript features. (Microsoft claims that IE 3.0 will support Java, but it has yet to materialize.)

Although ActiveX is cool and it does open the door to technologies such as the Microsoft NetMeeting collaboration application (available for free now, possibly bundled with Explorer in the future), it is still too early to tell what percentage of Web users (if any) will drop Navigator for Explorer. Most likely, some users will move over to Microsoft (especially when it becomes an integrated piece of the Windows 95 operating system late this year), but don't hold your breath if you are looking for any knockout punches in the fight for browser market share. System administrators and Web page designers will have to deal with supporting both browsers for some time to come.

> **Note:** NCompass Labs has developed an ActiveX plug-in for Netscape Navigator 2.x (and above). Basically, this helps Microsoft try to establish ActiveX as a platform that is accessible to a larger number of users than Internet Explorer would deliver by itself. That in turn, will help Microsoft convince developers to build ActiveX controls, and page designers to use those controls, as an alternative to Java applets. Visit the NCompass Web site at http://www.ncompasslabs.com/.

NT Server Internet Components

While Web browsers are at one end of the client/server transaction; server software stands at the other end. Microsoft feels that Windows NT and BackOffice are uniquely positioned to help them dominate the Intranet/Internet marketplace.

Take a peek at the server components in BackOffice that deliver Intranet/Internet functionality:

◆ Internet Information Server 2.0 is free with NT 4. This product is the key piece of technology that Microsoft hopes will help NT customers to build millions of Web sites. It offers a Gopher server, an FTP server, and, most importantly, a Web publishing server.

◆ A GUI Domain Name Server (DNS) is also free with NT 4 Server. Microsoft has recently announced its plans to merge the Internet DNS technology into the NTFS filesystem as part of the directory services war with NetWare.

◆ SQL Server 6.5 is the latest version of the enterprise database server that supports dynamic HTML page creation triggered by changes in the relational database.

◆ Exchange Server is the e-mail server and groupware application development platform that goes head-to-head against IBM/Lotus Notes and Netscape/Collabra Share.

Three-Tiered HTML Authoring Tools

Just as NT and BackOffice are designed to run the types of new Intranet and Internet server applications that are being developed around the world, Microsoft recognizes that Web page creation tools are key to the overall success of its product suite. Bill Gates and company have spelled out a three-tiered approach that looks to have at least something for everyone.

First, at the low end in both cost and features, are the series of Internet Assistant add-ons for the Microsoft Office applications. These applications include Word, PowerPoint, Excel, Access, and Schedule+. The Internet Assistants are all freely available at the Microsoft Web site (`http://www.microsoft.com`).

The current version of Internet Assistant for Word, 2.0, requires Word 7.0 for Windows 95. IA for Word allows you save word processing documents in HTML format or load and edit HTML documents. It also includes features to preview your HTML document, insert HTML tags, and even browse the Web, if you have a connection to the Internet.

Internet Assistant for Excel is a simple macro that allows you to save spreadsheets into HTML table format. Internet Assistant for PowerPoint accomplishes the same thing for your slide presentations.

The middle layer of the Microsoft Web authoring tools consists of FrontPage (recently acquired with their purchase of Vermeer, Inc.). As far as HTML editors go, FrontPage is a much more powerful and complete package than, say, IA for Word. FrontPage includes a personal Web server so that you can test your pages. In addition to a slick HTML editor, it also includes a Web site analyzer to help check for broken URL references in your HTML pages. Microsoft has stated the price of FrontPage will be substantially reduced from the level Vermeer was charging (analysts are predicting a street price of $99). Some reports indicate it will be available as an add-on to Microsoft Office.

Internet Studio represents the high-end of the spectrum of authoring packages. Pricing, feature details, and availability have not been released as I write this, but Microsoft has stated that it will go beyond HTML authoring. Given the positioning of FrontPage, I infer that Internet Studio will be a comprehensive package for creating enterprise-wide ActiveX Web pages and client/server Intranet *applications*.

ActiveX Redefines Client/Server Computing

In February 1996, Microsoft quickly renamed its technology for OCX controls to *ActiveX* in an effort to boldly take on Java. ActiveX is a hot topic, which you have probably already heard about before you bought this book.

ActiveX, VBScript (see Chapter 18, "Using Visual Basic Script on the Intranet"), and HTML are closely related. ActiveX controls can be placed inside Web pages to make them more dynamic. Because ActiveX is just another name for OCX, you can take any commercially available Visual Basic 32-bit extension control, such as a data grid or a stock ticker, and embed it into your HTML code (once the vendor upgrades the software to the ActiveX model). The ActiveX control will be downloaded to any client computer that retrieves your Web page.

How does the browser know how to display an ActiveX control? After all, ActiveX certainly isn't part of the HTML standard, not even the new HMTL 3.2 standard. The answer is that only Microsoft Internet Explorer 3.0 knows how to do it. Well, that's only true at first glance. Actually, Microsoft is making the technology available to other browser vendors who are porting it to Internet Explorer for Macintosh, and Microsoft has even teamed up with third-parties (such as NCompass mentioned previously) to provide it as an plug-in extension to Netscape Navigator (something that Netscape probably wishes wasn't workable).

Adding OCX controls to Web pages will transform client/server computing. It provides application developers with a whole new method to quickly build network applications. Visual Basic, PowerBuilder, Delpi, and C++ are all great tools, but none of those beat the ease of programming in HTML, especially when you consider that Web page creation tools are still only in their infancy.

VBScript fits in between HTML and the ActiveX control. VBScript is both a subset of Visual Basic and a powerful extension to HTML. VBScript is designed to be safe to run on the client Web browser; language commands that could be potentially damaging in the hands of a virus creator have been removed. VBScript is designed as a subset so that it is small and can be downloaded quickly from the server to client. VBScript is designed to compete with JavaScript (from SunSoft and Netscape) as an interactive Web page programming language.

> **Caution:** The question of whether VBScript is safe is still a debatable point. Some software engineers have devised ways for a malicious VBScript function to use OLE Automation to execute operating system commands on the client machine unbeknownst to the user!

When you place an ActiveX control, such as a gauge, on your HTML page, what happens when the user clicks it? The Web browser will fire an ActiveX event into your HTML code where you can provide custom code to process the event anyway you desire. For example, you could determine whether to load a different Web page or send a collection of form data to the Web server.

Microsoft has also announced a new product that it considers to be an outstanding example of what can be accomplished with Web technology and ActiveX. Microsoft is developing a new application (NetMeeting) that will provide real-time, worldwide audio and data conferencing over the Internet. See its Web page at `http://www.microsoft.com/intdev/` for more information.

> **Note:** Microsoft offers several mailing lists that may be of interest to Web page authors and Intranet/Internet developers. The following topics are currently available:
>
> ◆ ActiveX controls
> ◆ ActiveX scripting
> ◆ Code signing (trust verification services)
> ◆ CryptoAPI (cryptography for Win32 applications)
> ◆ DCOM (distributed COM-based programming issues)
> ◆ DocObjects (OLE document developers)
> ◆ Internet Explorer HTML
> ◆ VBScript
> ◆ WebPost API
>
> For more information and to subscribe to any of these mailing lists in either regular or digest form, visit this URL:
>
> `http://www.microsoft.com/intdev/resource/mail.htm`

> **Note:** NetManage offers a free package of ActiveX controls for use by Web designers and VB programmers. Be sure to check out this URL:
>
> `http://www.netmanage.com/`

C++ and Java Development Tools

In addition to selling application programs and operating systems, Microsoft has always been a vendor of programming tools. They started with Microsoft Basic almost 20 years ago, and they continue that tradition today with VBScript. Visual Basic does have its limitations, however.

Visual C++ is a very powerful environment for the creation of commercial PC software. Microsoft is in eternal battle with Borland for the king of the hill position in the C++ tools arena. To aid that effort, Microsoft has just released Visual C++ 4.1 and 4.2 with a new focus toward the Internet.

The following are some of the new features in Visual C++ that are targeted at Internet programmers:

◆ A new Class Wizard for creating an ISAPI DLL (Internet Server Application Programming Interface, Dynamic Link Library).

◆ C++ classes for Windows Sockets programming that treat complex TCP/IP data transfers as simple streams (CSocketFile, CAsyncSocket, and Csocket).

◆ Classes for the HTML, HTTP, FTP, and Gopher protocols and datastreams.

Jakarta is the code name for a new development tool from Microsoft that will function similarly to Visual C++. The difference is that Jakarta will develop Java code. Of course, Microsoft has to officially license Java from Sun first. Although Microsoft has business agreements with Sun, it remains to be seen whether Microsoft will drag its feet on this one in an effort to give VBScript a chance to catch up with JavaScript. No release date has been made public for Jakarta.

Powerful Application Programming Interfaces

Microsoft is making the following Application Programming Interfaces (APIs) publicly available for developers to help them build Internet-ready applications.

Winsock 2.0

This API provides TCP/IP UNIX-style sockets on Windows platforms. NT 4.0 supports the new Winsock 2.0 standard which allows application programs to be written transparent to the low-level network protocol. Winsock 2.0 will support AppleTalk and IPX/SPX, in addition to TCP/IP.

ISAPI

ISAPI is the Internet Services Application Programming Interface that Microsoft jointly developed with Process Software. Process has carved its mark on the Web via their full-featured and robust Purveyor Web Server for Windows NT.

I will discuss ISAPI a bit further in Chapters 19 and 20, but basically I can say here that it is a Windows DLL version of the Common Gateway Interface (CGI). It allows Web server extension programs to achieve much greater performance on NT than is possible with straight CGI.

CAPI

CAPI, or the Cryptography API, allows developers to call prewritten functions for encryption/ decryption of files and messages, and to transmit and verify digital signatures. CAPI is available in NT 4 (and soon in a Windows 95 service pack).

Sweeper or the WinInet API

It seems that Sweeper and WinInet API are practically synonyms for each other. Sweeper was apparently the code-word for this technology before it was released under the ActiveX umbrella.

So what does it do? It allows programmers to use HTTP, FTP, and Gopher to send and receive functionality without having to develop it from scratch on top of TCP/IP. It can be seen as one layer above TCP/IP and Winsock, and one layer below the application.

Security

Security is very important to the mainstream success of the Web. I already mentioned the Cryptography API above, but let me also touch briefly on some of the other security initiatives that Microsoft is either making or backing.

Code Signing

This is another feature that is built into Internet Explorer 3.0. The idea behind it is to let the browser user know which ActiveX and Java applications will be run on their machines *before* they are downloaded. The user can then choose to accept software from reputable developers or reject suspicious programs before they run.

SSL 2.0 and SSL 3.0

SSL stands for Secure Sockets Layer. Originally developed by Netscape, SSL has become a leading standard for credit card transactions between Web browsers and Web servers.

IIS and Internet Explorer include built-in support for both SSL 2.0 and SSL 3.0. If you wish to secure transactions on your SSL Web server, you must first obtain a digital certificate from a certificate authority as outlined in the IIS user's guide.

STT

The Secure Transaction Technology specification (STT) was developed by Visa and Microsoft for the purpose of secure credit-card transactions on the Web.

PCT

Here is a quote from Microsoft's own Web page (http://pct.microsoft.com) on their Private Communication Technology specification. PCT "...is designed to secure general-purpose business and personal communications on the Internet, and includes features such as privacy, authentication, and mutual identification. PCT enhances SSL with technology developed for STT, particularly in authentication and protocol efficiency. By separating authentication from encryption, PCT allows applications to use authentication that is significantly stronger than the 40-bit key limit for encryption allowed by the U.S. government for export."

SET

Secure Electronic Transactions (SET) is a payment protocol designed by Visa and Mastercard for Web merchants. It is getting very hard to keep up with all this, but I think that SET will supersede STT. Whereas STT was Microsoft and Visa vs. Netscape and Mastercard (who were backing SSL), SET is the fruit of Visa and Mastercard deciding to get together to avoid the possibility of having two Internet banking standards.

PFX

The acronym PFX is supposed to stand for *Personal Information Exchange.* (Hmmm, it looks like the marketing folks will do anything to get an X in there.) PFX was derived from Microsoft's work on STT and PCT.

This protocol proposal has been submitted to the W3C (World Wide Web Consortium) by Microsoft. The protocol is designed to let users transfer or carry personal data securely between different computer platforms. Internet Explorer 3.0 supports PFX.

TLS

The Transport Layer Security (TLS) protocol includes both PCT and SSL. TLS is being considered by the Internet Engineering Task Force as a potential standard.

Summary

This chapter has presented a quick overview of the vast array of Microsoft technologies aimed at the Intranet and the Internet. The discussion included everything from the Web browser to the application programming interfaces.

The next chapter, "Using Visual Basic Script on the Intranet," covers VBScript in much greater detail than was given in this chapter. I'll discuss the language elements and show you how to write VBScript into your own HTML pages.

18

Using Visual Basic Script on the Intranet

- ◆ The benefits of VBScript
- ◆ Integrating VBScript with HTML forms
- ◆ VBScript variables and operators
- ◆ VBScript flow of control statements
- ◆ Using ActiveX controls with VBScript

This chapter continues the theme of Part IV of the book, "Advanced Intranet Publishing," in which we are discussing advanced functions you can build that will capitalize on your Intranet. Visual Basic Script, also called *VBScript*, or *VBS*, is a tool that you can put to good use even if you don't consider yourself a programmer. As you will soon see, VBScript is not very advanced after all, and it integrates well with HTML. If you can learn basic HTML, you can learn VBScript and put it to good use building more creative, and more useful, Web pages.

VBScript functions as an extension to HTML. It is a subset of the commercial Visual Basic language. As I write this chapter, VBScript is only available in the beta release of Microsoft Internet Explorer 3.0. As a beta release, the browser is still somewhat shaky, but the final release should be stable and available by the time you read this.

This chapter will explore the benefits of using VBScript. If you are wondering why you want to bother with it at all, I will explain what you would be missing if you decided not to take advantage of it. I'll then discuss the details of the language, including how it integrates with HTML forms and ActiveX controls.

I apologize in advance for the shortness of this chapter. VBScript is a very rich language and there is so much that could be covered; it really deserves a whole book dedicated to the subject. Unfortunately, my publishing deadline is looming and only a quick overview of the language is possible at this time.

The Benefits of VBScript

Soon after hearing about the Java programming language (invented by SunSoft), most programmers quickly began to realize the striking possibilities that it presents for client/server application development on the Web. By December 1995, the Internet buzz about Java was becoming so heavy that some analysts began predicting the eventual demise of Microsoft because it was estimated Microsoft couldn't possibly compete with something so revolutionary.

Microsoft answered by saying that it would license Java in future versions of its own browser, Internet Explorer. But Microsoft also countered Java by creating (or you might say, renaming) an alternative language. Microsoft designed VBScript, and we should include the overall ActiveX strategy in this discussion, to combat the Internet rage over Java. In my opinion, Microsoft has an idea that is going to be very successful. Let me tell you why I think so.

First, VBScript is easy to learn. Many people first learned programming using BASIC. VBScript is a small subset of Visual Basic—a language that already boasts about three million worldwide users.

Additionally, VBScript is an excellent language with which to take advantage of hundreds of existing OLE controls (as the vendors of those controls move them to the ActiveX model). What is the basis for this statement, you ask? Let's start with the premise that Visual Basic itself is a very successful product, and that VB is already being widely used to develop client/server applications using OLE controls (and their precursor, VBXs). As easy as Visual Basic is to learn, it still isn't something that just anyone off the street can do. It takes time to learn client/server techniques, and it takes time to craft a GUI and get it working in the VB development environment (even as fast as the interpreter is). Having the ability to build certain classes of network applications in a Web page designer is certainly going to make that process easier.

VBScript is lightweight and portable to other operating system platforms (at least that is what Microsoft claims they have achieved). Assuming for the moment that this statement is true, consider the implications. It means that programmers will have a much easier time creating client/ server applications that run on numerous platforms. There will be no further need for expensive efforts to port a program that is tailored for one platform over to entirely different platforms. If VBScript is available in Web browsers on different operating systems, Microsoft and the browser vendors will have done your porting for you.

Today, VBScript, paired with HTML, is somewhat like a fourth-generation language. Although quite different from languages such as Delphi and PowerBuilder, VBScript and HTML are certainly head-and-shoulders above third-generation languages like C and C++. Currently, HTML authoring tools and editors are considered to be in their infancy. As better development tools become available for both HTML and VBScript, the ground rules of client/server application development are going to be radically altered for the better. I predict that HTML and VBS could eventually come to be known as fifth-generation programming languages due to the impact they will have on the pace of application development. Client/server application development is clearly going to become much more accessible and powerful than ever before.

Already, it seems obvious that Java is also turning traditional client/server programming on its head. Java has changed the rules of client/server development by making it so easy to develop true Internet-ready applications. Further, Java has wide industry backing, and SunSoft hopes to make it an open standard. Interestingly enough, Microsoft also hopes to make VBScript an open standard. It is giving away the object code, licensing the source code, and helping other browser vendors to port VBS to non-Windows platforms. Microsoft cites dozens of companies that have already thrown their support behind VBS and ActiveX. At the end of the day, it seems most likely that both Java and VBScript/ActiveX will succeed.

How to Learn More About VBScript and ActiveX

Here are several Web pages that you will want to visit to supplement the material in this chapter and the previous chapter. If you feel like you're hitting a stumbling block when you begin exploring VBScript in your own Intranet HTML pages, these resources should be able to lead you to the answer to any conceivable question:

◆ **Internet Explorer 3.0 Home Page**—This site is an excellent branch point for everything about ActiveX.

```
http://www.microsoft.com/ie/
```

◆ **ActiveX Control Gallery**—This page contains several ready-to-run ActiveX controls that you can embed into Internet Explorer 3.0 HTML pages. You can download them from Microsoft for free!

```
http://www.microsoft.com/appdev/controls/default.htm
```

◆ **Visual Basic Script Home Page**—This is the home page for everything you need to know about VBScript. It includes a link to an excellent VBS tutorial.

```
http://www.microsoft.com/vbscript/
```

◆ **Download the ActiveX SDK**—If you are thinking about inventing your own ActiveX controls, or if you just want to learn more about the inner-workings of OLE DocObjects, you'll need this Software Development Kit.

```
http://www.microsoft.com/intdev/sdk/
```

◆ **W3C Working Draft on HTML 3 Scripting**—Although this paper has a focus on JavaScript, it shows the techniques for adding scripting logic and event handlers to HTML.

```
http://www.w3.org/pub/WWW/TR/WD-script.html
```

Integrating VBScript with HTML Forms

Although VBScript is frequently discussed as the vehicle to manage ActiveX controls embedded in HTML pages, VBS can also be used without ActiveX controls. I'll present some VBS and ActiveX examples in a subsequent section, but for now, this section looks at the basics of VBS.

First of all, VBScript code goes inside ASCII HTML files. The VBScript code appears in the <HEAD> ... </HEAD> section of the HTML file. Further, VBS code is nested within HTML comments within the <SCRIPT> ... </SCRIPT> tags inside the <HEAD> section. If you think that sounds as if the code is being buried or obfuscated, you are probably right. But this is all necessary in order to preserve backward compatibility with existing Web browsers.

If you want to embed comments within your VBScript code, you can use the REM statement, which applies to a single line of code. Remember, HTML comments are in between <!-- and -->; that's different than VBScript comments.

The next thing to learn about VBS is that it can be tied to HTML forms. You won't have much need for VBScript if you don't have a <FORM> ... </FORM> section in your HTML file. Figure 18.1 shows a very simple VBS HTML file running in Internet Explorer 3.0 (beta). Notice that the HTML page contains a trivial form with one command button. When the button is pressed, a custom message box appears. This result is quite different from the usual result of HTML forms and CGI programming in which pressing the button causes the form data to be sent to the Web server, essentially uninterpreted by the Web browser.

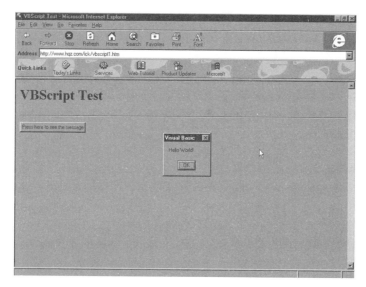

Figure 18.1*. A sample Visual Basic script shown in IE 3.0 (beta version).*

Listing 18.1 presents the VBS code for the simple HTML page shown in Figure 18.1. This file appears on the CD-ROM as vbscript1.htm.

Listing 18.1. The smallest Visual Basic Script page.

```
<HTML>
<HEAD>
<TITLE>VBScript Test</TITLE>
<SCRIPT LANGUAGE="VBS">
<!--
Sub Button1_OnClick
        MsgBox "Hello World!"
End Sub
-->
</SCRIPT>
</HEAD>
<BODY>
<H1>VBScript Test</H1>
<HR>
<FORM>
<INPUT NAME="Button1" TYPE="BUTTON"
        VALUE="Press here to see the message">
</FORM>
</BODY>
</HTML>
```

VBScript Variables and Operators

The only Visual Basic data type used in VBScript is the *variant*. The reason Microsoft chose to do this is that it significantly reduces the size of the VBScript language, making it faster to download. However, there is no major drawback to this decision because variants are capable of holding all the other basic data types, such as integers, strings, and floating point numbers (single and double precision).

In Visual Basic, a literal is a named constant value, either predefined (`True`, `False`, `Null`) or user-defined (such as `MAX = 100`).

VBScript also supports arrays of variables and collections of variables, just as in Visual Basic. Arrays can be indexed by integer values (using variants of course). Collections are analogous to an associative linked-list. By associative, I mean that you can give an item a name (key) when you insert it into the collection using the Add method. A collection is like a linked-list because the size of the collection grows dynamically as you add and remove items.

The following table lists the VBScript operators that can be applied to variables, literals, and constants in expressions.

Tables 18.1 and 18.2 list the various VBScript operators and their meanings.

Table 18.1. The VBScript arithmetic operators.

Operator	Meaning
+	Addition
-	Subtraction and Negation
*	Multiplication
/	Division
\	Integer Division
^	Exponentiation
Mod	Remainder Division
&	String Concatenation

Table 18.2. The VBScript comparison operators.

Operator	Meaning
=	Equality
<>	Non-equality
<	Less than

Operator	Meaning
>	Greater than
<=	Less than or equal
>=	Greater than or equal
Is	Object comparison
&	String Concatenation

In addition, VBScript supports the same logical operators as Visual Basic: Not, And, Or, Xor, Eqv (a bitwise version of And), and Imp (performs logical implication).

Assignment statements can be made to variants with either = or Let. The Set statement is used to assign object variables, such as ActiveX controls.

The Err object is built into VBScript. It allows you to track and handle run-time errors. It has several properties which you can test or set.

VBScript Flow of Control Statements

VBScript supports all the types of control flow statements that you need to create rich programs without resorting to GOTO (no, it doesn't even support GOTO). The following bullet list shows the major control flow statements in VBScript.

◆ **Do…Loop**—Execute the code within the block as long as the Loop expression is True. The conditional test is made at the bottom of the loop, so the loop will always execute at least once.

◆ **If…Then…Else…End If**—Test the If expression to determine if the Then block should be executed or the Else block should be executed. There are other variations of this statement using Else If and/or residing all on one line of code.

◆ **For…Next**—Execute the code within the block up to a specific number of times.

◆ **For Each…Next**—Execute the code within the block once for each item in the specified collection.

◆ **Select Case…Case…End Select**—Execute the code within the block headed by the value that equals the Select Case test expression.

◆ **While…Wend**—Execute the code within the block as long as the specified condition is True. The conditional test is made at the top of the loop.

In addition, VBScript supports both functions and procedures as subroutines. As you saw in Listing 18.1, a procedure is defined with the Sub keyword. Functions, which return a value, are introduced with the Function keyword.

Using ActiveX Controls with VBScript

Before you try to do any serious VBScript and ActiveX programming, make sure you check out the Microsoft ActiveX Control Pad editor. Currently, the beta version is available for free download from Microsoft at this URL: `http://www.microsoft.com/intdev/author/cpad/`.

The reason that you want to get your hands on this program is that inserting ActiveX controls into a Web page involves using very long OLE OBJECT identifiers as specified by the control vendor. The ActiveX Control Pad includes a tool to help you insert ActiveX controls onto your page without having to mess with the numbers.

It also includes a Layout Wizard for positioning the controls on the page and to assist you in writing the code for the event handlers. Figure 18.2 shows an example of the ActiveX Control Pad in action, so to speak.

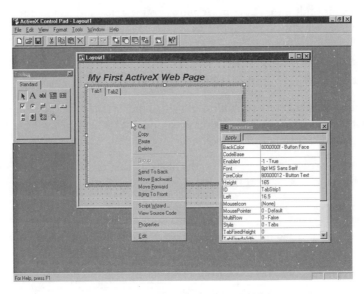

Figure 18.2. *The ActiveX Control Pad can create layouts and HTML documents.*

Although the ActiveX Control Pad program was rather quickly developed as a solution to the problem of many HTML programmers of using NotePad to write code, there are many more capabilities present in this program than I have discussed here. Now that Internet Explorer 3.0 is out, and ActiveX is gaining momentum, there will be a rush of other software development companies also building ActiveX controls and HTML editors that support them.

Summary

This chapter examined the evolution of the Visual Basic language into a client/server Web programming language. VBScript is currently available only in Microsoft Internet Explorer 3.0. But it is being freely licensed to other Web browser vendors, and Microsoft has demonstrated VBScript running in Netscape Navigator 2.0 (and greater) through the NCompass Labs plug-in technology.

VBScript can be tied to traditional HTML forms with or without embedded ActiveX controls. When ActiveX controls are embedded in an HTML page, VBS can be used to process the form data very extensively before the data is finally submitted to the Web server.

The next two chapters move to the server-side of advanced Intranet publishing. I begin the discussion of CGI and ISAPI by exploring the fundamentals of HTML form processing in Chapter 19, "Getting the Most Out of HTML with CGI." Then Chapter 20, "Building a CGI Database System," will return to the subject of Visual Basic and databases by presenting the full source code to a sample Web application you can build and customize.

CHAPTER 19

Getting the Most Out
of HTML with CGI

The Common Gateway Interface (CGI) is a standard that governs how external applications are interfaced with Web servers. The reasoning behind the invention of CGI is simple: without it, the HTTP specification and all Web servers would have become a patchwork of ad hoc extensions.

CGI provides a way to write programs that will run on the server when they are invoked by the client Web browser through HTML code. These programs can be written in the C language, but C is just one possibility. For a discussion of other options, see the section later titled "Choosing a CGI Programming Language."

At this point, the astute reader might have noticed that there are no fewer than four areas of programming prowess needed to get this dog to hunt: CGI, HTTP, HTML, and C (or some other programming language). And just for good measure, you might want to throw in the Win32 API and SQL, depending on what your Web program will do after you finish laying the necessary foundation.

And as if that is not enough, you'll want to consider writing your CGI program using the newer ISAPI (Internet Services Application Programming Interface) standard for better performance. The fundamentals of ISAPI are very similar to CGI, except that ISAPI programs are compiled as DLLs rather than EXEs, and they use pointers to memory blocks instead of stdin/stdout. This book does not substantially cover ISAPI; however, everything you learn about CGI can be applied to ISAPI.

The reason you will want to run this challenging gauntlet is that CGI and ISAPI open the door to great new opportunities. CGI/ISAPI programs are often associated with Web forms. When the user finishes filling out an HTML form and submits it, the data stream that is returned to the server is called the *form data*. Keep in mind that just because you send a blank HTML form to the client Web browser, nothing is going to happen with the form data when it is submitted unless you, the Webmaster, make it happen. The form data would just land in the bit bucket if not for CGI or ISAPI.

CGI/ISAPI is a necessity if you want to save the form data into a database on the server, for example. Or perhaps the form data should be e-mailed to the Webmaster or some other party. Maybe the intent of the form is to have some data faxed or e-mailed back to the client. Or the form could be used to obtain a database query from the user, which is then sent to a database engine before the formatted results are finally returned to the client as an HTML file. These are just some of the possibilities available to anyone brave enough to master the details of client/server Web programming with CGI/ISAPI. (There are tools that make it possible to do much of this without programming; I will tell you about several of them later.) Although all these things can be accomplished with traditional programming, doing it on the Web makes applications platform-independent, distributed, easier to develop, and easier to update.

The purpose of this chapter is to give you the fundamentals of CGI, and show you two simple CGI examples and one sophisticated and practical example. Because all the source code is on the CD-ROM, programming knowledge is not required, but let's not kid ourselves—it would be very helpful. If you don't yet know about programming, you might just want to skim this chapter to get a glimpse of the possibilities. On the other hand, if you want to utilize CGI on your Intranet, this chapter will be a guiding light.

Note: CGI programs are also called CGI *scripts* or *applications.* The reason they are called scripts is that they can be written in Perl, or at the command shell, in which case they are interpreted rather than compiled. When C or Visual Basic is used for CGI, the terms *CGI program* or *CGI application* are preferred to the term *CGI script* because those languages are not interpreted in the traditional sense of script files. Even shorter, some people just refer to all such things as *CGIs.*

CGI scripts are not to be confused with a new product from Microsoft named Visual Basic Script or a new product from Sun and Netscape named JavaScript. Neither JavaScript nor VBScript are necessarily associated with the Common Gateway Interface.

How CGI Works

Figure 19.1 shows a high-level overview of how CGI forms-processing works. There are many other details of HTTP and TCP/IP than what are shown here, but I omit those in order to concentrate on the basic concepts of CGI.

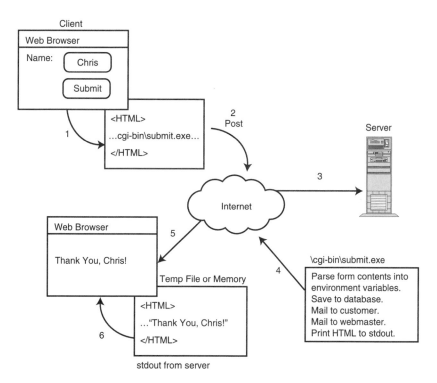

***Figure 19.1.** How CGI processes Web forms.*

The annotated steps corresponding to Figure 19.1 follow. (I assume you are familiar with the way an HTML file gets created and displayed in the Web browser, which is the point at which step 1 begins.)

1. After the user has entered the form data in the Web browser, he chooses the Submit button, which is coded between the <FORM> and </FORM> tags in the HTML file. The Submit button is a link to a CGI (or ISAPI) application on the server. For more information about HTML forms, please review Chapter 5, "What You Need to Know About HTML."

2. The browser uses the POST method of the HTTP protocol to send the form data to the server. The GET method could also be used, but POST is preferred for form data.

3. The data travels through the Intranet or the Internet and arrives at the server, which then passes the data to the CGI application.

4. In addition to parsing the form data and processing it as desired, the CGI application must write the HTML response that will be sent back to the client. The CGI specification says that the Web server should read the stdout device of the CGI application.

5. The server adds appropriate HTTP header information and sends the output of the CGI application back through the network as an HTML response file, which the Web browser receives in memory.

6. The browser interprets the HTML code and displays the results on-screen for the user. At a minimum, this file should usually contain some notification that the data was processed by the server, followed by a hyperlink to take the user back to the HTML page he was on before choosing the link to the form page. In other words, the file puts the client back where he was before he came to Step 1 of this list.

Caution: Allowing any person with a Web browser to execute applications on your server is a security concern. Ensure that all the CGI applications are isolated to one directory and that no one else has access to that directory. With Microsoft IIS, all CGI applications are kept in a directory called scripts under the server root (by default). Also, be careful about using public-domain CGI applications that have not been tested over time to be secure.

Choosing a CGI Programming Language

Nearly all Web servers conform to the CGI 1.1 standard, which is a protocol agreement between your application and the Web server. With most Web servers, CGI applications must be console-mode programs located within the HTTP data directory tree. By saying *console-mode*, I mean that CGI applications cannot be Windows API programs or GUI programs. However, Microsoft IIS is one of several HTTP servers that takes advantage of ISAPI. ISAPI permits you to write Windows DLLs for your CGI applications, and therefore you do have access to the full Win32 API, including ODBC functionality.

Of course, it is very unlikely that you would want to write a GUI CGI or ISAPI application, because that would imply that *you* (as the Webmaster) were going to sit at the Web server waiting to interact with every client that sent data to the server. Remember, the client never sees the CGI or ISAPI program—they will only see the HTML output of the program. Nearly all CGI and ISAPI applications process the form data as background tasks because there could be hundreds of transactions per minute (depending on how popular your Web server becomes).

Another major advantage of ISAPI over CGI is performance. ISAPI passes memory blocks between the server and the application. CGI relies on launching a new program to process the form data from every client, and it uses environment variables and disk files to pass data back and forth.

In UNIX, which is where the Web got its start, CGI applications are frequently written in C, Perl, or the UNIX shell command language. In Windows NT, you can use C/C++ or Perl with most servers and Visual Basic with some. (Well, you can use Visual Basic with any CGI Web server. I'll show you how in the next chapter.) Many Windows NT Webmasters run a public-domain Perl 4 interpreter for CGI and Web site statistics. Perl 5, which includes some nice object-oriented extensions, has recently arrived on the scene, and you should definitely give it consideration as a CGI tool on your Intranet. (See Chapter 29 for more information about Perl.)

Both Perl and C have their advocacy camps. Perl offers great file and string handling, and the code is fairly easy to write and modify. On the other hand, because C is a compiled language, it offers better efficiency, both from the optimization of the compiled code and the fact that the interpreter is not launched for every client submission of form data. In addition, many claim that compiled programs provide better security than scripts because hackers can more easily modify the text of a script just before its execution.

In this chapter, I use some DOS command language, some C/C++, and of course, some HTML. The first example uses a very simple DOS batch file. The second example is written in C. The third example, presented in the next chapter, is a practical application that shows you how to put C++ and Visual Basic together to build an HTML form that can save data into an ODBC database on the server.

It's okay if you don't plan to learn programming. Most of the examples are already compiled on the CD-ROM and will run without your knowing how to program. In this chapter and the next, I have used Visual C++ 4.0 and Visual Basic 4.0.

CGI Environment Variables

The server uses environment variables to pass information to the CGI application. The environment variables are set after the HTTP GET or POST request is received by the Web server (see the next section) and before the server executes the CGI application. Most environment variables are fairly standard from server to server, but be aware that some differences exist. Nothing stops the vendor of a Web server from adding nonstandard environment variables for use by their customers.

The CGI standard specifies certain environment variables that are used for conveying information to a CGI script. The following subset of those environment variables is supported by most HTTP servers. If this list seems confusing, don't despair; most CGI programs don't need to use all these environment variables:

CONTENT_LENGTH—The length of the content as given by the client.

CONTENT_TYPE—For queries that have attached information, such as POST and PUT, this is the content type of the data.

GATEWAY_INTERFACE—The revision of the CGI specification to which this server complies. The format for this variable is CGI/revision.

HTTP_ACCEPT—The MIME types that the client will accept. The format for this variable is type/subtype.

PATH_INFO—The extra path information, as given by the client. This variable enables scripts to be accessed by their virtual pathname.

QUERY_STRING—The information that follows the ? in the URL that referenced this script. This is the query information.

REMOTE_ADDR—The IP address of the remote host making the request.

REQUEST_METHOD—The method with which the request was made, such as GET, HEAD, and POST.

SCRIPT_NAME—A virtual path to the script being executed.

SERVER_NAME—The server's hostname, DNS alias, or IP address.

SERVER_PORT—The port number to which the request was sent.

SERVER_PROTOCOL—The name and revision of the information protocol this request came in with. The format for this variable is protocol/revision.

SERVER_SOFTWARE—The name and version of the server software answering the request. The format for this variable is name/version.

Other HTTP headers received from the client are available in environment variables of the form HTTP_*. For instance, the User-Agent header value is available in HTTP_USER_AGENT. Note that due to the rules of names in certain filesystems, - (dash) in the header names is replaced by _ (underscore) in the corresponding environment variable names. An understanding of the HTTP specification is probably a prerequisite to a full comprehension of the purpose of some of these environment variables.

Understanding Input/Output with CGI

The CGI application accesses information about how it was invoked through the environment variables initialized by the Web server; it reads any information supplied by the client (in a POST request) through stdin and sends output to the client through stdout. This process is pretty simple to understand, once you get the hang of it. (Isn't that how everything works?)

GET Versus POST

GET and POST are two HTTP methods of sending form data to the Web server. When you write a form in HTML, you should specify which HTTP method the browser will use when the form data is sent back to the server.

Listing 19.1 is a short block of HTML code that comprises a complete form. The line numbers are not a part of the HTML code. Note in line 2 that the form is using Method="POST". You could just as easily change this line to "GET". The main difference between GET and POST is that the CGI application will receive the POST data by reading the stdin device, whereas GET data would be received on the command line and in the QUERY_STRING environment variable.

Listing 19.1. A short and sweet HTML form.

```
1. <HTML><HEAD><TITLE>Simple Form</TITLE></HEAD><BODY>
2. <FORM Method="POST"
3. Action="http://domain\cgi-bin\prog.exe">
4. Your Name: <INPUT Name="user" SIZE="30"><P>
5. <INPUT Type=submit Value="Click here to send">
6. </FORM></BODY></HTML>
```

Usually, your forms will be much more complex than the one in Listing 19.1, which only contains one input field. Because many operating systems impose some limit on the length of the command line, it is usually best to use POST. On the other hand, if you know your form data is small, you can use GET.

CGI Command Lines

In the case of a GET request (or ISINDEX), the form data will be on the command line and in the QUERY_STRING environment variable. The command line will contain a question mark after the application name as the delimiter that marks the beginning of the form data. Suppose you change the HTML code in Listing 19.1 to use Method="GET", and the user types in the string User's Name in the text field named user.

The command line of the CGI application would look like the following:

`\cgi-bin\prog.exe?user=User%27s+Name`

The QUERY_STRING environment variable would look like the following:

`user=User%27s+Name.`

Your first observation is naturally going to be that this stuff looks somewhat strange. Your second observation is, hopefully, that the QUERY_STRING data appears somewhat more friendly looking than the command line data. To figure out what's going on with all those funny characters, recall from line 4 of Listing 19.1 that the input field was named user. Now that label is being sent back to you as the first word of QUERY_STRING. Everything after the equals sign in the QUERY_STRING represents the data that the user typed into that particular field. Because more than one field could be used, each one must be named uniquely in the HTML form and in the QUERY_STRING data that is sent back to the CGI application.

Remember that the example assumes that the user typed User's Name with no period on the end. (If he had typed a period, that would be another story—more about that later.) Checking the preceding QUERY_STRING above, notice that you almost have exactly what the user typed, except for the %27, which replaces the apostrophe, and the plus sign, which replaces the space character. HTTP calls for these translations because of operating system conventions for reserved characters in filenames. The same mechanism is used by HTTP to pass URLs, so the server needs to be able to distinguish between the two.

The percent sign is a hex escape character, and the two digits that follow it are used to indicate the ASCII code of a reserved character. The apostrophe sign has a hexadecimal code of 27. If the user typed a period, it would be replaced by %2E. Not all servers encode these characters because whether they are reserved or not depends on the operating system. For example, the apostrophe and the period are legal in some UNIX systems. The plus sign is simply the convention for encoding space characters. Another common translation is the dash character encoded as an underscore.

Finally, if there were other input fields in the HTML form, they would follow the data of the user field. Each name=value pair would be separated by an ampersand (&) character.

Summary of Seven Funny Characters

Table 19.1 is a quick review of the special characters you will come across in CGI. Some of these conventions make up what is known as URL-encoding.

Table 19.1. Special characters in CGI.

Special Character	Description
+ (plus sign)	Used in place of space characters in user input.
= (equals sign)	Used to separate the field name from the field value.
? (question mark)	Used to mark the beginning of the form data on the command line.
_ (underscore)	Used to replace dash characters.
% (percent sign)	Used to encode reserved ASCII characters, followed by two hex digits.
& (ampersand)	Used as the boundary between name/value pairs for each field in the HTML form.
# (number sign)	Used in URLs to indicate a section within an HTML document, sort of like a bookmark. This character is not strictly related to CGI; it can be used in any URL to an HTML document that contains an <A> tag with a Name attribute (called an *anchor*).

Reading from stdin

Recall that QUERY_STRING is not used for the POST method. Because POST is probably more typical, you need to understand how to read stdin to retrieve form data. (This is another reason why CGI programs are console-mode rather than GUI—GUI programs don't have a concept of stdin.)

First, the server will set the CONTENT_LENGTH environment variable to tell how many bytes to read from stdin. You must not read more than that amount. Then the POST-invoked program will read and parse the form data from the stdin device instead of the QUERY_STRING environment variable.

Whether you use POST or GET, have some standard routines in C or Perl to help you perform standard decoding. The C programs in this chapter include several useful functions for that purpose. Feel free to customize them and use them in your own programs. They are public-domain.

Writing to stdout

When the CGI application is done parsing and processing the input data, it must send a reply to the server. The server will forward the reply to the client after applying a header as per the rules of the HyperText Transfer Protocol.

The server will be listening to the stdout device of the CGI application while the latter is executing. The CGI program can generate HTML code on-the-fly or refer the server to another document that it would like to have sent instead. Either you want to compose an HTML document on-the-fly, or you want to refer to another document through HTTP, FTP, or Gopher anywhere on the Web. See the following section titled "A CGI Example in HTML and C" for all the details about composing an HTML response document from within the CGI application.

If you want the server to send another document that already exists, you can use the Location code. In C, you would execute a printf statement that looks something like the following:

```
printf("Location: ftp://FQDN/dir/filename.txt\n\n");
```

Because you must follow the header information with a blank line, the example has two newline characters.

> **Tip:** It is very important that your CGI program prints out an extra blank line after the HTTP header and before the contents of the document that follows the header. A missing blank line is a common source of trouble when trying to debug CGI systems.

How to Learn More About CGI

The granddaddy of all CGI information centers on the Internet is NCSA, the National Center for Supercomputing Applications at the University of Illinois. Full details of how to write CGI scripts are given in the CGI specification, which can be found online at `http://hoohoo.ncsa.uiuc.edu/cgi/`. You will find that NCSA has CGI material at all levels from beginning to advanced, as well as a CGI test suite where you can try the programs and see the code. At the time I am writing this, Version 1.1 is the latest CGI specification. It is not available as a single document, but consists of several hyperlinked pages maintained at NCSA.

For further information about CGI, check out these other resources:

◆ One of the best CGI and HTML documents available anywhere on the Internet is written by Michael Grobe at the University of Kansas. You'll find "An Instantaneous Introduction to CGI Scripts and HTML Forms" at the following URL:

   `http://kufacts.cc.ukans.edu/info/forms/forms-intro.html`

◆ For an introduction to HTML forms and CGI, see this URL (case-sensitive):

   `http://www.utirc.utoronto.ca/HTMLdocs/NewHTML/htmlindex.html`

◆ David Robinson has written an independent and detailed version of the CGI specification. Unlike the NCSA specification, his version exists as a single document (which makes it much easier to print), and it gives a description of all CGI environment variables. See this URL:

   `http://www.ast.cam.ac.uk/%7Edrtr/`

◆ Whether you want to post a question about a CGI roadblock you need help with or just pick up tips by reading the threads of others, the CGI newsgroup is definitely the place to be:

   `comp.infosystems.www.authoring.cgi.`

◆ Last but not least, don't forget to visit `www.yahoo.com`. Select Computers/WWW/CGI and browse the many resources available.

A Trivial CGI Example

There is a standard MIME type for plain ASCII text, `Content type: text/plain`. This MIME type is useful in a trivial but interesting example of CGI, which is often used as proof that the Web server and CGI are installed and running properly. The idea is to invoke a DOS batch file that echoes the values of the CGI environment variables on the server back to the Web browser. All you need to do is save the following text into a file named `trivial.cmd` (or copy it from the CD-ROM) in your `cgi-bin` or `scripts` directory (as configured in the Web server):

```
@echo off
echo content-type: text/plain
echo.
set
```

The set statement in this simple program prints the values of all the HTTP environment variables. The output is directed back to the Web browser. Now just write a line in your home page that links to `trivial.cmd` or create a new HTML file such as the following one, which is named `trivial.htm` on the CD-ROM:

```
<HEAD>
<TITLE>Trivial CGI Test</TITLE>
</HEAD>
<BODY>
<form action="trivial.cmd" method="POST">
<H2>Press the button to run the trivial CGI test.</H2>
<input type="submit" value="Go">
</FORM>
</BODY>
</HTML>
```

A CGI Example Using HTML and C

This section covers a complete CGI transaction, from server to client, back to server, and back to client. This example serves as a template from which you could build a more sophisticated CGI application. The CGI system you are going to build here starts with an HTML file that contains a form. When the user submits the form data, the server will determine that the Action attribute for the form refers to a CGI application. The server will start the application and send it the form data on stdin. Then the server will listen for stdout from the CGI application.

The CGI program is written in C. The program will show you how to retrieve the form data, parse it, and send back an HTML document. The HTML response is constructed within the CGI application because you should embed part of the form data in your response. You don't always have to create HTML on-the-fly from inside the CGI program, but doing so will make your Web pages more dynamic.

The Data Entry Form

To demonstrate CGI, you need to start with an HTML page that contains a URL pointing to a CGI application. Figure 19.2 shows how the data entry form appears in the Web browser as the user is filling it out.

Listing 19.2 shows the HTML code that gets the ball rolling with the sample CGI program. This file and the following C program are available on the CD-ROM if you want to experiment. Note that you will want to change the URL in the FORM ACTION variable to refer to your site (or use `localhost`).

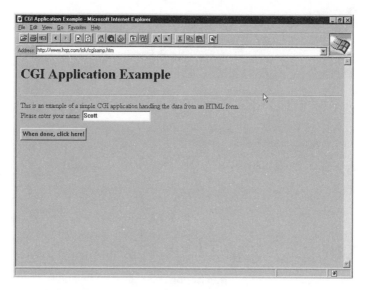

Figure 19.2. *The data entry form that the user fills out.*

Listing 19.2. The HTML code that creates the form.

```
<HTML>
<HEAD>
<TITLE>CGI Application Example</TITLE>
</HEAD>
<BODY>
<H1>CGI Application Example</H1>
<hr>
This is an example of a simple CGI application
handling the data from an HTML form.
<BR>
<FORM ACTION="http://www.hqz.com/scripts/cgisamp.exe" METHOD="Post">
Please enter your name: <INPUT NAME="name" TYPE="text"><p>
<input type=submit value="When done, click here!">
</FORM>
</BODY>
</HTML>
```

The C Code

Before getting to the C program that will process the form data, consider the output of the C program. Listing 19.3 is the HTML code that is sent back to the client after the server obtains it from stdout of the CGI application.

Listing 19.3. The HTML code that is written to stdout by `cgisamp.c`.

```
<HEAD><TITLE>Submitted OK</TITLE></HEAD>
<BODY><h2>The information you supplied has been accepted.
<br> Thank You Scott</h2>
<h3><A href="http://www.hqz.com/cgisamp.htm">
[Return]</a></h3></BODY>
```

Figure 19.3 shows the browser on the client side after the CGI application has finished processing the form data. Note in Figure 19.3 (and Listing 19.3) that the HTML response sent by the CGI application is customized for each set of form data; it includes the name that the user supplied.

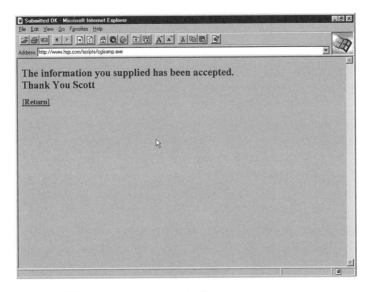

Figure 19.3. *The result of the CGI application as seen by the client.*

Listing 19.4 shows the complete C program, called `cgisamp.exe`, which is executed by the server when the client submits the form data. The following is a quick list of the five functions in `cgisamp`:

◆ `strcvrt`—Converts all occurrences of one character to another within a given string.

◆ `TwoHex2Int`—Called when a percent character marks an escape code.

◆ `UrlDecode`—Expands all the escape codes by calling `TwoHex2Int`.

◆ `StoreField`—Retrieves field/value pairs from the form data.

◆ `main`—Reads the form data from `stdin` and writes the HTML response to `stdout`.

Listing 19.4. The CGI application written in C language (cgisamp.c on the CD-ROM).

```c
/*************************************************************************
 *   File: cgisamp.c
 *
 *   Use: CGI Example Script.
 *
 *   Notes: Assumes it is invoked from a form and that REQUEST_METHOD is POST.
 *   Ensure that you compile this script as a console mode app.
 *
 *   This script is a modified version of the script that comes with EMWAC
 *      HTTPS.
 *
 *   Date: 8/21/95
 *   Christopher L. T. Brown   clbrown@netcom.com
 *
 *************************************************************************/
#include <stdio.h>
#include <stdlib.h>
#include <string.h>
#include <ctype.h>
#include <io.h>

char InputBuffer[4096];
static char * field;
static char * name;

/* Convert all cOld characters   */
/* in cStr into cNew characters. */
void strcvrt(char *cStr, char cOld, char cNew)
{
        int i = 0;

        while(cStr[i])
        {
                if(cStr[i] == cOld)
                        cStr[i] = cNew;
                i++;
        }
}

/* The string starts with two hex */
/* characters.  Return an integer */
/* formed from them.              */
static int TwoHex2Int(char *pC)
{
        int Hi, Lo, Result;

        Hi = pC[0];
        if('0' <= Hi && Hi <= '9')
                Hi -= '0';
        else if('a' <= Hi && Hi <= 'f')
                Hi -= ('a' - 10);
        else if('A' <= Hi && Hi <= 'F')
                Hi -= ('A' - 10);

        Lo = pC[1];
        if('0' <= Lo && Lo <= '9')
                Lo -= '0';
```

```c
        else if('a' <= Lo && Lo <= 'f')
                Lo -= ('a' - 10);
        else if('A' <= Lo && Lo <= 'F')
                Lo -= ('A' - 10);

        Result = Lo + 16 * Hi;
        return(Result);
}

/* Decode the given string in-place */
/* by expanding %XX escapes.        */
void urlDecode(char *p)
{
        char *pD = p;

        while(*p)
        {
                if (*p == '%')          /* Escape: next 2 chars are hex          */
                {                       /* representation of the actual character.*/
                        p++;
                        if(isxdigit(p[0]) && isxdigit(p[1]))
                        {
                                *pD++ = (char)TwoHex2Int(p);
                                p += 2;
                        }
                }
                else
                        *pD++ = *p++;
        }
        *pD = '\0';
}

/* Parse out and store field=value items. */
/* Don't use strtok!                       */
void StoreField(char *f, char *Item)
{
        char *p;

        p = strchr(Item, '=');
        *p++ = '\0';
        urlDecode(Item);
        urlDecode(p);
        strcvrt(p, '\n', ' ');
        strcvrt(p, '+', ' ');           /* Get rid of those nasty +'s */
        field = f;                      /* Hold on to the field just in case. */
        name = p;                       /* Hold on to the name to print*/
}

int main(void)
{
        int ContentLength, x, i;
        char *p,
                *pRequestMethod,
                *URL,
                *f;

        /* Turn buffering off for stdin.*/
        setvbuf(stdin, NULL, _IONBF, 0);
```

continues

Listing 19.4. continued

```c
        /* Tell the client what we're going to send */
        printf("Content-type: text/html\n\n");

        /* What method were we invoked through? */
        pRequestMethod = getenv("REQUEST_METHOD");

        /* Get the data from the client      */
        if(strcmp(pRequestMethod,"POST") == 0)
        {
                /* according to the requested method.*/
                /* Read in the data from the client. */
                p = getenv("CONTENT_LENGTH");
                if(p != NULL)
                        ContentLength = atoi(p);
                else
                        ContentLength = 0;
                if(ContentLength > sizeof(InputBuffer) -1)
                        ContentLength = sizeof(InputBuffer) -1;

                i = 0;
                while(i < ContentLength)
                {
                        x = fgetc(stdin);
                        if(x == EOF)
                                break;
                        InputBuffer[i++] = x;
                }
                InputBuffer[i] = '\0';
                ContentLength = i;

                p = getenv("CONTENT_TYPE");
                if(p == NULL)
                        return(0);

                if(strcmp(p, "application/x-www-form-urlencoded") == 0)
                 {
                        p = strtok(InputBuffer, "&");       /* Parse the data */
                        while(p != NULL)
                        {
                                StoreField(f, p);
                                p = strtok(NULL, "&");
                        }
                 }
        }

    URL = getenv("HTTP_REFERER");               /* What url called me.*/
    printf("<HEAD><TITLE>Submitted OK</TITLE></HEAD>\n");
    printf("<BODY><h2>The information you supplied has been accepted.");
    printf("<br> Thank You %s</h2>\n", name);
    printf("<h3><A href=\"%s\">[Return]</a></h3></BODY>\n", URL);

    return(0);
}
```

Notice the calls in the main routine to the C library function getenv. That is how the program can determine if the REQUEST_METHOD is equal to POST and how many bytes it should read by checking CONTENT_LENGTH.

Another very important point to make about the main function is that it must output a partial HTTP header to go with the HTML document that it creates. This line appears near the top of the function:

```
printf("Content-type: text/html\n\n");
```

You might want to add error handling later, in which case you would probably create an alternative HTML response document. The HTTP header would need to be printed in any case. The CGI convention requires that the header be followed by a blank line before the HTML code that is sent. That is why the printf statement includes two newlines at the end. Please forgive my frequent reminders, but this point is important.

The content type indicates a MIME encoding that tells the client browser that the data stream to follow is HTML code in ASCII format. There are several standard MIME encoding types. See the CGI specification for further information.

Testing CGI Systems

Getting CGI systems to work properly obviously requires the ability to integrate several sophisticated tools. And what should a good software engineer do when faced with the challenge of building a complex system? One proven approach is to establish clear milestones to reach the overall goal, build the software one piece at a time (preferably as black boxes with as few interfaces as possible), and test each module separately as you go to prove that the milestones are met successfully.

For example, test the HTML form independently from the CGI program. You might even take the time to build a test environment for the CGI application so that you can verify its input/output completely independent of any interaction with the Web server. Doing this could yield a great payback when it comes time to debug or enhance the system, especially if it is a large application or if it interfaces with a database. The goal is to reduce the edit/compile/link/test cycle down to as tight a loop as possible. A test environment that doesn't involve running the server, launching the browser, and filling out the form will yield significant time savings over the long run.

CGI Toolkits and Applications

Before trying to write your own CGI applications, consider letting someone else do it for you. This section discusses several CGI toolkits that are available on the Internet or the CD-ROM. Whether you are just counting visitors at your site, tabulating more advanced statistics, or running a customer support form, there is bound to be something here that will help you make your Intranet come to life.

CGI PerForm

CGI PerForm was designed to work with both Windows NT and Windows 95 and provide all the basic CGI functionality needed by a WWW site, without requiring C or Perl. With a simple command file, template file, and HTML form, you can create an e-mail feedback form, guest book, or even a ballot box—or perform all three of those operations at the same time and as many times as you want. For more information about CGI PerForm, visit this URL:

```
http://www.rtis.com/nat/software/
```

How CGI PerForm Works

You can break down an interactive WWW page into three pieces:

◆ The HTML form through which the data is typed in and submitted

◆ The Common Gateway Interface (CGI) application that receives and processes the submitted data

◆ The end result

CGI PerForm is one example of the CGI application that handles the incoming data and creates the result. A result can be a combination of more than one task or command. PerForm commands are discussed thoroughly in the online documentation that accompanies the product.

CGI PerForm uses a command file you create to determine what tasks it needs to perform on the data. A different command file is created for every interactive application needed. Each command requires certain key values in order for it to perform its task. A majority of the key values are filenames. Some of these files must already exist, such as a template file or a column file. Others are created by the command, such as a data file or the output file.

CGI PerForm takes all the incoming data supplied by the HTML form and stores it into a memory block. An HTML form supplies data in *name=value* pairs, for example, lastname=Smith. You can supplement the data supplied by the HTML form by plugging in hard-coded *name=value* pairs in the command file. These values go into the same memory block as the submitted data. You can hard-code values in your command file to hide them or to set defaults.

The next step is to use the data. You can save the data to a data file or a database or combine the results with a template file to create a confirmation message or a form letter to be mailed. The command can be performed as often as necessary with different key values. For example, you could save data submitted by a user into three different data files. These data files can have some of the same data as another, or two of them could be identical. You can also pass variables between command blocks to create unique files in which to store data at the user's request.

CGI2Shell 2.0

If you find yourself using a lot of CGI scripts, you'll like this little utility package from Richard Graessler of Germany. See this link for more information (and other utilities):

`http://rick.wzl.rwth-aachen.de/rickg/index.html`

The CGI2Shell applications are intended for Windows Web servers that do not support the execution of scripts without a corresponding shell in the command line of a `<FORM ACTION=>` or `<A HREF=>` tag.

The CGI2Shell Gateway is a set of programs that enable `PATH_INFO` to specify the name of a CGI script that will be executed with either the `POST` or `GET` method. Currently, the shells `Perl.exe` and `Sh.exe`, and the Windows NT command interpreter `cmd.exe`, are supported.

Using CGI2Shell

The CGI2Shell Gateway includes three programs, one for each shell it supports:

```
CGI2Sh.exe for Sh.exe
CGI2Perl.exe for Perl.exe
CGI2Cmd.exe for Cmd.exe (Windows NT only)
```

All you need to do is include the script with its path in the `PATHINFO` of the URL. For example:

`http://host.domain/progpath/CGI2xxx.exe/scriptpath/script.ext`

The shell programs must reside in the path or the same directory as `CGI2xxx.exe`.

CGIC

CGIC is a library of functions for CGI development with ANSI standard C written by Thomas Boutell. You can find more information about it at the following URL:

`http://sunsite.unc.edu/boutell/cgic/cgic.html`

EIT's CGI Library

Enterprise Integration Technology has created LIBCGI to assist programmers who are writing CGI systems in C language. The library consists of about 15 functions, and it is freeware. Originally written for UNIX as part of their Webmaster's Starter Kit, it has been ported to several other popular platforms, including Windows. As with several URLs mentioned in this book, I have not tried this product and cannot endorse it other than to suggest that you visit their site and have a look for yourself: `http://wsk.eit.com`.

Web Developers Warehouse

If you program with Borland C++ and don't mind paying for CGI and HTML tools, you should definitely drop by http://htechno.com/wdw/index.htm. A company called Specialized Technologies has developed a suite of products they call the Web Developers Warehouse. It includes three components: TCgi, HTML Objects, and Web Wizard. TCgi is a set of C++ classes for WinCGI, which works with the O'Reilly WebSite server and the FolkWeb server.

Visit their home page for more information. You can also try the demonstration programs, pay for the software electronically, and download it pronto.

Summary

The next chapter picks up where this one leaves off by showing you how to develop a functional CGI database application. The source code in HTML, Visual C++, and Visual Basic is ready to run from the CD-ROM, but the material is not for the faint at heart when it comes to programming. If you're ready to take a big step beyond static Web pages, read on.

CHAPTER

20

Building a CGI Database System

- ◆ Installing the CGI application
- ◆ How the HTML works
- ◆ Web Database programming with Visual Basic 4.0
- ◆ The C++ program
- ◆ The Visual Basic program
- ◆ The temporary .HFO file
- ◆ Examining the database with Data Manager

After being introduced to CGI and seeing a working (although not very useful) example in the previous chapter, you're probably eager to learn how CGI can really be put to work. This chapter shows you how to install and use a CGI application that is included on the CD. For those of you who want to understand the inner workings of CGI and HTML forms, I'll discuss some of the details of the program, which are written in C++ and Visual Basic.

When using forms in HTML, you need a CGI script or application to handle the contents of that form. You will find the source code and binary code for the programs in this section on the CD-ROM. Feel free to use the code as is or to customize it for your purposes. This CGI application is also useful if you know how to write HTML code but don't want to dive into CGI programming.

The HTML file used in this example is called `feedback.htm`. It enables a customer to send you comments about your Intranet. For lack of a better name, the first program, which is written in C++, is called `cgi1.cpp`. Just as unimaginative, the Visual Basic program is called `cgi2.bas`. The Visual Basic program is not mandatory. In other words, the C++ program is useful on its own. However, if you decide not to use the VB program, you will have to make a slight modification to the C++ program.

Installing the CGI Application

The list of files in Table 20.1 is what you will be working with in this section.

Table 20.1. The files to build the CGI system.

Filename	Description
cgi1.cpp	C++ source code for cgi1.exe
cgi1.mak	Makefile for Visual C++ 4.x
cgi1.exe	Intel binary CGI application
cgi2.bas	Visual Basic 4.0 source code
cgi2.vbp	Visual Basic 4.0 project makefile
cgi2.exe	Visual Basic program that writes the database
feedback.htm	HTML document that receives user input
cgi.mdb	Access database that saves the data

The C++ source code provided here is an enhancement to the source code that comes with the freeware EMWAC HTTP Web server for Windows NT. A RETURN tag has been added to the information dialog so that after your information is written to a file, you can return to the URL from which cgi1.exe was called. The nasty plus characters have been removed, so strings are now separated by spaces. Newline characters are now accepted.

To use this CGI database system, follow these steps:

1. Place cgi1.exe, cgi2.exe, and cgi.mdb in an executable directory for your Web server (for example, /scripts).

2. Place feedback.htm somewhere within the HTML document path of your Web server.

3. Provide a link to feedback.htm from your home page. You can use WebEdit to customize feedback.htm for your own purposes.

4. Try out the form from your own browser. After you submit the form to the server, it should run cgi1.exe. As it stands now, cgi1.exe will launch cgi2.exe and save the data in the database.

Recall from Chapter 5, "What You Need to Know About HTML," that CGI applications can capture only the form fields that you name in the HTML document. The cgi1.exe application captures the user data for the form field names that you establish in your HTML document (for example, feedback.htm) and writes them to a temporary file with the .HFO extension. Each temporary file contains one set of form data. The temporary file is a simple text file. The Visual Basic program that writes the data to the database deletes the temporary files. If you want to e-mail the temporary files using Blat, you will need to modify the Visual Basic program.

How the HTML Works

This section discusses the why and how of the CGI system. I refer to it as a CGI *system* because it requires proper integration of several languages and protocols, including HTML, C++, Visual Basic, HTTP, CGI, and ODBC.

Figure 20.1 shows a sample form, defined in HTML, that gathers comments from the user. When the user clicks the button labeled Submit Comments, the form will run the CGI application on the server, which will save the form data to a temporary file before passing it to Visual Basic.

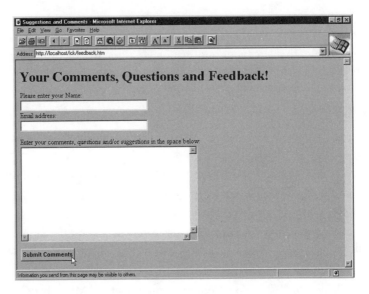

Figure 20.1. *Form processing screen.*

Listing 20.1 shows feedback.htm, which is the HTML code that creates the form and invokes the CGI application. To achieve the greatest portability among browsers, this code does not take advantage of any HTML 3.2 features.

Listing 20.1. This feedback.htm file sends form data to the CGI application on the server.

```
<HEAD>
<TITLE>Suggestions and Comments</TITLE>
</HEAD>
<BODY>
<form action="http://localhost/scripts/cgi1.exe" method="POST">
<H1>Your Comments, Questions and Feedback!</H1>
Please enter your Name:
<BR><INPUT TYPE=text NAME="name" SIZE = 40 MAXLENGTH=40>
<BR>Email address:
<BR><INPUT TYPE=text NAME="email" SIZE = 40 MAXLENGTH=40>
<P>
Enter your comments, questions and/or suggestions in the space below:
<BR>
<TEXTAREA NAME="comments" ROWS=12 COLS=60 MAXLENGTH=3000></TEXTAREA>
<P>
<input type="submit" value="Submit Comments">
</FORM>
</BODY>
</HTML>
```

The action attribute of the form is the URL of the CGI application. The action attribute of the sample form is as follows:

```
http://localhost/scripts/cgi1.exe
```

The scripts/cgi1.exe portion of the action attribute executes the first part of the CGI system on the server, cgi1exe. In this example, the method attribute is POST, which means the form data will be read from stdin by the CGI application. Notice the names of the input fields (name, email, and comments); you will be checking for those names in the VB program later.

Take another look at the <FORM> tag in Listing 20.1. Notice that the action URL indicates localhost. One of the rules of TCP/IP is that 127.0.0.1 is defined to be the localhost, or loopback address, meaning that this special IP address is always valid to refer to the current machine. The HOSTS file in your Windows directory should indicate that localhost is an alias for 127.0.0.1. This alias makes a convenient way to check your CGI systems on your server, even if you don't have a valid assigned IP address or you aren't connected to the Internet. You will have to modify the URL to refer to your actual server name if you expect the code to work in the Web browsers of your customers.

Web Database Programming with Visual Basic 4.0

Visual Basic includes very powerful capabilities for database, file, and string manipulation. And these features just happen to have a high correlation with a dream language for CGI. After you become familiar with VB, you'll see that this list is just the tip of the iceberg of its capabilities. For example, did you know that VB will let you send and receive e-mail on the LAN using MAPI (the Mail API)? Did you know that you can use VB to send a fax? VB programs are even used to control factory automation processes. Imagine using a Web form to automatically initiate a fax transmission, beep your pager, or build a customized pizza.

Pundits claim that VB is slow, but this just isn't true. Of course, VB is slower than a compiled language, but the point is that this *usually* doesn't matter. Before C/C++/Java programmers get in an uproar, realize that I didn't say *always*, I said *usually*. I can back that statement up with two principles that I have seen proven true in countless software development projects.

In the first place, the choice of algorithm is always far more important to performance than any other factor. One VB program can be a factor of 100 times slower than another VB program written to perform exactly the same task. And a C++ program can easily be written in such a way that it runs slower than a similar Visual Basic program. So before you criticize the speed of a language, first analyze the specific bottlenecks in the given program. Otherwise the conversation is meaningless. (By the way, the most likely kinds of programs where C++ will beat VB in benchmark tests involve compute-bound tasks where the CPU is heavily utilized. If you have a function which calculates a formula thousands of times in a loop, write it in C++. On the other hand, if you are developing a GUI client/server database application, the network and database software layers, like ODBC, are more important factors to the overall performance than is the language choice for the high-level application code. Obviously, hardware plays a critical role in performance too, but I assume that will be the same regardless of your choice of programming language.)

Secondly, with project schedules as condensed as they are on software developers and Information System Engineers, as soon as you identify the segment of your code that cries out to be optimized (evidence suggests that this code is often less than one percent of the total code), and assuming that your customers don't have more important things for you to be working on instead (like new features and enhancements), you can rewrite that function in C and put it in a DLL. This way, you get to retain VB for the things it does best, namely user interface construction and database connectivity, and tune only the sections of the program that need the boost. Isn't it better to get it working first and optimize it later?

Many Windows Web servers don't support WinCGI, which is a protocol invented by Bob Denny (author of the O'Reilly WebSite server) for building CGI applications in Visual Basic. Standard CGI requires a shell interface, but VB4 doesn't build that kind of console-mode application. This is unfortunate, but thanks to the infinite malleability of software, it's not insurmountable. You might call the program presented in this chapter a clever kludge (if you believe in the power of positive criticism). It allows you to use CGI with just about any Windows-based Web server and still take advantage of the database power of Visual Basic 4.0 (or greater) Profession Edition or Enterprise Edition.

The C++ program that is developed in this chapter parses the form data into a temporary file before it invokes the Visual Basic application. The VB program runs invisibly while it reads the temporary file passed in by the C++ program and writes the information to the Access database.

By the way, the C++ program is more like an "extended C" program because it doesn't use any object-oriented features. However, it is compiled with Visual C++ as a C++ program and it does use C++ style comments.

How Does the Application Work?

The application presented in this chapter has four pieces:

- The HTML form that invokes the CGI application
- The CGI application written in C++ that handles the environment variables and passes the form data to the Visual Basic program
- The Visual Basic program itself
- An Access database to store the data

Using Visual Basic and ODBC, you could just as easily connect to an Oracle database or any other database for which an ODBC driver is available instead of the Access database. I need not name your favorite database here because the chances are very high that you can obtain an ODBC driver for it. Once you have an ODBC driver, the rest of the story is all the same.

What does this application do when it is all done? As you saw in Figure 20.1, the HTML file captures user feedback about your Intranet. The CGI program then saves the data into an Access database, which you can query at your leisure. Writing the back-end program in VB opens the door to easy customizations in the future that could take full advantage of the Windows environment. For example, you could run other programs in Access or Visual Basic to process the collection of form data by sending e-mail in a batch fashion. If you run the second-stage programs offline (perhaps from another workstation) or on a daily or weekly basis, you can minimize the hit on system resources while the Intranet server is running. In other words, consider tuning the Web server to perform only the quick acquisition of form data, and save the data processing for later.

The program inserts the form data into a table in an Access database. Each database record includes a timestamp so that you can use a SQL query (in a separate program such as Access) to determine which records have been added within a given date range.

The main goal of this program is to show you the possibilities of CGI with VB. The sample application presented in this chapter is by no means robust. In particular, it lacks substantial error checking. You can easily extend this system in any number of ways. With HTML, VB, ODBC, and the Windows API at your disposal, you are limited only by your imagination.

The disadvantage of using two programs in this manner is that they must pass the form data in a temporary file. This takes more time than if only C++ were used or if ISAPI were used instead. Using two programs is going to be slower than using one program and that would in turn be slower than using one ISAPI DLL. But in the case of an Intranet, efficiency of server transactions is probably not going to be as key a factor as if you are running a Web site on the Internet. I'm not saying that you shouldn't care if it runs slow, but the primary goal should be to get a prototype up and running so that you can show it to your customers as soon as possible. Then you can collect their feedback, customize and enhance the program (and the HTML) based on their suggestions, and begin analyzing if actual performance is really considered lacking.

The Efficiency of CGI

CGI was invented from a command-line perspective in a UNIX environment. Unfortunately, having the Web server invoke the CGI application separately for each client request is not the most efficient means of processing form data on Windows NT.

Why is CGI efficiency important? The answer depends mostly on how large your Web site is. If you have only a few visitors per day, you don't need to worry about it. But if you are running a server with dozens of simultaneous client connections, you'll want your server to be tuned as tightly as possible.

The new generation of Web servers for Windows makes great gains in CGI efficiency by opening the door to ISAPI. Process Software, Ilar Concepts, Internet Factory, and Microsoft, among other vendors, already support this open specification. (Netscape and WebSite use other efficient CGI alternatives.) ISAPI (Information Server Application Programming Interface) allows developers to create 32-bit DLLs to run within the memory context of the Web server. Not only does the server avoid reloading the CGI executable for each client hit, but form data is passed into the application, and the HTML response is passed back, using pointers to memory blocks—thus saving a substantial amount of file I/O.

Although Visual Basic doesn't work with pointers as handily as C and C++, ISAPI programming in VB is probably no more complex than it is in WinCGI 1.2 or CGI 1.1.

Another alternative to CGI is SSI+ (Server Side Includes), which is supported by the WebQuest server from Questar. Only time will tell which of these techniques will ultimately prove to be the most effective. In the meantime, consider many factors when choosing your server, and then use the tools it offers.

The C++ Program

The C++ program is called cgi1.cpp. It is an enhanced version of the simple C program presented in Chapter 19, "Getting the Most Out of HTML with CGI." You recall that cgisamp.exe was used to parse the contents of an HTML form. The purpose for modifying the program in this section is to get it to parse the data slightly differently before handing it off to the Visual Basic program.

The C++ program creates a small temporary file each time it is invoked. See Listing 20.2 for the code. The following is a description of the functions in cgi1.cpp:

◆ The strcvrt function converts all occurrences of one character to another within a given string.

◆ TwoHex2Int is called when a percent character marks an escape code.

◆ UrlDecode expands all the escape codes by calling TwoHex2Int.

◆ StoreField retrieves field/value pairs from the form data.

◆ The main function reads the form data from stdin, saves it to CGIx.HFO, and writes the HTML response to stdout.

Listing 20.2. cgi1.cpp runs between the server and the VB program.

```
/****************************************************************
 *  File: CGI1.CPP
 *
 *  Description: This CGI program parses form data and invokes
 *  a Visual Basic program to save the data in an ODBC database.
 *
 *  This program assumes it is invoked by an HTML form.
 *  This program writes form data
 *  to a temporary file and then invokes the Visual Basic application
 *  that interfaces with the database.
 *  Ensure that you compile this script as an NT console mode app.
 *
```

```
 *   This program is public domain freeware.
 *   April, 1996
 *   By: Scott Zimmerman
 *
 ***********************************************************************/
#include <stdio.h>
#include <stdlib.h>
#include <string.h>
#include <ctype.h>
#include <io.h>
#include <time.h>

char InputBuffer[4096];        // Maximum amount of data user may enter

/* Convert all cOld characters in cStr into cNew characters.
*/
void strcvrt(char *cStr, char cOld, char cNew)
{
  int i = 0;

  while(cStr[i])
  {
    if(cStr[i] == cOld)
    cStr[i] = cNew;
    i++;
  }
}

/* The string starts with two hex characters.
** Return an integer formed from them.
*/
static int TwoHex2Int(char *pC)
{
    int Hi, Lo, Result;

    Hi = pC[0];
    if('0' <= Hi && Hi <= '9')
       Hi -= '0';
    else
       if('a' <= Hi && Hi <= 'f')
          Hi -= ('a' - 10);
       else
          if('A' <= Hi && Hi <= 'F')
             Hi -= ('A' - 10);

    Lo = pC[1];
    if('0' <= Lo && Lo <= '9')
      Lo -= '0';
     else
       if('a' <= Lo && Lo <= 'f')
          Lo -= ('a' - 10);
       else
          if('A' <= Lo && Lo <= 'F')
             Lo -= ('A' - 10);

    Result = Lo + 16 * Hi;
    return(Result);
}
```

continues

Listing 20.2. continued

```c
/* Decode the given string in-place by expanding %XX escapes.
*/
void urlDecode(char *p)
{
    char *pD = p;

    while(*p)
    {
        /* Escape: next 2 chars are hex          */
        /* representation of the actual character.*/
        if(*p == '%')
        {
            p++;
            if(isxdigit(p[0]) && isxdigit(p[1]))
            {
                *pD++ = (char)TwoHex2Int(p);
                p += 2;
            }
        }
        else
            *pD++ = *p++;
    }
    *pD = '\0';
}

/* Parse out and store field=value items into the temp file.
** DON'T use strtok here because it is ALREADY used by caller.
*/
void StoreField(FILE *f, char *Item)
{
    char *p;

    p = strchr(Item, '=');
    *p++ = '\0';
    urlDecode(Item);
    urlDecode(p);
    strcvrt(p, '\n', ' ');

    /* Get rid of those nasty +'s */
    strcvrt(p, '+', ' ');
    fprintf(f, "%s=%s\n", Item, p);
}

int main(void)
{
    int  ContentLength, x, i;
    char *p, *URL, *whocalledme;
    char datebuf[9], timebuf[9];
    char FileName[_MAX_PATH];
    char cmdbuf[_MAX_PATH + 30];
    FILE *f;

    // Turn buffering off for stdin
    setvbuf(stdin, NULL, _IONBF, 0);

    // Tell the client what we're going to send back
    printf("Content-type: text/html\n\n");
```

```c
// Uses a kludgy IPC method to pass form data to VB
for (i = 0; i <= 9999; i++)
{
    // Make a new filename
    sprintf(FileName, "CGI%d.HFO", i);

    // If the file exists, try again. Doesn't handle errors!
    if(access(FileName, 0) == -1)
        break;
}

// Open the file
f = fopen(FileName, "a");

// Check if open succeeds
if(f == NULL)
{
    printf("<HEAD><TITLE>Error: cannot open file</TITLE></HEAD>\n");
    printf("<BODY><H1>Error: cannot open file</H1>\n");
    printf("The file %s could not be opened.\n",FileName);
    printf("</BODY>\n");
    exit(0);
}

// Write to the file the URL which posted the form data
whocalledme = getenv("REMOTE_ADDR");
fprintf(f, "URL=%s\n", whocalledme);

// Write to the file the date/time of this hit
strdate(datebuf);
strtime(timebuf);
fprintf(f, "Date=%s\n", datebuf);
fprintf(f, "Time=%s\n", timebuf);

// Get the length of the client input data
p = getenv("CONTENT_LENGTH");
if(p != NULL)
    ContentLength = atoi(p);
else
    ContentLength = 0;

// Avoid buffer overflow -- better to allocate dynamically
if(ContentLength > sizeof(InputBuffer) -1)
    ContentLength = sizeof(InputBuffer) -1;

// Get the data from the client (assumes POST method)

i = 0;
while(i < ContentLength)
{
    x = fgetc(stdin);
    if(x == EOF)
        break;
    InputBuffer[i++] = x;
}
InputBuffer[i] = '\0';
ContentLength = i;

p = getenv("CONTENT_TYPE");
```

continues

Listing 20.2. continued

```c
    if(p == NULL)
    {
        fclose(f);
        return(0);
    }

    if(strcmp(p, "application/x-www-form-urlencoded") == 0)
    {
        // Parse the data
        p = strtok(InputBuffer, "&");
        while(p != NULL)
        {
            // Write the field/value pair to the temp file
            StoreField(f, p);
            p = strtok(NULL, "&");
        }
    }
    else
        // Write the whole data to file
        fprintf(f, "Input = %s\n", InputBuffer);

    // Confirm to client
    if(!ferror(f))
    {
// What url called me
        URL = getenv("HTTP_REFERER");
        printf("<HEAD><TITLE>Submitted OK</TITLE></HEAD>\n");
        printf("<BODY><h2>Your information has been accepted.");
        printf("   Thank You!</h2>\n");
        printf("<h3><A href=\"%s\">Return</a></h3></BODY>\n", URL);
    }
    else
    {
// What url called me
        URL = getenv("HTTP_REFERER");
        printf("<HEAD><TITLE>Server file I/O error</TITLE></HEAD>\n");
        printf("<BODY><h2>Your information could not be accepted\n");
        printf("due to a file I/O error at the server.</h2>\n");
        printf("<h3><A href=\"%s\">Return</a></h3></BODY>\n", URL);
    }

    // Close the file.
    fclose(f);

    // Run the Visual Basic program...
    sprintf(cmdbuf, "start cgi2.exe %s", FileName);
    system(cmdbuf);

    return(0);
}
```

One of the first things that main() does is to invent a temporary filename. It tries to use CGI0.HFO. If that filename exists, it will increment the number and try CGI1.HFO. This algorithm is pretty inefficient and it doesn't check for errors, but it serves the purpose so you can focus on the more interesting stuff.

The first item written to the temporary file is the URL from the REMOTE_ADDR environment variable. This variable tracks the client. The date and time follow on separate lines. All fields are on lines by themselves, and each field name is separated from its corresponding data by an equal sign. You need to keep these things in mind when you write the VB program.

This program ignores some error-checking, and it blindly assumes that REQUEST_METHOD is POST, so make sure you use that in feedback.htm or your own customized HTML that invokes this program.

The interesting thing about the code is that two output files are being written simultaneously. Remember, the CGI application is supposed to send some HTML output back to the browser so that the user won't get stranded on the Web. This task is achieved by the calls to printf, which write to stdout. The HTTP server picks up the stdout data, applies the HTTP protocol, and sends it back to the client.

Meanwhile, you still have to write the form data from the client into the temporary file before you launch the VB program. That is achieved by the fprintf calls. At the end of the program, cgi2.exe is launched through the system() call in the C standard library.

The Visual Basic Program

Now you need the VB program to pick up the form data and insert it into the database. This process executes fairly quickly, so you really don't need a user interface. In fact, you want the program to quit as soon as it's finished—with no user involvement at all. Remember, this program is only going to run on the server. I placed all the code in Sub Main and ParseField in the .BAS file to eliminate the unnecessary loading of a .FRM file. See Listing 20.3 for the VB code. This file is cgi2.bas in the \chapter20 directory on the CD. The VB 4.0 project file is cgi2.vbp.

Note: This program was developed using the Visual Basic 4.0 Professional Edition. The program will also work as is with the 4.0 Enterprise Edition, and presumably with VB 5.0. With very minor changes, the program could be made to work with the Visual Basic 3.0 Professional Edition.

The files on the CD do not include a setup program for this application. You must have Visual Basic 4.0 installed to get the proper DLLs and for OLE registration of the Jet engine to take place.

Listing 20.3. The VB program, which interfaces with the database.

```
' -----------------------------------------------------------------
' CGI2.BAS
' This program was written by Scott Zimmerman, April 1996.
' It is public domain freeware.
' -----------------------------------------------------------------
'
```

continues

__Listing 20.3.__ The VB program, which interfaces with the database.

```
Public Sub main()

    Dim szURL        As String
    Dim szDate       As String
    Dim szTime       As String
    Dim szName       As String
    Dim szEmail      As String
    Dim szComments   As String
    Dim db           As Database
    Dim rs           As Recordset

    ' Open the temporary file with form data and read it into memory
    Open Command$ For Input As #1
    Line Input #1, szURL
    Line Input #1, szDate
    Line Input #1, szTime
    Line Input #1, szName
    Line Input #1, szEmail
    Line Input #1, szComments

    ' Close the temporary file and delete it
    Close #1
    Kill Command$

    ' Open the database and the table
    Set db = OpenDatabase(App.Path & "\cgi.mdb")
    Set rs = db.OpenRecordset("table1", dbOpenTable)

    ' Add a new record to the table. Counter field is
    ' initialized automatically by Jet 3.0.
    rs.AddNew

    rs!When = ParseField(szDate) & " " & ParseField(szTime)
    rs!URL = ParseField(szURL)
    rs!Name = ParseField(szName)
    rs!Email = ParseField(szEmail)
    rs!Comments = ParseField(szComments)

    ' Update the table, close everything and quit
    rs.Update
    rs.Close
    db.Close
    End
End Sub

Private Function ParseField(szText As String) As String
    Dim k As Integer
    k = InStr(szText, "=")
    ' Return the substring following the equals sign
    ParseField = Mid$(szText, k + 1)
End Function
```

Almost all the code is in Sub Main. The command$ statement is used to retrieve the name of the
temporary file passed in by the C++ CGI program. Note that cgi2.exe assumes the order of the

fields in the text file written by the C++ program. This isn't robust, but again, that isn't the point. To modify the fields on the HTML feedback form, you also have to modify the VB code. The C++ code should be able to survive without modification if new fields are added to the HTML file, the VB code, and the database.

The Temporary .HFO File

The following is a sample file written by cgi1.exe before it is passed to cgi2.exe:

```
URL=127.0.0.1
Date=04/14/96
Time=10:54:13
name=Scott Zimmerman
email=scottz@sd.znet.com
comments=Thank you for building this Intranet!
```

Notice how each field of the form data has been parsed onto a line by itself with an equal sign serving as the delimiter for the VB program. The URL, Date, and Time fields are obtained automatically. The other fields correspond to data that the user fills out in the HTML form.

The temporary input file from the C++ CGI program is deleted as soon as you are through reading it in the VB program. Then the database is opened, and a recordset is created using the dbOpenTable parameter. This parameter permits you to write to the table. The table is called table1 (until you change it).

The fields in the table correspond to the data you capture on the form, as well as the URL of the client and the date/time the submission was made to the server. For each field, the table calls the ParseField function to retrieve the substring following the equal sign.

If you designate a key field to use AutoIncrement in Data Manager, the Jet 3.0 engine will automatically take care of incrementing the field for you as new rows are inserted. Therefore, you don't need to supply the value of the key field between the calls to AddNew and Update. See Figure 20.2, which shows the Edit Field dialog in Data Manager 32. Note the Counter checkbox. Only one such field per table should have that value turned on. It is only available for Long Integer type fields.

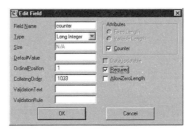

Figure 20.2. *The Edit Field dialog in Data Manager 32 showing the field named Counter checked to be of the counter type.*

Examining the Database with Data Manager

The database referred to by the Visual Basic program (cgi2.bas) is named cgi.mdb. The VB program assumes that it lives in the same directory as the Visual Basic program itself, which is also the same directory as the cgi1.exe program. The cgi1.exe program does not invoke the cgi2.exe program with a full path name, so they all should go in the \scripts directory. (Your Web server may use a different name, and it is also possible to put cgi2.exe in the PATH or even in the Windows directory.)

You can open the database with either Access 7.0, VisData, or Data Manager. The last two are utility programs that come with the VB 4.0 Professional and Enterprise editions. Access comes with Microsoft Office Professional. This chapter won't go into the steps to create the database because that information is readily available in the product documentation for Access and Data Manager. Table 20.2 summarizes the fields in the sample database.

Table 20.2. The fields and datatypes in table1 in cgi.mdb.

Field Name	Datatype
Counter	Long (primary key, required unique)
URL	Text, length 40
When	DateTime 8-byte variant datatype
Name	Text, length 40
Email	Text, length 40
Comments	Text, length 255

The field named Counter is the key field and is also marked as a Counter type in Data Manager. This means that you don't have to calculate unique values for it because VB will do this automatically when you execute rs.Update. See Figure 20.3 for the Data Manager Edit Index dialog showing the fields of the CGI table.

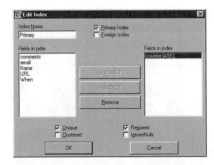

Figure 20.3. *The Edit Index dialog in Data Manager 32 showing the primary key field.*

As I've said, the program lacks several important error-checking features. For example, no check is made to ensure that the supplied text does not exceed the field sizes. The field sizes in the database should match the MAX attribute of the TEXT input fields in the HTML file. The VB program should probably be written to truncate longer text just in case the two sizes should ever become mismatched. As it stands now, the VB program would crash if the input text exceeded the database field size.

Summary

The next chapter gets into more of what you can do with databases on your Intranet. WAIS allows your customers to use a searchable database on the Web without your having to do any programming. You'll be amazed at how easy it is to use the EMWAC WAIS Toolkit with IIS to provide powerful search features on your Intranet.

21

◆

Indexing Your Intranet with WAIS

- ◆ Wide Area Information Server (WAIS)
- ◆ Installing the EMWAC WAIS Toolkit
- ◆ Indexing your Intranet with WAIS
- ◆ Other Web searching products for Windows NT

By now, you've made a good deal of data available on your Intranet—or at least you have some ideas about what you want to put on the Intranet. In all likelihood, your Intranet will eventually accumulate a substantial volume of data. The obvious next question is how are your customers going to be able to find anything among all your data? The equally obvious answer is for you to provide searchable indexes on your Intranet. You'll learn in this chapter how to enable your customers to both search your indexes and retrieve documents (or other data files) using their Web browsers.

This chapter talks about how WAIS works, how to install it, how to use it, and how to search with it. At the end of the chapter, I'll go over a few alternative indexing/searching technologies, including Excite for Web Servers. In case you haven't heard of Excite already, it is now available for Windows NT, it is coming on strong, and it's free!

Wide Area Information Server (WAIS)

WAIS, which stands for Wide Area Information Server, is a system for indexing large amounts of data and making them searchable over a TCP/IP network. It's misnamed, though, because it works just as well on a local network as it does over the Internet.

WAIS server software indexes data and responds to requests from WAIS clients to search the indexes and return a list of documents that match the search. Based on an ANSI standard for indexing library materials in computer systems (Z39.50), WAIS can form an important part of your Intranet. Because WAIS uses the Z39.50 protocol, you might hear the two terms used synonymously.

WAIS supports not only simple keyword searches, but also Boolean queries (for example, `thiskeyword and thatkeyword`) and even plain English searches. In addition, WAIS can do relevance searching—you can select part or all of a document that your WAIS search has found and ask for a new search based on the selection. In other words, WAIS will find more documents like the one it found.

WAIS was originally developed as free software at a company called Thinking Machines, Incorporated. Then the software was commercialized by WAIS, Inc., which is now owned by America Online (the Internet buying frenzy continues). At the time of this writing, AOL has not yet announced plans for WAIS, Inc. and its technology. Fortunately, WAIS software for Windows NT is available for free through EMWAC, and the good folks at Sams.net have arranged to include it on the CD-ROM with this book.

Note: In addition to the WAIS Toolkit, EMWAC has also developed a freeware Web server (HTTPS), Gopher server (GS), and SMTP server (IMS) for Windows NT. You can find more information about their highly regarded server software at this URL:

`http://emwac.ed.ac.uk/`

Although NCSA Mosaic has built-in WAIS client support, Netscape and Explorer don't. As a result, you must run a WAIS gateway on your Intranet to support users of those browsers. Fortunately, the EMWAC WAIS Toolkit on the CD-ROM serves this purpose nicely. You can use an HTML page as a front end to the WAIS search engine. The EMWAC WAIS Toolkit returns the results of the search in HTML format with matched documents as clickable hyperlinks. Once you learn how to set this up, it works beautifully. Web searching is definitely a slick feature to add to your Intranet. (And you will soon see it is not hard to set up at all.)

Figure 21.1 shows a demonstration WAIS search result for the keyword *address*. The results page is nicely formatted in HTML with hyperlinks to each of the located documents. WAIS has applied a best-guess score (maximum 1000) to each document for its potential value to the user searching for the keyword. Documents containing fewer occurrences of the word *address* are given lower scores. The highest scoring documents appear at the top of the list. The document with the search keyword contained in the HTML <TITLE> tag is given a perfect score. WAIS also displays the file size in bytes of each document, as that may help the user determine which hyperlink jump to take.

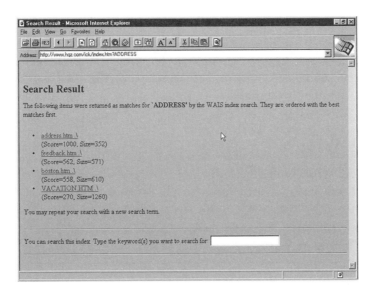

Figure 21.1. *The results of the WAIS search for the word* address.

The relative weighting of the found documents in the WAIS search results is based on a number of useful criteria, such as word frequency within the individual documents and the index as a whole. With multiword and Boolean searches, the weighting takes all the search words into account, so a document containing all your search words would get more weight than one that contained multiple instances of just one of them, for example.

If your Intranet is like most others, much of the data you'll want to index is in (or can be put into) plain text files of one kind or another. WAIS understands a wide variety of text formats. WAIS also knows about several kinds of image formats and can be coaxed into indexing them (or at least their filenames).

In addition, the package has special features that make it easy to integrate your data indexing into your Intranet, with a focus on Web-related capabilities. One major source of data that you may want to index is the data on your Web server itself. Finally, as if these capabilities weren't enough, you can teach WAIS to recognize and index new data formats.

Building a WAIS index is rather simple. The following is a quick overview of the steps involved in using WAIS (this process will be covered in more detail later in this chapter):

1. Build a WAIS index of all the HTML files at your site by using the program named `waisindex.exe`. WAIS creates several files that comprise your index. If you name the index `myindex`, for example, you will end up with files named `myindex.*`.

2. When using IIS, enable automatic WAIS searching by setting `CheckForWAISDB = 1` in the Registry.

3. Create a search page written in HTML in the same directory as the WAIS index and using the same base filename (for example, `myindex.htm`).

4. Include the `<ISINDEX>` tag in the `<HEAD>` section of the HTML search page and provide a link from your home page to this HTML document.

5. When a user loads the search page, he is prompted for a search keyword. After the user enters the word, the server automatically invokes `waislook.exe` and returns a list of matching documents. WAIS is that simple, and your Intranet users will love you for the added functionality it provides.

Installing WAIS

The EMWAC WAIS Toolkit included on the CD-ROM will help you create a database of all the text at your Web site so that users can search it by keyword. The creators of HTML designed the `<ISINDEX>` tag with this feature in mind. The `<ISINDEX>` tag causes the Web server to invoke a program named `waislook` to search a WAIS database and return links to the pages containing the search keyword. (The WAIS database is also referred to as an index.)

> **Note:** The European Microsoft Windows NT Academic Centre (EMWAC) has developed several excellent freeware programs for Windows NT. Programs that are written for Windows NT on the Intel platform will usually run on Windows 95 also. This is because both Windows NT and Windows 95 support the common Win32 API, which enables programs to call functions in the operating system in a consistent manner using 32-bit parameters for integers and resource handles.

Follow these steps to install the EMWAC WAIS Toolkit:

1. The WAIS Toolkit is distributed in four versions for the different architectures that Windows NT supports. Select the appropriate WAIS ZIP file on the CD-ROM for your processor. For example, the WAIS Toolkit for Intel is contained in the file `wti386.zip`.

2. Decide which directory you are going to put the tools in so you can unzip the .EXE programs directly from the CD-ROM to your hard disk using the WinZip program. Ensure that the directory you chose is on the path so that the commands may be executed from the command line.

3. Unzip the WAIS Toolkit. This action should leave you with the following files:

   ◆ The `waisindx.exe` program builds the index of documents on the server. Note in the EMWAC distribution that the name of the executable file was shortened from `waisindex` to `waisindx` for compatibility with older versions of Windows that only allowed eight-character filenames. You can rename this program from its 8.3 filename to `waisindex.exe` in order to match the EMWAC documentation.

   ◆ The `waislook.exe` file is the searching program invoked by the Web server when an HTML page includes `<ISINDEX>`.

   ◆ The `waisserv.exe` file is the Z39.50 searching server program. You won't need this file unless you plan to run WAIS clients. Users running Navigator and Explorer will depend on the server invoking the `waislook` program on their behalf.

   ◆ The `waistool.doc` file is the WAIS Toolkit manual in Word for Windows format.

   ◆ The `waistool.wri` file is the WAIS Toolkit manual in Windows Write format.

   ◆ The `waistool.ps` file is the WAIS Toolkit manual in PostScript and is ready for printing.

   ◆ The `read.me` file is a summary of features.

4. If you have installed a previous version of the WAIS Toolkit, remove it by deleting the old files or by moving them to another directory (which is not referred to by the PATH environment variable) for deletion after you have validated that the new version works correctly.

5. Determine which version of the WAIS Toolkit you have by typing these commands at the DOS Prompt:

```
waisserv -v
waisindx -v
waislook -v
```

The version number for each program will be displayed. Two version numbers will be shown for `waisindx` and `waisserv`; the first refers to the version of the `freeWAIS` code from which the programs were ported, and the second is the number of the Win32 version. As you can see in Figure 21.2, which shows the execution of those commands on my system, I am running version 0.73 for Windows NT. If the programs report a later version number on your system, you will find an updated manual in the files you unpacked from the ZIP archive (the information in this chapter would still be expected to work with few or no changes).

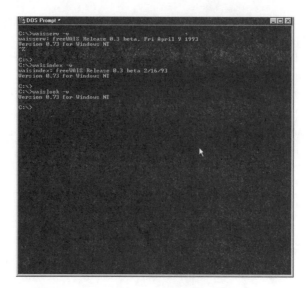

Figure 21.2. *The results of checking the WAIS version numbers.*

Indexing Your Intranet with WAIS

To create a WAIS database of the HTML files at your site, follow these steps: (Assume for the purposes of this discussion that d:\http is the home directory of your Web site.)

1. Make d:\http, or the HTML root, the current directory.

2. Execute waisindx (or waisindex, if you have renamed it to use long filenames), giving it parameters as shown in the following code. The -d parameter is used to name the index files which are created. The default name if no parameter is given is index, which I will assume is in use for the remainder of this chapter. The -r parameter tells WAIS to search all subdirectories. The -t (lowercase) parameter indicates the type of files being indexed. WAIS handles text files and HTML with ease. If you know all the files are HTML, WAIS will use the <TITLE> tags for the file headlines. The last parameter specifies the files that you want to search, which are, in this case, all HTML files in the HTML root directory.

   ```
   waisindx -d index -r -t html *.htm*
   ```

3. Observe the messages from waisindx to check that there are no errors.

4. Execute a dir index.* command on the d:\http directory to check that waisindx has created the seven index files, named index.* and described in the following text.

The following text describes the files created by waisindx:

◆ The index.cat file is the catalog of the indexed files, with about three lines of information for each file indexed. This is a text file.

- The `index.dct` file is the dictionary of indexed words. This is a binary file.
- The `index.doc` file is the document table. This binary file may contain several documents, depending on the type specified in the `-t` option.
- The `index.fn` file is the filename table. This is a binary file. The filenames stored in this table are supplied as the final parameters to `waisindx`. Thus, if filenames are supplied relative to the current directory (for example, `files/*`), they will be stored in the filename table in that form, and the resulting filenames from a database search will also be in relative form.
- The `index.hl` file is the headline table and a binary file. A *headline* is (ideally) a line of descriptive text summarizing the contents of a document. The headline is normally taken from the document itself. For instance, it might be the Subject line if the document is a mail message, the first line of the file, or the filename itself. Which it is depends on the type of the file, as notified to `waisindx` using the `-t` option. If you use `-t HTML`, `waisindx` will use the HTML `<TITLE>` tag to generate this headline.
- The `index.inv` file is the inverted file index. This is a binary file.
- The `index.src` is the source description structure. This is a text file.

Using `<ISINDEX>` with WAIS

Now that the WAIS index files are created, you need to modify your HTML code to take advantage of them. This is where the HTML `<ISINDEX>` tag enters the picture. Remember, the HTTP server is designed to automatically invoke `waislook` whenever it receives an `<ISINDEX>` request from the client.

This automatic invocation of `waislook` should not be taken for granted. I've only seen this work with three Web servers: Process Purveyor for NT, EMWAC HTTPS, and Microsoft IIS. Other Web servers, such as Alibaba, require a different procedure to take advantage of `<ISINDEX>`. I won't get into the details of that procedure in this chapter, but I can point you to Richard Graessler's home page, which contains thorough information about the topic. Mr. Graessler has written a very nice batch script that can be used on Windows NT to pass `<ISINDEX>` search parameters to `waislook` on Alibaba or other Web servers. He kindly provides the source code free of charge on his Web site at this URL:

```
http://rick.wzl.rwth-aachen.de/rickg/IsIndex/isindex.html
```

Because much of this book is based upon Microsoft IIS, I will assume you are using that Web server. In that case, there is a Registry setting that you must ensure is set properly. Follow these steps:

1. Start the Registry Editor and drill down to the following key:

   ```
   HKEY_LOCAL_MACHINE\SYSTEM\CurrentControlSet\Services\W3SVC\Parameters
   ```

2. Look in the right-side window pane to see if you already have a value named `CheckForWAISDB`. If so, and if it has a value of `1`, then IIS is ready to invoke `waislook`.

3. If you don't have a value named `CheckForWAISDB`, choose Edit | Add Value. Type in the Value Name and choose `REG_DWORD` for the Data Type.

4. After you choose OK, the DWORD Editor dialog box will prompt you for the initial value. Enter a value of `1`, and choose OK again.

5. Check that the value is entered correctly, and then exit from the Registry Editor. Now IIS will support `<ISINDEX>` searches using the WAIS Toolkit.

Note: These steps are not necessary with the EMWAC HTTPS Web server because it is capable of automatically invoking `waislook.exe`.

The next step is to create a new search page named `index.htm` that contains the `<ISINDEX>` tag in the `<HEAD>` section. Figure 21.3 shows how the `<ISINDEX>` tag is interpreted by Microsoft Explorer. The user is preparing a search for the keyword *address*, the results of which were shown earlier in the chapter. Listing 21.1 contains the HTML code for the sample page shown in Figure 21.3. You can find this HTML file on the CD-ROM.

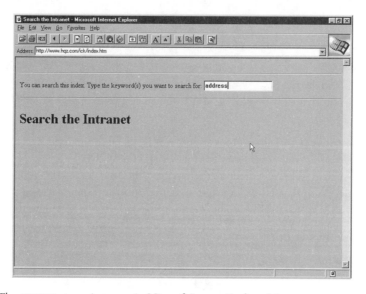

Figure 21.3. The `<ISINDEX>` tag as it appears in Microsoft Internet Explorer 2.0.

Listing 21.1. The code for `index.htm`, a sample HTML file that uses `<ISINDEX>`.

```
<HTML>
<HEAD>
<TITLE>Search the Intranet</TITLE>
<ISINDEX>
</HEAD>
<BODY>
```

```
<H1>Search the Intranet</H1>
</BODY>
</HTML>
```

Now you just need to provide a link from your Intranet home page to the new index file you just created. After you do that, your site will be searchable by keyword. Use your Web browser and give it a try.

Examining `waisindex`

Table 21.1 lists the `waisindex` command-line options, annotated to indicate which are required and which are optional. After this list, you'll find a bit more detail about each option that isn't self-explanatory.

Table 21.1. `waisindex` command-line options.

Option	Description
-a	Adds to existing WAIS index. Optional.
-d *database*	Specifies database name for WAIS index. Optional; defaults to `index.*` if -d not present.
-r	Recursively indexes subdirectories. Optional.
-mem *mbytes*	Specifies the amount of memory in megabytes to use in creating the database. Optional.
-register	The Windows NT version of `waisindex` cannot automatically register the database with the master Internet directory of servers. This option displays instructions on how to do it manually. Optional.
-export	Makes database network accessible, outside the Intranet. Optional.
-e *filename*	Logs errors in *filename*. Optional.
-l *number*	Sets log level (0 through 10). Optional.
-v	Prints the version of the software. Optional.
-stdin	Reads filenames to be indexed from standard input. Optional.
-pos or -nopos	Includes (or doesn't include) word position information. Optional.
-nopairs or -pairs	Doesn't include (or includes) word pairs. Optional.
-nocat	Doesn't create catalog files. Optional.
-contents	Indexes the contents, even if the document type is not normally subject to such indexing. Optional.

continues

Table 21.1. continued

Option	Description
-nocontents	Indexes only the filename, not the contents, even if the contents are normally indexable. Optional.
-keywords *string*	Uses *string* as keyword(s) in indexing. Optional.
-keyword_file *filename*	Takes indexing keyword from filename. Optional.
-x *filename1[,f2,...]*	Does not index these files.
-T *type*	Announces "TYPE" of the document. Optional.
-M *type,type*	Specifies multitype documents. Optional.
-t *type*	Specifies actual type of the files. Optional.

The first two options (-a and -d) control whether a new database is created or an existing one is appended to.

By default, waisindex will index only the files you specify. If you use the -r switch, it will recursively index all the subdirectories and files underneath the starting directory.

You can speed up waisindex by giving it a large -mem parameter. Expressed in megabytes, this parameter is the amount of your system's virtual memory (not physical RAM) to be used in creating index databases. Using too high a number here might interfere with the computer's other tasks, so be careful if your system is busy. Running your indexing jobs in off hours, when the system is less busy, can enable you to use more memory. If the default memory utilization (with no -mem specification at all on the waisindex command line) slows your system down, use this argument to limit the amount of memory used rather than to increase it. This option should only be necessary for indexing large Intranets.

The two related options -register and -export might seem similar, but they do entirely different things. In order for you to make your WAIS index database fully searchable by WAIS clients, you must use the -export option. This option modifies the database.src file, making it possible for stand-alone WAIS clients to access the database over a network. Web browsers or CGI gateway scripts like waislook don't need this information.

Using the -export option does not advertise your index database to the Internet. This is what -register does. In freeWAIS, the -register option creates and sends an e-mail message to two main WAIS index registries on the Internet. In EMWAC WAIS, this option only tells you how to advertise your index database. The effect is a public Internet announcement that your index is available to be searched from anywhere. If you don't want to make your index universally available, don't use this option. Also, if your network is not connected to the Internet or is behind a network security firewall, the -register option is unlikely to be of any use.

Two options, -e and -l, enable you to control whether your WAIS server will create logfiles of its transactions (all the searches that are done) on your index. In addition, you can control how much logging takes place. The first option (`-e` *logfile*) tells the server that you want a log kept in the file *logfile*.

By default, if you have logging enabled, the most verbose logging is done. To reduce the amount of information that's logged, use the `-l` option with a number between 0 and 9. (Level 10 logging is the default if `-e` is used alone.) The lower the number, the less verbose the logging. If you use default logging, watch the size of your logfiles to ensure that they don't fill up your disk.

Rather than typing in a list of filenames on the `waisindex` command line, you may want to use other command-line utilities to prepare a list of files for you based on some criteria. You can then feed that list to `waisindex` using the `-stdin` option.

One of the files created by `waisindex` is known as the *catalog file*. This file contains the headline of every document in a WAIS index database. If your database is large, this file can get quite large. It's really nothing more than a long list of the files in your database, annotated with a descriptive headline. Failed searches may result in the headline file being returned to your customer, and a long list of headlines may or may not be helpful. The catalog file is not required for the WAIS server to function or for your customers to do searches, so you can dispense with it if you're short on disk space by running `waisindex` with the `-nocat` option.

Ordinarily, `waisindex` knows that there are some kinds of files whose contents can't usefully be indexed. Examples include image files and other kinds of binary data. Based on the `-t` option, for example, `waisindex` will index the contents of several kinds of text files that it knows about. If, on the other hand, you'd like to inhibit content indexing of ordinarily indexable files, use `-nocontents`.

If you want to make sure that your WAIS index database contains specific keywords, even if some or all of the documents don't contain them, use `-keywords` *string* and specify the keywords on the command line, or use `-keyword_file` *filename* and specify them in a file. Your extra keywords will be added to the normal indexing. This feature is useful when indexing image filenames and other binary data.

The `-T` and `-t` options are confusing because they both appear to specify a document type. The difference is subtle but important. You can think of the two as specifying a document format and a document type, respectively.

The `waisindex` program has a built-in list of the document types it recognizes. You can get this list by entering the `waisindex` command with no options at all on your command line. For the most part, these are types of plain text files whose internal file format `waisindex` understands and can interpret. Examples include Usenet news articles and e-mail messages. The program expects such files to conform to the standard format of those kinds of files, with a certain layout and structure. Thus, the `-t` option deals with the format of documents—how they're laid out, what divides records, and the like.

As you'll also recall, Web servers and browsers know about a list of MIME data type/subtypes. This is where the `-T` option to `waisindex` comes in. Because WAIS is built to integrate into a Web, it has MIME hooks built in. When you index data with `waisindex`, you can use the `-T` command-line option to specify a MIME type that will be announced when your index is searched by a Web browser or CGI script. When a Web browser or CGI gateway script retrieves the document, the MIME type is returned, and your Web browser deals with it appropriately. Thus, if you index JPEG image files using `-T JPEG` on the `waisindex` command line, your customers' Web browsers will know to open the files they retrieve from your WAIS server as JPEG images.

> **Note:** In some instances, the `-T` and `-t` options appear to have the same file type specified. For example, because `waisindex` knows about GIF images, you might specify `-T gif` and `-t gif` on the same command line when indexing GIF files. Because the two options mean different things, their use isn't redundant.

> **Tip:** When using both the `-t` and `-T` options with `waisindex`, always put the `-t` option first on your command line. In some cases, `-t` may imply a `-T` because the overall default for `-T` is TEXT, so you may not need both options.

In connection with MIME types, the `-M` option to `waisindex` enables you to specify multiple file types in a single WAIS index database. Suppose you maintain copies of common word processing documents in several formats, including Microsoft Word, WordPerfect, rich text, and plain text. Using the `-M` option, you can index all these documents at once using a `waisindex` command line—something like the following:

```
waisindex -d mywords -M MSWORD,WORDPERFECT5.1,RTF,TEXT *.*
```

In this line, the multiple file types correspond to some of the additions you have made to the `mime.types` file on your Web server over the course of the last several chapters. Note that you must specify them on the `waisindex` command line in uppercase letters.

Indexing Images and Other Document Types

Most Web servers have more than just plain text documents on them. In particular, Web servers have HTML documents, images, and other multimedia files on them. So why not extend your WAIS index database to add these important files?

Suppose your Web server includes a directory tree containing not only the text files you've already indexed, but also one or more subdirectories containing HTML files. If the contents of your images aren't indexed, you may wonder what image indexing will add to your WAIS index database. Well, all the filenames of the GIF images in your Web server's file tree are indexed (along with any associated keywords you've added with the `-keywords` option) so that now you and your Intranet's customers can search for image files the same way you do keyword searches.

As you create more and more HTML documents, you'll collect more and more images; running `waisindex` on them enables you to manage them better. CGI gateway programs like `waislook` can help you and your Intranet's customers search for image files just as they can help you look for text files. If you have multiple Webmasters including customers setting up Web servers of their own for your Intranet, having a searchable, retrievable collection of images can be a boon. Everyone can share the same set of images, preventing duplicate work and giving your Intranet a common look.

As you've probably guessed, the technique of indexing filenames without indexing their contents, as just discussed with images, can be used for almost any kind of binary data on your Web server. You can index any set of binary files for easy search and retrieval, saving you the time and trouble of maintaining Tables of Contents as documents change.

> **Tip:** When using `waisindex` to index word processor, spreadsheet, or other data files, be sure to use the `-keywords` option to add key search words to your index. These documents' contents may not get fully indexed, so you'll want to use this important feature.

Using the same search form shown in Figure 21.3 (where the keyword *address* was used), you could obtain results showing not only the plain text versions of each file found, but also the original `.doc` file. Because your customers' Web browsers are already configured to use Word as a helper application (see Chapter 13, "Word Processing on the Web"), they can click the document they want and load it directly into Word.

Commercial Index-and-Retrieve Packages

A growing number of companies are coming out with commercial software packages for creating Web-searchable index databases for Intranets. The following sections sample several of the other commercial packages.

Fulcrum Surfboard

A long-time maker of full-text search technologies, Fulcrum, Inc. now has a Web-based product called Surfboard. Surfboard 2.0 for Windows NT can search both local and network indexes and can search multiple indexes in a single pass. You can use natural language, multiword phrases, fielded searches, wildcard word matching (such as `comput*` to match *computers*, *computing*, *computation*, and the like), and Boolean constructs. It also supports relevance searching. In addition, you can specify the kind of output you'd like from your search, with choices including listing or tabular arrangement, HTML, plain text, or document native format, and you have several choices for sorting. You'll find more information about Surfboard and other interesting Fulcrum products for Windows NT at this URL:

```
http://www.fulcrum.com/english/products/prodhome.htm
```

Verity Topic

Topic is another product suite consisting of eight products and including both an Enterprise and an Internet indexing/search engine. The former supports major office applications' data file formats, and the latter adds support for HTML documents on a Web. Both search engines support so-called fuzzy-logic searches, as well as concept, weighted, and Boolean searches. Following the overall structure of the Topic system, the Topic client is not a Web browser, but a stand-alone application, and is available for Windows NT. Figure 21.4 shows a demo of Topic searches. You can run the demo at this URL:

```
http://www.verity.com/demo/d/Topic_Demos/tisdemo.html
```

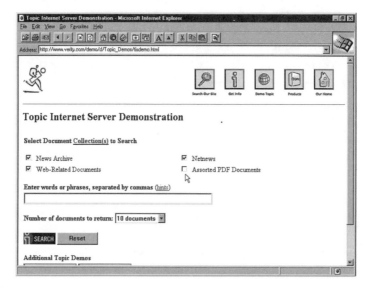

Figure 21.4. *The Topic Internet Server search demo.*

Architext Excite

Excite for Web Servers (EWS) enables users to search multiple database indexes and includes both concept and keyword searches. Queries can be natural language, with search results sorted by what Excite calls Confidence (similar to other weighted relevance searching). It provides a user-friendly fill-in search form (as do other packages mentioned in this chapter).

Excite's primary distinction is that it's available for no-cost download. You can retrieve it from this URL:

```
http://www.excite.com/navigate/download.cgi
```

Excite is available for Windows NT and several UNIX systems. The licensing document that comes with the downloadable package indicates that Excite can be used internally without any charge, although you are requested to register the package. (You need only supply your e-mail address to download it.) No support comes with the free package, but support contracts, which include future upgrades, e-mail, and phone support, are available for purchase. Currently, maintenance agreements for EWS are sold for $995 per year.

Excite supports "concept-based searching," which is a technology made possible by the way EWS goes through its indexing process. It uses probabilistic techniques to analyze the interrelationships between words within a collection of documents. This index supports concept-based capabilities such as finding relevant documents that do not even contain the words used in the query statement and improving the ranking of the returned documents so that the most important documents are shown to the user first, even when thousands of documents are found.

Currently EWS only supports ASCII and HTML documents, but Architext has stated that this restriction will be lifted in the near future. With what you now know about document conversion, that limitation can be considered an inconvenience, but not a show-stopper.

PLWeb

Another index-and-retrieval package for Windows NT, Personal Library Software's PLWeb, is available for no-cost 45-day evaluations to registered users. See `http://www.pls.com` for details of the offer. A demonstration is online there, but you may want to look at what some of PLS's customers are doing with the package. For example, Figure 21.5 shows AT&T's searchable Toll-Free Internet Directory at `http://www.att.net/`.

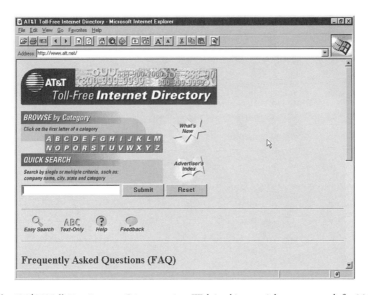

Figure 21.5. The AT&T Toll-Free Internet Directory gives Web junkies a quick way to search for 800 numbers.

Summary

Focusing on indexing and retrieving data on your Intranet, this chapter has covered general-purpose indexing packages that can be accessed using a Web browser. You've learned how to index your data and how to provide Web-browser interfaces to enable your customers to search and retrieve data from them. In addition, you've learned about a specialized database package that you can use to maintain an online corporate telephone directory for your customers. Finally, you surveyed the market of commercial software providing index-and-retrieval features.

The next part of the book, "Sample Applications," is geared toward typical business uses of an Intranet. The next several chapters will pull together all that you have learned about Web technologies and Web tools.

V
PART

Sample Applications

CHAPTER

22

Company Practices/ Procedures Manuals

◆ Using current electronic practices/procedures information

◆ MIME type/subtype setup

◆ Other kinds of data for your practices/procedures Intranet

◆ Sidebar: what you need to develop Web applications

◆ Indexing your practices/procedures data

◆ Imagemaps and your practices/procedures Intranet

Every organization, large or small, has hundreds of documents and other pieces of data that can be put on an Intranet for its customers. One major category of these is your company's practices and procedure manuals. Whether you have a formalized program of written standards for doing things or operate *ad hoc* much of the time, you undoubtedly have some documents that give instructions about how things are done. These instructions can range from the most mundane, such as how employees work or how vacation and sick time are recorded and reported, to the practical, such as company purchasing procedures, to the sublime, as in overall organizational policy statements on such large matters as corporate goals, employee diversity, or safety in the workplace. In this chapter, you learn how to integrate the information and tools presented earlier in this book and to make many of these documents accessible on your Practices/Procedures Intranet.

You also learn in this chapter about the use of graphical data and HTML *imagemaps* for your Intranet. This same general process of integrating the material from the rest of this book applies in the next several chapters.

Existing Electronic Practices/Procedures Information

If your company uses computers to create documents, you already have the foundation of your company's Practices/Procedures Intranet built. Your first task is identifying and locating these documents and getting them online on your Intranet so that they are easily accessible. You can find these documents in administration, engineering, human resources, and other corporate departments. You can also find them in filing cabinets.

The fact that paper copies of employee manuals, for example, are distributed to all new employees probably means there is an electronic original somewhere in personnel. Similarly, if your shipping/receiving department has written procedures for handling dangerous or delicate shipments of various kinds, in all likelihood you can find those procedures on somebody's computer disk in a word processor file. Although locating documents in this way might be a tedious, logistical problem, it's still possible, and what you find will provide the basis of your company's Practices/Procedures Intranet.

The main principles of this activity are those outlined in Chapter 3, "The Software Tools to Build a Web," with respect to the conversion of your legacy data for your Intranet. If you have electronic copies of documents available, you need to use what you learned in that chapter to move this data quickly onto your Intranet, making it accessible to your customers via your Web server and their browsers. When you have legacy data that's not in plain text format, you might need to use the conversion tools you learned about earlier. This might include using your applications' Save As feature to convert data into easily usable formats such as plain text. You can also use some of the other conversion tools covered in Chapter 3.

In addition, you might eventually want to use the Microsoft Rich Text Format (RTF) as an in-between while converting legacy data into HTML documents for direct use on your Intranet. Also, with more and more vendors, such as Microsoft, Frame Technologies, and Novell, adding direct HTML capabilities to their word processors and other packages, you can convert your legacy documents directly to HTML with almost no effort.

As you have learned, the basic setup of Web pages containing simple, clickable lists of available documents is quite easy. Adding a little subject matter organization is simple, too, using hyperlinks to create nested menu listings. In just a few minutes, you can present a useful list of available documents to your customers. To these ends, you should review basic HTML markup in Chapter 5, "What You Need to Know About HTML," and in Appendix A, "HTML and CGI Quick Reference," focusing on basic list markup, hyperlinks to other documents, and the jump-to-spot features of the language.

Tip: Use your operating system's basic utilities to get a leg up on the creation of simple HTML listings of documents. One way to quickly build a file containing the names of all the files you want to serve is to use the DOS prompt command-output redirection (for example, DIR > doclist.html). This captures the directory listing into a file. You can then edit the file to strip out unneeded directory listing details, add the HTML framework, add a few headlines, and add some list markup and hyperlinks. Your new Web page is ready to be sent to a Web browser, providing access to all the listed documents with a simple mouse click.

As suggested in Part I, you can come back to the skeleton Web pages containing your converted legacy documents once you have your Practices/Procedures Intranet running. Then you can refine them and add value by cutting in hyperlinked cross-references, graphics, and the like.

Monthly reports, for example, can contain clickable cross-references to other documents, statistical tables, spreadsheet data files, images, or even earlier months' reports (all with the same kinds of embedded links). This done, your customers can use their Web browsers to jump from one document to another, looking for answers to questions by following promising threads.

The more cross-references and hyperlinks you add, the more capabilities you give to your customers. A little later, you learn about indexing your practices/procedures documents to give your customers even greater opportunities to locate documents and information.

MIME Type/Subtype Setup

Even after you have successfully converted your legacy practices/procedures documents and created skeleton Web pages for accessing them, you will no doubt end up with a wide variety of document and data formats. You will probably have plain text files, word processor files, HTML documents, spreadsheets, graphics images, data files created by other office software applications, and others. At first, this might seem to be a confusing mess. However, you can confidently deal with this situation, using what you have learned earlier in this book, to organize the data and make it available in its native formats. After all, your purpose in building an Intranet is to pull together just such a wide variety of information resources and make them accessible using a single Web browser interface. All the information about MIME data types/subtypes and helper applications you have learned earlier in this book will help you as you make your practices/procedures information available.

As you recall from earlier chapters, enabling use of your word processor, spreadsheet, and such other office software packages as Web browser helper applications is a simple, two-step process:

1. Modify the MIME map on your Intranet's Web server(s) to add your new document types. With IIS, this information is stored in the Windows NT Registry. Other Web servers might store the MIME table in a configuration text file.

2. Configure your customers' Web browsers to deal with the newly defined MIME types/subtypes by defining helper applications.

Chapter 12 provides a thorough grounding in the subject of MIME data types/subtypes. Chapters 13 through 15 deal with a variety of common office software packages you might need to set up as Web browser helper applications. Now that you are putting specific documents and other data in place for real work on your Practices/Procedures Intranet, you might want to review that material so that you have the ticklish syntax of the MIME map and the Web browser Helpers dialog boxes down pat. If your customers use more than one Web browser, you need to understand the slight differences between Mosaic, Explorer, and Netscape in this area. Figure 22.1, showing setup of Microsoft Word as an NCSA Mosaic helper application, will no doubt bring this all back to you.

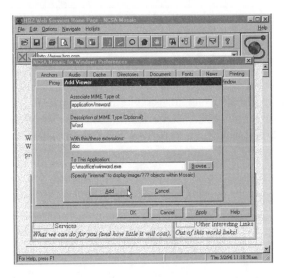

Figure 22.1. *The Mosaic Add Viewer dialog enables you to add new helpers based on MIME.*

Tip: You need to make sure the necessary helper application software packages are available to everyone on your Intranet, perhaps by setting up anonymous FTP services on your Intranet (see Chapter 9, "Adding FTP and Gopher Services") or by simply creating a shared subdirectory on the NT file server that everyone can map to from their workstation. This sort of infrastructure can save you a great deal of time that would otherwise be taken up with manual distribution of software around your Intranet. This way, if customers need a copy of a new helper application (or a new release of an old one), to download it they can click a Web page you have created with links to the applications. If you're trying to build your Intranet in phases and you don't have the time to organize it that well yet, at least add a sentence to your home page or send e-mail to everyone to mention the location of the helper applications that can be installed from the file server.

Once you have taken these steps, your Intranet's customers can use their Web browsers to retrieve and view your practices/procedures documents as necessary, regardless of their actual document format. As needed, helper applications are fired off as documents are accessed. For example, clicking hyperlinks pointing to Word files opens Word to display the files on-screen; Lotus 1-2-3 spreadsheet files work the same way. Having located the necessary document with which to answer their questions, customers are just a few steps away from saving or printing a copy of the document, via your Intranet, all without a trip to the personnel or engineering department where the document might have originated. (Hey, I've been in a large company where that would have saved a 15-minute walk to the copy machine.)

Other Kinds of Data for Your Practices/Procedures Intranet

There is virtually no limit to the kinds of information you can use on a corporate Practices/Procedures Intranet. You have already surveyed the legacy information you have available and put some of it up. You have merely scratched the surface so far, so consider a few more ideas.

Personnel and Employee Benefits Information

Your personnel department can be a gold mine for your Intranet when it comes to supplying documents of the sort you're looking for. I have already mentioned the idea of an overall employee manual, but many other personnel-related documents might also be useful:

- Employee work-related expense and travel-expense reimbursement rules and procedures.
- Job vacancy announcements and application procedures/requirements.
- Procedural documents on time-keeping, health benefits claims, retirement and pensions, use of company vehicles and other company equipment, and employee conduct.

The first two of these items suggest possibilities far beyond mere static documents your customers can read. Simple fill-in Web forms can be used by employees to submit their travel expenses for reimbursement or apply for a job opening, to give a couple of simple examples. This sort of thing can turn your Practices/Procedures Intranet into something interactive, something that does something. Each of these items can be accomplished through simple CGI or ISAPI applications that take the information customers enter into fill-in forms and pass it via e-mail to the appropriate employees for processing.

Although some security issues are involved in forms information processing (see Chapter 10, "Intranet Security in Windows NT"), you can implement this sort of thing quite easily. Employees won't have to deal with paper forms or spend work time for their pickup and delivery. Instead, customers' requests for expense reimbursements or job applications are sent when they click the Submit button in their Web browser, all without any trips to the photocopy machine or interoffice mail delivery.

> **Tip:** A potentially valuable Practices/Procedures Intranet resource in the personnel area might be an interactive pension calculator. Your ordinary pension benefits information Web page would include static information about the rules of eligibility and the mathematical formula for computing pension benefit amounts. Based on an HTML fill-in form and CGI script, such a calculator would enable employees to interactively enter their salary and years-of-service information and get back a pension estimate. Such a tool, easily implemented on your Intranet, can help an employee with retirement decisions, making multiple *what-if-I-worked-just-one-more-year* kinds of calculations without requiring them to take time away from their desk to ask for the same calculations from a human resources specialist. Furthermore, confidentiality is preserved.

Other Corporate Department Information

You can easily extend these ideas to other departments and activities in your organization. Here's a long, but by no means complete, list of possible procedural documents:

- Rules and instructions for telephone, fax machine, and copy machine use. I know my machine can do multipage, multidocument, double-sided, collated, stapled copies, but I can never remember how it works when I need it.
- Hard disk backup procedures.
- Precautions for network virus software, and how to install and use anti-virus software.
- Purchasing and contracting procedures.
- Equipment repair procedures.
- On-the-job safety rules and regulations.
- Building and grounds use and maintenance rules.
- Physical plant security procedures.
- Parking and traffic regulations.
- Procedures for operating manufacturing and other machinery.
- Laboratory procedures.
- Material Safety Data Sheets (MSDS) for chemicals and other potentially dangerous substances being used.

◆ Procedures for handling dangerous materials and dealing with spills or releases of them.

◆ Property-pass rules for employees and vendors taking company-owned equipment off site.

You can probably come up with an equally long list of other documents that fit well here. Where appropriate, fill-in forms enable customers to use their Web browsers to perform job functions, such as recording time off, ordering supplies, or requesting equipment repairs.

Figure 22.2 shows the simple vacation form you saw back in Chapter 5. This form, `vacation.htm` on the CD-ROM, could be easily adapted into an order-entry form for supplies or equipment. Depending on how elaborate you want to get, your CGI back-end script for the order form, or one like it, can e-mail the customer's order to data entry personnel in your Purchasing Department for hand-entry into your Purchasing system. It can also actually place the order into your corporate purchasing database system for processing, untouched by human hands. Again, there are security issues here, explained in Chapter 10, that you need to consider to ensure accountability in the area of purchasing.

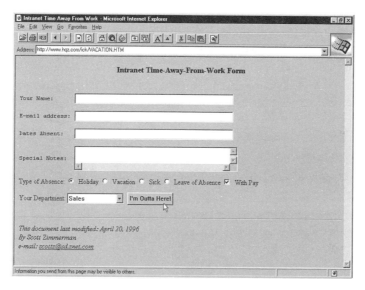

Figure 22.2. The vacation form, useful in its own right, could be easily adapted to an order form for supplies.

Similar forms, using HTML menus, radio buttons, and checkboxes, can be used for ordering everyday office supplies. Your CGI or ISAPI applications for all these kinds of forms can be pretty much the same script, with built-in options for sending the output of certain forms in one direction and directing others elsewhere. You can find basic e-mail scripts you can modify to meet your needs in just about every book you find on setting up Web services; you probably already have one or more of them. The Blat program on the CD-ROM with this book can be used to mail form data to a predetermined e-mail address for processing.

What You Need to Develop Web Applications

If you have heard about CGI from the UNIX world or from the early days of the Web, you might be wondering why I keep saying "CGI or ISAPI." As discussed in Chapters 19 and 20, ISAPI is a new kid on the block that uses RAM for interprocess communication between the server and the application, as opposed to the more disk-based approach of CGI. The goal of ISAPI is to run Web applications several times faster than is possible with CGI.

ISAPI was recently invented by Process Software and Microsoft and is available in both Purveyor and IIS. It is catching on, and many other Web servers are also offering ISAPI. If you're a Webmaster who is being asked to write Web applications, you also need to know that Microsoft Visual C++ version 4.1 now includes an ISAPI application wizard. All you have to do is click a few buttons and you get a DLL framework that works. You can then add extra functionality to complete the design. The Data Access Objects in Visual C++ might help you write the code that saves the form data to an ODBC database.

A CGI alternative that many claim is easier to develop (if you don't know C++, this is probably true) is Perl. Perl for Windows NT is on the CD-ROM. Perl scripts run quite a bit slower than ISAPI applications, but if your Intranet is not high traffic and your time to accomplish to the task is squeezed, you should definitely consider Perl. (Perl is also available as an ISAPI DLL.)

Chapter 19 lists other alternatives that might work without having to learn programming. If those tools don't work for you, be prepared for a learning curve if you have to write Web programs yourself.

Indexing Your Practices/Procedures Data

You're probably thinking this chapter has gotten ahead of itself. How will your customers locate answers to questions or locate specific documents? Surely they won't just have long on-screen lists of document names they have to browse through? Subject-oriented menus aren't always a big help either. As with the conversion of your legacy data, the answers to these questions take you back to material covered earlier in the book. In Chapter 21, "Indexing Your Intranet with WAIS," you learned about a variety of powerful tools for indexing data on your Intranet and, equally important, flexible tools for searching and retrieving Intranet data from the indexes created by them.

The ability to search for relatively complex text strings is an important feature of your Practices/Procedures Intranet. Similarly, keyword searches with Boolean capabilities are important also. Customers might not know exactly what they're looking for, and even being able to view document names might not be enough. Text-string and keyword searches become critical to customer searches for information. Note that the database here is one built with an indexing tool, such as WAIS or Excite. (See Chapter 21.)

Depending on the extent and nature of your library of practices/procedures documents (and other documents on your Intranet), you might also want to look at the Web-related relational database tools described in Chapter 16, "Linking Databases to the Web." This is particularly true because these packages are being extended to include many different kinds of data. The ability to create Web fill-in forms that interface with database engines via CGI scripts (or other means) enhances your Intranet and its capability of serving its customers.

Even if you have a preexisting full-text or relational database, hope isn't lost. Unless it's locked up without standard capabilities, you can just dump the data out to plain text files. As long as the data has an identifiable format, it can be run through a tool like WAIS, making it accessible via your Web browsers using fill-in forms. This enables you to continue to use the data you have accumulated in your application, and at the same time it frees you of proprietary data formats. With the outstanding capabilities of these search engines, you might find search-and-retrieval performance better than you had with your custom database—not to mention that nice, user-friendly Web interface.

Imagemaps and Your Practices/Procedures Intranet

The HTML *imagemap* capability can be an important part of your Practices/Procedures Intranet, adding interactive features to otherwise static documents. Imagemaps are graphical images embedded in Web pages that have *hot regions* marked off. Clicking such a hot region causes a predefined hyperlink to be accessed, taking the customer to another document or Web page. Clicking another hot region in the same image activates a different hyperlink, a third hot region, another hyperlink, and so on.

You can find imagemaps on many Web pages, including the Netscape home page, shown in Figure 22.3. The image in the top center of the page is a clickable imagemap, with six hot regions defined (Netscape Destinations, Company & Products, and so on). Moving your mouse cursor into one of those image areas causes the cursor to change from the standard arrow cursor to a pointing finger (not shown in this screen shot), giving you a tip-off that the image is an imagemap. The status bar at the bottom of Figure 22.3 indicates the hyperlinked HTML page pointed to by the cursor in the imagemap. Just click any of the regions to access the underlying hyperlink. Not all Web page imagemaps are as well-defined as this one, with clear delineation, but all work the same way. You should review Chapter 5 and Appendix A, or your other HTML documentation, for information on creating and using imagemaps.

For creating your own imagemaps, try Todd C. Wilson's Map This! software package, available on the CD-ROM. A sample Map This! session is shown in Figure 22.4. The package works by loading the graphics image, after which you select rectangles, circles, or polygons in the image for your hot spots. Once you have done that, you can use your mouse to drag your hot spots to size, and Map This! generates the setup file to create the imagemap. In this screen shot, you can see that the mouse currently lies within a polygon region referring to mountain.htm. Once your hot spot is selected, Map This! prompts for the URL of the underlying hyperlink. Continue to define hot spots in your image, and then save it when you're done. Map This! creates the necessary imagemap files for your Intranet.

Returning from the Map This! digression, let's continue the discussion of graphics imagemaps for your Practices/Procedures Intranet. Following are some practical ideas for your Intranet.

Figure 22.3. *The Netscape home page uses many clickable imagemaps.*

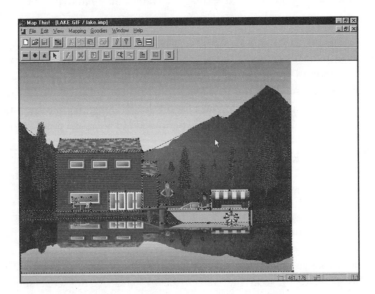

Figure 22.4. *Using the Map This! sample imagemap.*

Graphics Campus Map/Phone Book

If your organization occupies a large campus or building complex, you might want to help your customers navigate around the place via your Intranet, as well as looking for employee locations. The United States National Aeronautics and Space Administration's Johnson Space Center in Houston, Texas, maintains such a service for NASA employees and visitors, and it is accessible on the World Wide Web. They use a large graphics map of the Space Center campus. The map is useful in itself, because it shows where building, roads, parking lots, and the like are located. Both visitors to and employees of large organizations like NASA can use locator maps to find their way around, and more and more organizations are setting up such interactive, wherever-your-cursor-is-there-you-are maps on their Web servers.

In addition to the obvious value of such a map, the image has additional value because it's an imagemap. It provides direct, hyperlinked, Web browser access to a great deal of additional information about the Space Center. Clicking any building on the map, for example, takes you to a Web page specific to that building. On the building's Web pages, you see a photo of the building (good for helping the visitor identify the building), along with information about activities and NASA organizations in that building. Many of the buildings' Web pages accessible from the imagemap contain photos or other graphical images of building-related activities or facilities.

But wait, there's more! On each one of these NASA JSC building Web pages is a hyperlink labeled "Click here for building occupants." Selecting the hyperlink brings up a scrollable on-screen telephone directory for the people in that building. From there, the Web browser's Find feature (in Mosaic: File | Find in Current; in Explorer and Netscape: Edit | Find) can be used to locate an individual's name in the directory.

Blueprints, Engineering Drawings, and CAD Drawings

As the NASA imagemap example shows, there are many ways you can implement this tool on your own Practices/Procedures Intranet and many services you can provide with it. Campus maps like the NASA map can contain links to individual building imagemaps, with the individual maps further zoomable to show individual floors or even individual rooms. Your building services department might have imagemaps containing building blueprints—showing electrical, HVAC, and plumbing infrastructure—for use in building repairs or other service. Engineering drawings of industrial equipment or company products can be made available in the same way, with imagemap hot regions allowing for enlargements of individual portions of the drawings. Even your computer-aided-design (CAD) drawings can be turned into imagemaps.

Getting your paper blueprints or engineering drawings into electronic format might require a scanner, so be sure to save your scanned drawings in GIF or JPEG format, if possible. Many scanners save TIFF files, and Paint Shop Pro, available on the CD-ROM, can convert from TIFF to GIF. If you already have electronic CAD drawings available, you need to see whether your CAD software can export your drawings to one of the standard, Web-supported image formats, such as GIF, JPEG, PostScript, or Adobe Portable Document Format (PDF). You might find that your particular CAD package's image format is supported directly by Paint Shop Pro (or some other graphics utility program), and that you can turn your CAD drawings into a standard format for your Intranet. If all else fails, just search Yahoo (`www.yahoo.com`) for other graphics programs until you find one that runs on Windows and can handle your file format.

Along these lines (hmmm, no pun intended), you need to look at the FAQ document for the Usenet newsgroup `comp.lsi.cad`, where you can find descriptions of a wide variety of free and commercial CAD-related software that might be of use, especially if you're using an older CAD package. Possibilities include software to convert your existing CAD drawings to new formats, including those supported by Web browsers. You can find this at `http://www.cis.ohio-state.edu/hypertext/faq/usenet/lsi-cad-faq/top.html`.

Your Practices/Procedures Intranet need not be limited to blueprints and building maps. One idea is a schematic diagram for an electrical lock-out device (a device for preventing use of defective electrical equipment or equipment under repair). If you have electricians in your company, this and other procedural standards documents can be Web-accessible with little work on your part. Although your graphics images can be in any format supported by your Web browsers, diagrams can be created in the Adobe Portable Document Format (PDF) and then displayed in the Adobe Acrobat Reader as a helper application through the browser. Acrobat Reader is free software you can download from Adobe's Web site, `http://www.adobe.com/`. The package is available for Windows, DOS, Macintosh, and several UNIX systems. You can also find a new PDF reader for Windows 95/NT, Adobe Amber, which was in prerelease when this chapter was written.

Tip: You need to define Adobe Acrobat Reader or Amber as a Web Browser helper application before you can view PDF files found on Web pages. See Chapter 13, "Word Processing on the Web," for details on setting up helper applications.

Note: In late 1995, Adobe Systems acquired Frame Technologies, makers of the FrameMaker desktop publishing package. It seems logical to expect that Frame's products might incorporate direct support for Adobe PDF documents in the future. The no-cost FrameReader package can be set up as a read-only helper application for viewing native FrameMaker documents. In addition, Version 5 of FrameMaker includes direct HTML support for creating, saving, and viewing Web documents. Everything that rises must converge.

Yet another example of the sort of document you can place on your Practices/Procedures Intranet is a decision-making flowchart. Flowcharts can be applied to electrical devices in many endeavors, including computer programming, and you can surely find uses for them on your Intranet. As with the preceding imagemap example, you can explode portions of such flowcharts to reveal underlying details of the process.

You can see how you can make wide use of graphics images and HTML imagemaps on your Practices/Procedures Intranet. Web browsers' ease of use together with your graphics presentations can add substantial value to your overall Intranet. Having these sorts of documents and graphics available helps your customers meet their own job needs. This is particularly helpful because many of these kinds of documents are accessed only rarely. Having them immediately accessible saves the time that would otherwise be used in locating them and ensuring that the located copy is a current version.

Summary

This chapter dealt with the use of Web and Web-related technology to create a Practices/Procedures Intranet, incorporating much of what you have learned from the rest of this book. The chapter has focused on organizational documents and other information that spells out how your company does things. Large or small, every organization has standard operating procedures for many activities, just a few of which have been listed in this chapter. Documentation of those practices and procedures is a rich source of data for your Intranet, and you can easily put it at your customers' fingertips. Here's what you have done in this chapter:

- Considered the existing electronic practices/procedures information available for your Intranet.
- Determined the form(s) of that information.
- Learned how to put that information together so it's accessible to customers using a Web browser, putting what you have learned about MIME data types/subtypes and Web browser helper applications to work.
- Put what you have learned about Intranet document indexing to work to enable search and retrieval of this information, also using Web browsers.
- Surveyed a wide range of possible documents and other data for your Practices/Procedures Intranet.
- Used graphics images and HTML imagemaps to incorporate new special features in your Intranet.

The next chapter covers Intranet Help Desk applications. As with this chapter, the next one provides concrete examples of how you can integrate what you have learned in this book into useful and valuable features for your Intranet.

CHAPTER

23

Intranet Help Desk

- ◆ What does a Help Desk do?
- ◆ Existing Help Desk information
- ◆ MIME type/subtype setup
- ◆ Indexing your Help Desk data
- ◆ Help desk record keeping
- ◆ Giving your customers access to the Intranet Help Desk

Setting up your organization's Help Desk or Customer Service operation on your Intranet is a great way to enhance its efficiency, and an excellent practical use for your Intranet. In a Help Desk situation, it's important to get answers to customers quickly, whether the question is common or unusual. Keeping your Help Desk files on your Intranet can help your employees and customers find the right answer to questions most efficiently. Your Intranet can also help track problem reports and generate historical information about their solutions, making it easy to deal with the frequently occurring questions.

Setting up a Help Desk on your Intranet is likely to be one of your easiest Intranet jobs. Because you probably already have most of the pieces of an Intranet Help Desk already in place, all you have to do is creatively apply the information you have learned so far in this book. This chapter helps you see how easily this can be accomplished.

These objectives, as you can see, are the practical application of the information and tools found in the rest of this book. Your steps in putting your Intranet Help Desk together involve the following: analyzing and converting available data (Chapters 2 and 3); selecting appropriate network services and tools to implement your goals (Chapters 7–9); setting up MIME and helper applications (Chapters 12–15); and applying indexing and database tools (Chapters 16 and 21). You find this same general process of integration applied in this and many of the chapters in this part of the book.

What Does a Help Desk Do?

Although the answer to that question might seem obvious to many readers, professionals know it's still a good idea to lay out specifics. Doing so can help focus your Intranet Help Desk planning. Your first list might look like this:

◆ Receive and record telephone, e-mail, or other requests for help from customers.

◆ Research customer questions and provide answers to the customers.

◆ Track and update the status of trouble tickets (Help Desk terminology for the tracking records attached to trouble reports), for both internal and customer-reporting purposes.

◆ Monitor the quality of the Help Desk's activities, including both accuracy and timeliness of answers.

Intranet Context for Help Desk

Except for the physical taking of telephone calls, which can in large operations be partially automated by voice-menu systems, all of these steps can be performed using Web or Web-related tools you have learned about in this book. Let's revise the preceding list to add some Intranet context; *italics* show what's been added to each item on the list.

◆ Receive and record, *using a Web fill-in form front end to a trouble-ticket database*, telephone, e-mail, or other requests for help from customers.

◆ Research customer questions *using a Web fill-in form that interfaces with a searchable index or other database system* and provide *located* answers to the customers, *possibly via your Web browser's e-mail capabilities.*

◆ Track and update the status of trouble tickets, for both internal and customer-reporting purposes, *using a Web front end to your trouble-ticket database.*

◆ Monitor the quality of the Help Desk's activities, including both accuracy and timeliness of answers, *using a Web front end to your trouble-ticket database.*

Looking at this modified list, it might occur to you that you can add one more item:

◆ Give your Intranet's customers direct access to the Web-based Intranet Help Desk, so they can use their Web browsers to enter their own questions and/or search for problem solutions themselves.

By comparing this new list with the preceding one (which represents traditional Help Desk procedures) you can see yet another example of how easy and compelling an Intranet can be. Which Help Desk would you rather use?

What Is the Content of Your Help Desk?

Depending on the mission of your business or organization, your Help Desk can provide any of a wide variety of substantive information. What you provide is based on the perceived and expressed needs of your customers. Because you are probably involved with computers and networks (or you wouldn't be reading this book), it's no doubt easy for you to visualize a Help Desk for computer and network users—you probably already run one. Such an operation can provide answers to questions, such as how to use a software package, how to configure modems or printers, and so on. It can also take trouble reports on malfunctioning or inoperative computer or network hardware or software.

Help Desks are not limited to these narrow, though important, functions. Most large companies operate toll-free 800 numbers for customer support and questions about their products. You can call Proctor & Gamble, for example, with questions about toothpaste or other P&G products. Major furnace or air conditioner manufacturers refer you to dealers in your area for sales or service. Computer and computer software manufacturers also operate Help Desks for their customers. Of course, there are Help Desk databases of one kind or another underlying all of these operations.

Though quite simple, one of the most widely accessed Help Desk functions on the Internet is the package delivery form on Federal Express's Web server. Here (`http://www.fedex.com/`) you can check the status of your delivery using a Web fill-in form and CGI-bin script back-end. Figure 23.1 shows the FedEx Tracking Form. Just type in your FedEx Airbill number, and the system shows you the path of your package step by step through the delivery system, from pickup to final delivery, with date and time stamps. All of FedEx's competitors have set up similar services on the Web.

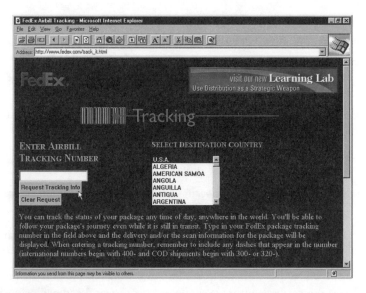

Figure 23.1. *Federal Express package tracking.*

Some organizations set up what might be called *Virtual Guy/Girl Friday* Web pages, with tips and information about doing odd jobs around the company. Such operations can cover a wide range of the kinds of miscellaneous questions that come up over and over again, such as who to call to get a broken desk repaired, how to ship an experimental widget, or how to get presentation booklets printed overnight. Your Intranet's Help Desk can be just as expansive or as limited as you want, with the information available subject only to your own imagination.

> **Note:** The *Virtual Guy/Girl Friday* function might well be implemented using USENET news or other means of communication and collaboration, such as Lotus Notes, Collabra, or other Intranet groupware. (See Chapter 27, "Collaboration on Your Intranet.")

Existing Help Desk Information

Help Desks get asked the same questions over and over again. These are your company's own Frequently Asked Questions, or FAQs. Your canned answers to these questions can form the foundation of your Intranet Help Desk.

In large part, the ease with which users can access the accumulated wisdom and experience of your Help Desk dictates how effective your operation is. Whether your Help Desk uses indexed file cabinets, shelves of tabbed three-ring binders, a sophisticated database system, or a less formal method to store answers to previously asked questions, your first task is to get these answers online on your Intranet so they are easily accessible.

The main principles for getting your legacy data online are those outlined in Chapter 3, "The Software Tools to Build a Web." In that chapter, you learned how to convert your legacy data into Intranet-usable information. If you have electronic copies of Help Desk documents available, you want to use what you learned in that chapter to move this data quickly onto your Intranet, making it accessible via your Web server and browsers. When you have legacy data that's not in plain text format, you might need to use the conversion tools you learned about earlier. This might include using your applications' Save As features to convert data into easily usable formats like plain text. In addition, you might eventually want to use Rich-Text format (RTF) as a go-between to convert legacy data into HTML documents for use on your Intranet. Now that vendors such as Microsoft and Novell have added direct HTML capabilities to their word processors, you can more easily save some legacy documents directly to HTML.

You can come back to your converted legacy documents once you have your Intranet Help Desk running. This enables you to refine them and add value by cutting in hyperlinked cross-references. This done, your Help Desk staff can use their Web browsers to jump from one document to another, looking for answers to customers' questions by following promising threads. The more cross-references you add, the more capabilities you give to your staff.

MIME Type/Subtype Setup

Even after you have successfully converted your Legacy Help Desk documents, you will no doubt end up with a variety of document formats, including plain text files, word processor files, HTML documents, and spreadsheets. This might seem a confusing mess. However, you can confidently deal with this situation using what you learned in Chapters 12–15. After all, your purpose in building an Intranet was to pull together just such a wide variety of resources and make them accessible using a single interface. All the information about MIME data types/subtypes and helper applications you have learned earlier in this book will help you as you make your Help Desk information available.

As you recall, enabling the use of your word processor and other office software packages as Web browser helper applications is a simple, two-step process:

1. Modify the MIME map on your Intranet's Web server(s). See Chapter 6, "Windows NT 4 Configuration," for tips on the Registry, and see Chapter 12, "MIME and Helper Applications," for information about MIME with IIS.

2. Configure your customers' Web browsers to deal with the newly defined MIME types/ subtypes by defining helper applications. Again, please review Chapters 12 and 13 for MIME details.

You need to add one more step to this simple outline: the creation of an HTML structure to lead your customers to the right documents. This can be done quite easily (as explained in the Tips in the previous chapter) without extensive knowledge of HTML.

Once you have taken these steps, your Intranet's Help Desk staff can simply use their Web browsers to retrieve and view your documents, regardless of their format. As needed, helper applications will open to handle requested documents.

For example, clicking a hyperlink pointing to a WordPerfect file opens WordPerfect to display the files on-screen. Having located the necessary document with which to respond to the customer's question, your Help Desk staff member is ready to close out the trouble ticket. It's just a few additional steps to provide not only the answer, but also a copy of the document containing it, directly to the user via your Intranet.

Indexing Your Help Desk Data

How, you're wondering, do the Help Desk staff locate answers to customer questions? Surely they don't just have long on-screen lists of document names to browse through? As with the conversion of your legacy data, the answers to these questions lead you back to material covered earlier in this book. In Chapter 21, "Indexing Your Intranet with WAIS," you learned about a variety of tools for indexing data on your Intranet and, equally important, tools for searching and retrieving data from the indexes. Those tools make it easy for your Help Desk staff to search out answers to customer inquiries using Web fill-in forms of the sort you have seen earlier in this book.

If your Help Desk data is already bundled into a commercial database application, you need to look at the Web-related relational database tools described in Chapter 16, "Linking Databases to the Web." The ability to create Web fill-in forms that interface with database engines via CGI scripts (or other means) will enhance your Help Desk's capability to serve its customers.

If you have built a custom text-based database application for your Help Desk, for which no tools are available, don't lose hope. You can probably dump the data out to plain text files, unless your database lacks support for standard export formats. As long as the data has an identifiable format, it can be run through WAIS, or some other indexing tool you find on the Internet, to make it accessible via Web browsers using fill-in forms. This enables you to continue to use the data you have accumulated in your application, at the same time freeing you of proprietary data formats. Further, with the outstanding capabilities of these search engines, you might find search-and-retrieval performance better than you had with your custom database—plus, your customers get a simple and familiar Web interface.

Help Desk Record Keeping

Unless your Help Desk operation is quite small and managed out of one person's back pocket, you're probably interested in keeping records of questions and their resolutions, trouble reports, and the like. You want substantive information about your Help Desk calls, such as the answers to questions customers have asked, so you can have them available the next time the same question arises. You also want timeliness and quality-control information about the way the calls were handled.

For example, was the answer provided on time, and with accuracy? Many Help Desks do this sort of tracking with paper forms, or with a computer program, which might or might not be integrated with the Help Desk substantive database itself.

It has probably occurred to you by now to wonder if you can put a Web interface on your Help Desk management and record-keeping itself. If you can provide your Help Desk staff (or everyone in your Intranet) the ability to search and retrieve documents and other data using their Web browsers, shouldn't it be possible to do your housekeeping (assigning and tracking questions or trouble reports, getting quality-control information, and the like) using similar methods?

The answer is, of course, "Yes." If you have already written CGI scripts that interface with fill-in forms and the index of your substantive Help Desk data, the same techniques you have used to retrieve data can also be used to enter and track its progress and to assign trouble reports to individual technicians. This can be done in as simple or as sophisticated a manner as you and the Help Desk team deem necessary.

You can do this either with an ISAPI or CGI database application or with simple, but limited, e-mail capability. ISAPI database applications can be purchased commercially (if you have the money), home-grown (if you have the time and skills), or custom-built using a hired-gun Web systems programmer (if you have the money, but not the time or the skills).

If you have the money, your choice to buy a commercial package or hire a custom programmer will depend on your specific needs and the level of functionality that you can find in a given off-the-shelf package. It is almost always cheaper to buy ready-made software than it is to build it yourself (or hire it to be built). The drawback is that ready-made software is usually less customizable than something you design yourself. A final point to consider; once you find a programmer with the right experience in Web technology and Windows NT, it will still take some time to design and finish the project.

Suppose you want to try the quick and dirty way via e-mail. Once you create one HTML form that you tie to the Blat program (on the CD-ROM), it sets your mind overflowing with other possibilities. You could use Blat to e-mail form data from a Help Desk call to the right expert who handles questions of a particular nature. Besides using it to assign support calls, here are some other uses (some of which might require CGI scripts):

◆ Use an HTML form and Blat to send e-mail to people who are responsible for the tracking of calls themselves.

◆ Send a confirmation e-mail message to the original sender of the message, perhaps with tracking or Help Desk staff assignment-control (trouble-ticket number) information.

◆ Send mail to a back-end program or other script that automatically updates your call-tracking database and/or makes trouble call assignments.

Giving Your Customers Access to the Intranet Help Desk

The preceding section on problem-tracking software for your Intranet was intended to do more than just acquaint you with the available software and its capabilities. It was also intended to lead you to the notion of making your Intranet Help Desk system accessible to all your customers via their Web browsers. Even in the problem-tracking software environment, which might not be fully aware of the Web's potential, there is widespread support for making it possible for users to enter their own problem reports. Most of the vendor packages have a graphical interface for users to enter problem reports. There are a number of reasons for this. Most of them are the same reasons that companies put voice-menu phone systems in place: to save time and staff costs.

Unlike the situation with such phone systems, however, which can make a customer feel depersonalized, direct user interface to problem-tracking systems can give customers more control over their problem reporting, and a better overall feel for the process. It might be true, for example, that a fill-in form on the customer's computer screen is the same one a Help Desk call-taker would fill in when answering the customer's telephone call. Still, there's a definite feeling of finality about clicking that Submit button, especially if the system gives you a confirmation message with a problem-tracking number, either on-screen or in an e-mail message.

Summary

In this chapter, you have learned how the information and tools described in the rest of this book can be stitched together for purposes of your Intranet Help Desk. Specifically, you have accomplished the following:

◆ Considered the nature, purpose, and substantive content of a Help Desk in the context of your Intranet.

◆ Considered what existing Help Desk electronic information is available to put onto your Intranet.

◆ Determined the form(s) of that information.

◆ Learned how to put that information together so it is accessible using a Web browser, putting what you have learned about MIME data types/subtypes and Web browser helper applications to work.

◆ Put what you have learned about Intranet document indexing to work to streamline search and retrieval of Help Desk information.

◆ Thought about maintaining Help Desk records for quality-control and related purposes.

◆ Opened up your Intranet Help Desk for direct access by your Intranet's customers.

In the next chapter, you use the same techniques used in this chapter to make ordering and inventory documents available on your Intranet.

CHAPTER 24

Ordering and Inventory

◆ Visualize your Intranet ordering and inventory application

◆ HTML forms

◆ CGI scripting for your Intranet ordering and inventory application

Like so many of the chapters in this part of the book, this one is about putting several of the things you've learned together to create something altogether new on your Intranet. In fact, most of this book is about the use of imaginative elbow grease to create wonderful things on your Intranet; there's more imagination than rocket science involved. The tools you've been learning in this book can be put together to bring off near miracles for your Intranet.

In this chapter, we'll talk about using some of the tools to create an ordering and inventory application for your Intranet. Keep in mind while reading this chapter that these techniques are generally useful on an Intranet, so you need not focus too closely on the ordering and inventory application used as an example.

> **Note:** Although this chapter is nominally about creating a specific order and inventory application for your Intranet, the ideas and techniques, including some important CGI scripting tips, aren't limited to this application. You'll be able to use them in other Intranet applications you build, even if you don't build this particular one.

Visualize Your Intranet Ordering and Inventory Application

Before going into a lot of implementation details, let's get a bird's eye view of the application. We'll look first at its basic purpose, then at the customer's view of it, and finally at the component parts of the application.

Purpose of the Application

Your Intranet ordering and inventory application's purpose is to provide your customers with Web-browser access to the underlying company ordering and inventory database. Specifically, your application will:

◆ Allow customers to place orders for in-house store items using fill-in forms and their Web browser.

◆ Generate e-mail acknowledgments of orders, including availability and delivery information on ordered items.

◆ Allow customers to query the underlying ordering and inventory database for order status and availability of items.

◆ Use customer account number information, entered by the customer in the Web order form, to debit accounts for the costs of ordered items.

◆ Consider the security aspects of the overall system.

◆ Update the inventory database when items are delivered.

I won't address specific information about the design of the database application underlying your Intranet application, nor any product-specific recommendations. It's assumed, however, that your in-place database is a relational database application capable of accepting input from HTML forms using CGI or ISAPI. Recall that Visual C++ 4.x includes both an ISAPI Wizard and an ODBC interface (actually two).

In addition, it's assumed the database tracks your inventory, accepts and verifies orders using user account numbers, debits user accounts for orders, and updates inventory once orders are delivered using predefined procedures.

This sort of database application is fairly standard in the corporate world, so details on setting one up aren't provided. If you don't already have such a database in place, refer to Chapter 16, "Linking Databases to the Web," for specifics on how a number of free and commercial databases work in a World Wide Web environment. It's not required that there be a specific Web interface to your particular database; you can always use the CGI mechanism to access it. But it's nice if there is.

The sort of database you'll need to implement the application described in this chapter depends on your organization's needs, anticipated level of use, and other factors. Small operations may be able to use a PC-based database, such as Microsoft Access, accessed using Visual Basic CGI programs from a Web server running on the same PC. (See Chapter 20 for an example.)

What the Application Might Look Like to the Customer

The primary view of your Intranet ordering and inventory application your customers will have is the one they see through their Web browser, of course. Figure 24.1 shows a simple HTML fill-in form for placing orders. As you can see, the form has spaces for customer name, account information, delivery information, and product and vendor information. There are also a couple of free-form text boxes for entering unformatted information. Later in this chapter, you'll see modified versions of this form with additional features that make it easier for your customers to order things. The form interfaces with a CGI or ISAPI program that processes what the customer enters, and then accesses the underlying database application to place the order.

Pieces of the Application You'll Create

There are several discrete parts of your Intranet ordering and inventory application. The first is the underlying database application, which we've assumed is already in place. You'll need to create the rest of the parts. Your first step should be to create the HTML fill-in forms for each of the major functions of the application. These functions include simple ordering, order status inquiry, and inventory search, so you'll want to build forms for each.

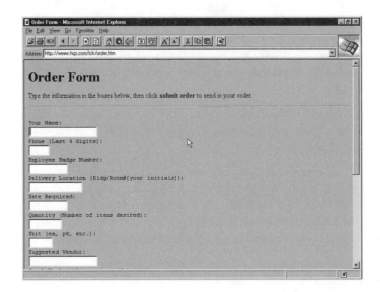

Figure 24.1. *A Web order form.*

Next, you'll create the CGI/ISAPI programs that underlie your fill-in forms. Although it's possible to write a single script with multiple options, you may want to follow the KISS (Keep it Simple, Stupid!) principle, at least at the outset, by creating separate, simple scripts for each of your forms. Doing so makes debugging substantially easier, and you can always steal from one script when you work on another. It's critical in crafting CGI/ISAPI programs that interface with database applications for you to have an intimate understanding of the way your database accepts and outputs data. As a result, your scripts need to reflect your knowledge of the database itself.

Finally, you'll want to put together an overall Web page (or set of pages) that neatly provides a single, easy-to-access interface to the application. Because HTML markup allows hyperlinks among documents, you can provide a top-level entry point, with branches to each major form accessible with a customer mouse click. Don't forget to provide a way back to the top from each major point in the application.

HTML Forms

Let's take a look at the code that creates the form shown in Figure 24.1. As you look at Listing 24.1, you'll notice that HTML markup is shown in all uppercase letters. You should be able to pick out the essential form markup and what it means by comparing the code with its rendering in Figure 24.1. For more information on HTML, see Chapter 5 and Appendix A.

Listing 24.1. The HTML code for the order form is in the file order.htm on the CD-ROM.

```
<HTML><HEAD><TITLE>Order Form</TITLE></HEAD><BODY>
<FORM METHOD="post" ACTION="http://intranet.yourco.com/CGI/order.pl">
<H1>Order Form</H1>
Type the information in the boxes below, then click <STRONG>submit
order</STRONG> to send in your order.<HR>
<PRE>Your Name:
<INPUT TYPE="text" SIZE=20 NAME=yourname>
Phone (Last 4 digits):
<INPUT TYPE="text" SIZE=4 NAME="phone">
Employee Badge Number:
<INPUT TYPE="text" SIZE=10 NAME="sitepass">
Delivery Location (Bldg/Room#[your initials]):
<INPUT TYPE="text" SIZE=15 NAME="location">
Date Required:
<INPUT TYPE="text" SIZE=10 NAME="datereq">
Quantity (Number of items desired):
<INPUT TYPE="text" SIZE=8 NAME="quantity">
Unit (ea, pk, etc.):
<INPUT TYPE="text" SIZE=5 NAME="unit">
Suggested Vendor:
<INPUT TYPE="text" SIZE=20 NAME="vendor">
Stock Number (Stores or vendors):
<INPUT TYPE="text" SIZE=15 NAME="stockno">
Description:
<TEXTAREA NAME="descript" COLS=60 ROWS=2></TEXTAREA>
Estimated Cost (per item):
<INPUT TYPE="text" SIZE=10 NAME="cost"><BR>
Additional Instruction or Information:
<EM>If this order exceeds your authorization limit, please indicate
your supervisor's name so it can be forwarded electronically
for authorization.</EM>
<TEXTAREA NAME="moreinfo" COLS=60 ROWS=2></TEXTAREA></PRE>
<HR>
<INPUT TYPE="submit" VALUE="Submit Order">
<INPUT TYPE="reset" VALUE="Clear Form to Start Over">
</FORM></BODY></HTML>
```

Analysis of HTML Form Example

Despite its length, this form is quite simple, with repeated use of just a few HTML form tags. Several fixed-size fill-in boxes are created using the <INPUT> tag, with the <TYPE> and <SIZE> attributes setting the type of input (text) and the displayed box's size. In addition, the <TEXTAREA> tag is used, with the <COLS> and <ROWS> attributes spelling out the dimensions of the free-form text box. Finally, the special <INPUT TYPE> attributes submit and reset are used for form housekeeping.

Also notice that the <VALUE> tag is used many times. In each case, the word inside the double quotes is used as a name for the information that is entered into the form. You may want to read these into a mental array, as you'll learn more about them later in this chapter, when we consider the CGI scripting that underlies your fill-in forms. For the time being, just think of the <VALUE> tag as a label for each piece of information requested by the form; the labels will be retained and passed to the CGI script when the customer submits the form.

As to the rest of the form, please note:

◆ The `<METHOD="post">` tag specifies one of two methods for sending data to the server via the script (the other is `"get"`). There is virtually no situation with respect to fill-in forms in which you would use `"get"`; using `"post"` should be your standard method.

◆ The back-end CGI/ISAPI program for the form is specified using the `<ACTION>` tag, as a Web URL, in this case `http://intranet.yourco.com/CGI/order.pl`. The filename extension `.pl` should tip you off to the fact this is a Perl CGI script.

◆ Standard HTML markup, with overall housekeeping tags (`<HTML>`, `<HEAD>`, and so on), as well as general text formatting, line-break, and horizontal rule tags.

◆ The actual text to be displayed to the customer when viewing the form.

Modify the Form to Add Choices

This form is a good all-purpose form for ordering any number of things. Although this is quite generic, because your Intranet Order and Inventory application is limited to a specific inventory, you may want to give customers access to a predefined set of choices, rather than requiring them to manually type in a text box the name of the item(s) they want to order. This makes customers' lives easier. It also makes the creation of your CGI scripts a lot less troublesome, because customers are not able to make typographical errors in text boxes. Let's look at Figure 24.2, which is a modified version of the form shown previously.

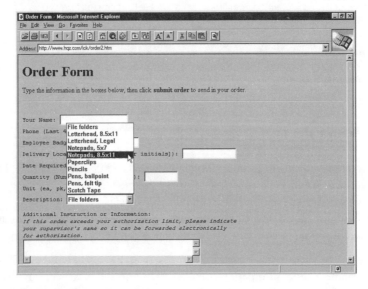

Figure 24.2. A modified order form with a pull-down item selection.

The first thing you'll notice about the modified form is the presence of a drop-down list of available items. Although the example shows a list of just a few office items, you can provide any menu of choices to your customers, who can select the item they want just by clicking on it. The menu is implemented using the HTML <SELECT> tag, with the <OPTION> attribute. You'll want to read the details of the <SELECT> tag and its several attributes in Chapter 5 and Appendix A. Here's the HTML code fragment which sets this up; it replaces the Description entry in the previous HTML document (Listing 24.1):

```
Description:
<SELECT NAME="descript">
<OPTION>File folders
<OPTION>Letterhead, 8.5x11
<OPTION>Letterhead, Legal
<OPTION>Notepads, 5x7
<OPTION>Notepads, 8.5x11
<OPTION>Paperclips
<OPTION>Pencils
<OPTION>Pens, ballpoint
<OPTION>Pens, felt tip
<OPTION>Scotch Tape</SELECT>
```

This HTML code is part of the file order2.htm on the CD-ROM.

As you can see from Figure 24.2, this is a substantial improvement over the previous form (Figure 24.1). Customers no longer have to manually type the name of the item they want. Instead, they can just select it from the pop-up menu by clicking the item.

You'll also notice the form has been simplified by removing the Suggested Vendor and Estimated Cost text-entry boxes. Presumably, when ordering office supplies, as this form does, you'll get all of them from a single source with known pricing, so you needn't trouble the customer for these two pieces of information. I've also gotten rid of the Stock Number box, because the customer does not need to know it when selecting from the pop-up menu. Finally, data entry fields have been moved up to the same line with the field label to ease right-to-left reading. Already, this first revision of the order form is much more useful. You should resist the urge during form design to ask the user for every imaginable tidbit of data. Users are generally more willing to use a less-cluttered form that is easier to zip through.

There's at least one major remaining problem with this form, however. Suppose customers want to order more than one item at a time. The current form allows only one item to be selected from the pop-up menu. If customers want to order something else, they'll have to reload the form, retype all the identifying information and select the next item. Another attribute to the HTML <SELECT> tag, however, resolves this limitation, with a three-word change to the HTML code. Just change the <SELECT NAME="descript"> line to read like this:

```
<SELECT NAME="descript" MULTIPLE SIZE=5>
```

This quick and easy change generates a substantially different-looking order form, as shown in Figure 24.3. As you can see from the product selections already made in Figure 24.3, the customer can now select multiple items from the scrollable menu. (Notice the scrollbar on the right.) The menu created using the `<MULTIPLE>` attribute is no longer a pop-up, as in Figure 24.2. It is now integrated right into the page, with five lines specified by the `<SIZE=5>` attribute. This revision appears in a complete HTML order form as `order3.htm` on the CD-ROM.

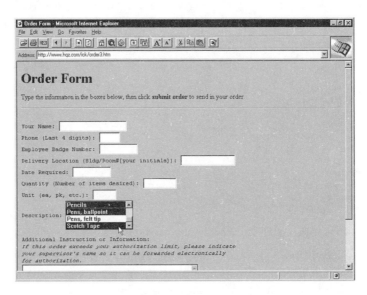

Figure 24.3. *A modified order form with scrollable item selection.*

Note: You'll also want to look at the `<SELECTED>` HTML forms attribute, which enables you to specify preset, default selections on pop-up and scrolling menus of the sort used in this form. In addition, as you'll learn from detailed HTML forms documentation, there are a number of other features you can use, including checkboxes, radio buttons, and hidden information useful for session tracking. Hidden information can be useful when the customer needs to fill in more than one form.

Advantages of the Modified Form to the Webmaster

The advantages of the modified form to the customer, with its scrollable menu of choices, are quite obvious. The advantages of the form to you are not so readily apparent, but are possibly even more important.

The main gain, besides the adoration of your customers, is that your CGI script that will process the form can now be much simpler. By removing the requirement that customers type the name of the item(s) they want and replacing it with clickable menu selections, you've eliminated the potential for customers' typographical and spelling errors. Because dealing with data entry mistakes is the bane of programmers everywhere, this change makes your scripting easier. You now have a set, predictable list of possible entries for the Description field of the form, and you no longer have to anticipate and deal in your script with every possible misspelling or typographical error customers might enter in the form. Also, a pre-set list of selections reduces the risk of a malicious user trying to subvert your Intranet's security by sending excessive, surprise, or dangerous text strings to a CGI/ISAPI program from a Web form.

> **Note:** While you're considering the security aspects of your fill-in forms and CGI scripts, you may want to look at the <PASSWORD> tag in HTML forms markup. It works much like an ordinary HTML form text box, but echoes a string of asterisks when customers enter their passwords (to escape the prying eyes of over-the-shoulder onlookers) rather than the actual password. The password entered by the customer is passed on by the form to the CGI or ISAPI program for processing, and the program can verify that customers are who they say they are.
>
> Further, your CGI/ISAPI program can use the network hostname of the computer from which the customer is entering information as another verification check by associating customer name, password, and/or computer hostname and checking them against an internal list of allowed matches. Recall that one of the standard CGI environment variables, listed in Chapter 19, "Getting the Most Out of HTML with CGI," is the network hostname of the customer's computer. Finally, you may want to limit access to the form itself, requiring a username and password before bringing up the form in the first place.

Creating Forms on the Fly and Making Them Smart

So far, the discussion of HTML forms has focused on pre-set HTML documents containing your forms. These are static HTML documents that you create with a text editor and serve with your Web server, just like other static documents. Your CGI/ISAPI programs, however, can create forms dynamically, and the ability to do so can be important to you. On-the-fly forms creation with a CGI/ISAPI program is done, essentially, by having the program generate valid MIME data type/subtype headers, followed by a stream of HTML markup. In Perl, for example, use the print statement to generate the necessary header and HTML output.

It may be difficult at first to distinguish a reason for preferring a static HTML document over a CGI/ISAPI program (or vice versa) that generates the same fill-in form. In this context, however, recall that Web interfaces to commercial database packages have the capability to make intelligent decisions about what to return to a customer and in what format. CGI/ISAPI programs can do the same thing. One reason you need the power to generate HTML dynamically is that Web browsers differ in their capabilities to render nonstandard HTML markup. Netscape, for example, has developed a set of semi-proprietary extensions to HTML its browsers support; in addition, the company has integrated advanced features of HTML table formatting to its browsers. If you've used another browser, such as NCSA Mosaic, you've no doubt encountered Web pages with such Netscape-isms and found these pages difficult, if not impossible, to view. A growing number of Web pages, however, are based on smart CGI/ISAPI programs that ferret out the name of the user's

Web browser and return an HTML document appropriate to the browser. This is quite simple to do, really. One of those standard CGI environment variables, HTTP_USER_AGENT, contains the name and release number of the user's Web browser.

Intelligent CGI/ISAPI program can use the HTTP_USER_AGENT environment variable with each run to identify each customer's Web browser and then return a document or form the browser can display properly. Similarly, you can use other CGI environment variables in your programs to make decisions and provide the appropriate document or form back to the customer. Recall that among these variables is the customer's computer hostname (REMOTE_HOST), numerical IP address (REMOTE_ADDR), and possibly, username (REMOTE_USER), as well as several others. Because your Intranet is by definition a closed group, with access limited to customers inside your organization, you can use predefined lists of users and hostnames in combination with these CGI environment variables to customize the documents, including fill-in forms, returned to customers by your Intranet order and inventory application.

CGI Scripting for Your Intranet Ordering and Inventory Application

The last couple of paragraphs jumped the gun on this section's subject matter—introducing some advanced CGI/ISAPI programming techniques in the context of dynamically generating custom HTML forms and other documents for different Web browsers. Before we get too far ahead of ourselves, let's take a few steps back and look at the CGI mechanism from a larger perspective and then focus back on your Intranet ordering and inventory application.

CGI Basics Revisited

Reduced to its most basic level, the CGI mechanism does two things. (ISAPI works essentially the same way.)

- ◆ It passes the information entered by a customer into a Web fill-in form to a back-end script or other computer program for processing.
- ◆ It returns the results of the program's run, in the form of HTML markup, to the initiating customer's Web browser for viewing.

For the most part, CGI/ISAPI programs use variables to pass and receive data using standard output and standard input. Each piece of information that a customer enters into a fill-in form is assigned to a variable for easy handling. The values represented by the variables are passed to the back-end program for processing, and results generated by the script are processed by the script and sent back to the customer's browser.

CGI/ISAPI programs can pass the variable information they get from the customer to application packages on your computer system, such as your ordering and inventory relational database package. For example, full-blown Structured Query Language (SQL) queries can be built from

Web fill-in forms. Customers enter (or select) SQL search criteria using their Web browser. All the features of HTML forms markup are useful here, including text boxes, pop-up or scrolling menus, checkboxes, radio buttons, and free-form text areas.

The back-end CGI/ISAPI program receives the customer's entries from the form as variables, reformatting the information into a legitimate SQL query. Next, the program passes the query off to the database engine using standard output and waits for a response. When the database engine returns the results of the query, the CGI/ISAPI program receives them as standard input. Recognizing the structure of the database engine's output, the program takes that data and reformats it into HTML. Finally, the HTML-formatted output of the results of the customer's query is returned to his Web browser for viewing.

Along the way, the CGI mechanism provides a handy set of standard environment variables for each transaction. You can use and manipulate these variables in your CGI/ISAPI programs to smarten them up further, allowing them to make decisions about Web-browser capabilities, user authentication, and a long list of other matters. Such decision-making enables you to customize the presentation of your Intranet Ordering and Inventory application.

The very same CGI/ISAPI program might, for example, serve clerical staff ordering office supplies and scientists ordering lab supplies. Based on the customer's userid, computer hostname, or other information from the list of standard CGI environment variables, the form previously shown (see Figure 24.3) can be dynamically generated, displaying a different list of available supplies for each customer.

> **Note:** For more detailed information on CGI programming, check out the NCSA Common Gateway Interface tutorial at `http://hoohoo.ncsa.uiuc.edu/cgi/overview.html`, where you'll find an archive of example scripts. In addition, there's a tremendous list of CGI-related resources, with access to many more example programs, at `http://www.yahoo.com/`.

Forms, CGI Programs, and Your Intranet Ordering and Inventory Application

Let's now trace the process of a transaction on your Intranet ordering and inventory application: looking at your forms, how the CGI/ISAPI program processes the data entered into it, and the results.

The Order Form

Having covered the background, let's fill out the sample order form and go over those parts of the HTML markup not analyzed earlier in this chapter. We deferred discussion of the numerous <VALUE> tags in the form's HTML markup. Let's now turn to these items. Take a look at Figure

24.4, which is the same order form as that shown previously but with specific order information filled in. All the data-entry boxes are filled in and a product selected.

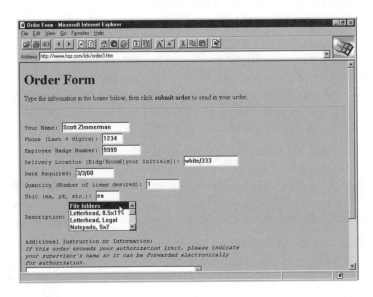

Figure 24.4. *Completed order form.*

Each of the data-entry boxes in the order form is now filled in. Table 24.1 shows each piece of information the customer entered in this order form, associated with the HTML <VALUE> label for that information used in the HTML form.

Table 24.1. Order form processing of the data entered by the user.

Label	Value
yourname	Scott Zimmerman
phone	1234
sitepass	9999
location	white/333
datereq	3/3/00
quantity	1
unit	ea
descript	File folders
moreinfo	No signature required for delivery

The heart of your CGI/ISAPI program for ordering these file folders is the manipulation and use of these nine chunks of information. The information from the fill-in form is passed by the program to the HTTP server, and then to the program, as a set of variables via standard input. (The details differ slightly if you are building or using an ISAPI DLL, but the CGI environment variables are essentially the same.) Your program, then, should expect to receive as standard input these nine discrete pieces of information.

Whether you're writing your CGI application in Perl, Visual Basic, or an ISAPI DLL in C or C++, you'll need to have it accept this information and deal with it. You can do this piece by piece, or by reading the standard input into an array. In the case of ISAPI, the data is essentially already in an array (you'll have a pointer to a memory block). In either event, your program can use these variables to generate a database SQL query/update or a request for a canned database procedure to run.

Finally, the program sends your request, containing the variable data in SQL format, via standard output, to your database engine for execution. Alternatively, you can call on the ODBC API and/ or the MFC DAO classes (if you are using Visual C++ 4.x) to interact with the database with superior efficiency. All of this processing between the browser, the server, and your CGI application will happen lightning fast. (You'll notice that the order in Table 24.1 isn't due until after the turn of the century, so there is no rush on this particular order for a single file folder.)

Note: C/C++ programmers use the term *white space* to refer to any number of space, tab, and newline characters.

Tip: Because several of these pieces of information are text strings containing white space, with more than one word in them, be sure to use appropriate quoting in your CGI/ISAPI program to handle them properly.

Your program needs also to expect to get data back from the database engine. Based on the input from the form, which is sent on to the database engine, the CGI/ISAPI program expects a specifically formatted response to the query, containing a specific number of chunks of data. Your program must know precisely how the output of the database engine looks, including record and field separators, to be able to parse it. Again, your program can read this information into an array for easy handling or deal with each piece of data individually. Whichever choice you make, the program now must reformat this variable information into HTML, with appropriate MIME type/ subtype header information.

Here's one way in which a Perl script fragment could acknowledge your customer's order:

```
print "Content-type: text/html\n\n";
print "<HTML><HEAD><TITLE>Order Response</TITLE></HEAD>\n";
print "<BODY><H1>Thanks for Your Order, $yourname</H1><HR>\n";
print "Your order for $quantity \"$descript\" has been placed.\n";
print "It will be delivered to \"$location\" and charged to your account ";
print "\"$sitepass\" on or before \"$datereq\"<HR>\n";
print "For information about your order, call the Help Desk\n";
print "</BODY></HTML>\n";
```

As you can see, the script has echoed back the customer's order essentials with some acknowledgment text and some cosmetic HTML markup to dress up the output.

Bells and Whistles

Now that you've gotten your basic CGI/ISAPI program to process orders, you'll want to add some useful features. There are any number of them, but here are a few ideas to consider. You'll undoubtedly think of others.

◆ Change the acknowledgment to a confirmation dialog by making your script output another HTML form with a single clickable Confirm Order button. This will change your CGI/ISAPI program so that its initial output is the acknowledgment/confirmation form. The customer's order would not actually be placed until she has confirmed it.

◆ Prompt the customer for a password and/or verify his name, account number and/or computer hostname against an approved list before accepting the order.

◆ Automatically route the order to the customer's supervisor via e-mail if the cost of the order exceeds a pre-set authorization limit.

◆ Generate e-mail to store personnel, actually placing the order.

You can apply these and other similar extra features as you develop additional forms and CGI/ISAPI programs for other functions in your Intranet order and inventory application. These can provide your customers with the ability to query the database for the status of an order, ask for inventory information on particular items or categories of items, browse the overall catalog of supplies, and the like. You can also create and use fill-in forms that are accessible only to store staff for use in updating inventory and customer account information.

Summary

In this chapter, you've applied much of the information you've learned in other chapters of this book to the practical task of creating an Intranet order and inventory application. This combination of HTML forms and CGI/ISAPI programming is a widely useful technique, so you'll want to consider its general lessons in creating other Intranet applications, not limiting your imagination to this particular application. In this chapter, you have focused on:

◆ HTML forms markup, with specifics for setting up order forms.

◆ The basics of CGI and ISAPI programming for your application, including some general CGI tips you can generalize to other applications on your Intranet.

◆ Interfacing your Intranet ordering and inventory application with your ordering and inventory database.

In Chapter 25, you'll see a similar process of integrating the information and techniques found throughout the book—this time for the creation of boilerplate document libraries.

CHAPTER

Intranet Boilerplate Library

◆ Preparing to serve existing documents
◆ Use of your Intranet boilerplate library
◆ Managing your boilerplate library
◆ Indexing your boilerplate library

Experienced word processors know one of the most valuable features of their word processing software is the ability to reuse documents, and parts of documents, without retyping them. For even the fastest typists, copying a paragraph, page, or an even larger part of one document to another makes words-per-minute measurements obsolete. Compared to typing a block of text from scratch, using the paste command is an obvious gain in efficiency.

Although virtually everyone who uses a word processor can profit from its cut, copy, and paste features to save time and typing, organizations that generate large volumes of similar documents will find the use of boilerplate text to be invaluable. In this chapter, we'll look at how two such organizations—the Public Inquiries Department of a Government agency and a law firm—can build an Intranet Boilerplate Library.

Your steps in putting your Intranet boilerplate library together involve assembly, analysis, and conversion of available legacy word processing documents. Then, just as you did in Part III of this book, you'll prepare to go live with the data on your Intranet by configuring the Web server MIME map; building an HTML page of document descriptions and hyperlinks; and configuring the browser helper applications. If you read Chapter 13, "Word Processing on the Web," you are already very familiar with these steps and I won't waste your time repeating them here.

Preparing to Serve Existing Documents

If you're interested in creating an Intranet boilerplate library, your organization is probably already running some sort of operation which reuses the same documents repeatedly. The example organizations in this chapter—the Department of Public Inquiries (DPI) and a law office—do. The former answers letters from the public or from legislators about government programs, often answering the same questions again and again. The latter assembles legal briefs and other legal documents, much of which are made up of boilerplate language.

In both cases, it's likely that a large number of reusable documents are already available for your Intranet boilerplate library. Your organization might or might not have organized this into a formalized process, so you may have to search out documents that can be used. Although you probably won't want to search customers' hard disks or fileserver directories for candidate documents, you'll want to encourage your customers to contribute information for your library.

Handling Word Processor File Formats

You'll recall from our earlier work that you'll need to get a survey of the word processors in use within your organization. If you determine that more than one program is popular, you'll need to deal with the file format issue on the Web server. You can do this in a couple of ways:

◆ Doing mass conversions of all your documents, using the word processor Save As feature, into each of the necessary document formats, resulting in two or more copies of each converted document.

◆ Selecting a common document format, such as the Microsoft Rich Text Format (RTF). (See your word processor documentation for its capabilities in this area.) This, too, involves using your word processor's Save As feature, but limits the conversions to just one format.

HTML Presentation on the Server

As you've learned, the basic setup of Web pages containing straightforward, clickable lists of available documents is quite easy. Adding a little subject-matter organization is simple, too, using hyperlinks to create nested menu listings and adding explanatory text to the pages. In just a few minutes, you can present a useful list of available word processing documents to your customers.

Obviously, this is an effective—but limited—way of doing business. The advantage of this approach is that you can get it up and running very quickly. Later in this chapter, I'll have a bit more to say about how you can better organize the Web site presentation to the end user.

Client Configuration

Client configuration has been dealt with in several earlier chapters, so I will address it here only by way of review. It boils down to two steps: 1) MIME configuration in the Web browser to reference the relevant helper application; and 2) the actual installation of the word processor helper application (for example, Microsoft Word). See Chapter 13 for step-by-step instructions.

Note: Some office applications support the notion of licensing and installing one copy on a server, as opposed to a full client installation on every desktop. The main advantages of this are that it saves disk space on the clients and the system administrators have an easier job configuring and upgrading the application. The disadvantages are that it takes slightly longer to load the application across the network and some applications don't distinguish individual user preferences based on a login ID. That can lead to a situation where say, I set the default file location to point to my drive, and then you override it by setting it to point to your drive. We would be in an endless loop unless the application stored user preferences on each client or identified user preferences which are stored separately on the server.

Once you have taken these steps, your Intranet boilerplate library's customers can use their Web browsers to retrieve, view, and interact with documents as necessary, just as they would with any other Web-page hyperlink. Customers' word processor helper applications are fired off as documents are accessed. For example, clicking hyperlinks pointing to WordPerfect files causes that program to start with a copy of the retrieved document loaded. Having located the necessary document, customers are all set to save, print, and edit the document for their own purposes. More importantly, for purposes of the Intranet boilerplate library, customers are able to use the downloaded documents as the framework for new ones, with boilerplate language intact. They'll even be able to assemble documents from multiple original source documents.

Note: Web browser helper applications, such as your customers' word processors, always operate on a copy of the original document. Your original document on your Web server remains unchanged until you change it. Customers can freely change the documents they've opened with a Web browser helper application for their own needs, all without touching the original.

Use of Your Intranet Boilerplate Library

Government agencies receive a lot of mail, including letters from the public, from legislators exercising constituent service and general legislative oversight, and from other government agencies. As does your Help Desk (see Chapter 23, "Intranet Help Desk"), your DPI gets repeated, similar questions and probably has a large library of canned responses to these common questions. You don't want to send an often-photocopied form letter in response to such questions, particularly to an influential legislator who may have control over your agency's budget. As a result, your DPI finds itself creating what it wants to appear to be original responses to these inquires.

In many cases, such responses are nothing more than a cobbling together of several off-the-shelf, stock paragraphs, with a few personalizing edits to make the letter look original. Your word processor's copy-and-paste function is a critical part of this process, but you might not have a way of easily finding the particular stock paragraphs you want, or an easy way of assembling those paragraphs into a completely new document.

In a way, law firms are like DPIs, in that they generate loads of documents consisting largely of standard, off-the-shelf language, and also develop altogether new documents that often include lengthy quotations from legal opinions, court cases, and other existing documents. Attorneys give cut-and-paste documents to clerks for typing, with text from prior briefs, photocopied pages from court decisions, and the like. Much of the text may have come from existing documents already online as word processor document files, and some court systems are making electronic copies of court documents available. It goes without saying that it profits the firm if the cut-and-paste documents can be assembled by the clerical staff from available electronic boilerplate.

High-volume DPI organizations and large government agencies (such as the U.S. Social Security Administration), which receive hundreds of thousands of inquiries a year, may be able to contract for an industrial strength document management system to meet these needs. Depending on its size and way of doing business, a law firm may need to do the same thing. Like other custom applications, these systems may come at very high cost. Although very large operations may require such custom document management systems, your Intranet boilerplate library can replicate most of their features at substantially lower costs. As with the data warehouse packages, you have trade-off choices between costs and capabilities.

The Boilerplate Home Page

Let's revisit an aspect of the boilerplate project that I touched on lightly above, namely the creation of what you might call its home page. This is just like any other Web home page, consisting of ordinary HTML markup, introductory text, graphics (if you want to include them), and a top-level set of clickable hyperlinks. For your word-processing staff, you may want to configure their Web browsers to start with this home page; if not, be sure to include a link to your home page on whatever startup page they use.

The hyperlinks on the home page may be organized in several ways. The best may be an organization by subject, with the home page main links leading down a hierarchy of subject matter that enables customers to perform a top-down search for documents matching their needs. For example, you might provide just ten or fewer broad top-level subjects with branches leading to more specific subjects. Although it's not a boilerplate operation by any means, take a look at the Yahoo Search Engine home page, shown in Figure 25.1, for a famous example of the hierarchical approach.

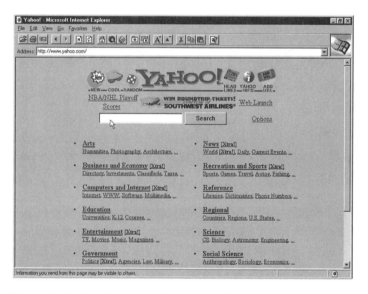

Figure 25.1. *The Yahoo top-level subject layout rises above a massive hierarchical structure.*

Walk Down the Subject Tree to Live Documents

Each of the Yahoo search engine pages presents a dozen or so very broad subject categories, such as Science & Technology or Business and Economy. Selecting one of these links takes you to progressively more specialized subjects within the general subject matter tree, finally leading you to individual Web pages and documents you can view with your Web browser.

Your Intranet boilerplate library can be laid out just the same way, with subject matter breakdown based on the documents in your own library. In fact, you can almost certainly port over the structure of your existing paper file cabinet, with top-level links representing, say, drawers—each one of which contains organized folders of individual documents.

The only difference between your Intranet boilerplate library and these search engine pages is that when customers reach the individual-document level and select a hyperlink, the document pops up in their word processor rather than in the Web browser. At this point, customers have a live document with which they can do more than just look. For example:

◆ They can edit, save, or print it with their word processors. (To save it, they need to have disk space on the client machine or a user directory on the server. The latter is easier for the system administrator to backup. Also, make sure you train the users how to subsequently retrieve the documents they save.)

◆ They can customize the stock language to personalize the boilerplate and to focus it the specific incoming inquiry.

◆ Perhaps more importantly, they can open whole new documents from within the word processor and then use the copy-and-paste feature to clip paragraphs of the stock language and paste them into it. The new document ultimately becomes the final response to the constituent's letter or the new legal brief. (Recall that the boilerplate documents they have downloaded are temporary copies.) Further, they can continue to open more boilerplate documents to grab additional text for insertion into the final document.

◆ They can use all the other features of the word processor software, including global search-and-replace, macro commands, graphic image insertion, tables, spreadsheet data, and the like, to further customize the new document for its intended purpose.

The last item in the preceding list deserves a bit more attention here. Your word processor can be custom-tailored to the needs of your Intranet boilerplate library operation. Besides the actual library of reusable documents you've created on your Intranet, you can also configure and share document style sheets and formatting templates; macro commands for inserting pieces of boilerplate too short to put in your library; custom spelling-checker dictionaries; and many other word-processing–specific facilities. Doing so not only adds efficiency to your operation, but it also brings about uniformity in the look of your documents and in the way they are produced.

Although it's true these things are not really part of your Intranet, they're commonsense means of streamlining the work that a boilerplate operation like a DPI or law firm does.

> **Note:** You may recall the discussion in Chapter 14 of the critical difference between spreadsheets saved as plain text (simple tabular rows and columns of numbers) and live spreadsheets (with formulae and macros already built-in). This same reasoning applies to custom document management systems. Being able to retrieve the text of a boilerplate

document on-screen may be one thing; being able to retrieve it directly into your word processor and use it immediately (with style sheets and macros attached) is something else altogether.

Documents and More Documents

Customers' Web browsers are still active after having retrieved a document into their word processors. As a result, there's nothing to stop them from popping back into the Web browser window and locating and retrieving additional documents. Unless your boilerplate library has all its stock paragraphs in just a few large documents (which would defeat many of your purposes), it's likely that customers will need to open several documents to retrieve all the necessary stock language to assemble their final documents. Continued browsing and retrieving documents, however, can result in multiple copies of the customer's word processor running concurrently. With some word processors, each new retrieval loads a new copy of the customer's word processor, not just a new document in the already-open copy of the word processor. This can result in a badly cluttered screen (and possibly badly confused customers). It can also result in out-of-memory errors.

It's possible to manage this multiple-document situation in several ways:

- Designating one of the retrieved documents as a master document and then copying and pasting from the others into it. The master document can ultimately be saved as a permanent file. This would be my recommendation.

- Closing the first downloaded document before loading another, as well as saving the new document under construction (into which customers have inserted boilerplate material) in a permanent location.

- Saving the several retrieved boilerplate documents to separate temporary files, closing them as you go, and opening a new, blank document into which they can be inserted one by one. This document, containing all the stock language from the others, can then be customized as needed.

Managing Your Boilerplate Library

Even the longest-lived, largest boilerplate operations will occasionally generate a completely original document. More frequently, though, incremental changes in stock language are made. In either case, it's important to ensure that new and revised documents get placed in your library so that everyone can retrieve them. Keeping your library up-to-date is important, and how you go about doing it goes back to some of the organizational choices you considered back in the early chapters of this book.

If your boilerplate operation is a large and/or critical one, with frequent document changes that must be put in place quickly, you'll probably want a Web server right in the department, with a local Webmaster to update the documents promptly, rather than relying on a central MIS department to maintain one for you.

Supervisors or others with the authority to update documents on your Intranet boilerplate library Web server can use facilities such as the TCP/IP File Transfer Protocol (FTP) to upload files to the Web server from their PCs or workstations. As you learned in Chapter 9, because you have the TCP/IP networking infrastructure to support World Wide Web services, you also have FTP and many other networking capabilities with which to supplement the Web services on your Intranet.

Netscape Navigator 2.0 even has FTP upload capabilities built in, so customers don't need to learn to use a stand-alone FTP client (such as CuteFTP). You can access this feature when browsing an FTP server by pulling down the File menu and selecting Upload File, but first you'll need to specify a username, and possibly a password, in the FTP URL. For example:

```
ftp://poweruser:password@ftp.yourcompany.com
```

The Netscape File Upload dialog box is shown in Figure 25.2. Note that if you attempt to do this with the Microsoft IIS FTP server, you must turn off the Allow only anonymous connections checkbox in the Properties dialog of the FTP service. File and directory permissions for the NT user account will also come into play, as you would expect.

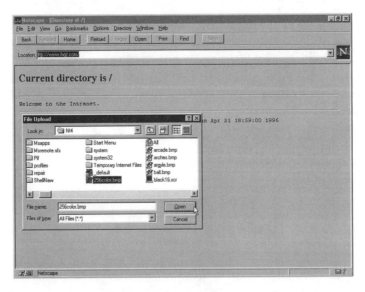

Figure 25.2. *The Netscape Navigator 2.0 FTP File Upload dialog.*

Tip: Because Government staff work is often reviewed by managers and legal documents by paralegals and other attorneys, you can use the FTP upload facility in Netscape, or in a dedicated FTP client program, to make draft documents accessible to reviewers, also using their Web browsers. Setting up a publicly writeable, shared review directory on an FTP server enables reviewers to download the drafts for review and edit them using their Web browsers, just as your customers download boilerplate documents. Pointing and clicking with a Web browser, the document is loaded right into your word processor.

Network drives can also be used to keep your Intranet boilerplate library up to date. If the system running the Web server shares its directory where your boilerplate files are located, supervisors running client workstations in that same domain can map the remote filesystem as a network drive and then just copy new documents over (using Explorer or the DOS prompt). This can even be accomplished across domains, provided that proper trust relationships are established between the Windows NT Server Domain Controllers. Connecting your client machines to shared drives on the Windows NT Server is absolutely the most convenient way for your customers to keep the files on the Web server updated on a regular basis. Files can be dragged and dropped in Explorer more easily than they can be uploaded via FTP.

Indexing Your Boilerplate Library

You could use a workaround, maintaining parallel plain-text copies of all your documents just for indexing. In such a situation, you'd index only the plain-text versions but somehow contrive to retrieve the original documents through custom CGI or ISAPI applications. This would be quite clumsy. A better alternative is to use waisindex on the originals. (See Chapter 21 for detailed information about WAIS.)

You can also index your RTF documents, if you're using RTF as a means of document portability among different word processors. RTF is a plain-text file format, much like PostScript or the Adobe Portable Document Format (PDF), with plain-text markup commands included right in with the document's text. As such, the full indexing power of waisindex will be available to you to index all your RTF documents (as well as PostScript and PDF ones). However, you may want to create your own waisindex stop files to exclude RTF-specific markup, such as font names and the like, from your indexes. Take a look at the bit of RTF that follows this paragraph, which is just one line from the top of a document, declaring the document to be RTF and specifying the available fonts:

```
{\rtf1\defformat\mac\deff2 {\fonttbl{\f0\fswiss Chicago;}{\f2\froman New
York;}{\f3\fswiss Geneva;}{\f4\fmodern Monaco;}{\f5\fscript Venice;}{\f6\fdecor
London;}{\f8\fdecor San Francisco;}{\f11\fnil Cairo;}{\f16\fnil
Palatino;}{\f20\froman Times;}{\f21\fswiss Helvetica;}
```

As you can see, there are a number of RTF-specific commands, such as the opening {\rtf1\defformat\mac\deff2, along with several font names, roman New York, modern Monaco, and the like. Because these font names contain words that might otherwise appear in your document text, you'll want to craft your stop list carefully. Otherwise, searches for words such as *New York* or *Cairo* will generate hits on the font names rather than on the substantive text; a search for New York, for example, might bring you back every single RTF document in your index.

As an alternative to extending your stop files, you can create waisindex document format description files that exclude the RTF or PostScript markup. These define the structure of your documents so you can do fielded indexing. You can then exclude all RTF markup codes from customer searches.

Depending on the extent and nature of the overall library of documents on your Intranet and your customers' indexing needs, you may want also to look into commercial full-text indexing tools.

Tip: With any commercial full-text indexing product, if you need RTF support, be sure to ask for specific details about how the product's RTF support works. As described previously with respect to waisindex, you'll want the package to exclude, or otherwise work around, all the RTF markup in your documents, so as not to get false hits in your customer searches.

Summary

In this chapter, you've seen a practical application for your Intranet, again combining several of the facilities about which you've learned. As you've seen in previous chapters, this flexibility, used in combination with your imagination, can result in significant added value for your Intranet. Creating an Intranet boilerplate library like the ones described in this chapter involves:

◆ Using your existing word processing documents to create a library of boilerplate documents on your Intranet's Web server.

◆ Converting documents to a common format usable in several different word processing programs, if necessary.

◆ Making your boilerplate library accessible to customers using a Web browser, putting what you've learned about MIME data types/subtypes and Web browser helper applications earlier in this book to work.

◆ Enabling your customers to search for and retrieve documents from your library using their Web browsers, bringing up retrieved documents directly in their word processor for editing and document assembly.

◆ Using the indexing tools about which you've learned in this book to create searchable indexes of your Intranet boilerplate library documents.

In the next chapter, you take the ideas discussed and illustrated in the past several chapters and create a completely new use for the Intranet. I'll show you how to put a new twist on a commonly used business application: the slide show presentation.

CHAPTER

Web-Based Training/ Presentations

◆ Simple slide shows
◆ Helper applications for training and presentations
◆ Simple Web-based training
◆ Multimedia presentations
◆ Designing your Intranet training

This chapter contains another series of example Web-based applications for your Intranet. In it, you learn about enabling your customers to conduct computer-based training courses and business presentations using World Wide Web technology.

You'll be able to use the information in this chapter in numerous ways, including setting up training for your customers in the use of your Intranet itself. As with the other examples shown, your customer's home base is his Web browser. In some cases, the customer's Web browser itself will be the means of the training or presentation; in others, Web browser helper applications will be called to perform the task, with the Web browser as the supervisor of the process. Overall, your Intranet can be an important part of your company's training and business presentation program.

In Chapter 27, "Collaboration on Your Intranet," you'll see some of the same facilities discussed in this chapter put to use in a different context. As you've seen frequently in this book, your Web-based toolkit is a versatile one, enabling you to use individual pieces of it in new and varied combinations to develop completely new ways of using your Intranet. What you learn about in this chapter is no exception to this.

Simple Slide Shows

The overhead projector and a stack of transparencies are the everyday tools of the professor, the salesperson, and the corporate executive. Laptop computers outfitted with special hardware and software to replicate the transparency are dragged to presentations. While the art of the slide show is advanced by such hardware and software, participants are still left sitting in the dark looking at transparencies that are all-too-often hard to see, and holding paper printouts of the slides that they can't read in the dark.

Wouldn't it be better if your customers could sit at workstations, or at their own desks, and see the presentation or training slides onscreen as it was meant to look? And, because this book is all about using Web and related technology for everyday work purposes, wouldn't it be great if they could do all this using their Web browser? Let's take a look at how you can have slide show presentations on your Intranet, using simple tools and your customers' Web browsers.

Slide Shows with Your Web Browser

With very basic HTML coding, you can put a slide show on the Web. Figure 26.1 shows a sample screen of a presentation that you might even be thinking about giving to upper management next week. You might think of it as sort of a "Poor Man's PowerPoint."

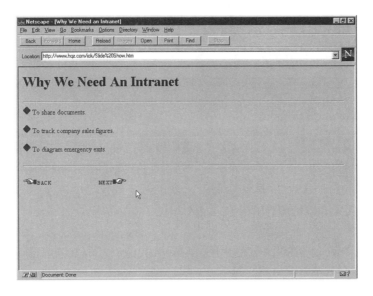

Figure 26.1. *Simple slide show prepared in HTML.*

The HTML code behind this simple screen appears in Listing 26.1. The filename is Slide Show.htm on the CD-ROM.

Listing 26.1. This basic HTML code can be used as a template to create simple slide shows on the Web.

```
<HTML>
<HEAD>
<TITLE>Why We Need an Intranet</TITLE>
</HEAD>
<BODY>
<H1>Why We Need An Intranet</H1>
<HR>
<IMG SRC="BL_DIAM.GIF">
To share documents.<P>

<IMG SRC="BL_DIAM.GIF">
To track company sales figures.<P>

<IMG SRC="BL_DIAM.GIF">
To diagram emergency exits.<P>
<HR>

<PRE WIDTH=132>
<IMG SRC="L_HAND.GIF">BACK                    NEXT<IMG SRC="R_HAND.GIF">
</PRE>
</BODY>
</HTML>
```

You'll notice that the HTML code in Listing 26.1 refers to a few GIF files. The bullet image and the pointing hand images are included on the CD-ROM. You could reuse the graphics and easily adapt the HTML code to serve as a template for your own slide shows on the Web.

> **Note:** If you adapt the HTML code to the Slide Show.htm file, don't forget to surround the <IMG> tags of the Back and Next buttons with <A HREF> tags hyperlinking to the appropriate documents in your presentation. It would also be a good idea to include an additional button on each screen to return to a Table of Contents document, like a slide show home page.

Important Considerations About Slide Shows

If you want to show a customer group how to use their Web browsers to search and retrieve text data, for example, you can prepare a slide show that runs through example searches with your explanatory slides written in HTML, containing hyperlinks to your Intranet's real fill-in search forms. The previously static slide show then becomes interactive. The ability to pause indefinitely, together with the hyperlinks contained in your training slides, gives your class the opportunity to actually use the services on which they're being trained, live and right in the classroom. And the instructor always has the ability, by controlling the return to the fixed part of the slide show or presentation, to bring students back from their interactive wanderings.

As you'll see in the next section, widely available Web browser helper applications for Windows can provide high-quality slide shows and presentations for your PC users.

Helper Applications for Training and Presentations

You can use a wide range of helper applications for Intranet training and presentation purposes, with your Web pages providing smooth access to various kinds of information that might be included in an overall curriculum. Let's look separately at a couple of very useful helpers, Microsoft PowerPoint and Lotus ScreenCam. Both are excellent packages that you can use for your purposes, but, as you'll learn a little later, your Intranet presents quite flexible training and presentation opportunities, and you won't want to limit yourself to just these two packages, or any other single package, regardless of how great they might be.

PowerPoint

In Chapter 15, "Other Client Applications on the Intranet," you learned how to set up the Microsoft PowerPoint presentation program as a Web browser application. For your training and presentation purposes, users can access and view PowerPoint slide shows easily, provided they have access to PowerPoint itself, or the read-only PowerPoint viewer available on this CD-ROM and at Microsoft's Web site, http://www.microsoft.com.

You may need to refer back to Chapters 12-15 for specifics on setting up PowerPoint datafiles as a new MIME data type/subtype on your Web server.

> **Note:** Microsoft has recently posted an announcement on their Web site that is of great relevance to the topic of slide shows and presentations on the Web. As you learned in Chapter 17, ActiveX is a new technology available in Internet Explorer 3.0 (and above) and as a plug-in for Netscape Navigator 2.0 (and above) that enables page designers to create truly interactive client/server applications on the Web. As proof of this concept, Microsoft is making available a free download of a beta ActiveX product that provides PowerPoint viewing directly inside the browser. They call it the ActiveX Animation Publisher & Player (two programs). The Publisher requires PowerPoint for Windows 95 or Windows NT. Check out this URL for more information:
>
> `http://www.microsoft.com/mspowerpoint/`

Once a customer has downloaded a PowerPoint slide show file and the application has started, she can view the slide show just as if it had been created on her own PC or as if she were sitting in a conference room. To start a PowerPoint slide show, pull down the View menu and select Slide Show. The resulting dialog box will prompt you for specifics.

Slide show presentations using PowerPoint as a Web browser helper application are an excellent means of self-paced training exercises. Customers can download and run them at their convenience, page through them, save or print individual slides, and so on. Using this mechanism in a group training room can, however, be a bit difficult to coordinate. In such a situation, each student independently downloads a copy of the same slide presentation and views it on his or her own workstation. Keeping everyone on the same page might present problems, but no more so than those that occur when presenters provide paper handouts of slides.

> **Tip:** A bonus to using PowerPoint as a helper application for presentations and training classes is that customers can use PowerPoint interactively during the presentation. While some users might get distracted by this capability, the ability to view the overall structure of a presentation in PowerPoint's Outline view mode can be useful. In addition, class or presentation participants have the ability to save or print the slides for permanent reference, or to steal material for use as models for other slide shows.

Lotus ScreenCam

As you may know, Lotus ScreenCam is a Windows software package which can be likened to your home VCR. Like a video camera, the ScreenCam recorder software records all on-screen activity on your PC, including mouse movements and clicks, the opening and closing of programs, and so on. It's frequently used to produce software demos and training sessions. The ScreenCam player plays back previously recorded ScreenCam sessions using the VCR metaphor, with start, stop, rewind, and fast-forward buttons.

Lotus has made the ScreenCam *player* freely available; you'll find it at Lotus' Web site, `http://www.lotus.com/intrprod/2142.htm`. (The ScreenCam *recorder* is not freely available, but must be purchased from Lotus; it costs about $100. However, I'm told that it is free with Lotus SmartSuite.)

Figure 26.2 shows the ScreenCam player in action in a demonstration of the Ami Pro word processor (also from Lotus). As you can see, the ScreenCam controller window in the lower right of the screenshot has VCR-like buttons to allow the demo to be played, paused, rewound, have new demos loaded, and so on.

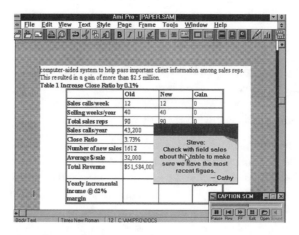

Figure 26.2. *Lotus ScreenCam playing a demonstration of Ami Pro.*

While ScreenCam can be run as a stand-alone application, as you probably expect, you can also set up the ScreenCam player as a Web browser helper application for your customers. Doing so enables you to use the package as a part of your Intranet training program to display sessions you record with the ScreenCam recorder or obtain from vendors. The configuration of the ScreenCam player as a helper application is much the same as that for other helpers:

1. Add a new entry for the ScreenCam player application to your Web server's MIME map in the Registry, like this (see Chapter 13 for the details on how to do this for IIS using RegEdit):

   ```
   application/x-screencam,scm,,5
   ```

2. Set up your customers' Web browsers to use the new MIME data type/subtype (`application/x-screencam`) and filename extension (`scm`) to call the ScreenCam player.

As with Microsoft PowerPoint slide shows, ScreenCam presentations and training sessions can be self-paced, run at customer convenience right from the customer's own Web browser. ScreenCam has important features not present in any slide show package, because the customer is viewing a complete session rather than frozen slides with screenshots. Every mouse movement, click, and screen change are shown in a ScreenCam presentation, while slides have a completely different purpose (the latter being more static, of course).

In a group training session, ScreenCam adds its advantages to those described with respect to PowerPoint, and your overall training program can profit from using it. You can use the ScreenCam recorder to provide training to your customers on the use of the various parts of your Intranet itself, and recording sample sessions in Explorer or Netscape for playback by customers, or in training sessions. The ability to pause, rewind, fast-forward, and the like using the VCR buttons is quite important because customers can go back to see earlier parts of the recording.

ScreenCam has, however, some features that might be considered both advantages and disadvantages compared to the other helper applications your customers might use. Most importantly, ScreenCam recordings are read-only. They can be viewed again and again but not changed in any way. Customers who view them can't save them to review later (although they can reload them with their Web browser) nor modify them for their own presentations as they can with word processor, spreadsheet, or PowerPoint datafiles.

ScreenCam, too, is subject to the whims of meeting participants or trainees, in that each customer, having downloaded his own copy of the demo recording, is free to fast-forward, rewind, and otherwise ignore the progress of the meeting or training class. Again, this happens in every presentation or training class ever conducted, regardless of the presentation media, and there's nothing at all you can do about it.

Finally, you should note that, with a room full of students downloading a ScreenCam recording from your Web server all at once, getting everyone's viewing of the demo synchronized can be a slight problem. ScreenCam recordings can be quite large, and download time over your Intranet may be affected by multiple simultaneous downloads in a classroom setting. Each session will start separately, and may well do so at different times. The stage of the demo that individual customers are viewing at any given time will differ unless you're able to get them all to pause the demo at the same place and restart it together.

Simple Web-Based Training

As it did with the first graphical Web browser and the leading freeware Web server, NCSA has also led the way in Web-based training with its outstanding Web-related tutorials. You'll find a list of them at this URL:

```
http://www.ncsa.uiuc.edu/SDG/Software/Mosaic/
```

You'll no doubt use these extensively as you set up and refine your Intranet and its capabilities, but you'll want to look at them in the context of this chapter's subject matter as well. Completely apart from their (very important) subject matter, the NCSA tutorials are great examples of how to use the Web as a training mechanism.

Another excellent (and relevant) example is the Microsoft Visual Basic Script Tutorial at this URL:

```
http://www.microsoft.com/vbscript/us/vbstutor/vbstutor.htm
```

As you can see from the VBScript tutorial in Figure 26.3, the student can simply follow the logical steps laid out at the top level to work his way through the course systematically.

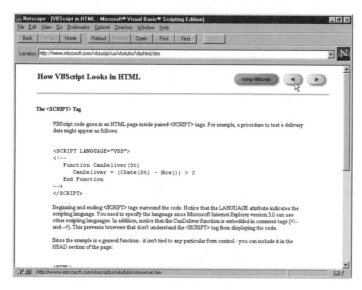

Figure 26.3. *The Microsoft Visual Basic Script tutorial is well presented.*

As you work your way through the VBScript tutorial, you'll find a nice, logical organization is followed consistently throughout. You'll notice that every page in the series contains a button back to the Table of Contents and to the previous and next training screen. Furthermore, the row of buttons appears identically at both the top and bottom of each HTML page. When I read through the screens, I found that I was occasionally scrolling up and down before going to the next page—and having buttons at both the top and bottom of long HTML pages proved to be a pleasant convenience.

Multimedia Presentations

The NCSA and Microsoft tutorials I just mentioned are great as a starting point because they show you the basics of how the Web can be used for training purposes. However, your Intranet is a multimedia system, with plain text, graphical images, sounds, video, and various other kinds of data accessible using the Web browser helper applications you've set up for your customers. This being the case, you won't want to limit your Intranet-based training and presentations to a single, text-based method.

Plain-text HTML markup with logically arranged hyperlinks, PowerPoint, Netscape Remote, Mosaic CCI, and ScreenCam are all great tools, but the overwhelming value of an Intranet like yours, as this book has hammered home repeatedly, is the ability to combine all these tools into something uniquely suited to your organization's needs. Using your Intranet as a training resource is no exception. There's absolutely no reason you can't use all of these tools as part of a single training session or presentation, picking and choosing each one based on its strengths at presenting the particular information you need to show at a given point in your presentation. Here are some things to keep in mind in putting together your Intranet-based training:

◆ While a plain-text slide may be good at one point in your presentation, a spreadsheet with a graph in it will be better than a slide with boring columns of numbers in another. Why limit yourself to slides, or go to the trouble of importing your spreadsheet into a slide, when you can just show the spreadsheet on your Intranet?

◆ If you're measuring process control in a factory, you may want to show in real time both video or graphical images of the process and a graphical visualization of the data being collected.

◆ A ScreenCam recording of an application being operated is great, but so is the ability for the trainee to get his hands on the application and run it himself. Use the wide array of tools you've implemented on your Intranet to give him both.

Designing Your Intranet Training

It's easy to get lost in the details of setting up a complex helper application and lose sight of the basics of training design for your Intranet. The glue that holds the training course together is, of course, the HTML documents that contain it. While this fact may be implicit in the last few paragraphs, it needs to be underscored here.

Like your training curriculum itself, your Web training pages need to be well thought out. Moreover, your planning needs to be done from a point of view that takes into account the important idea of using appropriate Intranet tools throughout a course. While this requires you to use an expanded horizon in planning your Intranet-based training, it also gives you incredible flexibility.

Using Web technology for training is superior to any other single technology, simply because you can use all those other technologies as you need them to form an overall Intranet training curriculum. If you need to show a picture to illustrate a point, for instance, add an image to your training page; a sound or movie, add an audio or video link; or a complex scientific application, add the application itself as a helper application.

If you have a corporate training staff, get them involved in your Intranet training. Professional instructors know, from being on their feet in front of students, how to design training curricula. Put your collective heads together to develop training that uses the capabilities of your Intranet to their fullest extent.

Summary

Training and business presentations using your Intranet have been the focus of this chapter. Your Intranet is an enormous potential source of training resources for your customers. Moreover, an Intranet, with all its multimedia capabilities, makes completely new ways of creating and executing training and presentations possible, because you can stitch together a wide range of training components. You'll want to give free rein to your imagination in putting together your Intranet's tools for these purposes. As a review, here's what you've done in this chapter:

◆ Learned about simple leader-led or self-paced slide shows for seminars, lectures, or business presentations.

◆ Learned about playing back recorded training sessions for individual or classroom training.

◆ Learned how the HTML markup language can be used to organize effective training Web pages for your Intranet.

◆ Learned about using Microsoft PowerPoint and Lotus ScreenCam as tools to build Web-based training and presentation applications.

◆ Learned about interactive training which allows customers to actually use the software about which they're learning.

◆ Considered all the capabilities of your Intranet for use in your training curricula.

In Chapter 27, you turn your attention to tools you can use to facilitate collaboration and cooperation among your Intranet's customers.

CHAPTER

◆

Collaboration on Your Intranet

- ◆ The different means of collaboration
- ◆ Simple, one-way collaborative activities on your Intranet
- ◆ Electronic mail as a collaborative resource
- ◆ Free-for-all collaboration
- ◆ Web-based annotation and conferencing
- ◆ Full-featured groupware for Web collaboration and communication
- ◆ Usenet news for collaboration and discussion

Along with the much-discussed Java, group collaboration using World Wide Web technology is one of the Web's most exciting possibilities. This is attested to not only by the fact that IBM's Lotus Notes product has been dragged kicking and screaming into Web integration, but also by the emergence of completely new products, built specifically for Web collaboration. After reviewing some simple and immediately available means of using your Intranet for group collaboration, this chapter will survey the world of Web groupware and give you some ideas of how you can put it to work on your Intranet.

The Different Means of Collaboration

It might be useful to begin this discussion by broadly categorizing the means of Web-based collaboration. Several may be defined as follows (although in practice, Web services more often than not cross these neat category boundaries):

◆ Simple, one-way information sharing, primarily through posting information on Web pages, including individual user home pages.

◆ Free-for-all Web resources, in which anyone is free to add comments and/or hyperlinks.

◆ Multidirectional conferencing systems of various kinds, such as Usenet newsgroups, e-mail distribution lists, bulletin board systems, even Web-based bulletin boards, and the like.

◆ True groupware applications, such as Lotus Notes, Microsoft Exchange, and Collabra Share, in which the preceding categories may be combined into a single monolithic application.

Simple, One-Way Collaborative Activities on Your Intranet

Leaving aside fancy groupware computer applications for now, let's remember that the most basic means of human collaboration and cooperation is simple, straightforward information sharing. People tell other people what they are doing, what they've learned, and so on. Learning by listening to what other people say about themselves and their activities is one of the most fundamental means by which we are educated and socialized—and by which we grow in our professional lives. Scholars and scientists write books to share information, and information distribution is the *raison d'être* of journalism.

Simple information sharing can form the collaborative core of your Intranet, and its value should not be overlooked in the glittery world of groupware. Indeed, online information exchange may be your most important tool. Let's therefore take a look at some simple but potentially powerful means of Intranet information sharing, beginning with user home pages.

User Home Pages on Your Intranet

In the introductory chapters of *Building an Intranet with Windows NT 4*, I emphasized the need for customer input in the design and content of your Intranet. As you'll recall from Chapter 2, "Planning an Intranet," one criticism of the centralized model of Intranet administration is that a bureaucratic process of Web-page approval places obstacles in the way of customers getting their own information out onto your Intranet. Looking at your Intranet from a high-level viewpoint, you've perhaps not focused on how individual users' home pages can contribute significantly to its overall value.

Perhaps at this point you're thinking of some of the personal home pages you've seen on the World Wide Web, full of adolescent bravado, bandwidth-eating images of CD covers, song lyrics purporting to state a philosophy of life, self-indulgent posturing, and hyperlinks pointing to similar drivel, and you probably wonder how such things can be a useful part of your Intranet. They can't. But what a 20-year-old college sophomore thinks appropriate for his university home page and what a working scientist, engineer, or other professional might put on a professional page are two completely different matters, and we're interested in the latter.

Users can be taught basic HTML markup in half an hour. Their personal Web pages can be copied to the main Web server, or an alias directory can be created on the Web server to point back to the users' workstations. Either way, the users don't need to learn anything about Web servers to make their pages available. This makes the language an excellent vehicle for information sharing on an organization's Intranet.

Whether they're office support staff or engineers, paraprofessionals, or scientists, your customers can easily create home pages to share their work with others in your company. Fancy graphics don't usually add much to Web page substance. Here are some possibilities:

◆ Scientists can share the results of their work with colleagues across the company, placing descriptions of their research on their home pages, together with underlying data, in a format accessible with a helper application. Word processing documents containing article or book manuscripts can be made available for viewing, while numerical data can be graphed on the fly, and other data can be seen with other helper applications.

◆ Engineers and draftsmen can place their CAD drawings on your Intranet for organization-wide viewing/sharing.

◆ Researchers of all kinds can provide links to summaries of their work, or to its details, regardless of its format.

It's hard to overstate the potential value to an organization of this sort of simple information sharing. In a business research environment, for example, the linking of a few important ideas can lead to breakthrough products or services. One researcher, stuck on a project, may find just the thing she needs on some other researcher's home page. Moreover, once the collaborative ball is rolling, customers will add hyperlinks pointing to other customers' home pages on their own pages, making the combined resources of many available to all.

Electronic Mail as a Collaborative Resource

You're already familiar with running a mail server on your Intranet (from Chapter 8, "Serving E-mail via TCP/IP"). Let's take a moment to think about the potential collaborative value of e-mail in your Intranet. E-mail distribution lists, run manually or with automated list servers, can be an important adjunct to your Intranet by providing another means of group discussions. And since the major Web browsers all have e-mail interfaces, it's easy to integrate e-mail into your Intranet.

If you expect e-mail to become a major part of your Intranet's collaborative efforts, you'll want to set up a means of retaining and retrieving messages. (You'll want to do this with your Intranet Usenet news articles too; I'll address this later in the chapter.) This will enable your customers to go back to mailing list archives and search for old messages that might have current relevance.

There are several ways you can archive e-mail messages:

◆ Use the public folder feature in Microsoft Mail or Microsoft Exchange Server.

◆ Charge someone with the responsibility of manually saving each and every message on your mailing list(s).

◆ Create a special user account on your system whose only purpose is to receive the mailing list traffic, then configure that account to automatically save all incoming mail in mailbox folders.

◆ Use an e-mail-to-netnews Perl script that will route all e-mail messages to a local newsgroup for posting as ordinary news articles.

In the latter example, you can then use news-indexing tools to index everything, since your e-mail traffic and netnews traffic will be merged into a single database. The Pro version of Eudora, as well as the enhanced version of the Microsoft Exchange client, include filtering features that can be set up to read all incoming mail to a user and automatically dispose of it in some way (based on criteria you determine). In this situation, you'd want the filter to automatically save all incoming messages on a mailing list to a file or directory, which can later be indexed.

Free-for-All Collaboration

The popularity of the World Wide Web, with thousands of new pages coming online every day, has generated the need for individual users to share new Web resources they've found or created. Since most Webmasters are busy people, often having job responsibilities over and above their Webmastering, ordinary users need a way to post hyperlinks to useful Web resources in a public place for others to see, without having to rely on a Webmaster or other system administrator to do it for them. (This is quite a different thing, of course, from users placing new hyperlinks on their own home pages.)

However, it doesn't take much thinking to come up with several significant reservations about implementing such a *free-for-all* Web resource. Leaving questions of appropriate content aside for the moment, the idea of a Web page that allows *just anyone* to add *anything they want* should bring shudders to anyone with the faintest sense of network security. Nonetheless, a large number of such services (and the CGI scripts to implement them) have sprung up across the Web. Major Web search services (such as Lycos, Yahoo, eXcite, and the others) allow users to fill in forms to have URLs added to the service.

Even taking these security concerns into account, though, there are good reasons for implementing a free-for-all page on your Intranet. Not everyone wants to create a home page of their own, but such people may still find useful resources they want to share with other customers. The ability to add URLs to such a page may, in fact, inspire these people to eventually create Web pages of their own as a contribution to your Intranet; certainly, these people shouldn't be discouraged from doing so.

From a collaborative point of view, browsing customers may want to be able to suggest links to those who do have home pages, complementing the information already there. If these folks can add a URL to a free-for-all page easily, they'll do so; if they can't, they may not bother to share their ideas. In any case, giving your customers free rein to add URLs to a free-for-all page can improve overall collaboration and communication on your Intranet. The question of appropriate content on a free-for-all Web page is, in this author's opinion, a management issue, not a technical one, and should be dealt with as such.

You'll find a long list of Web free-for-all links at `http://union.ncsa.uiuc.edu/HyperNews/get/hypernews.html`. This and several other such lists mentioned in later sections of this chapter are maintained by Daniel LaLiberte of NCSA, who may be the Web's foremost collaboration guru.

> **Note:** Web pages that collect *votes* of some kind or take *surveys* are a special kind of free-for-all page, as are pages that enable you to access some service or enter in a raffle after you've filled in a form with personal information such as your e-mail address or phone number. On the World Wide Web, many of these are thinly disguised marketing ploys, aimed at generating sales leads.

Web-Based Annotation and Conferencing

Almost as soon as the first World Wide Web servers and browsers came into use, people wanted some way to use these new tools for interactive conferencing. Being able to post documents is one thing; being able to respond to them in some way is quite another. Let's look at a couple of the results.

Web Interactive Talk

One of the earliest efforts at developing such a resource was the Ari Luotonen/Tim Berners-Lee project called Web Interactive Talk, or WIT, which was developed when both were at CERN. In WIT, discussions proceed according to traditional dialectic methods, with general topics and subsidiary proposals. Someone posts a document proposal, and then others are invited to post comments about the proposal in the form of agreements or disagreements.

WIT is primarily valuable as a pioneering work in the area of annotation and conferencing (and it's no longer being maintained by the authors, both of whom have left CERN), but you may want to look at it anyway. You can do so at http://www.w3.org/hypertext/WWW/WIT/User/Overview.html.

Matt Wright's WWWBoard

When I bought my iomega Jaz drive a couple of months ago, I was looking for the right SCSI device drivers for Windows NT. A friend of mine by the name of James Kirst, who knows all about SCSI and all about finding things on the Web, told me to check out the unofficial iomega Web page for threaded conversations at this URL:

http://www.stern.nyu.edu/~jwu/wwwboard/wwwboard.html

Not only did I find useful information about Jaz drives, but I also came away extremely impressed by the software used to run the board. The software is called WWWBoard. It is a Perl script written by Matt Wright. You can find more information about WWWBoard, and download the source code (as far as I can tell, it's free) at this URL:

http://worldwidemart.com/scripts/

Digital Equipment's Workgroup Web Forum

This section would not be complete without some mention of DEC's new collaboration package which runs on NT and DEC UNIX. *PCWeek* magazine gave version 1.0 of Workgroup Web Forum the Analyst's Choice Award in the February 26, 1996 issue comparing Web-based conferencing servers. Check out this URL for more information:

http://www.digital.com/info/internet/resources/applications/29.html

Microsoft's NetMeeting 1.0 Beta

Microsoft just recently announced a new product that could prove useful for remote teleconference meetings. NetMeeting 1.0 is designed to let several participants mark up documents in whiteboard fashion over the Internet. Microsoft used their own ActiveX Conferencing Software Development Kit to build NetMeeting. You can get more information about NetMeeting and the ActiveX Conferencing SDK, and download both of them for free from the Microsoft Web site:

http://www.microsoft.com/intdev/download.htm

Allaire Forums

A sample version of Allaire Forums is included with Cold Fusion on the CD-ROM with this book. Cold Fusion is a popular database interface to Windows NT Web servers all over the Internet. Allaire Forums is their new product which provides Web-based conferencing and threaded discussions. As usual, the clients only need to run a Web browser. Check out their Web site at

`http://www.allaire.com`

AEX About Server

The commercial About Server product (`http://www.aex.com`) provides forums for group discussions, much like Usenet news and other commercial groupware packages such as Lotus Notes, but at lower cost and with what AEX calls "tighter integration" with the World Wide Web. The product is available for several UNIX platforms, and they claim a Windows NT version will be available soon. Here are some descriptions of the forums in the About server:

◆ Accessible from Web browsers.

◆ Searchable by keyword, in both document title and text, author name, and date.

◆ Immediately accessible, in that your postings and responses to postings are made right away and are not queued for posting/propagation as in Usenet news.

◆ Subject to quite flexible security, allowing you to restrict access to all or portions of forums by username/password and other means.

◆ User configurable, so each user can customize his view of the available forums, much like traditional Usenet news kill files.

◆ Administered using a Web browser.

Demonstration versions of About Server are available from the AEX Web site. The user interface appears quite self-explanatory, with individual article hyperlinks, and indentations indicating article threads.

Open Meeting on the National Performance Review

A discussion of Web-based conferencing/annotation systems would not be complete without a brief look at the United States government's Open Meeting on the National Performance Review, reachable on the Web at `http://www4.ai.mit.edu/npr/user/root.html`. Here you can read various findings and recommendations of the NPR, which has been led by Vice President Al Gore, a major influence in the federal government's all-out plunge into the Internet/World Wide Web in the past four years.

As shown in Figure 27.1, the service is interactive, and you can add your own comments and questions. It's a bit clumsy, though, requiring you to enter your Internet e-mail address in a fill-in form, after which you're e-mailed a comment form to fill in and send back, also via e-mail. Moderators review submitted comments and questions, and not all of them are posted.

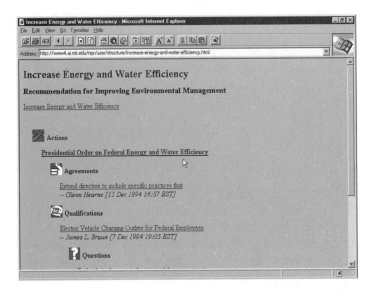

Figure 27.1. *The Open meeting on the National Performance Review lets you post ideas on the Web.*

Collaborative Art and Games

There are a large number of collaborative groupware art services on the Web. The basic idea behind all of them is that anyone can add Web resources to the picture, the work of fiction, or some other piece of creative work-in-progress. Image collages, for example, can be augmented by adding the URL to your own image on the Web; the next user will see the modified collage with your image added.

As another example, a novel can be entered at any page using a clickable imagemap. Once you're in, you can browse about the work or contribute to it by inserting your own text. Other collaborative groupware on the Web comes in the form of interactive single- or multi-user games or other creative *add-a-link* pages. The latter are modified free-for-all pages that have a theme of some sort. Users are free to add URLs (for images, other Web pages, and so on) that somehow advance the interactive fiction, enhance the art object, or otherwise contribute to the evolving entity that is that particular Web page. The beauty, if any, is in the eye of the beholder.

These examples, and others like them (again, see `http://union.ncsa.uiuc.edu/HyperNews/get/hypernews.html`) are useful not so much in their substantive content as in the possibilities they represent. After all, the World Wide Web is the world's largest vanity press, where anyone can post anything they want with no evaluation of its actual value. While you or your customers might not be interested in these particular endeavors, there is a wide range of possibilities for collaborative groupware for your Intranet, and these may be instructive as examples.

Full-Featured Groupware for Web Collaboration and Communication

The demarcation lines among free-for-alls, conferencing/annotation systems, and the more full-featured Web groupware are indistinct. Nonetheless, let's take a look at the latter. As with the previous sections, I'll start with some very simple ones. This will lead up to the more complex, full-featured groupware packages.

Lotus Notes

Almost from the beginning, the World Wide Web has been called, among many other things, "the Lotus Notes killer." You can see from the examples given so far in this chapter how this quip came about. After all, many of the Web tools about which you've learned in this book replicate some features of Notes. Whether it's simple information sharing via home pages, conferencing with Usenet news using a Web browser, Web-based e-mail, or Web-based annotation systems like WWWBoard, artful Webmasters can in fact provide their customers with most of Notes' features, at a tiny fraction of that package's considerable cost.

The downside of this replication is the lack of Notes' tight integration; however, being able to access the wide range of services Web browsers support may be integration enough for many. Making the choice between home-grown collaborative and commercial groupware on your Intranet can boil down to the following choice: Is the 10-15% of Notes' capabilities you miss with a homegrown set of applications worth the very substantial cost of the package?

IBM (the new owner of Lotus) thinks not. In early 1996, version 4.0 of Lotus Notes was released, outfitted with a whole raft of new capabilities, including World Wide Web browsing and authoring support, Usenet news access, and a lower (though still pricey) per-seat cost. Let's take a look at Notes R4, as it's called; you can be the judge of its potential value on your Intranet.

Notes R4 is, in essence, a document database. Users can search the database according to everyday criteria, and can also browse the database. Browsing can be done based on different views of the database, with the ability to step back and see high-level organization or dig in and see the details. Notes R4 databases can be replicated across an organization, over multiple servers, so all the employees in a far-flung company, including those on the road, have access to the same consistent information.

Integrated e-mail, group document annotations, collaborative functions, workflow management, and group scheduling are also featured. Built-in security features enable you to control access to authorized users at all levels of the database. Links in documents can be followed by pointing and clicking to other related documents. Users can create altogether new Notes applications using a set of graphical tools.

Finally, with Notes R4, IBM/Lotus jumped into the World Wide Web with what it hopes will be a "Notes-killer killer." Consider these features:

◆ Notes R4 databases are now browsable using ordinary Web browsers like Netscape, Explorer, and Mosaic because HTTP is now part of the Notes R4 server package.

◆ IBM plans to add Java support to Notes R4 in the future, while maintaining compatibility with its own scripting language, LotusScript.

◆ Even when viewing Notes R4 databases with a standard Web browser, Notes R4 document links work as Web hyperlinks.

◆ Notes R4 forms and database search facilities are also available when viewing Notes R4 databases from a Web browser.

◆ Web documents can be created and managed using Lotus InterNotes Web Publisher, then browsed with both the InterNotes Web Navigator Web browser and a standard Web browser.

◆ The InterNotes Web Navigator client supports HTTP and HTML, so it can be used to browse non-Notes Web pages as well as Notes R4 databases.

◆ InterNotes News integrates with Usenet news services via the Internet-standard NNTP protocol, but it adds support for Notes R4 database replication, hypertext links, and embedded objects, giving users enhanced news-browsing capabilities.

◆ The e-mail capability in Notes R4 supports the Internet-standard SMTP and MIME protocols to provide universal e-mail connectivity for Notes users.

> **Note:** You may want to look at Lotus' Web site, `http://www.lotus.com/`, where you'll find several detailed white papers about Notes R4, as well as some ScreenCam recordings.

Collabra Share

Among Lotus Notes R4 competitors, Collabra Software Inc.'s Collabra Share stands out. Despite the fact the package is a direct Notes competitor—providing integrated, collaborative groupware, with document-databases, e-mail, database replication, access to Usenet newsgroups, and even a Notes-compatible client for both Windows PCs and the Macintosh—this isn't the real reason the product has become important in the past year.

The real reason this upstart company has suddenly become worth mentioning here is not even that Collabra Share won the *PC Magazine* Editor's Choice award in late 1995 (although that must have been a big boost for the product).

No, what's really important is that Collabra Software, Inc. has been acquired by the Netscape Communications Corporation juggernaut, which has announced plans to integrate all of Collabra Share's features directly into the Netscape Navigator Web browser. Although Netscape says there will continue to be a stand-alone Collabra Share product for Windows and the Macintosh, and a Collabra server, and those products will continue to evolve, the next major release of Netscape Navigator will "incorporate fully the Collabra Share functionality." Given Netscape's dominance of the Web browser market, building in Collabra Share client support will undoubtedly provide a major boost to the Collabra server products, potentially to the detriment of Lotus Notes R4.

The acquisition should also help Netscape itself. Collabra Share supports integration with both Microsoft Mail and Lotus cc:Mail. The ability to use these popular and mature e-mail products within the Netscape environment should go a long way to help Netscape compete against the broad solutions these other vendors are pushing. It can be hoped that Collabra's Usenet news reader will be a major step forward for Netscape's netnews interface.

> **Note:** From the Collabra Web site (`http://www.collabra.com`), you can download Lotus ScreenCam recordings of Collabra Share in action as well as evaluation copies of the Collabra Share client software itself.

Microsoft Exchange

The long-awaited release of Microsoft Exchange Server finally happened in the Spring of 1996. It includes a very powerful Exchange e-mail client that goes far beyond the capabilities of the free Exchange client included with Windows 95 and Windows NT 4.

Naturally, the Exchange Server only runs on NT. Microsoft expects to use Exchange as a key piece of the overall BackOffice suite to demonstrate the viability of Windows NT for enterprise-wide solutions. Microsoft believes that BackOffice can take corporate networking the next step beyond what is possible today with NetWare, and that NT-based solutions are much easier to administer than UNIX. The May 1996 issue of *Byte* magazine features a cover story by Tom R. Halfhill comparing Windows NT to UNIX. One of the conclusions the *Byte* author reached is that Windows NT is clearly "off probation," given the continued advancement of its features, stability, and market acceptance since its release four years ago.

> **Note:** Speaking of magazines, another reference you will want to check-out is *NT Magazine*. The December 1995 issue carries the first of a two-part article by Tim Daniels comparing Collabra Share, Lotus Notes, and Microsoft Exchange. The article continues in the January 1996 issue. Further, the April 1996 issue includes two articles about Microsoft Exchange: "Migrating MS-Mail to Exchange" by Spyros Sakellariadis on page 66 and "Exchange SDK" by Tim Daniels on page 81.

In case you don't already know, BackOffice 2.0 (also just released) includes the following core components:

◆ Windows NT 3.51 Server—the network operating system. (Expect a new version of BackOffice as soon as NT 4 is released.)

◆ Internet Information Server 1.0—the HTTP, Gopher, and FTP server. (IIS 2.0 will be included with all copies of Windows NT 4 Server as soon as the latter is officially released.)

◆ SQL Server 6.5—the client/server database.

◆ Exchange Server 1.0—the integrated groupware and e-mail server.

◆ Mail Server 3.2—the predecessor of Exchange lacks groupware features.

◆ Systems Management Server 1.1—includes four main features: network protocol analyzer, inventory tracking of hardware/software on the clients, automatic push-installs of software on the network clients, and remote control of client workstations from a help desk.

◆ SNA Server 2.11—provides connectivity to IBM AS/400 mainframe environments.

Another powerful feature of Microsoft Exchange, and part of the reason that it is a competitive groupware solution for an enterprise, is the capability it gives developers to create GUI electronic forms tied to Visual Basic code. The true potential, and ease of use, of this feature is yet to be discovered by many organizations. If you get a chance to see a demo at a Microsoft-sponsored seminar, you might walk away wondering why anyone would want to develop client/server applications on any other platform. As a C++ and Visual Basic client/server developer myself, I can tell you that it is very impressive. (The only catch is that if you are thinking about building an application on top of Exchange, you will be subjected to criticism from plenty of potential customers who are already very happily committed to Collabra Share or Lotus Notes.)

> **Note:** For more information about Exchange Server, and all of the BackOffice components, see `http://www.microsoft.com/BackOffice/`.

Usenet News for Collaboration and Discussion

Besides electronic mail, Usenet news was probably the first groupware tool to be invented on the Internet. It's still a great means of online collaboration and discussion. Netnews might be called the Mother of All Computer BBSs, so great is its reach and breadth.

The idea was first developed in the 1970s, when computer researchers at a couple of universities in North Carolina wanted an open means of discussing and sharing ideas. The basic idea of Usenet, which is still pretty much what it's all about, is that people can post articles for others to see. *Articles* is a formal word, but you shouldn't think of netnews articles in any way like magazine or newspaper articles. Rather, an article can be anything anyone considers worthy of posting in an electronic forum.

Netnews articles range from treatises on TCP/IP networking to discussions of upcoming flying disc tournaments (`rec.sport.disc`) to comparative reviews of 4x4 truck tires. Once posted, a netnews article is available to anyone on the local computer system who might want to look at it. Article readers can also post follow-up articles in response to other articles, possibly starting a dialog or group discussion. The follow-up articles are also available to everyone on the system to read and, of course, respond to with further follow-ups.

Netnews articles may also be sent out from the local system to remote systems, where remote users can read/respond to them. Using a flooding algorithm, news articles that aren't purely local are distributed all over the Internet very quickly to thousands of systems serving thousands (possibly millions) of people who can read and respond to them. Usenet is almost infinitely divided, with more than 20,000 newsgroups in seven major categories:

- Computers (`comp`)
- Science (`sci`)
- Recreation (`rec`)
- Social topics (`soc`)
- Talk (`talk`)
- Usenet news itself (`news`)
- Alternative groups (`alt`)

Each newsgroup category is the tip of a vast iceberg of related newsgroups, subdivided into thousands of very specialized topics. Besides the major groups, you'll find `biz` (business), `bionet` (biology), `misc` (miscellaneous), and various local groups. Major Web browsers, such as Navigator, Explorer, and Mosaic, include the ability to post, read, and respond to Usenet news articles. You saw in Chapter 11, "The Web Browser Is the Key," how Netscape Navigator easily handles the job.

Netscape's netnews interface is substantially different from Mosaic's, and has gone through a number of recent changes; you may see something different by the time you read this book. An interesting feature of Netscape Usenet news interface is its capability to resize any of the three panes of the netnews window.

If you've spent any time reading Usenet news, you know how discussions often seem to pick up a life of their own. They often last for weeks as multiple readers post follow-up articles, then respond to the follow-ups of others. Although they frequently degenerate into personal insults, Usenet news threads (articles in a single discussion thread) can often be an important means of collaboration as consensus is hammered out in public discussion. You can use the same process to enable collaboration on your Intranet, with your customers using their Web browsers as news readers.

Note: Early in the book you learned about Internet Requests for Comments (RFCs) as part of the development of today's TCP/IP networking standards. The consensus-building that led (and still leads) to Internet RFCs is a good example of netnews collaboration through discussion.

How Usenet Newsgroups Work

Because you're running (or considering running) a netnews server on your Intranet, you need to know some basics about how newsgroups work. This background will allow you to set up Usenet-related facilities in your Intranet.

You'll recall the list above of the seven major netnews newsgroup categories (comp, sci, rec, soc, talk, news, and alt). Besides these major categories, there are many others, including regional newsgroups and, most important for your Intranet, local newsgroups. Before going into the details of creating and using local newsgroups, though, let's look at the way newsgroups in general work, using the seven major categories as examples.

As noted previously, there are major subcategories within each of the top-level newsgroups, and many of the subcategories are recursively subdivided into more categories. Eventually, the subdivision stops and individual newsgroups begin.

Given the penchant among netnews readers to want more and more specifically focused groups, you can imagine the near infinite subdivision of subject matter. Let's take a look at just one subcategory of the comp newsgroup category, where we will find newsgroups dealing with the World Wide Web. You'll find this subcategory within the comp.infosystems category (one of 70-odd first-level subdivisions of the comp category). Its name is comp.infosystems.www. You're probably already catching onto netnews' nomenclature, with newsgroup categories and subcategories named using periods to separate the levels. Thus www is a subcategory of the infosystems category of the comp top-level newsgroup category. Within the www newsgroup subcategory, there are eight further subdivisions (advocacy, announce, authoring, browsers, misc, providers, servers, and users).

Let's follow the comp.infosystems.www subcategory down one more step into the browsers category, where you'll find yet another four subdivisions, mac, misc, ms-windows, and x. Here, you've finally touched bottom and reached the last subdivision of this branch of the comp.infosystems.www newsgroup tree. Each of these is an actual newsgroup, devoted to Macintosh, miscellaneous, Microsoft Windows, and X Window World Wide Web browsers, respectively.

Your customers' view of the Usenet system reflects the way newsgroups are named. Figure 27.2 shows NCSA Mosaic's display of the newsgroup comp.infosystems.www.browsers.ms-windows. As you can see, this is a pretty plain, mostly text display of a list of news articles. Each article entry is a hyperlink, so clicking on one selects the article for display.

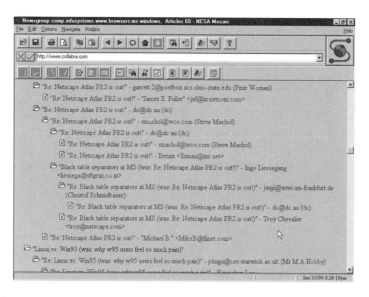

Figure 27.2. *The NCSA Mosaic newsreader.*

Rather than using a separate window to display a selected article, Netscape attempts to display all newsgroup information on a single screen, as shown in Figure 27.3. This busy screen is divided into three panes. The panes show:

◆ A scrollable, graphical display of the news server you've selected and its available newsgroups, in the upper left.

◆ A scrollable list of the articles in the currently selected newsgroup, on the upper right.

◆ The actual text of a selected article, in the lower half of the screen, with a scroll bar to move through the article.

The list of newsgroups in the newsgroup pane shortens the (often very long) newsgroup names, placing ellipses in the names. Unfortunately, the contraction method makes most newsgroup names unrecognizable, even to experienced readers. Even though you can resize the newsgroups window (click on the double vertical line, just to the right of the scroll bar and drag it to the right), the newsgroup names aren't expanded.

Note: The other two panes of the Netscape news window can also be resized by grabbing the double lines with your mouse and sliding left or right or up or down.

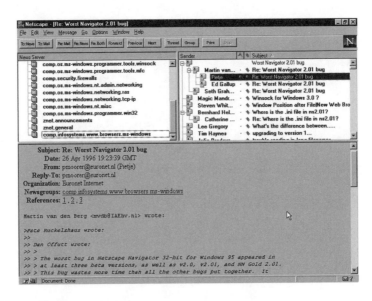

Figure 27.3. *Netscape Navigator news window.*

Creating Local Usenet Newsgroups on Your Intranet

It's important to note that Usenet news server (also called NNTP, for Network News Transfer Protocol) software provides for the creation of *local* newsgroups. You need not be a part of the Internet's Usenet system to run a news server. On the contrary, your netnews server can be entirely local, with your news articles not being sent anywhere outside your organization. All your customers can have access to your local Usenet news, and can use their Web browsers to read and respond to local news articles.

Normally, netnews articles get sent to the outside world, via your upstream newsfeed, from where they are sent on to netnews systems all over the Internet. Since you're using netnews as a local communication and collaboration mechanism on your Intranet, however, you'll agree it's not appropriate for your purely local newsgroups to get handled this way. Instead, you want them to stay inside your Intranet, where confidentiality and privacy are protected.

If you would like to try running your own NNTP server on Windows NT, you can download either a freeware or a commercial trial version at this URL:

```
http://www.netmanage.com/netmanage/nns/
```

NetManage also makes available the documentation for the freeware NNTP server, called NNS. They have enhanced the widely available NNS package and included it as part of a new commercial product they call the NetManage IntraNet Server for Windows NT. The server technologies they include in the package are

◆ Forum (this is the commercial NNTP server)

◆ DNS

- Web
- NFS file and print
- LPD
- Directory
- PC NetTime servers

> **Note:** By the way, the NetManage Web site is also quite interesting from the standpoint that they build a very competitive Web browser and now have a free package of ActiveX controls for use by Web designers and VB programmers. Be sure to check out this URL:
>
> `http://www.netmanage.com/`

Usenet News Server File Structure

Your Usenet news server stores news articles in a file tree that parallels the newsgroup subdivisions, with subdirectories for each category, subcategory, and individual newsgroups. Thus, the filesystem path to the `comp.infosystems.www.browsers` newsgroups, beginning at the top of your Usenet news spool, is `comp/infosystems/www/browsers`. The tree-structured system of directories and subdirectories parallels the subdivision of Usenet newsgroups. Within the bottom-level subdirectories, you find the actual netnews articles.

Files are named with a consecutive numbering mechanism, so when you do a directory listing of one of your netnews article subdirectories, you'll just see a list of numbers. The first article that created on your local system is placed in a file named `1`, the second, in the file `2`, and so on. These filenames are unique to your system, as they're created when users post articles or your system receives articles from other systems. The file named `7835` on your system will most likely not correspond with the file `7835` on any other system.

Configuring Your Web Browser for the Usenet News Server

All Web browsers require some initial setup for netnews. First, users need to define the Usenet news server to which they'll connect. Second, users need to select the newsgroups they want to read. The first of these is a quick, one-time thing, but the second is a potentially tedious process.

The major browsers use an essentially similar process for defining your netnews server. In Microsoft Explorer, for example, choose View | Options | News to configure the browser for your Usenet news server. You'll see the tabbed dialog as shown in Figure 27.4.

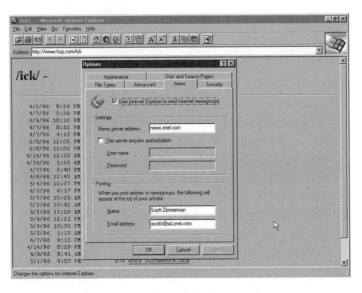

Figure 27.4. *News server configuration in Microsoft Explorer.*

There are several configuration items here, but you're concerned for the moment with only one of them, labeled News server address. Fill in the box with the name of your NT Server running NNTP (or NNS), or the name of your Internet Service Provider (ISP) news server (if you want to try out the real Usenet before running your own).

Click OK to return to the main window. To try the news service in Explorer, choose Go | Read Newsgroups. The resulting long list of newsgroups is rather poorly presented in Explorer 2.0. However, you can filter the list down to a more manageable level by entering a URL with an appropriate mask. For example: news:comp*.

Note: Be sure to check out the new Internet Mail and Newsreader applications from Microsoft for Windows 95 and Windows NT 4. These programs are currently available as free beta downloads from the Microsoft Web site (www.microsoft.com) and we can expect them to be well integrated with Internet Explorer 3.0 when all three are officially released. The Newsreader program is much nicer than the News feature, which is currently built into Internet Explorer 2.0.

Summary

In this chapter, you've learned how to put Usenet news to work on your Intranet. We also discussed several means of enhancing your Intranet through collaboration, and the tools you can use to make it happen. In summary, here's what this chapter has covered:

◆ Simple, one-way collaborative activities on your Intranet.

◆ Electronic mail as a collaborative resource.

◆ Free-for-all collaboration.

◆ Web-based annotation and conferencing, including NetMeeting and WWWBoard.

◆ Full-featured groupware for Web collaboration and communication, including Collabra Share, Lotus Notes, and Microsoft Exchange. This section also included a brief discussion of BackOffice 2.0.

◆ How Usenet news works, how you can use it for collaboration, how to obtain NNTP server software for Windows NT, and how to configure the browser to access the news server.

In Chapter 28, "Connecting the Intranet and Internet," you'll learn how to expand your Intranet services globally. This can be useful for your non-local customers who need to take advantage of the same facilities that are available on your local network.

CHAPTER

Connecting the Intranet and the Internet

- ◆ Configuring Windows NT as a router
- ◆ Internet robots
- ◆ Firewalls

Sooner or later, you are going to want to take advantage of what you now know about building an internal Web to help your organization establish a presence on the World Wide Web. Whether to help sell your products, share research, publish news, market software, provide customer support, or solicit customer feedback, a site on the WWW can help your organization further its goals.

Until recently, few people thought it was possible to run a decent Web server on Windows NT. I hope this book has convinced you, if it has done nothing else, how untrue that myth is. In fact, I have found Windows NT to be an excellent Web platform in terms of performance, cost, and ease of use. And if you want to build a Web site, without spending years learning about UNIX system administration, this chapter can help you get started.

The aim of this chapter is to go over a few assorted topics that you will likely come across when you connect your Intranet to the Internet. This chapter is by no means complete—whole books are written on the subject of how to build an Internet server. But few of those are devoted to Windows NT Web sites. One in particular is *Web Site Construction Kit for Windows NT*, written by Christopher L. T. Brown and yours truly. That book will provide you with a complete treatment of all aspects of building an Internet server with Windows NT 4.

This chapter will address using NT and a modem as a router, how to deal with Internet robots, and why you will want to consider building a firewall between your Intranet and the Internet. Most of the material in this chapter is not about running an Internet Web site; rather, it is about connecting your LAN to the Internet in the first place.

Configuring Windows NT as a Router

Let's say you want to connect a small Local Area Network (LAN) to the Internet using Windows NT, Remote Access Service (RAS), and a modem. Your Intranet customers are telling you that they all want access to the World Wide Web for research and software downloading, but you would like to avoid buying separate modems and phone lines for everyone. If you use Windows NT as a router, you only need to buy one modem, one connection to the Internet Service Provider (ISP), and one extra phone. Of course, bandwidth is a consideration, but you can always scale up to ISDN, Frame Relay, or T1 as your needs dictate. Let's be very clear about this; using a 28.8 Kbps RAS modem connection to the Internet does not make for a high-performance router.

If the idea behind this sounds appealing to you, be prepared for the fact that the path to success can be strewn with land mines. This section will present a summary of the steps that I took to make this work on my small LAN. The ideas presented will reflect my experiences, but they are based on advice from the Windows NT Webserver mailing list, conversations with experts (including my ISP), and assorted books and magazine articles (listed in the Bibliography).

Here is an overview of the various tasks that await you as you connect your LAN to the Internet.

◆ You need to obtain a dial-up PPP account with an Internet Service Provider in your area. Either get one subnet account that has at least twice as many IP addresses as you need for the number of client workstations on your LAN, or get one IP address in a separate range from a subnet having enough IP addresses to accommodate all the workstations on your LAN. I'll discuss this in more detail later.

◆ You need to hook up your modem through RAS and enable it to dial into your ISP as a stand-alone machine. Ensure that you can browse the World Wide Web from your NT Server.

◆ You need to configure your NT Server to redial the connection in the event of a disconnect or a server crash. You can use the SomarSoft Redial program for this.

◆ You need to install Network Interface Cards (NICs) in the server and in each workstation machine. Then select and install the appropriate network wiring between the NICs. This step is more a fundamental part of building a LAN than anything else. The workstations can be running Windows NT, Windows 95, or Windows for Workgroups. In the case of WfW, the Microsoft TCP/IP add-on pack must be installed separately.

◆ You need to adjust the Registry on the NT Server to function as a router.

◆ You need to configure the TCP/IP Address, Subnet Mask, and Default Gateway in each of the workstations. Ensure that the workstations can ping the NT Server.

◆ You need to adjust the routing tables on the NT Server to achieve the Internet connection for the workstations.

Once you have accomplished all this, you are ready to surf the Web from the client computers, as well from as the server.

Windows NT Registry Settings for the Router

Based on documentation from various sources, including the Microsoft TechNet CD, the following Registry parameters are a superset of what is strictly required for NT to function as a router between the LAN and the Internet. The reason I say "superset" is that your particular situation will determine whether or not you will need all of these. Future versions of NT may introduce other parameters enabling further optimization. Experimentation may be necessary to achieve the best results. All of the entries are documented in the Windows NT Resource Kit.

Now it's time to fire up RegEdit. To avoid repeating a large portion of the name of each value, I will tell you up front that they are all located under the following key:

```
HKEY_LOCAL_MACHINE\System\CurrentControlSet\Services
```

The following values can be found underneath this Services key. If they are not already present, you will need to add them as follows:

◆ RasArp\Parameters\DisableOtherSrcPackets = 0.

◆ RasMan\PPP\IPCP\PriorityBasedOnSubNetwork = 1.

◆ TcpIp\Parameters\IpEnableRouter = 1.

◆ TcpIp\Parameters\ForwardBroadcasts = 1. (This parameter is documented as unused on the Microsoft TechNet CD and its benefit in this scenario is unclear.)

Assigning Default Gateway Addresses on the LAN

The next trick is to assign one IP address to your RAS dial-up connection and a different IP address to each of the NICs on your LAN, including the Windows NT Server. It is very likely that you have already dealt with this issue as part of the overall configuration of TCP/IP on your Intranet.

Once you have assigned a unique IP address to each NIC on the LAN, set the Default Gateway on each of the client machines to the address of the NIC on the NT router. The Default Gateway of the NIC on the NT Server itself should be left blank. These steps are very important, so make sure that you apply them accurately. For reasons that I will get into in a moment, you must not try to take a shortcut by sending the client machine packets straight to the IP address of the RAS connection—the Default Gateway on the clients must be the NIC on the NT Server.

It might help if we develop a mental picture of what's going on here. Each machine on the LAN needs to be told where to send outgoing packets so that they will find their way out to the Internet. Otherwise, outbound packets would have no way to get off the LAN. The NT Server with the RAS connection is the gateway (or router). Since the NT Server is a dual-homed host (supporting a NIC and running RAS), packets from the NICs on the LAN that are sent to the IP address of the NIC on the NT Server will be routed by the NT box from its NIC over to its RAS connection. This will be accomplished within the TCP/IP software running in Windows NT. From there, the packets will travel through the modem to the ISP and on out to the Internet.

The Default Gateway of the RAS TCP/IP connection on the NT Server appears to be non-configurable in NT 4, but that is okay because RAS conveniently seems to assume that its Default Gateway is on the network it is dialing into, namely your ISP. For example, if you type ipconfig after establishing a RAS connection to your ISP, you will see that the Default Gateway is the same as the IP address assigned to RAS.

Assigning Subnets

Subnets can be a rather mysterious area of TCP/IP. The most important point about subnetting, as relates to this discussion, is that the IP address of the RAS connection must be in a separate subnet of the IP address of the NIC in the NT Server. That is why the clients cannot list the RAS IP address as the Default Gateway—because technically they can't see it.

TCP/IP Addressing

For all TCP/IP issues great and small I highly recommend *Internetworking with TCP/IP, Volume I, Third Edition*, by Douglas E. Comer as an excellent permanent reference book. There is no way I can possibly give a complete treatment of IP addressing here, so I'll just take a stab at the basics.

A Class C TCP/IP subnet can contain up to 254 separate IP addresses. The addresses are of the form X.A.B.C, where X, A, and B are fixed by the ISP, and C ranges between 0 and 255 for each machine on your LAN. For a Class C address, the X in the above address will always be greater than 192. X numbers less than 128 are Class A addresses. X numbers between 128 and 191 are Class B addresses.

Each of the numbers in a TCP/IP address consists of 8 bits, providing 256 possibilities, ranging between 0 and 255 in decimal. By convention, any TCP/IP subnet reserves the address with all zeros to mean the address of the network itself, and the address with all ones to mean the broadcast address. That is why each subnet may contain two fewer computers than the size of the subnet.

If you can afford to buy one IP address for your RAS connection and a complete (separate) Class C address for the rest of your LAN, you will have a very easy time connecting your LAN to the Internet. In that case, you will simply use a subnet mask of 255.255.255.0 for each IP address on your LAN. The subnet mask for RAS would also be 255.255.255.0 because it would already be on a different network segment.

If you want to perform a bit pattern subnet, things definitely get more involved. Let's suppose you have six client computers to connect to the Internet. You might think that you can get by with a subnet-8 account, as leased by many ISPs. But remember, you need one IP address for RAS, a different IP address for the NIC in the NT Server, and the all zeros and all ones addresses on the subnet will be skipped by convention (although in certain cases you can violate that rule).

In other words, you need a subnet big enough to hold a total of ten IP addresses. At this point you would think that all you need is a subnet-16, again an easy thing to lease from an ISP. Unfortunately, it's not even that simple. Remember, the RAS IP address must be in a different subnet. Each bit you use for a subnet divides the range of usable addresses in half.

You could divide the subnet-16 in half. Then you could devote the 0 through 7 subnet numbers for RAS—skipping the zeroeth address as the subnet address itself, you could assign the first subnet address to RAS (addresses 2 through 7 would be wasted). You would then give the numbers 8 through 15 in the higher subnet to the six client machines, actually skipping 8 and 15 as per convention. That would work except that we left out the NIC in the NT Server. Therefore, you would either need to step up to a block of 32 addresses or you would need to drop one client machine.

Whatever method you use, your ISP should be able to help you establish the bit pattern for the subnet mask on the clients. If you can't afford to go with a full Class C address for the LAN, the fourth *octet* in the subnet mask must be split into a binary number with zeroes used in the low-order bits for the number of addresses needed. The subnet mask on the RAS connection can simply be a Class C mask in all cases: 255.255.255.0. I believe that this is due to the fact that RAS always behaves as a LAN-to-WAN router, possibly allowing it to ignore the subnet mask.

Adding Static TCP/IP Routes for the Workstations

There is just one more step to get your LAN packets to travel out to the Internet. Actually, the purpose of this step is to let the data packets returning from the Internet find their way from the RAS connection on the NT Server over to the client machine that initiated the transaction.

You need to add static routes to the route table on the NT Server. This is done at the DOS command prompt using the route add command.

I'll explain this by example. Suppose you have given the NIC in the NT Server an IP address of 200.9.9.1 and the NIC address of the first client machine is 200.9.9.2. The procedure must be duplicated for each client machine.

The following command would provide a static route from the NT Server to the first client:

```
route add -p 200.9.9.2 200.9.9.1
```

The -p parameter specifies to add this as a persistent route. NT will store it in the Registry so it will be retained after subsequent reboots.

Finally, if you find that your client machines can ping Internet addresses by TCP/IP number only, but DNS name resolutions and Web browsing do not work, it could be that your ISP has not provided static routes on their end to pass network traffic into your RAS connection when the destination address is one in your subnet.

Internet Robots

World Wide Web robots, sometimes called *wanderers* or *spiders*, are programs that traverse the Web automatically. A robot's job is to retrieve information about the documents that are available on the Web and then store that information in some kind of master index of the Web. Usually, the robot is limited by its author to hunt for a particular topic or segment of the Web.

At the very least, most robots are programmed to look at the <TITLE> and <H1> tags in the HTML documents they discover. Then they scan the contents of the file looking for <A HREF> tags to other documents. A typical robot might store the URLs of those documents in a data structure called a *tree,* which it uses to continue the search whenever it reaches a dead-end (more technically called a *leaf-node*). I am oversimplifying this a bit; the larger robots probably use much more sophisticated algorithms. But the basic principles are the same.

The idea behind this is that the index built by the robot will make life easier for us humans who would like a quick hop to information sources on the Internet.

The good news is that most robots are successful at this and do help make subsequent search and retrieval of those documents more efficient. This is important in terms of Internet traffic. If a robot spends several hours looking for documents, but thousands (or even millions) of users take advantage of the index that is generated, it will save all those users from tapping their own means of discovering the links, potentially saving a great amount of network bandwidth.

The bad news is that some robots inefficiently revisit the same site more than once, or they submit rapid-fire requests to the same site in such a frenzy that the server can't keep up. This is obviously a cause of concern for Webmasters. Robot authors are as upset as the rest of the Internet community when they find out that a poorly behaved robot has been unleashed. But usually such problems are found only in a few poorly written robots.

Fortunately, guidelines have been developed for robot authors, and most robots are compliant. An excellent online resource for information about robots, including further information on which much of this material is based, see "World Wide Web Robots, Wanderers, and Spiders" by Martijn Koster, `http://info.webcrawler.com/mak/projects/robots/robots.html`. It contains links to documents describing robot guidelines, the standard for robot exclusion, and an in-depth collection of information about known robots.

Tip: The Internet community puts up with robots because robots give something back to all of us. A private robot, on the other hand, is one that you might customize to search a limited realm of interest to you or your organization. Private robots are frowned upon because they use Internet resources, but only offer value to a single user in return. If you are looking for your own Internet robot, however, you can check out the Verity Inc. home page at `http://www.verity.com/`. Please remember that one of the guidelines of robot design is to first analyze carefully if a new robot is really called for.

A good understanding of Web robots and how to use or exclude them will aid you in your Web ventures; in fact, it could help to keep your server alive.

Excluding Robots

There are lots of reasons to want to exclude robots from visiting your site. One reason is that rapid-fire requests from buggy robots could drag your server down. Also, your site might contain data that you do not want to be indexed by outside sources. Whatever the reason, there is an obvious need for a method for robot exclusion. Be aware, however, that it wouldn't be helpful to the Internet community if all robots were excluded from all sites.

On the Internet Web-related newsgroups and listservers, you will often see a new Web site administrator ask the question "What is `robots.txt` and why are people looking for it?" This question often comes up after the administrator looks at his or her Web access logs and sees the following line:

```
Tue Jun 06 17:36:36 1995 204.252.2.5 192.100.81.115 GET /robots.txt HTTP/1.0
```

Knowing that they don't have a file `robots.txt` in the root directory, most administrators are puzzled.

The answer is that `robots.txt` is part of the Standard for Robot Exclusion. The standard was agreed to in June 1994 on the robots mailing list (`robots-request@webcrawler.com`) by the majority of robot authors and other people with an interest in robots. The information on these pages is based on the working draft of the exclusion standard, which can be found at this URL:

`http://info.webcrawler.com/mak/projects/robots/norobots.html`

Some of the things to take into account concerning the Standard for Robot Exclusion are:

◆ It is not an official standard backed by a standards body.

◆ It is not enforced by anybody, and there are no guarantees that all current and future robots will adhere to it.

◆ Consider it a loose standard that the majority of robot authors will follow.

In addition to using the exclusion described below, there are a few other simple steps you can follow if you discover an unwanted robot visiting your site:

1. Check your Web server log files to detect the frequency of document retrievals.

2. Try to determine where the robot originated. This will enable you to contact the author. You can find the author by looking at the User-agent and From field in the request, or look up the host domain in the list of robots.

3. If the robot is annoying in some fashion, let the robot author know about it. Ask the author to visit `http://info.webcrawler.com/mak/projects/robots/robots.html` so he or she can read the guidelines for robot authors and the standard for exclusion.

The Method

The method used to exclude robots from a server is to create a file on the server that specifies an access policy for robots. This file must be named `robots.txt`, and it must reside in the HTML document root directory.

The file must be accessible via HTTP, with the contents as specified here. The format and semantics of the file are as follows:

◆ The file consists of one or more records separated by one or more blank lines (terminated by CR, CR/NL, or NL). Each record contains lines of the form:

```
<field name>:<optional space><value><optional space>.
```

♦ The field name is case-insensitive. Comments can be included in the file using UNIX Bourne shell conventions. The # character is used to indicate that preceding space (if any) and the remainder of the line up to the line termination are discarded. Lines containing only a comment are discarded completely and therefore do not indicate a record boundary. The record starts with one or more user-agent lines, followed by one or more disallow lines. Unrecognized headers are ignored.

♦ User-agent

The value of this field is the name of the robot for which the record is describing an access policy. If more than one User-agent field is present, the record describes an identical access policy for more than one robot. At least one field needs to be present per record. The robot should be liberal in interpreting this field. A case-insensitive substring match of the name without version information is recommended. If the value in the record describes the default access policy for any robot that has not matched any of the other records, it is not allowed to have two such records in the `robots.txt` file.

♦ Disallow

The value of this field specifies a partial URL that is not to be visited. This can be a full path or a partial path; any URL that starts with this value will not be retrieved. For example:

```
Disallow: /help
```

disallows both `/help.htm` and `/help/default.htm`, whereas

```
Disallow: /help/
```

disallows `/help/default.htm` but allows `/help.htm`.

Any empty value indicates that all URLs can be retrieved. At least one Disallow field needs to be present in a record. The presence of an empty `/robots.txt` file has no explicit associated semantics; it will be treated as if it was not present—for example, all robots will consider themselves welcome to scan.

Examples

Here is a sample `robots.txt` for `http://www.yourco.com/` that specifies no robots should visit any URL starting with `/yourco/cgi-bin/` or `/tmp/`:

```
User-agent: *
Disallow: /yourco/cgi-bin/
Disallow: /tmp/
```

Here is an example that indicates no robots should visit the current site:

```
User-agent: *
Disallow: /
```

Firewalls

If you intend to maintain an Internet connection and you truly want a secure site, you should consider getting firewall protection. A *firewall* can be software, hardware, or a combination of the two. Commercial firewall packages cost a lot more than loose change—usually the price range is anywhere from $1,000 to $100,000. If you are using NT, RAS, and a modem as a software-based router, then the first step in building a firewall is to change from a RAS-based connection to an Ethernet/router hardware-based connection.

> **Note:** For a much more thorough treatment of firewalls and Internet security, please see *Internet Firewalls and Network Security* by Karanjit Siyan and Chris Hare, published by New Riders Publishing.

There aren't yet many software-only firewalls for Windows NT, as most are based on UNIX. In the meantime, you might consider running a freeware version of UNIX for the purpose of including a firewall in your network.

> **Note:** If the cost of a firewall has you worried, consider a much cheaper and more secure solution. Namely, avoid connecting your LAN to the Internet Web server altogether. Obviously, there are drawbacks to this approach, but it is the most secure approach. For one thing, it assumes your client machines won't need a connection to browse the Web. For another, you have to use sneaker-net (hand-carried floppy disks) to modify your HTML files on the Web server. This inconvenience can be reduced by physically reconnecting the network cable to the back of the Web server machine for a limited time during the day when you need to access it.

A firewall usually includes several software tools. For example, it might include separate proxy servers for e-mail, FTP, Gopher, Telnet, Web, and WAIS. The firewall can also filter certain outbound ICMP (Internet Control Message Protocol) packets so your server won't be capable of divulging network information.

Figure 28.1 shows a network diagram of a typical LAN connection to the Internet including a Web server and a firewall. Note that the Web server, LAN server, and firewall server could all be rolled into one machine if the budget is tight, but separating them as shown here is considered a safer environment.

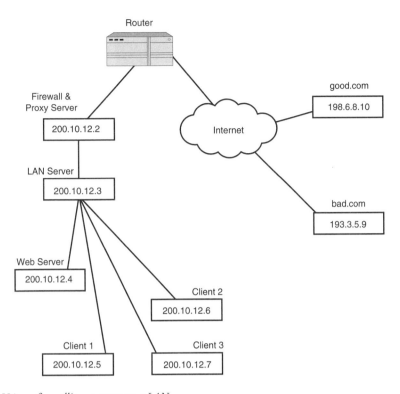

Figure 28.1. *Using a firewall/proxy server on a LAN.*

The proxy server is used to mask all of your LAN IP addresses on outbound packets so they look like they all originated at the proxy server itself. Each of the client machines on your LAN must use the proxy server whenever they connect to the Internet for FTP, Telnet, Gopher, or the Web. The reason for doing this is to prevent outside detection of the structure of your network. Otherwise, hackers monitoring your outbound traffic would eventually be able to determine your individual IP addresses and then use *IP spoofing* to feed those back to your server when they want to appear as a known client.

Another purpose of a firewall is to perform *IP filtering* of incoming packets. Let's say that you have been monitoring the log files on your Web server and you keep noticing some unusual or unwanted activity originating from IP address x.3.5.9. After checking with the whois program (available on the Internet, for example, at http://www.winsite.com), you determine the domain name is bad.com, and you don't have any known reason to be doing business with them. You can configure the IP filter to block any connection attempts originating from bad.com while still allowing packets from the friendly good.com to proceed.

> **Caution:** Many people think IP packet filtering is worthless if only implemented in software. They may advise you that packet filtering is useful only in a router or a hardware firewall solution that includes the capability to filter at the Link Layer, as opposed to the Network or Transport layers where the TCP/IP software operates. However, even if you do packet filtering via software, the trick is to filter based on both the source IP *and* the interface. That is, if a packet with a source address that is also an internal IP shows up on the external interface of your router (such as from the Internet side), you should drop the packet and have it logged for immediate attention.

Summary

This chapter has given you a brief taste of some of the issues involved in connecting the LAN to the Internet. This has by no means been a comprehensive treatment of the subject. I hope that it has been enough, however, to get you started with building your own site on the World Wide Web or in providing Internet access for all customers who need to go beyond the Intranet.

In the next and final chapter I will continue with the idea of building your own Web site by showing you a very handy Perl script that can be used to collect statistics of your visitors. When you think about it, you could even use the script on the Intranet. The chapter also provides a quick introduction to the Perl language and discusses other applications to which a Webmaster can apply Perl.

CHAPTER

29

Taking Advantage of Perl

♦ Obtaining Perl

♦ Learning Perl

♦ Web site statistical analysis

♦ WWWusage

♦ CGI forms handling with Perl

Perl is an interpreted language designed for scanning arbitrary text files, extracting information from those text files, and printing reports based on that information. It is also a good language for many Web site system management tasks. This chapter shows you how to use it for a few handy CGI scripts, including Web site statistics. Web site statistics are perhaps more relevant on an Internet Web site than on an Intranet—but whether or not you decide to put the information in Chapter 28 to use and connect to the Internet, you will still be faced with a need to automate countless numbers of server chores. If you take the time to learn Perl, you will find that it is an ideal employee for those tasks. And if you don't have time to learn Perl, you still win, because many Perl scripts which you can use as-is are available on the Internet.

For non-GUI systems programming, Perl fills the gap between low-level programming languages, such as C, and high-level languages such as AWK, SED, and the UNIX Shell. Although C is a very powerful language, it requires a steep learning curve to master. Perl does not offer the speed of a compiled language (like C), but it does offer very good string-handling capabilities and it is easier to learn. Most people with experience in any of the languages just mentioned will find Perl to be an easy migration.

Note: Here's some good news for those who like Perl but hate to give up performance. Hip Communications Inc., in Vancouver, BC, has recently announced `PerlIS.dll` for Microsoft IIS. PerlIS is an ISAPI version of the Perl interpreter, so the Web server is able to process Perl scripts at a greatly increased speed compared to traditional CGI. You can download the software and documentation for PerlIS and Perl for Win32 at this URL:

`http://www.perl.hip.com/`

Hip Communications maintains current versions of Perl 5.001m for Windows NT and Windows 95 using Visual C++ 4.x. PerlIS should have no problems running on the Purveyor 1.2 Web server from Process Software, and probably other ISAPI-compliant HTTP servers for NT as well.

WWWusage, which is available for free download at `http://rick.wzl.rwth-aachen.de/RickG/WWWusage/wwwusage.html`, is an excellent example of a powerful CGI script written in Perl. WWWusage was written by Richard Graessler to perform HTTP statistics on Windows NT. Christopher Brown, with whom I co-authored *Web Site Construction Kit for Windows NT* and *Web Site Construction Kit for Windows 95*, gets credit for the original draft of this chapter. Chris ported WWWusage to Windows 95, although Rick's latest version of the program for Windows NT is discussed here.

Note: Although Perl is an acronym for Practical Extraction and Report Language, like the names of many other program languages formed from acronyms, it isn't always written in uppercase letters.

Obtaining Perl

Perl comes in two versions: Perl 4 and Perl 5. Version 5 is the new kid on the block, and it comes with object-oriented extensions. Perl was invented on UNIX by Larry Wall. Keep in mind that Perl has always had strong roots on UNIX platforms, and most of the Webmasters who use it and post public-domain Perl source code work on UNIX. Fortunately, some nice folks have ported Perl to Win32 and made it available by anonymous FTP.

Dick Hardt of Hip Communications led the porting of Perl 5 to Windows NT/95. You can obtain the latest version of it from `ftp://ntperl.hip.com/ntperl/`. This site contains the Visual C++ source code for Perl, binary files, and documentation.

> **Tip:** If you plan to install Perl 5 on Windows 95, the batch files that come with Perl will not work. You will have to make three registry entries manually, as described in a file named `win95.txt` (accompanying Perl 5) that explains the process.

You can retrieve Perl 4 for Windows NT at the FTP site of Intergraph. Point your Web browser or CuteFTP (see Chapter 7, "Running the Intranet Web Server") to this URL: `ftp://ftp.intergraph.com/pub/win32/perl/`. You may want to download the file `ntperlb.zip` (if you only want the compiled version) or `ntperls.zip` (if you want the Visual C++ 2.0 source code). Using Perl 4 on Windows 95 requires a patch (which you can find at Yahoo) developed by Bob Denny.

Learning Perl

This book is already covering a great deal of information, and I don't intend to deluge you with a complete course on the Perl language. What this chapter does do is give you a quick introduction to the Perl syntax and show you how to put some Perl scripts to work so you can jump right in. For more information about Perl, please see *Teach Yourself Perl 5 in 21 Days, 2nd Edition* by David Till, published by Sams.

> **Note:** Much of the material in this section was generously contributed originally by Gary E. Major (Systems Analyst) at Seattle Pacific University. You can visit his site on the Web for the latest information:
>
> `http://www.spu.edu/tech/basic-perl/`

There's so much to cover and only one chapter to do it. I caution you that this material is not intended for those who are new to programming. In fact, I am going to take somewhat of a hit-and-run approach and present the material largely in reference format. The second half of the chapter contains a very useful sample application.

Symbols

Table 29.1 presents the most common symbols unique to Perl and their meaning.

Table 29.1. Common Perl symbols.

Symbol	Purpose
$	For scalar values.
@	For indexed arrays.
%	For hashed arrays (associative arrays).
*	For all types of that symbol name. These are sometimes used like pointers in perl4, but perl5 uses references.
<>	Used for inputting a record from a filehandle.
\	Takes a reference to something.

Script Components

This section lists the basic components of a Perl script. The first line of every Perl program is a required special comment to identify the file location of the Perl interpreter itself. For example:

```
#!/usr/local/bin/perl
```

◆ Comment lines begin with the # character.

◆ Commands end with the ; character.

◆ Subroutines are contained in braces, for example, `sub subroutine_name { }`.

This list shows the predefined data types:

◆ Scalars

Names begin with the $ character (for example, `$scalarname`).

Used for characters, strings, and numbers.

◆ Arrays

Names begin with the @ character (for example, `@arrayname`).

Individual items referenced: `@arrayname[n]`.

Used for lists of characters, strings, and numbers.

Note that the list can have a mixture of characters, strings, and numbers.

◆ Hashes (also known as associative arrays)

Names begin with the % character (for example, `%hashname`)

Individual items referenced: `%hashname{'key'}`.

Handles key/value combinations:

"Gary Major", "Systems Analyst"

"Phil Rand", "Senior Systems Analyst"

"E. Arthur Self", "Who?"

Special Variables and Characters

Table 29.2 lists several predefined variables and reserved characters in Perl.

Table 29.2. Predefined Perl variables.

Variable	Purpose
$0	Contains the name of the script being executed.
$_	Default input and pattern search variable.
$/	Input record separator, newline by default.
@ARGV	Contains command-line arguments. $ARGV[0] is the first argument.
@INC	Contains the list of places to look for scripts to be evaluated by the do or require commands.
%INC	Contains entries for each file included by the do or require commands.
%ENV	Contains your environment settings. Changes made affect child processes.
STDIN	Default input stream.
STDOUT	Default output stream.
STDERR	Default error stream.

Arithmetic Operators

Table 29.3 lists the common mathematical operators.

Table 29.3. Perl mathematical operators.

Operator	Example	Meaning
+	$a + $b	Sum of $a and $b
-	$a - $b	Difference of $a and $b
*	$a * $b	Product of $a times $b
/	$a / $b	Quotient of $a divided by $b
%	$a % $b	Remainder of $a divided by $b
**	$a ** $b	$a to the power of $b

Assignment Operators

Perl supports a rich array of assignment operators for many purposes. If the list in Table 29.4 seems overwhelming, try to stick to the easy ones and learn about the others after you have more experience with Perl programming.

Table 29.4. Perl assignment operators.

Operator	Example	Meaning
=	$var = 5	Assign 5 to $var
++	$var++ or ++$var	Increment $var by 1 and assign to $var
--	$var-- or --$var	Decrement $var by 1 and assign to $var
+=	$var += 3	Increase $var by 3 and assign to $var
-=	$var -= 2	Decrease $var by 2 and assign to $var
.=	$str .= "ing"	Concatenate "ing" to $str and assign to $str
*=	$var *= 4	Multiply $var by 4 and assign to $var
/=	$var /= 2	Divide $var by 2 and assign to $var
**=	$var **= 2	Raise $var to the second power and assign to $var
%=	$var %= 2	Divide $var by 2 and assign remainder to $var
x=	$str x= 20	Repeat $str 20 times and assign to $str

Logical Operators

The logical operators in Perl (shown in Table 29.5) are useful in If statements typical of nearly all programming languages.

Table 29.5. Perl logical operators.

Operator	Example	Meaning
&&	$a && $b	True if $a is true and $b is true
¦¦	$a ¦¦ $b	True if $a is true or if $b is true
!	! $a	True if $a is not true

Pattern-Matching Operators

Pattern matching is one of the areas in which Perl shows its strength. These operators, shown in Table 29.6, are very useful for string operations.

Table 29.6. Perl pattern-matching operators.

Operator	Example	Meaning
=~ //	$a =~ /pat/	True if $a contains pattern pat
=~ s//	$a =~ s/p/r	Replace occurrences of p with r in $a
=~ tr//	$a =~ tr/a-z/A-Z	Translate to corresponding characters
!~ //	$a !~ /pat/	True if $a does not contain pattern pat

String Operators

String operators in Perl, as shown in Table 29.7, are the mainstay of the language.

Table 29.7. Perl string operators.

Operator	Example	Meaning
.	$a . $b	Concatenate $b to the end of $a
x	$a x $b	Value of $a strung together $b times
substr()	substr($a, $o, $l)	Substring of $a at offset $o of length $l
index()	index($a, $b)	Offset of string $b in string $a

Relational Operators

The relational operators shown in Table 29.8 are essential to If and While statements.

Table 29.8. Perl relational operators.

Numeric Operator	String Operator	Example	Meaning
==	eq	$str eq "Word"	Equal to
!=	ne	$str ne "Word"	Not equal to
>	gt	$var > 10	Greater than
>=	ge	$var >= 10	Greater than or equal to
<	lt	$var < 10	Less than
<=	le	$var <= 10	Less than or equal to

Basic Perl Commands

Here are several predefined Perl commands that you will come across repeatedly.

◆ `print FILEHANDLE LIST`

Prints a string or comma-delimited list of strings to `FILEHANDLE` (`STDOUT` is the default).

Example: `print FILE "This is line 1\n", "This is line 2\n";`

◆ `printf FILEHANDLE FORMAT, LIST`

Prints a formatted string to `FILEHANDLE` (`STDOUT` is the default).

Example: `printf FILE "%s %d\n", "This is line", 3;`

`printf` formatting specifiers are as follows:

Conversion Character	Definition
`%s`	String
`%c`	Character
`%d`	Decimal number
`%ld`	Long decimal number
`%u`	Unsigned decimal number
`%ul`	Unsigned long decimal number
`%x`	Hexadecimal number
`%lx`	Long hexadecimal number
`%o`	Octal number
`%lo`	Long octal number
`%e`	Floating-point number in scientific notation
`%f`	Floating-point number

◆ `open(FILEHANDLE, EXPR)`

Opens a real file, `EXPR`, and attaches it to `FILEHANDLE`. Without `EXPR`, a scalar with the same name as `FILEHANDLE` would have been assigned the filename.

Example:
```
open(FILE, "this-is-a-long-filename.txt");
```

EXPR definitions appear in the following table:

Open as:	EXPR:
Read Only	`"filename"`
Write Only	`">filename"`
Read and Write	`"+>filename"`
Append	`">>filename"`
Pipe In	`"unix command |"`
Pipe Out	`"| unix command"`

- `close(FILEHANDLE)`

  Closes the file, socket, or pipe associated with `FILEHANDLE`.

  Example: `close(FILE);`

- `chop(LIST¦VARIABLE)`

  Chops off the last character of a string, `VARIABLE`, or the last character of each item in `LIST` and returns the chopped value.

  Examples:

  `chop($scalar);`

  `chop(@array);`

- `'unix command'` (these quotes are actually backtick characters)

  Executes the text within the backticks as if it were typed at the system command prompt. Example:

  `$date = 'date';`

- `&SUBROUTINE(LIST)`

  Executes a subroutine, which returns the value of the last expression evaluated. Subroutines can accept arguments through `LIST`. Subroutines are global and can be defined anywhere in the script, even in another file (Perl module). Example:

  `&printname($first, $last);`

Flow of Control Statements

- `if .. elsif .. else`

  Examples:

  ```
  if (Expression) { Block }
  if (Expression) { Block } else { Block }
  if (Expression) { Block } elsif (Expression) { Block } else { Block }
  ```

- `unless construct`

  Examples:

  ```
  unless (Expression) { Block }
  unless (Expression) { Block } else { Block }
  unless (Expression) { Block } elsif (Expression) { Block } else { Block }
  ```

- `while loop`

  Example:

  `while (Expression) { Block }`

- `until loop`

  Example:

  `until (Expression) { Block }`

◆ do ... until loop

Example:

```
do { Block } until (Expression)
```

◆ do ... while loop

Example:

```
do { Block } while (Expression)
```

◆ for loop

Example:

```
for (Expression1; Expression2; Expression3) { Block }
```

> **Note:** Expression1 is used to set the initial value of the loop variables. Expression2 is used to test whether the loop should continue or stop. Expression3 is used to update the loop variables.

◆ foreach loop

Example:

```
foreach VARIABLE (ARRAY) { Block }
```

> **Note:** VARIABLE is local to the foreach loop and regains its former value when the loop terminates. If VARIABLE is missing, the special scalar $ is used.

Perl Modules

A Perl module is a set of functions grouped into a package that deal with a similar problem. You can use module functions in a Perl script by telling your script the name of the module with the use command. For example, use CGI;.

One example of a Perl module is the CGI.pm module. This file includes functions that provide an easy interface to CGI programming, enabling you to write HTML forms and easily deal with the results. For more information about CGI.pm, visit its home page at http://www-genome.wi.mit.edu/ftp/pub/software/WWW/cgi_docs.html. This page has information about the functions available and examples of how they are used.

Executing the Script

To run a Perl program, you can type the script name at the command prompt. Here are several example commands that you can use for debugging scripts:

◆ To check syntax:

```
perl -c scriptname
```

◆ To generate warnings:

```
perl -w scriptname
```

◆ To check syntax and generate warnings:

```
perl -cw scriptname
```

◆ To run the debugger:

```
perl -d scriptname
```

Web Site Statistical Analysis

Two of the most common uses of Perl by Webmasters are statistical analysis and forms processing. This section and the next present two Perl CGI scripts that prove very useful for these purposes.

As a Webmaster, you want to know who's coming to your site, how often, and what they are doing there. To accomplish this, the examples use the Perl programming language interpreter and the WWWusage CGI application.

Actually, before getting into Perl, let's mention a very interesting tool that can help you chart your Web site statistics without requiring any custom programming. It will analyze your Web page usage based on your server log files. A company called Logical Design Solutions has invented a cool program called WebTrac. You can download the free program and give it a try. Visit their home page at `http://www.lds.com`.

WWWusage

WWWusage is a Perl script written by Richard Graessler (`rickg@pobox.com`) to analyze and calculate monthly usage statistics from log files generated by World Wide Web servers. This application is designed for use with Windows NT. Once the script is customized for your Web server (which is easy to do), WWWusage should work on any Windows NT system with NT Perl 5.001 installed.

WWWusage will generate a new statistics page each month and the output of WWWusage is easy to read. For more information about WWWusage and to download a free copy, please visit Rick's Web page. It also contains many other interesting resources and Perl scripts for Windows NT:

`http://rick.wzl.rwth-aachen.de/rick/`

> **Tip:** Remember that some Web server statistics tools require the Web server to close the log files before the files can be analyzed. This is true of IIS 2.0.

WWWusage will process HTTP access log files in the Common Logfile Format and output monthly statistics in HTML format ready for publishing on the Web. It creates reports on any or all of the following:

◆ Transfers by HTTP method (total)

◆ Transfers for each status code (total)

◆ Daily transmission statistics (total)

◆ Weekday transmission statistics (total)

◆ Hourly transmission statistics (total)

◆ Transfers by client domain—top level (top xx and total)

◆ Transfers by client domain—second level (top xx and total)

◆ Transfers by client subdomain (top xx and total)

◆ Transfers by client host (top xx and total)

◆ Transfers by file type (top xx and total)

◆ Transfers by file name (top xx and total)

◆ Total transfers to each remote identifier (total)

WWWusage does not make any changes to the access log files or write any files in the server directories (with the exception of two output HTML files per month).

Log File Formats

Gone are the days when every Web server used its own proprietary log file format (but for a few notable exceptions). Numerous formats made it very difficult to write general statistics collectors. Therefore, the Web community designed the Common Logfile Format, which will soon become the default, if it hasn't already.

The Common Logfile Format

Here is the format of each line in the logfile, followed by an explanation of each field:

```
remotehost rfc931 authuser [date] "request" status bytes
```

◆ remotehost—Remote host name (or IP number if DNS host name is not available, or if DNS Lookup of HTTPS server is disabled).

◆ rfc931—The remote logname of the user.

◆ Authuser—The user name by which the user has authenticated himself, or "-" if not available.

◆ [date]—Date and time of the request with time zone offset from GMT at end: [DD/Mon/YYYY:hh:mm:ss [+/-]HHMM].

- ◆ "request"—The request line exactly as it came from the client, using the format: "method file httpversion."
  - ◆ Method—Method can be GET, HEAD, POST, or none.
  - ◆ File—File contains the full file path and arguments of the requested file. The file path is either relative to the disk root or relative to the HTTPS document root.
  - ◆ Httpversion—Httpversion specifies the version number of HTTP specification, for example, "HTTP/1.0" for the current spec.
- ◆ status—The HTTP status code returned to the client (three digits) or "-" if not available.
- ◆ bytes—The content-length of the document transferred in bytes or "-" if not available.

> **Note:** Microsoft IIS does not write HTTP logfiles using the Common Logfile Format. However, IIS does include a simple command-line utility which can convert from the IIS format to the Common Logfile Format. You can then use WWWusage to process the results.

Some Web servers use a single log file. Some servers write logfiles which can be closed automatically (sometimes called *cycled*), others must be closed manually. Others have a single log file for each day, so that there is no need to cycle the log file.

Other Perl Statistic Scripts

Before we get to WWWusage, let's take a quick look at some other great Perl analysis scripts for HTTP log files. Just check Appendix C, "Resources for the Windows NT Webmaster," or search Yahoo for CGI or Perl.

- ◆ Roy Fielding's wwwstat. Works with Common Logfile Format under NT Perl, if some minor modifications are done to remove some UNIX NCSA HTTPD specifics.
- ◆ Steven Nemetz's iisstat. Works with both the Common and EMWAC Logfile Format under NT Perl.
- ◆ Nick Phillips's musage. Written for NT HTTPS and Perl. It works great with the EMWAC Logfile Format, but there are still some minor bugs with the Common Logfile Format.

Configuring WWWusage

Listing 29.1 shows the configuration section from the top of the file wwwusage.pl. All you need to do is read the comments in the source code to determine the modifications you need to make to customize the program for your site.

Listing 29.1. This excerpt of WWWusage shows the lines that can be modified for your Web site.

```perl
#!/cgi32/perl
#
# WWWusage - Perl script to calculate monthly usage statistics
# from log files
# generated by the Windows NT World Wide Web servers (https).
#
# Copyright (c) 1995 Richard Graessler (rickg@pobox.com)
#
# For the latest version, DOCUMENTATION and LICENSE AGREEMENT see
#   <URL: http://pobox.com/~rickg/rickg/wwwusage/wwwusage.html>
#
#     This program is provided "AS IS", WITHOUT ANY WARRANTY
#     (see License Agreement)
#
# Bug reports, comments, questions and suggestions are welcome.
# Please mail to
# rickg@pobox.com with the "subject: WWWusage" but please
# check first that you have the latest version.
#
# CREDITS:
#
# There are some other Perl logfile analyse scripts on the net:
#  Roy Fielding's wwwstat
#    <URL: http://www.ics.uci.edu/WebSoft/wwwstat/>
#  Nick Phillips's musage
#    <URL: http://www.blpes.lse.ac.uk/misc/musage.htm>
#  Steven Nemetz's iisstat
#    <URL:
# ftp://ftp.ccmail.com/pub/utils/InternetServices/iisstat/iisstat.html>
# Looking into these scripts helped me to write this script and
# there might be still some parts based on them.
#
# Requires timelocal.pl and getopts.pl which are included in the Perl
# disribution package.
#
# Thanks to the authors!
#


#####################################################################
#  Program internal variables (please do not change!)
#####################################################################
$VERNAME = 'WWWusage'; # Program name
$VERSION = '0.99';     # Program version
$VERDATE = '26 December 1995';  # Program version date


#####################################################################
#  Present setting
#####################################################################
# In Perl for Windows NT you can use forward slash (/) or double
# backslash (\\) in pathnames (e.g. C:/LOGS/ or c:\\LOGS\\). File
# and path names could
# be absolute(e.g. C:/LOGS/) or relative to current directory
# (e.g. ./LOGS/).

# hostname of www server (HTTPS)
$ServerName = 'rick.wzl.rwth-aachen.de';
```

```
# flag - specifies the logfile format
# 1 : common log file format,
# 0 : EMWAC HTTPS
$LogFormat = 1;

# file containing the country-codes to allow expansion from domain
# to country name
$CountryCodeFile = 'C:/www/alibaba/admin/country-codes.txt';

# Pattern used to recognise log files translated into a Perl regular
# expression, e.g. ('.+\.log' for *.log), ('ac.+\.log' for ac*.log).
# If your HTTPS have only one logfile simply set "access.log"
# Note: If you have more than one logfile the script assumes that the
#       alphabetical order of the filenames is the same as the
#       chronological order
$LogFilePattern = '.+\.log';

# directory containing external configuration files
# (without ending slash!)
$ConfigFileDir = 'c:/www/alibaba/admin';

# directory containing log files (without ending slash!)
$LogFileDir = 'c:/www/alibaba/logs/HTTP';

# filename (incl. path and arguments if necessary) of shell for
# unpacking archives. Note: If you use this feature please note
# that the archive contains only the logfiles for a single month
# and that you didn't analyse archives and normal logfile at
#       the same time.
$Gzip = 'gunzip -c';        # Gzip Format: *.gz, *.Z
$Zip  = 'unzip -p';         # Zip Format:  *.zip
$Tar  = 'tar -x -O -f';     # Tar Format:  *.tar

# WWWusage directory to write statistics reports
# (without ending slash!)
$OutPutDir = 'c:/www/alibaba/htmldocs/usage/wwwusage';

# WWWusage Error file name including path
$ErrorFile = 'c:/www/alibaba/admin/WWWusage.log';

# Filename without extension for HTML main output file
# (e.g. "WWWusage", "index" or "default")
$MenuFile = "index";

# Extension for HTML output files
$HTMLextension = "html";

# show top nn statistics in main output, the detail output
# contains all (e.g. 30)
$Top = 30;

# format of the output HTML page (0 = <PRE></PRE>, 1 <TABLE></TABLE>
$HTMLOutput = 0;

# flags - disable if you don't want that output
$DoDomain = 1;          # Transfers by Client Domain (top level)
$DoDomain2 = 1;         # Transfers by Client Domain (second level)
$DoSubdomain = 1;       # Transfers by Client Subdomain
```

continues

Listing 29.1. continued

```
$DoHost = 1;          # Transfers by Client Host
$DoFileType = 1;      # Transfers by File Type
$DoFileName = 1;      # Transfers by File Name (URL)
$DoHTTPSMethod = 1;   # Transmission Statistics HTTPS Method
$DoStatusCode = 1;    # Transmission Statistics Status Code
$DoDaily = 1;         # Transmission Statistics Day
$DoWeekdaily = 1;     # Transmission Statistics Weekday
$DoHourly = 1;        # Transmission Statistics Hour
$DoIdent = 2;         # Transfers by Remote Identifer
# NOTE for $DoIdent: For security reasons, you should not
# publish to the web any report that lists the Remote Identifiers
# (rfc931 or authuser):
# 0 : no display, 1 : real user name, 2 : cookie name

# flag - disable if you don't want to create the detail statistics
# to save time
$DoDetail = 1;

# flag - disable if you don't want to create links to your
# accessed pages
$FileNameHREF=0;

# user specific parameters for the TABLE tag
$HTMLTable = 'Border=2 CELLPADDING=8 CELLSPACING=5';

# user specific backgrounds for all returns. Here you can set
# all elements of the body tag which can appear between "<BODY ... >
# in HTML format.
$HTMLBackground =
  'BACKGROUND="/gif/bg0.gif" BGCOLOR="#63637b" TEXT="#ffffff" '
 .'LINK="#00ffff" ALINK="#ff0000" VLINK="#ffff00" HRCOLOR="#ff0000" ';

# user specific header for all returned HTML pages in HTML format
@HTMLHeader = (
 '<P><CENTER><A HREF="/image/ntrick.map"><IMG BORDER=0 HSPACE=10 ',
 'ALIGN=MIDDLE SRC="/gif/ntrick.gif" '
 'ALT="Rick\'s Windows NT Info Center"',
 ' ISMAP WIDTH=550 HEIGHT=44></A></CENTER></P>',
 '<H1><CENTER>World Wide Web Server Usage Statistic</CENTER></H1><HR>'
);

# user specific footer for all returned HTML pages in HTML formats
@HTMLAddress = (
    '<HR><HR><A NAME="Bottom"></A><A HREF="/image/address.map" >',
    '<IMG BORDER=0 HSPACE=10 ALIGN=MIDDLE SRC="/gif/address.gif" ',
    'ALT="Addressbar" ISMAP WIDTH=293 HEIGHT=31></A>'
);

# flag - disable if you don't want a detailed output on the console
$VerboseMode = 1;

# flag - disable if you don't want to see the skiped lines of
#  the logfiles on the console
$ShowSkippedLines = 1;

# flag - disable if you don't want to show unresolved addresses
$ShowUnresolved = 1;
```

```
# file containing DNS names
# (will be created and updated by the script)
$DnsNamesFile = 'c:/www/alibaba/admin/dns-names.txt';

# flag - to set the DNS lookup. Note: DNS lookup needs much time
#        and slow up the execution of WWWusage
# 0 : disable if you don't want to look up dnsname if ip address
# is given
# 1 : if you don't want to look up new dnsname but used the
# saved dnsnames
# 2 : if you want to look up new and old unresloved dnsname
# 3 : if you want only to look up new dnsname
$LookupDnsNames = 3;

# flag - disable if you don't want to sort the host list to save time
$SortHostList = 0;

# flag - disable if you don't want to encode filenames
$UrlEncode = 0;

# flag - disable if you don't want to detect on disk if filename is a
#        directoryor file. If flag is set, you should run the script on
#        your HTTPS machine
$FileCheck = 0;

# flag - enable it if you https automatically add a "/" to
#        slashless dirs (1 for EMWAC HTTPS, Netscape - 0 for Alibaba)
$DirWorksWithSlash = 0;

# real directory name of document root of the www server
# (without ending Slash!)
$DocumentRoot = 'c:/www/alibaba/htmldocs';

# list of configured "default/index" filename(s) for your HTTPS
@DefaultHTML = ('index.html','index.sht','default.htm');

# flag - enable to convert all filenames (URLs) to lower case
$FileNamesToLowerCase = 1;

# time zone information. Only necessary for EMWAC log file format.
# if not set it will be computed. Format: "+0100" or "-1100"
# $TimeZone = "+0100";

# exclude filter: optional list of IP addresses to ignore, please
# include ipnummer as well as dns name(s) in the list! IPnumber will
# be checked forward, DNSnames will be checked backward. Perl
# expressions are possible.
# (e.g. "137.226" for "137.226.*.*", "rwth-aachen.de" for
# "*.wzl.rwth-aachen.de")
# @IgnoreHost = ('137.226.92.10','rick.wzl.rwth-aachen.de');

# include filter: optional list of IP addresses to focus on, please
# include ipnummer as well as dns name(s) in the list! IPnumber will
# be checked forward, DNSnames will be checked backward. Perl
# expressions are possible.
# (e.g. "137.226" for "137.226.*.*", "wzl.rwth-aachen.de" for
# "*.wzl.rwth-aachen.de")
# @FocusOnHost = ('137.226.','wzl.rwth-aachen.de');
```

continues

Listing 29.1. continued

```perl
# exclude filter: optional list of paths/files to ignore. Paths
# will be checked forward from the beginning of the url filename.
# Perl expressions are possible.
# @IgnorePath = ('/gif/','/images/');

# include filter: optional list of paths/files to focus on. Paths
# will be checked forward from the beginning of the url filename.
# Perl expressions are possible.
# @FocusOnPath = ('/rick/');

# exclude filter: optional list of file extensions to ignore.
# Extension will be checked backward from the beginning of the
# url filename. Perl expressions are possible.
@IgnoreExt = ('gif','jpeg','jpg');

# include filter: optional list of file extensions to focus on.
# Extension will be checked backward from the beginning of the
# url filename. Perl expressions are possible.
# @FocusOnExt = ('.htm','html');

# Alias list for virtual paths.
# Format: '/aliasname/' => 'drive:/path/'
# Key: alias or pathnames relative to HTTPS document root.
# Value: pathnames relative to disk root.
# Do not include the $DocumentRoot (with its value '/'). This array
# does not make sense with EMWAC HTTPS because it doesn't
# support alias.
%WWWAlias = (
'/ALIBABA/', 'C:/WWW/ALIBABA/DOCS/',
'/ALIPROXY/', 'C:/WWW/ALIBABA/HTML/',
'/ICONS/', 'C:/WWW/ALIBABA/ICONS/',
'/IMAGE/', 'C:/WWW/ALIBABA/CONF/',
'/COUNTER/', 'C:/WWW/ALIBABA/COUNTER/',
'/CFDOCS/', 'C:/WWW/ALIBABA/CFUSION/CFDOCS/',
'/PERFORM/', 'C:/WWW/ALIBABA/PERFORM/DOCS/',
'/RICK/PERFORM/', 'C:/WWW/ALIBABA/PERFORM/OUTPUT/',
'/CGI-BIN/', 'C:/WWW/ALIBABA/CGI-BIN/',
'/CGIDOS/', 'C:/WWW/ALIBABA/CGI-BIN/',
'/CGI-32/', 'C:/WWW/ALIBABA/CGI-BIN/',
'/CGI32/', 'C:/WWW/ALIBABA/CGI-BIN/',
'/CGI-SHL/', 'C:/WWW/ALIBABA/CGI-BIN/',
'/WINCGI/', 'C:/WWW/ALIBABA/WINCGI/',
'/WINBIN/', 'C:/WWW/ALIBABA/WINCGI/',
'/DLLALIAS/', 'C:/WWW/ALIBABA/CGIDLL/',
'/ALIPROXY/', 'C:/WWW/ALIBABA/HTML/',
);

# List of used file types and its extensions. The extensions must
# be written in regular Perl expression. If @FileTypesSort is
# given it determine the search order.
%FileTypes = (
    'CGI Scripts', '(\/cgi32\/|\/cgi-32\/|\/cgi-shl\/)',
    'DOS CGI Scripts', '(\/cgi-bin\/|\/cgidos\/)',
    'WinCGI Scripts', '(\/wincgi\/|\/winbin\/)',
    'DllCGI Scripts', '\/dllalias\/',
    'Images', '\.(bmp|gif|xbm|jpg|jpeg)$',
    'Movies', '\.(mpg|mov|scm)$',
```

```perl
        'Archive Files', '\.(gz¦z¦zip¦tar)$',
        'HTML Files', '\.(htm¦html)$',
        'Imagemaps', '($\/image\/¦\.map$)',
        'Server Side Includes', '\.(sht¦shtm¦shtml)$',
        'Text Files', '\.txt$',
        'Binary Executables', '\.(com¦exe)$',
        'Script Executables', '\.(pl¦sh¦cmd¦bat)$',
        'Readme Files', '\/README.*$',
        'Directory Listings', '\/$',
        'Java Applets', '\.CLASS$',
);

@FileTypesSort = (
        'HTML files',
        'Images',
        'CGI Scripts',
        'Server side includes',
        'Java Applets',
        'Text files',
        'Directory listings',
        'DOS CGI Scripts',
        'WinCGI Scripts',
        'DllCGI Scripts',
        'Movies',
        'Archive files',
        'Imagemaps',
        'Binary Executables',
        'Script Executables',
        'Readme files',
);

# Response Codes taken from <draft-ieft-http-v10-spec-01.ps>,
# August 3,1995 Normally you don't need to change!
%StatusCode = (
        '200', '200 OK',
        '201', '201 Created',
        '202', '202 Accepted',
        '203', '203 Non-Authoritative Information',
        '204', '204 No Content',
        '300', '300 Multiple Choices',
        '301', '301 Moved Permanently',
        '302', '302 Moved Temporarily',
        '303', '303 See Other',
        '304', '304 Not Modified',
        '400', '400 Bad Request',
        '401', '401 Unauthorized',
        '402', '402 Payment Required',
        '403', '403 Forbidden',
        '404', '404 Not found',
        '405', '405 Method Not Allowed',
        '406', '406 None Acceptable',
        '407', '407 Proxy Authorization Required',
        '408', '408 Request Timeout',
        '409', '409 Conflict',
        '410', '410 Gone',
        '411', '411 Authorization Refused',
        '500', '500 Internal Server Errors',
        '501', '501 Not implemented',
```

continues

Listing 29.1. continued

```
    '502', '502 Bad Gateway',
    '503', '503 Service Unavailable',
    '504', '504 Gateway Timeout',
);

############################################################################
# END CONFIG
############################################################################
```

CGI Forms Handling with Perl

The WWW MailTo & CommentTo gateway is a Windows NT HTTP CGI Perl script. (Whew!) It enables you to send a message by SMTP and/or to log the message to a local file. You can check Rick's Web site for the latest and greatest (along with other resources and documentation) at this URL:

```
http://rick.wzl.rwth-aachen.de/rick/
```

Using the HTTP GET method, the script creates a predefined or user-supplied fill-out form with a self-reference by the action tag. After the form is submitted, the script will be executed a second time by the POST method to create the mail and send it by SMTP if mail is enabled, or save it in the comment file if comment is enabled.

The features depend on the configuration. The script can do any of the following:

◆ Send mail by SMTP

◆ Save mail in a comment file

◆ Load a follow-up URL to the client browser automatically when mailing is done

◆ Log all messages in a mail logfile

◆ Log all errors in an error logfile

◆ Log and append environment variable settings to mail or comment file

◆ Test the correct execution of mail-sending operations

◆ Notify the user if mail sending fails

◆ Create user-specific form files that are Perl scripts

◆ Use predefined and user-defined form fields

Installation

You need to put `mailto.pl` into your `scripts` or `cgi-bin` directory. Some HTTP servers use a different CGI directory for DOS CGI, Win32/NT CGI, or WinCGI binaries. If so, put the scripts in your Win32/NT CGI binaries directory, for example, the CGI32 directory. If your HTTP server does not support ALIAS, it must be in your WWW data directory or one of its subdirectories.

Now would be a good time to install Blat from the CD-ROM, if you have not done so already. (See Chapter 8, "Serving E-mail via TCP/IP," for more information about installing Blat.)

To install the WWW MailTo&CommentTo Gateway, you only need to modify the configuration as described in the following section titled "Configuring the Script." Beyond the simple configuration, the main issue is how to call it properly. This depends on how your HTTP server executes scripts.

If your HTTP server can execute scripts directly (for example, the Alibaba Web server), you can use HTML such as this:

```
<A HREF="http://rick.wzl.rwth-aachen.de/cgi32/mailto.pl">
```

If your HTTP server must execute a program binary (for example, the EMWAC HTTPS), you can use HTML such as this:

```
<A HREF="http://rick.wzl.rwth-aachen.de:8001/cgi32/perl.exe?cgi32/mailto.pl">
```

If you are unfamiliar with any part of the syntax of the above URL, please refer to Chapter 5, "What You Need to Know About HTML," for a refresher course. The question mark character is a special CGI marker indicating the start of the command-line arguments to be passed in the QUERY_STRING variable. (See Chapter 19.)

Alternatively, you can use Rick's CGI2Shell Gateway. In this case, you could do the following:

```
<A HREF="http://rick.wzl.rwth-aachen.de:8001/cgi32/cgi2perl.exe/
➥cgi32/mailto.pl?">
```

The last way is much easier if you want to specify parameters. See the following "Usage" section for more information about parameters.

Usage

First of all, you must create an HTML tag for WWW MailTo&CommentTo Gateway in your HTML document, which calls the script by the GET method. When called by the GET method, the script displays a standard e-mail form. Here is one example of the HTML code:

```
<A HREF="http://rick.wzl.rwth-aachen.de/cgi32/mailto.pl">Mailto</A>
<A HREF="/cgi32/mailto.pl">Mailto</A>
```

You can also include command-line parameters in the HTML tag where parameter is source, or one or more pairs of variables and values each separated by one ampersand. The variable and its value are separated by =. Note that all parameters must be HTML-encoded. That means that all spaces are replaced with plus signs (+). Also note that plus signs must then be specified in hexadecimal with %2B. Other HTML-reserved characters must also be encoded similarly.

The source parameter returns the script source code if source viewing is enabled and source is the only parameter. The pairs of variables and values could be all reserved variables except from and HTTPpage. These variables can be supplied in the GET request when linking to the mailto script. If you simply want your mail address to be given in the mail form as the default value, make your HTML look something like this:

```
<A HREF="/cgi32/mailto.pl?to=rickG@pobox.com">
```

If you want your default subject to be "This is a subject!", give the subject variable separated by an ampersand. For example:

```
<A HREF="/cgi32/mailto.pl?to=rickG@pobox.com&subject=This+is+a+subject!">
```

Notice that the subject must be URL-encoded.

Reserved Variables

Thereare several reserved variables that the script will check for explicitly.

◆ to—Defines a default mail address to send mail to. If mail is restricted to predefined e-mail addresses by the variable %defto (see the section on "Setting Default Values") and this address is allowed, it will be the default address.

◆ cc—Defines the carbon copy mail addresses (separated by commas). If mail is restricted to predefined e-mail addresses by the variable %defto (see the section on "Setting Default Values"), it will be disabled.

◆ From—Defines the mail address of the sender. If no value is given, the script tries to determine the address by looking for the CGI environment variables REMOTE_USER, HTTP_FROM, and REMOTE_HOST.

◆ Copyself—If the Copy to Self check box in the form is checked, the sender's e-mail address (from variable) will be added to cc.

◆ Subject—Defines the subject for the mail.

◆ Body—Defines the body text of the mail. There can be more than one body variable; they will be concatenated.

◆ Followup—Defines a followup URL to retrieve after mail is sent. If this variable is undefined, a default confirmation and "thank you" message will be sent to the client.

◆ Creator—Defines a default creator message. If this variable is set, the message given by "creator" will be added at the end of each mail.

◆ formfile—Defines the filename of a user-specific form file that will be used instead of the standard form. Because of security, the path and extension of the form file are defined.

◆ HTTPpage—Source URL, from which the mailto script is started. It will be automatically detected if your HTTP server supports the HTTP_REFERER CGI variable.

All of these variables (except `from` and `HTTPpage`) could be set to default values, which can protect against overwriting. All of these variables can also be set at the command line following the "?" (which will then be inserted into the CGI environment variable `QUERY_STRING`).

These reserved variables have a special meaning for the script and must be set by either the Webmaster or the user. With the exception of the `to` and `from` variables, all variables are set to default values if they are undefined.

For easy questionnaires, all other CGI variables will be logged after the body portion—regardless of whether the values are hidden or part of the fill-out form. Remember that the `GET` method is limited on the number of characters passed. The variable and its value are separated by `=`, different variables/values by `&`. Spaces are replaced with `+`; plus signs and other HTML-reserved characters must then be specified in hexadecimal with %2B. Every non-reserved CGI variable will be logged after the mail body in variable/value pairs. To use the user-defined variables, you need to first create a user-defined form.

Configuring the Script

Before starting to use the script, you must configure it. All configurable variables are in the first section of the script, as follows:

- ◆ `$mailprogram`—Filename of mail utility. If it is not in the path, you must specify the whole path.

- ◆ `$mailfile`—Location (including filename) of temporary mail file. If this variable is set, mail will be sent by SMTP.

- ◆ `$commentfile`—Location (including filename) of comment file. If this variable is set, mail will be written to the local comment file.

- ◆ `$saveenv`—Save environment setting. If this variable is set to 1, the environment variables will be saved to the comment file. If this variable is set to 2, the environment variables will be saved to the comment file and appended to the end of the mail file.

- ◆ `$timezone`—Set this to your local time zone (for example "MET" or "GMT+1").

- ◆ `$logfile`—Location (including filename) of application log file. If this variable is not set, no logging is done.

- ◆ `$errorfile`—Location (including filename) of error file. If this variable is not set, no error logging is done.

- ◆ `$source`—Location (including filename) of script file. If this variable is not set, source viewing is not possible.

- ◆ `$formdir`—Directory for form files. It must end with "/" or "\\".

- ◆ `$formext`—Extension for form file.

- ◆ `$HTTPsource`—Location of script file in HTTP format. The variable will be detected automatically if it is not set and your Web server supports direct script execution.

◆ `$libfiles`—Location of Perl libraries.

◆ `$ContactHTMLtag`—Contact URL for server/script problems in HTML format.

◆ `$HTMLBackground`—User-specific backgrounds for all returns. Here, you can set all elements of the `<BODY>` tag, which can appear between `<BODY ... >` in HTML format.

◆ `@HTMLHeader`—User-specific header for all returned HTML pages in HTML format.

◆ `@HTMLAddress`—User-specific footer for all returned HTML pages in HTML format.

Setting Default Values

You can set default values to all reserved variables (except `from` and `HTTPpage`) by configuring the default values with the `$def{}` variables in the script. All of these variables could also be found in the first section of the script. If the variable `$default` is set, these variables are fixed. They cannot be overwritten by given parameters to the script tag in an HTML page or the user input when filling out the form. If `$default` is not set, these default variables are used only if the reserved variables are not set by command-line parameters or user form input. For example:

◆ `$default`—If this variable is set, the default value (see `$def{}` variables in the following section) will be used and cannot be overwritten through script parameters or CGI input by `GET` method proceeding. If this variable is not set, the default values are used only if there are no other values.

◆ `$def{'to'}`—Default value for variable `to`.

◆ `$def{'cc'}`—Default value for variable `cc`.

◆ `$def{'copyself'}`—Default value for variable `copyself` (value 0 or 1).

◆ `$def{'subject'}`—Default value for variable `subject`.

◆ `$def{'body'}`—Default value for variable `body`.

◆ `$def{'followup'}`—Default value for variable `followup`.

◆ `$def{'form'}`—Default value for variable `form`. This is a form filename without path and extension.

◆ `$def{'creator'}`—Default value for variable `creator`.

Restricted Mail Addresses

You can restrict mail addresses to one address if you set the `def{'to'}` variable to an e-mail address and prevent overwriting of this value by setting the `$default`.

You can also restrict the to mail addresses to certain addresses by setting the `%defto` variable array. This variable can be found in the first section of the script. For this feature, you must run a separate copy of the script because the standard form always includes a selection list for the addresses.

User-Defined Forms

You can create your own forms without modifying the script. You must define form files, which are also small Perl scripts. You can create two kinds of form files. The first will be executed when the main script is executed with the GET method. It must create the form. If the second form exists, it will be executed when the main script is executed with the POST method (after the user submitted the mail). It is intended for preparing the mail. To use the form file feature, the first (GET) form must exist. The second (POST) is optional.

You can specify the name of the form with the predefined variable $defto{form}=form name inside the script or with the parameter form=form name. Form name is the filename of the form without the path and the file extension. The path, the GET, and the form extension must be configured in the script. If they are not configured, the forms will not be executed. This is for security reasons. The form files will be executed with the eval function of Perl. Therefore, use a separate path for the form files. If you don't do this, other files could also be executed!

Inside your form files, you can use all the variables and subroutines of the main Perl script. You can overwrite variables from the main script, for example $commentfile. You can even write your own mailto application.

CGI Form Handling in Perl

As mentioned before, another excellent use for Perl is writing code to manage the Common Gateway Interface (CGI) forms, which have become the mainstay of the World Wide Web for interactive communication.

cgi-lib.pl is a simple Perl library designed to make writing CGI scripts in Perl easy. Many Perl CGI scripts that you find on the Web use cgi-lib.pl. See Listing 29.2 for an example.

Listing 29.2. A minimal Perl application using cgi-lib.pl.

```
#!/usr/local/bin/perl
# minimal.cgi
# Copyright (C) 1995 Steven E. Brenner
# $Header: /cys/people/brenner/http/docs/web/RCS/minimal.cgi,v 1.2
#1995/04/07 21:36:29 brenner Exp $
# This is the minimalist script to demonstrate the use of
# the cgi-lib.pl library -- it needs only 7 lines
# --
# This is NOT intended to be a "typical" script
# Most importantly, the <form> key should normally have parameters
#like
#   <form method=POST action="minimal.cgi">
require "cgi-lib.pl";
```

continues

Listing 29.2. continued

```
if (&ReadParse(*input)) {
   print &PrintHeader, &PrintVariables(%input);
} else {
   print &PrintHeader,'<form><input type="submit">Data: <input name=
"myfield">';
}
```

Perl 5

Perl 5 adds many features to the language that space precludes full coverage of in this short introduction. Some of the more noteworthy enhancements are references, object-oriented extensions, general cleanup, support for modules, and importing.

Like any programming language, Perl will take some time to master. Alas, this is not a subject I can completely cover in this book. However, I can give you some information about where to look. This information will also tell you how you can quickly use existing Perl applications. The first thing you might want to do is check out these three text files that come with Perl:

◆ `relnotes.txt`—For general information about Perl for NT and how Perl for NT differs from Perl for UNIX.

◆ `status.txt`—For information on what features are supported.

◆ `registry.txt`—For information on using the registry access features.

To learn more about Perl, try the University of Florida's Perl Archive at `http://www.cis.ufl.edu/perl/`. Users in the UK might like to try something closer to home, such as the NEXOR Ltd Perl Page at `http://pubweb.nexor.co.uk/public/perl/perl.html`.

Here are a few other Perl resources on the Net; the last one consists of a few newsgroups dedicated to Perl topics.

`http://www.metronet.com/perlinfo/perl5.html`

`http://www.perl.com/perl/faq/`

`comp.lang.perl`

Summary

It has been a very educational experience writing this book. I hope it has been, and will continue to be, as useful for you as it has been fun to write.

You have chosen a very exciting time to be involved with Windows NT and Web technologies. I wish you continued success on your Windows NT Intranet.

PART VI

Appendixes

HTML & CGI Quick Reference

—by Lah Wah Ooi and Billy Barron

HTML

This reference guide marks the origins of all tags. Most browsers fully implement the HTML 2.0 tags correctly, which are marked in this guide as HTML 2.0. If a tag is marked as HTML 3.0, it's in the 3.0 release of HTML. However, the HTML 3.0 release isn't finalized and is subject to change. We used the latest draft available, which is dated March 28, 1995. Apparently, this single draft will eventually be a series of separate documents that will as a whole make up the HTML 3.0 specification.

> **Note:** At the time this book was going to print, HTML 3.2 was just announced by the World Wide Web Consortium. Unfortunately, it is too late to be covered in this appendix, but you can be pretty certain that it is compatible with HTML 3.0 features we describe here.

Netscape HTML Extensions means that the tag was invented by Netscape. Netscape Navigator might or might not be the only browser that supports these particular tags. *Sun* means that the tag was invented by Sun Microsystems for use with Java. Currently, HotJava and Netscape Navigator are the only browsers that support them. Netscape has created its own JavaScript-specific tags that currently can only be used by Netscape Navigator. More browsers probably will be available before the end of 1996. *Internet Explorer* means that Microsoft invented this tag and it's currently supported only by Microsoft's Internet Explorer.

Also, this is a quick reference guide, so only commonly used tags and attributes are listed. We have also added a few recently created tags that we expect will be popular in the future.

For more information on other HTML tags, see the following:

◆ Client-Side Image Map Draft
`http://ds.internic.net/internet-drafts/draft-seidman-clientsideimagemap-02.txt`

◆ HTML 2.0
`http://www.w3.org/pub/WWW/MarkUp/html-spec/`

◆ HTML 3.0
`Drafthttp://www.w3.org/pub/WWW/MarkUp/html3/CoverPage.html`

◆ Internet Explorer Extensions
`http://www.microsoft.com/windows/ie/ie20html.htm`

◆ Netscape Extensions to HTML 2.0
`http://home.netscape.com/assist/net_sites/html_extensions.html`

◆ Netscape Extensions to HTML 3.0
`http://home.netscape.com/assist/net_sites/html_extensions_3.html`

◆ Netscape Frames Extensions
`http://home.netscape.com/assist/net_sites/frames.html`

◆ Netscape JavaScript Extensions
`http://home.netscape.com/eng/mozilla/Gold/handbook/javascript/`

Special Characters

The following are the commonly used special characters. The full list can be found at `http://www.w3.org/hypertext/WWW/MarkUp/html-spec/html-spec_13.html`.

&	&amp
<	&lt
>	&gt
"	&quot

Structure

These tags define the structure of an HTML document. Although most browsers don't require the use of these tags, they're recommended for ensuring that HTML documents are always parsed correctly.

\<html>..\</html>

Purpose: Contains the entire HTML document.

Version: HTML 2.0.

Details: These tags are used at the beginning and the end of the HTML codes in a particular page.

\<head>..\</head>

Purpose: Contains other tags that describe the document in general.

Version: HTML 2.0.

Details: These tags should always come before \<BODY> and \<FRAMESET> tags.

\<title>..\</title>

Purpose: The title of the document goes within the tags.

Version: HTML 2.0.

Details: This is usually displayed in the title bar of the Web browser. However, a few browsers don't display this tag at all. This tag is highly recommended for all HTML documents and required according to the HTML 2.0 specification, though most browsers don't enforce this requirement.

\<base>

Purpose: References the absolute URL of the document itself and goes between the \<head>..\</head> tags.

Version: HTML 2.0, TARGET is a Netscape Frame Extension.

Attributes:

HREF="URL"	Specifies the absolute URL of the document itself.
TARGET="window_name"	Specifies the frame to which links in this document will be targeted.

Details: It's useful when you view the document with a file:// URL because the \<base> tag will reference the document to the correct absolute URL of the document.

`<body>..</body>`

Purpose: Contains the actual displayable part of the HTML document.

Version: HTML 3.0, `BACKGROUND` attribute is HTML 3.0; `ALINK`, `BGCOLOR`, `LINK`, `TEXT`, and `VLINK` are Netscape HTML 3.0 Extensions; `BGPROPERTIES` is an Internet Explorer Extension.

Attributes:

`ALINK="#rrggbb"`	Specifies the color of an active link.
`BACKGROUND="URL"`	Specifies a background image.
`BGCOLOR="#rrggbb"`	Specifies the background color if there is no background image.
`BGPROPERTIES=FIXED`	Specifies the properties related to the background. `FIXED` is the only one currently available, which means that the background shouldn't be scrolled.
`LINK="#rrggbb"`	Specifies the color of a link.
`TEXT="#rrggbb"`	Specifies the color of the text.
`VLINK="#rrggbb"`	Specifies the color of a link that has been visited by the user previously.

Details: This tag should come after the `</HEAD>` tag. It should never be used in the same document as a `<FRAMESET>` tag. `"#rrggbb"` is an RGB (Red-Green-Blue) value in Hex.

Style

These are logical style tags. It is recommended that these are used instead of the hard formatting tags in the next section.

`<A>..</A>`

Purpose: Specifies an anchor.

Version: HTML 2.0, `TARGET` attribute is a Netscape Frame Extension.

Attributes:

`HREF="URL"`	Specifies a link to another document. The other document is at the URL location.
`NAME="ANCHOR-NAME"`	Creates an anchor within this document so that a URL exists that can go to this exact location in the document.
`TARGET="window_name"`	Specifies which frame in a frameset that will load the new URL.

Details: Other attributes exist but are very infrequently used. Between the opening and closing tags, text that appears on the screen and describes the anchor goes there. In the case of the HREF attribute, this text is then highlighted as a link. If two or more shapes overlap, the one with a center closest to the point clicked will be selected. Valid shape specifications are listed in the following table.

default	Specifies the default link used when a spot on an image doesn't have a defined shape.
circle x, y, r	A circle with center at x, y, with radius r.
polygon x1, y1, x2, y2, ...	A polygon with sets of x,y coordinates that are the vertices of the polygon.
rect x, y, w, h	A rectangle with an upper-left corner at x,y with width w and height h.

<address>..</address>

Purpose: Contains any kind of address.

Version: HTML 2.0.

Details: It is typically displayed in italics and may be indented also.

<blockquote>..</blockquote> and <bq>..</bq>

Purpose: Contains a block of text quoted from another source.

Version: HTML 2.0, <bq> is HTML 3.0.

Details: Typically displayed in an italic font and/or with larger right and left margins. Both <blockquote> and <bq> are valid under HTML 3.0. However, use of the first is recommended because more browsers should know about it since it is in HTML 2.0.

Purpose: Specifies a line break.

Version: HTML 2.0.

Details: There is no closing tag.

<cite>..</cite>

Purpose: Contains a citation.

Version: HTML 2.0.

Details: Typically displayed by an italic font. Use <cite> for short citations. Use <blockquote> for long citations.

`<code>..</code>`

Purpose: Contains a segment of a computer program (code).

Version: HTML 2.0.

Details: Typically displayed in a monospaced font such as Courier.

`<em>..</em>`

Purpose: Contains words that need to be emphasized.

Version: HTML 2.0.

Details: Typically displayed in italics.

`<fn>..</fn>`

Purpose: Contains a footnote.

Version: HTML 3.0.

Attribute:

> `ID="identifier"`   Places an anchor associated with the footnote so that you can link to it.

Details: The HTML 3.0 specification recommends that these be displayed as pop-up notes whenever possible.

`<hr>`

Purpose: Specifies that a horizontal line (rule) goes at this location.

Version: HTML 2.0, ALIGN, NOSHADE, SIZE, and WIDTH are Netscape HTML 2.0 extensions attributes; SRC is an HTML 3.0 attribute.

Attributes:

`ALIGN=LEFT ¦ RIGHT ¦ CENTER`	Specifies the alignment of the line if the WIDTH attribute is used.
`NOSHADE`	Make a solid colored line and don't do fancy shading.
`SIZE=n`	Specifies the thickness of the line.
`SRC="URL"`	Specifies the URL of an image to be used as the rule.

WIDTH=n ¦ n%	Specifies the length of the line in pixels or a percentage of the screen width.

Details: There is no closing tag.

<kdb>..</kdb>

Purpose: Contains text typed by a user from a keyboard.

Version: HTML 2.0.

Details: Usually displayed in a monospaced font such as Courier. Used primarily in computer user manuals.

<marquee>..</marquee>

Purpose: Contains a marquee.

Version: Internet Explorer Extensions.

Attributes:

ALIGN= BOTTOM ¦ MIDDLE ¦ TOP	Specifies the alignment of the text around the marquee.
BEHAVIOR=ALTERNATIVE ¦ SCROLL ¦ SLIDE	Specifies how the marquee will move. SCROLL will scroll the text repeatedly around the screen like a stock ticker. SLIDE will slide the text in one side until it reaches the other side and then it stops. ALTERNATIVE causes the text to bounce back and forth.
DIRECTION=LEFT ¦ RIGHT	Specifies which side of the screen the marquee enters from.
HEIGHT=n ¦ n%	Specifies the marquee height in either pixels or percent of the screen height.
HSPACE=n	Specifies a horizontal margin in pixels.
LOOP=n ¦ INFINITE	Specifies the number of loops the marquee goes through.
SCROLLAMOUNT=n	Specifies how many pixels the marquee moves per redraw.
SCROLLDELAY=n	Specifies how many milliseconds between redraws.

WIDTH=n ¦ n%	Specifies the marquee width in either pixels or percent of the screen width.
VSPACE=n	Specifies the virtual margin in pixels.

Details: If you want to do this feature, but instead of Java-aware browsers, use `tickertape.java` or `ticker.java`.

\<note>..\</note>

Purpose: Contains an important note for the reader.

Version: HTML 3.0.

Attributes:

CLASS=CAUTION ¦ NOTE ¦ WARNING	Specifies the classification of the note.
SRC="URL"	Specifies an image to use along with the note.

Details: Without a CLASS attribute, the HTML 3.0 document recommends indenting the warning.

\<p>..\</p>

Purpose: Contains a paragraph.

Version: HTML 2.0, Attributes are HTML 3.0.

Attributes:

ALIGN= CENTER ¦ JUSTIFY ¦ LEFT ¦ RIGHT	Specifies the alignment of the paragraph.
NOWRAP	Specifies that the paragraph should not be automatically word wrapped. Line breaks should only occur at \ tags.

Details: Under HTML 1.0, the \</p> wasn't required. We strongly recommend that you use the closing tag.

\<pre>..\</pre>

Purpose: Contains preformatted text.

Version: HTML 2.0.

Details: Contains text that shouldn't be reformatted automatically by the browser. The text is displayed in a monospaced font, usually Courier, by browsers.

`<q>..</q>`

Purpose: Contains a short quote.

Version: HTML 3.0.

Details: Long quotes should use `<blockquote>`.

`<samp>..</samp>`

Purpose: Contains sample characters.

Version: HTML 2.0.

Details: Usually displayed in a monospaced font such as Courier.

`<strong>..</strong>`

Purpose: Contains text that should be strongly emphasized.

Version: HTML 2.0.

Details: Usually displayed in bold.

`<sub>..</sub>`

Purpose: Contains a subscript.

Version: HTML 3.0.

`<sup>..</sup>`

Purpose: Contains a superscript.

Version: HTML 3.0.

`<var>..</var>`

Purpose: Contains a variable.

Version: HTML 2.0.

Details: Usually displayed in italics.

Formatting

HTML purists recommend trying to use the style tags described previously and to avoid these tags whenever possible because they specify a fixed layout. The problem with this is that some browsers may not be able to display these. For example, the italics tag mentioned doesn't work with Lynx.

..

Purpose: Contains bold text.

Version: HTML 2.0.

Details: If bold is unavailable, the browser may select another representation.

<big>..</big>

Purpose: Contains text that should be displayed with a big font.

Version: HTML 3.0.

Details: Netscape's <font> tag can accomplish this, but this appears to be the standard.

<blink>..</blink>

Purpose: Makes text blink.

Version: Netscape HTML 2.0 Extensions (undocumented).

Details: This is possibly the world's most hated tag as it is irritating to many users. Its use isn't recommended.

<center>..</center>

Purposes: Contains items that need centering.

Version: Netscape HTML 2.0 Extensions.

Details: This is a much hated tag by much of the HTML community that recommends using the ALIGN=center attribute on other tags instead.

<font>

Purpose: Change the font size.

Version: Netscape HTML 2.0 Extensions.

Attributes:

SIZE=n   Specifies the font size. This can also accept a relative font size change with -n or +n.

Details: Font sizes range from 1 to 7. The default is 3.

`<i>..</i>`

Purpose: Contains italicized text.

Version: HTML 2.0.

Details: If italics are unavailable, the browser may select another representation.

`<nobr>..</nobr>`

Purpose: Contains text that must be on the same line.

Version: Netscape HTML 2.0 Extensions.

Details: To be used sparingly but can be helpful at times.

`<small>..</small>`

Purpose: Contains text that should be displayed with a small font.

Version: HTML 3.0.

Details: Netscape's `<font>` tag can accomplish the same task, but this appears to be the standard.

`<tt>..</tt>`

Purpose: Contains teletype (monospaced) text.

Version: HTML 2.0.

Details: If a monospaced font is unavailable, the browser may select another representation.

`<wbr>`

Purpose: Specifies where a word break can go.

Version: Netscape HTML 2.0 Extensions.

Details: Only for use within a `<NOBR>` element. It tells the browser where it can break if it needs to.

Headings

HTML has six different sizes of headings available. Some people recommend using them progressively in your document. However, most HTML documents use them randomly without following a pattern.

<h1>..</h1>,<h2>..</h2>,<h3>..</h3>,<h4>..</h4>,<h5>..</h5>,<h6>..</h6>

Purpose: Contains headings within the text.

Version: HTML 2.0.

Details: <h1> is the largest heading size. They get progressively smaller with <h6> being the smallest.

Lists

HTML supports quite a bit of flexibility in list types. They can handle anything from a simple numbered list to building an entire dictionary.

<dl>..</dl>

Purpose: Contains a definition list.

Version: HTML 2.0.

Details: A definition list contains terms as specified by the <DT> tag and definitions by the <DD> tag.

<dd>

Purpose: Gives a definition.

Version: HTML 2.0.

Details: Usually follows a <DT> tag and a term. <DD> has no closing tag.

<dt>

Purpose: Identifies a definition term.

Version: HTML 2.0.

Details: Usually followed by a term and then a <DD> tag with a definition of that term. There is no closing tag.

`<lh>..</lh>`

Purpose: Specifies a list header.

Version: HTML 3.0.

Details: This is placed after a `<ul>` or `<dl>` tag and before the `<li>` tag.

`<li>`

Purpose: Specifies the start of a list item.

Version: HTML 2.0, TYPE and VALUE are Netscape HTML 2.0 Extensions attributes, SKIP and SRC are HTML 3.0 attributes.

Attributes:

SKIP=n	In an ordered list, specifies that n sequence numbers be skipped in the list.
uSRC="URL"	Specifies an image to use as a bullet for this item.
TYPE=xxx	Specifies a change of type in the list type. *xxx* can be any of the choices from the TYPE attributes of `<ol>` and `<ul>`.
VALUE=n	Specifies the start element number of the list. For example, to start with 4 instead of 1. For ordered lists only.

Details: `<LI>` has no closing tag.

`<ol>..</ol>`

Purpose: Contains an ordered list.

Version: HTML 2.0, START and TYPE are Netscape HTML 2.0 Extension Attributes, CONTINUE and SEQNUM in HTML 3.0.

Attributes:

CONTINUE	Specifies that sequence numbers should continue where the last ordered list ended.
SEQNUM=n	Specifies the starting sequence number of the list. For example, to start with 4 instead of 1.
START=n	Specifies the starting sequence number of the list.
TYPE=A ¦ a ¦ I ¦ i ¦ 1	Specifies the type of enumerators used. 1 is the default, which is numbers. A is capital letters. a is lowercase letters. I is large roman numerals. i is small roman numerals.

Details: An ordered list is displayed as a numbered list by default. `<LI>` tags are used to specify where list items start.

`<ul>..</ul>`

Purpose: Contains an unordered list.

Version: HTML 2.0, the TYPE attribute is a Netscape HTML 2.0 Extensions. PLAIN, SRC, and WRAP are HTML 3.0 attributes.

Attributes:

PLAIN	Specifies that no bullets be used.
SRC="URL"	Specifies an image to use for bullets.
TYPE=circle ¦ disc ¦ square	Specifies the type of bullet to use.
WRAP = horiz ¦ vert	Specifies a multicolumn list. horiz and vert tell the browser whether to add items horizontally or vertically first. The browser determines how many columns are appropriate.

Details: An unordered list is usually displayed as a bulleted list of items by default. `<LI>` tags are used to specify where list items start.

Images and Sounds

HTML has quite a bit of support for images but relatively little for sound (and none for smell and taste!). There is quite a bit of debate over the future of image-related tags. In some ways, HTML 3.0 is heading one direction, but Netscape and some other companies are heading another. Much debate is sure to ensue. In this section, we have tended toward the Netscape tags because they are more widely used at the current time.

`<area>`

Purpose: Defines an area of a client-side image map.

Version: Netscape HTML 3.0 Extension, also in Client-Side Image Map Draft.

Attributes:

COORDS="x,y,.."	Specifies the vertices of the shape.
HREF="URL"	Specifies the URL that should be linked to.
NOHREF	Specifies that no action should be taken.
SHAPE=CIRCLE ¦ DEFAULT ¦ POLY ¦ RECT	Specifies whether the Shape is a circle, polygon, or rectangle.
TARGET="window name"	Specifies the frame in which the URL being linked to should be displayed.

Details: Must be used with a `<map>` block.

<bgsound>

Purpose: Specifies a background sound should be played.

Version: Internet Explorer Extensions.

Attributes:

SRC="URL"   Specifies the URL of the sound file.

Details: Currently supports au, midi, and wav file formats.

<caption>..</caption>

Purpose: Contains a caption for a figure.

Version: HTML 3.0.

Attributes:

ALIGN= BOTTOM ¦ LEFT ¦ RIGHT ¦ TOP   Specifies the alignment of the caption in relation to the figure.

Details: Only used within a <FIG> block.

<img>

Purpose: Specifies an inline image in the document.

Version: HTML 2.0, the BORDER, HEIGHT, WIDTH, HSPACE, VSPACE and the second version of the ALIGN attribute shown are Netscape HTML 2.0 extensions; the HEIGHT and WIDTH attributes are in HTML 3.0; USEMAP is a Netscape HTML 3.0 Extension and also in the Client-Side Image Map Draft.

Attributes:

ALIGN=TOP¦MIDDLE¦BOTTOM   Specifies how the image will be aligned compared with the text. TOP aligns the top of the image with the tallest item in the line. MIDDLE aligns the bottom of the text with the middle of the image. BOTTOM aligns the middle of the text with the bottom of the image.

ALIGN=LEFT ¦ RIGHT ¦TOP ¦   Specifies how the image will be TEXTTOP ¦ MIDDLE ¦ aligned compared with the text. ABSMIDDLE ¦ BASELINE ¦ LEFT puts the image on the left BOTTOM ¦ ABSBOTTOM margin and flows text around to the right. RIGHT does the opposite of LEFT. TEXTTOP is like TOP but uses the tallest text, not the tallest item. ABSMIDDLE is like MIDDLE but it uses the middle of the text. BASELINE is the same as BOTTOM. ABSBOTTOM aligns the bottom of the image with the bottom of the text.

ALT="text"	Specifies text that can be used as an alternative to the image if the image cannot be displayed.
BORDER=n	Specifies the thickness of the image border.
HEIGHT=n	Specifies the height of the image. Allows the browser to leave space for the image and go ahead and display the text.
HSPACE=n	Specifies how much of a horizontal margin to leave around the image.
ISMAP	Indicates that the image is a server-side image map.
SRC="URL"	Specifies the URL of the image.
USEMAP="URL"	Specifies the URL of the client-side image map.
VSPACE=n	Specifies how much of a vertical margin to leave around the image.
WIDTH=n	Specifies the width of the image. Allows the browser to leave space for the image and display the text.

Details: GIF is the most commonly implemented image format in browsers. JPEG is commonly supported (though not as much as GIF) and is a good alternative choice because it saves disk space and bandwidth. For an image map to work, the <IMG> tag must be surrounded by an <a>..</a> pair.

<map>..</map>

Purpose: Defines a client-side image map.

Version: Netscape HTML 3.0 Extension, also appears in Client-Side Image Map Draft.

Attributes:

NAME="anchor"	Specifies the anchor that can be linked to for this image map.

Details: The anchor needs to be linked to by a <img usemap="#anchor"> tag.

Forms

All HTML forms require a CGI program to be written to process the form. This means the use of these tags alone isn't sufficient to have a working form. HTML forms are primitive because it's not possible, without using JavaScript or Java, to check the validity of input while it's being typed.

<form>..</form>

Purpose: Contains a form.

Version: HTML 2.0.

Attributes:

ACTION="URL"	Specifies a URL that will process the form when completed.
METHOD=GET¦POST	Specifies the data exchange method with the action URL.

Details: With the opening and closing tags, there should be some other tags such as <input> or <textarea> to specific the fields of the form.

<input>

Purpose: Specifies a field for user input.

Version: HTML 2.0 (first TYPE attribute shown), HTML 3.0 (second TYPE attribute shown), all attributes except for TYPE are Netscape JavaScript extensions.

Attributes:

onBlur="function"	Specifies a JavaScript function to call when the field loses focus.
onChange="function"	Specifies a JavaScript function to call when the field loses focus and the data in the field has changed.
onClick="function"	Specifies a JavaScript function to call when this field has a mouse click.
onFocus="function"	Specifies a JavaScript function to call when this field gets focus.
onLoad="function"	Specifies a JavaScript function to call when all frames are loaded.
onMouseOver="function"	Specifies a JavaScript function to call when the mouse pointer is over this field.
onSelect="function"	Specifies a JavaScript function to call when the user selects some text in a text or textarea field.
TYPE=TEXT ¦ PASSWORD ¦	Specifies the type of field to be used. CHECKBOX ¦ RADIO ¦ IMAGE ¦ HIDDEN ¦ SUBMIT ¦ RESET
TYPE=CHECKBOX ¦ FILE ¦	Specifies the type of field to be used. HIDDEN ¦ IMAGE ¦ PASSWORD ¦ RADIO ¦ RANGE ¦ RESET ¦ SCRIBBLE ¦ SUBMIT ¦ TEXT.

Details: Because the explanation of these attributes is complex, we have broken them out separately below. A few of the uncommon ones aren't covered below. There is no closing tag.

`<input type=checkbox>`

Purpose: Specifies a checkbox that represents a true-false choice.

Version: HTML 2.0.

Attributes:

`CHECKED`	Specifies that the checkbox is checked by default.
`NAME="name"`	Specifies the name of the field. Required.
`VALUE="value"`	Specifies the value of the field. Required.

Details: You can have several `type=checkbox` items that have the same field name as specified by the `NAME` attribute. When you do this, you can create an `n-of-many` selection field.

`<input type=hidden>`

Purpose: Allows the HTML document to specify fields and values that the user cannot change.

Version: HTML 2.0.

Attributes:

`NAME="name"`	Specifies the name of the field. Required.
`VALUE="value"`	Specifies the value of the field. Required.

Details: A hidden field is not displayed to the user.

`<input type=radio>`

Purpose: Specifies a radio button representing a true-false choice.

Version: HTML 2.0.

Attributes:

`CHECKED`	Specifies that the radio button is checked by default.
`NAME="name"`	Specifies the name of the field. Required.
`VALUE="value"`	Specifies the value of the field. Required.

Details: You can have several `type=radio` items that have the same field name as specified by the `NAME` attribute. Only one of these may be checked at any time. This is how you can create a `1-of-many` selection field.

<input type=range>

Purpose: Specifies that the user must pick a numeric value within a range.

Version: HTML 3.0.

Attributes:

MAX=n	Specifies the upper limit of the range.
MIN=n	Specifies the lower limit of the range.
NAME="name"	Specifies the name of the field. Required.

Details: If either MAX or MIN are real numbers, real numbers are accepted as input. Otherwise, only integers are accepted.

<input type=reset>

Purpose: Specifies a button that resets the form to its initial state.

Version: HTML 2.0, SRC is an HTML 3.0 attribute.

Attributes:

SRC="URL"	Specifies an image to be used as the reset button.
VALUE="value"	Specifies the label for the reset button.

<input type=submit>

Purpose: Specifies a submit button.

Version: HTML 2.0, SRC attribute is HTML 3.0.

Attributes:

NAME="name"	Specifies the name of the field.
SRC="URL"	Specifies an image to be used as the Submit button.
VALUE="value"	Specifies the value of the field. If present, this also is the label for the button.

Details: The value of the NAME and VALUE attributes is that if you have multiple submit buttons, the ACTION URL can figure out which one was pressed.

`<input type=text>` and `<input text=password>`

Purpose: Specifies a field for the input of textual data.

Version: HTML 2.0.

Attributes:

MAXLENGTH=n	Specifies the maximum length of the field. The default is `infinite`.
NAME="name"	Specifies the name of the field.
SIZE=n	Specifies the size of the field on the screen. If the number of characters entered is greater than `SIZE` but less than the `MAXLENGTH`, the field will scroll. The browser chooses its own default size if one is not specified.
VALUE="value"	Specifies the default value of the field.

Details: The `NAME` attribute is required but all other attributes are optional. The only difference between `type=text` and `type=password` is that the users' keystrokes are displayed on the screen with `type=text` and aren't displayed with `type=password`.

`<option>`

Purpose: Specifies a list item in a selection list.

Version: HTML 2.0.

Attributes:

SELECTED	Specifies that the item is selected by default.
VALUE="value"	Specifies the value of the item.

Details: `<OPTION>` tags may only appear with a `<select>` block. Each `<option>` tag is followed by text that is displayed as in the list and also used as the value if a `VALUE` attribute isn't specified.

`<select>..</select>`

Purpose: Specifies a selection list.

Version: HTML 2.0, `DISABLED` is an HTML 3.0 attribute.

Attributes:

DISABLED	Specifies that the select list should be displayed, but not to allow the user to change it.
MULTIPLE	Specifies that multiple options may be selected at the same time. If it isn't specified, only one option may be selected at any given time.

NAME="name"	Specifies the name of the field.
SIZE=n	Specifies the name of options that are visible at any one time. If this is not specified, the browser chooses its own size.

Details: This is typically displayed as a scrolling list. List items are defined with the <OPTION> tag.

<textarea>..</textarea>

Purpose: Specifies a multiline text field.

Version: HTML 2.0, DISABLED is a HTML 3.0 attribute, WRAP is a Netscape HTML 3.0 extension, and the first set of attributes are Netscape JavaScript extensions.

Attributes:

onBlur, onChange, onClick	See <input> for the meaning of these onFocus, onLoad, onMouseOver, onSelect
COLS=n	Number of columns to be displayed on-screen.
DISABLED	Specifies that the text area should be displayed but no changes to it are allowed.
NAME="name"	The name of the field.
ROWS=n	Number of rows to be displayed on-screen.
WRAP=OFF ¦ PHYSICAL ¦ VIRTUAL	Specifies how word wrapping should be handled. PHYSICAL means word wrap on display and transmission. VIRTUAL means word wrap on display, but transmit line breaks only where the user typed them.

Details: If text appears between the opening and closing tags, it's the default value of the field. The COLS and ROWS attributes are used to determine the display size only. If the text is larger than the display size, scrollbars should be used.

Java and JavaScript

Java and JavaScript are languages that enhance the Web by making it more interactive. Sun and Netscape have invented their own tags for these languages. There has been some talk in the HTML community about replacing some of these tags with a new tag called <insert>, but no formal proposal has been made public yet.

`<app>..</app>`

Purpose: Includes an Alpha Java applet in a document.

Version: Sun HTML extensions.

Details: This only works for the Alpha release of Java and is obsolete. Use `<applet>` instead.

`<applet>..</applet>`

Purpose: Includes a Java applet in the document.

Version: Sun HTML extensions.

Attributes:

CODEBASE	Specifies the base URL or the directory that contains the applet.
CODE	A required attribute that contains the name of the applet class file.
ALT	Alternate text that will be displayed if the browser does not know how to interpret the `<applet>` tag.
NAME	Name or an anchor for the applet so that other applets on the same page will be able to communicate with the named applet.
WIDTH, HEIGHT	Required width and height in pixels of the area where the applet is going to be displayed.
ALIGN	Alignment of the applet with the same attributes as the `<IMG>` tag.
VSPACE, HSPACE	Blank vertical (above and below the applet) and horizontal (right and left sides of the applet) space in pixels around the applet. It's the same as VSPACE and HSPACE in the `<IMG>` tag.

`<param>`

Purpose: User-defined parameters that go within the `<applet>..</applet>` tags.

Version: Sun HTML Extension.

Attributes:

NAME="attribute of the applet"	Applet programmer-defined attribute.
VALUE="value"	Value of the attribute NAME.

`<script>..</script>`

Purpose: Contains a script.

Version: Netscape JavaScript Extension.

Attributes:

> LANGUAGE=JAVASCRIPT   Specifies the language the script is in. JavaScript is the only current option.

Tables

Tables are currently the most widely implemented part of HTML 3.0. They are powerful and extremely useful. The only negative is that table documents look very bad on browsers that do not support tables.

`<table>..</table>`

Purpose: Main table tag that wraps around all other table tags.

Version: HTML 3.0, BORDER=n, CELLSPACING, CELLPADDING, and WIDTH=percent are Netscape HTML 3.0 Extensions.

Attributes:

> ALIGN= BLEEDLEFT ¦ BLEEDRIGHT ¦   Specifies the alignment of the CENTER ¦ JUSTIFY ¦ LEFT ¦ RIGHT table. The difference between BLEEDLEFT and LEFT, and BLEEDRIGHT and RIGHT is that the regular versions are flush with the margins. The BLEED versions are flush with the window border. JUSTIFY scales the figure to cover from left to right margin.

> BORDER   Specifies that the table should have a border displayed.

> BORDER=n   Specifies that the table should have a border of the given width.

> CELLPADDING=n   Specifies the amount of space between the edge of the cell and its contents.

> CELLSPACING=n   Specifies how much space should be placed between cells.

> COLSPEC="column spec"   Specifies column widths and alignments.

NOFLOW	Specifies that text should not flow around the table.
NOWRAP	Specifies that the browser should not automatically break lines.
UNITS= EN ¦ PIXELS ¦ RELATIVE	Specifies what kind of units are used for COLSPEC and WIDTH. EN is a half of a point size. PIXELS is the number of pixels. RELATIVE is that each column is relative to the others.
WIDTH=n	Specifies the width of the table. Netscape allows this to be a percentage of the document width.

Details: A column specification is a set of column widths and alignment from left to right. Each column is made up of a letter specifying the alignment (C for center, D for decimal alignment for floating point numbers, J for justified, L for left, and R for right) and then a number specifying the width in the UNITS specified.

<td>..</td> and <th>..</th>

Purpose: Specifies table data and table header cells respectively.

Version: HTML 3.0.

Attributes:

ALIGN=CENTER ¦ DECIMAL ¦	Specifies the horizontal alignment within the cell JUSTIFY ¦ LEFT ¦ RIGHT DECIMAL and makes sure that decimal points are aligned.
COLSPAN=n	Specifies that this cell should span n columns.
NOWRAP	Specifies that the cell should not wrap the text within it.
ROWSPAN=n	Specifies that this cell should span n rows.
VALIGN= BASELINE ¦	Specifies the vertical alignment within the cell. BOTTOM ¦ MIDDLE ¦ TOP BASELINE guarantees that all cells in the same row share the same baseline. The meaning of the others are obvious.

Details: <td> and <th> must occur within a <tr> block. The major difference between <td> and <th> cells are that <th> cells are given a darker or larger font.

`<tr>..</tr>`

Purpose: Specifies a table row.

Version: HTML 3.0.

Attributes:

`ALIGN=CENTER ¦ DECIMAL ¦`	Specifies the horizontal alignment within the row. `DECIMAL` makes sure `JUSTIFY ¦ LEFT¦ RIGHT` decimal points are aligned between rows.
`VALIGN=BASELINE ¦ BOTTOM`	Specifies the vertical alignment within the cell. `BASELINE ¦ MIDDLE ¦ TOP` ensures that all cells in the same row share the same baseline. The meaning of the others are obvious.

Details: Must occur with a `<table>` block.

Frames

Frames are a Netscape invention. They break the browser screen in multiple windows, each of which contain a different HTML document. Unfortunately, navigation in Frames can be confusing and are disliked by many people.

`<frame>`

Purpose: Defines the size of a single frame in a frameset.

Version: Netscape Frame Extensions.

Attributes:

`MARGINHEIGHT=n`	Specifies a fixed top/bottom margin for the frame.
`MARGINWIDTH=n`	Specifies a fixed right/left margin for the frame.
`NAME="window_name"`	Specifies a name for a frame. This can be used to link to this frame from other documents.
`NORESIZE`	Specifies that the user isn't allowed to resize this frame.
`SCROLLING= YES ¦ NO ¦ AUTO`	Specifies whether or not the frame should have a scrollbar. `AUTO` means that the browser gets to decide whether there is a scrollbar.
`SRC="URL"`	Specifies the URL of the document to be displayed in this frame.

Details: There is no closing tag. Must be used within a `<frameset>` block.

`<frameset>..</frameset>`

Purpose: Defines a document as being a set of frames instead of an HTML document.

Version: Netscape Frame Extensions.

Attributes:

`COLS="columns_spec"`	Specifies the width of columns in a frameset. The specification is a comma-delimited list. Each element of the list can be a percentage, a pixel value, or a relative value. Relative values are specified as `*` (meaning 1), `2*` (meaning 2), and so on.
`ROWS="rows_spec"`	Specifies the height of rows in a frameset. See `COLS` for syntax.

Details: May not be used in the same file as the `<body>` tag.

`<noframes>..</noframes>`

Purpose: Contains an alternative view for browsers that don't support frames.

Version: Netscape Frame Extensions.

Details: Must be used within a `<frameset>` block.

Comments

A comment starts with `<!--` and ends with `-->`. Unfortunately, some browsers (for example, certain versions of Lynx) don't recognize comments. Therefore, though useful, the use of comments isn't recommended.

CGI

Common Gateway Interface (CGI) is an interface for external programs or applications to interact with information servers like the Webservers. CGI programs are commonly used to process forms, and they can be written in any language that can be executed on the Webserver such as C, C++, shell scripts, Visual Basic, Perl, and Tk/Tcl. CGI programs normally only reside in a special directory designated by the Webmaster due to security reasons. But some Webmasters use wrapper programs such as cgiwrap (UNIX) to safely allow Web authors to write and run CGI programs in a special directory under their home directories.

This section serves as a reference guide for commonly used CGI environment variables and headers. Version 1.1 of the CGI standard was used as the basis for this section.

Environment Variables

These are environment variables that are passed into CGI scripts. The last three involving REDIRECTs are specific to the NCSA HTTPD server and may not work with other services.

SERVER_SOFTWARE	The name and the version number of the server.
SERVER_NAME	The server's full host name, IP address, or an alias.
GATEWAY_INTERFACE	Revision of the CGI specification.
SERVER_PROTOCOL	The name and revision of the service protocol.
SERVER_PORT	The port where the server is running.
REQUEST_METHOD	The method of the request.
PATH_INFO	Extra information at the end of the path of the executing CGI script.
PATH_TRANSLATED	A translated version of PATH_INFO that has removed any virtual mappings.
SCRIPT_NAME	The full virtual path of the executing CGI script.
QUERY_STRING	Anything that goes after the ? in the URL that referenced this CGI program.
REMOTE_HOST	The hostname of the machine making the request to the Webserver.
REMOTE_ADDR	The IP address of REMOTE_HOST or the machine making the request.
AUTH_TYPE	The authentication method used if the script was protected.
REMOTE_USER	Login name of the user from REMOTE_ADDR if the user logged in via user-authentication.
REMOTE_IDENT	Login name of the user from REMOTE_ADDR if the remote host supports user identification.
CONTENT_TYPE	Content type of the data.
CONTENT_LENGTH	Length of the content given by the client.
HTTP_ACCEPT	The MIME type that the client accepts.
HTTP_USER_AGENT	The browser from the client.
HTTP_REFERER	The page that refers the client to this CGI program.
REDIRECT_REQUEST	The request for a redirect as sent to the server.
REDIRECT_STATUS	The status the server would have sent if it hadn't been redirected.
REDIRECT_URL	The URL that caused the redirect.

Headers for the Output of a CGI Program

These headers are HTTP headers. Your CGI program can return them to the browser as meta-information about the document being returned.

Allowed	Lists the requests that the user is allowed to use on this URL.
Content-Encoding	Encoding method.
Content-Language	ISO3316 language code with an optional ISO639 country code.
Content-Length	The length of the returning document.
Content-Transfer-Encoding	The MIME encoding method used on the returning document.
Content-Type	MIME type of the returning document.
Date	Creation date in GMT format.
Expires	Expiration date.
Last-Modified	Last modification date.
Location	Virtual path or the URL of the returning document.
Message-Id	Message identifier.
Public	Lists all requests that anyone can use.
Status	Returned status of the request.
URI	URI of the document.
Version	Version of the document.
Title	Title of the document.

Windows NT Web Servers

With the frequency that Web servers are hitting the market, it is hard to keep up with which ones are available and what features they provide. This appendix lists many (but not nearly all) of the Web servers that are available today. Christopher Brown and I have tested many of these servers and present reviews with a short list of our likes and dislikes.

A great online source of information on Web servers is Web Servers Comparison at `http://www.proper.com/www/servers-chart.html` maintained by Paul E. Hoffman.

SerWeb

This freeware Web server runs under Windows 3.1 or Windows NT. The server was written in C++ by Gustavo Estrella, and the source code is available as part of the software distribution.

`ftp://sunsite.unc.edu/pub/micro/pc-stuff/ms-windows/winsock/apps`

Web4HAM

This server was developed by Gunter Hille at the University of Hamburg. The product is in its early development (v 0.16) yet offers an easy installation.

`ftp://ftp.informatik.uni-hamburg.de/pub/net/winsock`

WHTTPd

This is Bob Denny's freeware Windows HTTP server. The operation and configuration of this server are documented with many HTML files. If you must run on Windows 3.x, you've got to check this server out. It is a very capable Web server, especially considering the price.

```
http://www.city.net/win-httpd
```

ZBServer

Written by Bob Bradley, this does double duty as a Web and Gopher server for Windows 3.1 and Windows 95. It is easy to install.

```
http://www.zbserver.com
```

Purveyor

Process Software Corporation, through an agreement with EMWAC, has enhanced the EMWACS Web server and turned it into a commercial product. Windows NT and Windows 95 versions are available. This was the first commercial Web server for Windows NT.

```
http://www.process.com/prodinfo/purvdata.htm
```

EMWAC HTTP Server for Windows NT

An excellent WWW server written by Chris Adie of EMWAC. You can't beat the price—it's free! On top of that, those who use this server hardly ever have any configuration problems to complain about.

```
http://emwac.ed.ac.uk/html/internet_toolchest/https/contents.htm
```

WebSite

An HTTP server for Windows 95 and Windows NT written by Bob Denny in cooperation with O'Reilly & Associates.

```
http://software.ora.com/
```

Alibaba

This is an HTTP server for Windows 95 and Windows NT from Computer Software Manufacturer in Austria.

SAIC-HTTP Server

SAIC has not yet announced plans to market or sell this HTTP server. The software was originally developed for internal use by Don De Coteau out of SAIC's San Diego, CA Information Technology Laboratory. It runs on Windows 95 and Windows NT.

```
http://wwwserver.itl.saic.com/
```

Netscape Communications and Netscape Commerce from Netscape Communications

Netscape Communications Corporation, the makers of the most popular Web browser, offers a standard Web server for Windows NT and a commerce version that supports SSL for encrypted secure operation.

```
http://www.netscape.com/comprod/netscape_commun.html
```

Ameritech Library Services' NetPublisher Demonstration Server

The NetPublisher Server provides the functionality of a Z39.50 server, a World Wide Web server, and a Gopher server all in one. The extended architecture has been designed to allow you to focus on the information you are serving, not how it is served. There is one source for all three protocols. Ameritech also offers a complete package of Web publishing tools.

```
http://netpub.notis.com/
```

Internet Factory's Commerce Builder

This is a pair of Web servers for Windows NT and Windows 95: Communications Builder and Commerce Builder. Features include multiple Web/domain support, authentication-based access control, a caching HTTP proxy, and an exclusive: Web-based, real-time chatrooms.

```
http://www.aristosoft.com/ifact/inet.htm
```

ILAR Concepts' FolkWeb WWW Server

This is a full-featured Web server for Windows 95 and Windows NT. A key selling point is its database connectivity, allowing you to publish your ODBC databases without writing a single line of CGI code.

```
http://www.ilar.com/default.htm
```

Folio Corporation's Folio Infobase Web Server

This is a Web server for Windows 95 and Windows NT.

`http://www.folio.com/`

Quarterdeck WebServer 32

Both the Windows 95 and NT versions of this Web server come in the same package. Quarterdeck WebServer 32 offers virtual domains and directory-level security.

`http://www.qdeck.com/`

FrontPage

FrontPage is much more than a Web server; it's a client/server GUI Web publishing package. Its client/server architecture supports authoring, scripting, and management of your Web site from your personal workstation, across your LAN, or even over the Internet.

FrontPage 1.1 is available for Windows 95 and Windows NT from Microsoft.

`http://www.microsoft.com/`

Microsoft Internet Information Server

This server is the principal focus of this book as it is now free with Windows NT 4.0. This server has outstanding security features and excellent performance. Its main drawback is that it is a little difficult to set up all the features.

`http://www.microsoft.com/`

WebQuest by Questar

This feature-rich HTTP server for Windows 95 and Windows NT offers many bells and whistles, including enhanced Server Side Includes (SSI+). It also has several very useful Web-related development tools for validation of directories, local and remote hyperlinks, and access control.

`http://www.questar.com/`

Windows 95 Web Server Reviews

We personally tested 11 of the Windows 95 servers listed above. The number of Web servers available for Windows 95 has more than tripled over the past six months, and we can only assume that this number will continue to increase rapidly. You will find that most of the Web servers on the market today offer a free trial period of 30 to 60 days.

1. **Purveyor Desktop WebServer 1.1**

   Likes: It is simple to install, runs fast, and has all the advanced security features for password-protecting files and directories by user or group. Of all the Windows 95 servers we tested, Purveyor and WebQuest had the best integration with the Windows 95 user interface (which bodes well for Windows NT 4.0 and its new Shell interface). An additional pull-down menu and button bar is added to Explorer for easy configuration. This is clearly a powerful server and the documentation is nothing short of excellent. Considering the quality of the Purveyor server for Windows NT, it comes as no surprise that Process has a fine Windows 95 server also.

   Dislikes: Doesn't support WinCGI or ISAPI (yet). However, Purveyor for NT does support ISAPI and Purveyor Desktop supports *buffered CGI,* which is similar to WinCGI.

2. **FolkWeb 1.1**

   Likes: This server has nearly all of the features of the big boys, and it is very affordable. The installation and operation couldn't be easier; it was literally up and running within seconds after completing the simple GUI installation. Outstanding technical support kept this server high on our list during testing. It supports image maps, CGI 1.1, and WinCGI 1.2—and has built-in provisions for ODBC databases.

   Dislikes: The online help system and the documentation are somewhat lacking. For example, the help doesn't include a Table of Contents.

3. **WebQuest**

   Likes: This is a nice Web server that contains a feature-rich set of Server Side Includes (SSI). The SSIs are so rich that you don't have to do CGI programming, not even for database access. Has very good server integration with Windows 95.

   Dislikes: A bit expensive for a Win95 Web server. In all fairness, the version we examined showed a few signs of it still being in the beta stage. Questar is banking on the SSI+ feature to extent that they don't support WinCGI or ISAPI.

4. **Internet Factory Communication/Commerce Builder Web Servers**

   Likes: Installed in a snap, and they give a 60-day trial; as a neat twist they added chat rooms to the servers so you have something like IRC built into your server; all in all, it's pretty slick.

   Dislikes: Running this server with just a few chat rooms will not only require a lot of network bandwidth, but also a huge amount of memory.

5. **Alibaba**

   Likes: Easy installation, good documentation, and a lot of nice features. We know of several well-known sites that use this server.

   Dislikes: No published price, you have to e-mail the authors for price information.

6. **WebSite**

Likes: This is packed full of features and utilities. After installation, you will have a new program group with several utilities to make your Web site maintenance easier: Home Page Wizard, What's New Wizard, Web View, Web index, Quick Stats, and the Image Map Editor. The installation is smooth, and you have the option to run from the desktop or as an NT service. This product runs on NT and Win95.

Dislikes: We found many of the utilities somewhat overwhelming and not very intuitive. Image mapping was not as straightforward as with the other servers. With the proper time invested in learning this package, it can be very powerful.

7. **ZBServer**

Likes: Easy to install, runs surprisingly fast, and supports WinCGI.

Dislikes: Lacked some of the advanced features and tools found in other servers.

8. **Front Page**

Likes: Lots of tools for Web publishing and Web page management. This is a good package for large corporate Web site management.

Dislikes: This 9MB package is more a Web publishing tool than a Web server.

9. **Quarterdeck**

Likes: Simple general purpose Web server.

Dislikes: Installation hard to follow and the server was hard to configure. The GUI did not perform well at low screen resolutions.

10. **SAIC-HTTP**

Likes: It's free and feature-packed. Nice file redirection and security features. It supports installing multiple HTTP servers on one NT Server. It also has a feature called external modules, which enables you to extend the functionality of the server. Modules (CGI scripts that reside in the modules directory under the server root directory) are automatically executed when the URL that is referenced matches an entry in the module mapping table.

Dislikes: This server was developed for Windows NT and is hard to configure to run on Windows 95.

11. **W4 Server**

Likes: $25.00 shareware.

Dislikes: You get what you pay for.

Windows NT Web Server Reviews

We personally tested multiple versions of several Windows NT Web servers. Some of the Web servers listed here have additional features that we have not covered in this appendix; please consult the product documentation or contact the manufacturer for full information.

Of the Windows NT servers that we tested, here is a list in the order that we rank them, with a brief statement of our likes and dislikes:

1. **Purveyor 1.2 for NT from Process Software**

   Likes: It is simple to install, runs fast, and has all the advanced security features for password-protecting files and directories by user or group. All the configuration is done from a Control Panel applet or an additional pull-down menu and button bar added to File Manager. Purveyor has full support to run as a proxy server. This is one smooth server.

   Dislikes: Doesn't support WinCGI (but it supports ISAPI, which is much better); and the logfile viewer is a slow application.

2. **Microsoft Internet Information Server 2.0**

   Likes: This product is free with Windows NT 4.0. The GUI installation is smooth. It supports ISAPI. It includes built-in ODBC database support with a very easy-to-use set of extensions to HTML. Its performance is ranked first among all NT Web servers and its numerous security features are tightly integrated with Windows NT.

   Dislikes: CGI support will leave you scratching your head. The only SSI it supports (in version 1.0) is #include. The security features are so strong that you might find yourself in a puzzle about why you can't view your own home page. Finally, it doesn't warn you if you don't have the RPC service running, which it requires. The online documentation is very plain in many areas that cry out for more details.

3. **HTTPS from European Microsoft Windows NT Academic Center (EMWAC)**

   Likes: Despite the fact that it's free, HTTPS is a very robust and easy-to-use Web server. It includes a good manual and has image mapping built into the system, so there is no need to call a CGI image mapping routine. We highly recommend this as a good starting point.

   Dislikes: It lacks the more advanced security features offered by commercial packages, such as exclusion by IP, file, or directory.

4. **Netscape Communications and Netscape Commerce from Netscape Communications**

   Likes: Both packages are very robust but take a little more time to install than the others. All server configuration and administration is done from a Web browser using forms. The Web browser approach to administering your Web server will appeal to anyone who wants to change server configuration remotely. It has a very nice server statistics viewer for monitoring server operation.

   Dislikes: We prefer a Control Panel applet for server administration instead of the Web browser approach. Setup proved to be somewhat time-consuming and hard to follow. If you use this server, do your homework prior to setup and installation.

5. **WebSite from O'Reilly and Associates**

   See the Windows 95 Web Server Reviews above for comments about this server.

6. **SAIC-HTTP**

   This product is expected to be freeware. It installed smoothly and was easily configured via the NT Control Panel. It also had nice file redirection and security features. It supports installing multiple HTTP servers on one NT Server. It also has a feature called External modules, which enables you to extend the functionality of the server. Modules (CGI scripts that reside in the modules directory under the server root directory) are automatically executed when the URL that is referenced matches an entry in the module mapping table.

   Dislikes: This is still a little quirky, but is definitely one product to keep your eye on.

APPENDIX

C

Resources for the Windows NT Webmaster

This appendix consists of dozens of Internet locations that I have found useful. These resources, organized by the following categories, can help you too.

- ◆ World Wide Web development
- ◆ Windows NT download sites
- ◆ Windows NT user groups and associations
- ◆ Informational Websites
- ◆ Internet server software
- ◆ Windows NT hardware compatibility information
- ◆ Windows NT newsletters and FAQs
- ◆ Newsgroups of interest
- ◆ Listservers
- ◆ About ISDN and Windows NT
- ◆ Business resources

The number of Windows NT resources available on the Internet grows everyday, so this list is by no means complete. If you have a question about running a Web server; however, you will almost certainly be able to find something in here that will lead you to the answer.

World Wide Web Development

From these two sites you will be able to find most of the WWW development information you need:

The WWW Developer's Virtual Library `http://www.stars.com/`

Bob Allison's Web Masters `http://gagme.wwa.com/~boba/masters1.html`

Windows NT Download Sites

Microsoft's Gopher `gopher://gopher.microsoft.com/`

Microsoft's Web Server `http://www.microsoft.com`

Digital Equipment Corporation `http://www.windowsnt.digital.com/`

EMWAC—Czech Republic FTP `ftp://emwac.faf.cuni.cz`

EMWAC—Czech Republic Gopher `gopher://emwac.faf.cuni.cz`

CICA Gopher Windows NT Directory—Index for CICA Gopher `gopher://ftp.cica.indiana.edu:70/11/pc/win3/nt`

The Coast to Coast Software Repository Windows NT Primary Mirror `http://www.acs.oakland.edu/oak/SimTel/SimTel-nt.html`

WWW Site for Native Alpha NT Tools & Utilities `http://www.garply.com/tech/comp/sw/pc/nt/alpha.html`

FTP Site for Native Alpha NT Tools & Utilities `ftp://ftp.garply.com/pub/pc/nt/alpha`

Somar Software—Many NT Security Type Applications & Others `http://www.somarsoft.com/default.htm`

Tucows Winsock Utilities `http://www.tucows.com`

Windows NT User Groups and Associations

San Diego Windows NT Users Group `http://www.bhs.com/sdug/`

International Windows NT Users Group `http://www.iwntug.org/`

Los Angeles NT/Microsoft Networking Users Group `http://bhs.com/winnt/lantug.html`

Rocky Mountain Windows NT User Group `http://budman.cmdl.noaa.gov/rmwntug/rmwntug.htm`

Interior Alaska Windows NT Users Group `http://rmm.com/iawntug/`

Northern California Microsoft Windows NT Users Group Information `http://www.actioninc.com/winntug.htm`

Stuttgart Windows NT Home Page `http://www.informatik.uni-stuttgart.de/misc/nt/nt.html`

European Microsoft Windows NT Academic Center—Czech Republic `http://emwac.faf.cuni.cz/html/emwaccz.htm`

EMWAC Information Services—UK `http://emwac.ed.ac.uk/`

Informational Websites

The Windows NT Resource Center `http://www.bhs.com/`

Rick's Windows NT Info Center `http://rick.wzl.rwth-aachen.de/rick/`

Windows NT Information `http://infotech.kumc.edu/winnt/`

iNformaTion `http://rmm.com/nt/`

Windows NT Information—Stuttgart `http://www.informatik.uni-stuttgart.de/misc/nt/nt.html`

Windows NT and NT Advanced Server Information `http://ms-nic.gsfc.nasa.gov/Titles/WinNT.html`

Windows NT Network Specialist `http://infotech.kumc.edu/`

European Microsoft Windows NT Academic Centre—EMWAC `http://emwac.ed.ac.uk/`

Windows NT Support Center—University of Karlsruhe `http://jerusalem.windows-nt.uni-karlsruhe.de/english.htm`

Mindspring Windows NT RAS Setup `http://help.mindspring.com/busi-d/nt/`

CSUSM—Windows NT File Archives `http://coyote.csusm.edu/cwis/winworld/nt.html`

Netherlands Windows NT `http://nt.info.nl/english/default.htm`

Yahoo Windows NT Page `http://akebono.stanford.edu/yahoo/Computers/Operating_Systems/Windows_NT/`

Internet Server Software

EMWACS Freeware Gopher server `ftp://emwac.ed.ac.uk/pub/gophers/`

EMWACS Freeware WAIS server `ftp://emwac.ed.ac.uk/pub/waiss/`

EMWACS WAIS toolkit based on freeWAIS 0.202 `ftp://emwac.ed.ac.uk/pub/waistool/`

EMWACS Freeware Finger Server `http://emwac.ed.ac.uk/html/internet_toolchest/fingers/contents.htm`

Windows NT Hardware Compatibility Information

Windows NT 3.5 and 4.0 Hardware Compatibility List `ftp://ftp.microsoft.com/bussys`

Windows NT Newsletters and FAQs

FAQ—Windows NT Administration `http://www.iftech.com/classes/admin/admin.htm`

FAQ—Windows NT by Dale Reed 4/15/95 `http://www.iea.com/~daler/nt/faq/toc.html`

MS NT FAQ `http://www.microsoft.com/kb/faq/backoffc/win-nt/`

Microsoft Windows NT Server Home Page `http://www.microsoft.com/ntserver/`

Windows NT Internet FAQ Part 1 of 2, available via FTP download `ftp://rtfm.mit.edu//pub/usenet-by-hierarchy/comp/os/ms-windows/nt/setup/`

Windows NT Internet FAQ Part 2 of 2, available via FTP download `ftp://rtfm.mit.edu//pub/usenet-by-hierarchy/comp/os/ms-windows/nt/setup/`

Windows NT FAX software FAQ—Courtesy of Walter Arnold `http://www.mcs.net/~sculptor/NTFAX-FAQ.HTML`

The Consummate Winsock Apps Page `http://cws.wilmington.net/`

Somar Software's NT Security White Paper (Highly recommended!) `http://www.somarsoft.com/security.htm`

Perl—Practical Extraction and Report Language 4/14/95 `http://www.cis.ufl.edu/cgi-bin/plindex`

Newsgroups of Interest

◆ `comp.os.ms-windows.nt.admin.misc`

◆ `comp.os.ms-windows.nt.admin.networking`

◆ `comp.os.ms-windows.nt.advocacy`

◆ `comp.os.ms-windows.nt.misc`

◆ `comp.os.ms-windows.nt.pre-release`

- ◆ `comp.os.ms-windows.nt.setup`
- ◆ `comp.os.ms-windows.nt.setup.hardware`
- ◆ `comp.os.ms-windows.nt.setup.misc`
- ◆ `comp.os.ms-windows.nt.software.backoffice`
- ◆ `comp.os.ms-windows.nt.software.compatibility`
- ◆ `comp.os.ms-windows.nt.software.services`
- ◆ `alt.winsock`—Discusses Windows TCP/IP
- ◆ `alt.security`—Discusses computer security
- ◆ `alt.security.pgp`—Discusses the Pretty Good Privacy program
- ◆ `comp.os.ms-windows.nt.misc`—Discusses miscellaneous Windows NT topics
- ◆ `comp.os.ms-windows.nt.setup`—Discusses Windows NT configuration issues
- ◆ `comp.os.ms-windows.networking.tcpip`—Discusses running TCP/IP in Windows
- ◆ `comp.risks`—Discusses computer security

Listservers

In addition to the informational sites above, these listservers are very valuable resources of information. You will receive an auto-reply telling you how to send messages to the list after you are a member.

- ◆ NT HTTPS: `http_winnt@Emerald.NET`. Enter `subscribe` in the subject line and leave the body blank.
- ◆ The International Windows NT Users Group (IWNTUG): `list@bhs.com`. Enter `subscribe iwntug` in the first line of the body of the message.
- ◆ The Beverly Hills Software Resource Center Newsletter: `list@bhs.com`. Enter `subscribe rcnews` in the first line of the body of the message.
- ◆ NT Consultants List: `list@bhs.com`. Enter `subscribe ntconsult` in the first line of the body of the message.
- ◆ UK NT listserver: `mailbase@mailbase.ac.uk`. Enter `join windows-nt firstname lastname` in the body of the message and leave the subject blank.
- ◆ UK Microsoft Back Office listservers: `mailbase@mailbase.ac.uk`. Enter `join ms-backoffice firstname lastname` in the body of the message and leave the subject blank.
- ◆ NT Lanman listserver: `listserv@list.nih.gov`. Enter `subscribe lanman-l firstname lastname` in the body of the message and leave the subject blank.
- ◆ `Webserver-nt-request@DELTA.PROCESS.COM`. Enter `subscribe webserver-nt` in the body of the message.

◆ DEC Alpha NT Listserver: To subscribe, send an e-mail to `majordomo@garply.com` with the body text of `subscribe alphant`. After you are subscribed, send messages to `alphant@garply.com`.

◆ Windows NT Perl Listserver: To subscribe, send e-mail to `majordomo@mail.hip.com` with the body text of the message saying `subscribe ntperl`.

About ISDN and Windows NT

See the Microsoft KnowledgeBase article: Q133704.

For general information about the PPP Multilink protocol or ISDN, see: `http://www.almaden.ibm.com/ciug/ciug.html` or `http://alumni.caltech.edu/~dank/isdn/`.

Business Resources

Here are a few sites that should be of interest to any business person building an Intranet or a Web site. See Yahoo at `http://www.yahoo.com` for other resources.

◆ The Small Business Administration: `http://www.sbaonline.sba.gov`

◆ Federal Government Information on the Internet: `http://www.wcs-online.com/usgovdoc`

◆ Stat-USA: `http://www.stat-usa.gov/`

◆ The World Wide Web Yellow Pages (includes a search page): `http://www.yellow.com`

◆ Yellowpages.com, another reference to online businesses: `http://theyellowpages.com/default.htm`

◆ Monster Board Classified Ads: `http://www.monster.com/`

APPENDIX

◆

What's on the CD-ROM

Installation Notes

On the CD you will find all the sample files that have been presented in this book along with applications and utilities needed to set up your site. Although this book is aimed at Windows NT running on the Intel x86 processor family, versions for the Alpha, MIPS, and Power PC of several applications are available.

Here you will find a listing of the applications contained on the CD and their locations. To install the software from the CD, run the setup program located in the root directory. This launches an interface that will allow you to install the programs and view the readme file. Each program's individual setup guides you through the steps necessary to finish installing the software. You will find that some files (with a .exe extension) are self-extracting archives. You can always reinstall the software directly from the CD-ROM without using the interface if necessary. Please check the \3rdparty directory on the CD-ROM for the following subdirectories.

\clients

- ◆ \eudora—Eudora Light v1.5.4 e-mail client, 16-bit and 32-bit.
- ◆ \explorer—Microsoft Internet Explorer v2.0 Web browser for Windows.
- ◆ \newsxprs—News Xpress v1.0b4 Usenet newsreader client application.
- ◆ \whois32—Whois v1.0b 32-bit Whois client application.
- ◆ \winftp—WinFTP v1.2 32-bit FTP client application
- ◆ \wsarchie—v0.8 16-bit Archie client application (32-bit version also available).
- ◆ \wsping—16- and 32-bit GUI application for Ping, Traceroute, and nslookup (16-bit version also available).

\graphics

- ◆ \acdsee—ACDSEE v1.3 is a fast Windows image viewer that supports BMP, GIF, JPEG, PCX, Photo-CD, PNG, TGA, and TIFF files.
- ◆ \psp—Paint Shop Pro 3.0 is a full-featured graphics editor and graphics file format converter for Windows.

\html

- ◆ \mapthis—An imagemap utility for creating map files.
- ◆ \webedit—WebEdit Pro, an HTML editor.
- ◆ \webtran—OEM version of Web Transit, a $99 value HTML editor.

\jazz

- ◆ Intranet Jazz—Intranet Jazz is a suite of client/server products which exploit Intranet technologies inside a corporate firewall. By JSB Computer Systems, Ltd.

\jdp

- ◆ JDesignerPro 0.9 beta—JDP is a complete Java client/server interface builder by BulletProof.

\perform

- ◆ CGI PerForm—The CGI Perform application.

\servers

- ◆ \cfusion—Demo version of Cold Fusion 32-bit ODBC database interface and Allaire Forums, a Web-based collaboration system.
- ◆ \emwac\gopher—EMWAC Gopher server.
- ◆ \emwac\mail—EMWAC Internet Mail Server.
- ◆ \emwac\wais—EMWAC WAIS Toolkit.
- ◆ \emwac\web—The EMWAC Web server.
- ◆ \folkweb—FolkWeb v1.01 is a Win32 Web server from ILAR Concepts, Inc.
- ◆ \postoffc—The Software.com Post.Office SMTP/POP3 Server.

\servers\tools

- ◆ \blat—Blat 1.5 is an NT send mail utility program (Intel).
- ◆ \hedit—Hedit, a Hex editor for Windows NT.
- ◆ \redial—Somar Redial for NT keeps your connection while using RAS.

\viewers

- ◆ Adobe Acrobat viewer

\winzip

- ◆ winzip95.exe—Winzip for Windows NT/95. You'll need this to unzip program files that use long filenames.

Please check the \book directory on the CD-ROM for the following sample files.

\book\chapter2

- ◆ The ABC Company Intranet Home Page.

\book\chapter5

- ◆ All sample files from Chapter 5 on HTML.

\book\chapter13

- ◆ Sample file from Chapter 13.

\book\chapter15

◆ Sample file from Chapter 15.

\book\chapter16

◆ Sample files from Chapter 16 on databases and the Web.

\book\chapter18

◆ Sample files from Chapter 18.

\book\chapter19

◆ Sample files from Chapter 19.

\book\chapter20

◆ The Visual Basic and C++ database programs in Chapter 20.

\book\chapter24

◆ Sample order entry HTML files from Chapter 24.

\book\chapter26

◆ Sample slide show files from Chapter 26.

About Shareware

Anyone who has ever tried to write a computer program knows it is a complex undertaking. This is especially true when you consider all the features that modern software must have before many users will even consider trying it. And as if the development process isn't tough enough, packaging, marketing, and distributing the program become another roadblock to the success of the software venture.

When you stop and think about it, you realize it is pretty amazing that the shareware concept solves all of these problems. Shareware is a *win-win* deal for both the developer and the user. Developers can concentrate on writing new code (which is what they usually do best) without having to worry about software packaging and distribution issues, and users can try the software for free before they decide if it fits their needs. That's not something you can easily do with shrink-wrap software.

But don't be fooled; shareware is not free! First of all, if a package is free, it will be clearly labeled as freeware, not shareware. Second, if the shareware author has taken his personal time to develop a program, with the hope that others will find it useful, he will have no incentive to enhance the program if nobody agrees to pay the registration fee. In other words, the user will lose out on a lot more than a few dollars because the program will age and cease to be compatible with other new technologies that will inevitably come along.

Shareware registration fees are trivial (typically under $100) and usually way less than commercial software that is of equal or lesser quality. If you decide that a shareware program is convenient, you are expected to follow the registration instructions that come with the package. You will get several benefits in return, depending on what the author states in a file named license.txt (or readme.txt). It usually includes a printed copy of the user's guide and a new version of the program which doesn't constantly prompt you with the reminder to register.

Unlike many software companies, shareware authors like to hear from their customers directly. You can usually reach them on by e-mail, or on the Web, or on a relevant list server or newsgroup. But keep in mind, they justifiably like to hear from paying customers the most. And I think they'd like to know that you heard about their program in *Building an Intranet with Windows NT 4.*

Bibliography

Books

Ablan, Jerry and Scott Yanoff etal. *Web Site Administrator's Survival Guide.* Sams.net, 1996.

Albitz, Paul and Cricket Liu. *DNS and BIND.* O'Reilly and Associates, Inc., 1994.

Brown, Christopher L.T. and Scott Zimmerman. *Web Site Construction Kit for Windows NT.* Sams.net, 1996.

Comer, Douglas E. *Internetworking with TCP/IP, Volume I Principles, Protocols, and Architecture. Prentice Hall,* Third edition, 1995.

Cowart, Robert. *Windows NT 3.51 Unleashed. Sams Publishing,* Third edition, 1996.

Dern, Daniel P. *The Internet Guide for New Users.* McGraw-Hill, Inc., 1994.

Graham, Ian S. *HTML Sourcebook.* John Wiley & Sons, Inc., Second edition, 1996.

Jamsa, Kris and Ken Cope. *Internet Programming.* Jamsa Press, 1995.

Lemay, Laura. *Teach Yourself Web Publishing with HTML in a Week.* Sams.net Publishing, 1995.

Miller, Mark A. *Internetworking: A Guide to Network Communications LAN to LAN; LAN to WAN.* M&T Books, 1991.

Morris, Mary E. S. *HTML for Fun and Profit.* SunSort Press/Prentice Hall, 1995.

Resnick, Rosalind and Dave Taylor *Internet Business Guide*, Second Edition, Sams.net, 1995.

Sant'Angelo, Rick and Nadeem Chagtai. *Windows NT Server Survival Guide.* Sams.net, 1996.

Stevens, W. Richard. *TCP/IP Illustrated*, Volumes 1 and 2. Addison-Wesley.

Stallings and Van Slyke. *Business Data Communications.* MacMillan Publishing, Second edition, 1994.

Zimmerman, Scott and Christopher L.T. Brown. *Web Site Construction Kit for Windows 95.* Sams.net, 1996.

Documentation and Manuals

"HTTP Server Manual" By Chris Adie of the European Microsoft Windows NT Academic Centre.

ISDN, a User's Guide to Services, Applications and Resources in California Pacific Bell stock number 9550.

JASC Paint Shop Pro Version 3. *User's Reference.* JASC Inc., 1995.

Purveyor For Windows NT. *User's Guide.* Process Software Corporation 1995.

Purveyor For Windows NT. *Guide to Server Security.* Process Software Corporation 1995.

Purveyor For Windows NT. *Programmer's Guide.* Process Software Corporation 1995.

Windows NT Resource Kit, Volumes 1 through 4. Microsoft Press, 1995.

Articles

Antaya, Doug. "Welcome to Wide Are Networking." *Technical Support,* February 1995: 37–39.

Ayre, Rick and Thomas Mace. "Internet Access: Just Browsing." *PC Magazine,* 12 March 1996: 100–147.

Ayre, Rick. "Intranet How-To: Setting Up Shop." *PC Magazine,* 23 April 1996: 151–158.

Bell, Mark. "TCP/IP Addressing Traps and Pitfalls." *Technical Support,* July 1995: 30–34.

Boyle, Padraic. "Your Defensive Line." *PC Magazine,* 23 April 1996: NE1–NE10.

Dachis, Jeff and Craig Kanarick. "Seven Steps to Dynamic Digital Design." *Web Techniques,* April 1996: 24–27.

Daniels, Tim. "Virus Scanners," *Windows NT Magazine,* October 1995: 55–58.

Davidson, Andrew. "Building an Internet Database, Part 1." *Web Techniques,* April 1996: 41–45.

Davidson, Andrew. "Building an Internet Database, Part 2." *Web Techniques,* May 1996: 53–59.

Derfler Jr., Frank J. "The Intranet Platform: A Universal Client?" *PC Magazine,* 23 April 1996: 105–113.

Duncan, Ray. "Electronic Publishing on the World Wide Web." *PC Magazine,* 11 April 1995: 257–261.

Duncan, Ray. "Setting Up a Web Server." *PC Magazine,* 16 May 1995: 273–280.

Duncan, Ray. "Publishing Databases on the World–Wide Web." *PC Magazine,* August 1995: 403–412.

Franklin, Carl. "Serving Up the Web." *Visual Basic Programmer's Journal,* April 1996: 22–34.

Friesenhahn, Bob. "Build Your Own WWW Server." *Byte,* April 1995: 83–96.

Gonzalez, Sean. "Internetworking." *PC Magazine,* 6 February 1996: 263–265.

Harvey, David A. "Sit Up Straight: Web Table Manners." *NetGuide,* February 1996: 91–92.

Jennings, Roger. "Piece Together Microsoft's Internet Puzzle." *Visual Basic Programmer's Journal,* April 1996: 42–45.

Kolsti, Peter. "Firewalls Keep Users From Kicking Your Apps." *Network World,* 13 November 1995: 61.

Lathrop, Jeffrey. "Build Your Own Web Site in Less Than an Hour." *Windows NT Magazine,* September 1995: 35–37.

Lemay, Laura. "Frames for HTML." *Web Techniques,* May 1996: 18–23.

Lemay, Laura. "Design Strategies for HTML Coders." *Web Techniques,* April 1996: 18–23.

Mendelson, Edward. "No Experience Required." *PC Magazine,* 10 October 1995: 203–219.

Metz, Cade. "The 100 Top Web Sites." *PC Magazine,* 6 February 1996: 100–142.

Microsoft Corporation. "Microsoft Internet Information Server." *PC Magazine,* 23 April 1996: NE34–NE35.

Nelson, Mark R. "Microsoft's Internet Assistant." *Web Techniques,* May 1996: 69–73.

Ozer, Jan. "Audio… Video… Live From the Web." *PC Magazine,* 23 April 1996: 100–145.

Pleas, Keith. "Visual Basic Script." *Microsoft Interactive Developer,* Spring 1996: 55–63.

Pompili, Tony. "Evolving Internet Security Methods." *PC Magazine,* 23 April 1996: 209–210.

Prosise, Jeff. "The Netscape Security Breach." *PC Magazine,* 23 April 1996: 199–200.

Scoggins, Steve. "The SLIP/PPP Route." *Windows NT Magazine,* September 1995: 21–25.

Siegel, David. "The Balkanization of the Web." *Web Techniques,* April 1996: 33–40, 73–74.

Sigler, Douglas L. "HTML Toolbox." *Internet World,* April 1996: 51–52.

Stark, Thom. "Internet Mail Is a MIME Field." *LAN Times,* 5 February 1996: 110.

Templeman, Michael. "Collision Course: Javascript and VB Script." *Visual Basic Programmer's Journal,* April 1996: 46–55.

Tropiano, Lenny, and Dinah McNutt. "How to Implement ISDN." *Byte,* April

Udell, John. "Web Design." *Byte,* March 1996: 91–94.

Venditto, Gus. "Dueling Tools." *Internet World,* April 1996: 37–49.

Yaari, Ronen. "Proxy Servers Without the Pain." *NetGuide,* February 1996: 93–94.

Internet Drafts

"Hypertext Markup Language 2.0" (Internet Draft) by T. Berners-Lee and D. Connolly, 1995.

"HyperText Markup Language Specification Version 3.0" (Internet Draft) by Dave Raggett, 1995.

"Hypertext Transfer Protocol HTTP 1.0" (Internet Draft) by T Berners-Lee, R. T. Fielding, H. Frystyk Nielsen, 1995.

Web Pages

"A Beginner's Guide to HTML," by National Center for Supercomputing Applications, pubs@ncsa.uiuc.edu http://www.ncsa.uiuc.edu/demoweb/html-primer.html.

"Building Internet Servers," by CyberGroup, Inc., http://www.charm.net/~cyber/.

"Clickable Image Maps," by Russ Jones, http://gnn.com/gnn/bus/ora/features/miis/index.html.

"iNformaTion," http://rmm.com/nt/ by Roger Marty.

"Publishing on the World Wide Web," by Gareth Rees, http://www.cl.cam.ac.uk/users/gdr11/publish.html.

"Rick's Windows NT Info Center," by Rick Graesslen, http://137.226.92.4/rick/.

"The Windows NT Resource Center," by Dave Baker, http://www.bhs.com/winnt/

"Windows NT Server White Papers," http://www.microsoft.com/ntserver/whtpap.htm.

"World Wide Web Robots, Wanderers, and Spiders," by Martijn Koster, m.koster@nexor.co.uk http://web.nexor.co.uk/mak/doc/robots/robots.html.

White Papers

"Advanced Internetworking with TCP/IP on Windows NT," by J. Allard 1993 Microsoft Corp.

"Microsoft Windows NT 3.5/3.51 TCP/IP Implementation Details," by Steve MacDonald 1995. Microsoft Corp.

Glossary

Access   A commercial desktop database for Windows developed by Microsoft. A runtime version of the database engine is included with Visual Basic.

ActiveX   The 1996 name for the OLE custom control technology invented by Microsoft. ActiveX and Java, open new possibilities for highly dynamic Web pages and Internet client/server applications on the Web. ActiveX controls, which are written in C, C++, or Java, can be controlled from within HTML code by VBScript. See also *OLE*. See also *Java*. See also *VBScript*.

American Standard Code for Information Interchange (ASCII)   A standard that encodes 128 common English characters by using 7 of the 8 bits in a byte. It also describes the file format of text files.

API   See *Application Programming Interface*.

Application Programming Interface (API)   The set of functions provided by the operating system as a service to programmers. Using an API is easier than having to develop the capability from scratch and helps to ensure some consistency across all programs that run on a given operating system.

Archie   This search utility keeps a database of FTP servers and the files that each has available. The Archie client queries the Archie server that keeps the database. Archie servers can also be queried by e-mail or by Telnet. There are a few dozen Archie servers on the Internet. This tool works best if you have some idea of the filename that you are looking for. It will return a list of domain names of anonymous FTP sites where the string you entered is contained within directory names or filenames.

ASCII   See *American Standard Code for Information Interchange.*

Asynchronous Transfer Mode (ATM)   A new data transmission technology that can deliver super-high throughput of 25 Mbps to 622 Mbps.

ATM   See *Asynchronous Transfer Mode.*

Backbone   Nationwide or international connections (usually T3 bandwidth) that provide the basic structure and IP packet routing on the Internet. Regional backbones (usually T1 bandwidth) provide the connections and IP packet routing for several local area ISPs.

Bandwidth   The difference between the highest and lowest sinusoidal frequency signals that can be transmitted across a transmission line or through a network. It is measured in Hertz (Hz) and also defines the maximum information-carrying capacity of the line or network.

Bridge   A network computer or device that contains two-link layer interfaces and listens to all packet traffic on both networks to determine that packets should be allowed to pass between the two.

Byte   See *Random Access Memory.*

C   C is a very popular general-purpose programming language invented in the late 1960s by Dennis Ritchie at AT&T Bell Laboratories.

C++   C++ is a very popular general-purpose and object-oriented programming language invented in the early 1980s by Bjarne Stroustrup at AT&T Bell Laboratories. C++ compilers will also accept most programs written in standard C.

Cairo   Cairo is the code name (made public for marketing reasons) of the next major release of Windows NT, currently expected to be beta tested in early 1997.

Canonical Name (CNAME)   See *DNS Alias.*

Cascading Style Sheets   Invented by Håkon Lie, CSS is a new addition to HTML 3.0, which allows page designers to have greater control over the rendering of a document. Browsers that support style sheets will allow font and color attributes to be specified. CSS1, the first phase of Cascading Style Sheets,.

CCITT   See *Consultative Committee for International Telephone and Telegraph.*

Central Processing Unit (CPU)   The microprocessor, or brain, which performs most of the calculations necessary to run a computer program.

CERN   The European Laboratory for Particle Physics (CERN) invented HTTP and HTML (which led to the World Wide Web) to share information among research groups. See also *World Wide Web.*

CGI   See *Common Gateway Interface.*

Channel Service Unit/Data Service Unit (CSU/DSU)   These are frequently packaged together as one device. A CSU/DSU is used for interfacing with a T1, Frame Relay, or ISDN line. In some cases, it is bundled inside of the router, such as the Ascend Pipeline router for ISDN. It serves much the same purpose for high-speed digital lines as a modem does for analog phone lines. (You could call it the digital analog of the modem.) It resides between your computer (or router) and the phone company data line that leaves your building.

Client-Pull   This is an HTML technique that tells the Web browser to repeatedly request a document from the server. The time interval, the number of requests, and the URL of the document to be retrieved, can all be specified by the page designer.

Client-Side Imagemaps   This is a new HTML technique that allows the browser to process hyperlink clicks within image regions without the server having to get involved. The advantage of this approach is that the browser can display the destination URL of a region when the mouse passes over it and some network traffic is saved because the browser can directly request the new document when a click is made.

CNAME   See *DNS Alias.*

Common Gateway Interface (CGI)   CGI is an interface for external programs to talk to the HTTP server. Programs that are written to use CGI are called *CGI programs* or *CGI scripts.* CGI programs are typically used to handle forms or perform output parsing not done by the server. See also *ISAPI.* See also *WinCGI.*

Common Logfile Format   The common logfile format is used by most Web servers to enter information into the access logs. The format is the same among all of the major Web servers, including Netscape Commerce and Communications servers, CERN httpd, and NCSA httpd. The EMWAC HTTPS does not follow the Common Logfile Format. Microsoft IIS comes with a tool for converting the IIS enhanced logfile format to the Common Logfile Format.

Consultative Committee for International Telephone and Telegraph (CCITT)   Regulates world-wide data communications standards. Recently renamed the Telecommunications Standards Sector, which is a body of the International Telecommunications Union.

Cookies   See *Persistent Cookies.*

CPU   See *Central Processing Unit.*

CSS1   See *Cascading Style Sheets.*

CSU/DSU   See *Channel Service Unit/Data Service Unit.*

DCOM   See *Distributed Component Object Model.*

Daemon   Pronounced *day-mon.* Any program that runs in the background waiting to be used by other programs. Also known as a *server.*

Data Communications Equipment (DCE)   DCE devices most often reside between the computer and an external data source. The most familiar kind of DCE device is the modem. The computer is usually considered a DTE (Data Terminal Equipment) device. Communications software running on the DTE (computer) must activate the DTR (Data Terminal Ready) signal on the DCE (modem) whenever the software and the computer are ready for further data transmission. The DTE and DCE are usually connected through an RS-232C serial interface and a UART.

Data Terminal Equipment (DTE)   See *Data Communications Equipment.*

DCE   See *Data Communications Equipment.*

DHCP   See *Dynamic Host Control Protocol.*

Distributed Component Object Model (DCOM)   The Component Object Model is the protocol on which OLE is based. DCOM is an enhanced version of COM, available in NT 4, which allows programs to share data with each other and provide services for each other across a network. Prior to Windows NT 4, COM was only functional between programs running on the same computer. You may sometimes hear DCOM referred to as *Network OLE* or *Distributed OLE.*

DLL   See *Dynamic Link Library.*

DNS   See *Domain Name System.*

DNS Alias   A DNS alias is a hostname that the DNS server knows points to a different host—specifically a DNS NAME record. Machines always have one real name, but they can have one or more aliases. For example, `www.yourdomain.domain` might be an alias that points to a real machine called `realthing.yourdomain.domain` where the server currently exists. DNS aliases are sometimes referred to as CNAMEs or canonical names.

DNS Name Servers   In the DNS client/server model, these are the servers containing information about a portion of the DNS database, which make IP addresses available to client resolvers that query the database across the Internet when performing a name lookup.

Document root   A directory on the server machine that contains the files, images, and data you want to present to users accessing the server.

Domain Name System (DNS)   A DNS is used by machines on a network to associate standard IP addresses (such as `206.43.105.233`) with hostnames (such as `www.hqz.com`). Computers normally get this translated information from a DNS server or look it up in tables maintained on their systems.

Dynamic Link Library   A file that contains a collection of subroutines or resources for use by Windows programs or other DLLs. Windows needs to load only one copy of the DLL into memory regardless of how many running programs will take advantage of it. Windows itself consists almost entirely of DLLs.

DTE   See *Data Terminal Equipment.*

Environment Variable   The environment table that exists for a program, such as the shell command processor, is a list of variables and their associated string values. Environment variables are used heavily by CGI and sometimes console-mode programs. They are rarely used by Windows GUI programs, except that ISAPI programs adopt and extend the CGI conventions.

Ethernet   Refers to the standard developed by Digital Equipment, Intel, And Xerox in 1982. It is the predominant standard in local area networks today. Ethernet uses the Carrier Sense, Multiple Access with Collision Detection (CSMA/CD) access method. Ethernet is also covered by the IEEE 802.3 standard.

FAT   See *File Allocation Table.*

FDDI   See *Fiber Distributed Data Interface.*

Fiber Distributed Data Interface (FDDI)   A high-speed (100 Mbps) network cabling technology that is immune to Radio Frequency Interference from other electrical sources and protected from the possibility of electronic eavesdropping.

File Allocation Table (FAT)   The file system used by MS-DOS through version 6.22. FAT is famous for the fact that it limits filenames to 8 characters with 3 characters for the file extension. Although the primary file system in Windows NT is NTFS, FAT is also available in NT for backward-compatibility. The file system in Windows 95 is a superset of FAT, called VFAT which permits long filenames.

File Extension   The last section of a filename that typically defines the type of file (for example, .GIF and .HTML). For example, in the filename index.html the file extension is .html. (.htm is also commonly used as the extension for HTML files.)

File Transfer Protocol (FTP)   A protocol that governs file transfers between local and remote systems. The programs that use this protocol are referred to as FTP clients and FTP servers. FTP supports several commands that enable bidirectional transfer of binary and ASCII files. The FTP server service in NT 4 is installed with IIS. Note that the client that comes with NT is a command-line version.

File Type   The format of a given file (for example, a graphics file doesn't have the same internal representation as a text file). File types are usually identified by the file extension (for example, .GIF or .HTML).

Firewall   A security device placed on a LAN to protect it from Internet intruders. This can be a special kind of hardware router, a piece of software, or both.

FQDN   See *Fully Qualified Domain Name.*

Frames   Frames are an HTML 3.2 feature invented by Netscape. Using frames, a Web page can be partitioned so that it displays several documents at once, each one in a separate window.

Frame Relay   A data transmission technology becoming more popular as a means of replacing expensive T1 leased-lines in wide area networks. Frame Relay and Fractional T1 can be purchased in units more appropriate for anticipated network traffic, can be scaled up or down over time, and can be used without predefining multiple point-to-point connections.

FTP   See *File Transfer Protocol.*

Fully Qualified Domain Name (FQDN)   Hostnames with their domain names appended to them. For example, on a host with a hostname www and DNS domain name yourco.com, the FQDN is www.yourco.com.

Gateway   A gateway is a network computer that is running software for more than one network interface. The gateway manages the flow of data between the two networks according to routing tables.

GIF   See *Graphics Interchange Format.*

Gigabyte   See *Random Access Memory.*

Gopher   The Internet program invented at the University of Minnesota for distribution of text files that are selected through character-based menus.

Graphics Interchange Format (GIF)   A cross-platform image format originally created by CompuServe. GIF files are usually much smaller in size than other graphic file types (such as BMP and TIF). GIF is one of the most common interchange formats and is readily viewable on many platforms.

Graphical User Interface (GUI)   This describes the method of interaction that a program offers to its user. A GUI permits mouse and keyboard control, as opposed to a command-line interface, which requires keyboard entry. Most Windows programs include a GUI with user-friendly buttons, menus, and scrollbars. Console applications can only be run in the NT Command Prompt window.

GUI   See *Graphical User Interface.*

Home Page   An HTML document that exists on the WWW server and acts as a catalog or entry point for the server's contents. The location of this document is defined within the server's configuration dialog.

Hostname   A name for a machine of the form machine.subdomain.domain, which is translated into an IP address. For example, www.hqz.com is considered a hostname or a Fully Qualified Domain Name. This machine, www can be either a unique machine (or host) in the subdomain (or network) or an alias (or CNAME) to another machine in the subdomain (or network).

HTML   See *Hypertext Markup Language.*

HTTP   See *Hypertext Transfer Protocol.*

HTTPD   An abbreviation for the HTTP daemon, a program that serves information using the HTTP protocol. UNIX-based HTTP Servers are often called HTTPDs.

HTTPS   In the PC world, HTTPS is the abbreviation for the HTTP server, a program that serves information using the HTTP protocol. Sometimes, HTTPS is also used as the designation for the Secure Sockets Layer specification, but this is more commonly referred to as the S-HTTP specification.

Hypertext Markup Language (HTML)   HTML is a formatting language used for documents on the World Wide Web. HTML files are plain text files with formatting codes that tell browsers, such as Netscape Navigator, how to display text, position graphics and form items, and display hypertext links to other pages.

Hypertext Transfer Protocol (HTTP)   The standard method for exchanging information between HTTP servers and clients on the Web. The HTTP specification lays out the rules of how Web servers and browsers must work together.

IDE   See *Integrated Drive Electronics.*

Imagemap   A process that enables users to navigate and obtain information by clicking the different regions of the image with a mouse. Imagemap can also refer to a CGI program called *imagemap,* which provides image mapping functionality in UNIX-based httpd implementations.

Industry Standard Architecture (ISA)   Defines the standard IBM PC bus.

Integrated Digital Services Network (ISDN)   Essentially operates as digital phone line. ISDN delivers many benefits over standard analog phone lines, including multiple simultaneous calls and higher-quality data transmissions. ISDN data rates are 56 Kbps to 128 Kbps.

Integrated Drive Electronics (IDE)   A standard disk drive adapter designed for the PC ISA.

Internet Services Application Programming Interface (ISAPI)   A new version of CGI using DLLs rather than external applications. ISAPI was invented by Purveyor and Microsoft to extend the performance of their Windows NT based HTTP servers.

InterNIC   The organization charged with maintaining unique addresses for every computer on the Internet using the Domain Name System.

Internet Protocol (IP)   The protocol that governs how packets are built and sent over the network. IP does not guarantee packet delivery or the order of delivery. TCP runs on top of IP to provide a reliable and sequenced internetwork communication stream. See also *Transmission Control Protocol/Internet Protocol* (TCP/IP).

Internet Service Provider (ISP)   The company that provides you or your company with access to the Internet. ISPs usually have several servers and a high-speed link to the Internet backbone.

Intranet   Most commonly used to describe a corporate network (LAN or WAN) that uses TCP/IP and related application layer protocols such as HTTP, SMTP, and POP3. An Intranet doesn't necessarily include a permanent connection to the Internet. Intranets can be used for publishing and sharing company documents internally, as well as for implementing custom-developed client/server applications within the enterprise.

IP   See *Internet Protocol.*

IP Address   An Internet Protocol address is a set of four numbers (4 bytes, or 32 bits) separated by dots, which specifies the actual location of a machine on the Internet.

ISA   See *Industry Standard Architecture.*

ISAPI   See *Internet Services Application Programming Interface.*

ISDN   See *Integrated Digital Services Network.*

ISINDEX   HTML documents that contain the <ISINDEX> tag can use a Web browser's capabilities to accept a search string and send it to the server to access a searchable index without using forms. To use <ISINDEX>, a query handler must exist on the server.

ISMAP   ISMAP is an extension to the <IMG SRC> tag used in an HTML document to tell the server that the image functions as an imagemap.

ISP   See *Internet Service Provider.*

Java   A new object-oriented programming language invented by Sun Microsystems. Java, which is based heavily on C++, is widely considered a very strong language for developing client/server applications on the Web.

Key   An entry in the NT Registry Editor that contains a unit of configuration information.

Kilobyte   See *Random Access Memory.*

Megabyte   See *Random Access Memory.*

LAN   See *Local Area Network.*

Listserver or **Listserv**   A server application that allows group members to broadcast e-mail messages amongst themselves. An individual sends a single e-mail message to the server, which in turn sends it to all the other members of the listserv group.

Local Area Network   A group of computers and peripheral devices that are wired together for the common good of all users. This is usually done in an office environment for the purpose of sharing files and printers. Typical LAN sizes range from 2 to 100 computers.

Mailto   An HTML element in the <A HREF> tag, which will open an e-mail client window in preparation for sending a message to the recipient specified in the HTML document.

MIME   See *Multi-Purpose Internet Mail Extensions.*

Multi-Purpose Internet Mail Extensions (MIME)   This is an emerging standard for multimedia file transfers on the Internet via e-mail or the Web.

Multi-Threaded   A programming technique that allows for more than one part of a program to be executing simultaneously on an SMP machine. Even on single CPU computers, multi-threaded programs can show the advantage of better responsiveness to user commands while a lengthy background process is running.

National Center for Supercomputing Applications (NCSA)   A research organization at the University of Illinois at Urbana-Champaign. NCSA is credited with the invention of Mosaic, the world's first graphical Web browser. Internet popularity has skyrocketed in the years since 1993 following the availability of Mosaic for desktop computers such as PCs and Macintoshes. See also *National Computer Security Association.*

National Computer Security Association (NCSA)   Provides a broad range of Internet and computer security advice and information. This NCSA is the registered owner of the NCSA trademark. See also *National Center for Supercomputing Applications* (NCSA).

NCSA   See *National Center for Supercomputing Applications*. See also *National Computer Security Association*.

Network News Transfer Protocol (NNTP)   This is the protocol Usenet runs to deliver newsgroups. There are thousands of newsgroups on the Internet. Each one is similar to a bulletin board devoted to a particular topic that its readers like to discuss.

NNTP   See *Network News Transfer Protocol*.

NT File System (NTFS)   This is the advanced file system that Windows NT provides as an option when formatting hard drives. The advantages of this system are long filenames, reduced file fragmentation, improved fault tolerance, and better recovery performance after a crash (as compared to DOS or OS/2).

NTFS   See *NT File System*.

Object Linking and Embedding (OLE)   The API developed by Microsoft on which much of the Windows NT 4 and Windows 95 user interface is based. Originally intended only to provide a means of treating documents as objects useable by other documents, it has since been expanded to include cut-and-paste functionality, the capability to program component objects from applications (including Web pages), store files and directories within compound files, and serve as the basis for distributed objects via remote procedure calls in the Cairo version of Windows NT.

ODBC   See *Open Database Connectivity*.

OLE   See *Object Linking and Embedding*.

Open Database Connectivity (ODBC)   The database-independent API developed by Microsoft to provide application developers with a portable means of writing database programs. Database vendors (such as Oracle, Informix, Sybase, Microsoft) supply low-level drivers conforming with the interface to ODBC.DLL. Application programmers make standard calls to ODBC.DLL to access any database regardless of its proprietary format.

PCI   See *Peripheral Component Interconnect*.

PDC   See *Primary Domain Controller*.

Peripheral Component Interconnect (PCI)   PCI is a local bus motherboard design from Intel. It is designed to compete with the industry consortium that developed VESA local bus (VLB.) It runs at half the speed of the main CPU, as opposed to a constant 6 MHz rate for the standard PC ISA bus and the VESA local bus. Its performance outshines VLB in many respects. It is becoming very popular in new Pentium-based systems.

Perl   See *Practical Extraction and Report Language*.

Ping   A TCP/IP program that is used to verify network connections between computers and to time how long packets take to traverse the route.

POP, **POP3**   See *Post Office Protocol.*

Post Office Protocol (POP, or POP3)   Defined by RFC 1721, POP3 is an application-level protocol designed to handle the mail at a local level. The POP3 mailbox stores mail received by SMTP (the routing agent) until it is read by the user. It also passes outgoing messages to the SMTP server for subsequent delivery to the addressee.

Point-to-Point Protocol (PPP)   An industry standard that is part of Windows 95 dial-up networking and Windows NT Remote Access Software (RAS) that allows you to connect to the Internet. Because it offers greater performance, PPP has widely replaced SLIP for remote Internet connections.

Port   A connection or socket used to connect a TCP/IP-based client application to your server. Servers are normally known by their well-known port number as assigned by the Internet Assigned Numbers Authority (IANA). The well-known port for HTTP is 80.

PPP   See *Point-to-Point Protocol.*

Practical Extraction and Report Language (PERL)   Perl is a programming language designed for scanning arbitrary text files, extracting information, and printing reports. Perl programs are called scripts because they are processed by an interpreter, as opposed to a compiler.

Protocol   A set of rules and conventions by which two computers pass messages across a network.

Proxy Server   A computer program that runs on a server placed between a LAN and its connection to the Internet. The proxy server software will filter all outgoing connections to appear as if they came from only one machine. The purpose for doing this is to prevent external hackers from knowing the structure of your network. The system administrator might also regulate the outside points to which the LAN users may connect.

RAM   See *Random Access Memory.*

Random Access Memory (RAM)   The physical semiconductor-based memory in a computer. One byte of RAM can hold one character, such as the period at the end of this sentence. One kilobyte (KB) holds 1024 characters. One megabyte (MB) of RAM holds one million characters (actually 1024 * 1024). Not counting graphics, this book consists of roughly 1,000,000 characters, or one megabyte. One gigabyte (GB) is equal to one thousand megabytes. Yes, that's a lot, and no, it isn't always enough. Terabytes (TB) are not discussed too commonly yet by ordinary folks, but just so you know, 1TB equals 1000GB.

Redirection   A system by which clients accessing a particular URL can be sent to a different location, either on the same server or on a different server.

Registry   The Windows NT and Windows 95 system database that holds configuration information for hardware, software, and users.

Resource   As it pertains to HTML, this refers to any document (URL), directory, or program that the server can access and send to a client that asks for it.

Request for Comments (RFCs)   The official documents of the IETF (Internet Engineering Task Force) that specify the details of all the protocols and systems that comprise the Internet.

RFC   See *Request For Comments.*

Robot   For our purposes, we are referring to software robots on the Web. These applications wander the Internet looking for Web servers and return indexing information to their host. Robots are most often used to create databases of Web sites. The Lycos Search Web page database is maintained by the Lycos Robot.

Router   This is a special-purpose computer used for connecting two or more networks together. Most routers enable you to create a physical connection between different types of networks such as Ethernet, Token Ring, and FDDI.

SCSI   See *Small Computer Systems Interface.*

Secure Sockets Layer (SSL)   This is a software interface developed by Netscape that provides for encrypted data transfer between client and server applications over the Internet. SSL, STT, SET, and S-HTTP (which is a secure version of the Hypertext Transfer Protocol) are all means of enabling secure commerce on the Web. A preferred standard is yet to emerge.

Serial Line Internet Protocol (SLIP)   SLIP is an industry standard protocol that encapsulates IP packets for transmission through modems. It is one of the available protocols when using TCP/IP with RAS.

Server   In general, refers to a computer that provides shared resources to network users. In some specific cases, related to the Internet, server refers to the TCP/IP application layer protocol server, such as HTTPS.

Server-Push   A CGI technique a server can use to continually update a document being sent to a client. A CGI application on the server sends a special HTTP document header to the Web browser so that a network connection will remain open while the completion of the data is sent.

Server Root   A directory on the server machine dedicated to holding the server program, configuration, maintenance, and information files.

Server-Side Includes   An HTML technique whereby the Web server parses a document before sending it to the client in order to find text sequences to be replaced by real-time information.

Service   A service is an executable object installed in the NT Registry database. A service can be started on demand or started automatically when the system starts up. No more than one instance of a given service can be running at a time.

SGML   See *Standard Generalized Markup Language.*

Simple Mail Transfer Protocol (SMTP)   A standard protocol in TCP/IP that determines how e-mail is transferred on the Internet.

Simple Network Management Protocol (SNMP)   A standard protocol in TCP/IP that determines how networks are monitored for performance.

SLIP   See *Serial Line Internet Protocol.*

Small Computer Systems Interface (SCSI)   Pronounced *scuzzy,* this is a type of hardware interface standard for computers and peripheral devices. It is general-purpose, but most often it is used for hard disk drives, CD-ROM drives, and scanners. SCSI is supported on many platforms. On Windows NT it is the preferred CD-ROM interface. SCSI and IDE drives and controllers can operate together in the same system. Up to seven SCSI devices can be daisy-chained together on one controller card (counting the card itself as one device). Although IDE (or EIDE) remains more popular for PC hard drives because of price, SCSI drives usually offer better performance—especially many of the new varieties of SCSI, such as SCSI II and Fast-Wide SCSI. A single Wide SCSI adapter can daisy-chain up to 13 devices.

SMP   See *Symmetric Multi-processor.*

SMTP   See *Simple Mail Transfer Protocol.*

SNMP   See *Simple Network Management Protocol.*

SSL   See *Secure Sockets Layer.*

Standard Generalized Markup Language (SGML)   This is ISO standard 8879:1986 for Information Processing Text and Office Systems. HTML is an application of this standard.

Style Sheets   Style sheets are an extension to HTML 3.2 to allow page designers to specify font and color attributes. See also *Cascading Style Sheets* (CSS1).

Switched-56   This is a circuit-switched technology with a throughput of 56 Kbps. It has been the middle-ground between analog phone lines and dedicated T1 lines prior to the development of ISDN.

Symmetric Multi-Processor (SMP)   A computer architecture in which more than one CPU is running and sharing memory simultaneously. This capability does not exist in Windows 95, but Windows NT is designed to take advantage of SMP hardware both inside the operating system and at the application level through the creation of separate threads using the WIN32 API.

T1   A data transmission medium capable of 1.544 Mbps. Lines can be leased for private or corporate use between two designated points. Some Internet Service Providers offer it.

T3   A data transmission medium capable of 45 Mbps. It is usually only in the Internet backbone or in large institutions.

TCP   See *Transmission Control Protocol.*

Telnet   A protocol where two machines on the network are connected to each other and support terminal emulation for remote login. A remote computer running a Telnet client application can execute any console based application on an NT Telnet server.

Terabyte   See *Random Access Memory.*

Timeout   A specified time after which a program should give up trying to finish an operation with a remote machine that appears to be non-responsive.

Token Ring   An IBM network arranged in a circular topology in which a circulating electronic token is used to carry the active packet. A node on the network must wait until the empty token passes by before it may insert a message onto the LAN. Token Ring is covered by the IEEE 802.5 standard.

Top-level Domain   The highest category of hostname classification, usually signifying either the type of organization the domain is (for example, .com is a company, and .edu is an educational institution), or the country of its origin (for example, .uk is the United Kingdom and .jp is Japan).

Transmission Control Protocol (TCP)   A connection-based Internet protocol responsible for breaking data into packets, which the Internet Protocol sends over the network. TCP provides a reliable and sequenced internetwork communication stream.

Transmission Control Protocol/Internet Protocol (TCP/IP)   The Internet protocols used to connect a world-wide internetwork of universities, research laboratories, military installations, organizations, and corporations. TCP/IP includes standards for how computers communicate and conventions for connecting networks and routing traffic.

UDP   See *User Datagram Protocol.*

Unicode   A 16-bit character encoding system that covers all the symbols in all the languages of the world and several currency, science, and mathematics symbols. Windows NT uses Unicode internally for all strings and filenames, and provides a set of Unicode APIs so that application developers can more easily build international programs. Windows 95 includes limited support for Unicode.

Uniform Resource Locator (URL)   Also commonly called a location. This is an addressing system that locates documents on servers. A client uses the URL to request a document to be viewed. The format of a URL is *protocol://machine:port/document*, though some parts of the full syntax are usually optional. An example, without specifying the HTTP default port number of 80, is http://www.hqz.com/default.html.

Uninterruptible Power Supply(UPS)   See *UPS.*

UPS   A battery-operated power supply connected to a computer to keep the system running just long enough to perform an orderly shut-down during a power failure.

URL   See *Uniform Resource Locator.*

User Datagram Protocol (UDP)   Runs on top of IP to provide more efficient, but less reliable, packet delivery than TCP. UDP is used for certain Internet programs such as Trivial File Transfer Protocol and Ping.

VBS   See *Visual Basic Script.*

VBScript   See *Visual Basic Script*.

Veronica   This gets its name from Very Easy Rodent-Oriented Net-wide Index to Computer-ized Archives. Veronica is a utility for searching gopher databases. It is accessed as a menu item displayed by a gopher server. The data returned by Veronica is displayed as yet another menu of gopher menu items that match the given search topic.

VESA Local Bus (VLB)   This is a popular type of PC local bus defined by the Video Electronics Standards Association. Most VLB machines can support two or three such devices. Peripheral cards in the VLB expansion slots operate with far less overhead than standard cards. It is most frequently used for EIDE hard-drive controllers or VGA display adapters—two devices that are heavily dependent on data throughput rates.

Virtual Memory   A software technique, often implemented in the operating system, that uses hard disk space to increase memory capacity beyond the amount of physical RAM present. Windows NT will automatically reload virtual memory from the hard disk into RAM at the instant that an application calls for it. This is not to be confused with a RAM Disk, which is a program that uses RAM to serve as a fast disk drive.

Virtual Reality Markup Language (VRML)   VRML is a draft specification that describes how to implement support for virtual-reality scenes on the Web. It builds on the foundation of HTML, but it is a new language. Like HTML, the language is not binary-restricted to any particular platform. With virtual reality support, clients are able to traverse 3-D Web pages.

Visual Basic   A point-and-click programming environment from Microsoft for development of Windows programs in the BASIC language. It is popular for its ease of screen design. It includes the Access database engine.

Visual Basic Script   An HTML scripting language invented by Microsoft. VBScript is based heavily on the syntax of Visual Basic, yet the former is far less functional so that it can be small, portable, and secure.

VLB   See *VESA Local Bus*.

VRML   See *Virtual Reality Markup Language*.

WAIS (Wide Area Information Server)   WAIS is a subset of the Z39.50-88 protocol that enables remote WAIS clients to conduct searches of server databases that have been prepared using a waisindex tool.

Win16   The 16-bit Windows API that was developed in Windows version 1.0 and extended through Windows For Workgroups version 3.11. It is 16 bits because it usually uses 2 bytes to represent programming objects such as integers, references to windows, and pointers to memory. Windows NT and Windows 95 support the newer Win32 API as well as programs written for the older Win16 API. See also *Win32*.

Win32   The 32-bit Windows API that was developed in Windows NT version 3.1 and extended through Windows NT 4.x and Windows 95. It is 32-bits because it usually uses 4 bytes to represent programming objects such as integers, references to windows, and pointers to memory. The Win32 API is a much richer and more robust API than Win16. In many cases, programs written for Win16 are very upwardly compatible with Win32.

WinCGI A new Common Gateway Interface for Windows GUI programs that doesn't require console-mode programs. Many Windows HTTP server packages include a reference implementation in Visual Basic that demonstrates the simple retrieval of CGI environment variables. See also *Common Gateway Interface.*

Windows 95 The desktop operating system from Microsoft for home and business application software running on PCs. Windows 95 is the all-in-one successor to DOS, Windows 3.1, and Windows for Workgroups 3.11.

Windows NT The portable, secure, 32-bit, preemptive, SMP, multitasking member of the Microsoft Windows operating system family.

Windows NT Server As a superset of Windows NT Workstation, Windows NT Server provides better centralized management and security, advanced fault tolerance, and additional connectivity options.

Windows NT Workstation The less expensive version of Windows NT. This version is intended for use as a desktop or personal operating system rather than as a central server for a workgroup or domain. NT Workstation 4.0 includes Peer Web Services, excellent networking support, and the ability to run DOS, Win16, and Win32 applications.

I

Index

W-Z

HTML in 10 seconds!*

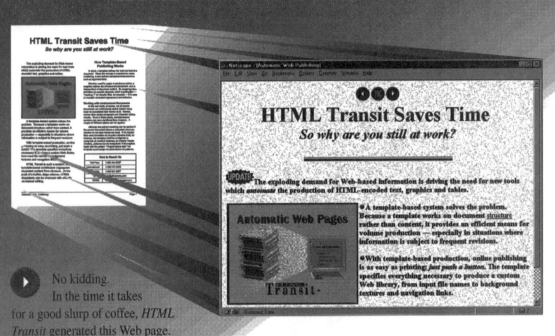

No kidding.
In the time it takes for a good slurp of coffee, *HTML Transit* generated this Web page.

Say hello to the template.

HTML Transit takes a new approach to online publishing, using a high-speed production template. It's fast and easy. You can turn a 50-page word processing file into multiple, linked HTML pages—complete with graphics and tables—in less than 10 mouse clicks. From scratch.

Customize your template—formatting, backgrounds, navigation buttons, thumbnails—and save even more time. Now in just 4 clicks, you can crank out an entire library of custom Web pages with no manual authoring.

Take a free test drive.

Stop working so hard. Download an evaluation copy of *HTML Transit* from our Web site:

http://www.infoaccess.com

Your download code is **MCML46**. (It can save you money when you order *HTML Transit*.)

Buy HTML Transit risk free.

HTML Transit is just $495, and is backed by a 30-day satisfaction guarantee. To order, call us toll-free at **800-344-9737**.

InfoAccess, Inc.
(206) 747-3203
FAX: (206) 641-9367
Email: info@infoaccess.com

- ▶ Automatic HTML from native word processor formats
- ▶ Creates HTML tables, tables of contents & indexes
- ▶ Graphics convert to GIF or JPEG, with thumbnails
- ▶ Template control over appearance and behavior
- ▶ For use with Microsoft® Windows®

HTML Transit is a trademark of InfoAccess, Inc. Microsoft and Windows are registered trademarks of Microsoft Corporation.
*Single-page Microsoft Word document with graphics and tables, running on 75MHz Pentium. Conversion speed depends on document length, complexity and PC configuration.

Teach Yourself JavaScript in a Week

— *Arman Danesh*

Teach Yourself JavaScript in a Week is the easiest way to learn how to create interactive Web pages with JavaScript, Netscape's Java-like scripting language. It is intended for non-programmers, and will be equally of value to users on the Macintosh, Windows, and UNIX platforms. Teaches how to design and create attention-grabbing Web pages with JavaScript, and shows how to add interactivity to Web pages.

$39.99 USA/$56.95 CAN   User Level: Intermediate-Advanced
ISBN: 1-57521-073-8   450 pages

Web Publishing Unleashed

— *Stanek, et al.*

Includes sections on how to organize and plan your information, design pages, and become familar with hypertext and hypermedia. Choose from a range of applications and technologies, including Java, SGML, VRML, and the newest HTML and Netscape extensions. The CD-ROM contains software, templates, and examples to help you become a successful Web publisher.

Price: $45.00 USA/$63.95 CAN   User Level: Casual-Expert
ISBN: 1-57521-051-7   1,000 pages

Creating Web Applets with Java

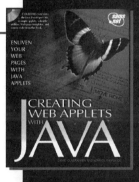

—*David Gulbransen and Kendrick Rawlings*

Creating Web Applets with Java is the easiest way to learn how to integrate existing Java applets into your Web pages. This book is designed for the non-programmer who wants to use or customize preprogrammed Java applets with a minimal amount of trouble. It teaches the easiest way to incorporate the power of Java in a Web page, and covers the basics of Java applet programming. Find out how to use and customize preprogrammed Java applets. Includes a CD-ROM full of useful applets.

$39.99 USA/$56.95 CAN   User Level: Casual-Accomplished
ISBN: 1-57521-070-3   350 pages

Java Unleashed

—*Various*

Java Unleashed is the ultimate guide to the year's hottest new Internet technologies, the Java language and the HotJava browser from Sun Microsystems. *Java Unleashed* is a complete programmer's reference and a guide to the hundreds of exciting ways Java is being used to add interactivity to the World Wide Web. It describes how to use Java to add interactivity to Web presentations, and shows how Java and HotJava are being used across the Internet. Includes a helpful and informative CD-ROM.

$49.99 USA/$70.95 CAN   User Level: Casual-Expert
ISBN: 1-57521-049-5   1,000 pages

Teach Yourself Netscape Web Publishing in a Week

— Wes Tatters

Teach Yourself Netscape Web Publishing in a Week is the easiest way to learn how to produce attention-getting, well-designed Web pages using the features provided by Netscape Navigator. Intended for both the novice and the expert, this book provides a solid grounding in HTML and Web publishing principles, while providing special focus on the possibilities presented by the Netscape environment. Learn to design and create attention-grabbing Web pages for the Netscape environment while exploring new Netscape development features such as frames, plug-ins, Java applets, and JavaScript!

Price: $39.99 USA/ $56.95 CAN   User Level: Beginner-Inter
ISBN: 1-57521-068-1   450 pages

Teach Yourself CGI Programming with Perl in a Week

— Eric Herrmann

This book is a step-by-step tutorial of how to create, use, and maintain Common Gateway Interfaces (CGI). It describes effective ways of using CGI as an integral part of Web development, and adds interactivity and flexibility to the information that can be provided through your Web site. Includes Perl 4.0 and 5.0, CGI libraries, and other applications to create databases, dynamic interactivity, and other enticing page effects.

Price: $39.99 USA/$56.95 CAN   User Level: Inter-Advanced
ISBN: 1-57521-009-6   500 pages

Teach Yourself Java in 21 Days

— Laura Lemay and Charles Perkins

The complete tutorial guide to the most exciting technology to hit the Internet in years—Java! A detailed guide to developing applications with the hot new Java language from Sun Microsystems, *Teach Yourself Java in 21 Days* shows readers how to program using Java and develop applications (applets) using the Java language. With coverage of Java implementation in Netscape Navigator and HotJava, along with the Java Development Kit, including the compiler and debugger for Java, *Teach Yourself Java* is a must-have!

Price: $39.99 USA/$56.95 CAN   User Level: Inter-Advanced
ISBN: 1-57521-030-4   600 pages

Presenting Java

— John December

Presenting Java gives you a first look at how Java is transforming static Web pages into living, interactive applications. Java opens up a world of possibilities previously unavailable on the Web. You'll find out how Java is being used to create animations, computer simulations, interactive games, teaching tools, spreadsheets, and a variety of other applications. Whether you're a new user, project planner, or developer, *Presenting Java* provides an efficient, quick introduction to the basic concepts and technical details that make Java the hottest new Web technology of the year!

Price: $25.00 USA/$35.95 CAN   User Level: All Levels
ISBN: 1-57521-039-8   207 pages

Netscape 2 Unleashed

— *Dick Oliver, et al.*

This book provides a complete, detailed, and fully fleshed-out overview of Netscape products. Through case studies and examples of how individuals, businesses, and institutions are using the Netscape products for Web development, *Netscape Unleashed* gives a full description of the evolution of Netscape from its inception to today and its cutting-edge developments with Netscape Gold, LiveWire, Netscape Navigator 2.0, Java and JavaScript, Macromedia, VRML, plug-ins, Adobe Acrobat, HTML 3.0 and beyond, security, and Intranet systems.

Price: $49.99 USA/$70.95 CAN   User Level: All Levels
ISBN: 1-57521-007-X   Pages: 800 pages

The Internet Unleashed 1996

— *Barron, Ellsworth, Savetz, et al.*

The Internet Unleashed 1996 is the complete reference to get new users up and running on the Internet while providing the consummate reference manual for the experienced user. *The Internet Unleashed 1996* provides the reader with an encyclopedia of information on how to take advantage of all the Net has to offer for business, education, research, and government. The companion CD-ROM contains over 100 tools and applications. The only book that includes the experience of over 40 of the world's top Internet experts, this new edition is updated with expanded coverage of Web publishing, Internet business, Internet multimedia and virtual reality, Internet security, Java, and more!

Price: $49.99 USA/$70.95 CAN   User Level: All Levels
ISBN: 1-57521-041-X   1,456 pages

The World Wide Web Unleashed 1996

— *December and Randall*

The World Wide Web Unleashed 1996 is designed to be the only book a reader will need to experience the wonders and resources of the Web. The companion CD-ROM contains over 100 tools and applications to make the most of your time on the Internet. This book shows readers how to explore the Web's amazing world of electronic art museums, online magazines, virtual malls, and video music libraries, while giving readers complete coverage of Web page design, creation, and maintenance, plus coverage of new Web technologies such as Java, VRML, CGI, and multimedia!

Price: $49.99 USA/$70.95 CAN   User Level: All Levels
ISBN: 1-57521-040-1   1,440 pages

Teach Yourself Web Publishing with HTML in 14 Days, Premier Edition

— *Laura Lemay*

This book teaches everything about publishing on the Web. In addition to its exhaustive coverage of HTML, it also gives readers hands-on practice with more complicated subjects such as CGI, tables, forms, multimedia programming, testing, maintenance, and much more. CD-ROM is Mac- and PC-compatible and includes a variety of applications that help readers create Web pages using graphics and templates.

Price: $39.99 USA/$56.95 CAN   User Level: All Levels
ISBN: 1-57521-014-2   804 pages

Teach Yourself Web Publishing with HTML 3.0 in a Week, Second Edition

— Laura Lemay

Ideal for those people who are interested in the Internet and the World Wide Web—the Internet's hottest topic! This updated and revised edition teaches readers how to use HTML (Hypertext Markup Language) version 3.0 to create Web pages that can be viewed by nearly 30 million users. This book explores the process of creating and maintaining Web presentations, including setting up tools and converters for verifying and testing pages. The new edition highlights the new features of HTML, such as tables and Netscape and Microsoft Explorer extensions and provides the latest information on working with images, sound files, and video, and teaches advanced HTML techniques and tricks in a clear, step-by-step manner with many practical examples of HTML pages.

Price: $29.99 USA/$42.95 CAN   User Level: Beginner-Inter
ISBN: 1-57521-064-9   518 pages

Web Page Construction Kit (Software)

Create your own exciting World Wide Web pages with the software and expert guidance in this kit! This kit includes HTML Assistant Pro Lite, the acclaimed point-and-click Web page editor. Simply highlight text in HTML Assistant Pro Lite and click the appropriate button to add headlines, graphics, special formatting, links, and so on. No programming skills are needed! Using your favorite Web browser, you can test your work quickly and easily without leaving the editor. A unique catalog feature allows you to keep track of interesting Web sites and easily add their HTML links to your pages. Assistant's user-defined toolkit also allows you to add new HTML formatting styles as they are defined. Includes the #1 best-selling Internet book, *Teach Yourself Web Publishing with HTML 3.0 in a Week, Second Edition,* and a library of professionally designed Web page templates, graphics, buttons, bullets, lines, and icons to rev up your new pages!

PC Computing magazine says, "If you're looking for the easiest route to Web publishing, HTML Assistant is your best choice."

Price: $39.95 USA/$55.95 CAN   User Level: Beginner-Inter
ISBN: 1-57521-000-2   518 pages

HTML & CGI Unleashed

— John December and Marc Ginsburg

Targeted to professional developers who have a basic understanding of programming and need a detailed guide, this book provides a complete, detailed reference to developing Web information systems. It covers the full range of languages—HTML, CGI, Perl C, editing and conversion programs, and more—and how to create commercial-grade Web applications. This book is perfect for the developer who will be designing, creating, and maintaining a Web presence for a company or large institution.

Price: $49.99 USA/$70.95 CAN   User Level: Inter-Advanced
ISBN: 0-672-30745-6   830 pages

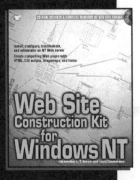

Web Site Construction Kit for Windows NT

— Christopher Brown and Scott Zimmerman

Web Site Construction Kit for Windows NT has everything you need to set up, develop, and maintain a Web site with Windows NT—including the server on the CD-ROM! It teaches the ins and outs of planning, installing, configuring, and administering a Windows NT–based Web site for an organization, and it includes detailed instructions on how to use the software on the CD-ROM to develop the Web site's content—HTML pages, CGI scripts, image maps, and so forth.

Price: $49.99 USA/$70.95 CAN   User Level: All Levels
ISBN: 1-57521-047-9   430 pages

Add to Your Sams.net Library Today
with the Best Books for Internet Technologies

ISBN	Quantity	Description of Item	Unit Cost	Total Cost
1-57521-039-8		Presenting Java	$25.00	
1-57521-030-4		Teach Yourself Java in 21 Days	$39.99	
1-57521-049-5		Java Unleashed	$49.99	
1-57521-007-x		Netscape 2 Unleashed	$49.99	
0-672-30745-6		HTML and CGI Unleashed	$49.99	
1-57521-018-5		Web Site Administrator's Survival Guide	$49.99	
1-57521-009-6		Teach Yourself CGI Programming with Perl in a Week	$39.99	
0-672-30735-9		Teach Yourself the Internet in a Week, Second Edition	$25.00	
1-57521-0681		Teach Yourself Netscape 2 Web Publishing in a Week	$39.99	
1-57521-004-5		The Internet Business Guide, Second Edition	$25.00	
0-672-30718-9		Navigating the Internet, Third Edition	$25.00	
1-57521-005-3		Teach Yourself More Web Publishing with HTML in a Week	$29.99	
1-57521-072-x		Web Site Construction Kit for Windows 95	$49.99	
1-57521-047-9		Web Site Construction Kit for Windows NT	$49.99	
		Shipping and Handling: See information below.		
		TOTAL		

Shipping and Handling: $4.00 for the first book, and $1.75 for each additional book. If you need to have it NOW, we can ship product to you in 24 hours for an additional charge of approximately $18.00, and you will receive your item overnight or in two days. Overseas shipping and handling adds $2.00. Prices subject to change. Call between 9:00 a.m. and 5:00 p.m. EST for availability and pricing information on latest editions.

201 W. 103rd Street, Indianapolis, Indiana 46290

1-800-428-5331 — Orders   1-800-835-3202 — FAX   1-800-858-7674 — Customer Service

Book ISBN 1-57521-137-8

Installation

Using the CD-ROM Guide Program

The CD guide allows you to easily navigate through the software on this CD-ROM. You can install software, read more information about products, run presentations, and more, with the click of a button.

To start the CD guide, click the SETUP.EXE icon in the File Manager or Program Manager. To navigate through the screens of this guide, click the navigation buttons at the bottom of the screen:

◆ Move to the next page

◆ Move to the previous page

Click the EXIT button to exit the program. You can also navigate using keyboard shortcuts:

◆ The Home key returns you to the initial screen.

◆ The right-arrow key moves to the next screen.

◆ The left-arrow key moves to the previous screen.

◆ Alt+F4 exits the program.

If you want to view the directory structure on this CD-ROM without having to run the *CD-ROM Guide* (in Windows 95), view the CD-ROM from Windows Explorer.

Troubleshooting Common Problems

The guide program for the CD doesn't run properly.

The usual cause of this is a damaged or dirty disc. Inspect the disc for possible flaws or defects, and clean it properly. You should also test another CD-ROM in your drive. This often reveals setup problems that are not disc-specific. If these procedures fail, you can contact us to get a replacement disc.

The programs run slowly or don't run properly.

Do you have at least the following amounts of RAM (memory)?

> Windows 95: 8MB
> Windows NT: 8MB

This might sound familiar, but Windows does not run well on anything less than these amounts. If you only have the minimum amount of RAM, the program might run slowly.

If you have a single-spin CD-ROM drive, the menu program and everything that's displayed in it will run slowly.

Contacting Us for Support

We cannot help you with computer problems, Windows problems, or third-party application problems, but we *can* assist you with a problem you have with the book or the CD-ROM.

Problems with other company's programs on the disc need to be resolved with the company that produced the program or demo.

If you're having problems with the software on the disc, here's how to get in touch with us. Please be prepared to give us information on your computer system and a detailed account of the problem you're experiencing.

> Internet e-mail: support@mcp.com
> If you're a member of an online services such as CompuServe, America Online, or Prodigy, you can send e-mail through your service.
> Mail: Macmillan Computer Publishing
> Support Department
> 201 West 103rd Street
> Indianapolis, IN 46290
> Telephone: (317) 581-3833
> Fax: (317) 581-4773

Visit us online:

> Internet World Wide Web (The Macmillan Information SuperLibrary):
> http://www.mcp.com/sams
> Internet FTP:
> ftp.mcp.com/pub/sams
> CompuServe:
> The keyword for our forum is SAMS (type GO SAMS). We are a part of the Macmillan Computer Publishing forum.